ROTH FAMILY FOUNDATION

Music in America Imprint

Michael P. Roth
and Sukey Garcetti
have endowed this
imprint to honor the
memory of their parents,
Julia and Harry Roth,
whose deep love of music
they wish to share
with others.

The publisher gratefully acknowledges the generous
contribution to this book provided by the Music in America
Endowment Fund of the University of California Press Foundation,
which is supported by a major gift from Sukey and Gil Garcetti,
Michael Roth, and the Roth Family Foundation.

SELECTED CORRESPONDENCE OF CHARLES IVES

SELECTED CORRESPONDENCE OF

CHARLES IVES

EDITED BY

TOM C. OWENS

UNIVERSITY OF CALIFORNIA PRESS
BERKELEY LOS ANGELES LONDON

University of California Press
Berkeley and Los Angeles, California

University of California Press, Ltd.
London, England

Frontispiece: Harmony and Charles Ives at West Redding, Connecticut, ca. 1946 (Halley Erskine)

Library of Congress Cataloging-in-Publication Data

Ives, Charles, 1874–1954.
Selected correspondence of Charles Ives / edited by Tom C. Owens.
p. cm. — (Roth Family Foundation Music in America imprint)
Includes bibliographical references (p.) and index.
ISBN 978-0-520-24606-5 (cloth : alk. paper)
1. Ives, Charles, 1874–1954. 2. Composers—United States—Correspondence. I. Owens, Thomas Clarke. II. Title.
ML410.I94A4 2007
780.92—dc22
[B] 2006102252

Manufactured in the United States of America

16 15 14 13 12 11 10 09 08 07
10 9 8 7 6 5 4 3 2 1

This book is printed on Natures Book, which contains 50% post-consumer waste and meets the minimum requirements of ANSI/NISO Z 39.48-1992 (R 1997) (*Permanence of Paper*).⊗

CONTENTS

ILLUSTRATIONS

ACKNOWLEDGMENTS

John Becker's letters are included by kind permission of Mr. Eugene Becker.

John Cage's letters are included by kind permission of the John Cage Trust.

Elliott Carter's letters are included by kind permission of their author.

Elizabeth Sprague Coolidge's letter is included by kind permission of Mr. Jeffrey H. Coolidge.

Aaron Copland's letter is included by kind permission of The Aaron Copland Fund for Music Inc., copyright owner.

Henry Cowell's letters are included by kind permission of the David and Sylvia Teitelbaum Fund, as successors to Henry and Sidney Cowell.

Lehman Engel's letters are included by kind permission of Jay S. Harris, Esq.

Henry F. Gilbert's letter is included by kind permission of Dr. Ellen Koskoff.

Lou Harrison's letters are included by kind permission of the Lou Harrison Estate.

Bernard Herrmann's letter is included by kind permission of Mrs. Norma Herrmann.

Charles and Harmony Ives's letters are included by kind permission of the American Academy of Arts and Letters.

John Kirkpatrick's letters are included by kind permission of the Reverend Daisy Kirkpatrick.

Gian Francesco Malipiero's letter is included by kind permission of the Fondazione Giorgio Cini, Archivio Gian Francesco Malipiero.

Carl and Charlotte Ruggles's letters are from the Charles Ives Papers, MSS 14, in the Irving S. Gilmore Music Library at Yale University. Used by permission.

E. Robert Schmitz's letters are included by kind permission of Jean Leduc.

Ruth Crawford Seeger's letter is included by kind permission of Mr. Kim Seeger on behalf of the Seeger Family.

Nicolas Slonimsky's letters are included by kind permission of Ms. Electra Yourke.

Peter Yates's letters are included by kind permission of Mr. Peter B. Yates.

INTRODUCTION

Charles Ives (1874–1954) wrote hundreds of letters during his life, and, taken together, they provide one of the most comprehensive sources of information about him, second in scope only to his music. The Charles Ives Papers preserve letters and drafts for letters to and from Ives that span a period from 1881 until after his death in 1954. As Ives aged, correspondence became his primary connection to the world and an important instrument through which he defined himself and shaped perceptions of his character and music. The collected correspondence gives us a perspective on the public and private man that even a close friend would not have had. It allows access broad and deep into his thought and character over time.

From the first letter, in 1881, we see Ives's energetic drive, his sense of humor and purpose, his tendency to be doing four or five things at once, and his relentless creativity. The letters from the 1880s show us Ives as a child balancing play, music, and family obligations. We see him in the 1890s as a college student carving out an independent identity, and we see the several roles that music plays in establishing that personality. The letters of 1907–8, between Ives and his fiancée, Harmony Twichell, provide the most personal glimpse of the composer as a young man and hint at the strength and depth of the relationship that sustained him personally and creatively through the rest of his life. Then there is a gap, a period from about 1909 until 1929, during which very little correspondence survives: Ives was writing his music. In the late 1920s and early 1930s, as his health suffered a serious downturn and he faced retirement from both insurance and composing, Ives forged an increasingly substantial link of communication to the musical world through his letters. He began to correspond and collaborate with E. Robert Schmitz, Henry Cowell, Nicolas Slonimsky, and other champions of modern music. He became a patron, a coconspirator, and eventually a father figure to this aggressively modernist and predominantly Americanist circle of musicians. And in this process, the character he presented in his correspondence changed. The letters also document the increased interest in Ives's music and its progressively wider acceptance by the musical community in the 1930s and 1940s. The volume of mail, both fan letters and more substantive correspondence, increased as Ives's health declined. The letters from the last years of his life show the importance of the friendships he had developed through decades of correspondence. And they provide a touching coda after his death in 1954: an outpouring of grief and sympathy for Harmony and an appreciation of his role in the musical and personal lives of those friends.

For several reasons, Ives's correspondence offers a particularly rich and detailed record of his activities after 1930. This was an especially difficult time for the Iveses: ill health forced his retirement from his life insurance firm, Ives and Myrick, and even though this meant that he finally had time to devote himself fully to his music, his condition prevented him from concentrated work on editing or promotion. He had stopped most composition by about 1927. Ironically, one of the most vexing problems for Ives, the deterioration of his handwriting due to a tremor in his hands, led to a boon for posterity. Faced with an ever-increasing volume of mail, the Iveses devised a system that would produce legible replies to the many requests and questions they received. Charles had always handwritten his letters or dictated them at his office to a stenographer who typed them. In the new system, he sketched pencil drafts for his letters on yellow legal pads. He wrote more clearly in pencil than in pen because he could bear down harder on the paper to reduce the effects of the tremor in his hand. The illustration demonstrates the variance between his contemporaneous pen and pencil hands. Ives occasionally commented on the difference between his pen and pencil writing. (See, for instance, Letter 147, December 1933, to Nicolas Slonimsky.) The sometimes drastic difference makes dating documents through their handwriting alone a problematic and difficult task.[1]

Ives rarely threw anything away, and his letter sketches are now the backbone of the collected correspondence. They show us Ives unfiltered and give a glimpse into the process of his thinking, especially in his multiple revisions and drafts for a single letter. Many of these sketches are included here in transcriptions and, in some cases, in facsimile, with their crossed-out lines and myriad revisions. When Ives sketched, he wrote in the voice of the person who would be drafting the final copy—usually his wife, Harmony, or their daughter, Edith. He referred to himself in the third person and enclosed direct statements in quotation marks. Many such letters begin, "I am ——," an abbreviated version of "I am writing for Mr. Ives, who is not at all well, and cannot attend to things nowadays as he would like to." The effect of this opening, usually in letters transcribed and signed by Harmony but composed by Ives, is one of mediation and distancing: she is a buffer between Ives and the recipient of the letter, a buffer required ostensibly because of his poor health. In this mediated correspondence, Ives developed exaggerated characters for all of the participants. Edith remained childlike and innocent, even after she married and had a child. Harmony was polite and reserved, friendly but proper. And Ives himself became the often ill and always reclusive, crotchety New Englander: "that ole' feller" who would toss a few good cusswords around as he complained about the "snake tracks" his pen made. This persona, the sheltered recluse who wrote proudly difficult and dissonant music that triumphantly refused to play by the rules of critical or stylistic categories, is still in many ways the best-known face of Charles Ives. And like the self-image created by his fellow New Englander Robert Frost, it is semifictional. It is no accident that many of the people who helped create and foster this image—those who promoted, edited, and performed his music—were in direct correspondence with him in the 1930s into the 1950s. The Ives of the letters became the basis for the legend that has grown up around the composer. Many of these people, even prominent figures such as Aaron Copland and important performers of Ives's music such as Radiana Pazmor, never met Ives in person. To them he existed entirely as a figure embodied in his music and the letters they received from Harmony. Almost none of them knew the extent to which these letters were in fact written by him.

Here is yet another paradox of Ives: the letters were a product of his physical isolation,

1. Ives commented on his differing hands in a memo from the 1930s or later (CIP Addendum).

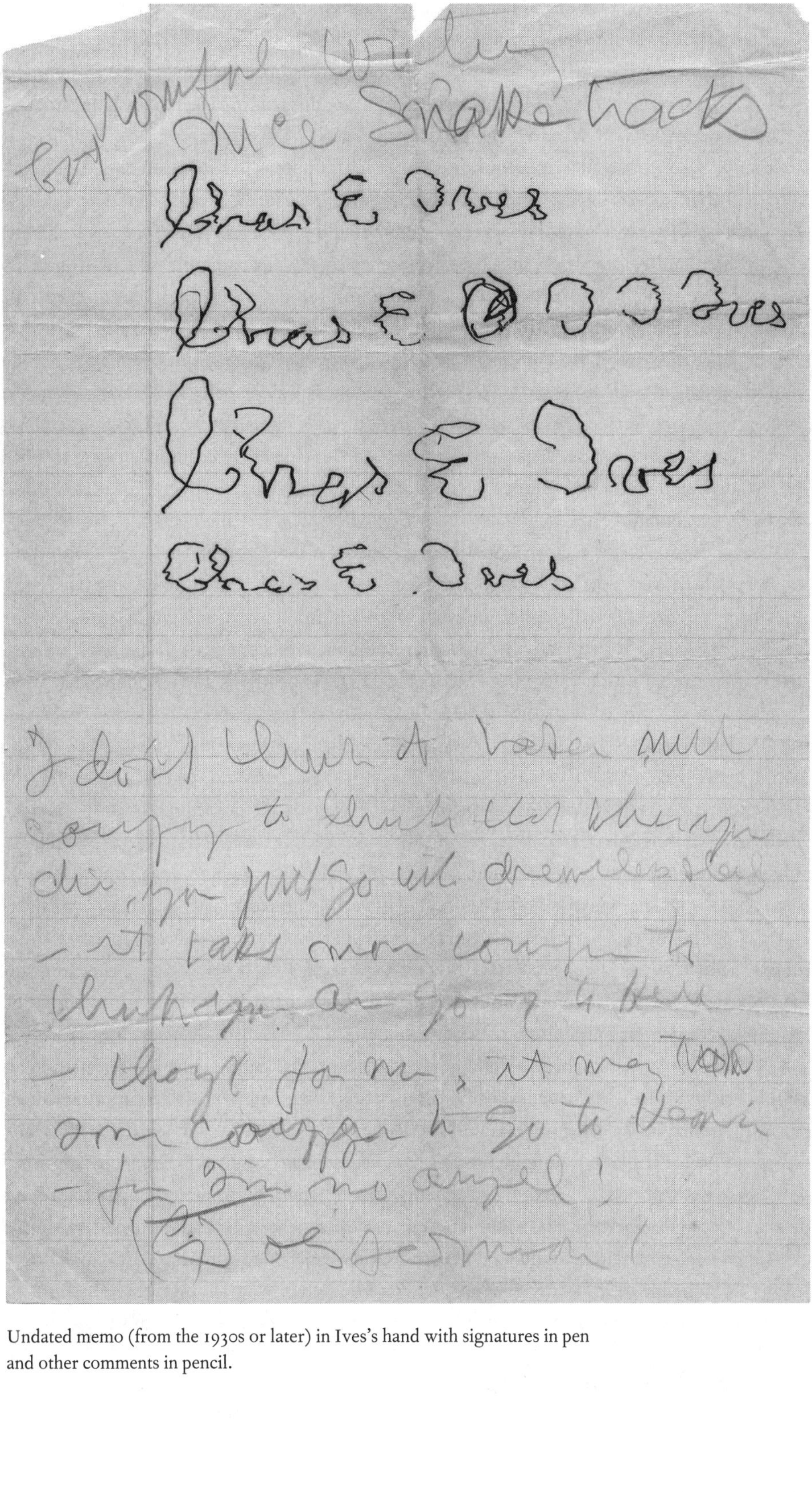

Undated memo (from the 1930s or later) in Ives's hand with signatures in pen and other comments in pencil.

but they were his connection to many people throughout the last twenty-five years of his life. Furthermore, the device of sketching and transcribing made him seem more isolated from the process of writing the letters and from the characters presented in them than he really was. The author of the vast majority of the words that flowed from Harmony's pen in these letters was Charles Ives.

One of the primary purposes for this collection of letters is to show the complex personality and character of the man who wrote both the letters and the music. To this end, I have chosen letters from throughout his life that illuminate Ives's personality, that document the composition and editing of his music, that show his friendships and philanthropy, that illustrate the state of his health, and that reveal his integral role in the new music community from the late 1920s until his death. I have tried to give a representational sample of the entire correspondence in terms of the number of letters to and from any particular person, but certain important figures such as Henry Cowell, Nicolas Slonimsky, and John Kirkpatrick loom just as large in this collection as they did in the career of Ives's music. I have also given considerable space to relative unknowns: people who wrote to Ives simply because they were touched by his music or had some tangential contact with him. Their insights about him and his works are often invaluable.

Because more letters survive from the 1930s and later than from the first forty or so years of Ives's life, most of the correspondence here is from the later years. Before the late 1920s, Ives had few professional contacts in music with whom he might exchange letters, so circumstance dictates the volume of earlier correspondence that survives. It has been my goal to include enough of the letters from across the entire scope of the correspondence to allow for the context and texture of the whole collection to be understood.

The letters included here are all housed in the Charles Ives Papers in the Irving S. Gilmore Music Library of Yale University. Most of them are originals; in some cases, however, the collection holds copies or transcriptions of letters that are in the possession of the recipients, their heirs, or other libraries. All transcriptions and copies are noted as such in the appendix. I have included many of Ives's sketches for letters, especially when there is no final copy in the Ives Papers. I do this primarily because I believe that the sketches are in many ways more revealing than the clean, final copies. Furthermore, the final wording of a given letter is regularly identical to the last sketch by Ives. By examining the sketches that show Ives's thoughts and revisions during the composition of his letters, we learn much more than we would by reading the finished copies only.

The Ives who emerges here is not the angry caricature of himself that he presented in his autobiographical *Memos*, which dates from the early 1930s, and which has so distorted the view of some modern critics of his character and music.[2] We rarely see this side of Ives, and when we do his anger is frequently cast as half-joking exaggeration. Often he balances angry outbursts with self-deprecating comments such as "so now I'll shut up." Although there are occasional instances of Ives's infamous and now anachronistic gender rhetoric, their rarity in the correspondence as a whole helps us understand them for what they are: a small, though significant, part of Ives's character.

Instead, we see a highly personal side of Ives through the eyes of his family. We see him

2. Charles Ives, *Memos*, ed. John Kirkpatrick (New York: W. W. Norton, 1972).

as the object of Harmony Twichell's ardent and devoted affection. We see him as the patron of Cowell's *New Music*, of Slonimsky's concerts in the early 1930s, of John J. Becker, and of many other composers and performers in the modern music community. We see him through the eyes of an admiring, almost reverent group of younger composers in the 1930s and 1940s such as Lou Harrison. And we see how he sometimes chafed at the restraint placed upon his music by editors and performers such as John Kirkpatrick, who wished to pin down the single finished form of pieces that had existed for so long in a creatively open-ended multiplicity of variants.

The Ives we see here is also much more connected and engaged with the world around him than the isolated figure made famous in the Ives legend. The sheer *volume* of the correspondence itself makes this clear. During the time that his music was becoming well known, while he supervised its editing and publication and as his declining health made it more and more difficult for him to take an active part in its promotion, he was in almost daily contact with an ever-increasing circle of friends, collaborators, acquaintances, and fans. This collection of letters tells the story of this surprisingly large group, and it presents a significant part of the story of modern music in the United States through the first half of the twentieth century.

Every effort has been made to reproduce all the letters exactly as they were written; misspelled and missing words, grammatical errors, and missing punctuation are corrected or supplied in square brackets only when the correction is necessary for the reader's understanding. The use of the word *sic* has been avoided except in a handful of instances. As the reproductions of Ives's sketches illustrate, it is not always possible to represent exactly in type what he wrote by hand. Some of Ives's letter sketches, especially in cases where he made multiple drafts or many revisions within the same draft, have been excerpted or condensed. Some inconsequential marks, errors, and revisions in the sketches have been omitted.

There are many who deserve my thanks and gratitude for their help in this project. I never had the opportunity to meet one of my most important collaborators, but without the herculean labor of John Kirkpatrick, who organized the correspondence, placed it in chronological order, and tracked down copies of hundreds of letters, this collection would have been quite different and much less rich.[3] George Mason University provided me with a grant and study leave to allow me to devote time to the book. Ken Crilly, Suzanne Eggleston-Lovejoy, and Richard Boursey at the Yale Music Library were always helpful and resourceful. My thanks also to the staffs of the Beinecke Rare Book Library at Yale and the Fenwick Library at George Mason University. Peter Burkholder was an invaluable help as always, and I am grateful for the advice and excellent scotch I received from Jim Sinclair on my visits to New Haven. Warm thanks also to John Halle and Marka Gustavsson, who were gracious and helpful hosts. I am

3. Indeed, Kirkpatrick's presence is apparent to anyone looking at the Ives correspondence because he inscribed the date of composition and occasionally other comments on the original letters themselves. These annotations are visible in some of the facsimiles included in this volume.

particularly indebted to Denise Von Glahn, H. Wiley Hitchcock, and the other, anonymous readers of this manuscript for their insightful suggestions on its shape and content. Special thanks as well to the students in my Ives Seminars at GMU and to Vinnie Oppido for his help with the musical examples. Also, the book is immeasurably clearer and better because of the amazingly perceptive, detailed, and conscientious copyediting of Ann Twombly. And, of course, my thanks are due to Mary Francis and Kalicia Pivirotto at the University of California Press for their hard work and guidance. Finally, I would like to express my deep thanks to my family, who have put up with my work and worry about Ives's letters for far too long; to them I dedicate this book.

• 1 •

CHILDHOOD, HOPKINS, AND YALE (1881–1903)

From his earliest letters Ives comes across as a strong personality, active in play, sports, music, and occasional mischief. The surviving letters from his childhood are addressed to his grandmother Sarah Ives, his aunt Amelia Brewster, and his father, George. Many of them were mailed from the beach house that the extended Ives clan occupied every summer in Westbrook, Connecticut. There life was a whirl of swimming, tennis, sailing, rowing, baseball, and croquet with his brother, Moss, his cousins, and his uncle Lyman Brewster. He also mentioned going to concerts and rehearsals and described traveling by himself, by train, to try out a particularly fine pipe organ. The professional side of his musical life also intrudes in these letters, as we see the young organist begging his father to help him find a substitute so that he can stay at the beach over the weekend rather than going home to play the Sunday service.

1. Ca. 10 September 1881, to Sarah H. Ives, Danbury, Connecticut[1]

DEAR GRAMA:

COME HOME AND SEE US. GIVE LOVE TO SARANE. I WOULD LIKE TO SEE COUSIN GEORGE'S PUNCH AND JUDY SHOW

GOOD BYE FROM CHARLIE.

[*Note in bottom margin:*] Received in Westbrook Sept 10 1881 by his grandmother Sarah H. Ives

2. 18 July 1886, to George Ives

Dear Papa

Mamma received your letter last night. I am very sorry you could not come Saturday and stay Sunday. I am having a nice time down here. Us boys have got an engine fixed up on the beach near the bath house, Mossie is the Conductor and brak man [brakeman], Joe

1. All of Ives's letters before 1893 were mailed from Westbrook, Connecticut, unless otherwise noted. Letter citations are in the following format: date, person(s) sending the letter to or receiving the letter from Ives, place of origination. See the appendix for a full list of the letters and their archival information.

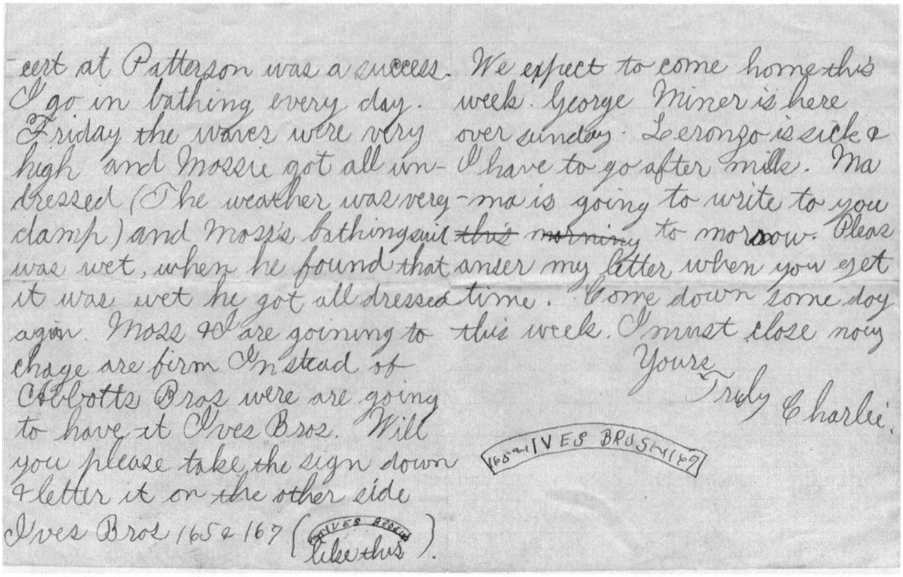
-cert at Patterson was a success. We expect to come home this
I go in bathing every day. week. George Miner is here
Friday the waves were very over sunday. Leronzo is sick &
high and Mossie got all un- I have to go after milk. Ma
dressed (The weather was very- ma is going to write to you
damp) and Moss's bathingsuit ~~this morning~~ to morrow. Pleas
was wet, when he found that anser my letter when you get
it was wet he got all dressed time. Come down some day
agian. Moss & I are goining to this week. I must close now
chage are firm Instead of Yours
Abbotts Bros were are going Truly Charlie.
to have it Ives Bros. Will
you please take the sign down
& letter it on the other side
Ives Bros 165 & 167 (like this).

18 July 1886, to George Ives, pp. 2 and 3.

King is the fireman & I am the engineer. I am glad the concert at Patterson was a success. I go in bathing every day. Friday the waves were very high and Mossie got all undressed (The weather was very damp) and Moss's bathing suit was wet, when he found that it was wet he got all dressed again. Moss & I are goining to cha[n]ge are [our] firm Instead of Abbotts Bros we[']re are going to have it Ives Bros. Will you please take the sign down and letter it on the other side Ives Bros 165 & 167 (like this) [*includes drawing of the sign*]. We expect to come home this week. George Miner is here over sunday. Leronzo is sick & I have to go after milk. Mama is going to write you ~~this morning~~ to morrow. Pleas anser my letter when you get time. Come down some day this week. I must close now

Yours Truly
Charlie

3. 14 August 1889, to George Ives

Dear Papa,

I have just received your letter I went to the mail in the rain this morning, and I had 30 letters and papers for the beach. We are all talking about the fires in Danbury. Mossie's hands are poisoned again but they are good deal better to day. We have just been rowing over to Monongutueseuske point in Mr. Cheneys new row & row boat. Uncle Lyman and I rowed and Moss and Mr. Theron B. stirred [steered?] We went 1 mi. in 16 min. Saturday the Westbrook base ball nine played the Essexes. The Essex asked me to play with them and I did, but the Essex got beat, 18 to 10. The Stannards Beach ball club asked me to pitch for them against the Clintons next Sat. Mamma wants to have you give $1 to the Parmelees to give to milkman Elwell to whom she owes. Please send last wks Youths Com. and this weeks, and the St. Nick. if it comes before we go. I can't write very well because I have to hold my sore arm up. I am going to play tennis now.

Yours etc.
C. E. Ives

P.S. I am going to the concert to night.

4. 20 August 1889, to George Ives

The blots were on this paper before I wrote but I took it because it was the best up here.

Dear Papa

We received your letter and the picture last night. Mossie just came home from Saybrook he went over on the cars and came back with the ponies. I play tennis most of the time down here. We played a set yesterday in which Lloyd and Sarane beat Uncle Lyman and myself. We play played [*sic*] croquet this morning. Mamma wants to go home Friday, but Aunt Milly wants her to stay because she is not very well but she wants to go home where she will have more to do. Why don't you catch the bug[2] Uncle Lyman and myself were going to have a boat race yesterday, to Salt Island and back but we didn't may be we will race Thursday or Friday. Uncle Lyman will try and get Mr. Cheny's new boat and I will take the old white round bottom boat that Cousin Howard had to row with when he went to ~~lake~~ school at Lake Mohegan. I don't know whether that is the right way to spell it and there is nobody here to ask as most of the folks have to sleep. Maybe it is spelled "Monheeghane." Capt. Brewster brought a pair of oars around this morning. The folks don't want to have me play ball much but yesterday morning Uncle Lyman, Miss Grout and Sarane, Lloyd, Moss and I played and Mr. Stevens umpired the game. Mr. Theron Brewster officiated as the solitary spectator. To morrow as Aunt Sil and her father were going to Salisbury, Uncle Lyman thought of getting up a party and go to Hartford and see the capitol and so forth. Some of the Whites and Demmings were going and Sarane, but they have given up going to morrow and I don't know whether they will go now or not. The Demmings are going home Friday. I don't want to go home. All the folks but Mamma want to have me stay as I am studying and Miss Hollister is gone as Mr. Morrow is and probably there will be no church Sunday and if there is Miss Hollister has made arrangements with Miss Moore to play for me.[3] The Seelys are going away this week and I can probably prac-

2. This is the first line of the second page; similar, seemingly unrelated lines appear at the tops of the third and fourth pages of the letter. The three lines read: "Why don't you catch the bug/ Why don't you catch the fire bug/ why don't you catch the fire fly."

3. Ella Hollister was Ives's piano teacher and the choir director at Second Congregational Church, Danbury, where Ives had taken the job as organist on 10 February 1889. He continued as a regular organist in churches in Danbury, New Haven, and New York from then until 1902. Jan Swafford, *Charles Ives: A Life with Music* (NewYork: W. W. Norton, 1996), 48–49; James Sinclair, *Descriptive Catalogue of the Music of Charles Ives* (New Haven: Yale University Press, 2002), 664.

tice on there piano. If I can stay over I will come home Monday. Aunt Milly has gone to Essex to get some Witch Hazel with Cousin Sarah. I am going in bathing now and perhaps Uncle Lyman wants to play tennis. I can serve overhand now.

Yours Truly,
C. E. Ives

• • •

These two letters, mailed in the same envelope, one from Ives to his paternal grandmother and one from his brother to their Aunt Amelia Brewster, embody the idyllic childhood world reflected in Ives's songs "The Circus Band" and "Memories." Topknot was the family cat.

5. 27 August 1889, to Sarah H. Ives, Danbury, Connecticut

Dear Grandma,

We arrived here last evening about 6:30. Papa was at the train to meet us. Our trunks were left in Hartford but they came this morning at 7 o'clock. Mamma went to Grandma Parmelee's to supper. Moss Papa and I came to the house and ate crackers and cheese bread & milk etc. When we got in front of your house the first thing we saw was Topknot on the front stoop and she came out to meet us. I went to Mrs. Martin's this morning. The chicks are all right. We have got the croquet set out and will beat Uncle Lyman when he gets home.

Yours Truly,
C. E. Ives

Moss got the blots on . . .

[27 August 1889, Moss Ives to Amelia Brewster, Danbury, Connecticut]

Dear Aunt Milly,

The first thing I saw when I arrived here was Topie cumming . She was so glad to see me that she kept agoin round in a circle. The morning an Indian show band parraded the streets and scared a pair of horses that came near running over Bobie Bennet, it said in the Evening News the [that] he cried but he didn't at all, he was not scared a bite [bit]. I suppose you heard about the Avrial property being sold and Mrs. Nichols fire. It had an account in the News about the boys stealing pears in your tree and how they all ran when a dog barked, but there was no dog that barked but Papa hollered, Get out of there. I close with love Moss

Charlie got the blots on.

6. 19 August 1890, to George Ives

Dear Papa,

Yours rec'd yesterday. I have just come back from Essex where I saw Dr. Hubbard, he put some new plasters on my hand. I think, the cut is very nearly healed Dr. says in a week I can use it as well as ever. If they are not satisfied with Mr. Gordon I would try and see Miss Smith, I don't think Mr. Gordon would care, I didn't exactly engage him for next Sunday I only said that I might be away. I might possibly come home myself but it would cost nearly four dollars to go and come. There is a Miss or Mrs. Traverse in Bethel that maybe could. I went sailing yesterday with Mr. Granis we went nearly to Madison. The waves are very large here to day and [I] think it is going to rain. Moss is now in bathing with Joe King. The Westbrook Band gives a concert to- morrow I imagine they are like M. N. C. Plese write before Sat.

Yours Truly,
Charlie

[*On the same page: a letter from Ives's aunt Amelia Ives Brewster to George Ives*]

Dear George,

Charlie's hand has prevented him from going bathing or rowing & he wishes to stay another week and he can if you can get anybody to play for him Sunday. The Mrs. Smith he speaks of is the one from Bethel I wish he had got her in the first place if you cannot get any body of course he will have to come home Saturday but I hope you will be able to. Mossie & I expect to come home the last of the week.

Millie

7. 31 August 1889 [1890], to Amelia Brewster (no envelope or postmark)[4]

Dear Aunt Amelia,

I left Bridgeport at 4:30 and got here in time for supper. I found all the folks very well. The first one I saw first, of course, was the cat. As soon as I left Uncle Lyman, I went to Mrs. Baker and she gave me a letter of intro. to Mr. Spinning. I did not find him home the first time but a lady said he would be home at one o'clock, so I went down to the park & stayed there about an hour. I had a sandwich and ice-cream for dinner. I found Mr. Spinning home after dinner and we then went up to his church (Presbyterian). I tried the organ which is (he says) the largest in the state and of course a very fine one. It has 60 registers. Uncle Lyman, I suppose has told about the tennis racket. I came down from the junction with the Merritts. As soon as Nelson saw Ned Tweedy & Moss at the Depot, he began to yell and dance, and made more noise than the cabmen and expressmen. I went to Sam

4. John Kirkpatrick dates the letter to 1890 on the basis of the opening date of Sam Harris's store, 30 August 1890. Ives, however, wrote 1889.

Harris' opening last night, after rehearsal, with some of the choir he has a fine store but not as large as I thought it would be. He (Harris) has a large picture of himself in the window and the American flag wound around it. They are running one horse car on the West St. road to day. Mrs. Sanford was worse Thurs. but better today. I will send the book in a registered letter. I used 33 miles and owe you $.66

Yours very sincerely,
C. E. Ives

• • •

Ives moved to New Haven, Connecticut, in the spring of 1893 and in April began studying at Hopkins Grammar School, which specialized in preparing students for Yale. Although Ives went to Hopkins because of his questionable prospects for making it into the university without substantial aid and effort, his letters suggest that studying often took second or third place in his crowded schedule. In these letters Ives's musical activities come into sharper focus: he was the organist of St. Thomas's Episcopal Church and also worked to improve his knowledge of harmony and his general musical ability. Particularly through his participation in sports during his days at Hopkins, Ives also began to lay the foundations of his social success at Yale.

8. 9 May 1893, to George Ives, New Haven[5]

Dear Father,

Yours just rec'd. I am in no particular hurry for the music etc. as there is quite a lot of good organ music in the church, and with that I brought with me I will have enough for 2 or 3 Sundays more. It may be a good scheme to fix the box as you suggest as I may not be able to get it all in the closet although it is quite large. I think the things had all better be sent to the church. I wrote Uncle Lyman yesterday telling him how the service etc. went. I had the most trouble with the chants and found the best way to learn them was to commit the music and then follow the words. They sing their hymns faster than I have been accustomed to and it is rather hard to get used to it. The nine goes to Bridgeport Sat. afternoon and so I will probably see George Clark etc. I sent the B[ase].B[all]. suit Sat. I have 2 receipts for the house and others from Brien & Co for Ba. B. suit. Tell Moss I am afraid the Academy & Co. Baseball teams will have rather hard time with B[ridgeport] but they may not. I am have to hurry as it is past time for dinner and will close with love to all yours truly,

C.

P.S. I think if you sent the box by freight it would be all right, and you can put the clothes in it that I will send back in the valise at the end of the week.

5. The remaining letters in this chapter were mailed from New Haven, Connecticut, unless otherwise noted.

• • •

Charles Bonney was the choirmaster and Ives's supervisor at St. Thomas's Church. Ives later remembered him as strict, demanding, and unpleasant, but in his letters home he kept quiet about this dimension of the relationship.[6]

9. 5 July 1893, to George Ives

Dear Father,

Enclosed please find check which I have rec'd from Mr. Bonney, and also receipt for rent of the room. I suppose Uncle Lyman told you I was going to the boat race, and I suppose you heard that Yale won as usual, although they had hard luck in the Base Ball Season [or series?]. The Hopkins B.B. pictures are done I have one for myself and will get one to send home if you wish they cost $1.25. Please tell me as soon as possible so I can get the order off. Garrison & Tritle have gone and so I have moved into the front room, which [is] much better in every way. I haven't seen Mrs. Porter yet as she is out of town and won't be back until tomorrow.[7] The services at the Ch. went smoother than I thought they [would], especially at the Choral Service Sunday before last, when I only left out "Amen." Last Sunday there was not any breaks as far as I remember. You ought to hear the choir sing "Alpha and Omega" Stainer.[8] When does mother and Moss expect to come to Westbrook?

Yours Truly
C.E.I.

• • •

Life in New Haven exerted a strong pull on Ives, and his letters home occasionally presented his hectic schedule along with apologies for not being able to visit more often. The following letter also shows that Ives himself worried about his prospects for entering college as planned.

10. 12 July 1893, to George Ives

Dear Father,

Yours rec'd this noon. Have just seen Mr. Bonney who says he don't know of anybody, now, who would play as and as it is the first Sunday for the choir it will be particularly hard besides he would have to have the rehearsal a week before as usual, although he may find

6. Frank Rossiter cites Harmony Ives as the source for his description of Bonney as "a martinet" in *Charles Ives and His America* (New York: Liveright, 1975), 48, 331n99.

7. Porter was Ives's first tutor in New Haven; Swafford, *Charles Ives*, 80.

8. Ives probably refers to Sir John Stainer's anthem "I Am Alpha and Omega."

Ives (left) with his Hopkins Grammar School teammate Miles, 1893. (H. Randall.)

somebody later but of course that would be too late. The ass't org.st. could not do it, as we will hardly be able to get him ready to play the hymns for August. I show him twice a week. He never had anything to do with an organ and so it is easy to show him. Mr. Bonney said I hadn't ought to take less than a dollar for the time so I get two dollars a wk from it. Even if I could go I don't see how I could get any time for the type writer, as I will have to study all the time if I get even 6 prelims off next Sept. They are marking very close this year as only 3 of my class passed and half of them flunked who were better prepared than I. I also heard that a pile of Andover fellows got left. It was lucky I didn't take mine. Any way please let me know about the plans as soon as possible.

Yours Truly
C.

• • •

In August 1893 Ives's uncle Lyman Brewster took him along as a secretary on a trip to the World's Fair in Chicago. Only a few tantalizing pieces of evidence survive to indicate what he may have seen and done at this watershed for American culture, which featured in its official and unofficial programs architecture by Stanford White, ragtime by Scott Joplin, and demonstrations of previously unimaginable technological wizardry.[9]

11. 22 August 1893, to George Ives, Chicago

Dear Father,

As soon as we reached Chicago, we went directly to the hotel and then to the grounds. Have just returned from West Va. State building, where the West Point Cadets had a dance. Heard Thomas' Orchestra with Hrr—Bazin as director. Will write in morning with better pen etc.

Yours, Chas

• • •

As Ives continued at Hopkins, his letters home sometimes reflect the tension between his father's desire to supervise his habits and activities and Ives's growing desire for independence. The following pair of letters sheds light on this submerged conflict and on the mundane de-

9. A letter of 1 September 1893 from Lyman to Amelia Brewster further describes Ives's visit to the fair: "Charley's task as 'Secretary of the Com. Commission' was not very onerous, about four hours in all. He is rejoicing in the prospect of hearing the famous French organist 'Guilmant' to-morrow on the Exposition grounds at 1. P.M. Charley says he is the best organist in the world & the papers seem of the same opinion. . . . You need have no apprehensions as to C's health. He has weighed at every stop & has found no deficiency in weight. If there has been any over-action it is in chewing gum—confined strictly to our room" (CIP, 33/1). Ives mentions Guilmant in a letter of 28 August 1893 to his father (ibid.).

tails of his life. In October Ives moved in with the family of his classmate Tom McIntire. Soon after, he wrote to his mother with requests for furniture and school supplies. The letter contains two indications of Ives's popularity and athletic achievement at Hopkins. First, he mentions that he has been named manager of the football team. Second, he notes that his new living arrangements should improve his opportunity for studying because the McIntire place is less convenient for his friends to visit.

Ives's postscript about his mother's handwriting is particularly interesting because of the relatively small amount we know about her. Letters to her are rare, and letters from her even rarer. In fact, she is seldom mentioned in the correspondence at all, even in the courtship letters when his fiancée, Harmony, describes meeting Ives's family.[10] As Stuart Feder has noted, Ives's aunt Amelia was often the subject of the attention one would expect his mother to receive.[11] The few letters that survive in Mollie's hand, which predate this one, are clear and legible, so one wonders if something had happened to her by the fall of 1893 that made writing difficult for her and whether this difficulty was related to the letter of 28 September 1894, in which George Ives wrote, "Mother has another new nurse."[12] If, as Feder conjectures, she was the victim of a debilitating physical or mental illness that was never mentioned within the Ives family, this enigmatic postscript perhaps indicates some of its effects.[13]

12. 30 September 1893, to George Ives (incomplete)

Dear Father,

Your letter rec'd yesterday noon. I enclose laundry bill and Mr. Bonney's check. I asked Mr. Bonney about trying voice last Tuesday evening after the rehearsal but he said wait until some time when we weren't both so tired. I think you asked in one of your letters how much time etc. I had for studies music and exercise. The studies take the most of the time. I have one now at every period in school and so it gives no time in school to study. Some days especially . . .

13. 4 October 1893, to Mollie Ives

Dear Mother,

Your letter just rec'd. I think the desk would be best with a plain wooden top but it don't make much difference if you have decided on the other. I would like a book case very much if you could possibly get one as the drawers would have to be filled with lots of other different things, besides books, which I have quite a number of. But if you don't think it would be worth while, why all right. Any way I wish whatever you do send you would send immediately. I haven't paid for the ch [illegible word] yet, as I only have about

10. See Letters 121–22.

11. Stuart Feder, *Charles Ives: "My Father's Song"* (New Haven: Yale University Press, 1992), 223.

12. See Letter 31.

13. Feder, *Charles Ives*, 227.

$4. left. I have bought 4 new books 2 of them 2nd hand, and some underclothes, etc. besides paying for the room rent at Crown St. and to Mr. Thompson but haven't paid for the board, which is $10.25. I will get the bill this afternoon, when I mail this letter. Tell Uncle Lyman I am studying Homer, which is not much harder than Xenophon, but takes more time. I also have German and I find what I studied with Father helps me a good deal. I can do very much more studying here than I could at the other, as it is not quite so handy for the boys, and Tom has to study a good deal himself. We both play foot ball in the later part of the afternoon, and so then all the rest of the time for practice and study. Tell Moss I was elected manager of the foot ball team, to-day. Why don't the D.H.S play the Betts Academy Stamford. I think they are a light team. I will send washing this Sat. as I didn't have enough to pay for sending last week. I wish you would send a Latin Grammar (Allen & Greenough) and also that ankle supporter if you can find it. I think it was in the beareau draw in Moss's room or in the closet. It is a white elastic bandage to go over the ankle. Please send this etc. as soon as possible.

Yours Truly
C.

P.S. I wish you would please get somebody else to write your letters as I can hardly make them out.

• • •

Football in the 1890s was not yet the domain of today's three-hundred-pound giants but it had its own ferocious violence, and players wore soft helmets and few pads. In the following letter to his father, Ives plays down the broken nose he suffered in one particularly rough game. George apparently didn't buy Charles's version of the story, however, as he seems to have forbidden his son to try out for the Yale football team the following year.[14] Ives's mention of the accounts of the game in the New York papers presages the exaggerated newspaper coverage of the famous 1894 game between Yale and Harvard, which featured the debut of the infamous, and later banned, flying wedge play, and in which a player was falsely rumored to have been killed.

14. 30 October 1893, to George Ives

Dear Father,

We rec'd your telegrams last evening and answered both. I suppose you thought I was nearly killed, as all the papers here had accounts of horrible accident and how we had to be carried off the field etc. etc. They say that there were accts. of it in N.Y. papers. Cheney got the worst of it as he broke his collar bone, but I just bruised the cartiledge of the lower part of the nose. It pains quite a good deal, but Doct. Cheney says it will be all right in a

14. See Letter 32.

week or so & will not leave any scar of deformity. The worst thing about [it] is that I have to go to him every day to have it dressed and so I am afraid his bill will be quite heavy but still it may not. I have to [go] around with a big plaster on so I try to stay in the house as much as possible. The McIntires are very kind, they won't let me go out for meals but have me eat with them. She says that she would always let you know if anything serious should occur even if I should not. I wrote to unc. Lyman yesterday and ask him to ask you to send the checks for my room rent and board. It will be 2 weeks to-morrow (Teus.) You can make them payable to me, or to Mr. R. McIntire and Mrs. —— Miller. I don't know the initials but I can find them out and fill them in. It is $35 in all or $15 of room and $20 of board. Please tell mother that the clothes all fit well. I send papers in wash. With love to all

Yours very truly
C

There was a choral service yesterday and they said that it went better than any service ever went before. Please excuse bad writing as I have to hurry to get to school in time.

• • •

George Ives's concern about his son manifested itself in a fairly regular stream of questions about his activities and well-being. George was particularly interested, as one would imagine, in his son's musical life but also in his level of physical fitness.

15. 19 November 1893, to George Ives

Dear Father,

Rec'd your letter yesterday and the washing Friday. The only questions that you asked that I haven't answered perhaps, was about the assistant organist, and what I did for regular exercises. The assistant is a young man about 20, he doesn't play much except hymns etc. I haven't had much to do with him yet. Since foot ball has stopped, I have been playing tennis pretty regularly. We use the Indian clubs nearly every night. I think I will be able to catch the 12:10 train Thanksgiving, I will have to leave Friday at 4:28. Tell Moss to get up a game for Friday. I would like to see the team play. Do you think you could get me a hat, and have it sent so I could get [it] in time to wear next Sat.[15] I would like a black one with a big brim and curl, like everybody wears here size 6 7/8. If you don't think that you could get it, can I get one here? I think I can get one that would do well, and and [not] not very expensive. You might get them to send one on trial if they do it. Four of us went hunting yesterday morning but didn't get anything. Uncle Lyman spoke when he was here about lending me some books for the bookcase. Will you please ask him if he has "The Reconstruction of Europe" or "Poole's Index" and if he has if he would send them so I could get them before the week is out. I have to hand in a composition on "United Italy"

15. By asking for a hat from Danbury, Ives was exploiting a hometown specialty. The town was a leading center of hat manufacture; Rossiter, *Charles Ives and His America*, 4–5.

by Mon. the 27th. Tell Grandmother I will write to her some time during this week. Ask Moss to write.

With love to all
yours very truly
C. E. Ives

• • •

The following letter shows Ives's desire to improve his ability and build his reputation as an organist. Dudley Buck (1839–1909) and his student Harry Rowe Shelley (1858–1947) were among the most important organ composers and players in the country in the 1890s. Though Ives did not intend to major in music when he went to Yale, his plans to play recitals and study with such nationally known teachers make clear his resolve not to foreclose on his future as a performing musician.[16]

16. 3 December 1893, to George Ives

Dear Father,

I reached here at twenty minutes of before seven instead of after, so had plenty of time. It snowed here last night and is raining to day, and as it was very bad walking, very few were out at church. Don't you think that after I have the pieces, that I could play at recitals, worked up sufficiently, it would be a good scheme to write Mr. Shelley, and see what arrangements I could make with him for a few lessons, in which I could play them over to him, and I also at the same time might finish up the harmony book. I might see him some time if he comes to New Haven, but I doubt if he comes up often. Do you think it would be best to get him or Dudley Buck. I think I can pay for the lessons myself, as the asst. org. [h]as spoken to me about my helping him, and said he wanted to start soon. He doesn't play much beside hymns etc. and knows nothing about an organ so I probably won't have much trouble in showing him. I think I can get along without a new over coat, if I get the buttons set over. And if you decide to get a dress suit, why wouldn't it be best to get a whole suit that either Moss or I could wear, as Moss if [he] should get one just for himself would get it a little large, as he will want [it] for several years, & if we should want it at the same time, I could used get along with the other pant and vest, and could borrow a coat. Please tell mother I bought my shoes and found my other glove have paid both bills, and will send receipt. Is Grandmother better Give my love to all.

Yours Very Truly
C

My cold is better.

16. See Letter 35 for further mention of study with Buck. No additional concrete evidence of Ives's study with Buck or Shelley survives.

17. 10 December 1893, to George Ives

Dear Father,

Your letter and wash recd yesterday, and the skates and knife earlier in the week. I told the express Co. to send for the wash yesterday afternoon, but they didn't come around so I will try to get it off early Monday morning. I send the library books with it. I saw Mr. Butler yesterday and he said he thought that he would go to Thomaston sometime this week, and would go over from there to Danbury. He said he would write you and let you [know] about the day, trains etc. I haven't written to either Buck or Shelly as yet will talk it over with Mr. Bonney first. I don't seem to be able to find my "Variations on America," I wish [you] would please look for it, and send it if you can find it. Enclosed please find check and receipt. Hope mother's cold is better.

Yours Truly,
CEI

18. 17 December 1893, to George Ives

Dear Father,

I won't have time [to] write much of a letter to day, as we begin our examinations tomorrow. I rec'd the two piano pieces and the America you sent. I went skating one day on lake Whitney, but the snow has spoiled it now. We have 3 weeks of vacation I am not sure of the time I can come, probably some Wednesday morning and go back Friday evening. I think Mac will come up with me, so please ask Moss to find out what is going on to entertain him with, any dances, etc. Did Mr. Butler get to Danbury? I haven't [heard.] Enclosed please find receipt of 2 bills which I paid. Will write again as soon as I find out when we will come.

Yours very truly,
C E Ives

• • •

New Haven, with its university and proximity to New York City, offered a much more diverse and exciting season of concerts and musical productions than Ives had known in Danbury. Here he mentions his interest in taking voice lessons and the prospect of attending a concert by the famed Italian soprano Adelina Patti.

19. 11 February 1894, to George Ives

Enclosed please find Check from Mr. B. $16.00

Dear Father,

Rec'd your postal asking for Library Book, which I sent with the washing yesterday. I sent them in two pieces, one a bundle and other the valise, which needs to be fixed before used again. I have not asked Mr. Bonney about voice yet, as he has been busy after the Tues. evening rehearsal, the time I thought would be best. I can't do anything more about recitals until after Lent. My clothes are in good condition, if they were not I would get them fixed. I haven't seen Howard Starr since. "Patti" doesn't appear here until the 16th I will try and hear her if I can. I think our vacation begins the week after Easter. We have a week. Send the "Music Leader" I think G. [probably Ives's friend Elisha Garrison] would like to see them. But didn't think Conn's papers were good for much. Please ask mother if she has any pair of black pants that I could wear for the rest of the winter as these are so shiny. If she sends any, ask her to put a big crease in them. Wrote to Uncle Lyman. Hope all folks are well.

Yours Very Truly,
C

• • •

With his duties as an organist and his active social life at school, Ives found it increasingly difficult to make time for visits home, a fact that aggravated the latent friction between father and son. The following letter presents a suspiciously long list of reasons he couldn't make it home during a short school break.

20. 20 February 1894, to George Ives

Dear Father,

Yours just rec'd. I suppose I can come home Wed. evening, but there is a card party which I would rather like to go and then Thurs the asst. organist wanted to have me play at the 4:00 Lenten service, which they have on every day in the week at which he plays, they have no choir, and use just hymns etc., and I could get out of it I suppose Then I have a debate Friday which I expected to work on almost all day Thurs. There is nothing in particular that I've to bring home except the music and bag, my clothes are not ready yet. And then if I come Easter, which is only about 3 weeks after. Of course if you think it best I will come. Of course I would like to see you all, but it is such a short time to Easter. Please let me know if you still think I had better come.

Yours truly
C.

21. 24 February 1894, to George Ives

Dear Father,

Have just written to Unc. Lyman. Received the "Eagle" to day. There is a choral service at the church to morrow. During Lent all the chants that are sung are founded on the Gregorian tones. The choir sing them in unison, and so I have to change the harmonies.

It is rather awkward to do as the air has to be kept on the top. The best way I have found to do is to use diminished chords in the same key, or go to the 1st ♭ or ♯ remove[d].[17] I knew that Mr. Bonney went to Bridgeport to give lessons. What is Mann Allen going to have for the musicale? This term ends the Thurs. before Easter and I will have 8 days. It is very cold here to day—the coldest this year. I hope all the folks are well with love to you all

Yours very truly
C

• • •

The following letter illustrates several themes that play through this section of the correspondence. Ives's application to be the organist at the New Haven Baptist church was rejected, and the letter begins with an attempt to explain the situation to his father; Ives also seems to have been trying to convince himself that things would work out for the best musically. One of his hopes, that he might be able to get the position at Center Congregational Church, was realized the following fall. More interesting is what this letter implies about the uncertain state of Ives's future plans for music and for college. It is clear that as late as the spring of 1894, he knew very little about the fledgling Yale music department, and he was still unsure about his prospects for getting into the college class for the following term. He had spoken to Mr. Fox, the rector at Hopkins, about the possibility of returning and seems to be trying to pacify his father so that he will allow him to continue with sports even in the face of uncertain academic progress. He was also trying to escape, at least in part, from his father's insistence that he take a tutor for his exams as soon as possible.

22. 29 March 1894, to George Ives

Dear Father,

Rec'd Uncle Lyman's telegram last evening and your letter this noon. I have finally managed to find Dr. Walker the chairman of the Baptist Ch[urch]. committee and he says that the committee have decided on a Mr. Hogson, I don't know how the name is spelled nor have I ever heard of him before, except that he was the one that offered to do it for nothing and was the one that Mr. Wheeler, the former organist criticized the most. Dr. Walker told me himself that this one knew some of the committee personally, and that may have had something to do with it. There are five on the committee and some of them weren't there at all at the trial. He said that he was very much pleased with my playing, etc. but that 3 were better than two. And from the way he said it, I didn't know but he meant that I had 2 & the other's 3. At any rate, I am satisfied that it was not just as Mr. Wheeler said, decided

17. Gayle Sherwood links this procedure for playing chants with Ives's *Nine Experimental Canticle Phrases;* Sherwood, "The Choral Works of Charles Ives: Chronology, Style, Reception" (Ph.D. diss., Yale University, 1995), 102.

by the merits. I think they will pay him something as they said that they wouldn't want an organist that would do it for nothing. It seems as if everything here was run that same way, by a "pull," and that is one of the reasons that I think it would be better for Unc. Lyman to see Prof. Stoeckel and the sooner the better, as I heard that he is going away again soon for his health, and that also, Jepson was going to Germany next fall to study, and that will probably leave the Center Church, and the asst. organist at Chapel open.

I am bound that I will not let all of these things interfere with my musical studies, in the end and if possible to take advantage of it, although it does make one feel blue, etc. I can't do so very much before examinations. The first thing I am going to get the best of is the harmony and counterpoint, which I ought to get through with out taking much time to it with Dr. Stoeckel. There is some kind of music course in college which I will look up. I think it can be taken with out any extra charge and may be substituted with other things. There are several other things I can do more at in the music line, for which I wouldn't have time for with the regular church. I think if anything the work at St. Thomas had a tendency rather to deaden that [than] to give ambition and I think that my aim ought to be now to improve in the things that I wouldn't have time to with the church work, and also to see and look out for some place in N.Y. for next year.

Haven't I enough money in the bank to pay what is necessary for my music lessons next fall?

I don't see now why things at school hadn't ought to go all right. I saw Miss Porter last evening the first chance I got, and she said that I ought to come out all right at Hopkins, that she will speak to Mr. Fox. He seemed to be all right today, and asked me how my arm was for baseball. (I think maybe that is one of the reasons he wants [me] to come back.) I don't quite see what you mean by the "appearances" it would make. It would be a means of regular outdoor exercise and won't take much time as I won't have to practice with the rest unless somebody else comes I feel as if I was needed to pitch, that is a position that there would be no danger in at all. I can tell more about [it] after season begins. Of course if you decidedly think it would hurt me very much, why I won't.

While I am [was?] writing the letter with the newspaper slip came. I won't let the N.Y. trip interfere with work but am very anxious to see what Wagner opera is. Please tell Uncle Ly. what I have said about school and Dr. Stoeckel etc., and will write him as soon as I find out anything definite from Mr. Fox. Give love to everybody.

Yours very truly,
C.E.I.

• • •

This lengthy description of a performance of Wagner's *Götterdämmerung* presents one of the earliest statements of Ives's highly individual musical aesthetics. It is particularly interesting to compare this statement with the comments on Wagner in Ives's *Essays Before a Sonata.*[18]

18. Ives, *Essays Before a Sonata,* ed. Howard Boatwright (New York: W. W. Norton, 1964), 72–73.

23. 1 April 1894, to George Ives

Dear Father,

Rec'd your letter last evening after I had returned from New York. I left here at 10:20 and reached the city at a little before one o'clock and went immediately to the theater in time to get a good seat in the family circle (top gallery) I could ~~hear~~ see quite well and could hear very plainly. I bought a libretto with both German and English words. I read the plot over thoroughly two or three times so I could understand and and [*sic*] follow the German words better. I could easily see what Wagner tried to [do]. You wouldn't notice the music or orchestra as it all seems to be a part of and go along with the action and story. I don't mean that you wouldn't notice it, because it is integral in the play but that it feels as if it was only made to help one pay attention to the action. I don't remember any particular piece or song that you would notice simply for the music itself unless it was the 'Song of the Rhine-daughter' at the beginning of the second act. There are some things though that don't seem exactly natural. For instance in one place, Siegfried is supposed to be greatly furiated at Brünhilde and she has a long song in which she is greatly excited and upbraids him, but he, instead of interrupting her, waits until the orchestra plays a long intermezzo and then begins, and there were several other places like that struck me as being rather unnatural, although there was probably some reason for it. They bring a horse on the stage, and it is supposed to be on the shore of the river but you hear his hoofs striking the timbers of the stage, which spoils all the effect. And then too the the [*sic*] using of so much horn, reed and kettle drums grows awfully tiresome towards the end. And about all I can remember of the orchestra now, is that it was all diminished chords, wholes, and trombone. Of course I don't mean to criticize but ~~there are just~~ this ~~things~~ is just as it seemed to me, but probably if I had studied it more ~~in the first~~ before, I would think differently. But any way the horse ought to have had some dirt to walk [on]. I wish I had time to study all of his operas. Everything all together is great, and you can see just what his idea was, and it seems funny that nobody thought of it before. Although it does seem that if the band beat more rhythm, or ~~melody~~ connected melody (you know what I mean) in his music, and if the action was more natural, and if the plot had more sense to it, as it is just a common fairy story, and when you think of it looks like a great deal of work over nothing, or if it was in fact in real history, or taken from some noted book, so that some educational benefit could be gotten from it. Will send program and libretto when I send wash, as I want you to read it all over and tell me what you think, and lieber Uncle Lyman.

The opera lasted until quarter past six and so when I got down to Prince Street, Mr. Crevling[19] had gone home but I was reassured very carefully by a clerk who said he would tell him I was in. Mr. Stan's store was also closed. I left at 8:01 and reached home at 10:20. Everything seems to be all right at school. Please ask Moss to get me one of those coaching hats, 6¾. Give my love to all.

Yours very truly,
C.

19. John Kirkpatrick transcribes this name as Cushing. His many transcriptions of and annotations on the letters are filed with the originals in the CIP. The John Kirkpatrick Papers contain additional material.

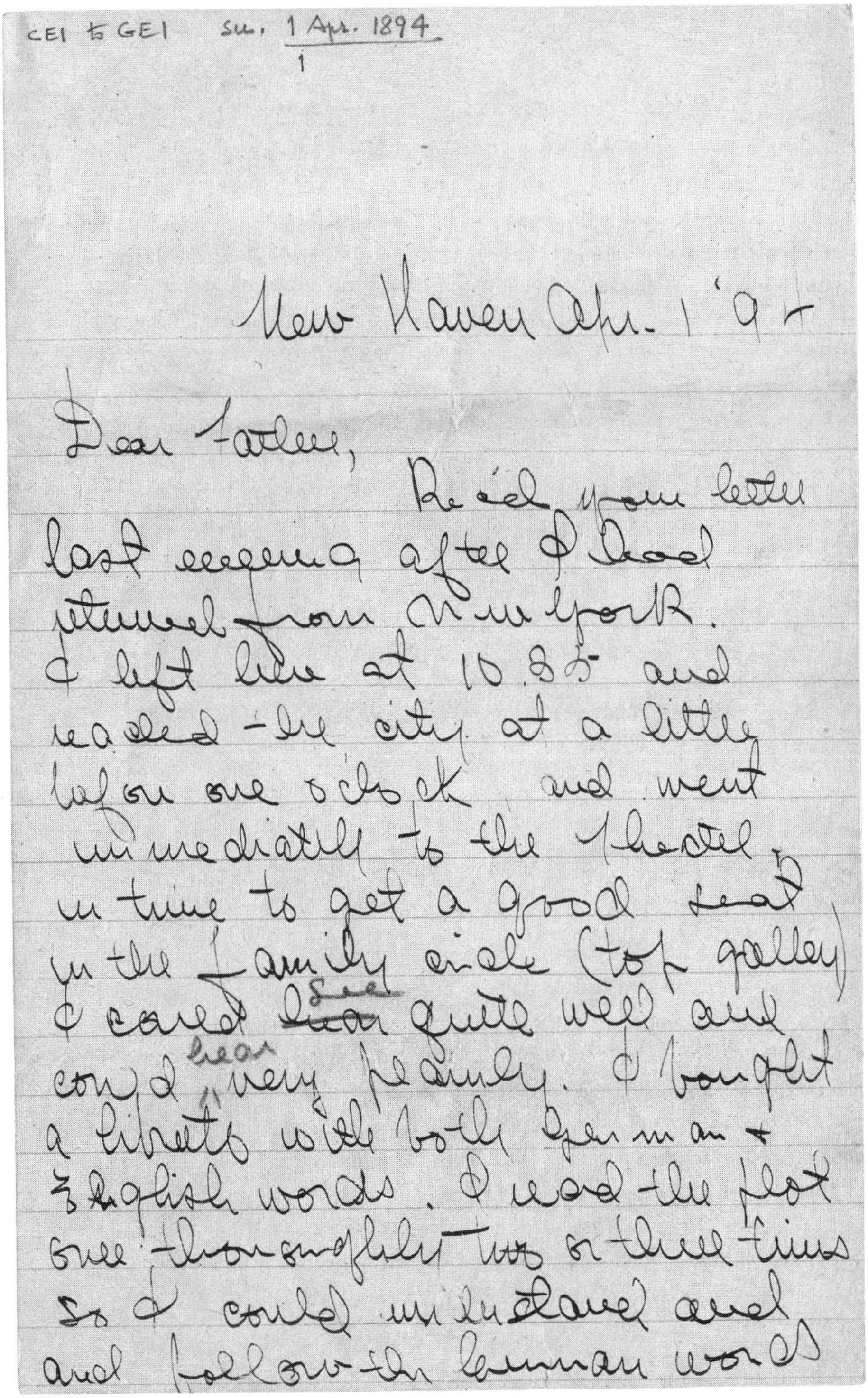

CEI to GEI Su, 1 Apr. 1894
1

New Haven Apr. 1 '94

Dear Father,
Rec'd your letter last evening after I had returned from New York. I left here at 10.35 and reached the city at a little before one o'clock and went immediately to the Theatre in time to get a good seat in the family circle (top gallery) I could ~~hear~~ see quite well and could hear very plainly. I bought a libretto with both German & English words. I read the plot over thoroughly two or three times so I could understand and and follow the German words

1 April 1894, to George Ives.

24. 12 April 1894, to George Ives

Dear Father,

I have just received your letter. Why don't you think that I don't understand your letters Maybe I don't write as if I did but I think I understand what you have advised and what I have got to do. You know after the first of May which is nearly here I can come up over Sunday. Of course if you writing won't do until then, I can come up some afternoon, and you might come down. The best I can do now is to study and exercise, with the church work. You know you said you had a way by which I could keep practice after organ is through with. I don't see how things could go better now either at church or school.

Please send hat as soon as convenient, as I described in a letter to Moss. I suppose he rec'd it although have not heard. Very bad weather here.

Yours very truly,
C

• • •

Anxious about being able to assist his parents in paying for his education as his brother, Moss, prepared to go to college as well, Ives worked conscientiously to find another job as an organist after he left St. Thomas's Church in April 1894. He was soon hired at Center Church, one of the most prestigious positions in New Haven, surely an indication of his talent as a performer,.

25. 29 April 1894, to George Ives

Dear Father,

I suppose Mother and Moss arrived from Stamford last evening, and told you about their Stamford visit etc. We finished the game in time to take the 6:20 train and reached New Haven at 7:30. We finally won 13 to 3. I expect to take the first [voice] lesson, as soon as Mr. Bonney gets settled. The service ended up in good shape today. I went to Center Church to see Jepson after service today but he had gone. If I need a tutor at all it will be in Greek, and the best time to have him would [be] right before the exam. Moss says that he is making arrangements by which he he [*sic*] expects to go to U. of P. [Pennsylvania] next fall. I wish I was doing something for my expenses. But I hope I will be again next year. It is a fine day to-day here. Archie was taken quite sick yesterday, and the doctor feared scarlet fever, but he is much better to day. Give my love to Mother and all. Please ask them to send clothes as soon as possible.

Yours very truly,
C

26. 2 May 1894, to George Ives

Dear Father,

The Letter with order rec'd this evening and one with 2 checks yesterday, and wash Monday. Well I have finally seen Mr. Jepson, and he says he will want me to play for him at Center Ch. in the mornings as soon as College opens next Fall, if one with whom he made arrangements with a long while ago can't do it and he says it is very doubtful if he can as since then he has accepted a pos. at Dwight Pl. and he is very doubtful if they will let him off for the mornings.[20] He said he hoped things would turn out so I could do it, as he didn't think so very much of the other fellow. He said he had heard of the organist at St Thomas but didn't know that I was the one, and was very glad I asked him. He didn't mention anything, but suppose he would give me ⅓ or ¼ of his salary which is $1000. I would have to be only at the Sunday morning rehearsal, and could do as I liked about Sat. evening. As he promised the committee he would be at the other rehearsals. They have a choir etc. He will let me know for sure some time this summer. I can have the organ to practice all I want.

Yours
C

27. 4 March 1895, from Charles W. Whittlesey[21]

Dear Sir:

The Music Committee of Center Church authorize me to offer you the position of organist under Dr. Griggs' directorship, for one year from May 1st 1895 at a salary of $200.00. If possible I would like to hear from you to-morrow and will then inform you how to get some of the money now due you for services. I will be in my office all day except between one and three or possibly 2:30.

Yours respectfully,
Charles W. Whittlesey

• • •

Though the experience of working for Charles Bonney left a bad taste in Ives's mouth, the ideas about a natural style of singing that he impressed on Ives during his voice lessons seem to have found an outlet in many of Ives's songs. The second letter in this group shows that these lessons were a source of conflict between father and son. Studying singing was not in itself problematic; George's concern seems to have been that all of Charles's extracurricular activities, particularly sports, took too much time away from studying for the impending Yale entrance exam. Charles responds by giving a detailed and defensive description of his daily routine.

20. This is probably Dwight Chapel at Yale.

21. The secretary of Center Church, New Haven. I include this letter here to give a sense of the scope of Ives's job at Center Church. Apparently he was employed ad hoc before March 1985.

28. 6 May 1894, to George Ives

Dear Father,

I don't see how Moss could have misunderstood my postal, as Mr. McIntire told me that he said he rec'd before starting. I said, as I remember that we would not play here anyway, probably would go out of town, and may not play at all. I waited as long as possible to find out what we would do. I am awfully sorry that he came. But Tom is going to write him to come and spend Sunday, next here. I hope he can come then. The hat is neat in looks & shape etc. but is altogether too big. I can't wear anything larger than 6 ⅞ and the smaller than that even, is better, even with a lot of paper it was too large. I wish he would try and get one same style but smaller size and bring it next week. I took first singing lesson Thurs. He didn't do much except try my voice. He said I had a good high tenor voice and also fairly low. Better than he thought I had. He told me to sing just as I speak, naturally you know. He said too I didn't have any bad faults. He says of what he knows of church com. that Dwight Pl. won't possibly let the organist off.

Yours very truly,
C

29. 8 May 1894, to George Ives

Dear Father,

Your last letter with envelope and paper just rec'd. I can't think of anything in my last letter that wouldn't do for the family to hear. Don't they know I am taking singing lessons, and if they there don't, don't you want to have them know? I don't remember writing anything about extra lessons in that letter, as I thought that you understood from what I have written before, that if I considered it necessary to have any tutors at all, it would be towards the end of the term, and I will look out and attend to that at the proper time. I use the technique every day and see more good in it than I did at first when I thought it didn't amount to much. I also exercise as you said every night and morning. I have succeeded in getting up about 6:30 every morning lately and get quite a little studying done then. I have been playing tennis for the last week or so, as I don't need to go to the field to practice with the nine except the day before the game. And don't see why ~~you insist why~~ you insist on blaming everything on ball, or at least because I didn't write a good letter last Sunday. I usually study in the evening until 9:30 or 10:00, and then go to bed. And this is the program as far as I can state it for the day. Mr. Fox has not complained to me at all for a long while, and I am sure he thinks I am doing all I can. I will try and write to Uncle Lyman soon about studies, but as much as I can say will be what we are studying, etc., and how I am getting along with them, (that is, as to what my opinion is.) but as to what Mr. Fox and the teachers think of course I can't say. Sunday after I had gotten lessons out of the way, I was working on a little song that I am trying to write for Garrison. I worked later than I expected to and then wrote that letter, I was rather tired and probably that was the reason it was so poor. I will try to have better ones in the future. I will attend to cash acct. and send next chance I get. If Moss would like to wait until May 19 (Sat.) there is a Yale-Princeton game which he might like to see. The last part of this letter is not written perhaps as well as I can, but hope otherwise it is satisfactory.

Yours very truly,
C.

30. 13 May 1894, to George Ives

Dear Father,

I took my second lesson from Mr. Bonney Thurs, he had me sing some of these Concone exercises, but of course paid most attention to the way I get the tone. He believes that singing is only an extension of talking, and makes me say a certain sentence and then sing it with the same kind of voice. I will need some money when my pants and shoes which are being fixed are done. It is also about time for another laundry bill. I will get a tutor if you think best, but I would hardly have time to do the lessons at school and his too. And I am pretty sure Mr. Fox will recommend me one. The base ball season is mainly at an end. I will send a letter to Moss by same mail.

Yours very truly,
C

• • •

Written only weeks before George Ives's fatal stroke, this letter seems to foreshadow the impending tragedy that would so change Ives's life. It also indicates some type of chronic health difficulty in Ives's mother. The letter is particularly touching when read in the context of the flurry of letters home from Charles as he excitedly prepared to begin his job as organist at Center Church and to start his studies at Yale.

31. 28 September 1894, from George Ives, Danbury, Connecticut

Dear Charles,

Was glad to rec've telegram. Want to know particulars but suppose you've been too busy to give details. As Mr. R. has gone to N.Y. I am to stay in the bank all day which will be the first day I have done so since last week Thursday. I feel awfully weak & shaky, but besides that & a cold & cough am about well I hope. Your mother and Moss each have colds. Mother has another new nurse, quite a young girl but starts off well. Rest are as usual. Send Draft for $5. as you must need that much at least by this time. Love from all,

Father

32. 30 September 1894, to George Ives (written on the back of Letter 31)

Dear Father,

Rec'd your letter with check last evening. I did rather need the check then as I had just found out that I had been admitted to the commons so early, and before I could enter I had to deposit ten dollars in the treasury as a security. As I understand it I can either let that go towards the board (which is $3.50 a week) or withdraw it again when I return the bond enclosed. Of course you will see where you are to sign, and then when you return it, I will fill it out fully in ink. We were about to move into our room in South Middle, when the Dean sent us word that they who had rented the room before Mullally[22] applied had changed their mind and as they were upper class men he had to give it to them, but he said there was a single room in the new Berkeley Hall which we could have until he got us something better although I think we shall be satisfied with that. The price is about the same but we won't have to pay for light, but steam heat is $12. a year, we also have the use of bathroom. We are not quite sure of this as it depends on whether the fellow who rented it, is coming back, but Prof. Wright thinks that he isn't and will let us know for sure by Tues. or Wed. If we take this room the only thing I will need will be a small folding bed and a few rugs and chairs. It has hard wood floor. Don't send trunk or anything until I send word.

Played at Cen[ter]. Ch[urch]. first time this morning, seemed to go very well. I am going to see Mr. Bonney to morrow and also get my music from St. Thomas' to Center. Began to eat at commons to day. I happened to get at same tables with Ned Tweedy. Rec'd Moss' papers. To read it, it would appear that I didn't often pass a successful examination (which is about right I guess) Ned is trying for foot ball team. Some of the fellows want to have me try, but of course have given up hopes of that. They some times get fellows together later in the season and play scrub games, just for the fun of it, Sat. afternoons, would like to play then if I get to it, and wish you send my football things, and also send heavy flannels, stockings shoes, etc. as I want to sell stockings and pants to some of the H.G.S. team. Haven't moved things yet from Macintires, will write when I know just where we will be.

• • •

College life seems to have boosted Ives's already frenetic level of activity, and his almost impressionistic letters reflect his desire to try to experience everything at once. This letter particularly reveals some of the musical opportunities Ives had as he entered Yale. The University Chamber Concerts were a yearly subscription series that featured performances by the nationally renowned Kneisel and Beethoven String Quartets. The Kneisel Quartet played a concert on the evening this letter was written, with the following program: Haydn's op. 76, no. 4, in B-flat, Jean-Marie Leclair's Sarabande and Tambourine, and Dvořák's op. 34 in D minor.[23] Later in the season the series presented quartets and other chamber music by

22. Ives's roommate, Mandeville Mullally.

23. *Yale Daily News*, 24 October 1894.

Beethoven, Haydn, Mendelssohn, Cherubini, Rimsky-Korsakov, and Brahms.[24] The *Yale Daily News* reported the program of the organ recital by Horatio Parker that Ives mentioned. It included works by Joseph Rheinberger, Alessandro Stradella, Wagner, Alexandre Guilmant, Théodore Dubois, Bach, and Parker himself.[25]

33. 24 October 1894, to George Ives

Dear Father,

Yours rec'd last evening. The man that makes them ought to know best about the cords The dis. between the window frames for pole or rod is 3 ft. 4½ in. I should think some colored stuff would [be] better than white, something like that in the music room. I have bought a ticket of Mr Hume[26] for the series of chamber concerts, this winter, Kneisel, Beethoven quartets etc. $2.50. Hope to hear the symphony concert Tues. When you get time please send Garrison some more lessons, if only a little. We can go over them together. Also please send the man[uscript]. of the march I was fixing just before I left. When you send the cushons, curtains, etc., please send my black hat, also. Have Thatcher Hoyt block it as he did Moss'. Have seen a good deal of Ned, Ebbie, and Bert Van, who also come over to the room quite often. I began playing football a little the other day I go out regularly, from 2–3 on Tues, Thu, & Fri, every week. The other days they have games. Its pretty good exercise as they make us run in and out to the field, which is little over a mile. There is not much fun in it, as I thought at first there would be, especially as I don't play in the games, but think I will keep it up for a while as I feel better for it. They take us in the gym. and give us a rub down after it. Mr. Parker gives an organ recital this evening in Battel [Chapel]. I have made arrangements with the blower for every day except Tues. and Fri., as I have recitations at that time. I send some old copies of the "Lit."[27] which Mullally's brother was editor, and which Mandeville will probably be on before he gets through his college course. If Moss wants to try to see what he can do, he might write something and hand it in under my name, which is all right. If he writes anything, it must be some, good sensible piece. He must know thoroughly what he is writing about, not only to have it sound good, but it must mean something, and above all it must be original but not in an egotistic way. Some little short stories are good, too. There is no harm in trying, as if it ~~don't~~ isn't published, they will return it with suggestions etc. The "Lit" is the best and largest paper in college, and to get on it is even a bigger thing than to make the football team (at least some consider it so).

Yours Very Truly,
C. E. Ives

24. *Yale Daily News*, 3 November 1894; 12 December 1894; 26 January 1895; 12 February 1895; 27 February 1895; 24 April 1895.

25. *Yale Daily News*, 25 October 1894.

26. Hume was Ives's tutor for the Yale entrance exams.

27. *Yale Literary Magazine*.

• • •

Almost as a balancing gesture against the dark premonitions of George Ives's letter, above, the following letter hints at a brighter future, as Ives mentions for the first time seeing the man who would one day be his father-in-law.

34. 29 October 1894, to George Ives

Dear Father,

I started a letter Sunday evening to you but left it before I had finished, to go over to Dwight Hall as Mullally wanted to have me go with him to hear the Rev. Mr. Twichell of Hartford. When I got back I couldn't seem to find it, and so thought I would [wait] until to day, and start a new one, although I found the other one between the leaves of a book where I had put it. We had an exam this afternoon so I had to wait until this evening before I wrote. Will try to get them off on Sunday after this. Rec'd Moss' letter Sat. We would both be glad to have Grandmother send us the "Out book" and will read it. There is a fellow who sits at my table at the commons, he asked me the other day, if I knew a Mr. Henry Hoyt in D[anbury,] that he was in his father's class '33 and had heard his father speak of him. His name is Bingham of Honolulu Sandwich Islands. I wore the overcoat Sunday, the sleeves are a little long, and maybe it is very little too short, otherwise it seems alright will keep until the other comes. Mullally has gotten a window seat from Mr. Crampton. It will be as for both of us, so he will let him have at wholesale price, let Unc. Joe send the bill to me and he will pay me. Mr. Butler's new address is #3–3–7 I copied the other one out of the directory. I wish the things could be sent as soon as possible. I see Nowell [Howard?] Starr quite often he was over here the other evening. I expect to write Grandmother and Uncle Joe soon, with love to all

Yours very truly,
C. E. Ives

Oct. 29

Please send march, music sheet paper & that book of B. Conwalls that Dr. Stoeckel used, Harmony.

• • •

George Ives's death on 8 November 1894 marked a stark turning point in his son's life. After this date there are few surviving letters to and from Charles at school. Letters like this one to his mother indicate that at least outwardly Ives continued much as before and that his musical ambition was still strong. The letter also mentions John Griggs, the choirmaster at Center Church, who became an important friend and musical influence.

35. 20 January 1895, to Mollie Ives

Dear Mother,

I rec'd your's and Aunt Amelia's letters. I finally found the landlady in and paid her $10.00. I told her about the mistake in the bill etc. and said she [would] make out another one and have it ready next week. The chairs haven't arrived yet, were they coming by express or freight, we suppose they would come by freight so we had a car man look out for them. I will say before I forget it that Garrison was much pleased with his hat, he says it fits him better than any hat he ever had. The commons bill was 15 weeks instead of 12. It began Oct. 13 Thur. which week I had to pay for as I went in before the 22nd. Mullally also owes about $6.00 as he went in on a guest ticket with me before he was admitted as a regular member. I spoke a little while ago about taking a few lessons this winter with Dudley Buck as I haven't had any lessons at all for quite a while. I think it almost necessary that I should and if I don't get any other good from it, just being a pupil of Buck's would be very helpful. I think I can go about every 3 wks until about March or April. I think he charges $4. a lesson. Mr. Griggs who advised me to do it has made arrangements for next Thurs. at 5 o'c. I can leave here about 1.30 and get back about 8.30 or 9 o'c. I have more time than I did, and no recitations Thurs afternoon. So I will go down any way next Thurs. unless I hear to the contrary from you.

Please ask Moss to go up to Izzie Raymond's and ask her for the copy of "Rock of Ages" which I wrote some time ago, and also ask Uncle Ly. for a copy of his song, "The Ocean and the heavens are arrayed in blue etc." I didn't send laundry as I had so few to send. Will send it next week. I enclose receipt from washing. With love to Grandmother and all

Yours Very Truly,
Chas

• • •

Ives graduated from Yale in 1898 but continued his association with many classmates and alumni. He lived with a number of recent Yale graduates in "Poverty Flat," a series of shared apartments in New York City, until his marriage. Letters from this time are very few. One scrawled draft, written to his future brother-in-law David Twichell in 1903, survives to give a sense of the rowdiness of Ives and his friends in the years just after school. The letter describes two trips. The first one was to Keene Valley, New York, with a Twichell family friend and Yale compatriot, Delano Wood, over Labor Day. The second was a trip to Pine Mountain, near Danbury.[28] Here also is a brief description of life in Poverty Flat.

28. See Mark Tucker, "Of Men and Mountains: Ives in the Adirondacks," in *Charles Ives and His World*, ed. J. Peter Burkholder (Princeton: Princeton University Press, 1996), 170–71.

36. September or October 1903, to David Twichell, New York

Dear Dave,

Why don't you occasionally write damn you anyway I hear good reports from time to time and hence the pyrimids.[29] Willis Wood spent a day with us recently & tells us you're in good form and an able foreman in the "wheez factory."[30] Del Wood took me to Keene Valley over Labor Day. We didn't seize any panthers, but had an agreeable time though am afraid I was a disturbing element being full of malaria . . . quinine and whisky at the time. YES. The flat is filled with 2 new dogs. Harry Farmer of Bart's class and Walter McCormack, a cousin of Vance.

Winter and Malony held a convention last evening. W insists upon more authority, that Malony's position is of the character of a secretaryship and not the vaunted idea in any sense of imperial treasurer or controller; that the bills be paid by him because when he don't want to, when he won't, then for just this reason, it can't be, because and why not etc. etc. A stenographer on the scene would have furnished Weber & Fields a 3rd act.

Bill takes it so placidly that my crys are most for Keyes, but for no real reason otherwise. Saw Morris Ely a while ago and says Joe is at present a good 2nd in the quarterback business I hope he keeps along through this season and doesn't get laid up.

We finally succeeded in placing that shanty on the mountain in Ridgefield, but did it unbeknownst to Aunt Amelia fearing adverse suggestions. It makes a good young camp. Geo Lewis went up with me last month taking Sat. afternoon off. What! We spent the night on the mountain. Having no curtains on the window, it took 2 hours of kind words to get the old scrinch to disrobe. He being afraid that some farmer's wives in the next house (about 3 miles down in the valley) would peek at him. He walked all day long in a circle among the woods and discovered an egg—that Benedict Arnold laid in the battle of Ridgefield. Remember me to Deac.[31] Is he with you and answer this soon.

Sincerely,
Chas E. Ives

29. This is the first of several references to the mysterious "pyramids" in the correspondence. See also Letter 369.
30. Twichell worked as a physician in a tuberculosis sanatorium at Saranac Lake, New York.
31. David and Harmony Twichell's older brother, Edward.

• 2 •

COURTSHIP AND MARRIAGE (1907–1908)

Ives met Harmony Twichell through her brother David, his classmate and friend at Yale. Although they attended the Junior Promenade together in 1896, the pair did not begin a serious courtship until the late summer of 1905, when Ives spent several weeks with the Twichells at Saranac Lake in the Adirondack Mountains of New York State. Harmony and her brother, a nurse and doctor respectively, worked in the tuberculosis sanitarium at the lake, and it was David, perhaps concerned about Charlie's health, who invited his old school friend up to take a break from his punishing routine of daily insurance work and nocturnal composition. The path that led to marriage in June 1908 was long, and the couple's pace along it was slow. Both were reluctant first to hope and then to admit that love was growing between them. On 22 October 1907 the pair took a walk through the woods near Farmington, Connecticut, and spoke of their love for the first time. Having finally declared their feelings to one another, they expressed their pent-up emotions in a flurry of letters, often two a day, filling in the time between their infrequent visits.

More of Harmony's letters to Charlie now survive: he later destroyed some of those he wrote to her. The remaining letters eloquently express the love and devotion that saw the pair through the trials they faced in their long and eventful married life. Ives likely proposed marriage that day near Farmington, although it was some time before they made the engagement public. As a prelude, a letter from the summer of 1907 shows the tone of the correspondence before the walk in the woods, which Ives called "the greatest event in the history of this Country."

37. July 1907, from Harmony Twichell, Henry Street, New York

Dear Charlie—

Thank you ever so much for the tickets. It happens that I am going up there any way tonight so I shan't have the pleasure of using your ticket but I think I will venture to give it to my Uncle who I am almost sure will want to go.

I'm sorry not to hear the Parsifal music with you again—but I've heard and seen very many nice things to remember with you.

I haven't minded the heat much today but it seems to make my handwriting even worse than usual—I hope you are having a successful trip to Stamford—

As ever sincerely Thanking you again—
Harmony Twichell

38. 25 October 1907, from Harmony Twichell, Hartford, Connecticut[1]

Friday Morning

just before we went down town

Dear—

I never wrote a love letter & I don't know how. If I don't write this today you won't get mail until Monday and I can't wait that long to have you see in my writing what you've seen these perfect days in my face—that I love you & love you & love you and no numbers of times of saying it can ever tell it. But believe it and that I am yours always & utterly—Every bit of me—

Harmony

• • •

Four days after their probable engagement, Harmony wrote a series of letters that she mailed together in the same envelope on 27 October. Consumed with thoughts of Charlie, she tried to express the intensity of her feelings through sheer volume of words.

39. 26–27 October 1907, from Harmony Twichell (postmarked 27 October)

Saturday Evening [26 October]

Only best beloved—

My dearest anything—Everything—I haven't any thoughts except that I love you and I've been thinking of all the "grandes passiones" in history and I know neither Francesca nor Beatrice nor anyone was ever more possessed than I am. I'm such a surprise to myself—and it's all You. My, what a time we've had and it's only the beginning. I went and did my errands after you left & made only one mistake so Providence was looking after me I think and then I went home & heard Dad & Mother talk about Andersonville.[2] Joe and I got all choked up hearing what they'd heard—no wonder Mother called them "splendid old heroes"—what they stood is beyond belief—almost. One funny thing Dad told me—It seems that several designs for the statue to be erected were sent in, among them one by Daniel French of a beautiful allegorical female figure and they were circulated among a good many of the old soldiers as Col. Cheney wanted to get their views of the subject—They didn't care for that one at all for they said "Why, there wasn't a single woman near the prison!" So it was rejected.

I wish it was last night and I had you—otherwise I am looking forward and it looks

1. All of Harmony Twichell's letters were mailed from Hartford, Connecticut, unless otherwise indicated.

2. Andersonville, Georgia, was the sight of the largest Confederate prison for Union soldiers during the Civil War. As many as thirteen thousand inmates died there owing to overcrowding, lack of food, exposure, and poor sanitation.

mighty good to me. Do you know how I love you and how perfectly I love you and how perfectly adorable you are altogether to me? I can never tell you how I feel when I kiss you—you are man and child and my best Beloved all together—

And now I am going to bed and I hope you are getting there early too for we have sat up very late. I hope awfully that you haven't found the business world upsetting—Good night and God bless you—Just as much as if vouchsafed I will be blessed too—yours always Harmony

40. 27 October 1907, Sunday morning (continued on same paper as Letter 39)

Annie found your pin in the china closet. I'll bring it to you.

Sue is going down town to church so Mother and I will be all alone in our seat this morning. I'm thinking how beautiful it's going to be to go and sit there and think of you—I have done it for months past and I should have gone on doing it all my life just the same without the happenings of the past blessed week but it's different & very difficult—no sweeter or dearer but more full of promise. I'm going to write Julie as soon as I finish this—She's got to have me there over next Sunday—I'll get a letter from you tomorrow morning I hope—I want it excruciatingly—I love you & love you & love you.

Harmony

Tell me just how you are—and your poor sore heels.[3]

• • •

The following letter reflects several dimensions of the growing relationship and Harmony's understanding of Ives's personality. The poem she mentions became Ives's song "Autumn." Most interesting is Harmony's touching description of her imagined communication with George Ives, whom she knew only from Charlie's descriptions. Thirteen years after his death, George remained a vital presence in his son's life, one that influenced even the relationship between him and his fiancée.

41. 27 October 1907, Sunday afternoon, from Harmony Twichell

Dear—

I wrote these lines down just as they came.[4] Of course, now I have the idea in any shape I can put it in to some other and it would be better rhymed or more rhythmical, wouldn't it? Do you think it seems like last Tuesday at all—from the cliff?

3. Jan Swafford has interpreted this postscript as a possible early indication of Ives's diabetes, which often leads to foot disease; Swafford, *Charles Ives*, 286.

4. Kirkpatrick speculates that Harmony included the poem that Ives set as "Autumn" with her letters of 27–28 October. It is on the same paper as the letter of Monday evening, 28 October, and may be what Harmony refers to here.

I found these Kodaks which may amuse you—haven't you any of yourself? Don't think you have to keep them. You will recognize Sarah Holter.

I've had a wonderful day only my feelings and thoughts are so much too much for my heart and brain that I don't know what I'm going to do. What do you think? In church I thought all of a sudden of your Father—so intensely that the tears came into my eyes and I thought how much I love him—actually as if I'd known him—I almost felt him and I am sure he knows all about this and how dearly I love you and that your welfare is my happiness—And I thought of other things I can't write about—I'll tell you my best beloved when I see you.

• • •

His relationship with Harmony was a source of stability for Ives during a difficult and pivotal time in his business life. In 1907 he was building his own life insurance agency, established the previous year with his new partner, Julian Myrick, as the industry as a whole sought to combat allegations of widespread nepotism and corruption made by the Armstrong Commission (1905–6).[5] Although Ives was not directly implicated by the commission, the ripples stirred by its investigation were undoubtedly a source of stress. The immediate cause of Harmony's comments about difficulties in business in the letter below was likely the failure of the Knickerbocker Trust Company, which had triggered a run on several New York banks and caused a significant drop in stock prices.[6]

42. 28 October 1907, Monday, from Harmony Twichell

I just got your letter—I'm sorry for all this business excitement but I'm not going to worry—only as you should, at least. It will surely quiet down soon. Harry Whaples told me about Bart yesterday—It's certainly too bad but might be far worse—Take care of yourself please—It's pouring today and I expect to spend a very quiet & peaceful day reading & thinking & making melody in my heart & praying things will go well with you. I must write you often of course if you write me very often the family will get on but I want to hear so much. I send you this extract from May's letter She can't have me at Litchfield—I think I'm pretty sure to get to Julie's Friday.

—Harmony

• • •

Music was an important subject of discussion between Harmony and Charlie; in a sense it was his contribution to their mutual desire to improve each other through their relationship.

5. Feder, *My Father's Song,* 179–80; Michael Broyles, "Charles Ives and the American Democratic Tradition," in Burkholder, *Charles Ives and His World,* 135–40.

6. The *New York Times* covered the story extensively as front-page news starting on 23 October 1907. See "Banking Troubles Hit Stocks Hard," p. 4, and "Knickerbocker Will Not Open," p. 1.

Harmony, in return, stimulated Ives's interest in literature and perhaps inspired the series of literature-themed compositions represented most famously by the *Concord* Sonata. This letter also alludes to Harmony's continued concern for Ives's health.

43. 28 October 1907, from Harmony Twichell

Monday evening—

Darling—

I am glad to see the Evening paper says the situation in NY continues to improve—Did it matter much that you weren't there last week?—I hope it didn't but our being together then was the most important thing in the world—this is Monday & a week ago Mr. Kuese [name barely legible] came and sang & we'd been driving & some of us sitting up the night before all night & we were very sleepy—and once I put my hand out and touched yours—do you remember? And felt as if I'd been a little familiar. And tomorrow is Tuesday "my fairest day."

If I come down Friday I think I will come on the train that gets to N.Y. at 9:30. If you can't come to it I'll telephone you as soon as I get in & we can meet somewhere later—Charlie, I loved your letter—every excellent word—Everything you will tell me interests me. Sue got tickets for Schumann-Heinke Wednesday night.[7] I shall be disappointed if she doesn't sing some of the songs you have sent me & so delighted if she does. I got you a book down town this morning—or ordered it. It is sort of diverting I think. Don't bother to send the "Elia"—you can give them to me when I come down.

I miss you all the time & feel how rich I was when I had you last week—to hear your voice & put out my hand & feel you—never mind. I have your love and that is everything after all—I was quite wrong when I said that it was a year ago that I knew I loved you It's been all the time just the same but I never said it right out to myself until a year ago & gloried & rejoiced in it—I believe it's really been since way long before the creation don't you? I think I've got that cold gone you were so anxious for me to have and I hope you feel happy about it.

Are you feeling better all the time & are you eating well? Tell me. I'm feeling so well myself I don't know what to do and I find myself laughing and conversing with everyone—people in shops & all—quite uproariously—I am afraid to go & see Aunt Sally [illegible word] again. Well, best beloved, I think of you & love you always & every inch of me—good & bad and all—I am thinking that as long as I had to love you how fortunate it is that you turned out so perfect a person. I hope things are going well with you—Good night & God keep you.

Harmony

7. Ernestine Schumann-Heink (1861–1936) was an alto who was best known as an interpreter of Wagnerian roles in Hamburg and London and later with the Metropolitan Opera. She was also renowned for her interpretations of art songs.

44. 29 October 1907, from Harmony Twichell (in the same envelope as Letter 43)

Dearest—

God bless us both—I just got a letter from Julie saying "come of course" so I'll be down surely. She also said she might very probably come up Thursday & go down with me in which case, we'd go on a later train—I'll have to let you know about that when I can. I'm glad things are looking a little better in N.Y. & am very glad, after your letter this morning that you were here during the worst instead of there, as you couldn't have done anything really—I suppose what you say about the contagiousness of the panic germ is very true—

You don't feel entirely well, do you? That's the only thing that worries me at all—I am so glad I'm going to see you soon.

Yours ever lovingly,
Harmony

• • •

Harmony's unbridled joy quickly bred impatience for the day when the two could be together. She touchingly tried to allay Ives's concerns, unsurprising in view of his uncertain business prospects, that he might not be able to support her adequately after their marriage. Here one senses the loneliness that Harmony felt in his absence, and one begins to understand the importance of the spiritual context in which she placed the relationship.

45. 7 November 1907, from Harmony Twichell

You darling & best beloved person in the world—I'm so glad to have a letter from you—My others are in my trunk & that hasn't come yet. I was utterly lonesome without even them. I'm glad I had the picture which I assure you lay very near my heart all night long.

Charlie dearest, I don't want you ever to do anything in regard to me that your best judgement doesn't recommend but I truly think it is best for us to be married as soon as we can—it's really a hardship for me to be away from you—I want to do the big things for you & all the little everyday things too and it isn't as if I hadn't always lived very simply—I shouldn't feel deprived of things I never wanted to have—I wouldn't mind feeling deprived but it just happens I couldn't for my wants are few & my tastes not fancy—If we were ten years younger it would be different too. When you can "get a line" on things we will talk it all over. But I really feel as if it were getting to be a duty to each other, as well as the most heavenly pleasure to be together. I'm not myself without you—I go lame.

When I got home last night I wished more acutely—what I'm always wishing subconsciously & acutely—that you were with me—The house was so quiet and peaceful & all the sort of thing that is worrying Howard and Bart[8] so far away & so much less

8. Harmony's brother Burton Parker Twichell.

important than higher & better things that it would have rested you as it did me—I do so hope we can make a home that will remind people who come to it of the same sort of things—I think we can for I truly believe the highest and best things are the most important & you do—that is why I can love you in the absolutely beautiful & sacred way I do—My best beloved my trip yesterday wouldn't have been bad if I hadn't been leaving you—

How I hated to and I'm glad you kissed me. I read the Schurz articles—they are interesting. Dad grabbed it as soon as he saw it and said it was just what he wanted for his evening reading—Morrie [name barely legible] had just come when I got here—we are going to make a grand effort to get Bart up here for Sunday. If he doesn't come we will all be furious at him. The sweater has just come—It was a shame to let it get so motheaten—I think I can get them out & darn the holes & then it will be a very useful garment.

Be sure & write me every day, even if it's only a line to say you are alright. My dearest I love you in every way as hard as my heart can—and it loves so hard it <u>aches</u> and even then doesn't do it <u>all</u> somehow or other

Good bye blessed one
Harmony

46. 8 November 1907 P.M., from Harmony Twichell

Dearest—

You must think I am very impractical to say the least to have written you as I have since I came from New York. What I really mean tho', is this—that I don't think we have to wait to have a whole house and a servant etc. to get married. I don't mean to be foolish about it but I am impatient to be with you—you dear.

I've been for a long walk and I am so tired I don't know what to do. I count the days until I am to see you again—best beloved. A week ago we were having dinner together weren't we?—and a week ahead I shall be looking forward to seeing you "tomorrow." I hope you are going to get up to Danbury tomorrow and that you will have a good rest & a pleasant time. You are in my heart & thoughts always.

Ever lovingly,
Harmony

• • •

A group of letters from November 1907 indicates that at the height of the correspondence, Charles was just as frequent a writer as Harmony and suggests that the number of letters from him to her that now are lost must have been significant. These letters highlight the way that Harmony almost immediately became a source of strength and healing for Ives.

47. 22 November 1907, to Harmony Twichell, New York[9]

Darling little old Harmony,

Another dark day outside but very bright inside—and that's all on account of Harmony—the only cause and reason for me now in anything and everything. Your letters are beautiful and have such a wonderful effect—so lasting and so strong. I wonder if it would be too much to ask you to divide your letters (because I don't like to ask you write two letters every day I know how much you have to do before you come to N.Y.)—but if you would just send me a line so I could have one to help me start the day then know all day that I'll find one waiting for me when I come home, It gives me courage and more ability all day long. Letters are weak substitutes for you—best beloved—but they're absolutely essential for me now. Could you do that until I see you? Just a line with your name would do—and a letter something else.

I'm sorry your aunts etc. annoy you. If it would be easier for you, just tell them. Tell any one you think best to if it will make it any less of a strain on you. I know it's much harder for you being home than it is for me anything that you want to do about anything will be what I want too. I can't tell you why it is that way but it is. Aunt Amelia enjoyed you so much I can tell by the way she acted. I'm sorry you didn't find her in—what right had she to be out in the rain? William James Cockle [name almost illegible] is sitting here waiting for me to take him out and buy him a cigar although it's not 7 o'c will take this up to the flat & finish this evening.

Home—such as it is—and find your letter here!—Harmony—blessed girl—how did you know I had to hear from you tonight, to make things endurable? When I started this letter and told you the day was dark I didn't mean that business wasn't as good as could be expected or that anything bad had happened—only meant that little annoying things had happened, as they always do and always will—business good or bad—lack of activity is the principal thing I guess that makes it hard. Our business I really think is on a sound basis, and is not suffering any more and not as much as most firms are. The hardest thing during the whole day is to feel that I haven't you—at hand—to get your encouragement in the morning and your sympathy at night. I wonder if that is selfish—it seems as though I were wanting you for something you could give me. Well—Harmony—I guess it's all one and the same thing By "twin lakes" laps one soul—and every bit of happiness and help I receive from you must be reflected back to you—That's one of the wonderful things about our love—we always understand each other and always will.

This is Nov. 22 a month after Oct 22 and the greatest event in the history of this Country though the populace doesn't know it—poor souls! Our wedding day can't be any greater than that—as we really gave all that was best to each other then—next time we are in Hartford let's try to go out to that wood road again and we must at least once every year. I'm thankful and grateful to God and everything that helped to make it possible for your dear mother and father to feel as they do about it all. I'd rather give up anything else in the world—except you—than to ever have them disappointed in me. Good night—God bless & keep you. I'll have to stop writing now or you may not get this in the first mail tomorrow.

9. All of Ives's letters to Harmony were mailed from New York City unless otherwise noted.

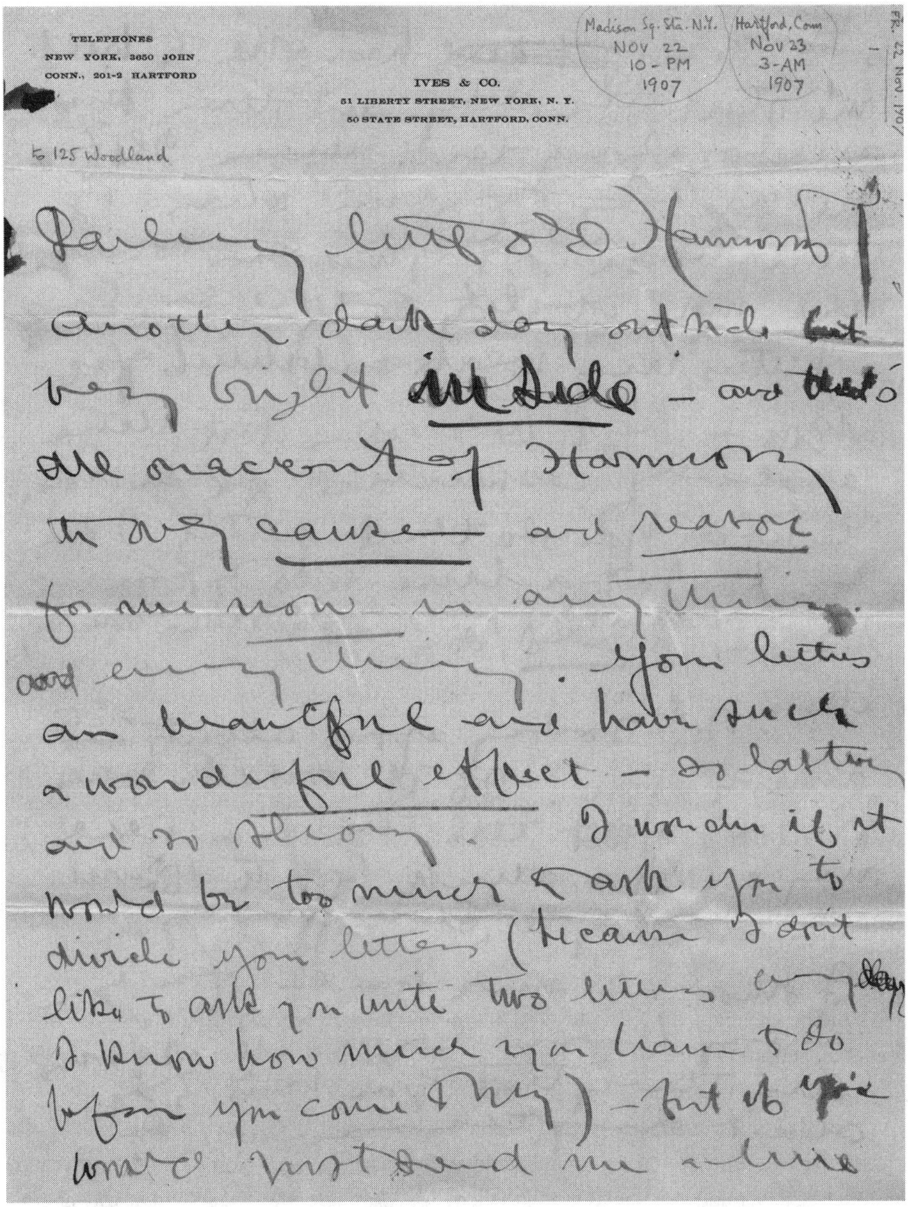
TELEPHONES
NEW YORK, 3050 JOHN
CONN., 201-2 HARTFORD

IVES & CO.
51 LIBERTY STREET, NEW YORK, N. Y.
50 STATE STREET, HARTFORD, CONN.

Madison Sq. Sta. N.Y. NOV 22 10-PM 1907
Hartford, Conn NOV 23 3-AM 1907

FR. 22 Nov. 1907

to 125 Woodland

Darling little Old Harmony

Another dark day out side but very bright in side — and that's all on account of Harmony the very cause and reason for me now in anything and everything. Your letters are beautiful and have such a wonderful effect — so lasting and so strong. I wonder if it would be too much to ask you to divide your letters (because I don't like to ask you write two letters every day I know how much you have to do before you come to N.Y.) — but if you would just send me a line

22 November 1907, to Harmony Twichell.

Did you get our book that we may put down all the perfect days?[10] Please start it Oct 22 and bring it to New York and will keep it together. God bless you, my dearest dearest and very best beloved,

Chas

10. The diary of important events that Charles and Harmony kept is now one of the primary sources of information on their life together (CIP, 45/7).

• • •

A month after they made their feelings know to each other, the couple began to tell close family of their plans, which were a surprise to no one. Harmony was also busy with preparations for moving to New York to work again as a nurse in the Henry Street Settlement, a community that provided housing, education, and health services to the poor on the Lower East Side of Manhattan.

48. 24 November 1907, to Harmony Twichell

Darling Girl,

I started to write you again last evening but it seemed so inadequate that I felt like starting over again this afternoon. I slept all this morning, we all did, it was very dark and raining and your special delivery came. It rather frightened me first—I thought perhaps they had sent for you from Henry st. and I had missed meeting you or something like that. I didn't realize that a special delivery stamp would insure a Sunday delivery or would have finished and sent the letter last evening that way. It's so kind and thoughtful of you to write me so that both ends of the day are easier and brighter for me. I'm going to try to write you in the morning as much as I can this week so you can get a letter at the end of the day as I do. But it's hard for me to write at the office there—as you can imagine—there's always somebody around and sometimes several and I don't know whether it's best for me to try to. Tues. noon—I['m] going to close my door and write no matter what happens—Aunt Sally—dear old soul—Thank her for me if you can. I wonder if she realizes what she gives us to be so interested and kind. We have a great deal to be thankful for—dearest—let's always try to let our friends know it and do what we can to deserve it. You do always and that makes me want to—and try to.

Bart has come in, and though it is raining wants me to take a walk Good bye will write later.

Sunday evening—Next Sunday at this time, I'll be with you—at least I hope you'll have the afternoon and evening free. If you can't we'll try to see each other at least for a few minutes during the day—and be thankful for that.

I heard from Aunt Amelia yesterday. She reached home safely and feeling well. She writes that she enjoyed you very much and hopes our friendship?—! poor soul—will bring as much real happiness to you as it will to all of us—I'm very glad she feels that way about it for your sake—If she felt differently it would of course make me feel sorry for her, because she was so incapable of appreciating you. I never heard her praise any girl before without handing out some kind of a—well—something that could be considered a little like a "knock" at the same time. She says that whenever the time seems best to us she will be so glad [to] welcome you to our Danbury home. Do write her. It will make her glad and happy.

We will take Aunt Dora across the city and do all we can for her—would she like to take dinner with us? Write to Dave and Bart, and let me know when you do so I can drop them a line too. How about Deac? I wish I could see him and tell him—next to Dave I think Deac was the first friend I had in your family, God bless him.

Let's start our book away back on that Sunday in July write whatever you can remember of everything from then on and bring the book to N.Y. and I'll try to fill in with whatever I can remember that you don't happen to.

I wrote your father yesterday—not much of a letter—just talked with him. I felt rather ashamed of the letter—as I express myself so poorly, but hope he will understand and not judge me by the words I use. I felt quite at home in writing him and didn't say anything in particular. There's only one thing to say any way—the whole and all of it is just based on one thing—truth. I hope he will read between the lines. I wrote not because I think it necessary but only because I wanted to. Please remember me to your mother—she knows and understands all—Thank God for that—Good night and God bless you. I love and love and love you.

Chas

49. 25 November 1907, to Harmony Twichell

How is your sore throat? Answer immediately!

Dearest,

Your Sunday letter which came to hand this morning was almost wonderful—it seemed to put me in the "right mood" to go through the day. You're always doing so much for me—I feel ashamed when I realize how little I deserve it. Harmony—You are always absolutely loyal and loving and gentle and always have understood me, from the beginning. I always felt that intuitively as you always seemed to understand. That was one of he most wonderful things about it all.

I always felt you did and it always seemed remarkable but very natural at the same time. Yes, dear little fellow, we must always be careful about our spiritual side. That is all a great part of our love—the foundation almost, a greater part than perhaps you know—Sundays are a necessity—at the same time they will be days that we can always be together every minute through the day.

Next Saturday and from then on I'll start to live again of course you'll let me know the train you'll take as soon as you decide, so there won't be any possible chance of my getting to the wrong train—

Leave as early as possible. Do you want me to do anything about your trunk or is there any thing in any way I can do for you?

I went over to the shop and took lunch with Bart in Williamsburg this noon. He had a good lot of orders which made him cheerful. We'll have to go over there again—it's just about a year ago, you went over there with me. It rained considerably and I took you back to the Holland House and bid you good bye, for sometime and felt very very badly, and felt as if I'd lost and left behind all that meant any thing real to me. I came back today by the ferry and saw How's clock—which made me think of those days last summer when I felt so much but couldn't tell you so as I can now. I love you, and know I have a real right to say so, and ought to. It's the only thing I want to say—it's the only thing I feel and everything else is a part of that. God bless you Harmony—darling—Next week this time I'll have you here.

Charles and Harmony at Elk Lake, New York, ca. 1909.

Please remember me to your mother often, very often and tell her and your father, too, what I feel but can't express.

God bless them both,
Chas

50. 26 November 1907, to Harmony Twichell

Tues noon! 12:15

Dearest, Dearest Girl!

Have just hung up the receiver and after hearing your voice without being able to be with you—I feel all wrong again. It was so kind and considerate of you to call me I didn't intend to give you that burden. I had to telephone this morning as I couldn't go through the day not knowing how you were. I rec'd two letters this morning—both of them beautiful and wonderful helps to me. Don't worry because the mail-man works on the wrong system, but I want this to reach you tonight.

With all my heart and love and all
Chas

This is not a letter, will write one later this afternoon.

• • •

In late November Harmony became ill and had to remain in bed at her parents' home in Hartford, Connecticut, for several weeks. This illness, to which Ives reacted in his letters of 25 and 26 November, is never identified in the correspondence. It struck Harmony's mother even more severely at about the same time and made it impossible for Harmony to keep her job at Henry Street, a position that would have allowed her to see Charlie regularly. This enforced absence, along with the fairly serious health threat, intensified her longing for him and deepened her religious understanding of their love as a force that would benefit everyone they knew.

51. 6 December 1907, A.M., from Harmony Twichell, Hartford, Connecticut

Darling—I feel so strongly what you say about our love being & bringing happiness into other lives besides our own—I know the joy & beauty of it can be communicated to others and that is what I long to do with it—to give out of my abundance that the world may be a little happier & better & I know I can be more to people than I ever dreamed I could—I haven't any feeling of wanting to shut this divine thing up into my own heart & life—I want every least person I come in contact with to feel its warmth & sweetness & I think they must—with no effort on my part. That is one of the blessed things about it. And my darling, all this because God has given me you to love.

The Dr. has just been & looked me all over & says I'm very healthy but I mustn't go to work at present—I'm going to telegraph the settlement and can you bring my trunk back with you? Check it on your ticket. I'm sorry to bother—I feel awfully disappointed but we must somehow arrange things to be very much together—Louise is just going down town & I'll finish & let her take this—I'll write Miss Hitchcock that I'll do any substituting or help out later if she wants me. Goodbye, dearest—

Your loving
H

52. 6 December 1907, P.M., from Harmony Twichell

Dearest—I can't think of anything much but of how glad I am that you are coming tomorrow. It means everything to me—The doctor asked me this morning if I had any "mental depression" & I said "no" very quickly but really if it weren't for you I believe I would have—I've been sitting up in the chair for two hours & feel better than yesterday—I got very tired yesterday—I feel so badly to think that our N.Y. plans are interrupted but maybe it's only an interruption—anyway I am glad that is decided for now. We have been laughing ourselves sick over Dad's going to Buffalo—he's so low in his mind over it & acts about five years old. Mother got so mixed up that she cut Louise a four legged pair of bloomers—she couldn't make out why she had so little stuff to make them of & pieced and planned all the morning & just came in to tell me why—It's dark & wintry but I've got a bright thing in my heart that defies anything—and to think I shall have it all my life only growing to be "more & more an absolute joy" as Dave says—there is no exhausting it is there? To live worthy of it—that is my life from now on and I cannot set a higher standard. How I love you, know it & believe it darling. It's a love that wants to hear & shall be for every day & it's a love pure heaven all the time—thank God I'm this way—It's a heritage I never thought I'd come into—the riches of the whole world & life—I think of all the old romances & understand them & see why they are important—the right kind of love is worth the best telling—I see why it's so powerful a theme since the beginning of time—It's the greatest thing in life—

Good night, My dearest,
H

53. 25 December 1907, from Harmony Twichell (possibly this is a continuation of an earlier letter; there is no salutation)

Christmas Afternoon

Your token came perfectly this morning, my darling, and I think it is very pretty and am truly delighted with it—I think you were a wonder to hit on it—I like it all & especially the fat tea pot—I am keeping it at my elbow & looking at it very often. Hannah came up to see me & admired it and hoped I'd "enjoy it"—and I do. Thank you dear lamb—Did you discern what my token was for? To put your collars in—I thought of something I am going to get you as soon as I can get about to choose it myself—I'll tell you what when you come. We all had a very nice Christmas—very quiet of course—I am wondering if you go back to NY tonight—I've missed you & long for you, beloved. Next Christmas we will surely spend together. I feel tired—I get scared sometimes about getting along so slowly, but I suppose it will come in time—I'm glad you think there's some purpose in it and I wouldn't give up our Sundays for well ones but I've had Enough almost—Well stop complaining Harmony! I know it would be nicer for you if I was "spry"—physically & mentally—my mind feels just about like my body you know.

Charlie, I think you are a wonderful person to have made these songs—I know some of them are lovely & [a page seems to be missing here]

[illegible: and?] very poor half life I'd have had to talk back to my maker & somewhere sometime he would have given me you I believe for he doesn't keep us out of heaven forever Darling how I love you—I thought afterwards that what I wrote you yesterday to say to yourself for me might sound like hyperbole but it wasn't anything but a plain truth for of course one's hope lies in what they are to become & what I am to become lies with you & what your love has brought me—All under the love of God of course—So it was simple to say I feel that—I feel it so keenly—

My beloved—I am going to find some things we can read next week & I hope to be down stairs so you can play me your songs—Sally came and is well—She is a dear child & we are glad to get her back—My heart is full of love & thankfulness—& for you, dearest dearest—how can I ever be thankful enough—

With my love & thoughts & prayers
Harmony

• • •

By spring Harmony had largely recovered her health, although her mother was still weak enough that her walking around outside was worthy of mention. The following letters demonstrate Harmony's renewed activity and indicate that plans for the wedding, which was about two months away, were well under way. We also see the importance of music for Harmony and get a glimpse of her collaboration with Charlie, probably on the song "Autumn." Her suggested changes in and comments about the text for the song make its autobiographical symbolism clear.

54. 1 April 1908, from Harmony Twichell

Sweetheart—

We are going down to So Manchester to see the Cheney exhibit It seems to be very famous—people coming from all sorts of places to see it. We four girls are going. I went to the concert last night & enjoyed it very much—I'm not sure that it was very good. Maud Powell played Traumerei as an encore & I felt almost as if it were the first time I'd ever heard it—I wondered while she played that anyone ever got disturbed or raved around—it was so beautifully peaceful. I've not heard from you yet, I hope to before the day is over Darling—I love you & live for you—my thoughts are always with you—I have got those verses about done but they don't fit your music very well & I must try & make them—If your music isn't as good as Mr. Schumann's my verses may do tho' they ought to be far better—I may write you again later—I don't know when we'll get back—[11]

Goodbye
beloved and lovely
with all my heart
H

55. 14 April 1908, from Harmony Twichell

Tuesday Afternoon

My Dearest—

It's so nice out we've all been in the yard including Mother—who walked around & inspected the vines & bulbs for quite a while. It is such a comfort to find her so much better. Louise & "Dutch" are sunning their hair—Dutch expects now to go Thursday. I will get her to try your song & see if she can say how it sings & I can tell you what she says. I've changed the last verse some & tho' it doesn't read as well [it] will sing better perhaps—I

11. She is probably referring to the translation she made of Heinrich Heine's "Die Lotosblume." Ives used her verses in "The South Wind," which is modeled after Schumann's setting of the Heine. See Sinclair, *Descriptive Catalogue*, 362.

don't want to leave out the word flower entirely for it's the only indication that She is a flower—Each year she greets him / For him for him alone Her flower in pure love's beauty / thro' her brief day hath shone—The first line is better anyway for the song isn't it?

Darling—we were together yesterday at this time. Every one of our times together has been a good time hasn't it? It is so entirely comfortable to be with you as well as the happiest time for me—I only rest perfectly with you—think of the completeness of living with you—together—I can't realize this wonderful thing is actually mine—My dear I love you so—

I hope you'll write about your interview with the janitor—of course you will—& asked him about the range & lighter colored paint & more heat—tho' we can ask those things later—and I wonder if you've found anything strange & queer about it.

Day after tomorrow I'll have you here, won't I? If you don't get here until 8:30 I will probably be at church when you come but will soon be back. I think that Waterbury train gets in at nine—Perhaps I'll meet you if I do—Tomorrow I'll write to Danbury. I'm glad you're going there & hope you will cheer up Aunt Amelia. I must write her—

It's around mail time—I wish I could say the love that is in my heart—and the happiness—I write about many things & over all the time feel that overwhelmingly but can't express it at all. You are my love—my darling so dear to me beloved. Good night & God bless you.

Yours beyond time & space
Harmony

56. 11 May 1908, from Harmony Twichell

Dearest beloved—

I've just time to send my love—my dearest love all my love & there'll be just as much after it's all sent. Dear heart—It's a lovely day & I hope you are well & feel like doing everything you have to.

Always yours
H.

• • •

The month before the wedding found Ives still fretting over problems in business, particularly the expansion of his office's territory to include New Jersey as well as New York and Connecticut. His descriptions of the difficulties he faced are much more humorous now, though, than they had been in the previous year. As the wedding approached, Ives's letters were filled more and more with the details of his and Harmony's increasingly shared lives.

57. 13 May 1908, to Harmony Twichell

My Best Beloved,

Am just back from Jersey—Newark and had one whirl of a day. The former manager whose place we took, came in with his lawyer—who by the way is suing the Co.—on what grounds I can't figure—although they took almost 2 hours trying to explain. Hoffman who's out for Hoffman listened as long as he could and then started writing letters—the lawyer after a long [illegible: meandering?] speech would wind up at the end of each effort—am I not right? And look at Hoffman. Harry usually answered—no—then seeing his error—prima facie—would jump around making 10 blots on his letter and shout "yes"—and then lose all interest until the next crisis came.

There's a good chance in Jersey, I think, and it is not quite as hard work as Conn. Am coming up to Stamford tomorrow and will reach Danbury and please girl—Dear heart—I must find you there. I'm so sorry your mother doesn't feel up to traveling yet but please come yourself if you can not very inconveniently. If you do you'll probably take the noon train from H. and reach D about 3. I plan to reach there about quarter past 5. And won't you drive over and meet me. Rocket isn't hard to manage—just talk to him and let him have a fairly tight rein. He's not afraid of the cars. It's almost half past five and I must go uptown. And I have a man to see for Hoffman in Harlem this evening.

June 16 seems a long long ways off—It's hard to resign to that extra week, but we must live and try to make things easier for others and I guess this is one of the ways.

I love you—my darling darling sometimes I wish you could get inside of me all and see and feel my heart and love for you. Tomorrow at this time I'll be with you.

Lovingly,
C

58. 20 May 1908, to Harmony Twichell

Darling Girl,

I stopped off at "our home" on the way down town this afternoon.[12] The paper all looks great. It's all on except one side of the dining [room] and will be finished tomorrow. All the rooms looked light and very salubrious—an especially clean aspect to it all. The paper in the front room, hall, and dining room seemed much lighter than it did in the sales-store—Harmony—we'll have a wonderful house. The dining room seemed about as light as the parlor and very very comfortable and it was dark and raining. The pansies and shrubs in the garden were more attractive than ever and very comforting. It did me 1000 lbs. of good to go in there and all the troubles of the day seemed to clear up after that. The front room seemed particularly airy and full of life and light and happiness and it was hard to leave. I called Mr. Callahan up this morning but couldn't get him and also stopped at his home, but didn't find him. I saw the janitor who said everything would be ready by the 1st

12. Their new apartment was at 70 West 11th Street.

of June to move in anything we wanted. I told him we expected to be in permanently by the 20th and that we would come down and make further arrangements soon after the first. He said that if we would tell him where we wanted the different things put he would have them in place before the 20th. He thinks it best to move the larger pieces in first—my piano—sofa-beds etc. and whatever goes nearest the floor. Also asked what we would put down on the hall floor—and if we wanted a layer to go underneath—also about curtains—didn't know exactly what to tell him about these but thought you could when we see him next month—and that that would be time enough—am I right? I think we can get all the things from Danbury down by the end of the first week—say the 5th or 6th—also the things from Grammercy Park.[13]—But do you think it safe to ship the linen and silver from Hartford until the 20th?

This letter sounds pretty full of business and responsibility—doesn't it? Well—anyway—don't let all of this weigh you down or worry—We'll get things to rights without much trouble.—We'll talk it over when I see [you.]

I leave tomorrow for Hartford—stopping in Stamford, Bridgeport, and New Haven and will get to H. by 9 o'c arriving promptly at eight. I'm going to stop at New Haven more as a matter of duty—know almost none of the undergraduates—but [two illegible names] and all the old Wolf's Head stand by's have asked me to be there—and as I haven't been to a tap day for years—am rather glad to go—especially as it fits in so conveniently.

My best beloved—how I love you—do you realize it all? It's just built right into me. I am completely happy all the time—though rather blue when I'm not with you, and to have a sunset go by without seeing you brings a hard and wrong feeling—only 19 days and all this feeling will be over and our perfect life for each other and for all our love will begin.

I enclose a good letter from Deac.

God Bless you,
C.

59. 25 May 1908, to Harmony Twichell

Only Darling Darling Darling—The hardest hours in my life were this morning after leaving you—but—girl—there will be only one more—"leaving time" and then I can never let a whole day go without being with you and seeing you and feeling the wonderful something that you give me, and which I feel more and more after days with you. Our days together are all beautiful—aren't they.

Willy and Wilky are both here and I'm pretty desperate—Willy is going up to dinner—so can't expect to get rid of him—lately this has been a pretty good time to write but not tonight young man.

I bought a straw [hat?] to day and Gen. Parker came in the store—congratulated me—looked foolish—so did I—and asked me to remember him to my better half.

We had quite a meeting at the Ives & Co. and almost 3 hours—we have to have another one in about 2 weeks—and F. Harris proposed the 9th—I got pretty diplomatic then—

13. Ives's last bachelor apartment was at 34 Grammercy Park.

some how—and made them fix it for next week. Did D [illegible] telephone me this morning. I got back to the office past noon so I didn't tell him I wouldn't see him today—Have written him and asked him to call for the telephone book.

Have found part of the addresses and will finish and mail them tonight. Some of them are not in the telephone book—probably live in the country—will send all I can tonight and telephone around for the rest tomorrow. Harmony—best beloved—I wish I <u>could</u>—I've tried to write very hard—came out wrong—I wish I <u>could</u> have a quiet place to write—I will before the week is out Good night How I love you and love you,

C

60. 26 May 1908, Tuesday, to Harmony Twichell

Darling,

Have just rec'd your dear lovely letter—what a wonderful help your letters are.

I enclose list with all addresses I could find so far. Hope to get the rest today, and will send them right [away.] Mother has just telephoned and I'm to meet her this noon. Good bye for now most dearly beloved,

C

2 weeks from to day—young man

—it feels about 2 years.

· 3 ·

CALL AND RESPONSE

(1911–1936)

One of the most important contributions of the correspondence as a whole is its revelation of Ives's efforts to bring his music to the public. The first glimpses we have of this long and ultimately fruitful effort comes in an exchange of letters with Walter Damrosch (1862–1950), the conductor of the New York Symphony. In 1910 and 1911 Ives sent Damrosch clear ink copies of the Second and Third Symphonies, ostensibly to find out if it would be possible to have the scores played in rehearsal and also in hopes of interesting the conductor in programming them. The group performed movements of the Second Symphony in a rehearsal in 1910, but Damrosch took no interest in either work. And despite repeated requests, he never returned the unique ink copies to Ives.

61. 14 December 1911, to Walter Damrosch[1]

Dear Mr. Damrosch:—

You were kind enough to say, at the time my manuscript was tried over last year, that you would look at it again later.

Since then I have finished another score in symphony form, which I think better in many ways than the former and would greatly appreciate your looking at it.

If similar arrangements could be made to have it played over at a rehearsal it would be a great help to me—at any rate I hope you may not find it inconvenient to let me show you the score.

The themes for the most part are suggested by tunes and hymns that have always been familiar to us New Englanders and for that reason I feel that it may be more interesting than the other.

Very truly yours,
CEI/ER

1. Unless otherwise noted, Ives's letters were mailed from his home or office in New York or from his country house in West Redding, Connecticut. The place of origin is noted only in cases in which it is important to the context or content of the letter.

62. 24 June 1915, to Walter Damrosch

Dear Mr. Damrosch:

About three years ago I sent you two manuscript scores.

Having heard nothing from you since I'm interested to know if you received them. They were delivered according to my boy to a maid at your residence.

Enclosed is a copy of the letter sent with them.

Will you be kind enough to let me know whether you have them or not, so that I may either send for them or have other ink copies made, as my copies are in pencil and getting indistinct.

Very sincerely yours,
CEI:JP

Enclosure.

63. 28 June 1915, from Walter Damrosch, Long Island, New York

Dear Mr. Ives,

The scores are very likely at my house but I shall not be there until October.

If you have orchestra parts I think you can arrange with the men in the orchestra to play your work through for you by paying them for their time. You can arrange the details through the Symphony office in Aeolian Hall next Fall.

Very sincerely yours,
Walter Damrosch

• • •

Hoping to recover the long-lost ink copies of the symphonies, which would have saved much editorial work, Ives resumed his correspondence with Damrosch in the mid-1930s. The pun on Damrosch's name that Ives uses as the salutation in the sketch below, which would have been adjusted in Harmony's transcription, reflects his considerably more sour opinion of the conservative conductor. It also recalls the self-critical marginal comment Ives wrote on the manuscript of his cantata, *The Celestial Country* (1902), "Damned rot and worse."

64. Ca. 1936, sketch for Harmony Ives to Walter Damrosch

Damnrot

I am writing for Mr. Ives as . . . [2]

As Mr. I remembers some 25 or more years ago, he sent to your home at East 62 st. the

2. This is a slightly longer-than-typical version of Ives's standard abbreviation for the first sentence in his mediated letters. Harmony would have transcribed the sentence as "I am writing for Mr. Ives, who is not at all well,

score of his 3rd Symph which had just been copied out at that time, and also he thinks but is not sure, that a copy of his 2nd sym was also sent.

These as he remembers were both clear ink copies which Tams had made & as only copies of these scores which can be found among his manuscripts are his own old copies in lead pencil, [in] some places almost illegible & somewhat difficult to make out, he hopes it will not be asking too much if you would be kind enough, when convenient, to have someone look through your library for them. And if they may be found we will have someone call for them if you will kindly let us know when and where they may be had.

Mr. I realizes fully that there is no responsibility whatever on your part for their return or safe keeping.

But if they could be found it would be greatly appreciated by us both.

• • •

Ives's health crisis of 1918 prompted his first significant effort to collect, edit, and distribute some of the pieces he had composed over the previous two decades. He paid for the engraving and printing of the *Concord* Sonata (1921), its accompanying *Essays* (1921), and *114 Songs* (1922). Ives sent copies of these to old friends and acquaintances, but the majority of the copies went to members of the musical establishment whom Ives picked by consulting membership lists of various musical institutions and the staffs of publications such as *Musical Quarterly.* This method produced a largely conservative audience for Ives's works, an audience, furthermore, that had no idea how or why it had been selected.[3] The result was a greatly varied set of responses to the publications, responses both approving and disapproving, some substantial, some perfunctory. The sample included here shows the variety of the replies Ives received and pays particular attention to the sides of this multifaceted conversation that continued longest and that were important in the later reception of Ives's music.

The first group of letters includes a variety of short responses to the works from people who were caught off guard by the works they received.

65. Ca. 8 March 1921, from John Spencer Camp, Hartford, Connecticut[4]

Dear Mr. Ives,

Please accept my thanks for your "Second Pianoforte Sonata" which came a few days ago. I have not had time to examine it as carefully as I hope to do, but can see that it is an unusual work, and a radical departure harmonically from even the present advanced harmonies. I am somewhat handicapped by not being able to play the work in the required tempi—as, in that event, I might, and probably should obtain a very different impression

and cannot attend to things nowadays as he would like to." All sketches are in Ives's hand unless otherwise indicated. See the introduction for a full discussion of the mediated correspondence.

3. It is unlikely that Ives knew much at this time of organizations that might have been more receptive to his works, such as the International Composers' Guild, which had formed in 1921.

4. Camp was a music critic with considerable local influence.

from the one obtained by slow playing. You have evidently aimed at impressionistic word pictures, striving to avoid the commonplace and trivial. Whether your musical inspiration has been able to meet the demands you have placed upon it is an open question, and one I should like to defer until I hear your sonata adequately performed. My present impression is that, in spite of the great amount of work you have put into this composition, the fundamental inspiration and glow are lacking. It is, however, a very interesting work. I question whether in the interest of musical beauty such an effect as you call for in page 25 is good. A 'strip of board' does not appeal to my sense of artistic piano music. As I have said before, however, my final judgment must be held in abeyance until I hear this work adequately performed, which I hope to do some day. Thanking you again for the opportunity of examining your most modern sonata,

Yours very truly,
John Spencer Camp

66. 9 March 1921, from Charles Wakefield Cadman,[5] Los Angeles

Dear Mr. Ives:—

I wish to acknowledge your kindness in sending me your second sonata with the essays. Why you call it "sonata" is not clear to me, however, since you have thrown over everything that the modern world calls music, why should you cling to the old term of "sonata"?

At any rate I want you to know I admire the cleverness of your essays, even though I cannot swallow or accept the philosophy in them. As for the "music", I confess with thousands of others who have seen it, that it is incomprehensible to me. I do not ridicule you, I do not critisise you, philistine-like, because it would do no good anyway, so all I venture to say at this time is that I hope you will find pleasure in the satisfaction of understanding what you yourself have set down in the seventy pages of your work! No doubt it took a great deal of time to prepare all that notation. You should be given credit for industry by even those who fail to follow you, and the reason why they fail to follow you (at least I speak for myself) is because your idiom is as much of a dark secret as Harvard English (whatever that is) would be for an Alaskan Indian! Upon looking over the work again, carefully, the thought struck me that even the diatonic note system might even be guilty of circumscribing your original—or intended—"expression"? Were you not, perhaps, trying to put into "form", expressions that were entirely (to use a term of our Theosophical friends) ASTRAL—with a modus operandi that granted only PHYSICAL possibilities? This is not sarcasm because I do not mean it as that—I am merely making this conjecture as a matter of psychological interest.

I am sorry that I cannot in any way comprehend your music. I would have to "hear" it AND WHAT IT MEANT TO YOU just as you "heard" it in order to grasp it. As it is, I "get" nothing but a disordered sea of sound and form, and hurting my ears, much the

5. Cadman (1881–1946) was a harmonically conservative American composer who was best known for his pieces inspired by or based on Native American music. Ives may have known of him through his articles in *Musical Quarterly*.

same, I imagine, as a very blatant cornet would hurt the ears of a canine friend. Perhaps in my next incarnation (if I have one) the "music of the future" may contain some of the elements you are searching after, but I don't think it will employ any diatonic system for getting its 'message' over. I make no prophecies of what it WILL be, because I know not.

I found the Epilogue in your Essays full of interest, and containing many things I agree to. But in the main, as I said previously, I cannot endorse your theories, not because I do not WANT to but because I CANNOT. It is not a case of perverse stubbornness, it is a case of mental incompatibility, while I recognize your right to your own freedom of thought—whether musical or otherwise. And I know you have given up the task (if indeed you ever entertained such a thought) of converting the present musical world to your theories or the form of your so-called musical thinking.

Thanking you for having the work sent to me, and with kindest regards, I am,

Cordially yours,
Charles Wakefield Cadman

67. 11 April 1921, to Charles Wakefield Cadman

Dear Mr. Cadman:—

Mr. Ives wishes me to thank you for your interesting letter acknowledging the receipt of his books, "Concord, Mass." etc.

Illness has prevented him from answering sooner; and keeps him from writing at present.

Respectfully yours,
for Chas. E. Ives
CH

68. 10 March 1921, from Walter Goldstein, New Orleans

My dear sir,

Your "Concord" Sonata, sent from Messers Putnam, was received several days ago, and I beg you to accept my thanks.

You will excuse a pardonable curiosity when I say that I am eager to know something of the author of the unusual work, and also eager to know how I came to be honored with a complimentary copy.

I have looked through your Sonata as carefully as is for me possible with so abstruse a work, and I am frank to say that I have not reached a stage of musical modernness that enables me to fathom your musical meaning. With the exception of orthodox passages in the "Alcott" movement, to me the sonata seems to be expressed in the Schoenberg-Scriabin-Ornstein idiom, the musicality of which is not yet comprehensible to me.

If you have the time and inclination, will you not satisfy my curiosity by letting me hear from you further concerning yourself, your First Sonata, and your subsequent work?

Very cordially yours,
Walter Goldstein

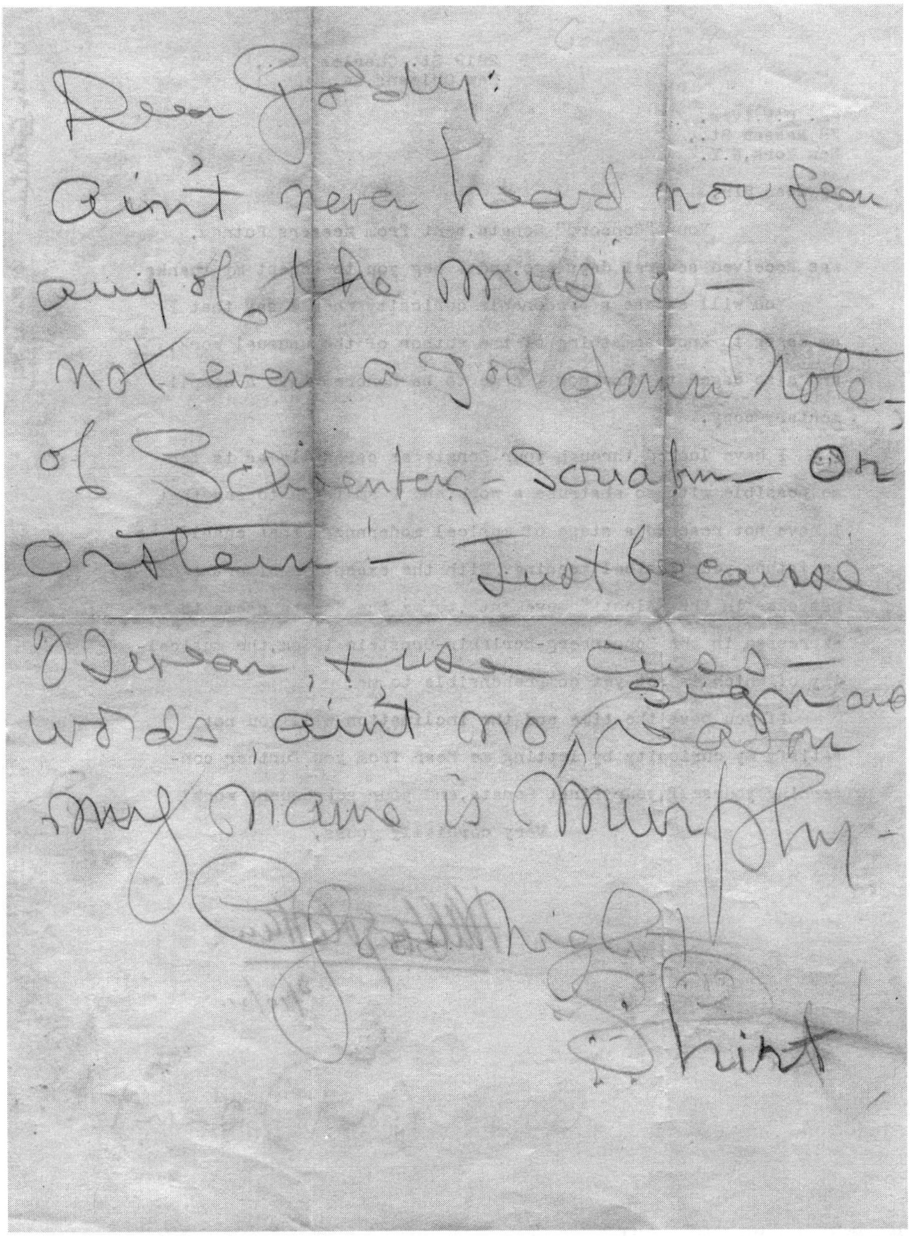

Dear Goldy:
Ain't never heard nor seen
any of the music—
not even a god damn Note—
of Schoenberg—Scriabin—or
Orstein—Just because
I swear, & use cuss-
words, ain't no sign and reason
my name is Murphy—
Good Night
Shirt

10 March 1921, sketch for Ives to Walter Goldstein.

69. Sketch for reply to Walter Goldstein on the back of his letter

[*At the bottom front of Goldstein's letter, Ives writes:*] "see over letter (not) sent!!"

Dear Goldy:

Ain't never heard nor seen any of the music—not even a god damn Note,—of Schoenberg—Scriabin—or Orstein—Just because I swear, & use cusswords, ain't no sign and reason my name is Murphy—

Good Night Shirt!

• • •

The following letters mostly respond to *114 Songs.*

70. 3 January 1922 [1923],[6] from George R. Falconer, New York

Dear Sir,

Please accept my sincere thanks for the volume of songs which you have so kindly sent.

The book was received on New Year's Day so that the year opened for me with song and music, I am sure they will often be sources of inspiration and good cheer.

Thanking you once again and wishing you a Happy and Successful Year.

Yours truly
Geo. R. Falconer

71. 8 August 1922, from William Ames Fischer, Oliver Ditson Company, Boston

My dear Mr. Ives:

I take pleasure in acknowledging the receipt today in perfect order of your unique book of 114 songs. I have only had time to glance at them and discover your keen sense of humor, both literary and musical. You must have had a lot of fun writing the music, doing it in your own way, exactly to suit yourself, unhampered by the thought of public, or publishers and their bread-and-butter "necessities." I trust that my copy is unique for song No. 17 is missing and pages 37–39 are blank.[7] Possibly this is a bit of delicate irony.

Yours sincerely,
William Ames Fischer

• • •

In the top margin of the following letter, Ives expressed a comic dismay at the apparent discomfort the songs had caused one recipient: he wrote, "from a 'well bred' lady!"

72. 9 August 1922, from Deane Dossert, New York

Dear Mr. Ives,

Your expensive publication sent to Mr. Dossert, reached its destination, but I am assuming the privilege of acknowledging its receipt. The truly gracious thing to do, would be to

6. Falconer must have miswritten the year, as the songbook was not completed and sent out until the summer of 1922.

7. Fischer's copy was one of the five hundred in the first printing of *114 Songs*, from August 1922. "Grantchester," song number 17, was omitted in these because Ives had not yet received copyright permission to use its text; Sinclair, *Descriptive Catalogue*, 658.

thank you in a few well-chosen words for having made us the recipients of your generous (?) volume. But curiosity impels me to ask, despite the adage about the "gift-horse", under what classification we became the beneficiaries of your housecleaning? Were we among the scrap-baskets, or the clotheslines? We have examined your work with care; music texts, foot-notes and appendix—and we have concluded that you are a man to be envied. Music to you has been a recreation and a pastime,—not—a means of livelihood. It is to be regretted that with your evident knowledge, your sense of humor, a certain vein of sympathy, and a fine appreciation of the best of literature, you do not really express yourself, but have striven to over-emphasize your technical ability. You have been clever—but not sincere. Although studio space is limited, the volume of songs will find a place there, if only for the amusement it has afforded us.

We hope you will continue to write, and that some day we will be able to purchase other of your songs worthy of you, and of real value to the literature of music.

Believe me, Very sincerely,
Deane Dossert
(Mrs. F. G. Dossert)

73. Ca. 3 April 1921, from Roland Diggle, Los Angeles

Dear Mr. Ives,

I wonder if you would be kind enough to send me a copy of your piano sonata. I should esteem it a token of great favor.

Yours sincerely,
Roland Diggle

[*Ives wrote in blue pencil on the bottom of the ca. 3 April letter after the receipt of the ca. 14 August one:*]

Copy sent \ no acknowledgement \ a regular Mus. Doc.![8] see 'left handed remark in another letter.—a sow? Belly weak sister! afraid to say what he thinks!

74. Ca. 14 August 1922, from Roland Diggle, Los Angeles

Dear Mr. Ives

Many thanks for your book of songs, I expect that ere long I should hear the newsboys of Hollywood whistling these plaintive melodies and I shall look forward to the arrangement for the ukelele and saxophone which I am sure a clamering public will demand.

Yours in the faith,
Roland Diggle

8. Diggle's stationery was engraved, "Roland Diggle, Mus. Doc." Ives added this comment to the letter after he received Diggle's letter of 14 August 1922.

75. 17 August 1922, from A. de Blanek, Havana

Dear Sir:

With great pleasure I have received the book of the very interesting songs which you so kindly had sent to me, and I desire to know my indebtedness to you and oblige—

Yours sincerely,
A. de Blanek

76. 21 August 1922, from Karl H. Eschman,[9] Granville, Ohio

My dear Mr. Ives:—

Permit me to express my appreciation for the volume of songs which you so kindly sent me. Their delightful whimsicalities interest me, and, although I have not yet read them all, I am sure I will return to many of them with pleasure.

I am somewhat at a loss to know whether the collection was sent to me in my "official" capacity—or for personal use. If the former, I must catalogue the book in the University Library. This I hesitate to do, for it might mean their loss to me. I am sure the library would be glad to have a copy for their files if they may obtain one, or I will place this copy there upon your instructions.

Sincerely yours,
K. H. Eschman

77. Ca. 21 August 1922, sketch for Ives to Karl H. Eschman

Karl H. Eschman

Granville O.

Thank you for the letter acknowledging the book of songs. This was sent to you personally—but if you think it is a volume that "may do" for a university library—it will be my pleasure to send on another copy. I was most interested in an article of yours in the Musical Quarterly in which you brought out the idea—forcibly and firmly, it seemed to me—that form in its larger fundamental sense—a kind of big rhetorical framework not necessarily made up of molds, regular irregular, is a dimension, too often unrealized,—a dimension [four illegible words]—and if one consistently tries to do only with it, the expression is quite likely [?] to come out in small canvases, and small designs.[X] This sounds as though I am trying to tell you what your essay was about—but writing you just started me thinking about it again.

If you have any collected writings published please tell me where I can get copies–[I] don't find them in Schi [illegible] list.

[X]Something like that in my mind from your article, though I haven't it before me.

9. Eschman was director of the Denison University Conservatory of Music, Granville, Ohio.

At any rate, I feel indebted to you, though to send you my music may not be a very generous way of showing it.

• • •

In its negative review of *114 Songs*, the *New York Sun* pointed out that Ives had offered to send a free copy to anyone who asked for it. *Musical Digest* reran the "free songbook" announcement, minus the critical review, in early September 1922. Ives replied angrily to the *Sun* that he was not seeking publicity, but these announcements generated an unexpectedly large number of requests for the book. As a result, Ives had a second printing made in April 1923 and subsequently had the collection *50 Songs* printed from the plates of the original songbook in order to fill requests.

78. 29 September 1922, from Bessie Bartlett Frankel, National Federation of Music Clubs, Los Angeles

My dear Mr. Ives:

In the September 4th issue of the Musical Digest I came across the enclosed notice.

If you still have copies for distribution I would appreciate it very much indeed if you would mail one to me. As I have no idea of the required postage I shall gladly refund that upon receipt of the volume.

Trusting that I am not too late in my request and thanking you—

Cordially yours,
Bessie Bartlett Frankel

[*Ives wrote in the lower left margin:*] "Wrote Oct. 8 / put on list."

79. 7 May 1923, from Mrs. Cecil (Bessie Bartlett) Frankel, Los Angeles

My dear Mr. Ives:

Please accept my sincere appreciation for the volume of beautiful and <u>difficult</u> songs which you so kindly sent me.

I should have acknowledged them ere this, only absence from the city prevented. I found them upon my return.

I shall take great pleasure in having a group of them presented before the American Music Optimists of Los Angeles next season.

Thanking you again for your courtesy and wishing you continued success—

Sincerely yours,
Bessie Bartlett Frankel

• • •

Leon Maxwell's response to *114 Songs* shows that even seemingly negative impressions of Ives's works, such as the one in Walter Goldstein's letter (Letter 68), led to greater dissemination and potential acceptance.

80. 4 December 1922, from Leon R. Maxwell, New Orleans

Dear Sir:

Mr. Walter Goldstein has shown me the volume of your songs. Some of them interest me exceedingly, and if you have any more copies of the volume available, I shall be glad to receive one.

Yours truly,
Leon R. Maxwell
Director, School of Music[10]

81. 11 December 1922, to Leon R. Maxwell

Dear Mr. Maxwell:—

Shortly after the first of the year, I expect to have more copies of the book of songs. It will give me pleasure to send you a copy.

Very truly yours,
CEI/MM

82. 21 January 1924, from Leon R. Maxwell, New Orleans

My dear Mr. Ives,

Early last year, you very kindly sent me a volume of your songs. I have looked over them with pleasure and amazement. Last Thursday I tried one of them out on an audience, and found that they apparently enjoyed it exceedingly.[11]

I enclose a program which I think you may wish to see. Thank you again for your generosity.

Yours sincerely,
Leon R. Maxwell
Director, School of Music

10. Maxwell was at H. Sophie Newcomb Memorial College, part of Tulane University in New Orleans.
11. Maxwell performed "Charlie Rutlage"; Sinclair, *Descriptive Catalogue*, 673.

83. 28 December 1922, from Caroline D. Hewitt,[12] New York

Dear Mr. Ives,

Your book with card of good wishes and generous appreciation touched me very deeply.

It is so little that we teachers can do for our children in comparison with the influence of a parent, but if we can only co-operate in our ideals and the training of their sensitive young minds, we sometimes have our reward in the sudden flowering of beauty in the child's soul. The outward expression of that beauty is often the most difficult to attain but it comes now and again as it did to little Edith last summer, and we stand amazed & repaid for all our labor of love and patience.

I shall take keen pleasure in reading your book for I am one of those who can "stand" essays and, perhaps I may have he pleasure of meeting you some afternoon and hearing the sonata which the essays helped to produce!

With many thanks, and good wishes for a very Happy New Year to you and Mrs. Ives,

Sincerely yours

Caroline D. Hewitt

84. 6 January 1923, from Mrs. Donald T. Baker, Long Island, New York

My Dear Sir:—

Due to my absence from home this week, the beautiful "Book of Songs", which came on New Year's Day, has not yet been acknowledged. I did not reply to your letter, received last September, because a reply then seemed unnecessary, but I feel I must thank you for the book.

It is such a peculiar incident and I consider myself fortunate to have been the recipient of a "gift copy." I think you were very generous to fulfill the obligation, which "The Evening Sun" certainly forced upon you. Personally I have benefitted by the error and want to say how much I enjoyed running thro' the book on New Year's-Night at the piano. The songs will be a pleasure to me and to others, I know.

I anticipate showing your music to friends in Panama with whom I am associated in "The Aucon Morning Musical Club." I presume you would have no objection to our using some of your compositions as part of our monthly meeting programs?

If you should visit the Isthmus, I shall be glad if you will let me know. It might be that my husband and I could help to make your stay interesting and pleasant.

I gave my mother's name when writing for the book, which was "free to anyone upon request." (Mrs. James G. Weeks)—I am staying here at present because of her illness—, but my home since my marriage, for the past ten years—is in Panama.

I want to tell you that I particularly liked your setting of "When Stars are in the Quiet Skies," a sweet old song, and liked very much "Two little flowers" and "To Edith" and

12. Hewitt ran the school that the eight-year-old Edith Ives attended in New York; Sinclair, *Descriptive Catalogue*, 673; Ives, Diary for 20 October 1922 (CIP, 45/7).

Longfellow's "The Children's Hour"—(I have a little daughter whose name is Edith, nearly six years old)

I like #9 (a&b), #16, #19, #44, "Watchman tell us of the night", #66, #67, and #100,—I note these from a casual playing over,—once only,—no opportunity since.[13]

With cordial appreciation of your kindness in giving this pleasure to one wholly unknown to you—I am—

Very Truly Yours—
Sarah G. W. Baker

85. 5 March 1923, from E. Linwood Lehman,[14] Charlottesville, Virginia

Dear Sir:

I was recently shown a collection of songs, the music of which you had composed. This music interested me a great deal and I was told that, altho the book was not for sale, you would send it upon application to you.

I am writing to ask you to be so good as to send me a copy of your collection. Altho I have not examined the book carefully I wish to congratulate you upon several of the selections that especially caught my attention.

Yours very truly,
E. Linwood Lehman

86. 18 April 1923, from Charles Ditson,[15] New York

My dear Mr. Ives:

I am in receipt of your very interesting looking volume for which I thank you. Although I have only been able to glance through it I shall take great pleasure in looking at it more carefully at my leisure.

Sincerely yours,
Chas. H. Ditson

87. 4 May 1923, from Muriel W. Humphrey, Middletown, Connecticut

Dear Sir,

Many thanks for the volume of songs you so kindly sent. They arrived while I was ill, hence the delay in answering.

13. The songs mentioned by number are "Duty" and "Vita," "Religion," "The Greatest Man," "Watchman Tell Us of the Night," "The Light That Is Felt," "Walking," and "A Christmas Carol."

14. Lehman was an assistant professor of Romance languages at the University of Virginia.

15. Ditson was the founder of Ditson and Company, music publishers.

I am still confined to my bed, so have not had the pleasure of playing them on the piano. It has been great enjoyment to me, however, to read them through and hear them, as well as I could, mentally. My husband has played some of them for me, and we both find them interesting. I should like very much to hear some of them well sung.

With many thanks,

Sincerely yours
Muriel W. Humphrey

88. 20 May 1923, from Percy Goetschius,[16] New York

My dear Mr. Ives:

I owe you an apology for not having sooner acknowledged your kindness in sending me a copy of your New England pfte. Sonata, and I herewith tender the apology most sincerely. Your Sonata, and the book, came to me at just this time of year, two years ago when I am extremely overburdened with many extra duties incidental to the closing of the school year, at the institute. As it would have been difficult for me to write to you at that time in an adequate manner, I postponed it, hoping to do it greater justice during the summer vacation to follow. The Sonata excited my deep interest, and the more I saw of it, the more I wished to see, before writing to you about it. So the time kept lengthening until I really felt ashamed to write—a curious psychological dilemma which you will understand. The recent receipt of your 114 Songs jogged my spirit back to reason, and I am now writing to thank you, very sincerely, for your significant gifts.

I wish you to know that I do not take your work lightly. I say, frankly, that I do not like this manner of sound-association, for I am too fully grounded in the habits (I admit that they are, to some extent "habits") of the classic methods. To my mind, these classic methods are correct ones [Ives adds between the lines, "for soft eared cissies and aural cowards!" with a frowning face] for I find them, in every detail, confirming the eternal physical laws which govern tone as well as stone. But I am not, in conviction, a heartless and brainless conservative, who recognizes the "Last Word" in anything that Bach, Beethoven or Brahms have said in tone—no, nor Ives. And therefore these newer methods, or experiments, interest me keenly. And, since I am absolutely convinced of your sincerity, and see many admirable evidences of that logic, which is a part of my pet physical law, in your work—note that I hesitate to call it "music," for I believe in accurate definition—I declare that these experiments of yours interest me particularly. As to your book, it is magnificent. I regard it as an ornament to any library—and my library is no commonplace Collection of Unread books.

With sincere thanks, and my very best wishes for your success,

I am cordially yours,
Percy Goetschius

16. Goetschius (1853–1943) was a composer and educator whose pupils included Henry Cowell and Howard Hanson. He was head of the theory department at the Institute of Music and Art in New York, which later became the Juilliard School of Music.

89. 25 May 1923, from Charles Holman-Black, Paris

Dear Mr. Ives

The American mail coming in has just brought to me the announced book of your compositions, which not following your letter, I had concluded was lost. I am glad to find it was not the case and I hasten to send a line to thank you for this collection of your works. I have glanced through the pages here at my desk on opening the package and am impressed with the originality and diversity shown in the compositions, believing a great pleasure is in store for me when I can give them study and likewise read them over at the piano. I thank you very much for this delicate attention of yours regretting only that the book did not contain a dedication. The printing and binding is in keeping with good taste.

With repeated assurances of appreciation and thanks believe me to be

Yours most sincerely
Charles Holman-Black

90. 6 May 1923, from Louis Sajous, Fraternal Association of Musicians, New York

My dear Mr. Ives:—

Upon opening the well printed and well bound copy of your "inspiration" of one hundred and fourteen songs and for which I thank you, I must confess that in opening the first page, I had a nauseous feeling, might I say a centipedial feeling or perhaps an astigmatized look into what might be a text book for the modern six.[17]

But my mal-aise was soon relieved, after reading your quotations that "they be not sung or given to students" I assure you that I shall strictly obey and bow to your will and judgement.

Your philosophy at the end of the book, is a classic, and should be read by all musicians; I appreciative [*sic*] it very much.

I am not sure that it must have been an oversight on your part, in not dedicating the book to George Chappell and the crew of the 'Kawa' much less the Village Nightingale, who, I am sure might do justice to your genius; again thanking you and with all well wishes for your future success, believe me

Sincerely yours,
Louis Sajous

17. Sajous probably means "Les Six," the group of French modernist composers (Arthur Honegger, Darius Milhaud, Georges Auric, Louis Durey, Francis Poulenc, and Germaine Tailleferre) whose works included *Les mariés de la tour Eiffel* (1921). Ives chose, in part, to invite such a reaction by placing the song "Majority," with its formidable tone clusters, as the first piece in the book, instead of the less intimidating "Evening," as had been his original plan. See Ives, *Memos*, ed. John Kirkpatrick (New York: W. W. Norton, 1972), 127.

• • •

Though the following letter is somewhat later than the others in this section, I include it here because it is a direct response to the *Concord* Sonata and *114 Songs*. It also shows how far afield Ives sent his scores. Ives's response to Malipiero sheds an interesting light on his knowledge of much earlier music.

91. 1 November 1928, from G. Francesco Malipiero,[18] Asolo (Treviso), Italy

Dear Mr. Ives

After your second Pianoforte Sonata and your 114 Songs (1920 & 1922) I never received anything further from you and I hope this does not mean that you never received my letters; if you have you must know your work interests me. If I am breaking the silence it is because I want to tell you about a certain endeavor which I hope may interest you, and very possibly your music loving friends.

I am working at editing and printing & publishing myself, by subscription only, the complete works of CLAUDIO MONTEVERDI, quite the greatest musician of Italy after Palestrina. His work is monumental not only by quantity but also by quality. Already I have brought out SEVEN VOLUMES and the EIGHTH VOL. is under press and will be ready for the new year. In order to be worthy of the contents I have devised an edition deLuxe on hand made paper of the very finest quality; it is a NUMBERED edition and there are only a limited amount of copies, 250 copies, printed of each volume. America has demonstrated the liveliest interest in this edition, and a great many Colleges and Universities have subscribed already, but I am seeking for just a few more subscribers in order to assure satisfactorily the fate of the enterprise. The volumes have come out fairly frequently and the first TEN volumes will be issued before January 1930; as I have said above there [are] 7 ready & printed, and the eighth is in hands of printer.

The Price of the first TEN Volumes is FIFTY DOLLARS

There will be afterwards SIX more volumes and these, considerably bulkier each volume, will cost SIXTY DOLLARS for the Six. Naturally as it is a numbered edition the subscriber MUST undertake the whole set otherwise the set would be wasted, it cannot be sold one at a time.

Thinking over the measure of the work that you give to Music it occurs to me that you might be interested in the study of the great Master. Let me add that this is the first time a Complete Edition of Monteverdi is offered to the Public. I hope to hear from you. I hope it will interest you, and also your friends.

Believe me Yours very sincerely
E. Francesco Malipiero

18. In addition to editing the works of Vivaldi and Monteverdi, Malipiero (1882–1973) was a composer of opera and instrumental music in a modern style.

92. 23 November 1928, to E. Francesco Malipiero

Dear Mr. Malipiero:—

Let me acknowledge and thank you for your letter.

A complete edition of Monteverdi is a thing that I should very much like to have. My father was a great admirer of Monteverdi and had me study some of the organ music when I was a young man. I remember of his speaking often of Monteverdi's remarkable pre-vision.

I take pleasure in sending the enclosed check for the first ten volumes and you will please let me know when the balance is due.

I wish you would visit America and play or conduct your music for us. There is need here of the influence of that rare Italian fervency, serenity and beauty.

I am sorry to say that your previous letters did not reach me. Perhaps our change of address may account for this.

Thanking you for thinking of me and hoping that I may have the pleasure of meeting you some day, I am, with best wishes,

Sincerely,
C. E. Ives

CEI/LG

• • •

Ives sent the *Concord* Sonata, *Essays,* and *114 Songs* to old friends and colleagues from Yale. Their responses range from appreciation of his development to surprise at the modernist Ives had become. William Lyon Phelps had been one of Ives's favorite professors at college and was probably instrumental in awakening the interest in American literature that manifested itself most conspicuously in the *Concord* Sonata and *Essays.*[19]

93. 17 June 1920, from William Lyon Phelps, New Haven

Dear Charley Ives:

I've just read your book (you were kind enough to send me) and I'm so proud of you! And this is the work of "Ives '98" my pupil and friend!

I read every page with keen interest and now I am impatient to have the sonata—when may that be?—are you by any chance coming to New Haven next week?

Your book is full of thought and inspiration—it came out of a rich, active mind—I can see how happy you must be and how you enjoy living.

You must reread Browning's "Charles Avison"—note the <u>stream</u> and how one favorite in music gives way to another.

19. Phelps (1865–1943) was Lampson Professor of English Literature at Yale University. He was an early and energetic proponent of the study of modern and American literature. See William Lyon Phelps, *Autobiography with Letters* (New York: Oxford University Press, 1939).

The theory however (mentioned in your book) not only fails to explain Bach and Beethoven but also Mozart and Handel—great revival old Handel has nowadays!

Be sure and send a copy of your book to the Yale Library—I suppose you did send one to Prof. Beers.

With hearty thanks and congratulations I am Gratefully yours,
Wm Lyon Phelps

94. 4 July 1920, from William Lyon Phelps, Huron City, Michigan

My dear Charles—

Your letter is fine! And I am happy to have it. Please lose no time in sending a copy of your book to Prof. Henry A. Beers, York Square, New Haven—He will love it, I'll guarantee that.

And send a copy to the Yale Library.

I am so glad you married one of Mr. Twichell's daughters—I don't know which one, but I know them all, and you are to be envied.

I am so glad her brother is to be the new Dean of Students at Yale: it is fine to have a Twichell hold office at Yale again.[20]

I await with eagerness your musical score—I shall be here till Sept. 28 or so—then New Haven—I am wild to see it and have someone play it over for me. I can't play any instrument tho I'm president of the N.H. Symphony—first thing I do when I get to heaven I shall learn some instrument—it will take all eternity, but I shall have time!

Your book is admirable—full of cerebration and full of a certain noble splendid high-heartedness, characteristic of all Twichells!

My affectionate greetings to her and to you.

Ever yours
Wm Lyon Phelps

95. 21 December 1920, to William Lyon Phelps

My dear Professor Phelps:—

Thank you for the comment in the "Alumni Weekly" and for sending it to me. You are generous in everything. I hope I may deserve your good opinion.

The copies of the sonata are still delayed. Schirmer promised to have them ready by Christmas, but they won't—not this Christmas.

There is one correction in the notice—I'm not a professional musician. I've been in business for twenty-two years and so am free to write music which nobody has to play. However, I'm going to send one of the first copies I get for you to practice

20. This was Burton Twichell.

on; but don't put that off until you get to the next world, as it has little of celestial beauty.

Gratefully yours,
CEI/HFM

• • •

The correspondence with John Griggs, Ives's old friend and the choirmaster from Center Church, New Haven, who had become a missionary in China, was the farthest-flung of Ives's life. Ives sent Griggs a copy of the *Essays*, and it must have been exciting to receive a response to his work from halfway around the world, especially from a person as important to him as Griggs. This is also one of the longest early responses to the volume, and Griggs takes Ives seriously even if he does not agree with him at all points. The importance of this friendship is obvious in the second letter, as Ives remembers the difficult times he faced in college after the death of his father. This letter offers an interesting take on the famously difficult relationship between Ives and his teacher Horatio Parker. The problem, Ives suggests, was not that Parker was too strict or unwilling to accept experimentalism in music. Rather, Parker segregated the spiritual and intellectual aspects of music. To Ives, for whom serious music was intrinsically imbued with both of these attributes, this was a grave fault. Ives's statements about what Griggs did not do—he did not impose laws or rules—may be an allusion to Parker's legendary strictness.

96. 27 August 1921, from John Cornelius Griggs, Canton Christian College, Canton, China

Dear Charlie Ives,

Letters are difficult out here at best, and the hardest to write are those in which one wants to say the most. Many times in the past two years I have purposed writing you but have always procrastinated till some imagined vacation leisure, because you are not such an easy fellow to write to. A man who puts out such a book as Essays Before a Sonata is not to be put off with chaff. You may think I am proposing a tremendous blast, but perish the thought. I have been away with Eleanor leading our brass band along the paths of glory, not leading in the directing sense but going along as a sort of chaperone and general encumbrance. Like almost everything in these two years it has been a unique chapter. Today I have been correcting a crazier typed transcript of my crazy account of our trip. Sometime when you can't sleep, try to read it.

We are living in the most convenient little brick and concrete house that was ever made. Our servants do almost everything that any servants could do for one and except for making a stand against the heat, these few weeks before college opens next month are pretty idle. I seem to excel in sleeping. I wish you could hear this minute the work men who are building the house next door sing and whistle Chinese tunes.

Eleanor has come along a lot with piano, having gained immensely in reading ability. It's a rather lawless progress of course, and I hope will be supplemented with something else later. Meantime it gives us as well as many others a great deal of pleasure.

This is Sunday morning now and I am feeling the relief of no service,—no Sun. School class. Sunday in term time is a riot of Sabbath breaking,—choir, bible study, students calling, I.M.C.A. alarms, sermons by some visiting brother, Chinese or English. I'm making a lot of good resolutions to cut out some of it next term and try to honor it as a day of rest but the human heart is desperately wicked and prone to sin and I am fearing that Satan will entangle me. I have been appointed Exploding Secretary of the Anti-Denominational League which has its headquarters at Bunk Bungalow Bankok and a total membership of one-and-his-wife. This is not a very good field here at this non-denominational college, but the work has been greatly blessed in my travels, and I have occasional opportunity to coruscate hereabouts.

Your "Emerson" and "Thoreau" seem to me really fine.—the former one of the most satisfying treatments of the subject I have ever seen. I wish I could talk with you, or rather hear you talk about the whole book. I feel in reading again these past few days that the whole thing is a book that stands on its own legs. I can't think [of] it as "Before a Sonata" or "Before—anything else. And here is just the tough drink of the "Prologue," tough because involved in that perennially tough and to me rather unnecessary inquiry which plagues all our music analyses,—the translatableness of music. I have stumbled and bungled over it all my life. You neither stumble nor bungle, but you seem faced in the direction of an ultimate "translatableness,"—a direction in which I can see no light.—Here's what I think I believe, only I can't say it, and I don't stop to think about it much when music really comes to me.

Art is a projection into a realm beyond the understandable. As such it is in the analyses of Lombroso, wrongly entangled with insanity.[21] That's one blind alley we will stop up at the start.

It is a recognition of the beyond toward which our racial evolution is strongly progressing.

Its recognitions are accomplished by an elation,—a straining of receptivity.

We cheapen this by calling it emotion and sometimes enjoy it so much that we stop right there.

The very essence of life is its boundlessness; not only a being but a projection,—not only an exploration but a striving for greater depths and heights than can be measured in either material or intellect. The actualities of life have always a penumbra of reachings outward. Here are the futilities of philosophy, the futilities of childrens' play, of our own diversions, the pattern of a piece of lace, perhaps even the mad whirl of the insects. The lure of these futilities is their promise of becoming the actuality of a larger and higher plane of existence. We do not have to wait till a future life to be startled by the unexpected realization of these other actualities, none the less actual when once we have lived them than those we can measure and describe. Man's halting picture of this projected plane is more than imagination,—it is his prophecy

Music is preeminent, (because of its aloofness from spoken word, material from form or temporal thought,) in piercing this realm and making of this prophecy a definite super

21. Possibly Cesare Lombroso (1835–1909), whose *The Man of Genius* (1891) investigates the intersection between genius and insanity.

realization, a living experience. Why insist on always turning it back to a review of the understood and past experience,—to the commonplaces of reason and intellect? Why demand that it should be always a review of yesterdays, or even of the impressions which yesterdays have brought? Why limit it to a record of reactions? Reactions, however precious or pleasurable ~~in themselves~~ are no more an end in themselves than is religion, but like religion are a means to a larger life. The stopping at the reaction point is the sensuous with its decadence, or working in the finer medium of the spirit, is the sentimental. Sentimentalism is a spiritual death, sometimes a pleasant and perfumed death but a real arrest of progress on the very stepping stone to things beyond. "Beyond where?" you say. O you know where, and know just as definitely as you know of yesterday's dinner for you have been there. We may not be able to describe it to one another but we can speak just as confidently of it, for the experience as glimpsed on the higher plane in music is not vague, but explicit, complete, self substantial, as easy of identification and memory as baldest fact or event and to some of us as precious. Only attempted translation into the terms of more ordinary fact is vague. The continually tempting and apparently less remote translation into the joy-love-sorrow formulas of emotion are even more vague and unsatisfactory. They start out pretty well, often victimizing composers themselves into using perfectly irrelevant program titles, but insulting, as soon as they are pushed to the least explicitness of detail, in a confusion which makes their value nugatory.

Thus Spake Zarathustra without knowing much of what he was talking about. Come and take a walk with me down to the river before lunch and see families living in their little row boats, the buffaloes, the rice, the leaning of the junk sails, the airplanes, the brown legged women almost up to their waists in mud as they set out the water chestnut plants, and across the river the hills behind the city the pagodas, the big bamboo victory arches for last evenings celebration of the successful Kwang Sai campaign. Really you couldn't put in a better six months than to come out here and visit us. Why not? If you don't do it now while you and your good wife are young you never will. With many pleasant recollections and with affectionate remembrance to you both from us all. Yours as ever,

John C. Griggs

97. Ca. 3 January 1930, sketch for Ives to John C. Griggs

Who ~~I feel should h~~ better deserves the blessings of good health and a ~~peaceful~~ untroubled old age than you.—that word "old age" I use quite ~~easily~~ readily now since I've begun my 56th year my last birthday—in fact I rather like ~~to use it~~ the sound of it—the sound ~~probably~~ more than the fact—I guess) ~~But~~ You have put into the lives of others "greater things than you ~~know realize~~ know"—and without trying to ~~and without knowing it—you remember~~ Dr. Bushnell's Unconscious Influence",—Every time we read it you are always standing around

I don't know as you remember, but when I came to Center Ch. ~~Under and with you~~ my father had just died. ~~I think~~ I went around looking & looking for some man to ~~fill help~~ sort of help fill up that awful vacuum I was carrying around with me. The men in the class—the tutors program etc. And [I had a] kind of idea that Parker might—but he didn't, I think he made it worse—his mind & heart were never around together,—You didn't try to superimpose any law on me teach me, or admonish me ~~or advise me or boss me~~ or say very much—but there you were and there you are now. (I ~~couldn't~~ didn't show how ~~I~~ or what I felt—I never seem to know how—except ~~some~~ when I get sort of mad) I long to see you again, and so does Mrs. Ives. I hope you and Mrs. G. will come east soon & make us a good long visit.

Mrs. I. & E. are well & having a fine time together this Christmas vacation. Edie entered F. [Farmington Academy] last Fall.[22] She likes it very much quite ~~well,~~ especially the coming home part (she says). She seems enjoys staying home, she reads & writes & sings & draws all day contentedly. The few dances & parties she has to go to, she takes quite philosophically apparently with a natural contentment. She is a very satisfactory person. No child has ever given her family more than she has us—and she is often quite amusing: Just now She feels the delusion of the intelligence test—and this afternoon she has been occupied with making some—they are quite funny—enclosed is one of them. . . .

• • •

Among those to whom Ives sent copies of *114 Songs* were his old Yale acquaintances, intimates, and fellow residents of "Poverty Flat," the series of shared bachelor apartments in which Ives had lived until his marriage in 1908. The following are several responses of those old friends to the songbook.

98. 12 October 1922, from W. Woods Chandler,[23] Simsbury, Connecticut

Dear Charlie,

Many thanks for the volume of songs which came just before I left for a vacation.

Since my return, have been rather busy, which accounts for my seeming neglect.

The other day, at the rotary club, I sat next to Lucius Barbour. [I] asked him if he had ever seen any of your writings and when he said no, I told him I would like very much to have him see this latest volume and also the one of piano pieces, which you sent to me a few years ago. As you know Lucius is very musical, so that you may be sure he will be very much interested.

For my part, the one thing that impressed me most, in looking over the songs, was to trace the development from College Days, down to the World War, then through that period and so on to the present. Looking at it in this way, one could the better understand the why and wherefore of present day development.

It is a marvel to me how you have found time to write so much and what is more how you have grown during all these years. Am so busy myself through the week that I get very little time for music except on Sundays.

22. Harmony Ives had also attended Farmington Academy.

23. Chandler entered Yale two years earlier than Ives and had preceded him at Hopkins Grammar School as well. The two shared interests in sports and music, and Chandler also worked as an organist during his years in college. He was more directly involved in the Yale Department of Music than was Ives and received a second baccalaureate degree in music in 1901.

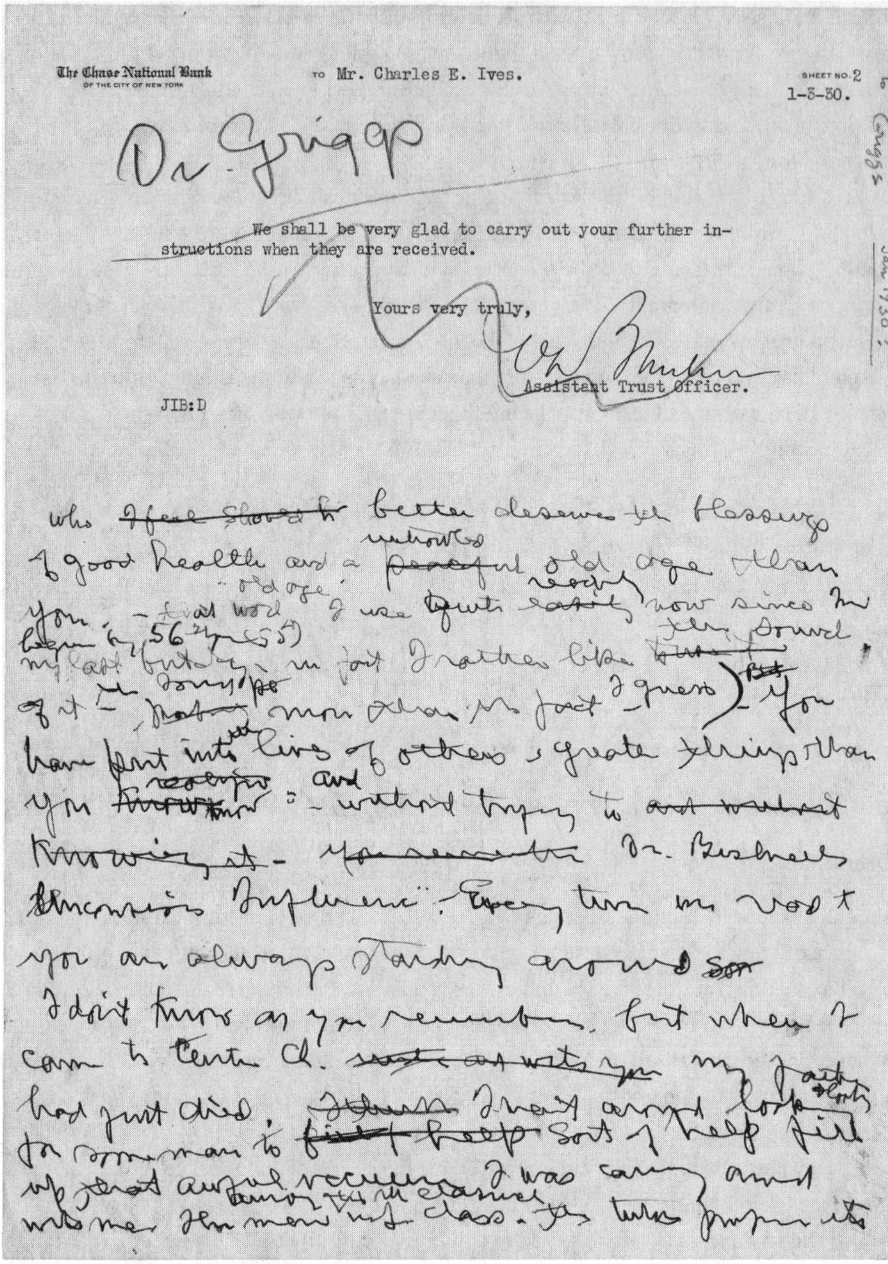
The Chase National Bank
OF THE CITY OF NEW YORK

TO Mr. Charles E. Ives.

SHEET NO. 2
1-3-30.

Dr. Griggs

We shall be very glad to carry out your further instructions when they are received.

Yours very truly,

Assistant Trust Officer.

JIB:D

to Griggs

Jan 1930?

3 January 1930, sketch for Ives to John C. Griggs.

About a year ago Joe Ensign had a letter from his classmate John Griggs, your old choirmaster, who is now in China. He wanted us to send him a lot of anthems which we did, but they were not such stiff, contrapuntal ones as he used to use in Center church.

Perhaps you will come to Simsbury some time now that Sue Twitchell is here at the

Walker School. If you do be sure to let me know for I should like to give you a good time.

Most Sincerely,
W. Woods Chandler

99. 16 November 1922, from Franklin Carter Jr.,[24] Greenwich, Connecticut

Dear Charlie—

The song book is a wonder! And while I appreciated the fact that you are essentially musical, I never before appreciated your breadth of poetical inspiration.

I am trying to sell the house with my eyes on another one to remodel for more room—Some time I hope we'll get you out here, but we feel the need of room at the present location.

Faithfully,
Franklin Carter Jr.

100. 19 March 1923, from Arthur (Pop) Baldwin,[25] Cleveland

Dear Dasher,[26]

I am very glad to have the possession of your book of songs, and to know of some of the work you have been doing these many days (and years) since I saw you last. Mrs. Baldwin is very interested in working up the music of your songs and we both (I listening) expect to enjoy them exceedingly. Pending learning the music, I can appreciate the verses. They are real, the kind that appeal to me! I take it the anonymous ones are yours, and they equally have a ring that appeals to me. Thank you very much.

I hope very much that I will see you in New Haven next Spring. Try and make it. It's our twenty fifth!

Sincerely,
Arthur (Pop) Baldwin

• • •

Henry Dwight Sedgwick (1861–1957) was an essayist, historian, and philosopher who was also a close acquaintance of the Iveses: they rented his house at 120 East 22nd street from

24. Carter received his LL.B. from Yale in 1903.

25. Baldwin graduated with Ives in 1898 and was a fellow member of the Wolf's Head secret society.

26. Dasher was one of Ives's several college nicknames; *Catalogue of the Officers and Graduates of Yale University in New Haven, Connecticut, 1701–1924* (New Haven: Yale University, 1924), 48; Henry Cowell and Sidney Cowell, *Charles Ives and His Music* (1955; repr. with additional material, New York: Oxford University Press, 1969), 35.

1917 through 1926. And, as Sedgwick mentions in the first letter below, Ives drew from Sedgwick's work in *Essays*.[27]

101. 5 May 1920, from Henry D. Sedgwick, Cambridge, Massachusetts

Dear Mr. Ives,

Your book has just come. What a nice looking book. My first feeling is envy. Thank you so much for sending it to me—I am going into the country in a few days & it shall be my traveling companion—and thank you for the compliment of quoting me. I am so glad to think that 120 is the house of the muses (this includes Mrs. Ives). I am sorry, however, to think that Thoreau is not on my shelves, unless you have put him there.

I hear that the book rack is at 109 E. 21—Thanks.

I look forward to the train & my book.

Sincerely yours,
H. D. Sedgwick

102. 10 March 1923, to Henry D. Sedgwick

My dear Mr. Sedgwick:

Under separate cover I'm sending a book of my songs. You'll see on p. 261 that I've taken the liberty of quoting you again. This sentence seems of rare beauty to us, Mrs. Ives & to me—when I'm somewhat aground I like to fall back on it.

In song #104, you'll recognize your "back yard" and the "Two little flowers"[28]

Sincerely
Chas E. Ives

103. 20 April 1923, from Henry D. Sedgwick, Cambridge, Massachusetts

Dear Mr. Ives,

You must indulge my surprise and pleasure on finding this very handsome book of songs here awaiting me, and also you must imagine my shame at knowing that the music is a sealed book to me. How I wish I could understand your songs, or more than that I wish I had a daughter to play things as you will hear Edith play these someday, singing too, I hope. It was most kind of you to send it to me, and I felt much flattered to see myself quoted. Thank you very much.

27. As Howard Boatwright points out in his edition of *Essays*, Sedgwick receives one of the few formal footnotes in the entire volume; see Ives, *Essays Before a Sonata, The Majority, and Other Writings by Charles Ives*, ed. Howard Boatwright (New York: W. W. Norton, 1961), xxii.

28. The "Two Little Flowers" of the song's title were Edith Ives and her friend Susanna Minturn. Ives composed the song while living in Sedgwick's house.

Edith and Charles Ives, 1924.

I think the musically endowed people are the only people I enjoy. I sometimes think that even at my age I will go regularly to concerts and at least have the joy of weeping with the violins, but I always find myself lacking in energy or too busy.

I am now running over in my mind all possible persons who can play and sing at least some of these songs to me. I congratulate you anyhow on doing what I am sure will be a great boon to your friends. You and Mrs. Ives must have had a very delightful time in the doing of it. I thank you again.

Sincerely yours,
H. D. Sedgwick

• • •

Ives also solicited opinions on his music more directly on a few occasions. Perhaps the most interesting instance of this in the correspondence involves Elizabeth Sprague Coolidge (1864–1953). She and Ives are intriguing parallel figures: although in remarkably different ways and with different agendas, both were substantial patrons of new music through the mid-twentieth century. The only documented contact between the two, which arose through Harmony's social acquaintance with Coolidge, resulted in a rather high-toned dismissal of Ives's music from Coolidge (who relied on the musical judgment of the orientalist composer Henry Eichheim) and a defensive but not unmeasured draft of a response from Ives.[29] Ives wrote the sketch in his own voice; he later wrote "not sent" on it in pencil.

104. 15 March 1921, from Elizabeth Sprague Coolidge, Lakewood, New Jersey

My Dear Harmony:

In accordance with your request I sent a copy of your husband's music to a friend in Boston, who is very interested in new work and modern ideas, and who has even given up writing in the European Idiom, and has recently been studying Asiatic music.

I sent it to him because I did not in the least understand your husband's work myself, and I thought that I could not judge of anything which to me was so foreign. I must confess that I found nothing in it which I liked, but there is so much now-a-days that I do not like because I do not understand it, that I did not wish to express my opinion about it.

I have today a response from this gentleman and it is not encouraging to Charlie's work. I do not want to quote him because I think it would hurt you, but you see I am trying to be honest in responding to your request, and feel it is more friendly to write in this way than not to write at all.

I do not know whether you are still in Quebec, but I hope that this will ultimately reach you and that your trip to Canada has proved a pleasant success.

I sent you today an invitation to hear some of the Quartet compositions which were sent to our competition last summer, and I thought perhaps you would be interested to come and hear them.

I am still in Lakewood as you see and am intending to stay here for a while. With kind regards to your husband I am, as always

Affectionately yours,
Elizabeth S. Coolidge

29. Eichheim's scathing criticism of the sonata is quoted in Cyrilla Barr, *Elizabeth Sprague Coolidge: American Patron of Music* (New York: Schirmer Books, 1998), 344–45.

105. Ca. 15 March 1921, sketch for Ives to Elizabeth Sprague Coolidge

Thank you for your letter to Harmony. If it isn't asking too much, I would like to hear all your Boston friend has to say about my music (I <u>still</u> call it that) He can't hurt my feelings—I've been called all the names in the criminal code. Favorable comment, to a great extent is negative—that is in effect, it sends one up too many "blind alleys." If I could see some of this man's music, any that is fairly representative of his main beliefs, I could probably tell whether his criticism will be of ~~any~~ value to me—as far as future work goes. But whatever he says <u>won't</u> be discouraging—that can only come from one source—you forgot that. However, don't bother to tell me what he says or who he is if you'd rather not. The whole thing, of course, is but an experiment—and it was not written prim [a small portion of the page is ripped off here, but it is likely that he wrote, "It was not written primarily to be played," as he wrote in Letter 111] . . . I thought ~~that~~ would be generally ~~sensed~~ understood. However I was surprised to find so many men were interested in a thing so repellant in form.

We had an interesting trip to Quebec. Dave and Ella are much better—they are to spend the summer with us in Redding.[30] Harmony is well and we hope to see you when the [illegible word] Quartet play in New York—though I still have to be careful & can't go out in the evening unless I can manage to be away from the office during the day.

Sincerely Yours,

• • •

Several recipients of Ives's mysterious gift scores responded at length. A number of these went on to become important figures in the growth of Ives's reputation as a composer and formed close friendships with the Ives family.

The American composer and critic Henry F. Gilbert (1868–1928) wrote this substantial and largely positive response to *Essays Before a Sonata* soon after receiving a copy in 1920. Like Ives, a New Englander, church organist, and proponent of American music, Gilbert was a prime target for his ideas, many of which did hit their mark with him. Ives's response to Gilbert shows his eagerness for contact and conversation with the larger musical community. His joking but oversensitive response to the suggestion that a good thinker must not be a good composer is an example of his tendency to use humor to deflect criticism and his inability to escape its effects.

106. 26 May 1920, from Henry F. Gilbert, Cambridge, Massachusetts

My Dear Mr. Ives,—

Before acknowledging the receipt of your book "Essays before a Sonata" I wished to read it through. It didn't take me long and I was much pleased both with the "substance" and very largely with the "manner." You must know that all these Concord people have been my intimate associates for the last 35 years—especially Thoreau and Emerson. Every

30. Harmony's brother and sister-in-law, David and Ella Twichell, lived in Quebec. Ella died of tuberculosis later in 1921. David would also succumb to it three years later. See Swafford, *Charles Ives*, 341.

stone in Concord is well known to me and has been for a long time. Of all these Concord folks Thoreau hits me the very hardest I think. The winds of Nature blow through my mind as they did through his, and then beside there is a kink of "sassy" non-conformity in him which tickles me muchly: a kind of will-be-myself-in-spite-of-hell sort of individuality which strikes a most sympathetic chord in me.

But there, I started in to talk about your book but when I find so much in it which is really mine I find it hard to "keep off the grass" of my own personality. You won't find me any "mush of concession" and there are some points in your literary manner (as well as some of your substance) which did not altogether please me. Other places there are in which you decidedly strike thirteen. You say (on pg. 56) "In music, in poetry, in all art, the truth as one sees it must be given in terms which bear some proportion to the inspiration." This is fine, to my mind pregnant with truth; to most minds an obvious platitude: but how few creative artists know it. Many a fellow with a comic-opera soul has made a miserable failure because he would write symphonies. On page 106 you say: "Perhaps the birth of art will take place at the moment in which the last man, who is willing to make a living out of art is gone and gone forever." This also hits me particularly hard. It strikes a most sympathetic note in my personality.

The characterization of Hawthorne in the first sentence or two (on page 46) is also excellent, and I enjoyed the whole of the Thoreau essay thoroughly. In fact I was very surprised to receive such a book from a musical composer. I showed it to a friend of mine (one of the Boston critics) and called his attention to certain striking passages. He was most interested and enthusiastic but said: "Depend upon it, this fellow is a bad composer—good composers are usually non compos mentis on every other subject."

Well I'll have to give you a rest (on account of the high price of paper). Thank you very much for sending the book. You directed it I notice, to the Music Dept. of Harvard University. I am only a "side show" there hired semi-occasionally to lecture. I hope to meet you some time in New York. A talk and a row with you over some of the substantive points in your book may help to mitigate some of the disagreeabilities of the modern Babylon.

Yours Sincerely,
Henry F. Gilbert

107. 28 May 1920, sketch for Ives to Henry F. Gilbert

Thank you for your letter. It is not easy for me to tell you how I appreciated the trouble you took to write me as you did and how the letter interested me—us, ~~for that matter~~ as Mrs. Ives, who ~~for years~~, has been (~~practically~~ my only) audience, critic and sympathizer for years shares my gratitude. We have read some of your articles (all we have seen) in the Musical Quarterly and other papers—Your "generosity" if I may call it that, towards art and life attracted me. Is there a book of your collected writings?—and where can I get it?

I had no ~~little~~ idea of jumping into print much less a book when I started these prefaces—but Mrs. Ives ~~has been~~ was getting somewhat tired of having all her closet room piled up with unseen MSS which I was always talking about showing to someone but never getting to it. There are many things in the book that should not be there—~~but when~~

~~one is pretty sure that his first book will be his last it [is] hard not to "nail" down some of the things that have been wandering around in his mind——— I suppose just to know that they're "down"~~ It may be well to throw some things out of the system, ~~at times~~,—but many should never land in a book.

Your friend, the critic, is wrong again I am not a bad composer. I'm a very good one (though it's inconvenient to have no one know that but myself!) And sometimes the family—our 6 yr. old daughter says she likes "to have the piano keys washed because it sounds like Daddy's music" However when the "Concord" copies are finished I'm going to send you one—(don't try to play it!) ~~But you will~~ You'll be spared this for some time—as it takes longer to correct proofs than I imagined,—and besides the ~~engraver's~~ mistakes make the music sound so much better (to others) that there are big decisions to make on every page. The 1st movement is impossible from many standpoints It's a long mass of experiments, which no one will ever play.—a self- respecting pianola would hesitate at the 3rd chord. "The Alcotts" is short and playable—but I ~~was~~ found myself pretty tired of it before the note was dry. The Thoreau movement perhaps measures up the nearest to what I wanted—but it is below something it should be!

You must come down to see us the first time you come to NY next Fall—I'm going to write and remind you of this as soon as we get back next Fall. Again, I want to thank you for your kindness in writing me—indeed, the whole family thanks you.

Sincerely Yours,
Chas E. Ives

• • •

Henry Bellamann (1882–1945), now best known as the author of the novel *King's Row* (1940), was another critic who gave serious and positive consideration to the *Concord* Sonata early on and one of the first of many friends Ives would find after he began to "throw" his music at the musical public at large (some of whom were pleased with what they caught).

108. 10 April 1921, from Henry H. Bellamann, Columbia, South Carolina

My Dear Mr. Ives:

Recently I received a copy of your second piano sonata. I have either you or your publisher to thank. I have just recently had time to go over it several times and I want to tell you how remarkable a piece of work it is. Miss Purcell, who is my assistant and who plays a great many modern works for the various lectures I give thru the year on such composers as Casella, Malipiero and Schoenberg, is very delighted with the sonata and we purpose making it the subject of an evening's lecture recital in our series for next year.

I should be very interested to know the first sonata and any other music of yours. May I have also any information you care to have gives [*sic*] audiences about you. I shall value any material you can give me to render an estimate of your music intelligible to the music club audiences to whom I speak thru the year.

An extraordinary work. One feels very happy to know that a creation of such calibre on an American subject may be done in America—tho I must say truthfully that I am not much interested in the geography of any work of art.

My sincerest and most interested congratulations and with every good wish I am,

Cordially,
H. H. Bellamann

109. Ca. 10 April 1921, to Henry H. Bellamann

My dear Mr. Bellamann:

I regret that Illness kept me, upon the receipt of your letter of April 10th, from doing nothing more than formally acknowledging it. I appreciate your kindness in writing and thank you warmly for your interest. Your proposal to include the Concord Sonata in your lecture-recital programs shows more courage than most musicians care to show. But I am afraid it (at least the first two movements) will arouse little enthusiasm with most audiences (except perhaps in the form of refined abuse or expressive silence). The first movements I find are severe tests for the listener as well as the player. But it is not so difficult to make the "Alcott" and "Thoreau" acceptable to the average audience. Possibly passages from the Emerson or Hawthorne movements selected in ways that may suggest themselves to you could be played separately,—without losing too much of the general impression which I've tried to present,—for instance, in the "Emerson", his free-sweeping way of throwing one from the many-colored aspects towards the underlying thought—the breadth of his philosophy. However, I want you and Miss Purcell to feel free to make any changes or revisions which meet your best judgment; there are some passages that were not exactly intended to be played literally—at least by two hands.[31] I shall be much interested to know what comes of the adventure. If your efforts in my behalf meet with enough success, that is, artistically (measured by your standards—not necessarily by that of others, the press or the audience) possibly Miss Purcell and you may find it practicable to give the lecture in New York sometime. If later you should think this advisable I would insist upon seeing that you are both adequately compensated for your time and efforts, and also paying all the expenses. However, this is just a thought that occurs to me while writing—it may not appeal to you at all.

Perhaps by this time you have decided that to undertake my music will be a too arduous and thankless job,—perhaps you have already relegated me to the "bench"; but in any event I am grateful for the interest and sympathy of one who I hear has done much valuable and unselfish work for the advancement of serious music in this country. Thanking you again for your letter, I am

Sincerely yours,

P.S. Under separate cover I am having sent a copy of the "essays" which were intended to be a "part with the music", whether for better or worse is an open question.

31. Here Ives refers to the origin of the "Emerson" and "Hawthorne" movements as orchestral scores. The piano concerto version of "Emerson" has been reconstructed by David Porter and recorded by Alan Feinberg and the National Symphony Orchestra of Ireland, conducted by James Sinclair (Naxos CD8.559175).

110. 4 July 1921, to Henry H. Bellamann

My Dear Mr. Bellamann:

Thank you for your letter of June 28th; I was very glad to hear from you. There are several mistakes in the copies of the "Concord" pieces. I expect to have time in a week or so to go through and correct them—will then send copies on to you.

It is generous of you to be interested and willing to try out this score; and I hope your efforts, in some measure, may be justified—at least, from your point of view. I have no printed matter about myself, outside of class-books, business notices etc., but the enclosed copy of a letter which I've sent to some who have made inquiries may give you enough,—it was written in a hurry and I've been too busy or too lazy to change it.

Most of what work I've done is in manuscript:—some early organ fugues, cantatas etc.; 4 violin sonatas; 3 symphonies, 2 suites ~~sets of~~ for orchestra; 1 string quartet; and about 250 songs—75 or 80 of which, are being published this fall (under one cover).

The first Piano Sonata, which you kindly ask about, was written about 6 or 7 [sketch has "7 or 8"] years ago. In some ways, it seems satisfactory enough to keep—in other ways doubtful; so I thought it best to put it away and haven't looked it over for about 5 years. Perhaps when something in hand, now, is finished, I'll get it out and see how it measures up.—whether it will seem worth sending you, I don't know.

I've said enough about myself and will stop—but not without thanking you again for your interest,—which we (Mrs. Ives is the better part of whatever I try to do) are grateful for.

Sincerely yours,
Chas E. Ives

• • •

The letter that Ives mentioned to Bellamann was the following one to Edwin Stringham, who was the music editor for the *Rocky Mountain News* in Denver.

111. 22 June 1921, Ives to Edwin Stringham

Dear Mr. Stringham:

At this late date may I acknowledge and thank you for your letter of April 3rd. Illness kept me from writing at the time, though I had copies of the "Concord Books" mailed to you then,—which I hope you received.

You ask for a history of my life, education and ideals. I was born in Danbury, Connecticut, went to public schools there; and received a groundwork in music from my father, who believed that all families should be raised on Bach and Beethoven. I graduated from Yale College in the class of 1898,—while there taking the elective courses in music under the late professor Horatio W. Parker, open to students in the academic department. Since then I have been in business in New York and am a member of the above firm. I played in the Danbury churches while a boy and was organist of Center Church, New Haven, for four years while at college. The following three years was organist and choirmaster of the Central Presbyterian Church, 57th St., New York City.

One's ideals are not so easily disposed of in a letter. A general idea of what I like to believe some of them are may be found in the "Essays" and I hope in the "Music." One of them—perhaps it is little more than a notion, for I find many do not agree with me,—is that an interest in any form of art should not be strapped down,—and money dug out of it, where that is possible. From some experiences several years ago, it seemed that to have a manuscript played or published usually required some kind of compromise;—so have been trying to work things out in my own way; and I imagine have been freer to do so than if I had remained in the profession. The Sonata you ask about is an experiment which perhaps goes too far. It was not written primarily to be played—at least with two hands. This is the first of a series which I propose to have similarly printed and thrown at the music-fraternity—chancing that a few might be interested. In this way you see no one has to buy the music, sell it, play it, or listen to it—except with both eyes open; there is no audience to throw things at the performer (or composer!); the artist does not have to risk his reputation, nor the publisher his capital, and the musical public is left in peace to work out its own salvation (whatever that means), and I to do the same without disturbing anyone but the neighbors. As a newspaper man I imagine you won't take this too seriously.

There is no objection to your making any comment in your columns, if you think it advisable to make any—but it is by no means necessary that it be favorable to be satisfactory to me.

Thanking you again for your interest and courtesy in writing me, I beg to remain,

Respectfully yours,

• • •

Another long-distance response to Ives's works came from Arnold Capleton, an Englishman teaching in Czechoslovakia. Although Capleton played a tiny part in the story of Ives's music and its acceptance by the musical community, the inclusion of his letters gives one a sense of the variety of people who wrote to Ives.

112. 18 April 1921, from Arnold Capleton, Prague

Dear Sir,

I borrowed your work "Concord Sonata" from my friend Dvorak the composer, to whom you sent a copy, & being interested in it have been propagating it here; but of course with a borrowed copy one can do little or nothing, and no one who is so taken up with himself will do less I should be glad if you could let me have a copy of your work and any others you may wish to propagate.

Yours faithfully
Arnold Capleton
(Prof English)

113. 24 June 1921, to Arnold Capleton

My dear Professor Capleton:

Permit me to acknowledge your letter of April 18th recently received and to thank you for your expressions of interest in the "Concord" Sonata. Another copy, as you request, has been mailed to you today. Later in the year I expect to have more copies ready and possibly a collection of songs which I will take pleasure in sending you,—you are quite welcome to dispose of them in any way you see fit.

I am gratified to have found a sympathetic friend in your new country which we Americans have great admiration and respect for.

The music in question is not the kind that is readily accepted with enthusiasm—it is but an experiment, which may in many places go too far—nor is it intended that it all be taken literally. Some musicians are willing to see what I am trying to do but some resent the work as a kind of infringement on their prerogative. It is the first of a series which I propose to have similarly printed and thrown on the music-fraternity—whether they like it or not.

Let me thank you again for your interest in my behalf.

Hoping I may some time have the opportunity of recompensing you for your trouble, I beg to remain

Sincerely yours,

114. 15 August 1921, from Arnold Capleton, Schloss Tloskov, Prague

Dear Mr. Ives,

I am spending part of my holidays at the above castle and have been very lazy, hence my not having till now acknowledged the receipt of your Sonata and book, which came slightly battered to hand. However, I am glad of the delay, for only yesterday I read with great interest your Epilogue and to-day I put aside sloth and studied 'Emerson.' There is much that appeals to me strongly in the essays. It is difficult to speak about the music, because words are so futile where the abstract and spiritual enter in.

You will no doubt gather that I am an Englishman. I am a first-rate pianist, playing everything from memory, also a composer and liable to turn into one of those 'silent musicians' who write nothing, for I don't know which direction to take. I began an opera music and text last winter but had to put it aside because I found that what with my other duties it was too much of a strain for my nerves. Composing is all very well, but if one can't find a publisher, publishers being necessary tyrants, there is not much encouragement. I don't ask for money, but just a little recognition, which one doesn't get unless one is prepared to write twaddle on the one hand or the conventional modern stuff on the other. So much for myself.

It will interest you to hear that in your Essays you express yourself in a manner in which I do very often myself. So there must be something in common between us. As regards your music this much I can say: I know what you want to say, and it is a vast improvement on modern conventionalism with its fantastic titles and mechanical throwing in of fourths and fifths in order to try and "be funny." But can it be said? And if so, is it not too much for a player, a human player that is? If only there were some other medium! I admire your courage. Further as I have often said—"most "hyper-modern" music might emanate from one and the same pen." Which cannot be said of yours, which has a distinctive note of its own. Which is no flattery, as I for my part am by no means a "modernist." I say that if a man has something in him, his soul can show itself through the old means, and it is the soul which counts, the poetry, not the medium. In Brahms one can find all possible composers Beethoven, Schubert, Schumann etc., and yet there is always Brahms there. The great mistake of the moderns is that music is for them not the soul to be expressed but the manner of expressing it. Chopin is for them the "Czerny school." If you lay a composition before them and they glance at it and find no bald fifths & fourths in it, then they toss it aside. If one writes something new in spirit in the simple form say of a Mozart, then it has no worth.

One generally thinks that in America everything is the "Dollar" I see this is not so in your case. And yet without the almighty dollar you would not have been able to publish. I wish I had a few dollars to publish some of my stuff. For after all one writes music that it may be heard, however much one may feel the necessity of writing something. I wonder how many of those who write because they "must," would feel such a keen necessity for doing so if they were placed in a desert island without any hope of an audience? I think not many. After all one writes for an audience, and to give pleasure in one form or another. I use the word pleasure in its very widest biggest sense.

I leave here to morrow. My address . . .

Looking forward to seeing more of your work, & with the intention of showing your sonata around

Yours sincerely,
Arnold Capleton

• • •

Clifton J. Furness (1896–1946), who first wrote to Ives after receiving the *Concord* Sonata, became a close friend. Furness specialized in the works of Walt Whitman and shared Ives's interests in music, transcendentalism, and American literature. For Ives the interest of a literary scholar in his prose, as well as his music, must have been gratifying. The pair also discussed works by Schoenberg and Scriabin in their letters, and from them it is clear that Ives knew some of the Russian composer's works in the early 1920s. The relationship between Ives and Furness was important: it was Furness who introduced Elliott Carter, then his student at the Horace Mann School, to Ives. Below is Furness's preliminary response to the *Concord* Sonata.

115. 15 August 1921, from Clifton Furness, Indianapolis

My Dear Mr. Ives:

One day last spring I was very surprised to receive a copy of your Concord Sonata, addressed to me in care of Northwestern University. I took great pleasure in presenting it, both to classes in modern harmony, and in esthetics and criticism. Needless to say, it aroused a storm of comments. I wish that you might have been a mouse in the corner!

For my own part, I must confess that I was completely non-plussed by it for some time—altho I am an ardent devotee of Schoenberg, and keenly alive to all new phases of the great fundamental problem of art-expression. Your work has, however, from the first fascinated me, with the charm of the unknown, perhaps. The Alcotts, in particular, has grown upon me, but I am perfectly frank to say that certain moments, especially in the opening movement, are a sealed book to me. I should very much welcome any further light on interpretation.

You will notice by the enclosed programme that I have taken the liberty to present your work in public.[32] I was much interested in the reaction of the audience. Some took it very seriously—others giggled. One man, an artist of some repute, who is not generally responsive to music, openly expressed his admiration.

I notice that this is a "second sonata." I should like very much to see the one which preceded it—also the essays designed to accompany the Concord Sonata. I shall hope to hear further from you, and shall certainly look you up when I come to New York, probably in the near future. Believe me

Your sincere fellow-seeker in the quest
Clifton Joseph Furness

116. Ca. 15 August 1921, sketch for Ives to Clifton Furness

Furness,

Let me thank you so warmly for your interesting letter & the program. You are more courageous than many musicians—a man takes unpleasant chances when he puts my music in front of an audience. It (that is the Concord music) is more or less of an experiment and one that goes too far in some ways—the first two movements—particularly so. It is but an attempt at piano transcendentalism—The Transcendentalists as I hear them, are ever [illegible word] out in speculative thought, approaching infinite & to the unknown based on "innate ideas"—which in themselves are not always easily accepted.

But there are many things, ~~especially in~~ or the way I've tried to say them, which I don't entirely agree with now—and that can hardly be hinted at by 10 fingers—in fact the first 2 movements are harder to play than to understand To express, one is better to wander away from what 10 fingers can do—for instance The principal aim in the Emerson, to express the sweeping way in which he throws the various aspects around the . . . [this sentence is incomplete] In trying to catch something of this, unconscious departures too many & too few from what 10 fingers can do.

The "Emerson" would express, but does very modestly the breadth of his philosophy & sweep of his thought as it throws the many sided aspects of his thought around it. I hes-

32. Furness performed "The Alcotts" in a lecture recital on 3 August 1921. This was the documented premiere of the movement. See Sinclair, *Descriptive Catalogue*, 672.

itate to encourage ~~or to expect~~ anyone to play this movement (or the 2nd for that matter). The reception it will get from most audiences (or auditors for that matter) will not balance the time & effort in preparation. The Thoreau is more practicable & can be made more readily acceptable.

I'm glad to send you (under separate cover) the Book of Essays which go with this music. I think this may give you enough of what the music tries to do and I won't bother you with a longer letter.

I greatly appreciate your kindness & the interest you have shown. I hope you will let me know when you are in NY. I would be very glad to see you. We will be there all winter.

Let me thank you again!

Sincerely,
Chas

117. 11 October 1921, to Clifton Furness

Your manuscripts, which I am mailing back to-day, were read with much interest and often with pleasure—rather always with pleasure, but in varying degree.[33] I say, we, as Mrs. Ives shares my interest in work of this kind. The appeal of the sketch in biography is immediate. Its dramatic touch, it seems to me, is well sustained and it has a strong kind of frankness, which is not a common virtue in biography now-a-days. Perhaps, if it were suffused with "a reticence which kindleth imagination," as some Victorian has said (I forget who), it might gain in some ways.

The "Brahms" is fine,—it has a buoyant stride and reminds me of the way he first 'got me.' I enjoy him now more than ever, he stirs me but in a different way perhaps,—more as a personal friend; I sit back and let him carry me high but with less exertion on my part. I'm not inclined to parallel Whitman and Brahms altogether the way you do. Both, as you say, are swept by the great universal impulse, but Brahms doesn't let his personality get in the way of his expression. Whitman, it seems to me, tells us with wonderful power of the great life values of everything in life and out of it, of the way he enjoys roast beef, but he likes to squeeze all the blood out of it himself; he doesn't let us have enough hand in it. Whenever he wants us to know how human he is, which is quite often, he becomes somewhat of a "loud talker,"—I'd take his word for it with less effort on his part. I dare say in a great deal of this I am wrong. I have read Whitman very little lately, and I'm probably prejudiced; Mrs. Ives says she doesn't like the over- human leer in his face.

I am ~~mighty~~ glad you were kind enough to send me your work. I hope you will let me see more of it and also that I will have the opportunity of meeting you personally.

33. Furness had sent Ives several essays on music and literature. Ives's response concerns the essay on Johannes Brahms.

* * *

Capleton wrote Ives again upon receiving *114 Songs* in 1923. It is unlikely that Ives ever sent him a photograph so that Capleton could "examine his forehead." Although Ives's interest in mysticism and ideas such as phrenology was slight at best, the transcendental cast of the *Concord* and *Essays* attracted many correspondents who, to use Capleton's words, "reach[ed] the mystical Borderland of the Occult."

118. 10 December 1923, from Arnold Capleton, Prague

Dear Sir,

I am writing to express to you my best wishes and compliments of the season. I also wish to tell you of the interesting hours I and my wife have had with the sonata and the Book of Songs you so kindly sent me. Without being in agreement with all you try to say, it at the same time affords me much pleasure in informing you, without flattery, that the close of "Thoreau" is for me one of the most wonderful things in music which I know. In it you reach the mystical Borderland of the Occult.[34] You use the same wonderful music in the Song Book, headed with a quotation from Thoreau. How the words express the music and vice versa! Of the songs my favourites seem to be "Two Little Flowers" and "Like a Sick Eagle." I think a Cor Anglais might sing the latter better than a voice. Perhaps my taste is bad, but I have a natural predilection and gift for melody. Your essays are equally interesting to me. There is one thing I can't understand. That supernal close of yours to Thoreau has a strange almost physical effect upon me: it gives me as it were the beginning of a headache (although I don't suffer from headaches); it has often run through my head for hours, and yet I feel it to be dangerous for me. The music is perfectly easy for my fingers and supremely clear for my mind, and yet the effect upon me can be such an one as that produced by, say, some occultistic séance! And yet there are people who find only a horrible noise in it. And yet again sometimes when I play it my wife begins singing the music or whistling it.

I have just received two orchestral works of mine "De Profundis" and "To Eternal Melody" back from Zemlinsky the conductor. Suk the conductor had taken up the first work with enthusiasm and promised to give it at a series of concerts. After the first concert he became insolvent, so it was all up. Suk said he would leave Prague for America this autumn. I gave him a card of introduction to you. He is a good musician, and has lost a fortune on music, which speaks for his idealism. But he seems to be an unreliable sort of chap.

Being interested in heads, at the risk of seeming vulgar I am going to ask you to send me your photograph. I want to "examine" your forehead. If I can find one I will enclose a photo of myself.

Being poor, and now married, I have lowered my standard for the time in music, and in

34. Capleton was interested in spiritualism and mysticism as well as music; he translated Karel Weinfurter's *Man's Highest Purpose* into English (London: Rider, 1930).

the hope of making some money I am composing an operetta to an English text and lyrics also written by myself. But it will be rather a 'classy' musical comedy. Could you tell me if there is much chance for such things in America. Perhaps you are in touch with the right people. My aim is to make a bit of money, buy a bit of land and get back to Nature, in which case if I wrote at all I trust I should write to please myself as I have hitherto done. Do you happen to know Mr. Samuel Thurman of the Metropolitan Opera House? He was my pupil for English. I sent him a simple song in the hopes of getting it published. Where it is now I don't know.

With greetings from me and my wife
Yours sincerely,
Prof. Arnold Capleton
English Lector on the Prague Techn[ical] Highschool

P.S. I find no photo for the present. What is the opinion in America about the Bollschevich atheist Bishop William Brown of the American Church? I have had some correspondence with him.

· 4 ·

HEALTH

(1907–1954)

The correspondence offers extensive documentation of the state of Ives's health, especially from about 1930 until his death in 1954. There is also more fragmentary evidence from earlier periods, such as the year leading up to his marriage in June 1908.[1] The nature and extent of Ives's health problems during and after his period of active composition have posed a vexing series of questions for biographers and students of his music.[2] Ives suffered from diabetes, for which he was eventually treated with insulin injections by about 1930; we do not know when the disease first developed. Ives also had at least three significant health crises that provoked great concern among his family and business associates. The two in 1906 and 1918 have been called heart attacks in the Ives literature because this was the term the Ives family used to describe them.[3] The episode of 1929 was not so labeled by Ives, but it was serious enough to keep him away from work for a period of months and to prompt his reluctant retirement from business in January 1930. This chapter presents, in part or in full, many of the surviving letters that describe aspects of Ives's illnesses. These letters are of several types. The most common ones, which I have mostly excluded, mention the composer's ill health in a general way in the context of an apology for his inability to meet with someone or to correspond at length. Often this statement was a part of the explanation for the fact that Harmony answered the bulk of the mail sent to Ives after 1930. Even for correspondents who expected the communication to flow through Mrs. Ives, the general declaration of Ives's inability "to attend to things as he would like" was standard—essentially a part of the salutation. Indeed, the ubiquity of this formula in the letters makes these general statements about Ives's health an unreliable gauge of the relative severity of his condition. The more important and revealing letters are usually written to close associates or friends and contain details of the timing, severity, or symptoms of a particular episode or "slump."

The first group of letters with substantial references to Ives's health are the courtship let-

1. For instance, it is unclear if the reference to worries over Ives's health and frequent checks of his weight in a letter home from Lyman Brewster during their trip to the Chicago World's Fair is related to Ives's later health problems. See note 9 in chap. 1.

2. Gayle Sherwood provides an overview of the various theories concerning Ives's health and offers a convincing case that his nervous disorder would likely have been understood as neurasthenia in "Charles Ives and Our National Malady," *Journal of the American Musicological Society* 54, no. 3 (Fall 2001): 555–84.

3. Henry and Sidney Cowell, whose biography of Ives is the most directly based on personal contact with him, write that the attacks left Ives with "permanent cardiac damage." Cowell and Cowell, *Charles Ives*, 76. See Letter 403, in which Edith Ives Tyler describes her *mother's* heart condition as poor.

ters from 1907–8. It is not clear whether the problems Harmony mentions are related to Ives's more serious latent conditions.

119. 17 October 1907, from Harmony Twichell, Hartford, Connecticut

I'm so sorry, Charlie, that being sick is what kept you yesterday—I thought it was lots to do perhaps. I hoped it was something nice anyway. Please let me know right away again how you are or have Bart or someone—I'll really be worried and uncomfortable if you don't or better yet get well & telegraph you'll come any day or time. The family is small & there is lots of room. If you'd come here & get well we'd like it.

I'm awfully disappointed—these days are so heavenly. I've always called this time of year the peace of God, to myself—the Earth has done her year's work and seems to be resting and these days seem to be a grin of approval—[4] But I shan't enjoy them now until I know about you—I hope you haven't got anything that is going to take time—Please Charlie, let me know right off & don't be sick—

Yours as ever
Harmony

If you are going to be ill any time do get a nurse or go to a hospital—A household of men isn't any place to be sick in, say what you will.

120. 13 January 1908, from Harmony Twichell, Hartford, Connecticut

Darling—

It was very pleasant to get your letter from home & Aunt Amelia's with it—They made me feel as if I had a place there.

This has been a very gray day & Louise & I both feel very glad for writing We rode around in a chair this morning for a while & I went out this afternoon again and sat & watched the water & the people for about an hour—Louise couldn't get up enough energy to do even that. We eat & sleep so well I can't tell why we are so slow about getting our strength back. . . .

Aunt Amelia says you seem very well— She says she thinks you have a tendency to work too hard that is a very bad thing & that you can't be too careful of your health & she adjures me to be very careful of mine—poor soul, she says she has always known [?] the limitation of delicate health—I suppose that is why its value appears so great—I quite agree with her & do you keep just as well as you are now. . . .

Your loving
Harmony

4. Note the similarity of this part of the letter to the text of Ives's "Autumn," for which Harmony would write the poem about a year later.

121. 30 January 1908, from Harmony Twichell , Danbury, Connecticut

My Beloved— My dear dear beloved—

I love you in almost another whole new way since I've been here with you in your own home & among your own people—the ways are all the same things but my heart sees farther & feels tenderer than ever tho' I hadn't supposed it could but this love is such a revealer—all the time—Dear dear heart I'm so glad you are mine to love & to cherish & to be happy with &, please God, to try & comfort when you need that & to be my comfort, beloved & that you are & will be and oh so much besides—Everything—you are my way thro' life & its happiness & strength & beauty—so dear to me & so beloved & such solid gold.

Aunt Amelia & I went to walk this afternoon time up & down the street in the sun. I was glad she felt like going out & now we are just up from our naps. I slept about an hour & I missed your coming in afterwards. Your uncle Joe is here now & he wants me to come in there—I have just been writing Dad & thinking how good a thing it is that this new way of life that shows so plain to me is just a continuation of the old way that has been familiar & sweetest & best to me—there is no wrench from anything I have—Only a refilling [?] of the very best of all. The love you have given me and the love you have wakened are all heavenly, dear.

Keep well & be a little careful—You don't know how badly it makes me feel to have you not all well—It's so hard for me to let you go even for a few hours—Good bye my heart's beloved my dear & darling

Harmony

122. 31 January 1908, from Harmony Twichell, Danbury, Connecticut

My dear lamb—

I miss you & want you so—I have such a feeling of loss about the time we must be apart—my beloved, my darling you are so dear so wonderful to me—I've just had my nap & I am writing you before dressing to go up to your Uncle Joe's to tea. He was here late yesterday and when I went out to mail your letter, he & I went together & I walked home with him & stopped on the way to see the library—We had a nice walk & talk—he's so nice. I am not being visited too much & am really enjoying myself ever so much—I'm glad I stayed for I think that I am more satisfactory to visit with when you're away. I can pay a little more attention to what is said to me—I think of you all the time darling in this place where you were little—Aunt Amelia tells me awfully amusing things about you—my dear beloved love.

We went & heard about Dr. Bushnell—some things I was very glad to have explained about his theology—I can see so plainly, the more I hear of him, how much he has been my father's teacher & leader—I am so happy that it makes you happy to have me here—I hope your head is better—it worries me. It's bad enough to be away from you when you are fully well and almost unendurable when I know you aren't perfectly so. I wish you would get to feeling alright before you go back again this time. . . .

Good bye darling my whole heart goes to you.

Harmony

123. 6 February 1908, P.M., from Harmony Twichell, Hartford, Connecticut

My beloved darling heart—

I call you all these things a thousand times a day grinning, and always with my heart close to yours & my cheek against yours & my soul in yours I think. I love you love you love you. It makes me so anxious to have you not well—It seems as if I couldn't stand it to be away from you when you're not perfectly well—If you are going to be sick you've got to let me marry you & get you well—when you come Saturday, dear, if you still feel that way you have to tell them at the office you may be away some time, can't you? & then stay until you are well—it's poor economy of yourself to be going on this way and I feel sure it's because you are tired & sort of bankrupt of nervous energy & you don't take time to lay in more than about a two days store with just a Sunday off. Dear Lamb—it makes me feel so badly How I wish I had you evenings, to love you and hold you and try and make your head feel better & put you to sleep by & by & not to leave you—there's nothing for me but that. . . .

My room is a different place to me from what it used to be—You are here & the memory of our hours here is wonderful—and day after tomorrow you'll be here again beloved—We'll come up here Saturday evening if you want to & you shall do the fire building and then, if you are tired you must be my couch & let me sit by you & read or not read as you choose. We don't expect anyone for Sunday I'm glad to say. I wish I knew how you are now my beloved love. Goodbye I love you beyond this world and any of its ways of telling you so—

yours forever
Harmony

124. 11 March 1908, from Harmony Twichell, Lakewood, New Jersey

Dearest heart—

I am getting so impatient to get to you—I haven't heard yet from Kate Goodrich—I thought I would this morning—If she is away & I can't go there I suppose I better stay here until Saturday & then come over & meet you.

It seems pleasant to think of you walking thro' Henry St. I have a feeling of attachment to that neighborhood that is strong—I suppose it is largely because it is all so connected with thoughts of you. I used to start out there mornings having seen you the evening before or going to see [you] feeling so happy & so much readier to work & give sympathy than I'd every felt in my life before. And then our Tuesdays were perfect—I can't think of a mar on one of them except for the last one—It seems to me I didn't think once that day. I loved you too then darling but—I didn't dare "let go"— our love & friendship has all been so sweet & beautiful & happy—and has transformed common things into beauty & will never cease. I wish the days would go easier for you—I wish we were married & that I could be with you—Aunt Amelia says she wishes we were too—She worries me about you. I really think if I saw her and not you most of the time I'd begin to think you on the verge of a nervous collapse. You yourself seem very healthy & good & lazy too, at the right time—I don't worry at all when I'm with you for I think you are willing to take life easy with me—that's my disposition—you were bad, tho', about writing her or anyone that time you were in Hartford almost three years ago—she told me how worried they all got. Well, dear child, that's long ago. Darling boy, I love you & feel your love & want it. Have you ever felt that you saw and knew my love for you & you knew your own for me? I wish you might & feel & believe its strength & devotion—have you dear? I think I haven't quite that myself—I feel your love I know I may ask anything of it and sometimes I almost get inside it—as it were. I think that may be a revelation that is in store for us as life goes on & experience brings each of us a fuller knowledge of the other's power of loving & character—I don't mean that you don't know me all now—you do—but capacities & natures will grow & deepen I hope with life & more & more darling we'll have knowledge of each other's soul & each other's self.—I think it's the most wonderful thing—an impossible thing I should have said if I hadn't felt it—to have such an insight into another person's actual self—to have a sympathy that can do away with all the frills of convention or misunderstanding or concealment, I mean one's natural instinct to conceal what is very sacred or intimate—I am that way with no one else beloved—not even with mother—I know she understands absolutely but I've had lots of feelings I couldn't talk to her of—we are both reserved with all our affection with you only have I ever had this unreserve that is freedom, my beloved, my own dear heart—I love you—I'm afraid & I want your arms to cry in. . . .

Goodbye my beloved
with all of me
Harmony

• • •

In this letter, written eight years after their marriage, Harmony's tone of concern about Ives's health resembles that in the letters from 1907–8.

125. 8 June 1916, from Harmony Ives, Hartford, Connecticut

Darling—

I hope & suppose that your not telephoning this morning means that you felt alright & went to N.Y. I felt miserable to have you away from me & not feeling perfectly well. I hope you had a good time & kept yourself comfortable—Dad had the best night he has had yet & I think we may consider him convalescent. He seems more like himself tho' his eyes look big. I think we will get to Danbury Sat. at 1:15—It's a better train than the later one—If you can't meet us have Mr. Collins will you? I feel rather used up & shaky myself. I suppose because I was very anxious for a few days & I haven't had a good sleep once since I've been here. The baby wakes at five—or before—She is well & good tho'.[5] I will go up now & sit with Dad while his energy holds out.

Bye darling love
H

• • •

In 1918, at the height of World War I, Ives volunteered to serve on a civilian ambulance crew in support of American troops in France. The required physical examination for the position found unspecified but apparently serious problems that foreshadowed the health crisis that struck him on 1 October and caused him to miss almost a year of work.

126. 4 September 1918, to C. C. Whittelsey, Assistant Personnel Secretary, YMCA Ambulance Corps

My dear Mr. Whittelsey:—

I have your letter of August 30th asking for my medical certificate.

Shortly after making application to the Y.M.C.A. I was examined by Dr. Bradshaw, one of the staff here. He seems to think that there are a couple of medical points to be cleared up before approval. I know that there is nothing whatever the matter with me except that I have been at business steadily for some time with no let up. I have decided to take two or three week's vacation, and am sure that I can give a clean bill of health before the end of the month.

I do not think it unfair to ask that my application, after the medical examination is in, take precedent over applications made later than mine.

In reply to your second question I have enlisted for six months service in France, exclusive of the time required going and coming.

Very truly yours,
CEI/MVM

• • •

On the page for 1 October 1918, Harmony wrote in her diary that Ives became ill and was unable to work all that winter.[6] In fact, this episode, which has traditionally been described

5. Harmony refers to their two-year-old adopted daughter, Edith, who began living with the family in 1915.
6. Harmony Ives, Diary, 1918 (CIP, 45/7); cited in Ives, *Memos,* 331.

as a heart attack, kept Ives away from the office until the following September and prompted a trip to Asheville, North Carolina, which was well known at the time as restorative resort.[7]

127. 19 November 1918, Julian Myrick to Rockland Tyng, New York Board of Taxes and Assessments, New York

Dear Sir:—

I beg to enclose herewith assessment of my partner, Mr. Charles E. Ives, together with an affidavit made by him as to:

First: The fact that he is a resident of Redding, Connecticut, and

Second: He is confined to his house and has been for some time past and cannot appear before your Board in person in order to swear off these taxes.

I trust, therefore, that with the enclosed notice and affidavit on proper form, his name will be stricken from your records.

Very truly yours,
JSM/HFM

Encs.

• • •

By the summer of 1920 Ives had been back at the office for several months, but his health was still fragile and a cause for concern among his coworkers.

128. 2 August 1920, from Julian Myrick, New York

Dear Charlie:—

The Eastern Underwriter man was in to-day and I told him you wanted a week longer to prepare your article. He said it would be satisfactory to them if they would be sure to have it next week.

I have also consented to take another page of advertising in their "Gold Book" at $75.00. What would be your idea on the advertising matter to insert?

Glad to hear that you are feeling better. Take your time about coming back, and do not take any chances.

With kind regards, I am
Very sincerely,
Mike

7. Stuart Feder, a medical doctor, finds little evidence in Ives's surviving medical records that the 1918 episode was technically a heart attack (myocardial infarction). Feder, *Charles Ives*, 285–87.

• • •

Ives mentions the limits his condition imposed on him in the following letter to Henry Bellamann.

129. 9 January 1922, to Henry H. Bellamann

My dear Mr. Bellamann:—

We were interested to hear about the Atlanta Recital. It must have been more or less of a strain on you both to give a whole evening to a work of that kind. I have felt less tired after digging potatoes all day long, than in an afternoon trying to get some of that music into the fingers. Please ask Miss Purcell to accept my thanks and appreciation and I hope some day I may hear her play. I realize what you have done,—so much so that it is hard to thank you adequately, perhaps I can when I can see you, but—probably not.

We were disappointed not to see you during the holidays; but don't wonder that Mrs. Bellamann dreads New York climate, (—climates, 10 below yesterday, 50 above tomorrow,) and we hope she is much better by this time. Perhaps towards spring you may feel more like coming North.

From what I have heard, the Mac Dowell Colony must be a satisfactory place to work in. If you go there, you must stop off and see us at Redding. We've found plenty of solitude there—especially since the doctors have stopped me from active farm work. You can have the pick of all the writing tables, including the camp bench in the woods.

I showed your verses to Professor Phelps Wm Lyon, Lampson prof of Eng. Lit at Yale. He was much interested and spoke especially about your delightful "sense of color"; but he is so rushed at this time of the year that he didn't go into detail as I hope he will later. I couldn't find the "Broom" at Brentanos but have ordered it, I assume it is in the December issue. The songs are in the hands of the engravers and have been for some time—but at the rate they're sending me proof sheets, it will be late in the spring before the book is ready.

I am, with best wishes,
Sincerely,
Chas E. Ives

[*In Ives's hand:*] If you have a program or two on hand, I should like one—also any press notices—but don't go to any trouble about it The Sonata [*Concord*] was played in London recently—by whom, I don't know.[8]

8. No information about this London performance survives.

• • •

Julian Myrick's comments in this letter imply both that Ives had another serious health episode in the summer of 1926 and that such illnesses were not particularly uncommon.

130. 22 June 1926, from Julian Myrick, New York

Dear Charlie:

I am glad that you have decided to stop trying to come down until you have gotten back to nearly your normal state and hope that you will not attempt it again until you find yourself in that condition.

The invitations for the dinner went out last Friday and we are getting to a considerable number of favorable responses. Send along any suggestions which you may have or anything which I may say at the dinner.

The paid-for business up to this morning is $2,266,000. It looks as though we ought to go, at least, a little more although the business slowed down last week and is not very lively right now. Otherwise, everyone is very well.

Sincerely,
JSM

JSM: EBC

• • •

In the summer of 1929 Ives faced the illness that forced his retirement the following January. His absence from the office required that business be conducted by letters such as the one from Julian Myrick below. Myrick's tone about his partner's condition resembles that of 1926. Ives finally decided to retire not because of a markedly more serious condition but because of the accumulated effects of a generally worsening chronic illness.

131. 5 June 1929, from Julian Myrick, New York

My dear Charlie:

I am enclosing herewith a subscription card, copy of a Deed of Trust, describing the American College of Life Underwriters and a booklet concerning the Edward A. Woods foundation.

I was one of the people that inaugurated the American College and at the Convention in Detroit last year I put the firm down for $500. If you agree, you might fill in the subscription blank and draw a check to the foundation for $250.00 and I will do likewise. This, of course, is exempt from taxation.

Everything is going well here. We made a slight increase for the month of May both in the Full Year and Initial. A copy of the statement sent to the press is attached hereto. Business has slowed down a little bit but everyone is working hard and we are trying to have a big June.

The company has increased its limit from $350,000 to $500,000 on one life. I guess that is about all the news.

Don't bother to come back until you feel absolutely sure that you have regained your full strength.

Give my regards to Mrs. Ives.

Very sincerely,
JSM

• • •

About two weeks after Myrick's letter, Ives describes the onset of the 1929 attack in a letter to T. Carl Whitmer. The symptoms Ives mentions, shortness of breath and possible tachycardia, are intriguing in view of the diagnosis mentioned in Letter 133, below.

132. 18 June 1929, to T. Carl Whitmer

Dear Mr. Whitmer:

When you were with us in N.Y. last winter, I meant to have asked you about the work at Dramamount and tell you that I wanted to be of some help in it, if I could in some way. I intended writing sooner but about the middle of April I ran into one of these bad spells, (slow breath—hard—pump etc.) And haven't been able to do anything—business, music or correspondence, am getting around now though the doctors say I'll have to go slow all summer. . . .

• • •

By July Ives had decided to retire, and he sketched a long and unusually specific letter to Myrick in which he describes his condition. Most interesting in this account is that he divides his illness into two parts: the "usual physical condition," presumably diabetes, and an additional mental depression that his doctor called "a kind of n x." This enigmatic abbreviation strongly suggests that Dr. Wells's diagnosis was neurasthenia or nervous exhaustion.[9] Harmony had used similar terms when she fretted over Ives's health in Letter 123, back in 1908.

Myrick's reply to Ives also shows that he understood the origin of Ives's illness to lie in a depleted stock of nervous energy, which was held to be the primary cause of neurasthenia.

9. Neurasthenia was a general term for a disorder that was thought to stem from a depletion of its victim's mental energy. It manifested itself in a wide variety of symptoms, including excitability, heart palpitations, lethargy, and depression. The disorder was widely diagnosed up through the first decade of the twentieth century and struck even such famously robust figures as Theodore Roosevelt. This letter bolsters Sherwood's claim that Ives's condition would have been understood as neurasthenia; Sherwood, "Charles Ives and Our National Malady, 557–58.

133. Ca. 22 July 1929, sketch for Ives to Julian Myrick

Dear Mike:

H[armony] wants to acknowledge receipt of the Trustee check that Watson forwarded—And I want to send the enclosed check for any extra ~~personal~~ expenses, as traveling, luncheons, etc. that you had paid personally. I remember just before I left you gave a luncheon to the field club men—If the enclosed isn't enough for these items please let me know. If it happens to be more please keep the bal[ance] till needed. It's an uncomfortable enough feeling to be drawing full profits and not be able to be on the job, without having you put to any expense which I don't share in. That's one reason it's a relief to have the future plans settled as they are and it's also well to have ~~a little~~ some time for readjustment. I realize fully now that I could not keep going for another year,—but though I always want to do anything I can to help you & the office ex-officio from next year on ad-infinitum. My main regret is entirely one of sentiment—for you ~~not for~~. but as Harmony says, we may have more time to see each other than we have in the last few years.

I don't know exactly what to say about myself. For 3 or 4 days at a time, I feel quite well, then come periods when I certainly don't. However, I ~~know that~~ I'm ~~gradually~~ better than I was ~~in May~~ during the last two months in NY, when I was apparently in worse shape than I thought. I couldn't do anything physically or mentally. Wells said it was a kind of n x over the usual physical condition and is trying to get the weight up etc. I won't ~~go into~~ bother you with more details except to say that I couldn't possibly have written a letter as long as this a month ago and so I hope to be able to get down for a few days at a time when you are away, the last of August or Sept. and by Oct. I want to be able to finish strong on the home stretch just for the satisfaction ~~of doing~~ of it if nothing else. It won't have any great effect on the year's bus[iness]. I have some things in mind to suggest for the fall, but haven't got down to work on them yet—~~hope~~ expect to soon.

I hope you are keeping well and not taking on so much that you're kept under a strain.

Please give the enclosed note to Joe and Miss G. Edie & Harmony are in fine shape this summer. They send kindest regards to you and the family,

Sincerely,
Chas

134. 22 July 1929, from Julian Myrick, New York

My dear Charlie

I can't tell you how much I appreciated your letter. I had of course realized for some time that it was now most unfair to you and yours to have you continue in the business but it was just one of those possibilities that had to be put off as long as possible. When the decision was made & since then I am free to confess that I do not get the same joy or zest out of the work that I did before & I only wish that I had put by enough so that I could retire with you.

I can't contemplate any other partner than you, however, I suppose like most everything it will work out & I hope for the best for us all.

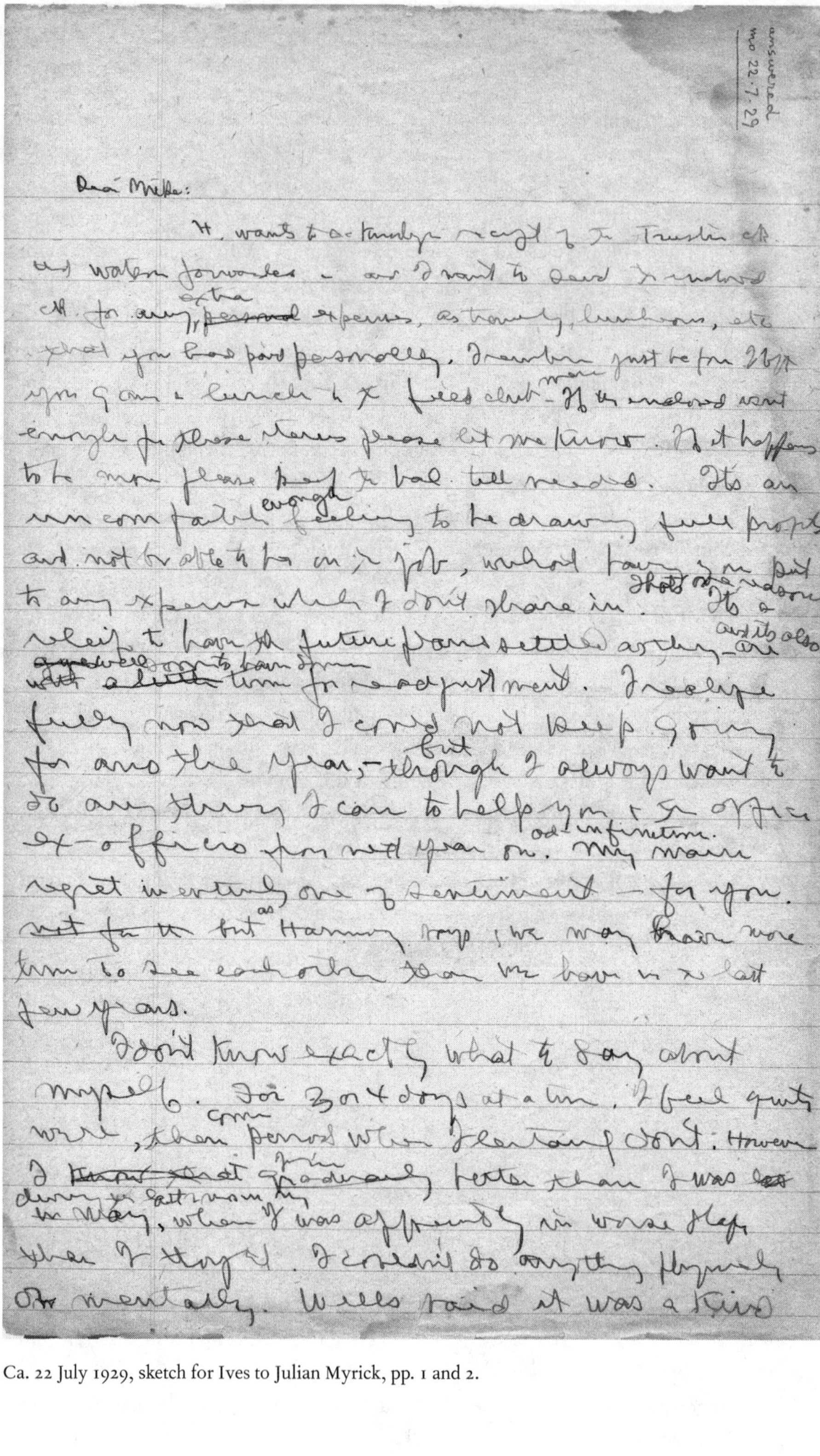

answered
no 22.7.29

Dear Mike:

H. wants to acknowledge receipt of the Trustee ck. and water forwarded — as I want to send the enclosed ck. for any extra ~~personal~~ expenses, as traveling, luncheons, etc. that you have paid personally. I remember just before [illegible] you gave a lunch at the [illegible] club — If the enclosed isn't enough for these more please let me know. If it happens to be more please keep the bal. till needed. It's an uncomfortable enough feeling to be drawing full profits and not be able to be on the job, without having you put to any expense which I don't share in. It's a relief to have the future plans settled as they are and it's also [illegible] time for readjustment. I realize fully now that I could not keep going for another year, — but though I always want to do anything I can to help you & the office ex-officio from next year on ad infinitum. My main regret is entirely one of sentiment — for you. ~~not for~~ But as Harmony says, we may have more time to see each other than we have in the last few years.

I don't know exactly what to say about myself. For 3 or 4 days at a time, I feel quite well, then come periods when I certainly don't. However I [illegible] gradually better than I was during the last warm [illegible] in May, when I was apparently in worse shape than I thought. I couldn't do anything physically or mentally. Wells said it was a kind

Ca. 22 July 1929, sketch for Ives to Julian Myrick, pp. 1 and 2.

[illegible] on [illegible] & over the nervous physical condition
and is trying to get the weight up etc. —
I won't ~~go into~~ bother you with more details
[I couldn't possibly have written a letter as long as this 2 mos. ago]
except to say that I hope to be able to
get down for a few days at a time when
you are away, the last of August or Sept.
~~I want to~~ and by Oct. I want to be able
to finish staying on the home stretch
just for the sake of ~~doing~~ of it
[it will have any great effect on] of nothing else. you know. I have some things
in mind for the fall ~~work~~, but haven't got
down to work on them yet — ~~hope~~ expect to soon.
I ~~do~~ do hope you are keeping well
and not taking on so much that ~~keeps~~ your days keep
you under a strain.

Please give the enclosed note to Joe & Mrs. G.
Edie & Harry are ~~[illegible]~~ in from their [illegible] [illegible]. They
~~[illegible]~~
send kind regards to you & the family.

Sincerely
Eva.

I agree that the best part of our partnership was the affection & confidence in which we always held one another & I like to think that this relationship resulted in our having had a good influence on many individuals & organizations that it has been our duty or pleasure to work with.

If we had known as much then as now we would have no doubt taken a S.A. [stand alone?] contract but I doubt we are as good at bargaining as we are at working & believe in what we undertook & in the old Mutual that we have served for the best part of our lives. I presume there is no one or group very grateful but that cannot take away our own joy in friendship & the opportunity we had to work together & develop the largest as well as the most respected agency of its kind in the country. I will certainly try in carrying on never to let down the good will & reputation we have built up together.

Thanks for the check I am careless on records as to what I spend on business & otherwise sometimes it is very hard to apportion so it is hard to say if it is too much or not but I hadn't thought of your contributing, so it is very satisfactory, if agreeable to you, so it stands.

I think it would be most unwise for you to attempt to come back before you return to town for the winter & then you must be most careful not to over do again. I will take a winter vacation. I hope to be able to see more of each other but N.Y. is a terrible place to live in & see friends & the rush of demands at the office has always been almost beyond belief. . . .

My main worry is that you should take care of yourself & not do anything to overtax your strength & nervous energy again.

My best to Harmony & Edie

Affectionately,
Mike

135. Ca. 22 July 1929, sketch for Ives to Julian Myrick

I don't know quite how to thank you for your very kind letter. I appreciated it very deeply and so did Mrs. Ives. If I'd as much sense as she, I would have resigned some time ago. I ought to have known better than to have tried to stick it out this year. and during the last 6 mos. or so months, it['s] been so obvious that I could not go on, that even I could see it. One of the reasons partly that I didn't "come to this sooner" was that for certain periods I seemed quite alright, and felt I could go on forever. But lately these times have been shorter and farther apart. This last bad spell hasn't been so much due altogether to the physical condition—it's been more of a general running down.—and there's been a kind of depression that I can't account for. . . .

• • •

The next two letters provide more details of the symptoms Ives faced in 1929. Ives also stated that this episode was a recurrence of his previous illness rather than a new disease.

136. 30 December 1929, to T. Carl Whitmer

Dear Mr. Whitmer:

We are always glad to see your handwriting on the outside of a letter—and on the inside too. I hope you are quite well again now and I gather you are from your letters. We were much interested in Mrs. Whitmer's outline for the art visitors & young students Sometimes I think it must be a greater art to draw the young towards it and in the fine way she does, than to be an artist (every one is an artist—if you ask them first!) I wonder if Mrs. Whitmer will send us another copy a friend of ours borrowed it a while ago and still borrows it. We were disappointed in not seeing you this summer and in not being able to get to Dramamount. I haven't been good for anything in some while. Last spring an acute condition of my old trouble set in. I haven't been anywhere or to the office for over 6 mos. but am better now & hope to get going soon. But the serious things aren't the meanest things—a neuritis in both arms came along last summer, (probably caused by the other trouble) and I couldn't touch the piano for 4 months and now only with 2 fingers, and only recently have been able to write. I've never had such a depressing time. It's good to sit down and think music in silence part of the time but not all of the time. However I hope to be able to make a little noise for you when you come to N.Y. for your annual visit—which we are looking forward to—& which we expect without fail—and we hope Mrs. Whitmer may be able to come also this year—& next year.

With best wishes to you both from us for the new year & all the new years

I am
Sincerely
Chas. E. Ives

137. 16 January 1930, to Nicolas Slonimsky[10]

Dear Mr. Slonimsky:

Thank you much for your letter. I greatly appreciate what you say and that you feel the music is worth playing. It doesn't seem right that you should be placed in so much uncertainty about carrying on the concerts—it is work that should not be circumscribed. The Boston Symphony Directors ought to lend more of a hand, if only from their sense of duty to music in Boston—(we won't say from their sense of music). However anything that's any good works out slowly—usually I suppose.

I was very sorry not to go to your concert Sunday, but I have not been able to get out at all recently. Was glad to see that the critics were favorably impressed—and I hope you felt the same way. Your comment in the "Transcript is very interesting & so well put. It seems to me that Mr. Rosenfeld's interest in words is keener than his judgment of music. Probably I ought not to say that as I know very little of the music he talks about. Something I

10. An uncompromisingly modernist composer and conductor, Slonimsky was the first to conduct works by Ives in Europe. He became a close friend.

read of his some years ago rather gave me that impression. When you come to N.Y. again I hope to have the pleasure of seeing you.

I am, with kind regards,

Sincerely
Chas. E. Ives

• • •

By February Ives felt well enough to receive guests at Redding. Nevertheless, the neuritis in his hands persisted.

138. 17 February 1930, to Nicolas Slonimsky

Dear Mr. Slonimsky

I must write just a line to tell you what a fine time I had yesterday—it was quite a memorable occasion, for me, at least. It was good of you to come. Mrs. Ives & I will expect you in 2 weeks, we would like to have you stay with us while you are here—but you must do whatever is most convenient for you, you must be here part of the time, at least—and all the time if you can. We want you to feel free to come and go as you would in your own home.

I can't write as I would like to, the lame hands make it bad So good-bye for a short while.

Sincerely
Chas. E. Ives

You left your baton here. It feels rather etherial so I won't mail it as it may be broken, unless you want me to.

• • •

Here Myrick links Ives's inability to work and his diabetes, a subject of personal and professional interest to the two men.[11] Letters 139, 142, and 144, below, suggest that the insulin treatments Ives began to receive around June 1930 were of significant benefit, even though they did not completely alleviate his symptoms.

139. 21 June 1930, from Julian Myrick, New York

My dear Charlie:

I was delighted to receive your note of the 18th and very glad that somebody has finally put you on insulin. Personally, I do not see why, with all the medical knowledge we have here in New York—the Rockefeller Foundation, the work they are doing at Johns Hopkins

11. See Letter 144, below.

and in Boston—that you can't be built up and have your strength restored even though you might have to take it quiet.

The reason you have not been able to work on your music is because you haven't had the strength to give it the necessary energy and concentration.

Your note was the best news I have heard in a long time and I do hope you will get the best there is to look after you and not putter around with a lot of men that haven't the up to date information at their disposal. I know I can help you in this respect, if you will only let me.

Very sincerely yours,
JSM

JSM: EBC

140. Ca. 30 September 1930, to Julian Myrick

Dear Mike:

The page from the "Eastern Underwriter" with your fine thoughts of me was unexpected—and also a good deal undeserved. It was thoughtful and generous of you to remember our past and me as you did. Not many men would be as big minded as that—or would bother themselves about an old and useless partner. Harmony says it is typical of you—of your friendship, fine mind and heart that you've always seemed more like a member of the family than a business partner—and she's right! Every way—Reading it makes me feel less low in mind than I do sometimes. I wish you would retire before long and let me get even with you.

I hope you and the family are keeping well—and that you got in a good vacation—I bet you didn't. I would have written before but about the middle of August I had a kind of bad time though up to then was going well—however I'm better now. We hope to be able before long to go up to the mountains for a little change—Harmony is pretty tired from her job as housekeeper nurse and chauffeur and needs a rest—ever yours,

Chas—

141. 30 September 1930, Harmony Ives to Julian Myrick

Dear Mr. Myrick,

I must tell you how fine I think your appreciation of Charlie—He is an extraordinary man and what he has done in the two fields of business & music shows unusual brain power doesn't it? He is so modest he thinks little of himself and I am just glad to have you say in public what <u>you</u> think—and you know him so well. I am sure no two partners ever arrived at the end of a long partnership with truer regard & respect for each other than you two. Charlie has had a good summer on the whole but he hasn't the grip on things yet I hope to see him have again—we are going off next week for a short vacation for <u>me.</u> I want to shake housekeeping for a week or two! I hope your family have had a good & happy summer. Edith has been fine & is a great comfort—

I would like to have a few copies of that article to show the family—do you think Will [Verplank] could get a dozen copies & tear out the page? Many thanks for that & many other things

Sincerely yours
Harmony Ives

142. Summer or fall 1930, from Mrs. E. Robert Schmitz, Paris

Dear Mrs. Ives

We received your very nice letter and are happy to know that Mr. Ives has found the insulin a good relief for him and is in good shape. We were disappointed not to see you before sailing. . . .

143. 13 January 1931, to T. Carl Whitmer

. . . ; They say that Dr. Joslin[12] knows more about diabetes than any man in the world—but potentially he doesn't know as much about it as I do—he's never had it—that's the way with these doctors & music critics. . . .

144. 29 January 1931, from Julian Myrick, New York

Dear Charlie:

I was delighted to receive your letter and to know that you had decided to go up to Dr. Joslin. I feel sure that even though he says your case has been handled well that he will be able to make some improvement.

I am also glad that you struck up such an acquiantanceship and there are lots of things about these sugar cases that Life Insurance Companies have to learn and men like Joslin have to help us in determining some method whereby we can tell the good ones from the bad ones outside of a blood sugar curve and it will have to be simplified in some way. If you get a chance you might talk to him about it.

We will be about $500,000 behind our paid-for business as to January of last year. Would have gone over but for one of these sugar cases—George Hurd, who has had sugar off and on in his specimens since 1915. He looks as well today as he did then, kept the same weight and went to Dr. Mosenthal where he had a blood sugar curve made in 1925, took longer than two hours to come back to normal but in 1928 he had another one made at the New England Mutual, came back alright in the two-hour time and went to

12. Dr. Elliott Joslin was a highly regarded specialist in diabetes who pioneered the use of insulin to treat the disease. Founded in 1898, his research center and clinic are now affiliated with Harvard University.

Dr. Mosenthal again this year and came back in the two-hour time. Dr. Mosenthal's diagnosis of the case is that it is not diabetic but as having a low threshold—whatever that means.

It looks to me as though we are discarding too many good cases that show an occasional trace of sugar which is due to a dietary condition or nervous excitement or the other things that go on in a person's life that causes a slightly elevated blood pressure, trace of albumen or sugar but which clears up right away when they are under normal conditions.

As you will remember, we used to decline everybody that had a trace of albumen in two or more specimens but now they are put on the quantitative test and unless a person has more than that they are not declined. As a result we have made great progress in that respect and think we have Dr. Bradshaw to thank for that improvement. We are also disregarding the functional heart murmurs where we used to decline them but the sugars have not yet been solved and our selection now is worse than it was twenty years ago yet the medical profession apparently knows more about it.

I am glad that Mrs. Ives is attending the lectures about the diabetic diet. I will be interested to hear about it.

I am sorry I did not get to hear the concert here in New York but Marion and Mrs. Edwards went. They both took great pride and pleasure in your piece.

I am sure that you are doing the right thing and my only advice to you is do not be in a hurry because I believe, in Dr. Joslin you have the best man in the country and hope that you will have the patience to stay as long as he wants you to and when you leave do exactly as he tells you.

Of course one can't help getting angry once in a while but I do it less often now than I did twenty years ago—the business strain of course keeps up but I try to throw it away after five o'clock but have been having quite a time recently on account of the medical department and other situations which you know about.

With kind regards, I am
Sincerely,
JSM

• • •

The correspondence with John Becker (1886–1961) provides an excellent overview of Ives's health in the 1930s.[13] Becker, who was an uncompromisingly modernist composer, became a good friend and corresponded frequently with Ives during the decade; their close working relationship ensures the availability of numerous descriptions of Ives's health problems, which were substantial and not an excuse to avoid the demands placed on him by the growing interest of the general musical community.

13. Final copies of all of the correspondence from Ives to Becker are preserved in typed transcriptions made by John Kirkpatrick from the originals lent to him by Evelyn Becker after her husband's death. The CIP also includes photocopies of many of the original letters.

145. 29 April 1931, Harmony Ives to John Becker

My dear Mr. Becker

Mr. Ives has been waiting to write to you for some time but has not been feeling at all well lately and I want to send you word from him that he will write you before long. He has been very deeply interested in your music and feels in strong sympathy with your way of thinking. It was a relief to him to have someone write about a subject that is so important and so neglected as you did in your article "The Fine Arts and the Soul of America" which Henry Cowell gave him a while ago.

He will send you copies of some of his music very shortly with some photostats of manuscripts which are being made now.

He wishes you success in the cause you have undertaken & hopes to write you before long—With his best wishes I am

Yours sincerely
Harmony T. Ives

146. Ca. 6 April 1932, Edith Ives to John Becker

Dear Mr. Becker:—

Father has not been well, & as it is difficult for him to write, I am acting as his long-hand stenographer.

We all enjoyed your visit so very much, & look forward to seeing you again. Did you ever run into "Paul & Virginia"—or just Paul? He seems to be a bashful fellow even eluding Sarah's valiant Bookstore scouring![14]

I forgot to give you the little Christmas Carol for John, & have asked Daddy to let me enclose it in this. The extreme immaturity of it ought not to tear the envelope, although it may later cause those of any musical talent to tear their hair over the hopelessness of these "Pseudo- intellectuals"(?)! By this, therefore, you can tell that I did listen to your lecture, even though my outward appearance seemed touched with the effects of dropsy. . . .

Daddy says he is very glad to hear that Mr. Goossens liked your music so much, & he is sure that it will be played.[15] If he can be of any use in the matter of getting the parts ready, please let him know. We were all glad that the Philadelphia Orchestra played Mr. Cowell's "Synchrony"; it was well received by those who had "ears to hear." Mr. Cowell left Monday for the West; his plans were somewhat changed, & he is afraid that he will not get to St. Paul.

If all goes well, we are to sail on May 4th, & Daddy will let you know our foreign address as soon as we get settled over there. He wants to be remembered to Mrs. Becker &

14. *Paul and Virginia* was a didactic novel by Bernardin de Saint Pierre (1771); it was widely read in translation even into the early twentieth century.

15. Probably the English conductor Sir Eugene Goossens (1893–1962), who had been working in the United States since 1923.

the children & says that knowing you & having your friendship is something he is very grateful for. We send affectionate greetings to you all,

Very sincerely yours
Edie Ives

P.S. Father has a printed list of works, with the dates, wandering somewhere within the sahara of his papers, & will send it to you as soon as he locates it. Also, he asks you to be sure & have the second edition of the "Soul of America" printed as he suggested.

• • •

In 1932 the Ives family took an extended European vacation on the recommendation of Ives's doctors, who felt that travel might improve his condition. A number of letters from this time make passing reference to his health—for instance, in the context of describing plans for travel. Excerpts from several of these are below; the complete letters may be found elsewhere in this volume, as noted. In mid-June, a month into the vacation, Ives wrote a letter to Lehman Engel that was transcribed by Edith. Its first paragraph indicates that the trip was preceded by a downturn in Ives's health: "I am acknowledging your letters to my father, one of which came after we left. He is somewhat better, but it is still difficult for him to write, so I am acting as his longhand stenographer."[16] By July the Iveses had settled into a quiet life in the English countryside and were preparing to sail for Germany and the next leg of their journey. Feeling somewhat better, Ives wrote to Nicolas Slonimsky to apologize for not being able to see him in New York because of the illness: "Dear N.S. Am. Ambas! / I felt very, *very* badly in not seeing you again that time in N.Y. I was just about in the end of one of those ——, —— low sloughs, when a man can't do anything & doesn't know it—couldn't eat, sleep, think, or even cuss moderately!"[17]

In June 1933 the vacation was nearly complete, and the family had returned to England in preparation for sailing back to New York. Though the health effects of the trip had largely been beneficial, Ives still occasionally experienced episodes of the tremor and vision problems that would plague him for the rest of his life. He alluded to these difficulties in a letter to John Becker: "I would have written before but my arms & eyes have bothered for a spell."[18]

Ives had been back in the United States for some months in December 1933, but he was still hampered by episodes that required him to cease all activity. In the following letter to Slonimsky, he relates these "slumps" to overwork and overexcitement. The letter also concerns changes Ives wanted in the edition of *Three Places in New England* that Slonimsky was preparing.[19]

16. From Letter 234.

17. From Letter 243. Ives often called Slonimsky an ambassador for American music after his Parisian premieres of *Three Places in New England* in 1932.

18. From Letter 260.

19. Slonimsky's edition of the chamber orchestra version of *Three Places* was published by Birchard in 1935. See Sinclair, *Descriptive Catalogue*, 40, for full details.

147. December 1933, to Nicolas Slonimsky

Dear Padre—[20]

I would have written before but have been somewhat out of shape for the last few weeks, and am still kept on "the back" most of the time—too much "riting, talkin', playin' & cussin'" they say!

Thank you much for what you have done, & also Mr. Birchard. Am sending the enclosed ($200) ck on account.

I'm not sure I'd make any changes in the score—the drum part at beginning of II movement, I wrote that way, so the "down beat" bass drum, would go along as they play it on main beats not after beats.

On page 27—think it might be easier for Drum & Piano to play, as it is written, or both ways might be printed. Would also keep 2nd viola here.

There are 2 or 3 places (short phrases only), where it might be better for Horn than Tp't. But I will look it through again in a few days & write more. Generally speaking, I don't like to change any thing after once finished. But you may be right. We can tell better when we see the proofs.

It was fine to hear that Mrs. Slonimsky had such a success in Pittsburg.[21] We do hope to see you both—wrong—you 3, soon after we get to N.Y.—but we may stay here till after Christmas.

Our love to Electra and you all

as ever sincerely
Chas E. Ives

Please excuse, "paper, pencil & ritin" as you see there is no "tremolo" with nice pencil . . .

• • •

In the summer of 1934 Ives again sailed to England in search of restful and restorative surroundings. As the following letters make clear, the voyage was essentially prescribed by his doctors.

148. 4–5 August 1934, to John Becker

Dear John:

Don't bother to send the "Gen B" score to me—anything that J.J.B. does is good enough for me.[22] I guess from your letter that I didn't tell you that we had decided to sail over to England & stay there for 2 mos. or so. Mrs. Ives backed up by all the family plus the M.D.s

20. Ives began to address Slonimsky as "Padre" after the birth of Slonimsky's daughter, Electra, in 1933. See also Letter 149.

21. Dorothy Adlow Slonimsky frequently lectured on art and art history.

22. Becker was working on an orchestration of "General William Booth Enters into Heaven." See Letters 150–51.

decided that it [is] the best move to make now—an' I hope it is—the trip over before worked well health-wise—the tests, counts, etc. have not been satisfactory to the Dr.—etc. and we are sailing next week. . . .

149. 7 August 1934, to Nicolas Slonimsky

Dear Padre:

I've been on the point of writing you for many days back—but I'll have to admit for some time I didn't seem to be able to keep in decent shape—and had to give up about everything—it's humiliating & makes me mad.

Mrs. Ives has decided, & backed up by all the family plus the M.D.'s that the best thing to do now is to sail over to England and stay there for 2 or 3 months—anyhow for good or for otherwise, we're going to sail on Aug. 10. . . .

It has been such a disappointment not to see you this summer—and Electra and her mother, but we must have a family reunion when we get back.

It must have [been] a joy to you to have your family complete again—and to hear first hand from Russia and your Brother and old friends.

Everybody seems to like the records—you did a good job—a hard one—I appreciate all you have done deeply—and "I take off my hat"[23]

I've been wondering if I owe Birchard & Co anything?—let me know when you hear. The data etc. for the little "brochure" (is that spelled OK? My Irish is bad!) will be sent in a few days from the office typewriter. It has,

(1) a short biography paragraph (including name & date of birth")

(2) a list of compositions etc.

(3) Digest of Comment.

Beside these—the "Verses & program story" in re "The 3 Places in N.E." which are printed in the score might go in, and I suppose whatever (but short) forenote the publisher thinks ought to be made—but please No Picture. of me or any nice man anywhere!

The digest of Comment has been arranged in preferential order by one who thinks he knows—but I suppose . . .

(Dear Mr. Slonimsky: I am now writing for daddy. Here is a hug for . . . [*the rest of the letter is missing*]

• • •

The 1934 trip was ineffective, and the family returned to the States in October, after only about two months. As he wrote in two letters to Becker during the following winter, Ives was still experiencing episodes that affected his mobility, breathing, writing, and, increasingly, his sight as well.

23. Slonimsky had recorded "In the Night" from the *Set for Theatre Orchestra* and the "Barn Dance" from *Washington's Birthday* for *New Music*'s recordings series the previous May. See Sinclair, *Descriptive Catalogue*, 83–84, and Letters 274–78.

150. December 1934, to John Becker

Dear John:

You are right about adequate rehearsing for recordings— & that orchestra is much better than a piano for the phonograph. I've never heard a decent piano record. I didn't know that the recording of the song "Gen. B" had been definitely decided upon.—& after getting your letter I found out that it had already been made & put in the circular. I haven't heard it nor do I know the singer—though H. says she sings well.[24] Later on, when your orchestra gets going again—with you at the "bat" & "hitting them out" again, you will be a great help to Henry's recordings—if not my song, there will be many possibilities for the things they have rehearsed & others—but don't try to do much before you feel stronger. I do greatly appreciate your interest & work on that Gen. B" score—what you have done is a very great help to me—and it is worth all & more of the enclosed.

I should have written before but have been going through a bad spell—had to stay on my back, couldn't breathe, write, or cuss—for a while. Mrs. Ives asks me to ask what book John Jr. would like for Christmas—another Babar? Give our love to all the family—& we do hope that bad health & bad days are about over.

Ever yours
Chas E. Ives

151. 27–29 January 1935, to John Becker

Dear John:

. . . Your score came—it is a very good job,—you have taken a great deal of time & trouble—& I much appreciate it.[25]

I think that there will have to be a trombone part—more Bass Brass is a necessary part of a thing like this—I could indicate in a general way—also, a snare drum is too much for Chamber orchestra—indoors—just a small Bass Drum—or tympany (tuned out) is enough & it keeps up the beat all through—as the whole thing is but a kind of Street March—

Tues:

I tried going over the score yesterday, but for the last month or so have been going thro' a kind of bad spell, couldn't breath[e], etc.—(not unusual) but during those times, my eyes go blurry if I use them much—After 20 min. have to wait for an hour or so,—so it takes me a week to do some thing that ought to take an hour. However am getting better, and

24. Ives's comments on the difficulty of recording a piano well are fascinating in view of his general disdain for recordings. One wonders if he was thinking of his own experience with recording "Transcriptions from Emerson" in May 1933. The recording of "General William Booth Enters into Heaven" was made by Radiana Pazmor and Genevieve Pitot for New Music Recordings on 5 December 1934. See Sinclair, *Descriptive Catalogue*, 387, and Letters 285–89.

25. Ives refers to Becker's orchestration of "General Booth."

will send it back in a week or so. You may not think so but your work is a valuable help to me—and you've got to let me do my part.—which the enclosed Ck. is for—is just for value received. & have another job for you when you are ready—

Love from all of us to all of you
Chas

• • •

In July 1933 Becker lost his job teaching at the College of St. Thomas in St. Paul, Minnesota. In the two years that followed, he and his family faced a long string of missed or illusory opportunities and rumors of jobs or performances that did not pan out. As the previous letter implies, Ives helped Becker out financially by paying him to edit and prepare works for performance. Indeed, Ives also intervened in Becker's behalf more substantially by giving him the money to avoid a threatened foreclosure on his mortgage.[26] In the following letter, while sympathizing with Becker, Ives alludes to his own health problems.

152. March 1935, to John Becker

Dear John:

Am sorry to be such a bad letter writer,—but we were glad to hear from you & see your newspaper interview—what you say is to the point & well said—and the dissonance solution and the need for mental development in the listener—(especially those lily pad—lady birds—in charge of too many college orchestras, & dress suits,—emasculating art for money!) = make it easy for the soft ears!! Percy!

I'm sorry haven't been able [to] go over the 'Gen. B.' score & get it back—my eyes and other conditions have kept me from doing anything—but last few days have been better and expect to get it off soon—any way you have done a good job with it.

We think you're quite right in not getting in the music mess in N.Y. either in dance radio band or other work. From what we see and hear, there's more after 1 job here than in any other place. A friend of mine in the N[ational] B[roadcasting] Co.[27] says it's depressing to see so many good musicians out of jobs—men with good reputations & recommendations—and even those with a pull. He says don't encourage any one but your worst enemy to come to N.Y.—at least at present. Some good opportunity is bound to come up in your own part of the country—as Henry says, from your good record & fight in the past & your growing reputation—and I think he is right.

I would feel better if you will let me help out a little every month until a steady job comes along or things get better. Anyway I'm going to, no matter what you say. One thing

26. See Becker to Ives, 29 August 1935 (CIP 27/4). Ives's success in life insurance provided him the money to make such substantial contributions to Becker, Cowell, and many others. His income was substantial even after his retirement.

27. The friend was probably George Roberts, his longtime copyist, who worked at NBC.

I know—you would do the same thing for me, if fate had happened to cast us in each others shoes.—Now be a good boy—& don't cuss—except when you hear a lillypad singing to an eggplant!

Goodbye for tonight. With love from us all to all of you
as ever,
Chas. E. I.

• • •

This undated letter to Cowell from the late spring of 1935 is one of Ives's strongest protests against his persistent "slumps." The following letters to Becker document his slow recovery from this particularly difficult time.

153. Spring 1935, to Henry Cowell[28]

Am just getting out of one of them g—— d—— slumps and haven't been able to write—or do anything much—I guess music and I are parting company—can't see it—can't hear it most of the time—eyes and ears blur—It makes me—wild—it's the Creator's fault—not mine!—is that right? Now I'll shut up this fool talk! Keep well out side of that no advice! Will write a better letter soon The enclosed just for the general fund or whatever you think best.

Love to you from all of us
Ever your
C.E.I.

154. 8 June 1935, to John Becker

Dear John:

We thank you for sending the book and the poem. Mrs. Ives read me Tyrbyfill's fine—high aimed poem—your music will keep the high places high—& raise the others upwards.

Please send whatever you want photostated to the Quality Photoprint Co. 521–5 Ave—have written them about it.[29]

I do hope you are feeling better & that things are going better—I'm gradually getting over this last bad slump—not all dead yet . . .

With love to all & from all
Chas E. I.

Will write more soon

28. All letters to Cowell in the CIP are photocopies.

29. The Quality Photoprint Studio made photographic reproductions, mostly for businesses; Ives often used the company to obtain copies of his own music or, as in this case, to help composers such as Becker have copies made.

155. Ca. 17 June 1935, to John Becker

Dear John:

We are sorry you have to be away from home—and in Chicago for a summer month, to make it worse—Mrs. Ives was a nurse in hospital work there years ago & knows what a hot day is there—& sends you her sympathy.

I am proud to have you dedicate any of your music to me—whether it's your best or worst best (which is better far than the best-best of most men) makes no difference—it's from you! Thank you—we all thank you.

Hope to send you the Gen'l Booth score back soon—my hands are getting somewhat steadier—though you may not believe from this nice writin' Good luck—

With love from us all
Chas E. I.

156. 3 September 1935, to John Becker

Dear John:

Both your letters at hand—It's fine about the new lecture possibilities. The enclosed letter,[30] which Mrs. Ives copied for me, I hope will be what is wanted—if not let me know.—it's the way I feel—anyway. . . .

Have had a little set-back a few days ago—& eyes, hands, etc. a little off again—So haven't been able to go over the "Gen'l B" score—but will soon.

Love to all
Chas E. I.

157. Ca. 18 September 1935, to John Becker

Dear John:

I hope Autumn is bringing better health & opening up in better ways—I've been sort of on the bazoota for the last month or so—but am better now. . . .

Haven't been able to get at "Gen. Booth" score but hope to soon—Had to look over some pages of songs that Henry is going to publish next month—principally because its little more than a job of printing from the old plates—& 2 which couldn't get copyright permission in the old book & 2 written since.[31]

Henry ought to publish some of your songs before long.

Forgive this —— Letter.

We all send love to you all

ever yours
Chas E. Ives

30. Ives enclosed a letter to be used in the promotion of Becker's musical lectures.

31. This is *Eighteen Songs, New Music,* 9, no. 1 (October 1935).

158. 15 October 1935, to George F. Roberts

Dear Mr. Roberts:

We will be very glad to see you all Saturday,—& will arrange good weather. Please bring my copy of score,—as there is none here—I hope it will be one of the days I can see the notes—
Best wishes to all—

Sincerely
Chas E. Ives

159. November 1935, to Nicolas Slonimsky

Dear N.S.P.:[32]

We all send kindest wishes to Electra and her mother and father; we hope you all have kept perfectly well.[33]

I'm sorry to report that I haven't been able to attend to those various things you wrote me about last summer. For some time past haven't been in shape to do anything I want to—As for music, sometimes for days at a time—can't see it, hear it or play it—not even a nice wrong note! But am getting somewhat out of this spell & hope soon to be more like a human being. May things go well with all of you.

Best wishes again
ever yours
Chas E. Ives

160. Ca. 2 November 1935, to John Becker

Dear John:

We were all glad to hear the news.[34] It's about time politico-sap woke up and did a masculine job! When do you start? Mrs. Ives says she hears the salaries are always slow in starting in the Gov. Jobs—and the first month is the hardest—So just to feel a little better am sending the enclosed. God bless you & your heaven sent wife & the good children! We [are] back in Babylon[35]—Just happen to be in one of those slump-attacks—so will write more when I can get up again—

ever yours
C.E.I.

32. Nicolas Slonimsky Padre, one of Ives's many nicknames for the conductor; see also Letters 147 and 149 and note 20, above.

33. Ives often referred to his correspondents' families by mentioning the names of their young children.

34. Becker was hired as music director of the Minnesota division of the Works Progress Administration. See Becker to Ives, 30 October 1935 (CIP, 27/4).

35. The Iveses typically stayed in Redding until November before returning to New York City for the winter.

161. Ca. 17 November 1935, to John Becker

Dear John:

Thanks for your letter. It's fine to think of you & yours as being more free from that tough strain you've been under so long,—and hope things are starting well. Haven't any copies of the songs here—as I left the last one I had in Redding—but Henry is having some more sent on, and will be glad to send you one, with a few "snake tracks . . . His Mark!

Am getting over a little bad spell and will write more later.

Love to all of you from all of us.

Ever yours
Chas E. I.

• • •

Though the treatment Ives received from Dr. Elliott Joslin did not bring about the dramatic improvement in his symptoms that he must have hoped for when he first consulted the eminent physician in 1930, Ives was clearly grateful for his help, as the following two letters illustrate.

162. 21 January 1936, from Dr. Elliott Joslin, Boston

My dear Mrs. Ives—

Dr. Cook has just told me of the receipt of your check of $100. for the George F. Baker Clinic Guarantee Fund—completing your entire pledge of $500.

I want to thank you too. In this fund and in the clinic I take great pride because it has all gone as planned. Sometime I would like to show you about it. From it directly and indirectly radiate many activities.

The new insulin is far better than has been announced.

Sincerely yours—
Elliott P. Joslin

163. Ca. October 1936, sketch for Ives to Elliott Joslin

Dear Dr. J

Thank you for your letters ~~of Oct 18~~ . . . You ask if I am well happy & keeping up with the next man. I am still living on this planet—I can swear to that—whether I can do as much for my age as the next man [illegible]—you have to ask me who the next man is!

And I can say there is no man happier than I am.

I have to take only a small amount of insulin.

—So you see I am well!

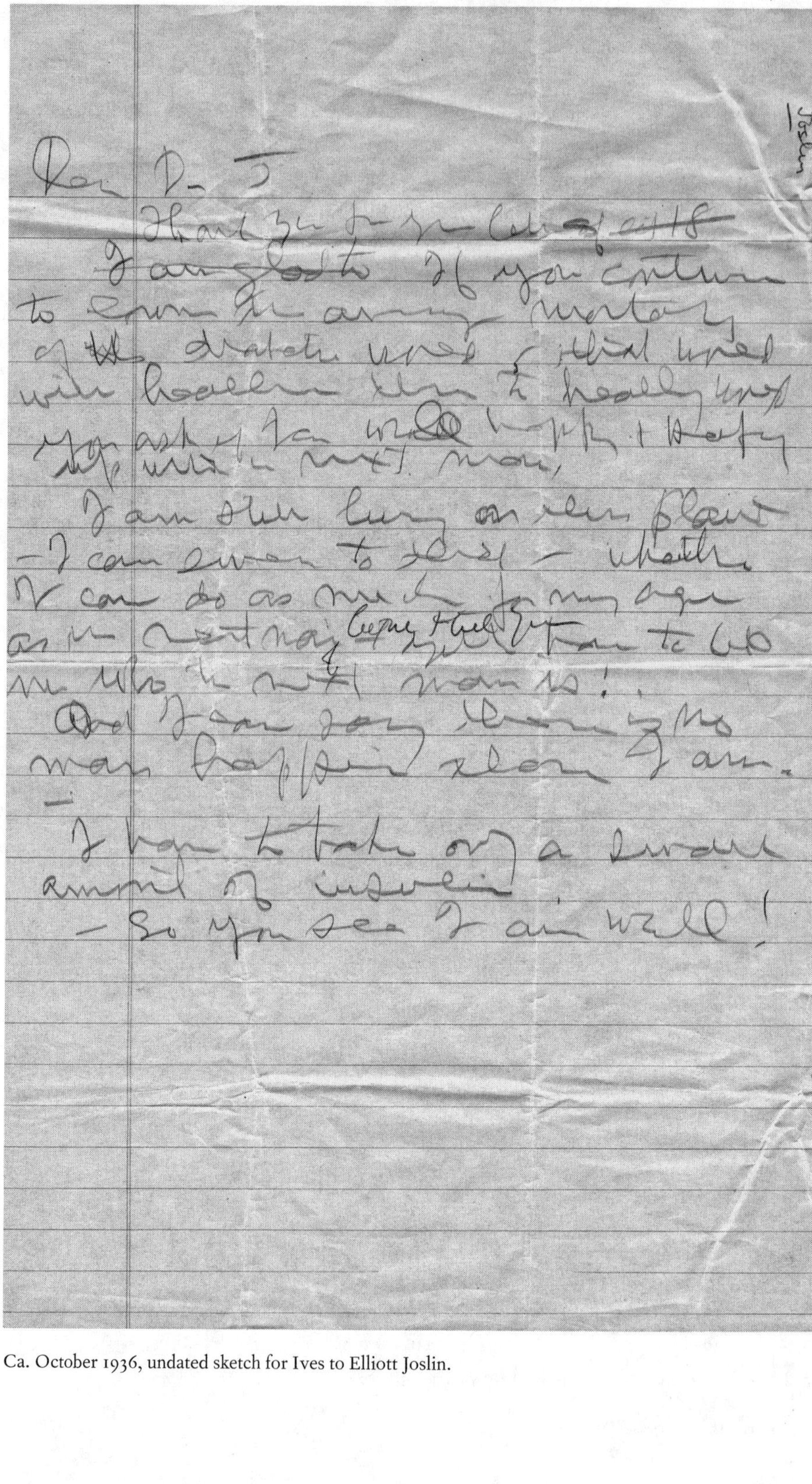

Joslin

Dear Dr. J

~~Thank you for your letter of [illegible]~~

~~I am glad to~~ If you continue to [illegible]

[illegible]

[illegible]

[illegible]

I am still living on [illegible]

[illegible]

[illegible]

[illegible]

And I can say [illegible] man happier than I am.

I have to take [illegible] a [illegible] amount of insulin

— So you see I am well!

Ca. October 1936, undated sketch for Ives to Elliott Joslin.

164. Ca. 3 July 1936, to John Becker

Dear John:

I'm a poor correspondent, I know—am sorry, but haven't been able to do anything for some while, write or see well—however am now getting somewhat out of that slump.

Take a good rest on your vacation—don't bother with music—at least not "Gen'l B"—there's no hurry about that. But take Bruce Cowell up into the North Country and see him lasso a Buffalo. Edie has been away—and will write Mary Cecelia[36] soon.

Our love to all of you—

ever yours—
Chas E. I.

Don't have any copies made of the 2nd Piano Sonata—Have found 2 whole copies and 1 with only a page out here.

• • •

The following draft and letter to Slonimsky are possibly the only examples in the correspondence in which Harmony Ives censored the content of a letter she transcribed from her husband's almost illegible drafts. As such, they invite a more lengthy examination. The sketches are largely a reaction to two letters noting the lack of an American audience for Ives's music that Fred Goldbeck and Marc Blitzstein had written to the French music journal *La Revue Musicale*.[37] Ives read the letters in pencil transcriptions Slonimsky had sent to him on 18 June; these contained only sections directly related to his music. Blitzstein's letter, titled "The Young Americans in Music," seems to have been the prime offender in Ives's eyes. It presented Ives as a case study in the lack of an audience for modernist music in America:

> Perhaps the most tragic example is that of Charles Ives, the magnificently endowed New England musician, who since 1921 has completely stopped composing. His *114 Songs*, his choral, orchestral, and chamber works, reveal an audacious and profound talent and extraordinary prophetic vision. In 1905 Ives already employed dissonances and stylistic procedures surprisingly like those of the Debussy of *Préludes pour piano* and of the Stravinsky of *L'Histoire du soldat*. He is a true original who launched into his music bursts of ideas which will require many years for history to understand. But a composer, even if he is a genius, cannot write only for himself, without an audience, he is without support; he becomes isolated, eccentric or like Ives, despairing, he no longer composes.

This passage provoked an extreme response that reflects Ives's tendency to direct his anger at a stock set of targets.

The first paragraph of the sketch answers questions in Slonimsky's letter directly. Ives

36. Ives refers to John Becker's children, Bruce Cowell Becker and Mary Cecelia Becker.

37. Marc Blitzstein, "The Young Americans in Music," *La Revue Musicale*, no. 163 (February 1936): 145–48; Fred Goldbeck, "Musiciens Américains à la 'Spirale,' " *La Revue Musicale*, no. 165 (April 1936): 293.

apologizes for not being in contact; he has been in a slump that has impaired his vision and possibly his ability to concentrate.[38]

The angry tirade occasioned by the remarks in *La Revue* occupies the bulk of Ives's drafts for the remaining paragraphs of the letter. Characteristically, Ives redirects Blitzstein's criticism of the American audience onto a more specific group of music and culture professionals personified by Arturo Toscanini, William Randolph Hearst, and Warner Brothers. This step has two consequences: it exonerates the audience at large of purposeful indifference and focuses Ives's attack on what he believed to be the cause of American apathy toward modern music, commercialization and subsequent laziness. Ives was of two minds about the taste of the American musical public. He trusted in the infallibility of the majority and in the innate goodness of the common man and, thus, could not write off the entire concertgoing public.[39] Instead, he blamed a small unrepresentative but powerful group for deceiving the common music lover: the prominent figures of the culture establishment, epitomized here by Toscanini.[40] Ives's argument is that an audience that has been fed only "mush" will come to think that only "mush" will do, thus enriching the "mush-makers." That Ives would choose to argue thus is not surprising in view of his proclamations concerning his own decision not to participate in music on a professional level—that is, in order to make money.[41]

Although Ives brings Toscanini into the discussion as an example of a purveyor of the musically easy, his specific criticism of him takes a different form. What is fascinating about Ives's attack on Toscanini is the fault he finds with the Italian master's conducting and what it reveals about Ives's own musical preferences. Ironically, Toscanini failed as a conductor of Beethoven because he was *too modern:* he did not keep with earlier nineteenth-century performance practice. To Ives, Toscanini was a "stopwatch," a "clicking machine," a "little metronome," who played Beethoven's notes precisely but conveyed nothing of the spirit of his music. This angle of attack puts Ives in the same camp with the earlier and quite different critic of Toscanini, Giuseppe Verdi.[42] Both accused Toscanini of imposing a sort of tyranny over the music by rigidly conducting it in such a way that its essence was lost. This criticism of Toscanini points out a clear rift between the spiritualistic modernism of many of the ultramodern composers and the highly rationalistic version of the movement most prominently

38. It is possible to relate the term slump, which Ives often used to describe his periods of increased illness, to two areas of his life. Though the word is closely connected to the baseball imagery Ives often used, it is also specifically linked, in American usage, to business and especially to the stock market. The *Oxford English Dictionary* cites American usage of the word in this context in 1888 and notes that it was still current in the 1920s. Both contexts resonate strongly with Ives's life.

39. For Ives's ideas on the rightness of the common man, see Rossiter, *Charles Ives and His America,* 135, 159.

40. Ives railed against Toscanini on other occasions as well, as evidenced by Slonimsky, *Music since 1900,* 4th ed. (New York: Charles Scribner's Sons, 1971), 118; and Ives, *Memos,* 125.

41. See especially Ives, *Memos,* 130–36.

42. For Verdi's criticism of Toscanini, see his letter to Ricordi, 18 March 1899. As Judith Tick points out, Ives was not alone among American musicians in his criticism of Toscanini: Daniel Gregory Mason, Carl Ruggles, Edgard Varèse, and Virgil Thomson are several of the various other critics who took a similar position; see Tick, "Charles Ives and Gender Ideology" in *Musicology and Difference: Gender and Sexuality in Music Scholarship,* ed. Ruth Solie (Berkeley: University of California Press, 1994), 104.

associated with Stravinsky.[43] Ives's use of this argument is revealing. First, his statements emphasize the idea that, for Ives, the spirit or "substance" of a work does not reside entirely in the notes. And second, though the circumstances that provoked Ives's anger are firmly anchored in the reception of modern music (Ives's own music and that of the other composers championed by Slonimsky), Ives responds in nineteenth-century terms. Just as Ives often used the character Rollo, a literary child of the 1830s, to vent his frustration at the negative reaction to his works, he reflected his preference for a nineteenth-century interpretive style in his anger over this twentieth-century circumstance. Certainly, Ives's taste in conducting was less of reach into the past than his use of Rollo or his adaptation of Concord transcendentalism; nevertheless, the trend of using the interpretational strategies of the previous century—not to mention the popular tunes, hymns, and so on—in his twentieth-century context continues in Ives's Toscanini argument.[44]

A third, obvious element in Ives's invective is the use of gender and class stereotypes. The first of these is an almost infamous aspect of Ives's rhetoric, but the use of class in a polemic sense has been less thoroughly discussed.[45] It is important to note that though velvet and silk imply effeminacy, they are also indicators of wealth. Ives uses this rhetoric in a context that was clearly set up to accommodate it: he is, after all, talking about the commercialization of music, about the conjunction of music and money. Those who provided the money to further the careers of the culture professionals were also in line for criticism. One must recall that this is the class to which Ives himself belonged; his language itself shows the anxiety this fact created for Ives. This anxiety reveals itself in Ives's desire to keep anonymous his substantial financial contributions to aid in the performance and production of modern American music.[46]

165. Ca. 18 June 1936, sketches for Ives to Nicolas Slonimsky

NSP

You are a good boy—Thank [you] very much for your good letter and the French paper notice. I would have written before but haven't been able to do anything, play or see any music for a long time—but am getting somewhat out of that slump—& hope to be able to attend to things before long. And will write you in more detail about the things you have suggested ought to be done just as soon as I can use my eyes & work for longer periods.

The French article was right about American audiences 'conventional& stupid' but

43. Carol Oja discusses the spiritualistic dimension of American modernism at length in *Making Music Modern: New York in the 1920s* (New York: Oxford University Press, 2000).

44. Ives seems to have made a distinction between interpretive style, in which he preferred a romantic elasticity of tempo, and repertoire, where he felt that certain "comfortable" works had been repeated to the point that they had become a sort of musical sedative, and in which his taste was obviously more modern.

45. For a discussion of Ives's use of gender rhetoric see Tick, "Charles Ives and Gender Ideology," 83–106.

46. For an example, see Peter Yates to Charles and Harmony Ives, 1 October 1944, reproduced in Burkholder, *Charles Ives and His World*, 257–58.

(it's) they (not) are not wholly to blame—'commercialized sap' flowing like tape worms around their emasculated ears'—Emasculating America for money—that's the root of the snake—also the nice ladies hypnotized by those permanent waves (in Toscanini's 2 arms—) the $75000 Massage boy) play even easy, get the money almost as bad is the way the lady-birds fall for that $75000 masseur' that old stop-watch, ~~adding~~ clicking machine, little metronome 'Arthur Tascaninny' with his 'permanent waves' (in both arms) he hypnotizes the nice boys in purple coats & the silk ladies—& gets their money! He makes Beethoven an Emasculated lily-pad—he plays the notes B. wrote down—plays it nice, even, up-down precise, sweet pretty tone, cissy-sounding way—not the <u>music</u> of Beethoven. He makes it easy for bodily part of the box-sitting sap & gets the money! He isn't quite good enough to be as bad as the Radio (the movies, & phono is [illegible—possibly "bis," as in business] in the process) in emasculating art for money. He can't make Beethoven be a 'liar'—it takes Warner Bros.—Hearst, etc. to do that. A Nation Mollycoddled by commercialized papp—America losing her manhood—for money—Whatever faults the puritans—they were men—& not effeminate!! Wake up America—kill somebody before breakfast

[*Sketch 2*]

What the French article says about American audiences—conventionalized & soft-headed etc.—a large part of them are, but many of the audiences of younger people are independent & stronger minded.—The older ears are the worst—but it's not altogether their fault—They have been fed so long on commercialized sap—and lady-bird sounds, over and over again—what else is to be expected. And this commercialized sap is made worse by the Radio, movies & phonograph—it flows. . . .

The men and ladies who have made the most money out of music, whether composing playing singing or conducting—are the ones who have kept music too much an emasculated art—They do the same thing little more or little less than a barber, who massages faces—he makes them feel a little better, a pleasant physical sensation, for ~~the time he~~ a little while—etc etc—& that's about all they do—though the barber may stop a pimple—but the music-commercialists don't even do that—they ~~but grow~~ sometimes encourage pimples in the musical-brain parts!

• • •

Although the sketches above were written in the first person, as if Ives intended to send a cleaned-up or overtly transcribed copy to Slonimsky over his own signature, Harmony wrote the letter that was sent, and it ignores Ives's drafts almost entirely. Such a recomposition by her is not to be found in any other surviving letter. The irrationality and venom of the sketches, and the slump that produced them, wore on her to an extent that is evident here. The candid discussion of his physical disability and personal tone of the letter show how difficult taking care of Ives had become for Harmony.

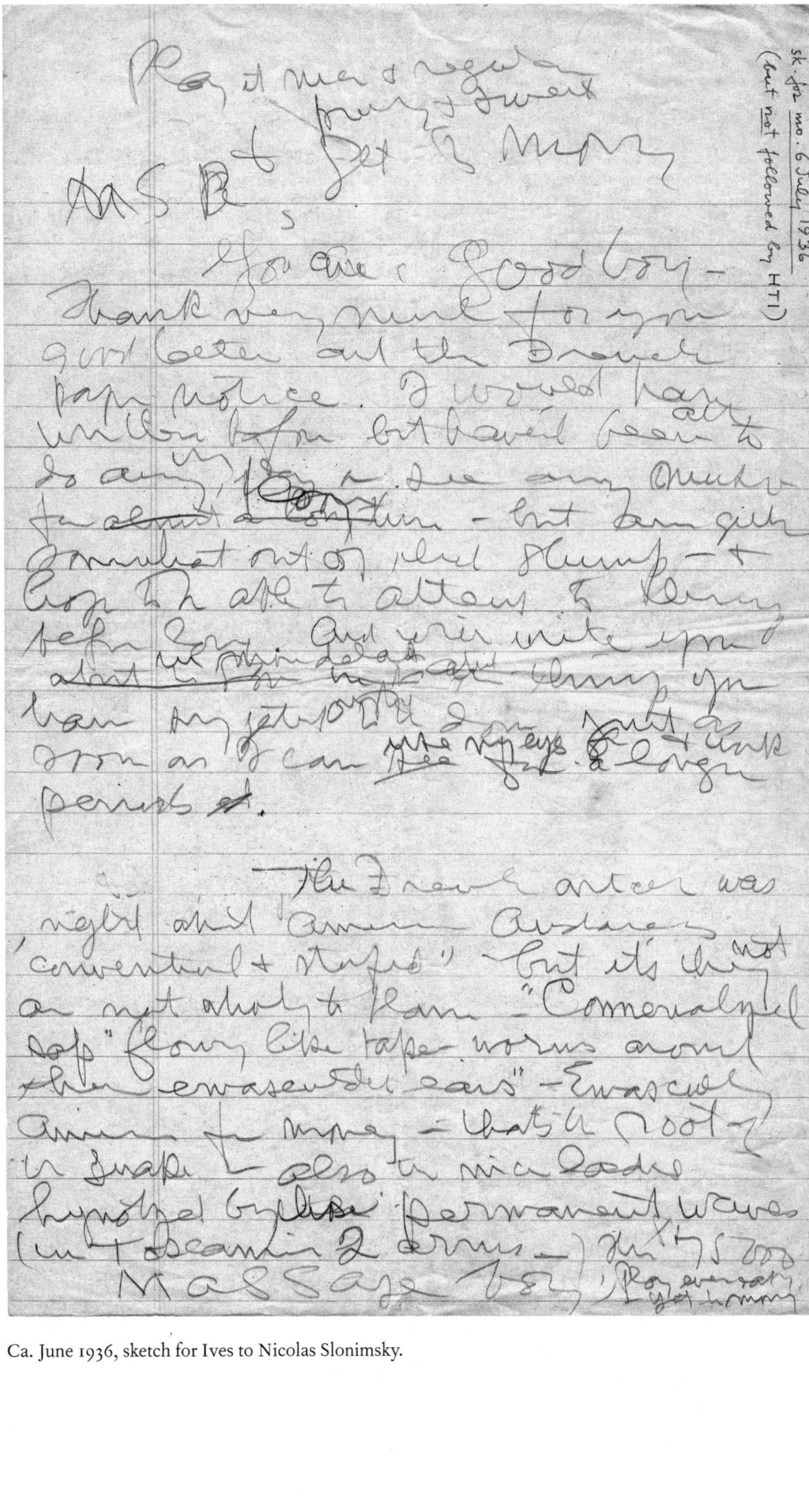

Ca. June 1936, sketch for Ives to Nicolas Slonimsky.

166. 6 July 1936, Harmony Ives to Nicolas Slonimsky

My dear Nicolas—

We were glad to get a line from you & to know you are all well—I can imagine that Electra's conversation is most diverting.

We have been here since early may. Mr. Ives isn't feeling very well—I get a little discouraged about him tho' he got a very good report from the doctor before we came away as to his physical symptoms. He says to send his love to you and to say that when he can he will get the work you want—the violin sonatas. He has been working over his Browning score—some of it was lost & much of [it] nearly illegible & it has been a lot of work to get it in shape even to be copied. He can work only for a short time at a time as his eyes allow little strain. He would write for himself but his handwriting is so bad that he hesitates to. He really has many trials and is very uncomplaining.

We were interested to see the excerpt from the French paper. Of course the writer had his own idea which he wanted to bring out. It wasn't lack of audience & appreciation that made Mr. Ives stop composing. It just happened—the War & the complete breakdown in health. He had worked tremendously hard in his quarry all those years & exhausted the vein I suppose. I am always hoping he may open up a new vein & he may—His ideas are by no means exhausted, but there are the physical disabilities to be contended with. He is such a wonderful person—he has such strength of <u>character</u> and will & sense. In all family troubles & decisions & problems he is the one they all come to.

Well I didn't intend writing so much, but you are a friend and I get rather pent up.

I am Yours as ever sincerely
Harmony T. Ives

• • •

In the spring of 1937 Ives continued to face episodes of tremor, shortness of breath, and lethargy. His vision was also deteriorating, as he implies in the following letters to John Becker.

167. 1–5 March 1937, to John Becker

Dear John:

. . . Tues. A.M. Expected yesterday to have Edie's help in writing, but she is sick again this A.M. and Mrs. Ives is in Hartford taking care of her sister who has been very ill—why doesn't "the Creator" make better human bodies!!—Can you see this—I can see the Blot! Will finish on the other side this afternoon.
Friday: Yesterday, thought I'd get a stenog. to come in so I could write a decent letter—but had one of those short of breath days & couldn't talk, except when flat on back—so will finish with paw—later on when I can sit up & dictate will send you a good letter . . .

168. January 1938, to John Becker

Dear John:

Have been on a down slant for most 2 months. I wanted to send a line at Christmas—but haven't been able to write—breathe or get up & do anything right—until a few days ago. That g—— d—— sap! Who said you were a defeatist—composer—is a musical half-wit—or a liar—you are a great composer—to Hell with the lilly-ears!

Please let the enclosed go towards publishing your "Sonata"—don't bother about the subscriptions.

God bless you—your wife & dear children

Love from all of us to all of you

Ever yours
Chas

• • •

Three years after Radiana Pazmor recorded "General Booth," Ives wrote to her, via Edith, to thank her for her work on it. His excuse for not writing sooner, that he could not hear sustained tones well, is interesting in view of his 1934 correspondence with Becker about the sound quality of the piano in recordings.[47] References to difficulty in hearing begin in the correspondence around 1935—for instance, in Letter 153 to Cowell, in which Ives lamented that he and music were "parting company." By 1937 he seems to have accepted the hearing distortion as a permanent affliction and decided that he should wait no longer to respond to Pazmor.

169. 14 October 1937, Edith Ives to Radiana Pazmor

My dear Miss Pazmor:—

I am writing for my father as he is not well.

Ever since you made that splendid record of the "General Booth" song of my father's, he has been wanting to write you, but has kept putting it off in hopes that he could hear it himself. He has an ear trouble which bothers him and makes it difficult for him to hear—especially sustained tones. As this condition seems to be getting no better, he wants to have you and Miss Pitot know that he greatly appreciates what you have both done. He has heard from many friends and musicians who speak in great appreciation of the singing and playing in the record.

Father sends you his best wishes and a great many thanks—

Sincerely yours,
Edith Ives
(For Charles E. Ives)

47. See Letter 150.

• • •

In May 1938 the Iveses sailed to England, again at the recommendation of family physicians. Ives described the reason behind the trip in a letter to Schmitz: "Greetings to you all from London—we came rather unexpectedly. Everybody including the doctors (who are usually right especially when they're wrong) seemed to think an ocean sail would be well for us—(personally Redding has it on Europe!)—We'll be home before the end of summer and will hope to see you in the fall. . . . Please excuse these snake tracks—I can't see 'em well enough to see ~~know~~ how bad they are—not my fault—Creator's!"[48] Ives is more explicit about the motivation for the trip in a letter to Becker.

170. 30 June 1938, to John Becker, London

Dear John:

Your letter was forwarded to Scotland. The usual delays, & should have been answered sooner.

I will write to Mr. Kondolf when Scriba Editha comes in—you're used to my snake tracks—but a stranger might not make 'em out—not yet. We sailed rather unexpectedly—was in a rather uncertain condition for some time before. I had one of those usual, chronic low swings, am used to them, but this lasted longer than usual—but Mrs. Ives has been in quite a serious condition—it worried me—the doctors were afraid of a bad nervous breakdown. She has been under a constant strain with my condition for the last ten years or so—and during the last year her two sisters have both been seriously sick—one had to go to a retreat—And this & many other things—many of her old friends have been in so much trouble etc. in one way or another the doctors felt she must be kept quiet & have a rest from all this. And it is a relief to say she is getting much better. We'll probably be back before the summer is over.

I do hope things are going well with you and your dear ones.

Don't worry if they don't play your music in a N.Y. concert. I don't think it makes much difference whether they do or not—for there are too many "lilly ears" in N.Y. They want cissy-coddle music,—easy to play easy to listen to, and easy to sell—yours isn't—you're a man!

But you've got to let me help out a little in those travel expenses to N.Y. which you shouldn't have been subjected to—so grin & bear it.

We all send love to you all

ever yours
Chas E. I.

• • •

The family returned to Redding in July, and the voyage benefited Harmony especially. The following September Ives suffered another serious health setback, which Edith described as

48. For the full text of the letter and a facsimile of Ives's draft, with slightly different wording, see Letter 267.

a heart attack. The prescription of quiet and lack of mention of any trip to the hospital or other unusual medical intervention in response to the attack supports the idea that the family used this term in a general way to refer to Ives's slumps, perhaps especially the ones that were accompanied by chest pains or palpitations.[49] Thus, the term would be equivalent to Ives's own description, "slow breath—hard—pump" for his symptoms.[50]

171. 11 October 1938, Edith Ives to John Becker

Dear Mr. Becker:—

We were so sorry to hear of Mrs. Becker's illness and Bruce's asthma, and do hope they are better now.

We had a very pleasant summer in Scotland and England, although the weather was not as kind to us as it might have been! Mother is much better for the trip, and so was Daddy until three weeks ago, when he had quite a bad heart attack, and has had to be quiet ever since.

He thanks you for sending the piano sonata—he hasn't been able to read it very well on account of his eye condition, but says he knows it is good, strong music.

We all send out love—and please give my special remembrances to Mary Cecelia.

Sincerely,
Edith

172. 16 October 1938, Edith Ives to Lehman Engel

My Dear Mr. Engel:—

I am sorry to say that about three weeks ago my father had a very bad heart attack. He is better now, but has to keep quiet,—he is sorry not to be able to attend to things, and not to have written you sooner.

He says if you will just do anything you think best about the music to be published, it will be alright with him.

We expect to be back in New York before long, and when father has a good day we will telephone you, and father hopes you will be able to come up. He will be very glad to see you again, and says that then he would like to go over with you a business matter he has in mind, which may, he hopes, be of some help in the work of both publications.

My mother joins us in kindest greetings.

Sincerely yours,
Edith Ives
for
Charles E. Ives

49. Compare with Letter 181, which does describe an emergency trip to the hospital by ambulance.

50. See Letter 132.

• • •

By the end of the 1930s Ives had become less active as a correspondent even though the total volume of mail he received continued to increase. The following letters and excerpts are representative of the discussion of his health concerns from this period. Impaired vision that was due to cataracts and distorted hearing are the most commonly cited problems. In the face of these difficulties he kept his sense of humor and resolution: in a sketch for a letter to the composer Dane Rudhyar, he wrote, "Mr. I says he hasn't yet been able to say conclusively which is worst for mankind—bad health or bad music!—but both cause profane words."[51]

173. Ca. 27 July 1939, to John Becker

Dear John:

Just a scrawl to let you know that I'm still out of Purgatory—near it for some months back—but getting up now again.

But here is some family news! Edie is to be married this week! To George G. Tyler—a young man we have known well—& have a great respect & confidence in—and a fine kind of character.—Mrs. Ives & I feel that it is "God's will" and that it will be a happy marriage—and their's a good & useful life.

It is to be just a small wedding—only a few of the family.

Edie greatly enjoyed seeing Mary Cecelia.—we are going to try to get her to come up & see us as soon as things quiet down again.

Love to all
Chas E. Ives

Hope you can see these snake lines—I can't—

174. 17 January 1941, Harmony Ives to Evelyn Becker

Dear Mrs. Becker,

Edie wants you to know that they received & enjoyed the bucket of sweet cookies so much! They were in Florida for two weeks from Dec. 20th as George had two weeks of his vacation left over from last summer & were only back a week when George came down with the flu, as so often happens, & is still in bed & quite weak & miserable. So Edie has been very busy & has not had time to write. I divide my time between them & my own duties.

Mr. Ives hasn't been very well—he has such poor nights. He has plenty to do trying to get things in shape and correspondence and of course his failing eyesight is a great trial. However, he is still able to be funny—I don't know what we should do without his sense of humor.

51. For the full text, see Letter 348.

We are sorry Mr. Becker hasn't been so well either but I judge the boys are fine and I can imagine that three lively boys occupy your time & thoughts completely. . . .

175. March 1942, two sketches for Harmony Ives to Joseph Szigeti[52]

Szigeto

We thank you for your kind letter. Mr. Ives was surprised to receive the Times check—as he did not send the marginal notes to the Times & did not know that they were to be published. He is very glad to endorse the ck. to the Myra Hess Fund,[53] and it is enclosed as we have not her address.

Mr. I greatly appreciated your making the record[54]—but for the last 2 years his hearing has been somewhat impaired—In sustained notes especially in high register a blurring makes it difficult to hear well.[55] But I know he would be deeply impressed by yours if he could hear it.

We have heard from many who greatly enjoyed your fine playing of the sonata.

[*Sketch 2*]

Szigeti

I am ——

Mr. Ives has just heard for the first time your record of the 4th sonata. He couldn't hear very distinctly on account of his ear condition, but he heard enough to know that you got caught the spirit of the music & of those out-door days—wonderfully. He feels that you expressed it all deeply strongly naturally, & beautifully . . . ;,

He doesn't know how to thank you both adequately, but he deeply & sincerely appreciates all you have done & he hopes some day to have the opportunity of doing something in return. ~~We have heard from many who were thrilled by your fine playing.~~

176. 6 September 1943, Edith Ives Tyler to John Becker

Dear Mr. Becker:—

I am writing for Father as he is not well. He thanks you very much for your copy of the score just received. Sorry to say his eye condition has been worse lately, and he cannot see

52. Joseph Szigeti (1892–1873) was a Hungarian American violinist who was an important performer of contemporary repertoire from the 1930s until his retirement in 1960.

53. This probably refers to the Musician's Benevolent Fund, a British charity that was funded largely from the proceeds of concerts given by the pianist Dame Myra Hess during World War II.

54. Szigeti and the pianist Andor Foldes recorded the Fourth Violin Sonata for New Music Recordings on 14 February 1942; Sinclair, *Descriptive Catalogue*, 157.

55. This letter places the onset of Ives's hearing disorder somewhat later than is implied in Letters 153 and 169. Perhaps the condition had worsened in the early 1940s.

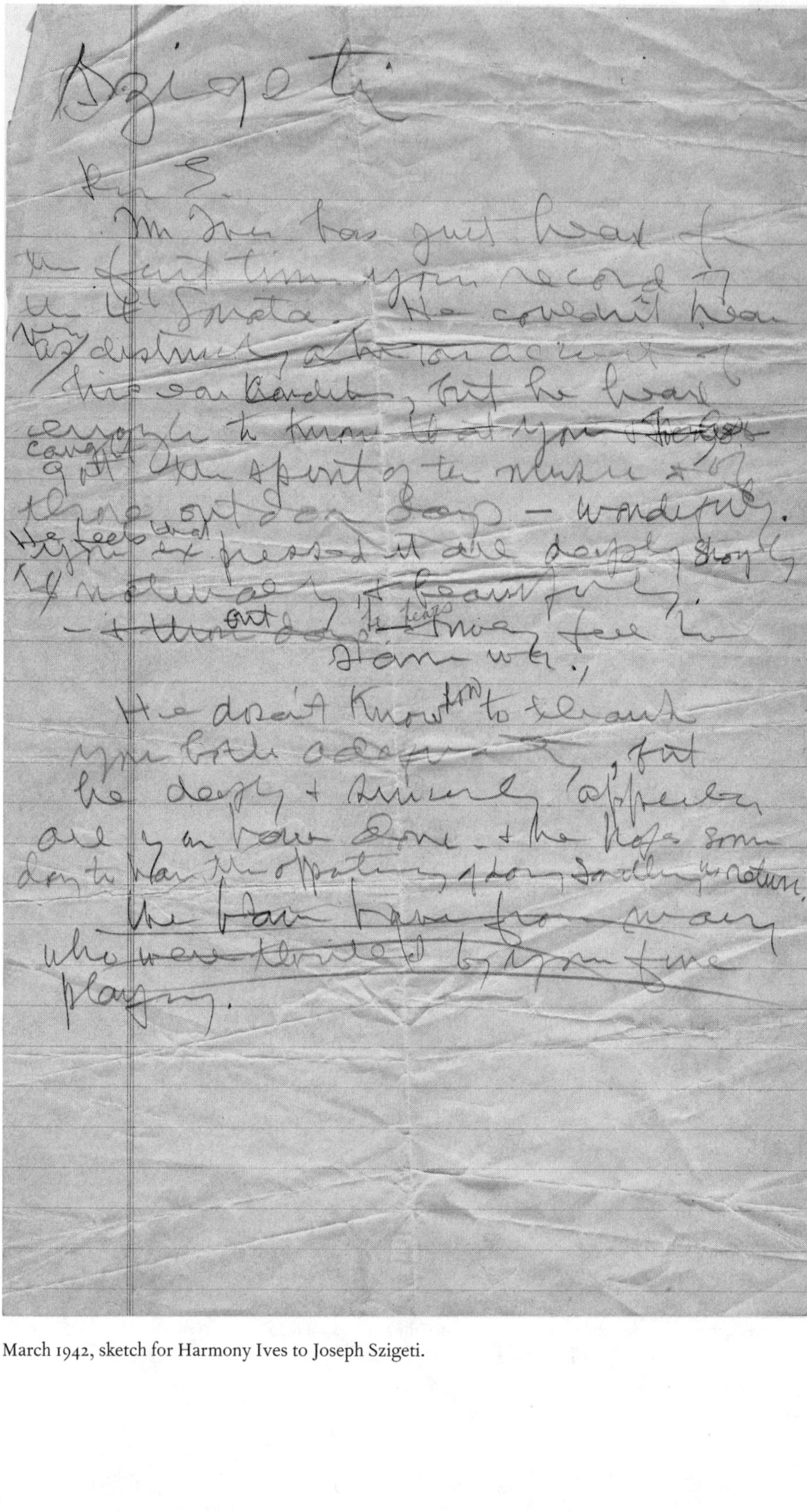

Szigeti

Dear S.

Mr Ives has just heard for the first time your record of the 4th Sonata. He couldn't hear very distinctly on account of his ear trouble, but he heard enough to know that you caught the spirit of the music & of those old days — wonderfully. He feels that you expressed it all deeply, strongly, naturally, & beautifully, — as he knows ... them.

He doesn't know how to thank you both adequately, but he deeply & sincerely appreciates all you have done — & he hopes some day to have the opportunity of doing something in return.

We have heard from many who were thrilled by your fine playing.

March 1942, sketch for Harmony Ives to Joseph Szigeti.

small notes, especially in lead pencil. He will have an enlarged photostat copy made which he may be able to make out. As there is no particular hurry about this, he will wait until he is better before trying to go ahead with it. He greatly appreciates all you have done. . . .

• • •

In the 1940s Harmony began to write more of her letters on he husband's behalf in her own words, seemingly without relying on a sketch by him. Her voice is distinct from the one that Ives used in the sketches he drafted for her.

177. 16 March 1944, Harmony Ives to Charlotte Ruggles, New York

Dear Charlotte—

We had such a lovely Christmas card from you & Carl—we just loved it! It is too bad to meet so seldom people we love as we do you—We didn't come in town 'til Christmas time & are planning to go to Redding again Ap. 15th. Charlie isn't very well & gets awfully blue and indignant about his failing eyesight. He had some correspondence last summer with Lou Harrison who did some copying for him—in one letter Mr. Harrison says "I consider you with Ruggles, the two most important composers of this century" Charlie loves to be bracketted with Carl. . . .

178. 2 April 1944, Harmony Ives to Carl Ruggles, New York

Dear Carl—

Thank you for your reply to my inquiry as to the disposition of the "Sun Treader" Photostats—I have told Mrs. Stevenson to forward them by express as you said.

We were very interested to hear of Sharon Ruggles's advent. What a pretty & unusual name!—We have no grand child and are missing some fun I know—

We are going to Redding shortly and shall be glad to. Charlie says he knows the music is grand but he can't see it well enough to get it all—When we get to Redding & his big magnifying glass he will try again—his failing eyesight is a heavy trial.

Our best to you and Charlotte & to Micah's family too

As ever
Harmony T. Ives

179. Ca. 10 September 1947, sketch for Harmony Ives to Friede Rothe[56]

Friede F. Roth 135 w. 56

I am writing for Mr. Ives as he is not at all well. He is very sorry not to see Mr. Arrau, whose interest in his music is much appreciated. He has a bad heart condition and the doctors say he must keep quiet and should have no interviews.

The 2nd Edition of Concord Sonata will probably be ready in a month or two and Mr. I will be glad to have a complimentary copy sent to Mr. Arrau. In this edition there are some playing explanations, some of which may lessen the difficulties—at least Mr. I hopes so.

Please give Mr. Arrau Mr. Ives's kindest wishes, and tell him how much we regret not seeing him.

Cordially yours

180. Ca. 4 May 1949, sketch for Harmony Ives to Norris A. Pynn

I am writing for ——

He regrets that he cannot nowadays, attend to things as he would like to—also he has a cataract condition in both eyes and cannot see well enough to look over manuscripts. But by your letter he feels that you are one of those strong personalities who are not afraid to stand up & think for themselves,—with a natural originality. . . .

• • •

This letter contains the first mention of the hernia that would eventually contribute to Ives's death of a stroke in 1954.

181. 15 November 1950, Harmony Ives to Carl and Charlotte Ruggles, New York

Dear Carl & Charlotte,

We loved Carl's letter—very characteristic I should say. We came from Redding last Sunday and hated to leave it was so lovely—the bare trees give us back so much that is smothered in their foliage.

Charlie did have to go to the hospital—hurry trip with the ambulance & all—but nothing had to be done as the doctor manipulated the hernia which was giving the trouble, back into place—this happens every once in a while & is a trying experience all around—I have been the really sick one as I had a sharp gall bladder attack three weeks ago & find it hard to get my strength back but I shall.

56. Rothe, who was Claudio Arrau's agent, wrote to Ives on 10 September to tell him that the pianist would like to meet with him to talk about the *Concord* Sonata.

We like to think of you as still in Arlington—it is noisy here & so crowded—I go out very little & Charlie only by dark!—It is no kind of life but physically easier than by ourselves in Redding where so much has to be gone for & done by ourselves—lots of things I like to do & used to do easily come hard now—so we should be thankful we have this place and a good maid.

Glad to hear that "Organum" is being conducted by Stokowski in Houston—of course you know the Philharmonic here is to do Charlie's 2nd Symphony in Feb.—Bernstein conducting. I suppose we shall be in misery.

Our love to you both & we shall be seeing you—
Charles and Harmony

182. 9 July 1951, Harmony Ives to Nicolas Slonimsky, West Redding

Dear Nicolas

When I come across a word like "gluosity" I think of you & must submit it tho' you are doubtless familiar with it—in Boswell's Johnson.

Mr. Ives is having a siege of the troublesome virus pneumonia—He has been going on four weeks in bed,—not very sick but running a slight temperature that augments if he tries to get up and attend to matters demanding his attention. Oh! These theses writers with their questionnaires—often asking for an answer by return mail

We hope you are all well—We were so interested to know that Electra is at Barnard—next season I hope we shall see her—last winter I wasn't well and ended up with an operation for gall stones—am very well now.

Our love to you all
as ever sincerely
Harmony T. Ives

183. 16 September 1951, Harmony Ives to Carl and Charlotte Ruggles, West Redding

Dear Carl & Charlotte,

Thank you so much for sending us the copy of Vermont Life—we were glad to see it and thought it pleasantly and tastefully written—those things can be so awful. Charlie was very happy, as he always is, to be linked with Carl—the characterization of Charlotte is delightful and the quotations from Carl fine & interesting—

We have had our usual quiet summer—Charlie had a tedious attack of virus pneumonia in the early part which kept him in bed five weeks—He wasn't very sick but got a temperature if he did anything but stay in bed—He surrendered gracefully after the first two weeks. . . .

184. 19 March 1952, Harmony Ives to John Becker, New York

Dear John

We are sorry to hear of your disabling illness.

We have been going slow all winter and I am specially bad about letter writing—Charlie isn't very well and finds it just about more than he can do to attend to the things that must be done. We have seen Henry only once—he is in Baltimore three days a week & always busy. Sidney [Cowell] had a serious operation but made a good recovery—I have tried over & over to get her by telephone since she got home but unsuccessfully. Carl & Charlotte have been in New York all winter and had a lot of virus illnesses—we had one very pleasant tea time with them. They don't get around much & we don't at all. My news isn't very bright colored but that is the way & not only with us old ones—Edie & hers have had their usual winter ailments—George had a kidney stone attack & Edie a painful bursitis & Kit the sore throats etc. of childhood.[57] At present all are on their feet.

Indeed you will be lonely when your last boy goes off—Evelyn will feel it greatly. We are certainly living in times that try one's soul—but they are interesting and great with such important questions—if we can only produce the men who have the answer—we dread the coming campaign—America at about its worst.

The enclosed is a belated Christmas remembrance—Charlie was too used up at Christmastime to attend to anything—We hope your book can be resumed before long—the interruption is hard to bear.

With our kindest wishes to you all
As ever
Charles and Harmony Ives

185. 24 March 1953, Harmony Ives to Carl and Charlotte Ruggles, New York

Dear Carl & Charlotte,

I feel so badly that we haven't been able to get together with you.

Charlie doesn't feel able, really, to see anyone. I tell him he is "the can't man"—I tell him to get up & he says "I can't get up"—(he does) I say "do eat" & he says "I can't eat anything" & if I suggest his seeing anyone he says "I can't see anyone"—and I just haven't the strength to overcome his inertia—There isn't anything specially wrong except his approach & he of course does feel weak & miserable— . . .

186. 2 January 1954, Harmony Ives to John and Evelyn Becker, New York

Dear Evelyn & John,

We were glad to hear from you tho' your news wasn't very gay—We have had a somber autumn too—Charles isn't well—he has slowed up very much & hasn't seen anybody—

57. George and Edith Ives Tyler and their son, Charles Ives Tyler, whose nickname was Kit.

not even Henry or Carl Ruggles—he & Charlotte spend the winter months in New York—Arlington too cold in a cellarless house.

Edie has been in hospital for weeks—She had a small cyst removed from her breast which didn't amount to much but they kept her on for radium treatment & the doctors just seem to string it along. She goes home for a night or two now & then. It is hard on George & Kit. They have an excellent woman who comes at noon every day & takes charge of Kit but George has to get him off to school early, that with spending evenings with Edie make a long hard day for an awfully busy man. George's mother & sister came on for Christmas & his mother will stay on which is a big help to all of us—of course I've tried to have Kit here to lunch often but he is too much for me when I must devote my day to Charles.

Your package came & Edie is going to love the geographical note paper—& Kit will pour over the book. Edie wants me to thank you for both herself & Kit—you will hear from her some day tho' maybe not soon. She says she has twenty three notes & seven letters to write! That is Edie all over—always swamped—

I know it is hard for you parents of three young men—Just now the idea of a war doesn't seem popular anywhere but in these perilous times anything can happen. We go out not at all.

With our warmest best wishes for a good new year
as ever yours
Charles & Harmony

·5·

COLLABORATORS AND CHAMPIONS (1923–1933)

The publication and dissemination of the *Concord* Sonata, *Essays,* and *114 Songs* were the first steps in the process of introducing Ives's works to the musical public. Because of the unusual method of distribution, to say nothing of the unconventionality of the music itself, much more work remained to be done before most musicians would take Ives and his works seriously. A small group of performers, conductors, promoters, and critics appreciated or became curious about the music, and it was these people who began to correspond with Ives and to bring his works to light.

187. 22 January 1923, from Clifton Furness, New York

Dear Mr. Ives:

The date of the "Pierrot Lunaire" Schoenberg concert has been changed to February 4, (Sunday week) in the evening. Will you be in town, and would you care to go? I understand that there is to be a rehearsal (semi-public) on Sunday morning) to give members the opportunity of a second hearing—on the theory, I suppose, that they should have an opportunity to recover from the first shock! Perhaps you would rather go with me to the rehearsal than to the whole concert, if the other numbers in the programme do not interest you particularly. I enclose announcement of the other numbers. The Schoenberg, at least, will be worth hearing, I'm sure. Carl Engel, of the Music Library of the Library of Congress, gave a very interesting diatribe on it yesterday afternoon. I would have asked you to venture it, but anticipated a bore—on the contrary, He dropped some really stimulating ideas, about which I'll tell you when I see you. I hope you will be able to go.

Sincerely,
Cliff Furness

P.S.—I have under headway a real piano piece—Liberation !

• • •

One of Ives's earliest supporters was E. Robert Schmitz (1889–1949), a pianist, conductor, and promoter of modernist music. Schmitz, who had immigrated to the United States from France in 1918, was the founder of the Franco-American Music Society and an important contact with the world of the musical avant-garde.[1] He also became a personal friend. Through Schmitz, Ives made some of his first steps into the wider public musical arena.

188. 4 October 1923, from E. Robert Schmitz, New York

My dear Mr. Ives,

It has been a great pleasure for me to have this meeting with you.

I somehow feel that I have to tell how gratifying to me, it has been to find your spontaneous collaboration.

I am looking forward with anticipation to our next meeting. Meanwhile, please let me propose your name for membership in the Franco-American musical society as this will help keeping in touch with the work. Dues: [$]5 a year. And the enclosed blank once filled need only be returned to me so that I exist as "proposer"—

If you have a copy of your earlier work (you spoke of) I would love to have it to look at while on tour and it would reach me through my New York address. If not possible to make copy, I shall wait until our next meeting.

Yours most sincerely,
E. R. Schmitz

189. Ca. 4 October 1923, sketch for Ives to E. Robert Schmitz

My dear Mr. Schmitz:

Thank you for your letter and for preparing my membership in the society. Am sending the application & ~~fee ck~~ fee. It was a great pleasure & a help to me to meet you.—and interesting to find a man and a ~~professional musician~~ with such a comprehensive range ~~so interested and not only in his career. This is not a critique of the professional artist for I've known almost none—that is personally.~~

The earlier piano ~~pieces~~ sonata, ~~I have in mind~~ is ~~all~~ in lead pencil—I looked over it ~~last~~ yesterday Sunday. Two movements ~~go would~~ won't have to be changed at all—only copied in ink—they seem to go as they stand. The 1st movement will have [to] be compressed and revised; the 3rd movement cut out all together—it's too involved. It may take a month or two to get it in shape. The whole is a kind of adventure—in a state of mind of 10 or 15 years ago—in different fields than the 'Concord Sonata.' Most of it is a rough-hewn kind of a thing—but I am not going to soften it up. ~~I may see you again~~

The Fine Arts "Co" office is one of the most interesting places I've been to for some time. It ~~seems to be~~ is more of an educational art exhibit than a store. There must be ~~hundreds~~ many people (like myself) who know nothing about it and who ~~should be brought~~ would like to be brought in touch with it.

You will let me know when I may see you again

1. Oja, *Making Music Modern*, 179.

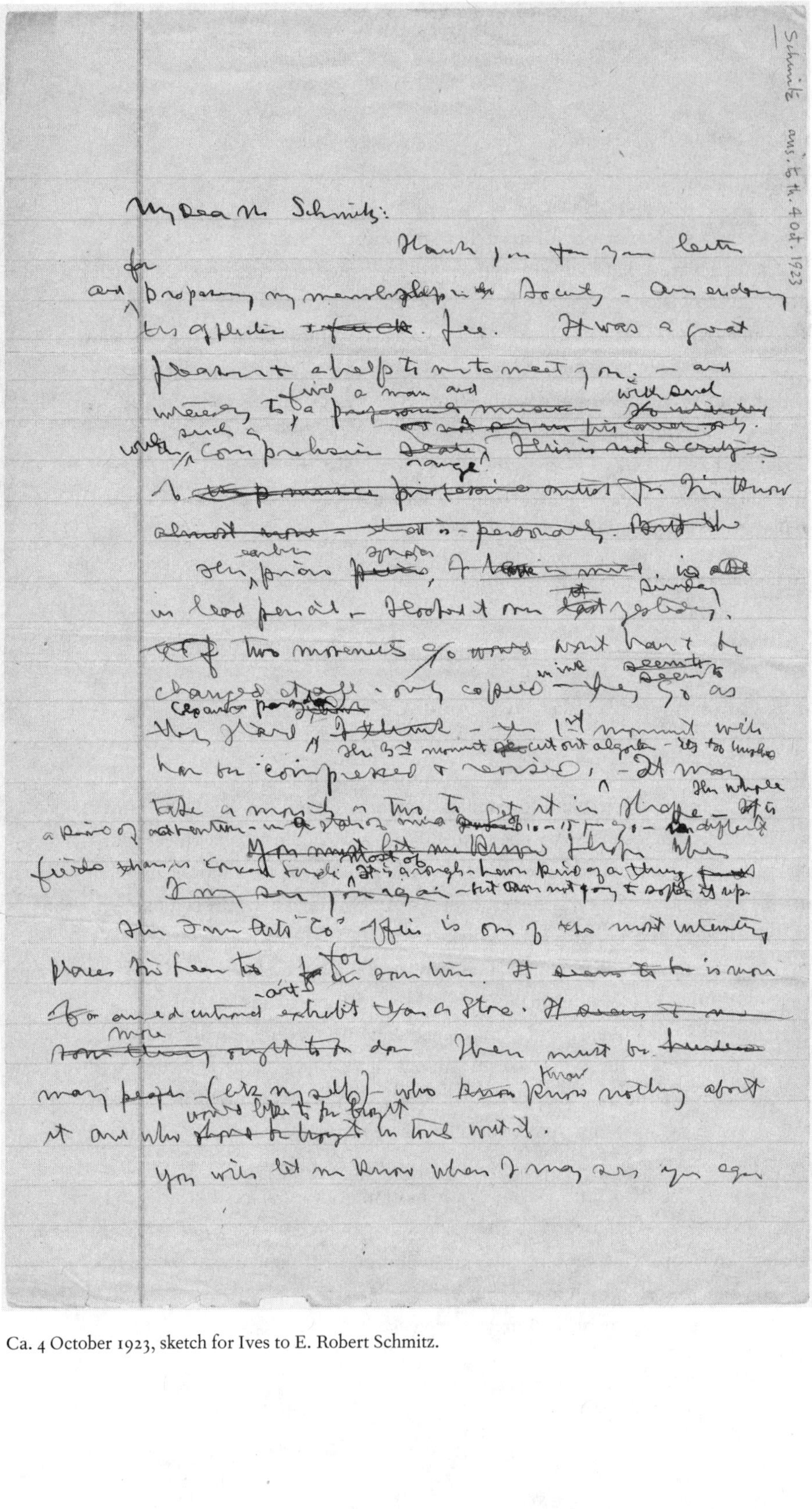
Schmitz ans. 5 th. 4 Oct. 1923

My dear Mr. Schmitz:

Thank you for your letter and for proposing my membership in the Society — and enclosing the application [illegible] fee. It was a great pleasure & a help to me to meet you — and interesting to find a man and a professional musician with such a comprehensive range [illegible]

The earlier piano sonata [illegible] is in lead pencil — I looked it over Sunday yesterday. Of two movements [illegible] won't have to be changed at all — only copied — they go as they stand [illegible] — the 1st movement will have to be compressed & revised — the 3rd movement [illegible] — It may take a month or two to get it in shape — the whole [illegible]

[illegible]

The Fine Arts "Co" office is one of the most interesting places I've been to for some time. It is more of an educational art exhibit than a store. [illegible] There must be many people (like myself) who know nothing about it and who would like to be brought in touch with it.

You will let me know when I may see you again

Ca. 4 October 1923, sketch for Ives to E. Robert Schmitz.

• • •

The next letter contains a number of revisions for Ives's article "Some 'Quarter-Tone' Impressions," which appeared in the *Franco-American Music Society Bulletin* in March 1925.[2] The letter is a kind of microcosm of Ives's tendency to revise, which manifests itself in the correspondence, especially after 1930, when Ives began to write sketches of his letters to be transcribed by others, and in the multiple versions of many of his compositions. The analogy here is particularly strong because, as would later be the case in the second edition of the *Concord* Sonata, he is deciding to restore passages from an earlier version of the work that he had previously cut.

190. 9 December 1923, to E. Robert Schmitz

Dear Mr. Schmitz:

In the copy of the article about Quarter-Tones sent you last week (for the next issue of the "Pro Musica Quarterly"), it seems to me now that a paragraph, and parts of others, which were in the first copy, but omitted last, would probably be better left in, as they perhaps help to bring out more fully the underlying idea that the use of quarter-tones is but one of the ways by which music may be less encaged by some of the restrictions of custom and habit. Will have a complete copy made later, but in case there may be some hurry to start printing, am including them separately here.

2nd Paragraph—Page 3—"We approve certain things, not because there is any natural propriety in them, but because we have been accustomed to them, and have been taught to consider them right; we disapprove certain others, not because there is any natural impropriety in them, but because the are strange to us, and we have been taught to consider them wrong."

2nd Paragraph—Page 6—"Chords of four or more notes, as I hear it, seem to be a more natural basis than triads. A triad, it seems to me, leans toward the sound or sounds that the diatonic ear expects from hearing the notes which must form some diatonic interval. Thus the third note enters as a kind of weak compromise to the sound expected." . . . "(It is assumed here that a chord is a division of the octave though later on perhaps greater periods than an octave as a unit for larger, and newer scales may come as a natural development.)"

The figures measuring the ratio of vibration numbers or difference of overtone beats, may be somewhat out of place in a short article like this, but possibly not.

Page 10—"In this connection, it may be out of place here to refer to something that has been bearing itself in on me for much longer than a few years.

The drag of repetition occurs in many phases of art. In music, this drag is often caused by a structure built primarily on a progression of chords not necessarily the same but of

2. Although Ives refers to the journal as the *Pro Musica Quarterly*, the society and its journal did not adopt this name officially until 1925, after Ives's article had been published. Perhaps the name had been used unofficially previously.

the same relative intervals, and seems more and more to hold up that organic flow which we feel the need of—it halts us so severely that a resort to other material is almost forced on us."

Page 12—Section III was entirely omitted, but would suggest that it be included as follows:

"The contribution of Quarter-Tones to rhythm may be in their ability to relieve the monotony of literal repetition.

A shift to a quarter tone chord or tonality seems to drive in on the ear in a way somewhat similar that changing instruments do[es]; they may vary ~~with the base on the pulses~~ more as in changing passages. And in a rhythmic cycle or series of uneven periods pure quarter tone chords alone or in a short phrase of definite tonality used alternatively with the same in pure diatonic intervals, etc. seem to clarify and widen the general rhythmic scheme."

Page 13—"An interesting effect (the manner of which is may be probably more physiological /psychological? than musical) may be obtained by striking a chord on both pianos, made up of a series of whole tone triads on say C, C♯, D, D♯, distributing them upward through three or four octaves. In this way all the twenty-four tones are caught and in a chord not especially harsh. If the pedal is held, as the sounds die away a composite is heard in rhythmic waves similar to the sounds in the resonance when the twelve note chord, at the beginning of the Piano Piece (2nd Abolitionist Riot" in Boston in the 50's) is held with the pedal. This chord is distributed through three octaves less a whole tone. It was written out in the margin—with some indication of its vibration ratio—difference of the overtone beats, but not completed.

Well, now I'll stop and lift the pedal—let you have a let up from all this. If it's going to make much trouble, let the shorter copy with ommissions be used—the shorter, the better, ~~for most of the fellows~~ sometimes.

Our best wishes to you all,
Sincerely,

• • •

The correspondence with Carl Engel reflects the early stages of the distribution and recognition of Ives's works. Engel wrote asking for copies of Ives's printed music for the Library of Congress. Ives's reply challenges the notion that he was isolated from the music world, at least in 1924.

191. 27 March 1924, to Carl Engel

My dear Mr. Engel:—

Let me acknowledge and thank you for your note of the 22nd. I am very glad, indeed, to send you the books which you ask for. This is the only music of mine that is printed—the "Violin Sonatas" are in manuscript.

Can't you induce Mr. Sonneck to put the "Musical Quarterly" on a monthly basis?[3] In three evenings we have read it through and most of it re-read. Then you keep us waiting for three months.

According to my way of thinking, there should be more of this, or more magazines of similar character in this country.

Sincerely,
CEI/MM

[*In Ives's hand:*] books sent March 31st / "114" "Concord Sonata" & Essays / (in one package parcel post)

• • •

This letter, in particular, demonstrates the extent of Furness and Ives's discussion of Scriabin and implies that both men knew the works of which they wrote very well.

192. 6 April 1924, from Clifton Furness, Evanston, Illinois

Dear Mr. Ives,

I'm sending the program notes from the Boston Symphony about Scriabin "Reverie Poème," thinking you might be interested in some of the information. The quotation from Rosenfeld reiterates the "Venusberg" stigma about the "[Poème de l'] Extase." Perhaps it has some foundation, but it seems to me that the critics who fulminate that as [the] final verdict thereby convict themselves of being incapable of apprehension beyond the physical aspect of music for they miss totally the point of the introduction of "sensuousness"—the way in which Scriabin transcends this (or as you said, builds out of it) is the point and purpose of the whole work. Those who label the thing in its entirety by the opening have not crossed the threshold of its meaning.

Of course I wished very much for you to be there, except for one thing. The reading Monteux[4] gave it seemed to me wholly inadequate, in comparison with Damrosch's "L'Extase." It may have been partially due to the composition itself, of course, since it is naturally a bit anti-climactic after the one we heard last week, but it seemed to me that he took almost all of it at a deadening tempo. There was not the fire and ebullience requisite for Scriabin in his symphonic vein. Monteux seemed to conceive it more as I do the piano things—did not lay on the colors thick enough—seemed to be trying to paint in oils with aquarelle techniques. He drew out the tempi until you could see and feel gaps in the tonal fabric. There was not the rich warp and woof of sound, the dynamic tightened-up mass of tone as in "L'Extase" Perhaps better say, the fluid sound came in spurts, rather than in one

3. Oscar Sonneck, a pioneering student of American music, was a vice president of G. Schirmer and the editor of *Musical Quarterly*. Engel had worked with Sonneck at the Library of Congress and succeeded him as editor of the journal.

4. Pierre Monteux (1875–1964) was the conductor of the Boston Symphony from 1920 until 1924.

continuous stream—wave, flood, whatever it was that seethed out and drew one in like the suction of a whirlpool in "L'Extase." I think Scriabin had not found out completely in this the secret of using all the instruments to augment one another, as in the later work,—he is more interested in countering themes against each other, leading individual voices—not so much mass movement in which each separate atom of sound merges indistinguishably into the whole—or is the seeming difference in effect due to the greater strangeness, newness of the thematic & harmonic material in the later work. I don't know—this is just my impression.

At any rate, whether I was wholly satisfied or not, the audience were as before enthusiastic. They demanded [?] really just as with "L'Extase" and it was spontaneous and for the piece itself I felt—not put on just for the occasion as perhaps was the last "hand," a tribute to Monteux on his farewell appearance. A friend of mine who was there, and dislikes "modern" music (except [Charles Griffes's] "The White Peacock") said, "you know I liked that Scriabin thing in spite of myself!" You see, I think Scriabin's ultimate acceptance is inevitable.

Miss Heyman[5] gives an all-Scriabin piano recital at Aeolian Hall next Sunday evening. Several of the late works including the VIII sonata and the last set of Preludes that you liked. I have complementaries. Will you and Mrs. Ives join me?

Sincerely,
Cliff Furness

• • •

Ives met Elliott Carter when he was Furness's student at the Horace Mann School in New York. The letter of recommendation that Ives wrote in support of Carter's application to Harvard demonstrates both his appreciation of the younger musician's budding talent and his penchant for thumbing his nose at authority.

193. Ca. early 1926, to the dean of Harvard College

[*In Ives's hand across top in clear script:*] letter to Harvard Dean in re Elliot Carter

Carter strikes me as rather an exceptional boy. He has an instinctive interest in literature and especially music, that is somewhat unusual. He writes well—an essay in his School paper—"Symbolism in Art" shows an interesting mind. I don't know him intimately, but his teacher in Horace Mann school, Mr. Clifton J. Furness, and a friend of mine always speaks well of him—that he's a boy of good character and does well in his studies. I am sure his reliability, industry and sense of honor are what they should be—also his sense of humor which you do not ask me about.

5. Katherine Heyman (1877–1944) was a composer and pianist who specialized in Scriabin. Ives subsidized her performances of Scriabin in Paris in 1927. See Letter 197.

194. 19 February 1927, from Elliott Carter, Cambridge, Massachusetts

Dear Mr. Ives,

I am very sorry that I was unable to come to see you that Sunday afternoon nor later to hear your symphony. As I am interested very much in your music I would like to hear it once instead of having to work over it to make it sound at all.

I wonder if it would be possible to have a few more records made of your violin sonata—or is the stamp lost? Recently I have been greatly interested in recordings. I have records of "Pelleas and Melisande," "Pacific 231," Stravinsky's "Petrouchka," "Fire-Bird," "Ragtime," as well as Scriabine's "Poem of Ecstasy"—only to mention the moderns. I find the victrola a great help in studying Beethoven and Brahms. Unfortunately very little good Bach has been done.

I am sending you a very interesting magazine dealing with recordings entirely. In it, this month, has appeared an account of private recordings. I wonder if Pro-Musica could not have a department for recording its more popular modern works. "Pierrot Lunaire," and other things are waiting to be done as well as some Scriabine.

The subscription record idea seems a very good one (at least to me) and would help in the understanding of modern music.

I wish it were possible to start a modern music group here in Boston—it has never been done though we hear a great deal from Koussevitzky.

I am coming to Miss Heyman's concert Sunday evening Feb 27. I hope I shall see you there.

Sincerely yours,
Elliott C. Carter Jr.

• • •

In the late 1920s Henry Cowell (1897–1964) and Nicolas Slonimsky (1894–1995) became important figures in the career of Ives's music. The correspondence richly details the working and personal relationships among this unlikely trio. Cowell was the tireless composer, conductor, performer, propagandist, and champion of "ultramodern" music. In 1927 he founded *New Music*, which published the second movement of Ives's Fourth Symphony in January 1929, and which subsequently became one of the most important sources for his music. Slonimsky, an expatriate Russian, was also an aspiring young conductor and modernist; he gave the American and European premieres of *Three Places in New England* (Orchestral Set no. 1) in 1931. The letters below document the first contacts among the three as they developed a network of musical, financial, and personal support and friendship. The tone is formal at first. Cowell and Slonimsky were looking for a patron and becoming increasingly interested in Ives as a composer. Ives seems amazed at the level of interest in him and his works and throws himself into the role of champion of modernism.

These letters provide details of the early working relationship between Ives and Cowell, including arrangements for regular funding of *New Music* by Ives, and the provision that he would pay for the extra costs of publishing the second movement of his Fourth Symphony. This dual system of contributions was standard in the years that followed. The conversations with Cowell and Slonimsky also provide a window into Ives's life and interests. His invitation to Cowell to attend a concert of Ravel with him and his description of a concert in which Cowell's "Banshee" was performed further demonstrate that Ives was not as isolated from the musical world in the 1920s as has commonly been believed.

195. 27 July 1927, from Henry Cowell, Menlo Park, California

Dear Mr. Ives:

I am hoping that you will be interested in becoming a subscriber to "New Music" of which I enclose an announcement. I also hope that you may feel like offering some compositions for consideration for publication in "New Music," and I further hope that you will do the New Music Society of California (which publishes New Music) the honor of allowing it to use your name as a member of the advisory board. There is no obligation attached to this position. The society is altruistically favorable to the furtherance of newer ideas in music, and gives concerts in San Francisco and Los Angeles, of modern works.

Sincerely yours,
Henry Cowell

196. 16 August 1927, to Henry Cowell

Dear Mr. Cowell:—

Thank you for your letter and enclosures.

I shall be glad to serve in any [way] that I can in the work. Your idea of a circulating music library via a magazine of unsaleable scores is admirable—and a needed move. If the plan does nothing more than make possible a freer exchange of opinions, it will be of value, it seems to me.

I was sorry to have been laid up last winter when Mr. Nicolaric telephoned; but shall hope to see you when you are again in New York.

I am with best wishes,
Yours sincerely,
Chas E. Ives

CEI/LG

• • •

Ives's correspondence with Katherine Heyman, a pianist and composer whom he met through Clifton Furness, is typical of the early stages of his contact with sympathetic musicians. In this letter he plans to send a score, possibly the "Emerson" Transcriptions, to Heyman, who was performing in France. Heyman specialized in Scriabin, and here we find more evidence of Ives's familiarity with, and appreciation for, the Russian composer's works. We also see the beginnings of Ives's financial support for the performance of contemporary music. Typically, he deflects any potential objection by Heyman to his philanthropy by saying that it is intended for Scriabin's music, rather than her.

197. 9 September 1927, to Katherine Heyman

Dear Miss Heyman:—

I hope you had a favorable trip over and did not meet the storm that blew the horse off of our barn. You must find it interesting to be back in Paris again. A letter from Mr. Furness in Florence says he is on his way to France—you have probably seen him by this time.

The copy had plenty of mistakes in it and was not very clear at that. Before having it photographed I am waiting for a man who has done good work for me. He expects to be back in about two weeks. With it, I will send "The Book of Essays" and Bellaman's magazine article. You may find them of some help but perhaps not much.

I came across in an old Musical Quarterly an article by the English Antcliffe, about "Prometheus" and "Scriabin"—though you may have seen this.

I did not find out from Tam's what they charged you for copying but I want to send the enclosed to cover this and ask you to use the balance towards any clerical or other work that Prometheus may need done.

Mrs. Ives and Edie would want to send remembrances if they knew I were writing and we all wish you success in your "Adventure"—not the success you deserve but that Scriabin does—you can't object to this.

Let us hear when you will of the "Pilgrim's Progress." I am, with best wishes,

C. E. Ives

• • •

John Kirkpatrick (1905–1991) began his relationship with Ives, as did countless other correspondents, with a letter requesting a copy of the *Concord* Sonata. This simple letter led to a lifetime of devotion to Ives and his music. Yet Ives was slow to warm to the pianist, and for years the two knew one another only through letters. It is perhaps an indication of the deterioration of Ives's health in the 1930s that it was so long before he and Kirkpatrick met face to face, even though they lived only a few miles from one another for much of this time. Both Cowell and Slonimsky, who began to work closely with Ives in the late 1920s, quickly became his personal friends as well as important musical allies. Kirkpatrick, with whom Ives began steadily corresponding in December 1933, did not meet Ives until May 1937, and he did not sign letters to Ives with only his first name until March 1945.

198. 7 October 1927, from John Kirkpatrick, New York

My Dear Mr. Ives,

Would I be troubling you too much to ask you how I could obtain a copy of your Concord, Mass Sonata? Miss Heyman showed it to me in Paris before I left. I must admit that I feel as yet only the more diatonic Alcotts, but I would love to study the work further.

I am an amateur musician on the brink of becoming a professional, and very much interested in almost anything concerning American music. I enclose the program to prove it.

Hoping to hear from you soon,

Yours sincerely,
John Kirkpatrick Jr.

• • •

When Ives sent Kirkpatrick a copy of the first edition of the *Concord,* he also promised to send along copies of the "Emerson" Transcriptions, which would give the pianist his first glimpse of the thicket of versions, revisions, and sources of the sonata that he would spend the rest of his life untangling.

199. 10 October 1927, to John Kirkpatrick

Dear Mr. Kirkpatrick:—

Let me acknowledge your letter of October 7th and thank you for the interesting program.

Under separate cover I take pleasure in sending you a copy of the book and ask you to accept it with my compliments. But perhaps what Miss Heyman referred to was a transcription of the first movement which is in more playable shape than some of the printed score. As soon as I can get to it will have a few photographic copies made and shall be glad to send you one.

I am, with best wishes,
Very truly yours,

200. 16 October 1927, from John Kirkpatrick, New York

My dear Mr. Ives,

I received the Sonata yesterday, preceded by your very kind letter. That my feeling of gratitude is far above my powers of expression is the sort of thing I imagine you are used to hearing, so I will spare you my attempts.

I don't yet understand Emerson's "prose,"[6] but have hopes thereof, adore the Alcotts, and am very impatient to see how Thoreau sounds with his flute.

Hoping to be able some time to thank you in the flesh, I remain
Yours truly,
John Kirkpatrick Jr.

6. In the first edition of the sonata, sections of "Emerson" were designated as prose and verse.

201. January 1928, from Elliott Carter, Cambridge, Massachusetts

Dear Mr. Ives,

These examinations are something of a waste of time and they have taken me away from my music. Before they began I wrote two more songs and planned partly another movement of that string quartet.

I am getting together some fellows up here to play it and also that violin sonata of yours. I have not had time to look it over but it looks very good so far. I have not tried to fit the Emerson movement together yet. But that violin sonata seems to me to have that quiet emotionality which is the real inspiration of music. Music should be admitted to have an effect on people and more that has a good effect should be played. Your violin sonata seems to make ideals and serenity sprout out of one as Brahms and Bach do. Furness has played Emerson for me and I think it is wonderful too. I have always wanted to hear you play these and possibly learn some of them (as much as my poor technique would allow). And then too those in *New Music*. That is a great thing. Henry Cowell deserves much praise. I can hear some of "Men and Mountains" but Rudhyar's Paens are good but they seem a little too majestic, too much of his own greatness taken for granted.

Anyhow, thank you very much for all these, they will last long and mean much. More, now, than I can say and certainly more than I have yet discovered.

Elliott C. Carter jr.

• • •

In January 1928 Ives provided funding for a quarter-tone piano that the composer and performer Hans Barth (1897–1956) was having designed and built by George Weitz of the Chickering Piano Company.[7] Ives had been interested in having such an instrument built since at least 1925, and it is clear from his letters that he intended to compose for it, although his work with it was limited.[8] His declining health in January 1929, when the piano was completed, may have deterred him from much new composition. Ives's secretary typed the following letters from Ives to Barth from his dictation.

202. 11 January 1928, to Hans Barth

Dear Mr. Barth:—

Confirming our recent conversation, it will be understood that my property interest in any future value of the Quarter-Tone piano which the Chickering Company is now making will be limited to the proportion of the amount I have invested ($500) to the total cost; that

7. Sinclair, *Descriptive Catalogue*, 237.

8. See Letter 206; the introduction to Letter 212; and Ives to E. Robert Schmitz, 30 July 1925; E. Robert Schmitz to Ives, 3 September 1925; E. Robert Schmitz to Ives, 15 March 1926; E. Robert Schmitz to Ives, 5 April 1926 (all in CIP, 30/15).

I shall have the right to a reasonable use of the piano for my personal work; that Mr. Barth shall have exclusive right to use this piano for public performance during the first year after completion; that the piano shall not be sold or any interest in it transferred without the consent of all the owners.

The above seems advisable as a matter of business though we understand each other, I think, perfectly in this matter, ~~and that~~ we have undertaken the ~~manufacturing~~ building of this piano primarily so that ~~this piano~~ it may be of help to each of us in ~~our~~ his work in Quarter-Tone composition and it will be used as a serious contribution to the development of Quarter-Tone music in general, and ~~that it shall~~ not be ~~used~~ as a means of exploiting anybody or anything.

Sincerely,

[*Handwritten:*] Rent eventually to earn $500

203. 6 February 1928, to John Kirkpatrick

Dear Mr. Kirkpatrick:—

Under separate cover I am sending you a photographed copy of some transcriptions of a movement of the sonata you asked me for last Fall. I think, perhaps this is what Miss Heyman had in mind when she wrote you.

These pieces cover the principal sections of the movement and are in more playable shape. There are some revisions and changes and also some things from the original plan in which I had in mind more instruments than the piano and which were left out of the printed score.

With these I am sending a copy of an early violin sonata.

Please accept them with my compliments, I am
Sincerely yours

204. 28 February 1928, from Henry Cowell, New York

Dear Mr. Ives:

I have received the enclosed letter from my printers in the west. It seems to leave the field open to succeed if one wishes! Please let me know whether you wish to take advantage of a possible special price and service by the Chicago house?[9] It might be well to start to begin procedures, as the engraving of your work will doubtless take some time.

The Pan American Composer's Association, of which I spoke to you over the phone the other day (and whose minutes you are doubtless receiving) proposes to give some concerts in April in New York, and would like to have your "Emerson" performed, if you are

9. Rayner, Dalheim, and Co., a firm associated with the Pacific Music Press, regularly did engraving and printing for *New Music*.

agreeable. Have you in mind any pianist who could play this? Otherwise we though of asking Mr. Richard Buhlig to play it.[10]

Was so very sorry I couldn't go with you to the Ravel concert only the fact that I had to play kept me from it.

I hope that we may visit again soon, as our visit the other evening was the greatest sort of pleasure.

Highest regards to you and Mrs. Ives,
Sincerely yours,
Henry Cowell

205. 10 April 1928, from Henry Cowell, New York

Dear Mr. Ives:

I forgot to take the program notes and press clippings of your symphony when I hurriedly had to leave this afternoon. Please hold them for me 'til Thursday.

The prospect of having some regular backing for New Music and the Pan American Association overcomes me with a joyful feeling. The really greatest pleasure in life is to have means to be able to work toward the furtherance of the general good of the best in new music, for me!

Cordially,
Henry Cowell

P.S. My address in California, where I will arrive about May 5th, is simply Menlo Park.

The address of the music engraving firm in Chicago is Raynor, Dalheim and Company, 2054 West Lake Street, Chicago.

I enclose a prospectus of the dance program for Sunday evening. Sorry not to send you tickets, but they have not offered me any, and I do not like to ask for them.

• • •

Ives feared that the engraver would balk at the notational difficulty of the second movement of his Fourth Symphony, and, indeed, Rayner, Dalheim refused the score, which was eventually engraved in New York by Herman Langinger.[11] The catalogue mentioned below was a proposed list of compositions by members of the Pan American Association of Composers. It was never completed.

10. Richard Buhlig was a pianist with a well-established career who had studied with Ferruccio Busoni; he sometimes performed in concerts Cowell organized in California.

11. Sinclair, *Descriptive Catalogue*, 18. See Letter 207.

206. Ca. 24 April 1928, to Henry Cowell

Dear Mr. Cowell:

I've just mailed the score (22 pages) and the enclosed letters to Rayner-Dalheim Co. ~~It doesn't~~ does look pretty bad—but it's the best I can do. We expect the usual "howl" before they get to work. As you say it depends more or less on the engraver's state of mind.I hope they won't throw it out ~~altog~~ altogether. Whatever you can do in its behalf I will appreciate.

We all enjoyed the dance-concert last week (some of it.) The "Banshee" was the most vivid—its only fault was its brevity—is that a fault? Let me hear from you when you can—sincerely,

Chas E. Ives

The duration of the pieces I gave you for the catalogue are not very accurate—I find,—will try to make a better estimate, as soon as I can get to it. It may be just as well to put in all the 1/4 tone pieces. The 1st is for a 1/4 T. Piano (one player only) & the 2nd is more the rhythmic side. They don't pretend to be much more than studies of the situation from 3 different angles.

207. 12 August 1928, to Henry Cowell

Dear Mr. Cowell:

Thank you for the letters. I appreciated your interest (and so does Mrs. Ives) and for including me in the 4 specimens—It's all well done, the estimates are clearly put and interesting—not a common virtue. Mrs. Ives is very much impressed and delighted with the way you write. There is an economy and tenseness that drives the reader along. To our way of thinking the Chavez piece, in Pro Musica is one of the best written criticisms we have seen recently—incidentally those about Schoenberg & Honegger about the worst. So many of the present writers seem more interested in words than thoughts (assuming that every word is not always a thought—not yet—even to the wise).

I'm glad "Pro Musica" & <u>New Music</u> are beginning to co-operate. It seems to me perhaps later on some plans of benefit to each may be worked out—for instance printing manuscripts that are to be played at the chapters or at other concerts. I suggested this to Mr. Schmitz in writing.

There is one thing certain—in fact, two things certain (this sounds like a theosophist)—"<u>New Music</u>" must be kept going—and we will keep it going—if you can't get enough outfielders we'll go through without them and I think before a great while we'll have the bleachers with us—and perhaps the umpire.

I have you to thank for getting me to get out a couple of old (not sores) scores which I'd thrown into the discard. You remember last winter, we were talking about something involving them. You said you thought that the mechanical or perhaps artificial had its part—that is a natural part. It seems so the more I think of it. I looked over these scores a few years ago, when getting the song book in shape and they looked stiff—rather mathematical—if I'd played them over & got them back in the system a little, as I did recently, I should have copied them out and used them (I don't know on whom)

In some ways, considering the subject matter they seem quite worthwhile. I'll play them for you next winter.

A little while ago a Mr. W. G. Moorehead asked me for some of my music, saying that he is to lecture on modern music. He wrote from the Harvard Club and I take it, is connected with the Music Dept. there. I suggested that he get in touch with you and gave him your address, and also sent him a few of your piano pieces and the string quartet (with thunder stick). He seems serious in his interest. Perhaps you know him. His address is 206 Detroit Street Xenia Ohio.

The engraving of the score can not be finished for the October number. I saw the engraver yesterday. He says it will be impossible. Only 5 plates are done & he has worked steadily (he says). We went through the situation thoroughly and it seems his points are well taken. He thinks there will be about 75 or more plates and then I may not have much time to correct them. I'm sorry about it.

I sent a half dozen or so song books to you last week and some of the photostats this week. There are none of the "Sonata" copies (complete) left though Schirmer thinks they may have some in their stock room—if so I'll send some. If you give any of the "Emerson" movement out, I'd rather like to have you tell the "consignee" that it doesn't stand exactly as it might. There are many places that aren't down quite as it ought to sound—that is as I usually—(not usually but occasionally catch it when it's right) and in several places—for instance in last part of the last section the version seems to change according to the mood the previous part has gone in. As soon as I can get a chance to practice a little I want to make a record—it will clear some things up—perhaps. But I feel sometimes that an experience never can be caught again literally or even told again—any more than a "space of life—be it a moment" can be lived again. But we won't talk about that now! The evil unto the day! Also music may resent going down on paper!

The enclosed are a couple of subscriptions ($75) that are due about this time and I want to transfer them to New Music or "Pan Am" as you think best. Where they have been may do more harm than good. One was a music settlement house—more of a feeding place for "commercial musicians" than music. The balance is for renewal of 4 Xmas present subscriptions [*gives addresses for "Miss Russ Johnson, Mr. David Talmage, Elliott Carter, Clifton Furness, & 2 for me."*]

This is a long Sunday letter I hope you can read it. Mrs. Ives and Edie send remembrances

Sincerely,
Chas E. Ives

208. 20 August 1928, from Henry Cowell, Menlo Park, California

Dear Mr. Ives:

Your letter is all but a visit with you! It is really wonderful to be able to so closely express yourself in a letter—I never can. I am glad you like my articles—in them I sometimes get going!

Sorry the plates will not be ready for the October issue, but I will put in Ruth Crawford instead, and save the symphony for the January issue. I suppose there is no danger that the plates will not be ready by then?

Thank you very much for the check—you are a lifesaver for "New Music," as we had no funds to do the really necessary summer circularization, to try to fill up the gap left by subscribers who will not renew. Now we can do it nicely, with this check! I feel that I am fortunate indeed to have found someone who shares with me the feeling of the vital necessity of this publication. I will send the subscriptions to the addresses you sent.

I have arranged to have portions of your Emerson played at a concert of the New Music Society on Sept. 20th in San Francisco by Georgia Kober, a Chicago pianist of note, the president of the Sherwood Music School, general headquarters, and one who was the first to play Debussy in Chicago, as well as many modern works. She has also played my works.

I am also sending copies of your Emerson to Miss Winifred Hooke of Los Angeles, Arthur Hardcastle of Los Altos, Calif., Miss Deme Denny, of Carmel Calif. All of whom I believe will play it, and sending the songs to Mr. Reuben Rinder, of Mayfield, Calif. (Cantor of the San Francisco Hebrew Temple, and a very good singer) and to Miss Alma Williams, of San Jose. She sings modern works, and she is writing a book on the progress of music, and I am getting her to include your contributions to music as a part of her text.

I am glad to hear that you plan making some records. I think it is a fine idea, and hope to have some of them if you get them made. I should be delighted to have the opportunity of presenting your work from them.

With most cordial regards to your wife and daughter,
heartily yours,
Henry Cowell

• • •

On 19 September 1928 Arthur Hardcastle presented the first documented performance of "Emerson" from the *Concord* Sonata in a concert sponsored by Cowell's New Music Society in San Francisco. Ives worked to help support Cowell in return by lobbying E. Robert Schmitz to have the New York Pro Musica sponsor a lecture by Cowell.[12] Edith Ives was fourteen years old when this letter was written.

209. 11 October 1928, to Henry Cowell

Dear Mr. Cowell:

I owe you and Mr. Hardcastle a debt of gratitude—you, one that's not easy to express. I should have written sooner but about the middle of last month I got laid up just as I was planning to get 2 weeks vacation. They kept me on my back till a few days ago & I haven't seemed able to do much but am around now & expect to be back at the office in a week or so—I also rather wanted to find out more definitely about the engraving. They sent me some proofs yesterday up to p. 44 about 2/3 done. I should say and I see no reason why it

12. Through Ives's aid, Cowell gave many lectures at Pro Musica chapters. Rita Mead, *Henry Cowell's New Music 1925–1936: The Society, the Music Editions, and the Recordings* (Ann Arbor, Mich.: UMI Editions, 1981), 105.

won't be finished in another month. Will let you know more exactly when I can get down & see them. Haven't done much correcting yet but it won't take long once I get down to it. The work seems well done.

I hope you've had a satisfactory summer. I would like to hear your lectures. It seems to me that ~~they ought~~ Pro-musica ought to have you give them in New York—Am going to speak to Mr. Schmitz about it.

Mrs. Ives and Edith send remembrances to you. Edie has turned from the piano to "singing."—She sings "Hark Hark & hark" more sweetly than the lark—You will let me know if there is anything I can do for you.

Very sincerely yours,
Chas. E. Ives

I haven't any picture for the magazine—but I thank you for the article very much.

• • •

The publication of the highly complex second movement from the Fourth Symphony was the most ambitious and expensive project *New Music* had ever undertaken, and Ives and Cowell wrote frequently to discuss editorial and financial arrangements for the piece. Here Ives's roles as composer, patron, and advisor and Cowell's roles as editor and promoter come to the fore.

210. 24 November 1928, from Henry Cowell, Menlo Park, California

Dear Mr. Ives:

Thank you for your letter. It is a real pleasure to have word from you, and with due consideration, I find no trouble reading your script! I shall follow your suggestion about wording the title page, and the heading of II is very good, of course, for the inside. Too large a title is not essential! The idea is good to show that it has been played, in the notes—particularly considering the difficulty of the cross-rhythms.

Many thanks for the check for $100.00. It is a god-send. I shall, as we agreed in conversation in New York, be forced to ask you to undertake all extra expenses connected with your symphonic issue. These may be considerable, as the edition is so very much larger than any we have tried, and the whole system of mailing will have to be altered, and the copies sent out flat, and the postage will be very high. The printing will be more than usual also. I believe a number of surplus copies should be printed, so you (and I) can have some on hand, and if you are willing, I think it would be a good idea to send complementary copies to all conductors of important orchestras that are not our subscribers already.

Owing to the drop in subscriptions, which was to be expected, as many of the initial subscribers did not know how "steep" the music was to be, an edition of five hundred will cover everything, and give a few to spare. New Music is in rather a bad position, and it has been through your checks through the summer that have made possible its continuance. Right now with the majority of our renewals in, (and the October issue of this year paid for) we have $175.00 in the bank. Not counting your $100.00 of today. I believe that I can get enough new subscribers through personal efforts on my tours, to pay the summer bills when they fall due, and am not so worried, as New Music has always lived from hand to mouth. If you can help see us along through the forthcoming issue, containing your score, we should sail along.

However, I have in mind something else—You gave me a sum of money to apportion between New Music, and the Pan American Association for Composers. I apportioned $125.00 to the latter, and have been holding it for them, pending the time they show some action, and need it. However they have been inactive, and Varèse, the president, has moved permanently to Paris, and Chavez has, I understand, resigned, thru some lack of interest. The catalogue of composers' works we were to print has not been begun,—because my most strenuous efforts have not called forth their lists from all of our composers, and it seems foolish to print an incomplete list. I regret to say, that I believe the lack of success of this organization is because certain composers blocked any action, thru jealousy that other composer's works would be presented to conductors! I think some working plan may be found for the association later, and all the troubles ironed out. In the meantime, it seems to me that New Music needs the $125.00 more than the Pan-American, and if you give me your permission, I will turn it over. Say frankly whether you think it would be best, or whether you would prefer to have me continue to hold the funds for the Pan-American.

The Copland-Sessions concerts in New York are to do my String Trios on December 30th.[13] I may not be in the East yet then but hope so.

Heartiest greetings to you and your family,
Henry Cowell

211. 31 January 1929, from Hans Barth, New York

My Dear Mr. Ives,

I thought you might be pleased to know that the quarter-tone piano is finished. If you should care to see it will you call me sometime soon and we can arrange a convenient time for both of us.

With kindest regards and best wishes,
Sincerely yours,
Hans Barth

• • •

The arrangement mentioned in the following letter must be Ives's quarter-tone version of the Ragtime Dances for Two Pianos; Barth played the first movement, Largo, in concert with

13. Cowell's "Paragraphs" for Two Violins and Cello, performed by Hans Lange, Arthur Schuller, and Percy Such at the Little Theatre, New York City; Oja, *Making Music Modern*, 375.

a second, unknown pianist on 9 April 1929.[14] He apparently did not use the quarter-tone piano in this performance. Barth did, however, perform the Largo on that instrument in a Carnegie Hall concert on 23 February 1930.[15] The "Notes" Ives mentions making for *New Music* are his "Conductor's Note" and commentary for the Fourth Symphony, part of which was later reproduced as "Music and Its Future" in Cowell's book *American Composers on American Music* (1933). Barth was not mentioned directly in the article as published by Cowell.

212. 1 April 1929, to Hans Barth

Dear Mr. Barth:—

I have stopped in to see you several times but you were out. The last time I left a copy of the quarter-tone piece arranged as you wanted.

I hope things are going well with you. It seems to me that you ought to do something immediately about the patent rights. The big piano companies ought to feel somewhat ashamed of their lack of interest, enterprise and generosity. In some notes I've had to make for the "New Music" magazine, am referring to your efforts and sacrifice in building the piano as an illustration among others of what some of the large institutions and foundations might do but don't. Will send you a copy when it is printed.

Whatever I've done to help, I am glad to consider just as a contribution in a cause we both believe in. I don't want to have you feel under any obligation to me or to return the money which you said you might want to do if the piano was a success commercially. I am glad to relinquish to you any part of its ownership I may have. All I want is to be able to work with it occasionally. I hope you will get adequate benefit and satisfaction from your labors.

Hoping to see you soon, I am
Very Truly Yours,

• • •

Cowell engineered the first contact between Ives and Slonimsky, which centered around the preparation and subsequent performance of a newly arranged, small-orchestra version of *Three Places in New England*. Cowell's interest in and support of his music seem to have stimulated Ives's desire to have his music performed. Rescoring and revising the entire Orchestral Set no. 1 required considerable musical effort and editorial work.[16] Ives's health, however, was at a low ebb in July 1929. That month he decided to retire from insurance, effective 1 January 1930, and wrote to his partner about his inability to work since February 1929.[17] In view of the seriousness of the medical condition that forced the obviously reluctant Ives to retire from insurance, it is remarkable that he decided to take on such a large project.

14. Sinclair, *Descriptive Catalogue*, 237.
15. "Hans Barth Gives a Unique Recital," *New York Times*, 24 February 1930, 24.
16. Sinclair, *Descriptive Catalogue*, 42.
17. See Letters 133–35.

213. 14 July 1929, sketch for Ives to Nicolas Slonimsky[18]

Last spring Henry Cowell told me that you had been kind enough to ask for a score of mine which your orchestra might play. I should have written before but have been "laid up" for some months back and haven't been able to attend to things—even correspondence; also was not sure I could get anything ready by next fall, as all of my scores are for larger orchestras.

But I have one which I got out the other day and played for Henry Cowell who liked it & thought it should be played and could be, with some revision reducing it to the chamber group. The 1st & last movements lend themselves quite readily but the 2nd which has some old "brass-band town-tune" things in it has a considerable brass part. But I remember, this (in part) was first played by a theater orchestra, as a kind of topical march. They made it quite well with only a cornet & trombone,—a piano taking off the rest of the brass. So, I think, it can be brought down with the help of a piano part. At any rate I'm going ahead with it on this basis & should have it ready to send you in September. I am glad to do this any way and you must not feel at all obligated to play it. You may not like it and even if you do, you may not think it advisable or practicable to present,—that will be quite alright. This score was written quite some years ago & won't loosen up much of a modern "sword-swallower"—but the subject matter, I feel, justifies its existence. It has some colloquial spots which the older generations of New Englanders (including mine) will get. But please feel free to do whatever you think best with it.

I have heard with pleasure that you & your organization are making a valuable contribution to music and to Boston. I wish I could hear it & am also very glad "New Music" will publish some of it soon.[19]

Henry Cowell left last week for California after spending a few days with us. You will like to hear his experiences abroad, especially in Russia. He is a courageous "advance guard" all in himself. I tell him he is a better ambassador than some of our more famous ones.

Hoping to have the pleasure of meeting you before too long, I am with best wishes,

Sincerely yours,
Chas. E. Ives

I understand from H.C. that the score should be for,

1 flute, clar, oboe, bassoon

1 trumpet, horn, trombone

1 percussion player, & 10 strings

18. The letters to Slonimsky in the CIP are photocopies.

19. *New Music* published Slonimsky's "Studies in Black and White," for piano, in October 1929; Mead, *Henry Cowell's New Music*, 585.

• • •

By August 1929 Ives, Cowell, and Slonimsky were thick with plans for performances of Ives's music and promotion of what they called "the cause" of new music. But Ives's health became progressively more problematic. The neuritis mentioned below, aside from keeping Ives from the piano and slowing his progress as an editor, caused a persistent tremor in his hands that made shaving nearly impossible, and so he grew his beard for the first time. Indeed, the correspondence with Cowell demonstrates the severity of Ives's health problems in the late 1920s. Ives first mentioned being kept "on his back" on doctor's orders for three weeks in a letter of 11 October 1928 (Letter 210). On 3 December he mentioned missing a Pro Musica concert (probably the 14 November Town Hall concert on which Anton Rovinsky played "The Celestial Railroad") for the same reason.[20]

The "German concert" to which the following letter refers was a program of American music for the Berlin chapter of the International Society for Contemporary Music (ISCM) that Cowell had proposed to Ives in a letter of 14 April. Planned for the fall, the concert seems never to have materialized. As indicated here, Cowell visited the Iveses in early July 1929, just after he had returned from a European tour. The check Ives mentions in the closing of the letter was his return of the amount he would have been sent as a musical contributor to *New Music* under the system of fees to be paid to composers that Cowell had recently proposed for the publication.

214. 28–29 August 1929, to Henry Cowell

How are you? I hope you're able to get in some long periods of work and that the piece with the various orchestrations is going well—I think you will open up many new things with those ideas. I've been thinking about what we discussed before you left—or rather just after you came—(your brief visit was like a prologue & coda in one measure.)—that there should be some fee given to the composers in "New Music" even if only nominal & inadequate, is more advisable than having none. It seems to me that it is not only a decent thing to do, but that it may help to increase the feeling of permanency in the work. I gathered that you feel somewhat this way.—The contributors will understand that it will not affect your original profit-sharing plan (that's a big word for our profits to date)—but you "never can tell who Willie is until you hear him eat" And as they know there have been no profits yet, just a word, if you think it will, in that connection—that the fee is but from a (small) fund which friends of the idea of the publication, its aims etc. have been glad to contribute, or something of that sort, if you think best, so there will be no misunderstanding of the situation. Only I would prefer ~~not~~ to have only you know that it comes from me. Am enclosing a check for $200 for the 1st—2 years i.e. 8

The above are only suggestions (—be that as it may!)

I'm sorry to report that I haven't been able to do anything much since shortly after you were here. I was [*parenthetical comment written in the top margin of a new sheet of different paper*] (letter paper seems scarce on my desk—excuse this) just getting back into shape, when an

20. Ives to Cowell, 3 December 1928 (CIP, 28/1).

attack of neuritis in both arms came along about 6 weeks ago. Can't play & have only been able to write for about a week. The doctor says I must keep away from the piano for another month. This is bad enough for me, but for you it would be a calamity. I hope you may escape anything like this. It gets on the nerves and depresses me, (sometimes). It's all right to sit down & think music for a while, but after a month of that one wants to hear a few man-size sounds. So I'm way behind in what I wanted to do. I don't know what to do about the German concert. I thought I could get some of the old scores for strings etc. and from which some of the songs came but can find only one as yet, & it's quite indistinct. I don't think it worth while just to send the song books—They won't use them as they are—however I might send a couple & tell Herr Vogel I'll send more later. I can copy well enough now & ought to have the rearranged score (for Chamber O) ready for Slonimsky by Oct 1—& will send one of these to Germany. Had a nice letter from Mr. Slonimsky. [*Lower left corner is torn off.*] . . . swick Canada. Also sent a sonata [?] . . . Ives wants to be remembered, Edie . . . for a week. . . . Sincerely,

Chas. E. Ives

Sometime you must compose a Rhapsodic ode & dedicate it to your great grandfather Dixon. I imagine you get some of your idealism & courage from him. He had it on most of the Yankee abolitionists. They didn't have to give all of their substance to the cause, though some of them furnished a little blood & a black eye sometimes.

In making out the enclosed check, I forgot that I was one of the contributors to N.M. in first 2 years, so just credit this to the 9th or beginning Oct. 29

If you don't think the fee plan best charge this up to surplus—in the general fund.

In writing to composers, I think it may be alright to say that the fee is from the operating expenses,—what you and I contribute is part of that—you give time, physical and mental energy and I wampum.

215. 31 August 1929, from Henry Cowell, Menlo Park, California

Dear Mr. Ives:

I have been running back and forth twice to Los Angeles, to play concerts, and cannot remember if I wrote to thank you for sending on the score and book, which I did not carry, but allowed you to send on instead. I lent the book to Hardcastle, and he is full of enthusiasm—says that there is more in a sentence in it than in the whole of a better class magazine. He also heartily approved the conductor's note. I am delighted to find someone who shares my own spontaneous enthusiasm over your attainments, without having even the bias of meeting you! I looked at your score again, and it seemed really grand. I wish you would send a copy to Adolph Weiss, for consideration by the Conductorless Symphony—they are planning to do a lot of American Music (Carl Ruggles "Portals" on Oct. 26th) and although the rhythmic problems would be great for them to handle at once, I think they should know of it. Weiss's address is West 69th St. New York City.

I am quietly at home now, and working on a new piano piece. I have several in mind.

Also an orchestra piece. I got together the material for my new circular, and have sent it to my manager, for printing and distribution. He seemed to think it might cost more than $200 to send out many copies of the circular, as well as printing it, but said that he was so much interested in my new notices that he would finance any extra cost himself. I also wrote a new circular for New Music, and am trying to get a hold of the Pro Musica mailing lists again.[21] I am going to do a lot of work to get the subscription list up again. It went down when I was in Europe, and was not home to attend to it.

I will send you my Russian article, which appeared in the New Republic. I believe this gives a fair resume of my activities since returning. If you feel like it, I wish you would write me.

Affectionate greetings to you and your family,
Henry Cowell

216. 5 September 1929, from Henry Cowell, Menlo Park, California

Dear Mr. Ives:

I have just sent you a letter, and our letters must have crossed.

It is perfectly grand to have your sudden and unexpected assistance in donating funds toward paying the composers—I have had it in mind, ever since the first, but could never see how it was to be done; and I certainly hated to have to follow the usual policy of having to ask them to give their work for nothing, as is practically the usual policy among publishers. You have no idea which what a warmth of feeling I will divide the fund you sent among the composers of the first two years—some of them need the money badly enough, I happen to know.

I will assume that since you donated the amount, you will be exempt from a share in the division, and divide it among the eight composers of the first two years, Ruggles, Rudhyar, Weisshaus, Ornstein, Chavez, Crawford, Weiss, and Copland.

• • •

The following letter reveals the extent to which *New Music* depended on Ives's support for its day-to-day operations. In fact, as was the case here, Ives often had to step in with additional resources beyond his regular contributions.

217. 15 October 1929, from Henry Cowell, Menlo Park, California

Dear Mr. Ives:

I forgot whether I wrote you about the finances of New Music. I have been in the hospital, and in the illness, left out many things I was to have done. I am better now, and should be out of the hospital in another eight days.

21. These lists would have been a valuable resource for *New Music* because of the comparatively large membership of the society, 3,500 in 1928. See Oja, *Making Music Modern,* 180.

When I went to deposit the check for $200.00 which you sent for the use of sending $25.00 each to the past contributors of New Music, I found that there was a balance of about $60.00 (approximately) and the bills for the October issue had to be paid. I was therefore forced to use the $200.00 for the October issue bills, and will give the $25.00 each to the composers from the $500.00 check, dated Nov. 15th, which I am keeping for New Music from you. Since Oct. first, new subscriptions and renewals have been pouring in at a very encouraging rate, and it would seem that there will be no further financial difficulties for some time. It is only your support that keeps New Music running; it could never have survived this your [*sic*] without your aid.

Arthur Hardcastle is playing your Sonata, and perhaps also the jazzy shorter piano piece of which you gave me a copy or so, at the first New Music Society concert here, which will be on Dec. third.[22]

I hope to hear that you are well, and that you are working on your composition; that you have put some fine old works into form.

I had just completed a longish new piano work before I got sick, and have spent some time copying it here; I will begin scoring it as soon as I can, because I think it would make a good orchestra piece. Did I tell you that I am invited to play one movement of my Concerto on April 26th with the Conductorless Symphony Orchestra in New York? They are playing Ruggles "Portals" sometime very soon after you receive this letter—I think Oct. 23rd.

Affectionate greetings to you and Mrs. Ives and "Edie."

Henry Cowell

• • •

Throughout the early 1930s, Cowell and Slonimsky continued to champion Ives's music with both notable setbacks and successes. Among the former was the plan for Slonimsky to conduct *Three Places in New England* at the eighth festival of the International Society for Contemporary Music in Liège, Belgium, in September 1930. The work, however, was rejected by the body's international selection committee.[23] Ives's reaction in the letter below provides a window into the character he projected in his correspondence. Ives began by discussing a vacation to Richmond, Virginia, and plans for the publication of a set of his songs in *New Music*. Turning to the rejection of his piece, Ives writes, "and when they ask for more American beauties,' we can say 'Nix on that stuff—you know me Al!'" Ives alludes to the famous tag line in Ring Lardner's 1914 book, *You Know Me Al: A Busher's Letters*.[24] With this phrase Ives takes on the role of the novel's main character, Jack Keefe, the small-town pitcher who

22. This is probably "Potpourri," an arrangement of the ragtime material from the First Piano Sonata. Cowell mentions the piece by this title in a letter to Ives of 27 March 1928 (CIP, 28/1). Ives also sent the piece to E. Robert Schmitz, who referred to it by this title. See Schmitz to Ives, July 1928, and Schmitz to Ives, 20 August 1928 (both in CIP, 31/15).

23. For a list of pieces included in the festival, see Slonimsky, *Music since 1900*, 513–14.

24. Rossiter, *Charles Ives and His America*, 224n135; Ring W. Lardner, *You Know Me Al: A Busher's Letters* (1914; reprint, New York: Charles Scribner's Sons, 1960).

makes the major leagues and describes his exploits in a series of letters home. The transformation is a masterstroke, for it allows Ives, a former pitcher himself, to assume the voice of the archetypical common American. Lardner portrayed Keefe as sincere but not too bright and as a naturally masterful pitcher able to hold his own, mostly through raw talent and instinct, against Hall of Famers such as Ty Cobb and Christie Mathewson. He is the unsophisticated country boy who gets the better of those who are more worldly—an image that must have appealed to Ives.

By speaking in Keefe's voice, Ives can respond to European criticism of his music with the voice of the American people. By extension, the rhetoric acts to cast even domestic detractors of his music as "un-American." The full sense of Ives's aside is clear in one of Jack Keefe's many uses of the line: "If he ever talks to me like he done him I will take a punch at him. You know me Al."[25] Ives might well have wanted to punch the jaws of a few committee members; by using Keefe's phrase he constructs a system in which he would have the support of, and in which he would be acting as, the common man in doing so.

The aside to Al occurs as Ives implicitly distinguishes between "true" and "false" forms of American music. Ernst Krenek's jazz opera, *Jonny Spiel auf*, had premiered in 1927, and Ives implies that it is a "counterfeit" American music—in direct contrast to the "substance" or reality projected by the Keefe figure. Cowell shared Ives's negative opinion of the opera; in 1929 he reviewed it under the title "Why the Ultra-modernists Frown on Krenek's Opera."[26]

Ives's letters, as a whole, project a complex self-image that could be fully known to no single correspondent. And a substantial part of this created character derives from the recurring subjects and ideas in the letters. One of these is the sometimes exaggerated political commentary that was also important in Ives's essays and song texts. The idea that the rejection of Slonimsky's ISCM bid was a result of Warren G. Harding's presidential victory in 1920 and the subsequent failure of the United States to enter the League of Nations shows both Ives's sense of humor and the increasing importance of politics in his thought.

218. 17 April 1930, to Henry Cowell, Richmond, Virginia

Dear Henry:

We had day trip down but not a bad one—it was interesting to watch the brown gradually turn to green—this is quite a beautiful place and an agreeable change from N.Y. It reminds me of Virginia. This old house hasn't changed since the civil war, but there is a mansion just as well.

I meant to have mailed you the enclosed list for the books before leaving. I wish you would send 2 tickets for the concert to George A. Lewis: Yale Club, Vanderbilt Ave, NY and also if you will [a] program for the conductorless Symp concert to Mr. & Mrs. James S. Cushman, 815 5th Ave.

25. Lardner, *You Know Me Al*, 33.

26. Henry Cowell, "Why the Ultra-Modernists Frown of Krenek's Opera," *Singing and Playing* 4, no. 2 (February 1929): 15, 35; cited in Bruce Saylor, *The Writings of Henry Cowell: A Descriptive Bibliography* (New York: Institute for American Music, 1977), 5.

I have talked to him about your music:—They might be quite a help to the cause, if I can arouse an interest.

If you read the words to the songs, there is a line that ought to go in, the 1st, "The New River"—after "dancing halls & tambourine" ~~should go~~ "human beings gone machine" should ~~go~~ be there too. I cut this out in the book—I couldn't stand that hand organ phrase repeated again.

It seems to me it would [be] better to read the text before each song—I think a some ~~little~~ pause is needed between—and save the Indians from getting mixed up in Ann St, How[ever] it makes Lit Dif do what comes easiest.

The action of the "non-contemporary society of music & commercial Travelers"[27] is a good one—for our vanity. It will be well I suppose, not to throw anything else at these we can be good sports, as the man said when the undertaker came in.—and when they ask for more American beauties" we can say "Nix on that stuff—you know me Al!"—and Johnny spiel auf will put it to American music. In a new country like ours, children should be obscene and not heard.—But the real cause of the situation is the Republican Party, they ~~wouldn't~~ let kept us out sing in the L of N chorus, & we are still out.

With that I will go out and look over 'Patrick Henry in Libby Prison' We'll be back toward the end of next week.

Sincerely,
Chas. E. Ives

• • •

In the following letters we see the progression of Ives and Slonimsky's friendship as well as their efforts in behalf of modern music. Slonimsky's request that Ives contact the music correspondent of H. L. Mencken's journal, *American Mercury*, shows the Russian drawing Ives into the mainstream of modernist discourse. Although small, the magazine was a central voice in the movement, and without Slonimsky it is doubtful that Ives would have made this potentially important contact.

In return, Ives gave Slonimsky material support. In the spring of 1930 Slonimsky was in the process of reserving Town Hall to present *Three Places in New England* the following January, and Ives sent him $100 on 30 May to reserve the booking. The ensuing discussion (see Letter 221) of what should be on the program for the concert provides insight into Ives's ideas about the reception of his music at a time when most of it was still little known. There is more discussion of the ISCM committee decision, and Ives continues the running political joke of associating it with the League of Nations. Even though he was receiving few visitors, Ives asked Slonimsky to visit him in West Redding, which he eventually did on 18 August.

27. Ives refers to the International Society for Contemporary Music.

219. 9 May 1930, from Nicolas Slonimsky, Jamaica Plain, Massachusetts

My dear Mr. Ives:

I was sorry to miss you in New York, but I expect to make the trip before the end of the month, and hope to see you this time.

I am in correspondence with the Judson office in regard to the Town Hall date; the booking has just opened , and I hope to secure a Saturday Evening or Sunday afternoon in January 1931. Of course, I shall let you know the moment I hear anything definite. I was thogoughly [*sic*] disgusted with the verdict of the International Committee. At least, if they could not see the significance of your score, they might have selected the second or third best. As it is, well . . . committees will be committees.[28]

May I ask you a favor? The man in charge of the Music Dept. of the AMERICAN MERCURY is interested in your songs, and would like to write about them, particularly about the Wilson and Lincoln ones. If you have a copy to spare, may I ask you to forward it to Dr. Isaac Goldberg, 65 Crawford Street, Roxbury Massachusetts.

I have not made my plans for the Summer yet. I don't believe, my European trip will materialize itself under the circumstances. It is more than likely that I will remain in Boston, possibly getting away for a week or two.

I hope you had a good vacation in Virginia and that you feel rested and in good spirits.

Cordially yours,
Nicolas Slonimsky

• • •

In the following letter, Ives makes the puzzling comment that problems in business had kept him from making suggestions on orchestration for Slonimsky in a copy of *114 Songs*. This suggests that Ives had asked Slonimsky to do orchestrations of some songs well before he actually worked on choral editions of "December" and "The New River" beginning in about January 1934. More problematically, Ives had retired from insurance officially in January 1930 and had done little at the office for months before that date.[29] Perhaps he continued to consult on matters in which he had been involved. There is occasional business-related correspondence between Ives and his partner, Julian Myrick, throughout 1930, but nothing indicates that he was involved in the daily affairs of the firm. Indeed, there seems to have been little direct contact between Ives and the firm that summer.[30]

A second interpretation of Ives's comment about business difficulties is that he was using them as a general excuse to disguise his poor health at the time. Perhaps Ives had been in the business world for so long that he continued to use the phrase to describe general hard

28. Slonimsky, *Music since 1900*, 513–14.
29. See Letters 133–35.
30. See Letter 140.

times. Though we know that he felt well enough to attend the performance of Cowell's piano concerto in New York on 26 April, the summer in general seems to have been a low point.[31] In September Harmony Ives gave a guarded estimate of his condition: "Charlie has had a good summer on the whole but he hasn't the grip on things yet I hope to see him have again."[32] Still, it is odd that Ives, even faced with severe illness, would have used such an excuse with Slonimsky, who was already familiar with his medical problems and who, along with Cowell, was in closer contact with him than almost anyone outside his immediate family at the time.

220. 27 May 1930, to Nicolas Slonimsky

Dear Mr. Slonimsky:

We are up here now for the summer—and I'm afraid we missed you again in New York.—but Mrs. Ives and I hope you may find it convenient to come down here and see us sometime this summer. I suppose it's too early to know just what your plans will be, but we expect to be here right along.

It's too bad you won't be in France this Summer especially as your mother is there,—

Thus, you see, how the virtuous sins of committees and men, (assuming committees are men) throw their long shadows o'er innocent humanity". But we won't be cast down by the fall of this Inter Rational committee—& they may see Casey driving his own hearse some day! Personally I put it up to the Republican Party of ours—it's just one of the many hard-boiled, old-lady, soft stuff things they are to be responsible for—they kept us out of Geneva—and you can't blame Europe for wanting to keep us out of everything—except their hotels.

I hope things are going well with you and just as soon as you want me to do anything in any way about the concert, please let me know.

I wrote Dr. Goldberg, saying I was mailing the book of songs, but as I looked for one to wrap up, I found there were no complete copies here—only those that I'd cut single copies from. So some of the pages are missing—but not that many—I will send him one [of] these now & a complete copy later—as soon as I can get hold of one. I think next fall I'll get some more printed perhaps adding some others.

I hope to get off the one to you with the suggested orchestration, within a few days—It just happens that so many problems came up in business recently that had to be handled that I've had but little time for anything else but hope to have more time from now. Hoping to see you surely before the summer is over, I am,

Sincerely yours,
Chas E. Ives

31. Ives to Slonimsky, 28 April 1930 (CIP, 32/1).

32. See Letter 141.

• • •

The following gives a particularly casual impression of Ives's life in West Redding, Connecticut. It also suggests that Ives was not always incapacitated even during his slumps. He still enjoyed the outdoor life that the farm provided him. Ives's aside about "my little pool" is a reference to Slonimsky's song of that title.[33] The final topic of the letter is the program for Slonimsky's Town Hall concert. Ives responds to Slonimsky's suggestion that the pieces chosen shouldn't be "unadulteratedly modern lest we scare away the gentler part of our patronage."[34]

221. 8 June 1930, to Nicolas Slonimsky

Dear Mr. Slonimsky:

We're very glad you will make us a visit—it will be fine to have you here. It won't do you any harm to get away from the routine, Boylston st. & city noise. This is a good place to rest if you feel like it or to work if you feel like it or to meditate in or all three at once. Bring some old clothes and your bathing suit—on a hot day you may like to dive into "my little pool" (—but it has nothing on yours.)

We're a little uncertain about the last part of June—we may have to be away for a few days—but how about the first week in July—or if more convenient for you the 2nd week—suit yourself—only be sure to come.

There used to be a way of getting down via Boston & Albany RR to Pittsfield and down the Housatonic div.—but probably the best way now is to come down the main line to So. Norwalk, & we will meet you there. If you are to go to N.Y. first there are several good trains up here—we're about 60 miles from N.Y.

I didn't have in mind, so much scaring away the "gentler part" of the audience, by the quality of the program, (they will have to stand for that) as by the "quantity" If they get too much they go home "groggy."

Have just gone through the book of songs and will mail it today. Some of the pages are gone. I can't seem to find any more whole copies.

Sincerely,
Chas. E. Ives

• • •

In the early 1930s Ives increasingly worked to promote performance of new music and continued his association with E. Robert Schmitz. Indeed, the Ives and Schmitz families became somewhat close, and Edith Ives and Monique Schmitz kept up their own correspondence. The following sketch, full of Ives's characteristic rewriting, also mentions a lecture tour for which the pianist Anton Rovinsky had sought Ives's support in April 1930.

33. Slonimsky, *Music since 1900*, 1323.
34. Slonimsky to Ives, 5 June 1930 (CIP, 32/1).

222. Ca. July 1930, sketch for Ives to E. Robert Schmitz

Dear Mr. Schmitz:

We were disappointed not to see you all, before you left—but we didn't think you were going so soon—in fact, we only knew that you were back in N.Y. through Monique's letter to Edie, which came while she was at school, and only shortly before yours—we feel relieved to know that the Orient didn't pull your health down as much as it might, and it was fine to hear that the trip was so successful musically. I'm sorry to know that Pro Musica is not exactly in a normal state—but its just going through what most everything else is—too much "Hoover + Prosperity"—minus the latter. Our business and all business has been in a mess—its just a matter I guess of "treading water," till things come back and most people have a queer notion that automobiles and feather beds are necessities—and that music isn't—so they cut out a $5 subscription in order to go abroad—there was a man once who in hard times cut down on his budget by giving up going to church—until after the offertory! So you see "Pro Musica's" experience is just a comment on human nature.

[*The next sketch page reworks the same content.*]

[*Upper margin:*] too much Hoover & Prosperity—Prosperity is not so bad, even if it does bankrupt everybody—but Hoover has a face—"talks—

[Page 2]

there was also a man, once, & you may not believe it who in a good year put in $1. a Sunday when the plate came around—in a bad year would take out $.50 a Sunday when the plate came around.

I'm sorry I can't do what I would like in this ~~work—this budget adjusting is I suppose a tiresome thing~~—but I hope the situation is only temporary I do want to help in the "scholarship" ~~work.~~ If I send a ck just after Aug 1—will it be in time?

Rovinsky has written & talked to me about a plan he would like to have Pro Musica's cooperation.[35] I told him I would take it up with you. I think it something that should be carried out. But I asked S.K. about it a while ago & he said with things as they are it was impossible.[36] R wants to lecture & play among the chapters, giving a program which he has taken great care in preparing—showing the development of America & also a survey, as he puts it of European and American Crosscurrents etc. He sent me the enclosed program marking general ideas on the back. I told him I could not give much encouragement but I would write you.

I hope the summer's work goes to your satisfaction we shall hope to see you all in the fall and that you are all well. Mrs. I is well & I feel about the same—that is, I do, when I don't make a fool of myself which is an easy thing for me to do. Edie has been in the [illegible word] hospital, but is better now

35. See Rovinsky to Ives, 30 April 1930 (CIP, 31/9), in which he proposes a concert series for Pro Musica.
36. Perhaps Ives refers to Sigmund Klein.

• • •

In the next two letters, the conversation about Slonimsky's Town Hall concert continues, and the cost of the concert is set. The final detail to be settled is whether the new pieces on the program (Ives's Orchestral Set no. 1 and pieces by Cowell and Carl Ruggles) should be repeated on the second half to allow for better audience comprehension of the difficult and unfamiliar works and, if so, how the repetition should be announced. The "special insert" Slonimsky mentions was an announcement of the repetition to be included in the concert program. The large number of programs and fliers Slonimsky had printed indicates the grand scale of the publicity that he hoped to garner from the concert.

This pair of letters highlights the different personalities of the two men as well. Slonimsky's determinedly lighthearted approach to criticism contrasts with Ives's evident and voluble anger, even though his outburst is couched in humorous exaggeration that sarcastically employs his insurance man's penchant for percentages. His antipathy to the business side of music and to what he considered the immoral subjugation of musical content to desire for financial gain surfaces in a sudden tirade against the Victor Record Company, which Slonimsky had been soliciting to record the concert. Although Cowell, as a music instructor at the New School for Social Research, and even the instrument inventor Leon Theremin were enlisted to argue the case for the recording, it was not made.[37]

223. 24 December 1930, from Nicolas Slonimsky, Jamaica Plain, Massachusetts

My dear Mr. Ives:

Thank you for your fine letter, which I appreciate immensely, as sentiment, but, of course, cannot see myself as anything better than one of the few who have had a chance to get acquainted with your music and consequently have become champions of your work. It somehow offends my sense of proportion to believe that I have done something for you whereas the reverse, greatly intensified, is the case.

It is too late to insert a mention of the fact that your score was made over for Chamber Orchestra at my request. But it is clear from the context, dates, etc. The printers will ship the 2500 copies to your representative today or early tomorrow, with special delivery stamps and everything to insure speedy delivery. The flyers (1500) will be included in the shipment. I have instructed them to send 500 extra copies of the corrected edition and 100 flyers direct to your address.

My manager has written to the broadcasting company which rules the air above New York City. Alas! The ether is all taken up, and they cannot do anything for us. The reports from the Victor Company are hardly more encouraging. They reply in a formal fashion to the effect that all the commitme[n]ts are made by themselves, and that while they do not doubt the ability of the Chamber Orchestra of Boston, they cannot have any records made

37. Slonimsky to Ives, 4 January 1931 (CIP, 32/2).

by us right now. Of course, the letter is worthless as expression of reality, and my manager is writing them again offering them BUSINESS,—so many records garanteed to be sold etc. This ought to wake them up.

I have engaged the extra bass player; also a second violinist will play the percussion in your work. We shall have six violinists beside him, which will afford an even distribution of the divisi parts in the last movement, 2 violas, 2 Cellos, as originally planned; one Flute, Oboe, English Horn, Clarinet, Bassoon, 2 Horns, 2 Trumpets, Trombone, one percussion player (the second alternating on second violin), pianist. I cannot find Jasser's address, but I am sure you can get it through Henry who is due shortly anyway. If you are reluctant to ask Jasser yourself, I shall take the steps to locate him. There's plenty of time. Our rehearsal in New York will take place in Town Hall, Friday, January the 9th, at 10:30 A.M. The first rehearsal here is fixed for Dec. 26, the second sometime next week. There will be three rehearsals in all; the players charge $5.00 for each rehearsal, which is reasonable, and $20.00 for the concert, which is high. I have failed in trying to reduce their fee; they point out that in order to play the concert they will have to stay in New York overnight, or pay the Pullman berths on the night train. I can see that, but this would not account for more than $5.00 each. However, we shall have to submit and pay their regular price, which is, as I have previously mentioned, $35.00 per man. There will be Twenty Four players, not counting the pianist, which makes $840.00. This plus the 720.00 of the fundamental contract would be well within the originally specified sum of $1500; the printer's bill will constitute the unforseen expenditure. My manager tells me that the printing of 10,000 copies of the program and 1500 Flyers will cost about $300, not counting the postage and the mailing expenses. About 3000 copies will be mailed on this end—out of this number 1500 will go to all colleges, school and musical institutions in the country. As propaganda, it is of inestimable value. I understand that my manager will put a full-page advertisement in the Boston Symphony program-book at his own expense, but there will be an extra ad in the New York Symphony program (that is the program-book of the Boston Symphony when they play in New York) which will entail some $50.00 extra. However, I okayed it on my own responsibility, seeing that out of the six thousand people who hear the Boston Symphony in New York there may be an appreciable number who will be interested in our concert.

If luck is with us, we may draw enough to offset all this additional expense, so that the actual investment would not exceed the original figure of $1500.00. But this is in the lap of the gods. . . .

Mr. Laurent, the Flute-player, tells me that he cannot possibly learn the Riegger Suite within these few weeks; besides he does not find it very grateful [graceful?] for the instrument. It is just as well—the program will be lightened, and will be reduced to the original form, as outlined last Summer. I offer the enclosed form for the special insert. Please amend it as you think fit, and let me know your opinion.

Mr. Philip Hale, the "dean of American Critics", gives us a fine send-off. As all old men (he is 74) he is cynical, but apparently my notes caught his fancy. I was vastly amused by his comments.

I had a flattering letter from Lawrence Gillman about my Transcript articles. I am writing him, asking him to come to our concert. I hope he will comment on the program in his Sunday column. There is no finer advertising than this kind of comment,—even though it be cynical and slightly ironical. Why, even history is being written in our times with a cynical side-glance. We must take it or leave it. At least, no one can say that our concert, or our program, is dull.

I will be in New York on Wednesday, January the 7th. I will immediately get in touch with you (sometime around 5 o'clock in the afternoon).

My best remembrances to Mrs. Ives and Miss Ives. I hope Miss Ives will stay in New York for the Concert.

Sincerely,
Nicolas Slonimsky

224. 26 December 1930, to Nicolas Slonimsky

Dear Mr. Slonimsky:

Thank you for your card & letter and enclosures. Edie is singing your Christmas card. It seems to me ~~it might~~ there is no particular hurry in having the notice of the repetitions printed. Henry will be here Sunday & I'll find out how he feels about it. Personally, I should just say that these will be repeated & let it go at that—with possibly a paragraph to the effect, that as these things happen to [be] made to a great part of new materials in general structure, rhythm, harmony etc. which may not be easy to get on the first hearing, ~~they have~~ they are repeated.

Also, I don't know that we ought to assume if a listener stays to hear something repeated, ~~that he is~~ it is a sign of his approval—it may be just the opposite—or at least a willingness to give it another chance.

Radio"! Art & business all bitched up together. 91 3/8% (I like to be precise) of all radio & phonograph records—are "subaceous cysts" and soft ones at that—and they sell—though if a 3 yr. old is always fed candy for breakfast he will always be a 3 yr. old—the oatmeal market will die. The letter from the Victor Co. "All commitments are made by themselves" = unnecessary statement!—just look at their G—— D—— soft headed lists!—94 5/8% "ta ta" stuff. However, in a day or so I'm going to see how [I] can get in touch or at least take a crack" at both the "ether & Victor."

Please don't worry about the concert either the business part or wrong note part—I'll try to see Mr. Jasser or is it Yasser![38]

Hoping to see you soon,
Hastily,
Chas. E. Ives

• • •

As plans for the Town Hall program took shape, work on the revised version of *Three Places in New England* continued as well. Here Ives reacts to changes in the score proposed after the first rehearsal. Ives's flexibility seems to be in part a reflection of his gratitude at having the work performed; his response also reveals the influence of his experience as a performer and

38. Ives refers to the pianist Joseph Yasser.

his sharp appreciation of tone color. The note for Mr. Handley, Slonimsky's agent, acknowledges receipt of the programs for the premiere of the Orchestral Set, scheduled for 25 January in Boston.

225. 30 December 1930, to Nicolas Slonimsky

Please tell Mr. Handley that the circulars came OK Thanks

Dear Mr. Slonimsky:

Yours just at hand. Take out the oboe, by all means, in 1st 2 measures p. 27 before H; these notes were originally for a 2nd flute (ad. Lib.

At "O," p. 39, do as you think best. Perhaps if the V.s & piano could pound ~~theirs out~~ the waltz out somewhat it might do. I used to find if 2 counter tunes in about same register were played by 2 brass instruments the contrast was sometimes lost. However the quality of the trumpets seem different today than when I played one. But do anything in this or other places you think advisable.

Will see you tomorrow—come right up—if convenient—but call up anyway. Will let you know about the repetition notice, as soon as I see Henry—He has not come yet.

Hastily,
C.E.I.

• • •

As interest in and knowledge of Ives and his music increased in the musical community, the volume of requests for his music grew. The following is an example of what would eventually become a substantial part of Ives's overall correspondence. Morton Gould (1913–96) was a musical prodigy and, as an eighteen-year-old, was already established as a composer and performer when he wrote to Ives.

226. 7 July 1931, from Morton Gould, Richmond Hill, New York

Dear Mr. Ives,

Although I am personally unknown to you I am taking the liberty of writing in reference to your compositions.

I might identify myself by stating that I am a young pianist and composer and have been giving and will continue to give next season concerts in New York and out of town, among which will be a planned series of Modern Music lecture recitals with Mr. Felix Deye and Dr. Alexander Russel, and by referring to the "Musical America" issue of Feb. 25, 1931, which contains an article about me on page 44. I am in sympathy with the new school and my compositions (which are being published by Schirmer's are in that idiom. In my piano I have just concluded a course with Mr. Harold Bauer, and am looking for contemporary American compositions for my next season's programs.

I am particularly interested in your "Concord" piano sonata and Violin Sonata. Would it be an imposition on my part to ask for copies of these compositions, along with any others you might think suitable or representative of your style?

I would also like to meet you so that you might get a better idea of the work I do and I could discuss your compositions with you. Any date that you might make would be agreeable to me.

Thanking you,
Sincerely,
Morton Gould

• • •

Ives remained a trusted advisor and supporter of Cowell's *New Music* even as his own music received more frequent performance and preparing it for performance took more of his time. Here Cowell calls on him in both capacities, and this letter and Ives's reply again indicate his indispensability to the publication, for which, at times, Ives provided as much as one third the total financial support.[39] The airmail to which Cowell refers was a $100 check to help pay off debts from the 1930–31 *New Music* publication season. The letter from Universal was a rejection of Cowell's proposal that they distribute *New Music* in Germany. *New Music* eventually made an agreement with Edition Adler for the "Teutonic rights."[40]

227. 13 July 1931, from Henry Cowell, Menlo Park, California

Dear Mr. Ives:

Your wonderfully prompt Airmail came this morning. The check is a life-saver! I am so delighted to have it.

I received the enclosed letter from the Universal Edition today also, after so long a time, so that is out for the present. Shall I try the Heinrichshofen Verlag, the firm with which I have made a contract for New Music to take over the Teutonic rights, or shall I let the matter drop until later? Maybe the Universal would take it if I offered to wait. Wish you would give your advise!

Adolph Weiss writes me that Arnold Schoenberg offered his piano piece opus 33a to us (New Music) at a fee of $100. Here is where I would welcome your advise some more. I think that about once a year, we might do some European work, as we did the Webern last season; and it gives New Music a very high standard to have represented, only the very best of the Europeans. Also, it seems to me that it is an opportunity to catch a man like Schoenberg between tie-up contracts—he has always had one with Universal. The fee is very low, as such things go. Stravinsky would charge $5000! Still, I hate to pay for material from Europe, while I am forced to offer nothing to most of the men who write for us. What do you think?

Love to you and your folks,
Henry

39. Michael Hicks, *Henry Cowell, Bohemian* (Urbana: University of Illinois Press, 2002), 134.
40. Mead, *Henry Cowell's New Music*, 170.

228. 19 July 1931, sketch for telegram to Henry Cowell

Henry Cowell

Menlo Park Calif

Would accept Schoenberg's offer. Will send fee. Keep original plan for Vienna Concert. Will write soon.

C. E. Ives

• • •

Probably written in the fall of 1931, the following two undated and fragmentary sketches for a letter to Ives's Yale classmate Ashbel Barney reveal Ives reaching out to his potentially powerful network of social connections. Indeed, the sketches expose the depth of those seldom tapped resources; the extravagantly wealthy Barney became famous for buying a French château and having it torn down, shipped to New York, and rebuilt there. Ives's salutation recalls their rowdy student days and perhaps the lingo of D.K.E., a fraternity to which both belonged at Yale.[41] Ives wrote to Barney because he believed that the New York Philharmonic was looking for a new conductor and had discovered his old friend's name on its board of directors. Ives made the case for Slonimsky. These sketches highlight the change in Ives's musical and personal identity since college. There he had been seen primarily as a church organist and a writer of vernacular music—a jovial musical prankster who wrote the musical *Hell's Bells* for his junior fraternity and who improvised works such as "The Yale-Princeton Football Game." This Ives was far from the champion and composer of modern music he had become by the early 1930s. In writing to Barney, Ives had to bridge the two worlds and seems to have had trouble doing so. These sketches imply that the letter may never have been sent—or at least that it was reworked in a copy that does not survive.

229. Ca. 1931, sketches for Ives to Ashbel Barney

It's been long since I've seen you—a generation's time almost

Dear Ashbel:

You God Damned old puss—how in hell are you—Zabatoh Zwinkle Angick!

~~How have you been~~ How are you? ~~all these years?~~ It seems years long since I've seen you and it has been ~~about~~ a generation's time almost. It's a comment on the life of today—how little one sees of old friends living almost in the same acre—but it is greatly my fault.—I've been able to get around but little for several years—and I wouldn't be writing

41. Note the similarity of Ives's nonsense outburst in the salutation to the lyrics of a song sung during meetings of the Skull and Bones secret society: "Nap dang pizzle wing linkmem ragdam"; quoted in Alexandra Robbins, *Secrets of the Tomb: Skull and Bones, the Ivy League, and the Hidden Paths of Power* (Boston: Little, Brown, 2002), 133.

you now if I hadn't seen your name on the Philha[rmonic] board—and I would have called you tried to see you instead of writing if I had been well enough to. I ask (want) your help in a matter that I among many others think important. And if it is not possible for you to do anything in the premises, will you be good enough to let me know to whom I may write. It's a thing that I've felt you should hear something about, and now that Toscanini sore arm" makes it a good time to talk of the Phil Sym are asking for substitute conductors and seem to be falling back on those who in the opinion of many exponents of the younger musicians, from letters I've received and experience today, is making the Philha more of a perfunctory thing than a power that it might be in the vision & life of today.

The enclosed will give you, better than I can in a letter, what it is about.—please read it over carefully and if it doesn't interest you, may I ask you to give it to some of the directors [who] might give it consideration etc. . . .

[*Ives breaks off and begins a different paragraph. He writes a congruency sign to show that this is a reworked continuation from somewhere—there is a similar sign in the second page.*]

. . . Slonimsky, before coming to this country to conduct the Boston Symphony Chamber Orchestra, (he is now a naturalized citizen) thought there must be some mature indigenous Amer music (other than Jazz) and started out to find it. The enclosed program and reviews of his Paris concert ~~reflects this idea~~ give some idea of this interest, of his work, and of him. He is a remarkable musician in many ways. ~~He is the only conductor, I know of~~ He is one of the few young conductors in this country who can read or play a difficult modern score, not in the familiar usual European idioms (habits of writing). Even if not permitted to include any modern American scores he ought to be invited to conduct at least one concert. You will find that he will play Bach, Beethoven, ~~and the classics~~ and the other classics with strength, directness, ~~without~~ and mastery, that ~~does~~ takes one higher than the usual sensuous, perfunctory way of the more famous men.

After his Paris concerts of last spring he was surprised to find so much interest in his programs and conducting, ~~after that~~ and as a result he was engaged immediately to conduct 2 gala concerts of the Paris Philharmonic this winter, 2 concerts with the Berlin orchestra, and also concerts in Madrid, Budapest, Vienna, and Prague. All of these he was requested to present Amer works—in which Am[erican] music would be at least ½ the program. To give a good part of the program to Am music. There may have been instances, but I know of none, where any American orchestra has shown a similar, or any interest for that matter. . . .

[*There is no continuation of this part of the letter. The reverse of the second page starts the letter over and runs in very much the same wording up through "I wouldn't be writing to you now . . ." It then stops. On the bottom third of this page is a passage labeled "end of letter":*]

I rather hesitate to send all of the enclosed clippings and notes, as my music is involved, to some extent in them, but I have nothing else just now at hand. However, at any rate you may be interested to see it.

Don't bother to send these back. It is somewhat presumptuous I feel, to bring all this to you, and ask your help, especially at this time when there are so many things to be done that may be more important that may need your attention. Please don't let me put you to any trouble. . . .

[*On top of the other side of the second page Ives reworks his first paragraph again:*] and I'll admit I wouldn't be writing to you now. I suppose if I hadn't seen your name among the directors of the Phil Orch. It is about a matter that many think should have been taken up long before this, but at this time, when the Phil is calling on guest conductors, during Toscanini's illness, I feel that I ought to try to do something now in the premises. The enclosed will give you, better than I can in a letter, what the moment is . . . [*This continues in much the same wording as before and then trails off.*]

• • •

In 1932 Cowell and Slonimsky, with Ives footing the bill, commissioned the Russian inventor Leon Theremin to design and build an instrument, the rhythmicon, which could play extremely complex and multilayered polyrhythms. Cowell wrote a piece called *Rhythmicana* for the instrument, but it was not widely performed.[42] The following letter discusses some of the flaws of the instrument and sheds light on Ives's view of technology, which is not as negative, in this case, as is usually assumed. The demonstration of the instrument took place at the New School in New York on 19 January 1932.[43] Ives's acquaintance with Theremin also explains the appearance of a part for his more famous, eponymous electronic instrument in the Fourth Symphony and suggestions for its use in the Orchestral Sets nos. 1 and 2.[44]

230. Ca. 13 January 1932, to Nicolas Slonimsky

Dear N.S.A.—this doesn't mean "no swearing allowed" nor "no silence aloud"[45]

I had a long talk with Henry the day after you left. I told him what I told you about the "Rhythmicon" situation as I had got to thinking about it after our meeting—and we went into it from all angles. It relieved my mind to know especially the new one, would really be nearer to a instrument, than a machine. There will be a "lever" that can readily change the "tempo" by the player and also the "tones" etc.

It wasn't so much the question of having another made—as I think it ought—it will be improved, transportable and "studied out"—but the main question is whether it is the time to present it at Paris—& if so how is the best way to do it. Henry feels as I do about that—and after the demonstration at the "New School" next Tues we can know better how to act.

I sent the initial ck. to Mr. Theremin yesterday—& he's started the building. It will be yours & Henry's—I just want to help—and sit under its "shadow" on a nice day.

42. Mead, *Henry Cowell's New Music,* 189.

43. CIP, box 40, scrapbook 2, 59.

44. Sinclair, *Descriptive Catalogue,* 42.

45. Ives's salutation was probably intended to be Nicolas Slonimsky Ambassador, a nickname Ives started using after Slonimsky's Paris concerts featuring American music. See, for example, Ives to Slonimsky, 20 October 1931 (CIP, 32/2), and Letter 243.

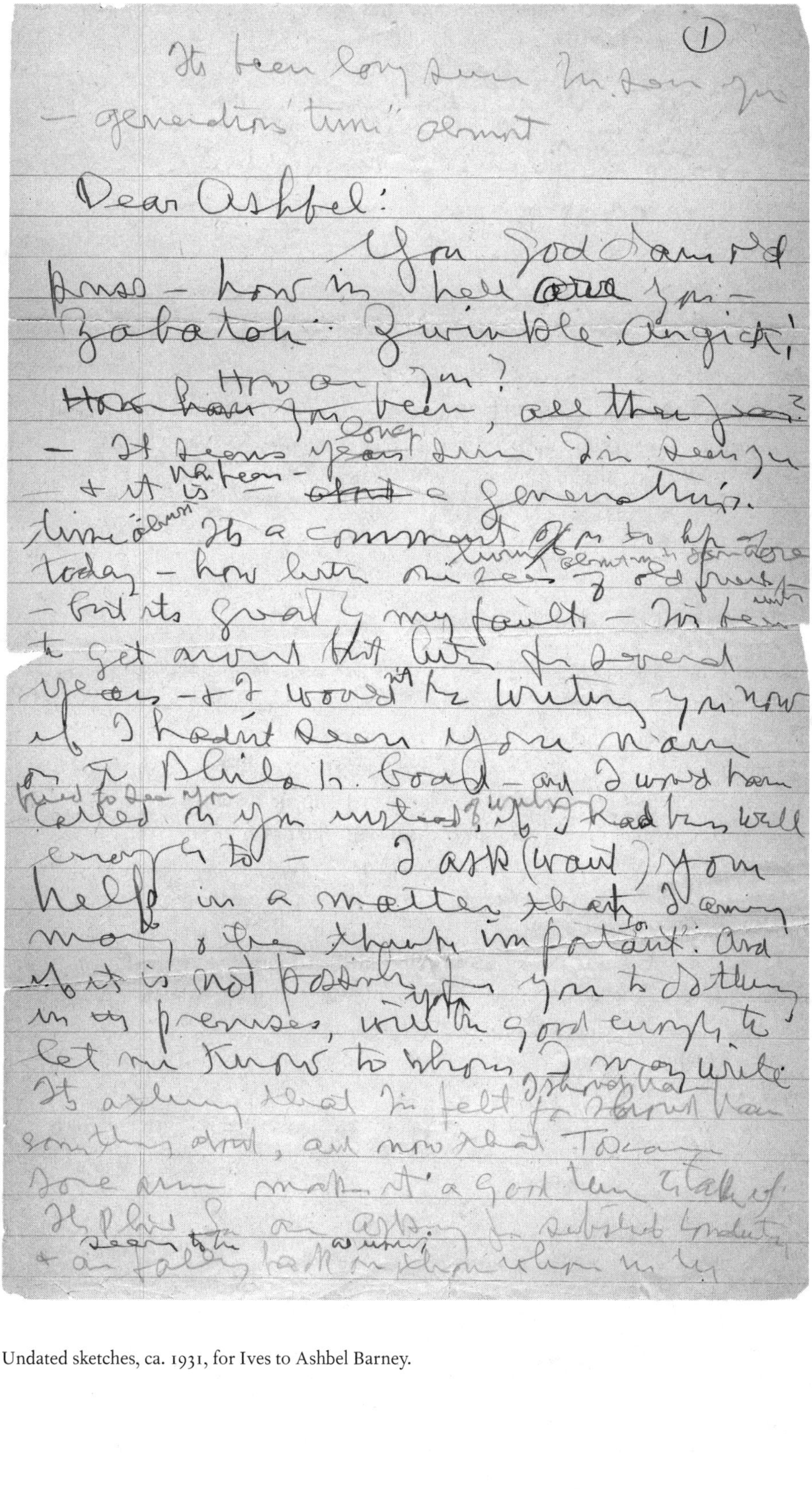

Its been long since I'm seen you — generations' time almost

Dear Ashbel:

You God damned old pussy — how in hell are you — Zabatch: Zwinkle, Angick!

How are you? ~~How have you been, all these years?~~

— It seems long since I've seen you + it is nineteen — ~~about~~ a generation's time almost. Its a comment on the life of today — how little one sees of old friends — but its greatly my fault — I've been unable to get around but little for several years — + I would not be writing you now if I hadn't seen your name on the Phila. Board — and I would have tried to see you / called on you instead if I had been well enough to — I ask (want) your help in a matter that I [illegible] think important. And if it is not possible for you to do this in my premises, will you be good enough to let me know to whom I may write

[illegible]

Undated sketches, ca. 1931, for Ives to Ashbel Barney.

I was glad to hear that you feel better about the 3 other pieces of mine at the Paris concert. Good clear parts are made. It can be put like this:

"Three Pieces for (Large) Orchestra"
I "The Cage"
II "The 4th of July"
III "An Elegy"

Hoping to see you both soon,
Sincerely yours,
Chas. E. Ives

• • •

Ives's involvement with the Pan American Association of Composers led to his contact with the Cuban composer and conductor Pedro Sanjuan, who presented the Cuban premiere of Ives's "Washington's Birthday" from the *Holidays* Symphony in July 1932.

231. 15 February 1932, from Pedro Sanjuan, Havana

Dear Mr Ives:

Yours of Feb 7th has just been received and in answer to same I am pleased to inform you that I shall be glad to have the copies in question made here just as soon as the copyists finish some important work they are now doing for me.

I am looking forward to the pleasure of receiving the extra copy of the score you say you are having sent to me, hoping to be able to conduct same about the month of May or at the latest June as we have already all programs' set as far as April.

So far I am unable to inform you as to the price of the copy work, but shall do as soon as I know and thank you in advance for your kind offer regarding the disposition of whatever balance may be left.

I appreciate very much your efforts as well as the Pan-American towards the end of my going up there to conduct, not only Cuban music but any other Pan-American music as well. Do you think this might take place soon?

At next March's concert the Varèse's "Integrales" will be performed for the first time in public: I hope it will be a success.

I am looking forward to the pleasure of meeting you as well as Riegger and Weiss and with best wishes from Roldan and Caturla and very best regards from myself, I beg to remain

Most sincerely yours,
Pedro Sanjuan

232. 9 August 1932, from Pedro Sanjuan, Havana

Dear Mr. Ives:

My delay in writing to you has been due to the fact of my waiting to have some interesting news to let you know.

The "Washington's Birthday" was performed in our concert of last July, I enclose programs and articles on same, and feel sorry these critics are not up to the level of your beautiful work. Actually we lacking down here real musical critics and the only one up to standard, Francisco Ichaso, is engaged at present in newspaper work of a different kind and lacks his musical section. Anyway your work aroused enormous interest in the audience and the orchestra rendered it with great gusto.

We are leaving for Europe on the 20th inst and after some time in Madrid I intend to go to Paris and I hope to see Varèse up there.

The financial standing of our Philharmonic Orchestra is frankly bad, due to the general economical crisis of the country, and it follows the impossibility of achieving any artistic labor of importance. This is the reason of my taking a long vacation, awaiting better times, while I see what can be done in Europe. However I will never reject my former plans of working for the advancement of the musical interest of our Pan-American cause. This will not interfere with my going this year to New York to conduct, as I told Cowell, just for the expenses. As rate of exchange with Spain is so low it wouldn't be much difference in travel expenses from Spain to the States as compared with rates from Havana.

Am taking along "Washington's Birthday": I hope to perform it in Europe on first suitable opportunity as it is a work I regard highly.

I intend to stay in this same address up to the 19th inst when you may forward your answer. As soon as I settle down in Madrid I shall get in touch with you immediately. . . .

Congratulating you, I am
Sincerely yours,
Pedro Sanjuan

• • •

On 1 May 1932 Aaron Copland accompanied the baritone Hubert Linscott in a performance of seven songs by Ives at the Yaddo music festival in Saratoga Springs, New York. This proved to be an extremely important event in the career of Ives's songs because of the positive critical and audience response it generated. The songs, which previously had been treated derisively if at all by critics, became some of Ives's most respected and frequently performed repertoire. The performance at Yaddo also prompted a new generation of supporters to contact and work with Ives. One of these was A. Lehman Engel (1910–82), who became a champion of Ives's choral works with his group, the Madrigal Singers, in the late 1930s and 1940s. When Engel first wrote Ives in January 1932, he proposed including the *Concord* Sonata in a series of lectures on modern music that he and his pianist, Hortense Monath,[46] were planning. Ives's letter, below, responds to this suggestion.

46. Her married name was Mrs. S. A. Hirschman; see Hirschman to Ives, 10 April 1940 (CIP, 30/8).

233. 4 May 1932, from Lehman Engel, New York

My dear Mr. Ives:

This is merely a line to attempt to tell you how very much I enjoyed your songs which were performed at the Yaddo Festival. It gives me a great thrill to consider the life work of one who has struggled so diligently and so alone and who now is beginning at least to be seen for his true worth. I consider the songs really great and real American contributions to music literature. I feel sure that they were among the most impressive works heard at our festival.

Hoping that someday I may have the pleasure of meeting you with all sincere admiration, I am

Cordially,
A. Lehman Engel

234. 16 June 1932, first sketch and letter from Edith Ives to Lehman Engel, London

Dear Mr. ~~Lehman~~ Engel:

Thank you very much for your ~~kind~~ letter. I greatly appreciate ~~deeply~~ greatly your interest and your kind expression & etc. When we get back next year I hope to be of some help in to be able to take a more active part in the work & also having the pleasure of (knowing) meeting you personally.

It is good of Miss Monath & you to consider playing something of mine—but to play the whole 2nd Sonata is a long and rather hard job for any pianist & for most listeners it seems, ~~usually I have found.~~ If she thought best, I might suggest that one or two of the shorter transcriptions of the 1st movement & the last mvt "Thoreau" with perhaps the short Alcotts might be played. The first 2 movements of this sonata, as they stand in the printed book, are for the most part a reduction for piano from a concerto. ~~The last 2 movements are o.k. & as they were originally for piano, as they stand.~~

The transcriptions are nearer and more practicable to play. . . .

Mr. Emil Hanke (at his office room 309) or 711–5 has photostat or original copies of most of my music—& will be glad to let you & Miss M. have whatever you may want ~~would like~~.

The II mvts of transcriptions and the Thoreau movement after it go well enough—might be enough for a concert. They go well enough. Even these as they are in copy are not exactly as I play them & as soon as I can get to it, I want to make a few phonograph records—which might help a little in playing[47]

[*On back of page in pencil:*] He thanks you for the kind letter & is sorry it did not come before, as we will probably not be back til next year.

47. Ives did in fact make such a recording, Ives Plays Ives, reissued by New World Records in 2006.

[*Edith's letter as sent (all Ives to Engel letters are photocopies):*]

My dear Mr. Engel:—

I am acknowledging your letters to my father, one of which came after we left. He is somewhat better, but it is still difficult for him to write, so I am acting as his longhand stenographer. He says:

"Thank you very much for your letters & their kind expressions. I deeply appreciate your interest. When we get back next year I hope to be able to be of more active help in the work, & also to have the pleasure of knowing you personally.

It is good of Miss Monath & you to consider playing something of mine. To play the whole second sonata is a long & rather hard job for any pianist—& for most listeners, it seems. If Miss Monath thought best I might suggest one or two of the Transcriptions of the first movement with the last movement in the printed book "Thoreau." The first two movements of this Sonata, as they stand in the printed book, are for the most part a reduction for piano from a Piano-Concerto score. The transcriptions are nearer and more practicable to play. Mr. Emil Hanke at his office—room 309—711 5th Ave (Plaza 1900) has photostat & what copies there are of most of the music, & he will be glad to let Miss Monath & you have whatever you may want of the piano or other things.

I'm sorry to say that the trouble with too much of the piano music is that the copies are not altogether as they are played—that is, as I play them, & also there are some things, mostly detail, left out that were in originally. There are also about the right number of mistakes. The second transcription & the "Thoreau," are the most entire,—whatever mistakes there are I can readily correct in the margin.

I've had in mind for some time making phonograph records of some of these piano movements—and will, as soon as I am able to play again, which I hope to soon. These might be of some help (though perhaps not much) in making some places clearer than in the written notes; and also save time in getting the general "gist," or at least the general play of things & playing that I had in mind.

Let me thank you again for your letter, & I am indeed grateful for your interest. Please extend my thanks & best wishes to Miss Monath.

Sincerely yours
Miss Edith Ives
for
Chas E. Ives

• • •

Ives seems not to have fully trusted Aaron Copland (1900–1990), whom he saw as a proponent of a French-influenced, neoclassicist ideal of American music in competition with the one he, Cowell, and the Ultramoderns were promoting. Ives was, however, grateful to him for presenting his songs at Yaddo, as the following letter demonstrates.

235. 21 July 1932, to Aaron Copland, London

Dear Mr. Copland:

I want to write you,—if just a line—to tell you that I appreciated greatly your playing some of my songs. If they went well—it was due to the way you and Mr. Linscott handled them. I am grateful to you both; please thank Mr. Linscott for me.

But the way you stood up in "Congress", and had your say from "within" "out" gave added substance to the whole festival. Not exactly all critics are "lily pads"—but too many are.

With appreciation, best wishes,
Yours sincerely,
Chas. E. Ives

When we get back we are looking forward to the pleasure of meeting you personally—and I hope then to be able to be of some help in the work in any way I can.

• • •

Ives's correspondence with the mezzo-soprano Radiana Pazmor shows the dynamics of the relationship between the composer and performers of his works in the 1930s. The letters offer a wealth of concrete information on performance of selected songs and demonstrate the influence of Ives's reputation as an isolated and "diffident" composer on the reception of his works by potential performers.

236. 29 July 1933, from Radiana Pazmor, Middlebury, Vermont

Dear Mr. Ives,

Since the beginning of the summer I have been trying to get some recent songs of yours to sing in San Francisco. The enclosed letter from Henry Cowell (which I should ask you please to return to me) will tell you how important it is for me to have them. I am under the impression that those published by the Cos Cob Press are not among your latest productions. I know that you are extremely diffident about allowing performances of your songs, but really I am intelligent and I hope you can feel that you may entrust to me with a reasonable degree of safety the interesting task of singing some of them.

My voice is a sort of mezzo contralto but it is quite supple and I have a very good range, singing many songs in the mezzo soprano tessitura.

I am leaving for California a week from tomorrow and am very eager to have the songs to study in the train.

I hope very sincerely that you will not feel obliged to disappoint us, and shall feel honored if you will accede to our request.

Sincerely yours, with great admiration and respect,
Radiana Pazmor

The concert in question is to be given for the New Music Society of San Francisco.

• • •

Apparently, Pazmor's name stimulated Ives's propensity for wordplay. As in the letters to Lou Harrison, below, the final copies would have used standard salutations.

237. Ca. 29 July 1933, sketch for Ives to Radiana Pazmor

Radiater
Paddyassmore:

Dear Cig

Thank you very much for your letter. I'm very glad to send what songs I have here to you, ~~and~~ hope they reach you in time

There are no more complete copies of the ~~larger~~ book ~~of songs, but am very glad to send you what I have here, and I hope they reach you in time.~~ but I found also there were some ~~extra~~ separate copies of some ~~single of some separate~~ songs ~~for the pianist~~ which are enclosed. ~~I'm sending these not the complete book.~~ If you find any of them suitable, I shall appreciate it greatly to have you sing them. I'm not exactly diffident, as you say, about having them sung; it's rather, the unpleasant position process of pulling singers "in wrong" with ~~their audiences~~ most everybody & ~~the world in general. However that was some years ago—there has been much~~ less of that lately. However that is less usual now, than it was some years ago (accompanists over

Sometimes a pianist ~~make~~ can "yawp" better than ~~they~~ he can play—but Henry Cowell knows where to get a good pianist.

If you should like any of the songs and sing them, I would feel myself fortunate. I am with best wishes

[*Second page of sketch with revisions to paragraph on pianists*]

sometimes ~~but often~~ accompanists will make a ~~"fuss"~~ at times and refuse to play—~~they can "yawp" better than can play~~

Some ~~pianists~~ of them ~~can~~ will "yawp" better than they play.

238. 10 August 1933, from Radiana Pazmor

Dear Mr. Ives,

"General Booth" is great and I'm going to sing it if I can persuade the accompanist to struggle with that manuscript! My part is fairly clear but I can't for the life of me figure out the very last phrase. Could you be so kind as to let me know what these notes are? Also from what book you took the text? There is one place that I cannot quite figure.

I am wondering if the turned down pages mark any special favorites of yours or if they are someone's else. The material is so rich that it is difficult to decide on a group. The songs are so diversified both musically and textually that there is no danger of monotony at any rate. I am very eager to begin work viva voce upon them.

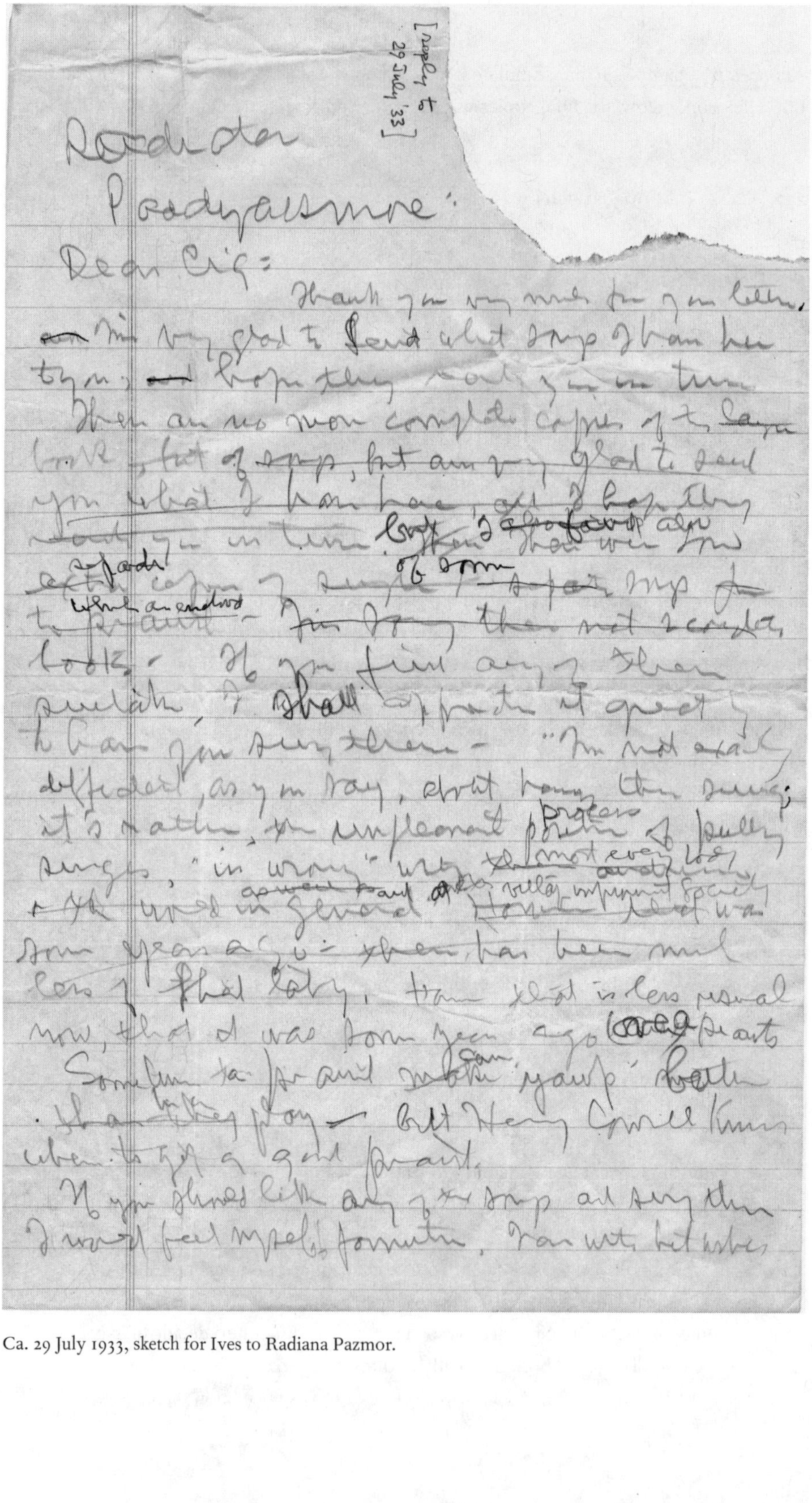
[reply to 29 July '33]

Ca. 29 July 1933, sketch for Ives to Radiana Pazmor.

I was very much interested in your remarks at the end of the book. There is in them much food for thought, much concerning which I have questioned for years without ever coming to a fixed opinion.

I hope you don't mind my writing, it's out of a growing enthusiasm that I write. Please excuse the Pullman scrawl, a bit worse than usual.[48]

Sincerely,
Radiana Pazmore

• • •

When Aaron Copland wrote inquiring about Ives's songs for a proposed article in *Modern Music,* Ives responded at length.[49] Copland's questions centered on the volume *Fifty Songs* (actually, fifty-two songs) that Ives had had reprinted from his *114 Songs* in 1923. He also referred to the *New Music* volume of *Thirty-four Songs,* which was published in October 1933. Ives's standard sketching process is more transparent in this letter: the voice projected is Ives's and Harmony is the acknowledged transcriber.

239. 10 October 1933, Harmony Ives to Aaron Copland

Dear Mr. Copland

Let me acknowledge & thank you for your letter to Mr. Ives. He is not well and as it is difficult for him to write I am taking his reply for him—

Sincerely,
Harmony T. Ives

"It is good of you to write about the songs & and I greatly appreciate your interest.

In answer to your questions:

(1) The book of 50 was printed about two or three years after the larger book as there were not many of the latter, had to send to some who, I imagined, weren't musically interested but asked for copies principally because the book was not sold.

(2) Why so many were deleted

I don't remember exactly—probably to give a cross section. It was reprinted in a hurry—Why was 'Where the Eagle' omitted—don't know.

(3) Why postscript omitted—

probably to save space, cost of reprinting & trouble to the reader!

(4) Does your attitude in postscript still hold good?—

<u>Yes</u> except possibly in some details.

(5) Why did you include certain songs written in 1921 in the back of the volume with the earlier ones?

48. Pazmor wrote from the train she was taking to California.

49. Aaron Copland, "One Hundred and Fourteen Songs," *Modern Music* 11, no. 2 (January–February 1934): 59–64.

As I remember a mistake of the binder and partly mine.

The trouble with some of my songs is that they were not originally written as such—at least not for one nice voice & piano. Several were arranged when the book was published and some of these were reduced and weakened in the process. For instance, the first song ['Majority'] was originally for a large chorus and orchestra and contained two sections omitted in the book arrangement. This was composed several years before the book was published. Perhaps you would like to see the original manuscripts. I have some photostats here, which I am sending you under separate cover and will have more made of the others and sent to you shortly.

Some of the songs were adapted from old scores composed with no idea of transmigration—as 'Tolerance, 'The Housatonic at Stockbridge' and those from symphonies, sonatas etc. But some of the others were thought of in terms of a song for a solo instrument, quite often for basset horn, cornet, English horn, etc.—with a few other instruments assisting. I got this habit I think for two reasons. My father was a musician and played about every instrument he could lay his hands on—the cornet, french horn, and basset horn the most. He could get as near Schubert with these as Bispham would with 'his'[50] He once gave a song recital with the basset horn as the chief singer. The words were handed around to the audience for them to sing silently with him.

Secondly, when some of these songs were written most [of] the singers in those days it seemed to me were good-voiced, soft headed & stunted-eared. They would make such a fuss about the intervals etc. that if I wanted a song sung I'd have to write one I didn't want sung.

I suppose a note should have been made in the book as to the source, date, etc of the original score instead of just the time of the arrangement—but I didn't take the trouble to do it. This has been done in the edition Henry Cowell is publishing this October and occasionally more of the score is put into the piano part.

In this connection I wrote Mrs. Wertheim, as I remember, about a year ago in answer to her letter saying that the Cos Cob Press were publishing some of the songs.[51] I explained the above and said that as some of the original scores might be published some note to this effect ought to be made, as a man might sometime buy both thinking that they were different things & when he found they were the same pieces he might not feel quite right about it. Whereas in my book which was not going on the market this point would make little difference. I asked Mrs. Wertheim to send the proofs to me but they were not sent.

There are songs that ought to have gone into the former book but for one reason or another didn't—for instance 'General Booth'—Macmillan Co. would not give copy right permission. There is one "Soliloquy" Henry is now publishing that ought to have gone in but did not because about that time I was getting tired of the whines of the 'old ladies.' One of these told me that he considered this song was an insult to all respectable singers and musicians & I probably felt there were enough insults in the book without it. Henry is also including an early song ['Song for Harvest Season']—it isn't much of a song but some what amusing showing a boy's experiment in 'four keys at once.' There are some songs

50. The American baritone David Bispham (1857–1921).

51. Alma Wertheim; see Wertheim to Ives, 20 August 1932, and Ives's sketches for a reply in CIP, 32/12.

composed since the book was published they might be mentioned just to make the article complete but I haven't them here and would just about as well have them passed up as somehow, nothing that I have done in the last ten years or so seems much good to me.

In starting I didn't intend to bother you with such a long letter but I think that some of the above facts you should be familiar with—If there is anything further that I can do please let me know.

Thanking you again for your interest I am, with best wishes
Sincerely yours,
Chas. E. Ives"

· 6 ·

TRAVEL

(1930–1938)

Both because of the clearly local qualities of many of his works and because of the indelible image of Ives as the crusty New Englander, it is hard to imagine him anywhere other than New York or Connecticut. Yet the Ives family took four long trans-Atlantic trips to England, Scotland, and the Continent. The first, to England, was between 30 July and 13 September 1924. No letters survive to mark this trip. Most of the correspondence that describes travel dates from the 1930s. The examples included below round out our understanding of Ives as a person and also provide a glimpse of his interaction with Harmony and Edith.

The following letter provides one of the few indications of the strain that caring for Ives placed on the rest of his family, particularly his wife. The letter also contains one of the few reactions by Ives to the performance of music by another composer. Although he says little about the unnamed work by Thomas Tallis, his comment on the piece itself and on the atmosphere created by the specific sound and setting of the performance is quite suggestive about his participatory and place-specific approach to music.

240. Ca. 12 October 1930, to Nicolas Slonimsky, Château Frontenac, Quebec

Dear Mr. Slonimsky:

Your letter came just when we were leaving. We didn't intend as much of a trip as this—but Mrs. Ives seemed pretty much tired out with the long job of housekeeper, chauffeur, nurse and general care taker—and needed a rest. We will probably stay around here until the latter part of the month depending on how we feel and will probably stop over for a little family visit at Williamstown Mass. on the way back. I'm sorry not to be more certain as we want to see you in Redding again. But if that isn't possible we'll hope to see you in N.Y. the first part of November. Will write when our plans are more certain.

This city on the cliff, the country about and the waters in the river all seem beautiful to us. Looking at the inscriptions on the monuments and "boite a rubat" and all the children only 2 years old and speaking French—make us feel in a foreign land—& we are. We went to the old English church this morning—The "Plain Chant" and Canticles sung by every body in unison, each one making a little music of his own to Mr. Tallis—may stand as a point of departure into collective composing—or the universal lyre" I will now stop this and say good-night.

Mrs. Ives sends kindest regards.

Hoping to see you soon
Sincerely,
Chas. E. Ives

241. 17 September 1931, to Nicolas Slonimsky, Kedgemakooge Rod and Gun Club, Nova Scotia

Dear Columerica:

You're back, I guess, about now, from shooting the buffalo—and with robes & scalps—and if not,—it's quite alright—too. I hope you had a satisfactory time & found Henry well—& sitting on the end of his summer symphony—loafing.

We came up here for a boat ride—& it seemed great to us, to get back to the wilderness, a log cabin & living with the moose," again—and we're staying longer than expected.

Am sending the enclosed—according to your instructions—Some Tombstone inscriptions,[1] pieces, to be or not to be, played—and—(A) "face"—and when I look at it—I apologize to "Igor S"—and for any thing I may have thrown at any face anywhere—when is a man, not a man—(ans.) = When he has his picture taken. The sins of his forbears—all—& posterity—"it is their Day," unprepared & sour—However this [is the] last picture I'll ever have taken—so I'll stop talking.

We all send best wishes to you both—and shall hope to see you both soon—will probably be back some time next week.

As ever, sincerely
Chas. E. Ives

I wrote to Mr. Sanjuan, as you directed—if you haven't heard from him—it is not my fault.

We expect to see Henry around the 20th As we intended to be away only a few days, we didn't have the mail forwarded. So if you've sent anything to be answered,—will attend to it as soon as I get back.

• • •

In 1932, 1934, and 1938 the Ives family took three long European vacations with an eye toward improving Ives's health. As Gayle Sherwood has noted, this "cure" was a typical treatment for neurasthenia.[2] Whether Ives's physician had this in mind or not, the trips he recommended varied in their effectiveness. As was the case at home, Ives's health oscillated between

1. Ives refers to songs of this title by Slonimsky.
2. Sherwood, "Charles Ives and Our National Malady," 562.

highs and lows. The European trips did produce many memorable occasions for Ives and his family, and these led to some remarkable letters. The first trip lasted from 12 May 1932 until 6 July 1933. It was the longest of the three, and the Iveses traveled to England, Scotland, Germany, France, Switzerland, Italy, Sicily, and back to England before returning home.

242. 15 April 1932, sketch[3] for Edith Ives to E. Robert Schmitz

Dear Mr. Schmitz

Father has not been well, & as it is difficult for him to write I am acting as his long hand stenographer. We were all sorry to hear that you won't be able to come east this month as it means that we probably will not see you for quite a while. We expect to sail on May 4, & will be in England & Scotland for a few months, later on leaving for France, Italy, and possibly Germany. If all goes well, we will not get back until next spring. Father and I have never been on the continent so we think it is about time we completed our education!

Father wants to thank you for your letter & enclosures; he isn't quite sure whether it is the melodies for trumpet and piano you want, or the book of songs, but he is sending you copies of both. Some of the trumpet pieces are from an old score for trumpet, violins, saxophones & piano which were also arranged for voice and piano, & put into the songbook later. Daddy says a good trumpeter with "plenty of breath" & also a good pianist (also with strong breath) will make these go along well. Father is sending some enclosures for Pro Musica & a program or two that you may like to see.

We all send
Very sincerely

P.S. Father can find no complete copies of the large book of songs, but is sending one from which a few numbers have been taken out for single copies.[4]

243. Mid-July 1932, to Nicolas Slonimsky,[5] 18 Half Moon Street, London

Dear N.S. Am. Ambas!

I felt very, very badly in not seeing you again that time in N.Y. I was just about in the end of one of those ———, ——— low sloughs, when a man can't do anything & doesn't know it—couldn't eat, sleep, think, or even cuss moderately!

3. Here is an example of a sketch produced from dictation. The writing is in Edith's hand, but the style and content clearly mark this as a sketch by Ives, who later made corrections to it in his own hand. Though Ives often mentions using a stenographer to write letters, there is limited evidence of this practice in the archives. This is not surprising: dictated letters would be less likely to leave behind preliminary drafts than letters Ives sketched by hand.

4. Schmitz had written asking for a copy of the songbook for an upcoming performance of songs in a concert by the Los Angeles chapter of Pro Musica. Other composers on the program were Harris, Copland, Cowell, and Sessions. See Schmitz to Ives, 8 April 1932 (CIP, 31/16).

5. A portion of this letter is excerpted in chap. 4.

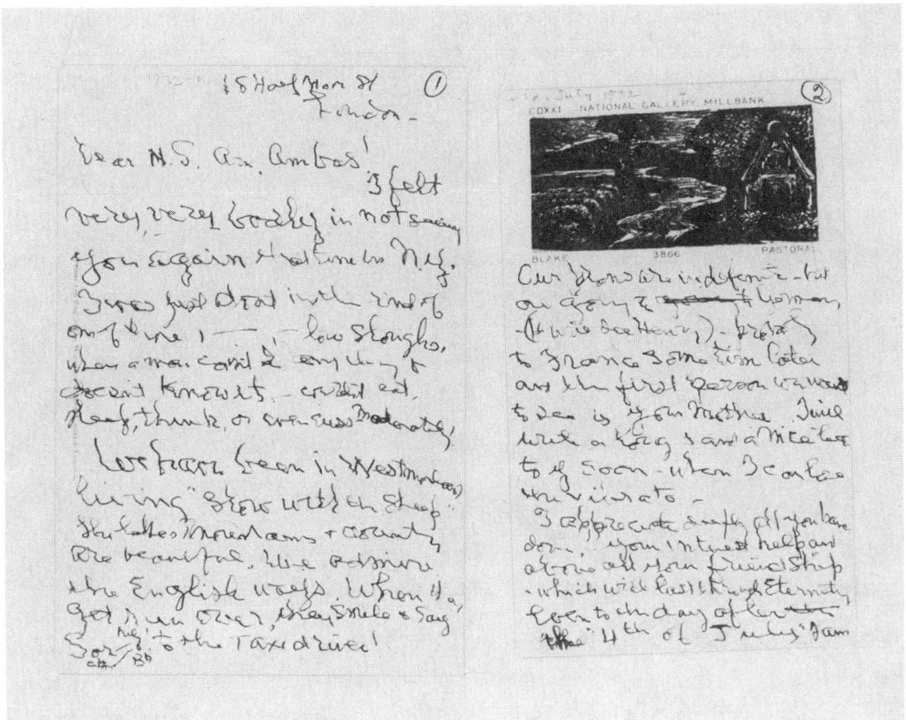

Mid-July 1932, to Nicolas Slonimsky.

We have been in Westmorland living "slow with the sheep" The lakes mountains & country are beautiful. We admire the English ways. When you get run over, they smile & say Sor—ry (C#–B-natural) to the taxi driver!

Our plans are indefinite—but are going to Germany (& we'll see Henry)—probably to France some time later and the first person we want to see is your mother. I will write a long & nice letter to you soon—when I can lose the vibrato.

I appreciate deeply all you have done, your interest help and above all your friendship—which will last through eternity even to the day after the "4th of July." I am glad to report that I am much better than I've been for some time. You see I have a remarkable doctor in N.Y. (He's no good when you're sick)—but when I told him on leaving, that I was going to take a pint of ale every night, he said "Don't do that—Remember 3 pints a day keep the doctor away & drink good ale when you can." He was quite right. Eat, drink, and be merry for tomorrow we live on Main St." . . .

Sincerely,
Chas. E. Ives

244. 15 August 1932, postcard to John Becker, Burg Reichenstein, Germany

Remembrances for you all. We are going up the Rhine, from Wiesbaden where we have been for a while. The southern German countries are beautiful, & the old towns. I hope things are going well with you. Will write some more as soon as I can lose this "vibrato" Mrs. Ives & Edie send affectionate greetings to you all

Chas E. Ives

• • •

Nicolas Slonimsky's mother wrote one of the only known descriptions of the Iveses traveling in Europe, after they dropped in on her at her Paris home in September 1932. She recounted the visit in an excited letter to her son, who translated it and forwarded it to Ives.

245. 19 September 1932, from Nicolas Slonimsky

. . . A long P.S.

Just as I was mailing this, the letter-carrier came, and brought me this enthusiastic report from my mother about your visit with her. I translate it in full:

Sept. 10. My dear Kolinka (this is a pet name for Nicolas), day before yesterday I had an extraordinarily pleasant and interesting surprise—the visit of the Ives couple. I am over-enthusiastic about them, and I only regret that I have not a 25-year old son or grandson, who would marry their daughter. I didn't meet her, but I suppose she is just as charming as her father and as beautiful as her mother. The miracle was the way we made each other understood. Mrs. Ives speaks a little French, more than your sister's English, and he understands a little German. But little comprehensible as our words were, our gestures were quite understandable, and these gestures expressed my greatest joy and pleasure at meeting in person somebody whom I seemed to know so well from your descriptions. Only you never mentioned their only daughter. And on their part, they were probably interested in meeting the mother of Nicolas, about whom you told them. Time and again, he would shake both my hands and say something in English, and I was only saying: Thank you very much. Now I am determined to learn English, otherwise I cannot get along with your most charming friends.

The most charming thing they did was this. The first time they came in the daytime when I was out buying food. They got to Ditia (pet name of my sister). Ditia, not knowing that it was the Ives, received them formally as she would receive some unknown American friends. Ditia asked them to stay a little, telling them that I would come soon. They, not knowing who Ditia was, left after waiting, and only on the stairs Ditia found out that it was Ives. Then Ditia asked them to wait some more, foreseeing my complete despair at having missed them, and it was then that she said she was your sister. Ives stirred and asked whose sister. Well, sister of Nicolas. Then Ives came back grasped her hands and shook them several times. As luck would have it, I was not in a hurry to get back and several times sat down on the bench to catch my breath. When I finally arrived, Ditia said the Ives had been there, and now had left. I was terribly upset and disappointed. She comforted me with the words that the Ives were going to Switzerland but would be back in Paris on their return trip.

That night we went to see your much-vaunted Shanghai Express in the movies (awful stuff). All of the sudden I am called,—the Ives are downstairs. I jumped and instantly ran to the exit, and there were Mr. and Mrs. Ives speaking to me with an enchanting smile on their lips, greeting me in an incomprehensible tongue. Right away, we turned the cab home,—it was fortunate I had time to buy something,—prepared tea, fruits, wine, and began to talk. I chattered all the time expressing my delight at meeting them. Mrs. Ives spoke of your talent, and Mr. Ives showed how you produce various criticisms out of your pocket. We spent some hour and a half very pleasantly, I think they had a pleasant time, too. He looked over all the photographs, even the one with the broken nose, and explained that he, too, had a broken nose.[6] Of course, we spoke of Dorothy,[7] too,—naturally, what else do you suppose? He found resemblance between you and Ditia, particularly, the eyes, and she emphasized your resemblance to me. To make a long story short, in spite of our microscopic knowledge of English words, thanks to some French of Mrs. Ives and the German of Mr. Ives, we managed to understand each other and parted as great friends. I kept repeating: "Thank you very much," and my request to come have dinner with us on the return trip. I was so excited, I grew red in the face, and he paid me a gallant compliment and told me he didn't believe I was 75. In a word, we received a full pleasure. Of course, they asked why I am not coming to America, but I explained that I don't belong with the newly-wed, but when Nicolas and Dorothy come to be a threesome, then I would go to be the fourth. She seemingly liked the explanation very much, and translated it to him, and he smiled with his gentle sympathetic smile. Even before I was always in love with Americans, all Americans I met seemed extremely charming and thoughtful but the Ives are over-charming and more than merely sympathetic. She is so beautiful, here stature, her profile, her eyes, her smile. But he with his delightful way to laugh so joyfully simply enchanted me. I also paid him a compliment saying that there is one language that everybody understands,—it's the language of his music.

246. Mid-October 1932, to Nicolas Slonimsky, Interlaken, Switzerland

Dear Mr. Slonimsky

We were in Paris and saw your mother. She has all our votes—Paris, only a few! Your mother is a remarkable character! We see where you get your "envoie"—"go," the best ways you have. It was interesting to meet your sister. She is fine and reminds us of you.—And Dorothy Adlow Slonimsky! How they like to talk about her—it reminded me of my old Aunt Amelia—who said "Now that I know your wife—I have some hope for your future life." We should both have congratulations—you have mine!

I hope some of the plans for another invasion may work out. From what I hear—and from Henry, Adler, etc., there is a great interest in the work, but a great deficiency in all other departments,—but I feel we must try to keep the work going as well as we can until times get better. I don't know enough of the situation in detail to propose anything but will do all I can when the opportunity comes.

6. See Letter 14.

7. Slonimsky's wife, Dorothy Adlow Slonimsky.

To play "Washington's B.D." in N.Y. as you propose, seems to me much the best! I hope the players don't give you too much troubles—or flat tires.

Have you ever been in Zwitzerland? Well,—I have!—for a month! And we think seriously of staying on till 1974. We are in a little place just out of the village—nobody around but 2 goats & the "yungfrau." Traveling doesn't seem to agree with us, and we may stay here for some while—perhaps go to Italy later.

Mrs. Ives & Edie send love to you both—

Sincerely,
Chas E. Ives

247. Ca. November 1932, letter on two postcards to Carl Ruggles, Interlaken, Switzerland

Dear Carl:

This is another great country for men (you) & mountains. We've been here most of the fall in a little place just out of the village with the "Jungfrau" above.[8] We find that traveling much doesn't agree with us exactly & have been to not many places, staying mostly in the country. Saw Henry in Berlin also Mrs. Adolph Weiss.[9] Were in Paris for a short while on our way here. Would you like to have me give you some nice advice?—When traveling don't go to Paris—go to Macy's—but when looking around for a place in eternity—this would do quite well. We do hope Mrs. Ruggles is much better. Please give her our kindest remembrances. Keep well—I long to see you.

Chas E. I.

248. 22 October 1932, to Clifton Furness, Interlaken, Switzerland

——— Do you ever meet Slonimsky in Boston? I have known what an able man he was, but I'm astonished to find what a remarkably outstanding man he is over here. All the critics: musicians modern and "agin" it—think he is a kind of natural wonder. Especially in Berlin and Paris. Some of the men who played under him say that Furtwangler, Toscannini & others could not do what he does. It is his "ear-mentality" I think—almost uncanny. Yet he has that other side—the human, and emotional—I hope Boston will give him a chance some day—why does the running of music always seem to get into the hands of the old ladies!—and "blue stocking" girls![10] Slonimsky draws but a "sour bow" with them—he isn't always polite to them! He isn't afraid of anybody and he has a very active mind—a bad combination sometimes—before the "sufficient and properly dressed." However he will win out sometime—even in Boston.

8. Ives refers to the photograph in the postcard he used to sketch the letter.

9. Adolph Weiss (1891–1971) was the secretary of the Pan American Association of Composers and a player in the Conductorless Orchestra, which performed works by Cowell and other modernists.

10. This is perhaps a reference to the old Yale football song "Harvard Has Blue-stocking Girls, Yale Has Blue-stocking Men."

249. 20 November 1932, sketch for Edith Ives to E. Robert Schmitz, Interlaken, Switzerland

Dear Mr. Schmitz:

We hope you are all well—It is long since we have had word from you. Our plans changed somewhat, after writing you from London, we went to the Lake country, Westmorland & Scotland instead of going to Paris. Traveling does not agree with us exactly—I would have been content to [visit] a few places—mostly in the country. We were in Paris for a little while before coming here—and have stayed in this great outdoors most of the fall.

I hope things have gone well with you—and as you would want. . . .

250. 22 November 1932, Edith Ives to John Becker, Interlaken, Switzerland

Dear Mr. Becker:—

Daddy wants me to thank you very much for your letter, & it will give him great pleasure to attend to the Gugenheim matter just as soon as the papers come.[11] He wrote to you a month or so ago about the New York lectures & thinks you have probably received the letter by this time. He was most pleased to see the good article about you in the magazine, & greatly appreciated you including him in the articles that you are writing. He would write to you himself, but his hands shake, & it is difficult for him to write—also it makes him mad!

Right now we are in an orgy of packing—getting ready to take a villa in Taormena. When we get there, I shall write you a nice long letter; a thing I have been meaning to do for some time. . . .

Interlaken is perfectly beautiful at this moment of writing. The mountains are being eaten alive by flames in the form of autumnal trees, & the vivid color combined with the dazzling snow peaks, is enough to drive an artist into eating his paint brushes with despair. As to the sensation of exhilaration in the air—Matthew Arnold can describe it better than I: [*Here she quotes Arnold's "Parting" in full.*][12]

Please give my love to everybody—especially the latest addition! Does he like aeroplanes, or do you think he would enjoy the thunder of the avalanche more?

Very affectionately
"Edie" Ives

251. December 1932, to Nicolas Slonimsky, Taormina, Sicily

Remembrances to you both from the family.—best wishes for the new year—& many of them—but of course, not too many! We are in this country of great beauty—living in a little stone hut, on a side hill, overlooking the Ionian toward the foot of Italia" We hope to stay here till spring. We hear you did heroic work at the last concert—against the opposi-

11. Becker had asked Ives for a recommendation for a Guggenheim grant.

12. Matthew Arnold, "Parting," in *Empedocles on Etna*, 1852.

tion of the Union & the "Premature Comment" girls It is much appreciated You see I'm getting so I can write (almost nice) & will send you a nice long letter soon, writin' regular.

C. E. Ives

252. Christmas 1932, to T. Carl Whitmer, Taormina, Sicily

Dear Mr. Whitmer:

We all send Mrs. Whitmer and you best holiday wishes & remembrances from Sicily. We came down from Switzerland, slowly through Italy—& expect to stay on here till the spring. Taormina is a place of great beauty—the foot of Italy across the bay—Etna in the distance—& down the hill the ruins of a Greek Theater—where Aeschylus said something 400 B.C.—think of saying anything in 400 B.C.—that's more than we can do! Keep well in Dramamount.

Sincerely
Chas. E. Ives

253. Christmas 1932, sketch for Edith Ives to Bernard Herrmann, Taormina, Sicily[13]

Dear Mr. Herrmann,

We all send you best wishes for the holidays & remembrances from ~~us all &~~ Sicily. We are in this place of great beauty; ~~on a side~~ with Aetna in the horizon & a Greek theater and over ~~with the past, farther away from away from the future.~~ Father is better, but his hands shake when he writes, & it makes him mad. He wants to thank you deeply for your kind remarks about American music including his, which you made at the meeting last summer. It has helped to gain serious interest in the movement. He greatly appreciates what you said & thanks you sincerely for it. It was good to know that it was that Mr. Moross's music was played, & so successful—& we hope some of yours will be played soon—Daddy thinks it will. We probably will not be home for six mos or more, but shall look forward to seeing you again then—

With kindest greetings from us all
I am

254. December 1932, sketch for Edith Ives to Jerome Moross, Taormina, Sicily (on the same sheet as Letter 253)

Dear Mr. Moross—

We all send you best wishes, remembrances, & congratulations.

We were delighted to know that your music was played & so successfully. When we get

13. Ives began corresponding with the composer Bernard Herrmann (1911–1975) in 1932.

back we shall hope to hear some of it. Daddy says that at every concert some of the music of the younger composers should be heard & he thinks it will be & also published.

Daddy is better, but his hands bother him, so I write for him.

This is indeed a country of great beauty & "so a joy forever." The best part of traveling is not traveling but staying in a place like this. We hope to be here until spring. It is uncertain when we will get back, but will hope to see you when we do.

255. 8 January 1933, postcard to Mary Bell, Taormina, Sicily

Dear Miss Bell:

I want to thank you for singing the songs in the Hamburg concert. You did remarkably well, from the accounts Henry sent us. I greatly appreciate your interest and help. We are now living under an olive tree in a little stone cabin—(the Italians are polite & call it a "villa") on a side hill, overlooking the "Ionian" & we see (sometimes) the sun rise over Greece! Kindest remembrances from us all & also to Frau Schmolke![14]

Chas E. Ives

• • •

In the following, Ives writes to Slonimsky from Sicily, and the setting sends him into a comical pidgin Italian laced with a few half-remembered bits of Latin left over from compulsory study at Yale. Most of the letter is Ives's pleased response to José Rodriguez 's article "An Old Lady Gets Three Shots in the Arm," a review of Slonimsky's concerts of ultramodern music with the Los Angeles Philharmonic. The remarks that Rodriguez had "something to say" and was "convincing and dignified" are high praise from Ives. That he tempers this serious assessment with verbal slapstick is typical of his writing style, especially with Slonimsky. The letter closes with a reference to Dorothy Adlow Slonimsky, who was an art critic and teacher.

256. 5 February 1933, to Nicolas Slonimsky, Taormina, Sicily

—io—TE Saluto Signore!

"Buona Bonaparte de Batone"

—and you are a good boy, even if you shoot old ladies in the Elbow. You have been doing great work—and the Los Angeles battle was an extraordinary feat—a literal triumph for you. I'm glad they speak of your courage as well as your genius—Questo mi piace—and all the family who read with enthusiasm the tributes to your Napoleonic Forelock,[15] your Rostrumic-Authority, your imagination to say nothing of your Riding-master" ability.

14. Else Schmolke ran a guesthouse in Berlin where the Iveses had stayed, along with Bell and Henry Cowell, to whom Schmolke had at one point been engaged to be married. As she was unable to leave Germany, the wedding never took place. Hicks, *Henry Cowell, Bohemian*, 128.

15. Penned by a Los Angeles critic, this was Ives's favorite description of Slonimsky's hair. See also Letter 259 and the introduction to Letter 269.

That article "An old lady gets 3 shots" etc. is one [of] the best of its kind we have ever seen. He "Jose R" writes as though he were writing to get something off his chest & not to fill up a newspaper column. In spite of its play of comedy, it is convincing & dignified:—of a man who thinks & thinks for himself & a literary "something" besides—Everybody in Boston aged over 38 years 6 mos ought to read it.—but "Parla troppo presto!

It can't be long now before you get a permanent job with some big orchestra, we hope in the East—you've done so much for practically nothing—it makes me mad—and Mrs. Ives too. "Mi dia una hatto! Though many a true word lodges in the teeth, & though it's a long road that has no saloon, thou'l be there with Aurora!—non posso aspetto tanto!!

It was good to know that the Pan. Am. concert has been arranged for the 1934 Italian Festival. "Guggenheim" or not you will have to be there—even if we have to train a nice eagle to fly you over. Vogliamo anche un salotto.—when you're there—swatta di wappo, non troppo!

We are on a side hill of "lemoni" & "biancheria"—have you been in Sicily?—that is, early in the morning?—The sun comes out of Greece over the Ionian—which is quite all right & then a nice breeze over Calabria, brings it to your eye—but with it lemons, figgimendetti & madaringall on the other eye! Mi mandi un barbiere alle otto.—But this is a place of great beauty—& we can lead a quiet, "peasant" kind of life which agrees with us. When the sun shines it is as our June—When not it is like "election day, and Republicans! It is the color—buona mollo—in everything & every where that makes the scenery here—There are many artists here—no musicians—Lo voglio molto forte!

It looks now as if we would not get to France again—and it will be a disappointment not to see your mother again[. We] will probably stay here until the first part of March or so, & then go to some of the Italian cities for a while & may sail back from Naples—or possibly a boat to England & back that way—desidero un sigaro—forti—When you write again it would be best to mail to the London address, c/o Guaranty Trust Co. 50 Pall Mall.

We hope you have both kept well, and not too tired with the season's work. Edie when talking with some of the artists here—often refers to your wife (ex quotation) with great admiration. molto bene—we all send kindest remembrances to her—

Signore, io TE Saluto—ancora—e—ancora!

Feb 5 '33 (ex diebus CEI [*written like the impression a signet ring would produce and with a face at the bottom*]—"scribes Romanis"
401 B.C.

One of the best things about that the 'Old Lady' etc. article is that it backs up what Henry has been saying all along—about the whole movement.—though if the portraits of all the Pan Am's had been continued around the page—it would have had it on any school of Design—non cosi buono—.

257. 28 February 1933, to Mary Bell, Taormina, Sicily

Dear Miss Bell:

The enclosed I thought was going in a letter Edie was writing you some time ago—I find she didn't send it—so I am. We are still in Sicily but expect to go up through some of the Italian cities soon, and then sail to England & be there for a month or so & then home in

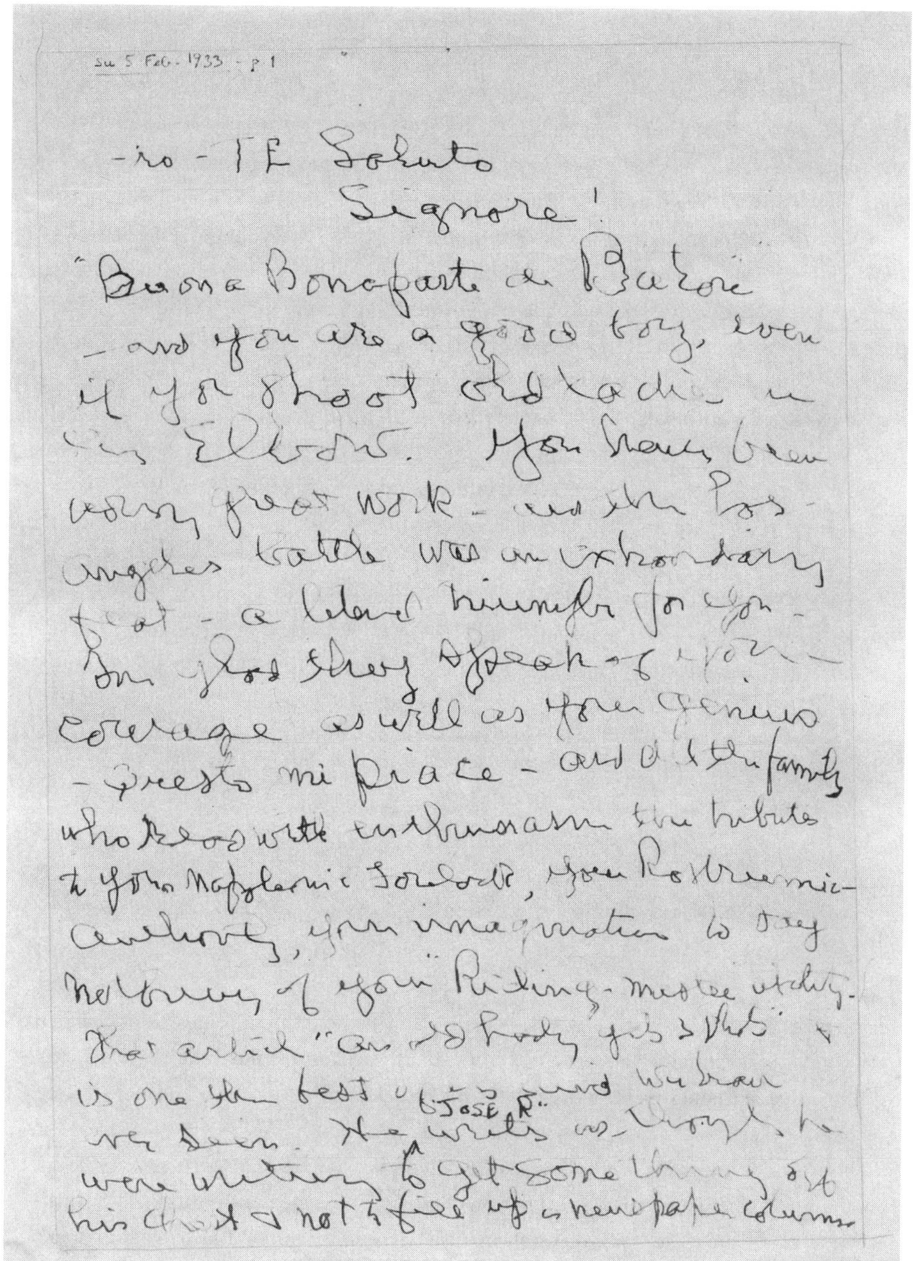

5 February 1933, to Nicolas Slonimsky.

June or about.—We are sorry not to go to Germany again—but I'm afraid we are poor travelers—We hope it won't be long before we shall see you in New York.

With best wishes from the family

I am

sincerely

Chas. E. Ives

258. 28 March 1933, Harmony Ives to John Becker, Rome

My dear Mr. Becker,

Henry Cowell sent us a copy of your article on Mr. Ives and I want to tell you how much Mr. Ives appreciates your writing it and how pleasant it was to me to have him presented as you did it—mentioning his truly great qualities so warmly. You will know how much it means to me after so many years of lack of appreciation to have younger men of insight & sympathy write about him. Mr. Ives asks me to ask you to send copies of the article to the three people whose addresses I will add at the end of my letter[16] & he would like a dozen copies reserved for him until he gets back to Redding, Connecticut, c/o Richard G. Ives at any time & Mr. Ives could send you a cheque for them later.[17]

We have had a good year & fortunately kept well. Sicily wasn't so successful as we had cold, unpleasant weather most of the three months we were there. Now we are enjoying Rome's brilliant sun & seeing so much to interest and stir us that the days are too short. We go on tomorrow to Florence, thro' Assisi & Perugia and Sienna—don't those names thrill one?

We hope you and your family have kept well & that the baby flourishes. Edith sends her best wishes to you. She is enjoying her "History of Art" class in the actual.

With warm regard from Mr. Ives & myself & renewed expression of appreciation I am

Yours always sincerely
Harmony Ives

259. May 1933, to Nicolas Slonimsky, London

Dear "Nap"—con Forelock:

Thank you very much for your letters,—which we all enjoyed. Our plans were changed somewhat—we wanted to see more of Italy—but travelling around, hotels, etc. don't seem to agree with me somehow—so we came more directly to England. Will probably stay here, "quiet & slow" until we sail—probably in July.

I hope things are going well with you. When do you get back from Russia and are you going there? Is Russia a musical nation—like Italy—I mean—is Russia a musical nation?—or do they like nice voices!—and is a "Serenade" good? I hear from Henry occasionally—he is now in Menlo Park and says that America is "a Musical Nation! (—out there)—I didn't intend to get this old subject in this letter—but an article in an English paper this morning "Are we a musical nation" brought it! I'm sorry. There is nothing in a musical nation—not even music!—for a nation is only a nation—but a good cigar is et al!

16. There are four addresses appended to the letter: William Lyon Phelps, the *Yale Alumni Weekly*, Julian A. Ripley, and J. Moss Ives.

17. This is Ives's nephew.

It seems a long time since we've seen you—and it is. I hope next year things will work out better for all of us. Just now it seems a bad time for carrying on "the work"—all armies are apparently out of "breath & supplies"—but another year we must resume.

It was a disappointment not to get through Paris again & see your mother—Mrs. Ives says she hopes she may be spared—till we may have another visit with that "Grande Dame"

We all send kindest wishes to you both and hope you have both kept well

Yours as ever
Chas. E. Ives

P.S. Am not sure, but think before leaving I told you that in cleaning house preparatory to being away so long, I found several of the old scores, etc.—from which some of the songs were taken—I had forgotten some of them or thought they were not kept—so before arranging any songs it would be better to wait until we can get together again & look over these old manuscripts. I also found some other things or parts of them—that might do for short—chamber pieces, some of only 4 or 5 instruments—among them were a set of half dozen pieces called "Cartoons" "A 3 minute Yale-Princeton Football Game" "Gyp the Blood & Hearst! which is worst?" "The Gen. Slocum Disaster" "Mike Donlin at the Bat" etc. "Central Park in the Dark" Some of these on topics of those days—but why not! "D.K.E. & Phi. U. Calcium Light Night Yale Campus

When we get back will have Hanke copy what he can—they were mostly in lead pencil, some rather indistinct—I think you will like some of them—one thing they won't take much rehearsing & only a very few players.

In looking these over, I was impressed with this—that I now have good advice for young composers—"If you write anything you think is good, copy it out in ink"—"If you write anything you think is no good, copy it out in ink!

Auf wiedersehen—but not yet—"Good bye"—and if you go to Russia come back before sunset—for it's long since we've seen you around the table.

260. June 1933, to John Becker, London

Dear Becker:

I hope now you are better and that erysipelas has quite walked off. You have enough difficult problems to handle without that one of bad health besides—but that is only temporary—only a foul ball—you're now batting .460 again. Mrs. Ives wrote you when we received your "article" how very greatly we appreciated what you said, and I want to send just a line to thank you directly and sincerely. I would have written before but my arms & eyes have bothered for a spell.

We are in England again, where we will stay until we sail home the first of next month. We've had a good year on the whole reviving—interesting—sometimes— But we will be glad to turn again home. America is quite a good place—even for Americans,—to be in.

You must let me send the enclosed just to help out a little in the incidentals etc., which are always more than expected, in the work you are doing & in connection with the concerts. There are always more parts to copy, rehearsals & extras, as well as printing, postage etc. that mount up to more than one will estimate—and I know——I've been through it. You will understand—and let me do whatever I can, at any time.

Edie asks me to tell you that Sarah received an honor scholarship, at the end of her first year in Barnard. Mrs. Ives, Edie, and I send our very kindest remembrance to you & Mrs. Becker and to the Children, including B[ruce] Cowell B.—ad cogitando—

I am, sincerely
Chas E. Ives

261. July 1933, to T. Carl Whitmer

Dear Mr. Whitmer:

Back again—under the right tree, the cat sleeping on the hearth—the wind's in the right place & so are we!

You and Mrs. Whitmer must come over soon,—it will be fine to see you again

For the next week or ten days I have to go into the city more or less for sessions with doctors, dentists etc. & don't always know ahead the days I'll be here—but after first of the month when the Dr's get through with me—or rather when I get through with them, for they never get through with you—I'll call you up—and we hope you can get over here—it's long since we had a family meeting.

Mrs. Ives & Edie join me in best wishes,

Sincerely
Chas. E. Ives

• • •

In the late summer of 1934 Ives again sailed for England in an attempt to revive his health. As he writes to Henry Cowell, he is somewhat dubious of the prospects for the voyage.

262. June or July 1934, to Henry Cowell

Dear Henry:

We have decided to sail over to England & stay there probably 2 months or so[18] The only drawback to going now is that we won't see you again as soon as we had expected this fall. But Mrs. Ives and others of the family & backed by doctor, seem to think it's the best thing to do now. I'll have to admit that I haven't been getting any better to say the least, for some

18. See Letter 148.

time, and the trip before seemed to do us all good. Anyway for good or otherwise we are sailing Aug. 10 on a 10-day one cabin boat. . . .

263. August 1934, to Henry Cowell, on the S.S. *Pennland* en route to Scotland

Dear H:

On our way, in the middle of the ocean—but still on board. This is a slow ship, which we like—and am beginning to learn how to sleep and eat again.

Suppose it won't be long before you are starting east again. It's a real disappointment that we won't see you in Redding—and we hope the fall work will go well with you. Just before leaving Unc. Sam got quite decent & sent me some hundred dollars—saying I'd paid too much income tax some while ago. —So it seems to me that "N[ew] M[usic]" is the place for that—Give my best to Becker if you stop there, he is doing good work under great strain—& so are you!

—with our best to you ever,

sincerely
Chas. E. Ives

264. 12–16 August 1934, to John Becker, on the S.S. *Pennland* en route to Scotland

Aug 12

Your letter came almost at the moment we were leaving the house for the wharf.

We are now off the "Banks" & the Gulls are giving us up. We stopped a[t] Halifax this A.M.—a slow boat which we like—and I'm beginning to know how to sleep again,—& join [?] all good sailors.

Tues. Aug 14

A N.E. wind this morning—a good rock—& out of sight of land.

Thank you for being willing to take care of "Gen B[ooth]" score If you want I will look it over.

Perhaps I might think of something from the old score that might go in—but I really don't think it will make much difference—if it were ever published in future years, I could go over it then—John B's way will be alright for me.

Aug 16

A fog through the night—the ship's fog horn whistle a low tuba—around low G or G-flat—& sharp when the wind blows.

Am glad you think the "W.B" ["Washington's Birthday"] will go well—There are minor things I might suggest—I played it some years ago & having no bells or Jew's H[arp]—played these on a piano & seemed to go well enough—a piano can kind of slide up taking off a "J.H." Also had a small drum with snares taken off, play in the Barn Dance, an even quarter-note beat throughout the part—which makes it sometimes on the beat &

sometimes on after beats, which sounded well & also helped the men get the rhythms more decisively—hit them rather than slur them "pretty" Anybody could play this drum, without notes—Young John could—even Toscaninini! However do anything you think best. One other thing & I'll stop suggestin'. The title "Washington's Birthday" when played separately (without the whole holiday set) seems to cause misunderstanding—people think it has to do with Mt Vernon—national history, etc.—when in fact it hasn't any thing to do much with "George" except that he made a "winter holiday."

I'd call it on the program just "A Winter Holiday"—"in the country" or "in the Back Woods" if you thought best. And the program notes should be printed for the audience—under wise [*sic*] the "take offs" of the "old songs" at the end & jigs etc. don't make much sense. It's just an attempted picture of a country boy's Holiday—program music may be a low form or reason—but that's what this piece is—eat it or not—!

By all means have your friend in the orchestra do what copying is necessary—please give our love to all the Beckers, big and little.

Ever yours,
Chas. E. Ives

I find I can just as well send the enclosed now as later. It will help more now extras parts etc. So many incidentals.

265. September or October 1934, to Henry Cowell, England

Dear Henry:

We are in the Cheshire Country—Chester Cathedral in the distance—have good weather & some fine scenery, but the trip hasn't worked out especially well, healthwise as we hoped, & are coming back sooner than planned—probably in a month or so. I can't tell exactly now but will say, at least, will arrange $300. for your work at the school, etc. between now & the end of the year—and I hope more. The enclosed [check] am dating Oct. 16 to be on safe side—& the rest probably in November or so.

Please give our best to Frau Schmolke.[19] We will be sorry if we don't see her before she leaves. Hoping things go well—ever yours

Chas E. Ives

• • •

The last European trip, in the summer of 1938, came at a time when both Charles and Harmony were in poor health.[20] Like the previous trip in 1934, this one was limited to England and Scotland and featured little of the touring and sightseeing that marked the grander voyage of 1932–33.

19. See Letter 255 and note 14, above.
20. See Letter 170.

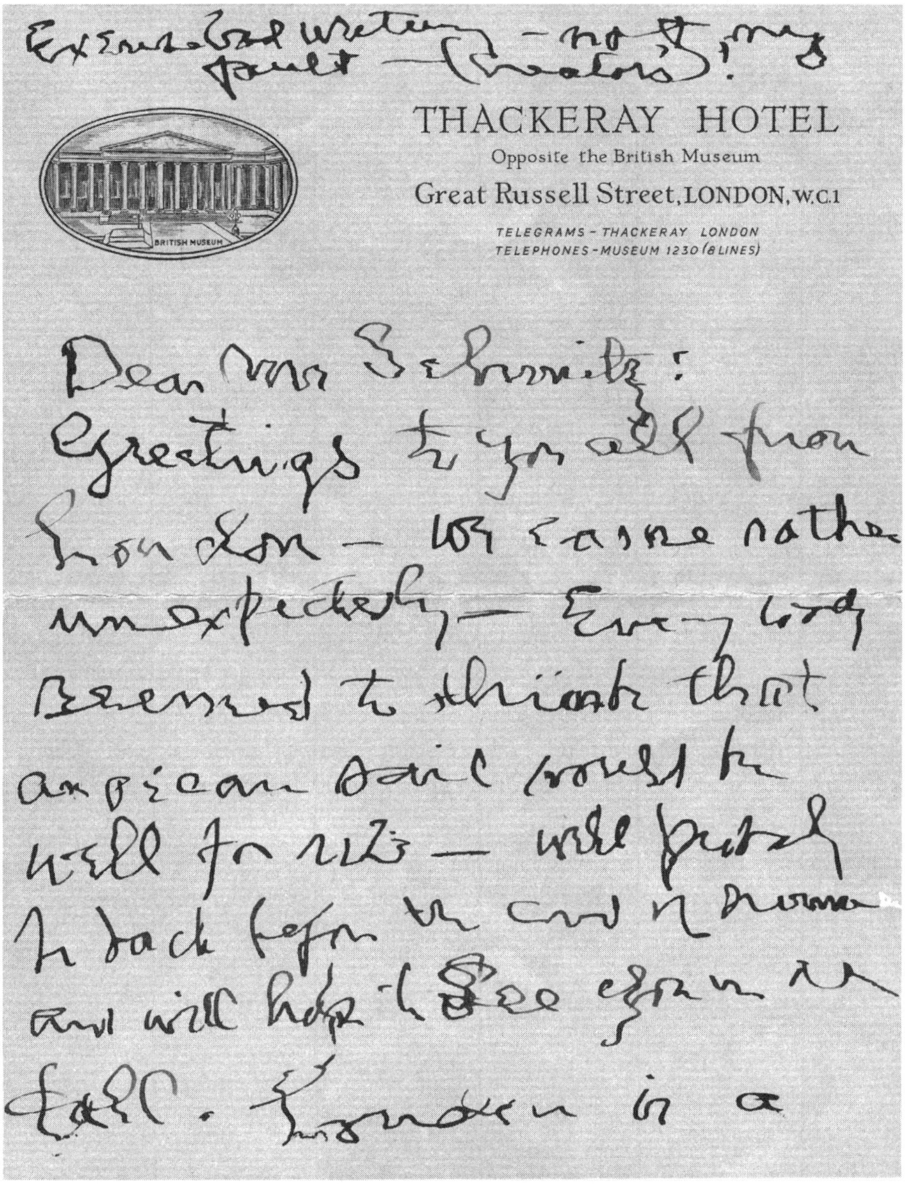

Excuse bad writing — not my fault — (Creator's)!

THACKERAY HOTEL
Opposite the British Museum
Great Russell Street, LONDON, W.C.1
TELEGRAMS - THACKERAY LONDON
TELEPHONES - MUSEUM 1230 (8 LINES)

Dear Mr Schmitz:
Greetings to you all from London — We came rather unexpectedly — Everybody seemed to think that an ocean sail would be well for us — will probably be back before the end of summer and will hope to see you in the fall. London is a

22 June 1938, first sketch for Ives to E. Robert Schmitz.

266. 9 May 1938, Harmony Ives to Charlotte Ruggles

Dear Charlotte,

Carl's note—so characteristic & so delightful—made us happy. We are so very glad to hear of his improvement & the likelihood of his being "better than ever."[21] I hope the la-

21. See Letter 344.

bor of deciphering Charlie's note won't be too much for him!—Charlie is frightfully used up—he tried seeing a few people & it just doesn't work.

We are sailing for Glasgow on the 18th so won't be in Redding until later in the season. I imagine that except for Carl's illness you have had a good winter. We think [the Ruggleses' son] Micah's plan excellent—good for him. We have had a marvelous month of April—sunshine & warmth & the vegetation ahead of anything I ever remember—now we begin to need rain.

I hope you will have a good trip home and that your summer will be a good one.

With our love & best wishes

As ever yours
Harmony Ives

267. 22 June 1938, to E. Robert Schmitz, London

Dear Mr. Schmitz:

Greetings to you all from London—we came rather unexpectedly. Everybody including the doctors (who are usually right especially when they're wrong) seemed to think an ocean sail would be well for us—(personally Redding has it on Europe!)—We'll be home before the end of summer and will hope to see you in the fall.

London is a "nice" place for "nice" music!—Rollo says—(you know those Rollo lilies who write nice pieces about nice music in the newspapers). 5 columns to say Toscannini played that nice C maj-Sym "real nice"—but Rollo forgot to say that it was the 587629th time Tossy had played it—and he knew every note "real nice"—Believe it—or "note"!

I do hope things are going well with you, and that the summer classes will be all you deserve them to be. I am very glad to send the enclosed. Mrs. Ives & Edith send kindest remembrances to Mrs. Schmitz and Monique.

Please excuse these snake tracks—I can't see 'em well enough to see how bad they are—<u>not my</u> fault—<u>Creator's!</u>

· 7 ·

EDITORS AND PERFORMERS (1933–1944)

Throughout the 1930s and 1940s Ives continued to work with many of the musicians who had begun to champion his work. He also developed important new relationships with the musicians who inquired about him or his scores. As performances of his works became more common, the pace of organizing his manuscripts and editing them for performance and publication picked up. Meanwhile, Ives's health continued its cyclic pattern of good periods followed by slumps in which work on music and almost all activity became nearly impossible. As he entered his seventh decade, however, his overall health declined, and he became even more reliant on editors such as John Kirkpatrick and Lou Harrison.

The following selection of letters focuses substantially on important figures in this part of the story of Ives's music. Along with Kirkpatrick and Harrison are George Roberts, Ives's trusted copyist, and Radiana Pazmor and Mordecai Bauman, who made some of the first recordings of Ives's songs. Others who appear are the musicologist and composer Charles Seeger; the composers Wallingford Riegger and Lehman Engel; the conductors Serge Koussevitzky and Artur Rodzinski; and E. Power Biggs, the organist who performed Ives's "Variations on 'America'" in 1948 for the first time since Ives himself had played it nearly fifty years earlier.

· · ·

John Kirkpatrick resumed his correspondence with Ives in 1933. Although it would still be several years before he performed the entire *Concord* Sonata, his interest in Ives's works was growing and his desire to edit them for performance becoming more distinct. The partial copy of *114 Songs*, mentioned below, belonged to Aaron Copland. It was incomplete because Ives had removed individual songs from several of his copies of the songbook. Later, when there were no more intact copies, Ives sent out several of these incomplete ones along with his regret that a complete copy could not be found.

268. 11 December 1933, from John Kirkpatrick, Greenwich, Connecticut

My dear Mr. Ives,

Perhaps you remember me as the friend of Miss Heyman to whom you so generously sent a copy of "Concord, Mass." with the essays back in 1927.[1] My gratitude grows

1. Kirkpatrick refers to the pianist Katherine Heyman; see Letter 197.

with each degree of penetration. I am slow at these things and still play only the "Alcotts."

Last night at the Dalcroze Institute, Henry Cowell told me that you were in America, at home in West Redding, which I was very glad to hear, as I imagined you were still in Europe. I would like very much to see you some time.

I shall have the honor to accompany "Where the Eagle . . . " next Sunday at the League (Ada MacLeash is to do the same group of songs as at Yaddo). So I have for the moment Aaron's incomplete copy of the *114 songs*, and though I have often played at them before, I must say that this renewed acquaintance has been quite a revelation.

I have even been copying them out.—it all started a couple of months ago when I got so put out with the page turning in the Indians (Cos Cob ed.) that I copied it out just to see what it sounded like when you got it all together,—and as I hardly ever copy anything without a few orthographic changes, a whole set of problems was opened up before I could decide what I thought was the clearest way to write it down (No changes in note values—just what you might call the optical presentation). So it's gone on that way and I've done 13 of them. I imagine it's the sort of thing everybody's been bothering your music with for a long time, and that you're not particularly interested in it, being occupied (thank God) with its inner substance and creative development,—but still I suspect you might be amused to see the pretty frames I've drawn around them. The Things our Fathers Loved came out particularly well.

Miss Heyman is here in Greenwich for the Winter. We were discussing the songs day before yesterday—with enthusiasm.

Cowell mentioned you were moving in to town next month. How long will you be at West Redding? I thought I might drive up some day, if that would be convenient.

Hoping to have the pleasure of meeting you some time soon, I remain with best wishes,

Yours very truly,
John Kirkpatrick

• • •

As Ives's collaboration with Kirkpatrick began in earnest, he continued to work closely with Nicolas Slonimsky. The next three letters center on the preparation of the Orchestral Set no. 1 for publication. After a critic in California commented on Slonimsky's "Napoleonic forelock," Ives, who enjoyed both the humor and the conquering heroic power conveyed by the image, began opening letters to him with "Dear Nap," or "Dear Nap—con forelock."[2] Their jokes aside, these letters focus on substantial corrections in the proofs for this work. Ives wrote in great detail on editorial problems caused by his myriad sketches and revisions and by his tendency to change his mind at the last minute. Slonimsky complicated matters by insisting that the passage in "Putnam's Camp" in which two bands pass one another be notated in different meters rather than in the highly syncopated but monometric notation Ives originally used. That Ives would eventually compromise on the notation of his own piece shows his flexibil-

2. See also Letters 256 and 259.

ity, his respect for Slonimsky, and his desire for publication. At the end of Letter 269, Ives returns to the idea of having Slonimsky edit and orchestrate the choral versions of "December" and "The New River" that the two had discussed in passing as early as 1930 (see the introduction to Letter 220). These editions were completed and performed on 15 April 1934.[3] The programming suggestions that Ives makes prefacing the discussion of these two works show both his sensitivity to affect and his practicality in consideration of required rehearsal time and resources.

269. Ca. 3 January 1934, to Nicolas Slonimsky

Dear Nap:

I take my pen?[4] in hand to write you a long tiresome letter about why A is quite natural & 2/4 nice but wrong—but Happy New Year—first—to you all!

The engraver, when he sees my marks on the proofs of the II movement, which I'm mailing you today—may get quite sore & I wouldn't blame him. I should have gone through this especially the strings before it was sent to him. I've done the best I could, to straighten it out—& I hope you & he can make out the corrections etc. For instance:

(1) If div. bow marks up & down are in one measure & then only the "up" in the next, the "down" players might not know what to do always—keep on—or stop—All these things I've tried to fix with the least trouble to the engraver. But he may know of a better way.

(2) If the parts are to be made from the score, as you suggested all the marks, ff, [*decrescendo*], rit. etc. etc will have to go in each staff—a great many are in—but not all—for instance the "rallen—" just before (G).

(3) In II movement, a piccolo often plays with the Flute sometimes "unis," sometimes, oct. higher. I tried to show this by a "note" over Fl part. But a separate (in II) "Pic" part should be made for the player.

(4) In some places, an extra player on the piano is better—so have put at beginning Piano (for 2 players ad lib)—the passages, etc. can be suggested in the conductors note, to go with parts—I do[n't] like too many observations in score.

#(5) Horn parts were all left out on pages—53–54 (didn't try to copy them in engraver can take them from the photo score

(6) 2 measures before Q, would put in the regular parts (not the "ossia"—or both

(7) At H.P 35,—where the 2 bands play, Your plan of the separate time for each is a good and great improvement. But I think it is important to show in score, where each fits into the other—so have kept piano as it was, with dotted lines up to show how II orches stands with I.

(8) Have kept the first 5 meas of II as it was, so the drum parts, will keep B[ass] D[rum] on main beats,—the rest of the orchestra miss the beats.

There are other things but can't think of them now. When they send the corrected

3. Sinclair, *Descriptive Catalogue*, 310.

4. Ives was writing in pencil and probably included the question mark to make a joke out of the figure of speech.

proofs back, I wish they could be with black notes on white paper, these white notes blur my eyes—& I can't work as steadily as on the white and black, which is not very steadily at that. Am not starting over the III proofs for a little while—to give the eyes a let up.

What concert is to be in March, which Varèse spoke to you about? It's very good of him to have you play something of mine. I might suggest 2 short but active songs & the quiet—At Night (Theatre orchestra

(1) The New River (p 42 Henry's edition (about 40 seconds)

(2) December P. 40. (About 30 seconds

(3) "At Night" ["In the Night"] 3rd movement Theater Orches Set (New Music Edition (about 2 minutes)

This gives a contrasting group—short (about 4 minutes) not many players, not many rehearsals, & not very expensive!

The "December" ought to be sung by 3 to 10 fat basses (raucous voiced) & the (New River) by 1 or 2 men or 1 man & a lady (top A#). "At Night without a voice.

But the "New R" & "December" will have to have the old scores copied and parts made (you have I think photos, of these which you might look over. When we get back will have this done. As I remember there are some measures in the old scores that are rather indistinct, but not many—& it won't take long to have copies made. Also I think "New River" takes 2 saxophones, but one & a Trombone would do it.

Good night,
C.E.I.

• • •

Slonimsky's reply gives a clearer picture of the editing process for this work and shows his tenacity in holding onto his bimetric scheme, which was tied directly to his ability to conduct simultaneous, separate meters. The conversations with Schoenberg mentioned here may have been one of the influences that prompted him to characterize Ives as "a great man."[5]

270. 5 January 1934, from Nicolas Slonimsky, Boston

Dear Mr. Ives:—

Your proofs of the second movement arrived today. All your corrections are very clear, and there will be no trouble, except (and through my fault) before Q, where I took out the 11/8 measure, believing that the optional cut was intended as definite. However, a page can be inserted, and the two preceding measures broadened in print so that the extra page will consist of the three measures of the horn and the trumpet before Q. I will speak to the engraver, and I hope it can be done. There is no difficulty, of course, in printing the Ossia parts as in the score.

5. On 17 November 1953 Gertrude Schoenberg sent a memo in which her late husband had called Ives "a great man—a composer" (CIP, 31/17).

I suggest the enclosed compromise in that famous place where two bands clash with the second viola. I fear that if the piano is adjusted to the main rhythm, then the entire idea of conducting two rhythms will have to be abandoned,—the piano being the mainstay of the second rhythm, as in the fourth of July. You may think I have an awful nerve arguing with you about your own work! But such is the fate of composers, philosophers and pathfinders, that their followers and interpreters end by telling them what they ought to do! In my eager desire to be a 100% Ivesite, I am obsessed by the demon consistency, asking myself, "if there are two separate rhythms in the Fourth of July, why not here?"

I will await your reaction to the version as in the enclosed two pages, before giving these particular pages to the engraver. It seems to me that by printing the "adjusted" part below the piano part, all ambiguity will be avoided,—also the pianist can follow either part, according to whether the conductor beats two rhythms, or one. If only the original notation is printed, the pianist, (who usually plays from the score) will not be able to follow the second rhythm at all, or will have to write out the second rhythm part—which would mean trouble at rehearsals, etc.

I restored the second viola as it was in the original.

Two more questions: 1) 2 bars before K, I would take E-flat out of the bassoon part,—[*he gives an example, D against E-flat, with the second circled and marked, "out"*] this is the only place where two bassoons are required, which seems unnecessary. I also took out one bassoon note in the beginning of the third movement in order to make the work playable with one bassoon only (in case of performance by a chamber orchestra).

2) Two bars before S, in the right hand of the piano, shouldn't there be an E instead of an F?—easier to play, also it will help the E of the second violins and the oboe.

When do you expect to be in New York? I'd like to time my trip to New York as soon as you are installed there. We will settle all the remaining problems concerning the proofs, and also go over the orchestrations of your songs (which I will submit to you then).

Arnold Schoenberg is in Boston,—he is teaching at a conservatory here. He gave a lecture yesterday, speaking in German and in a sort of Austrian English with French words,—I acted as chief interpreter and had a grand time. Dorothy had a good time, too, watching the show. Schoenberg has seen your scores in the New Music Edition,—he also read my Berlin criticisms, although he was not present at the concerts. I will show him the proofs of the Three Places,—he seems genuinely interested in your works. Hope to get him to visit Electra,—he is here with his wife and small daughter, and he talks like a human being not only about music.

Electra sends her regards. She is getting terribly fat,—she weighs over 16 pounds,—and she is not quite 5 months of age. Dorothy is lecturing in Providence,—She is very successful.

Greetings to the family
Nicolas Slonimsky

P.S. Please, don't work too hard on the third movement, but do let me know if the enclosed pages are o.k. (That is with an ossia line for the piano.)

• • •

The extent to which his health forced Ives to rely on editors like Slonimsky is clear in this letter. Ives's nephew Chester was his brother Moss's youngest son. He lived with the Iveses at 164 East 74th Street for several months in 1934.[6]

271. 11 January 1934, to Nicolas Slonimsky

Dear Interpreter for tongues & Sounding Brass (not the Psalmist kind—but all nice music)

Do you beat 2 rhythms when interpreting a lecture? We would have liked to have seen the setting. We're back in this gas-grained city. If we didn't have this house on our hands, we wouldn't come attall [*sic*]. When are you coming down? We hope soon—only we're sorry but just now, as our nephew is living with us & in the only spare room—but we're having a room fixed for him in the attic (my floor), which Mrs. I thinks will be ready about the first of next month—as they have to run heating pipes, etc. up—but if you come down now—the next time you must stay with us.

Am returning the 2 pages—This (ossia piano) way is good, I think would go ahead with it.

Haven't started going over the III yet. Haven't been quite in shape for a week or so & getting back to this "circus" doesn't help. Will you please ask them to send me another proof of the III in black & white (& charge it to me)—after I look at those white notes on green for about 10 mins, they all start to move around—like "rice" in green "soup" to my eyes—but you are a good boy to take so much trouble and we hope to see you soon.

Our love to all the family and Electra and Matre and Padre.

C.E.I.

I haven't seen anybody yet—& won't until I can get up to—an 84 + a quarter note—except you.

• • •

In a sense John Kirkpatrick's timing couldn't have been better: just as Ives was forced to rely increasingly on editors and interpreters for his manuscripts, the pianist became more and more interested in performing, editing, and understanding Ives's works. Their collaboration became the most substantial one of Ives's later years.

272. 5 January 1934, from John Kirkpatrick, Greenwich, Connecticut

My Dear Mr. Ives,

I was very happy to receive Mrs. Ives's letter last month—please thank her for me—and very sorry to know that you are not well. You have my best wishes for a happy new year and speedy release from bodily ailments.

6. For Chester's recollections of life with his uncle, see Vivan Perlis, ed., *Charles Ives Remembered: An Oral History* (1974; reprint, New York: Da Capo Press, 1994), 84–88. See also Letter 318.

I still go on making pretty copies of the songs—and that activity has lately spread itself to certain passages of Emerson—in fact I have decided quite resolutely to learn the whole sonata, and am going at it in regular piano-practice-fashion, which I have never done before except for the Alcotts. A few passages in Emerson still elude me as to their rhythmical nature—in this connection I quote from your letter of Oct. 10, 1927:—"But perhaps what Miss Heyman referred to was a transcription of the first movement which is in more playable shape than some of the printed score. As soon as I can get to it will have a few photographic copies made." Do you happen to have one handy? and could you send me one? I imagine it would clear up many of my uncertainties. I remember seeing Miss Heyman's copy in Paris (last time she came back, she left many things there intending to return shortly, but has been here ever since—I was in the same quandry [*sic*])—and at that time I hadn't achieved any intimate contact with the piece so didn't study it particularly. I would like to play some of it for you as soon as it begins to sound.

Hoping to have the pleasure of making your acquaintance sometime soon, I remain, very truly yours,

John Kirkpatrick

• • •

Although Ives had promised to send Kirkpatrick the Four Transcriptions from "Emerson" years before, he actually did so early in 1934. The degree to which they differed from the printed sonata movement baffled Kirkpatrick, who prized order and believed that it was the duty of the performer to arrive at a single, fixed interpretation that best suited the intentions of the composer of any work he intended to perform. The variety in Ives's treatment of musical material in the multiple versions of "Emerson" left the pianist at a loss and stimulated his desire to discuss the piece with Ives.

273. 18 January 1934, from John Kirkpatrick, Greenwich, Connecticut

My dear Mr. Ives,

I have been meaning to write you ever since the arrival last week of the sumptuous copy of the 4 Transcriptions from Emerson. I am deeply touched that apparently you had the copy specially made, and also quite sorry to have put you to that trouble. My delay was simply that I wanted to say something about it, and I must confess being quite mystified as to the significance and relation of the arrangements to the original.—evidently I hadn't realized the extent to which your music may be considered in a state of flux, so to speak. Emerson had always seemed a perfectly satisfactory piece, having come to that degree of focus where its form becomes recognizable and strong,—in fact I consider it one of the most interesting modern variants of the old sonata machine, just as valid as Liszt's or any other. So it was rather a shock to find it could so readily be dismembered and reassembled by its own maker. It all opens up a great many avenues of consideration which I would like to have the pleasure of discussing with you sometime.

In the meantime let me thank you deeply and enthusiastically. I am sure it will prove as rich for progressive penetration as its original. Please accept my continued best wishes that your full health may be soon restored.

Very sincerely,
John Kirkpatrick

• • •

The following letter to Cowell shows Ives's dedication to Slonimsky even as it acknowledges some of the latter's faults as a conductor, exposed in a performance of "In the Night" and Ruggles's "Portals" at a concert in New York's Town Hall.[7] This letter also contains the genesis of the plan to make a recording of works by Ives and Ruggles.

274. 27–30 April 1934, to Henry Cowell

Dear Henry:

I would have written about the concerts etc.—before, but have been in a kind of rotten dark [?] for a month or so, can't seem to do anything that I want to—except cuss—We're going to Redding this week & that will help. I didn't get out to the concert or rehearsals—I can't make out whether they were good or bad—Mrs. Ives & a few others I've heard from are not very enthusiastic.—Nicolas S. had as usual too much of a job at the last minute—all players nervous singers frightened—too long a program etc. but the thing that made me sorest is that no records could be made.

In order to have something done at once, we suggested while Carl Ruggles was here on 1 side 4 ¼—Ruggles "Angels" 2 m[inutes] & my "In the Night" 2 m other side Roldan[8]—but something about the combinations [of] players [and] time (I don't know the details) & also both Carl R. & Becker, and also Nic. S. thought it better to have a whole side to both Carl R's and to mine, instead of crowding them on one—Roldan can be done later when the different instruments are together.

So it has been decided to do as soon as possible

1 side Lilacs Ruggles about 4 min

Other side 2 mins Barn Dance from Holiday Symphony 2 mins In the Night Ives

These are going to be done & done right—and as soon as possible, probably in a week or two. The $200 that Riegger has may not cover this job and whatever more is needed I might as well give to Riegger directly and we'll just charge it to the "surplus."

7. In a letter to Becker (excerpted in Letter 148) Ives elaborated on Slonimsky's performance. Its chief fault was that the main melody in the horn was played a fifth too low because the part was notated at pitch rather than in the standard horn transposition. This explains Ives's concern about the part in Letter 277, below. Interestingly, Becker, who was at the concert, didn't notice the mistake; he wrote to Ives on 16 April that Slonimsky had done "In the Night" very well.

8. Ives refers to Amadeo Roldán, the Cuban violinist and composer.

Monday

Started this letter Friday—I had to knock off yesterday & Sat. [on] account of my eyes. I'm sorry it takes so long to get a letter on its way. I hope things are going well & that "Sun Treader" is up on his way. If the records cost only $200,—there will be at least $100 probably $150, of surplus a/c which is the balance after the records). I can send after may 15.

What I know of the Pan Am situation is mostly hearsay—Have not seen Varèse for 2 months or so. I couldn't see Weiss's enthusiasm for him at first—& now Weiss can't see it apparently. There are 2 matters (more of principle, than procedure) that I as a member of the association, will take up with him directly—probably this week. I also hear there is a big deficit—poor management—they (V[arèse] & R[iegger]) will have to take care of that themselves—Carl R was in last week we had a fine time cussing out the elements [?]

Sincerely,
Chas. E. Ives

• • •

Wallingford Riegger (1885–1961) coordinated the recording of pieces by Ives and Ruggles described in the previous letter. Ives acted as patron and musical advisor to Riegger as he hired the conductor and decided on repertoire for the record. Stubbornly loyal, Ives insisted that Slonimsky conduct his pieces and subsequently provided extra money for him to be compensated fully for the job.

275. 10 May 1934, from Wallingford Riegger, New Music Quarterly Recordings, New York

Dear Mr. Ives:

After much debating and a vain attempt to get Eugene Goossens for the recordings, I at last decided on Charles Lichter. Lichter was the concertmaster on our 2 concerts and moreover has done considerable conducting himself. He knows the works—better than Slonimsky, I am convinced, and moreover is in direct touch with all the men. He has conducted the group before and says he will be able to get the strings in an extra rehearsal.

The point is this: it is impossible to get the men for less than minimum rates, and the lowest possible estimate for the number of men and the hours of rehearsing would bring the expense of the musicians to $350. In addition to this there would be the pay of Lichter himself, who as contractor should receive twice as much as one of the players, in other words $50, for which he would do the conducting.

So far I have not been definite about his going ahead, altho he has the scores and parts, as I wished to find out whether you thought you would undertake this—

Please let me know at once, as the thing should be done next week if at all, some of the men intend to leave the city after that.

I have great confidence in Lichter. He is very musical and Varèse intends to have him conduct a concert for the Pan Ams in the Fall.

As for the records—your two numbers would be on one side, and Lilacs and I think

"Toys" on the other. "Toys" (Ruggles) was sung last year by Judith Litante very well, I thought, and would fill out the record very well.

Hoping to hear from you soon, and that you are having a good rest, I am

Sincerely—
Wallingford Riegger

276. 13 May 1934, sketch for Ives to Wallingford Riegger

Dear Mr. Riegger:

Your letter came yesterday & also one from Henry C—which says, Henry writes. . . .

I don't like to go back on N. Slonimsky after all the good work he has done—just because he ~~don't~~ happened to be in a batting slump in our concert. And I don't feel I know enough about the doctor to give orders. The one advantage in having the concert master of the men do it, is that he (as you say) knows the men & can get more rehearing out of them which is <u>all important.</u> Nicolas might conduct the "Barn Dance" which he knows, & is more difficult [?] for a stranger & the other man Lichter do the rest—as Carl R. apparently has it in for NS, ~~or as Henry~~ & you & Weiss might take a hand, if you would like it, which I do not know. I think with Henry NS ought to have his name on our record—at least. Another thing as that Mrs. I & I remember, & also something that Henry said—Carl R may not want the song "Toys" on. I think it important to be sure that he does. ~~Perhaps~~— as we ~~remember~~ recall he said something to make us think that he wasn't exactly ~~enthusiastic~~ satisfied with "Toys" as such. He may have another short piece he [would] rather go in.

All the above are just suggestions—based on the premises, which I don't know all about.

277. May 1934, undated and incomplete sketch for Ives to Wallingford Riegger

Dear Mr. Riegger:

The ~~mail & telegrams are slow in getting here, but hope you got my~~ letter in time.

In writing Sunday, I forgot to say that who ever conducts that "In the Night" should see that the horn part is played right—that is—the notes written are <u>actual</u> pitch. If you think it necessary, you might get somebody to copy it transposed for the F. horn & send me the bill.

(1) Also on the 3rd staff from the top marked I think—(X)—(I haven't a score here) is a part for one or two violins (con sor), a harp & a flute (which plays small notes (loco)—this is just one of the "night sounds" & should appear as such & <u>not</u> played heavily—

—Weiss, I think, played this part with 2 V's "off stage" & he got the effect, I heard. Those playing the part should see the score sent sat[urday] playing from this if possible—Weiss says he has copies.

(2) Also—In one of the scores, there is a violin part, written in lead pencil 2 m [illegible] throughout. 2 violins play this con sordini (see parts). This was in the M.S.S. score as one of the "night sounds" but left out of the published score. (It shouldn't have been).

(3) Also, the line, solo cello beginning of hymn on bottom of 3rd page ~~I think,~~ suggests the hymn "Abide with me" should be distinctly here, ~~slightly~~ over all ~~the rest~~ but not "loud" It wasn't heard last time. A trombone with a good lip (who knows how to play quietly yet clearly, may be used with the cello. However the conductor ought to know (position of the players etc.) ~~how to do it~~ best—the size of the room has something to do with it—I played some years ago, in an outdoor concert & found the trombone a help (muted went well (If no organ basses

The whole piece is but an attempt to get a simple picture of darkness, silence, the loneliness of an old man who has lost everything but his faith & night sounds perspective sounds and sounds in perspective

I'm sorry to bother you with all this detail—but it may save time in the end.

I hope so.

The piece is but an attempt to get a short picture of

& represents the loneliness of

(basses should be sustained and substantial but not loud

P.S. The other piece Barn Dance about 1.45 min I think, should go first on the record—Nicolas S understands what is to be played—but it may be just as well to write it. It starts at L (after measures ending the ~~slower~~ first & slower part of the first movement) then a pause & the dance starts allegro & plays through second page about half down the page & stop on a chord just before the ~~coda of~~ Andante & coda. I'm quite sure, the beginning & end is marked in the score sent you. It's a rough dance & the strings should fiddle it, not "play it too nice" and the accents ~~should~~—they kind of dig into—down bow & not glide into "pretty" you know what I mean. It runs around 132 = quarter note or faster. This is from a movement of what I called originally a "Holiday Symphony"

This is Washington's Bir

4 movement Washin B

Decoration

4th July

Thanksgiving

278. 16 May 1934, from Wallingford Riegger, New Music Quarterly Recordings, New York

Dear Mr. Ives:

The records have been made! On one side your two numbers, (the Barn Dance first) and on the other "Lilacs" and "Toys"—Had to put Toys on as there was not time to work up another ensemble number of Ruggles—that is the time could not be taken from the rehearsal of the other three numbers. Even as it was, we ran an hour overtime (which I am trying to negotiate)—

1. Transcription of the horn part of "In the Night."

Monday I wired Slonimsky, who arrived this morning (Wed.) and conducted your two numbers—very ably, I thought—Lichter did the Ruggles, and Judith Litante and Henry Brant (piano) did "Toys"—

Your numbers sounded very well as they were played back—In spite of several attempts (3 proofs were made) the horn player began his 6/8 time as follows: [*see example 1*] in spite of the fact that he played it o.k. while rehearsing. Later on, however, he got into the rhythm.

As a whole the things went very well, and will certainly sound gorgeous—We were at it this morning from 8:45 till one o'clock and the men were very serious and enthusiastic—Nicolas certainly went at the thing like a past master—

Will let you know about the price of the whole thing (the painful post mortem) as soon as I've had it out with Lichter, which will be tomorrow A.M. So far I have not paid out anything, altho when I wired Slonimsky I said "expenses paid"—I felt I should at least do this. I imagine I should send him ten or 15 dollars—don't you think?

Very sincerely,
Wallingford Riegger

• • •

George F. Roberts helped prepare much of Ives's music for publication. A copyist with a clear hand and the inclination and ability to decipher Ives's scores, Roberts developed an easy working rhythm with Ives and a personal friendship as well.

279. Ca. 12 May 1934, to George F. Roberts

Dear Mr. Roberts:

I was sorry not to have seen you before we left, but for the last month or so, I wasn't in very good shape & had to keep on my back & so couldn't do much. Would like to start in again & the first is a little score ("Luck and Work" 3 p 25 in song book) for Basset Hr. Fl. Violin Piano & Drum am enclosing a piano and voice arrangement from the song book—and when convenient if you will call the Quality Photostat Co—they will send you a positive of the MSS. score. I think it is fairly clear, and whatever part or measure isn't—just mark it—& I'll copy it out clearly. There's no hurry about [it]—but as I have so much ahead I like to get started.

Also, I had spoken to Mr. Van der Molen sometime ago, about having him copy the score to the "Fugue"—movement #3 in my 4th Symphony—The Quality Co. will also give you a positive. If you will look it through, & straighten out any places that may give Van der Molen trouble & then give it to him I would appreciate it—as I haven't his address. The "Fugue" is not difficult, and most of it is plain I think

Don't forget that I owe you for a part.
We hope your little daughter is now home again, happy and well.

With best wishes
Sincerely,
Chas E. Ives

• • •

The following excerpt from a letter was typed, likely at Ives and Myrick, and saved among Ives's papers. It reveals a fascinating missed connection between him and the world of popular music. Ives's pencil comments emphasize the way that the saved letters were a scrapbook for him. Martin worked at the Florentine Bindery, a firm that did work for Ives.

280. 15 May 1934, from Charles Martin, New York

My Dear Mr. Ives:—

. . . The writer mentioned to Mr. George Gershwin that we were doing some work for you, and he said he was very much interested in your compositions and would like to meet you. Mr. Gershwin lives at 134 East 72nd Street, and his private telephone number is Butterfield 8–7797. The writer feels sure that he would be very glad if you would get in touch with him. . . .

Yours very truly,
Charles Martin

[*In pencil in Ives's hand:*] Mr. Martin came in later in the year I think when we were at 164—and said that he was sorry that [I] didn't call Gershwin—as G said my music has been a help to him—had known it from several years back.

[*On the back, in the same hand:*] Bill Verplanck told me, shortly after I left the office, that Geo. Gershwin telephoned—Bill answered for me said Gershwin said he had gotten more out of my music than of any other especially new chords and new rhythms and that he wants to ask about more copies etc. and that it had been a great help to him.

• • •

Ives's response to Aaron Copland's article on his songs in *Modern Music* (January 1934) shows his happiness at the increased attention his music was receiving and his firm philosophical convictions.[9] That Ives wrote directly to Copland in his own voice and hand is unusual by 1934 and probably indicates the importance he attached to the correspondence.

9. See Letter 239.

281. 24–28 May 1934, to Aaron Copland

Dear Mr. Copland:

I want to thank you for your article in the "Modern Music" magazine. I saw it only when we came back last month.

You put things well and say what you think—and I appreciate what you say—even as to my faults which you don't want glossed over—you are quite right—I have plenty of them, God knows, and so do I sometimes—especially when I wake up in the night.

But when you say I glorify the business man, you're wrong. I was paying my respects to the average man (there is one) in the "ordinary business of life," from the Ashman down to the president—among whom, it seemed to me, there was more open mindedness and fair fighting than among musicians.

The songs would have done probably, as well, without that rear end glossarybo. I was taking a day off from the logic of the mortality tables,—to ride a few whim bolts, and throwing some "over-hand slants" around—some of which have more truth than logic;—and some of them I could have put much better if I had left them out.

I hope sometime to have the pleasure of meeting you. We were in NY a short while this winter, but I was not well and they kept me on my back most of the time and could do but little as I would. Hoping to see you before another year goes by.

—With best wishes to you and for your creative work, I am, Sincerely yours

Charles E. Ives

• • •

As his works attracted the notice of Copland and other prominent figures in the musical community, Ives continued to work with George Roberts to prepare scores for performance and publication. Such work was spurred on by the increased interest of conductors such as Serge Koussevitzky, to whom Copland had shown some Ives scores.

282. 15 June 1934, to George F. Roberts

Dear Mr. Roberts:

Thank you for your letter and copy—It is <u>very well</u> done.[10] Your suggested scoring for the strings is good—but [I] think 3 violins as in the old copy had better be kept,—as this piece is listed in the "<u>New Music</u>" catalogue as for "3 Violins" etc. Have put on a separate sheet the last 4 measures, using the I V. to help out the piano in a few chords and as I remember it was originally played—was a kind of after-sound chord at the end & have made an extra measure at end as in old copy. The pedal is lifted at end of measure before last & F [natural] etc. held pp by hand in piano—there are a few [accents] & phrase marks to go in. After

10. This was Roberts's copy of "Luck and Work" for flute, basset horn, three violins, piano, and drum. See Letter 279, above.

this is done, will [have] the Q. Co send you photostats of 2 other pieces—The song part of one—"Like a Sick Eagle" is enclosed. You must send me the bill for the work as it is ready & don't forget the previous one for the part.

We are very glad to hear that your little daughter is home & gradually improving—we hope she continues. I am, with best wishes

sincerely yours
Chas E. Ives

am sending the copies back in separate mail to Valley Stream.

283. 28 June 1934, from Aaron Copland, Lavinia, Minnesota

Dear Mr Ives—

Thank you for your very kind letter about the article. I'm sorry if I misquoted you on the subject of the "business man." It served my purpose so well that I must have misread its meaning.

Has anyone told you of the performance of some of your songs at at League of Composers Concert in March with Julius Huehn, baritone. I wish you could have witnessed the enthusiasm of the audience.

I have talked with Mr. Koussevitzky about the possibility of a performance of one of your scores and hope something comes of it. At any rate I intend to keep the issue alive with him.

I hope you won't forget to get in touch with me on one of your visits to New York. I should very much enjoy knowing you personally. I can always be reached c/o Cos Cob Press 209 W. 57th St.

Cordially Yours,
Aaron Copland

• • •

Meanwhile, John Kirkpatrick continued his slow conquest of the *Concord* Sonata and sent periodic progress reports on it. His desire to edit Ives's works was also growing.

284. 12 July 1934, from John Kirkpatrick, Greenwich, Connecticut

My dear Mr. Ives,

I have at last got to the point where I can play Emerson end to end—not that I have by any means decided just how I would like to play it—but at any rate it's a first stab at it and I would like very much to play it for you and have your opinion on what to do to certain passages before going ahead with any more memorizing. Today I finished my working copy of it, so to speak, on the same principle as the "pretty pictures" of the songs that I mentioned last fall. (Or more exactly the first state of the working copy).

Would it be too much to ask if I could drop in on you some day at West Redding?

I can't tell you what satisfaction this beginning of an accomplishment gives me. My regard and admiration for the work has grown immeasurably with each degree of penetration and it is a great joy to be on the brink of being able to make it manifest to others. In fact that has already started—yesterday in town I played George Antheil as much of Emerson as I could remember and he confessed he didn't know that American music that wonderful existed, and that its acquaintance was a real inspiration to him. (I don't think that's betraying his confidence)

I look forward with impatience to the time when I can do the whole sonata. In spite of its length I see no reason why it shouldn't be perfectly satisfactory as a composition and hold interest.—if not it would be the fault of the presentation.

Hoping to have the pleasure of meeting you some day soon, I remain

Very sincerely yours,
John Kirkpatrick

• • •

As the correspondence with Wallingford Riegger suggests, the mid-1930s witnessed the first substantial efforts to record Ives's music. The pianist Genevieve Pitot accompanied Radiana Pazmor in performing and then recording "General William Booth Enters into Heaven" late in 1934. The four-and-a-half-minute limit of a 78-rpm record was a serious obstacle in the path to a recording of "Booth." Ives's response to Pazmor's request that cuts be allowed shows his deference to performers.

285. 9 November 1934, from Radiana Pazmor, New York

Dear Mr. Ives,

Pitot and I are doing "General Booth" on a program for the Pen and Hammer Club (communist) at the New School on the 17th. At the same time we are working on it for the record. Last time we succeeded in getting it down to 4.45—Which leaves still 15 seconds to be eliminated. It's pretty difficult but I've set my heart on doing it. Would you possibly consider shortening two places: the long repetition of the "blood of the lamb" phrase just before the "cantabile" section, and the repetitions of "round and round," at the end of that section? I know you want a certain definite effect in both those spots but if it comes to a choice between shortening there and giving it up, there is no doubt in my own mind as to what I myself should do. It occurs to me that the very end could be cut just a bit Supposing we let the size of the record determine the ending? I mean, just go on and if a measure happens to be cut off, never mind? I wish we might meet, the three of us, and work it out together. Are you possibly going to be in town within the next weeks? Pitot and I are rehearsing Tuesday, Thursday, and Friday at two, chez elle, 133 West 10th St.

You probably know that we sang Gen. Booth for Henry's class [at the New School] one evening and that it was acclaimed. I am curious to see what it [*sic*] effect it will have upon a not particularly musical, but otherwise intelligent, public—next week. I mean Pitot and I are if possible more enthusiastic about it than ever.

Can you answer this soon? I hope I'm not too much bothering. I hope too that you are better. Are you always to remain a disembodied handwriting to me?

Sincerely,
Radiana Pazmor

286. 13 November 1934, Edith Ives to Radiana Pazmor

My dear Miss Pazmor:—

My father asks me to acknowledge and thank you for your letter. He thinks that the places you mention in the song are the best parts to cut down, and he is quite willing to have you do whatever you think best in the matter.

He is greatly appreciative of your interest and singing,—and wishes to thank Miss Pitot for playing.

I am writing for father as he is not well—

with best wishes
I am sincerely yours
Edith Ives
for Charles E. Ives

287. 1 December 1934, from Radiana Pazmor, New York

Dear Mr. Ives,

Henry Cowell is as you probably know leaving a week from now for California. He phoned me yesterday that he would like to have me make the record of "General Booth" before he goes. I am very fortunate in having secured Genevieve Pitot to play the piano part. We are eager to have it done as nearly as possible as you want it. We will have our last rehearsal on Wednesday afternoon. Can you possibly be here? I believe you are planning to come to town soon as hope that you can do so in time to give us your almost indispensable advice.

I have not yet thanked you for the elegant copies you sent me, expecting as I did that you might be in town any day. It is a great pleasure to have them and to be able to sing the song at last correctly. Only today I met Varèse by chance and he asked if there were a setting of it for small orchestra. I do hope you are going to make it

Pitot and I are prepared to give you any hour you may find most convenient on Wednesday afternoon, only hoping that it will not be very late.

Sincerely,
Radiana Pazmor

P.S. I almost forgot to ask about an error on p. 3, 2nd staff 2nd measure, should not the second note, G♯, be a quarter note? Will you please let me know about this and about Wednesday as soon as possible?

[*In Ives's hand, above the postscript:*] The last note A natural in the measure you ask about is a quarter note.

288. 3 December 1934, Edith Ives to Radiana Pazmor

Dear Miss Pazmor:—

My father is not well and is not able to come to New York now. He wishes to thank you very much for making a record, and says that if you just sing it in your own way it will be quite alright—and well sung. We expect to stay here until after the holidays and will hope to have the pleasure of seeing you in January.

Sincerely yours,
Edith Ives
for
Charles Ives

P.S. The last note A-natural in the measure you ask about should be a quarter-note.

• • •

On a sheet enclosed with the following letter, Ives gives performance times for several songs: "'Gen Booth' 4:10–4:20 / march about 132 / adagio 66; 'West London' 2:10, 'Immortality' 1:30, 'At Sea' 1:00, 'Walt Whitman,' 0:45, 'White Gulls' 2:00, 'Swimmers' 1:25, 'Rainbow' 2:00, 'Ann Street' 0:30, and 'Luck and Work' 0:30."

289. December 1934, sketch for Ives to Radiana Pazmor

the tempo question / I've been trying to take about as usual / —without overly hurrying—& the first time is 4:10 / —the next 4:20.

Pazmor

How are

H.C. has written me that the song, takes more than 4 ½ minutes in recording ~~It is probably my fault in marking the march in Allegro moderato.~~

~~As~~ I've just played it over ~~twice~~, & trying to take & without taking it hurrying it any faster more than usual or trying not to; the 1st time was about 4.10 & the other 4.20. I feel that I took the march time at 132 = quarter note running it up to around 144 = quarter note at the "molto animato" p. 5—(1) It was my fault in ~~marking th putting~~ marking ~~Allegro~~ mode[rato]—after allegro "~~Vivace assai" would have been nearer right~~ But However you may not like to take it at that.

HC asks me to suggest other contrasting songs that could be sung together in nearly 4 ½ min. and I ~~am enclosing~~ have marked suggestions a few pairs on the enclosed sheet. They are all from the Edition of 34 songs which H. published in NM in Oct. & you probably have copies but as there are several, I will have one sent you.

I appreciate the trouble you & Miss Pitot have taken & hope if records are made they will be to your satisfaction. I would have written before but have been waiting till I can ~~getaround to~~ playing again—I haven't been well & at times it is difficult for me to play—as well as write.

• • •

Among the ultramodern composers, Carl Ruggles (1876–1971) was the closest to Ives in age and regional identity. Although Ives did not share Ruggles's anti-Semitic and intolerant views, the two men had enough in common, musically and personally, to become natural friends. Ives also clearly respected Ruggles as a composer working in a kindred style.

290. 15 December 1934, from Carl Ruggles, Arlington, Vermont

Charles Dear:

Henry [Cowell] was up here for his lecture at Bennington College, and told us you had returned to N.Y. I'm glad we'll be together soon. Micah is going to the University of Miami, Florida for the winter term, beginning Jan. 2. And Charlotte and I will be in N.Y. until spring. There is no point in trying to live here in the winter months. It's so cold and difficult to heat the house.

I'll be giving you a ring very soon now. Deepest love to you and yours.

Always,
Carl

P.S. I hear you are composing. Fine!

• • •

In the summer of 1935 Ives asked George Roberts to copy out several songs for that fall's issue of *New Music*. In the following letters Ives mentions his songs "Requiem," "A Farewell to Land," "On the Antipodes," and "Aeschylus and Sophocles," which were published in *Eighteen Songs* that October. Roberts was also working on the "Harvest Home" Chorales for Ives in 1935.[11] Ives trusted Roberts, who was familiar with his manuscripts and style, and his instructions to him are somewhat cryptic. One wonders what Roberts's reaction was to Ives's reassurance that Roberts could "probably make out" what was wanted in the scores. As usual, in each letter Ives includes greetings and concerns for Roberts's family, to whom he had a

11. Sinclair, *Descriptive Catalogue*, 261.

close attachment. At a time when his health problems made visitors to West Redding increasingly rare, Ives encourages the Roberts family to visit regularly.

291. Early June 1935, to George F. Roberts

Dear Mr. Roberts:

Am sending under separate cover, the photo of the old song to Stevenson's "Requiem." I've tried to make some bad measures plainer—but not sure—most of it I think you can probably make out. The echo parts in last page were the most indistinct—& the notes in the ink lines are to be smaller than the others—Measure 16—should go in as it stands & have copied it over,—think the marks crossing it out were meant for something else.[12] In measures 21 to 25 have used the lower Bass parts in L.H.

This [is] one of the Songs that is going to be published next fall & the engraver writes that they would like to start in as soon as possible. So you don't have to bother about the "estatic" [aesthetic?] looks of this copy—as long as it is plain to the engraver. When it is ready please send your copy to the "Q photo Co" & ask them to send it on to me with the orig. Whatever corrections there are, I can probably fix them—and send it on to engraver—without bothering you.

We hope Janet & her father and mother, are keeping well—& will hope to see you all here before long.

With best wishes,
Sincerely,
Chas E. Ives

When the 2nd Chorale is ready for me to go over, just have the Photo. Co send it with the orig.—& then I'll send it back to you & the 3 can then be bound together.

292. 20 June 1935, to George F. Roberts

Dear Mr. Roberts:

It was fine for us to see you all here last Saturday & to see Janet looking so much better. You must all come up again before this summer goes far, & Edie will give Janet a ride in the boat, if she doesn't want to swim.

It has occurred to me, that to make the idea of that "Farewell to Land" song more visible, would be to have the piano notes especially in the beginning written actually, & not with 8va—as I wrote notes with the bass not 8va basso but actual notes as I wrote them with added staff lines—When the songs are ready please have photo of your copy made &

12. Ives probably means that he was using the song as a source for another piece but did not want to use that particular measure. No such setting survives.

ask the Photo. Co to mail the positives & my copy to me & I'll get them back to you straight away

our best to all
sincerely,
Chas. E. Ives

Please excuse this —— —— writing, Mrs. Ives is waiting to go down to the P.O.[13]

293. 24 June 1935, to George F. Roberts

Dear Mr. Roberts:

Thank you for sending the songs—they are well done—The corrections are mostly things I left out or wrote wrong—You will make out my marks, I think, don't bother to send corrected copies back to me, but please ask the Q. Photo. Co to mail the corrected positives of both songs to: Golden West Music Press 368–9th St. San Francisco Calif.

What little there may be to correct, I can easily do when the engraved proofs come back. There's nothing to be added except please put the dates in bottom of last page, in small print.

There's no hurry about the Chorale, when it's done, I'll give you a little vacation, which I guess you're glad of. Please don't forget to send the bill, for value well rec'd and appreciated—

Our best to Mrs. Roberts & Janet

Yours
Chas E. Ives

—am sending back copies under separate cover—same mail.

• • •

In the following letters, Ives gives Roberts instructions for the preparation of "Aeschylus and Sophocles," which he refers to as the Greek song, and "On the Antipodes." The letter of 10 July demonstrates the complexity of the tasks Roberts faced in making copies from Ives's various and fragmentary sketches and manuscripts.

294. 10 July 1935, to George F. Roberts

Dear Mr. Roberts:

When I wrote you last I didn't expect to bother [you] more during the hot months—I thought then I would shelve those 2 other songs, I showed you.—but now have decided to include them in those to be published next fall.

13. Ives regularly wrote to Roberts in his own hand, but the apparently rushed writing in this letter is especially messy, even for him.

Am sending one, today, by registered mail—as part of it is the old lead pencil-copy done over in ink, (with Edie's help) and have no other copy, so don't want to take any chances of losing it. It is for voice, piano, & a string Quartet (optional). The string parts, I think best to keep on 2 staves (under the piano), the I, II, [*treble clef*], Viola/Cello [*bass clef*]. This will make fewer pages, & also easier to play it on the 2nd piano if necessary. In engraving this will have the 2 S.Q. staffs, smaller than the piano—but it isn't necessary to do this in your copy. As there are no whole notes the up stems will show I. V. & Viola & down stems II & Cello. The voice part doesn't start until measure #9. & that part for 3 measures #9–10–11, is copied on an attached slip.—On the following pages, the voice part is in the right place

Am sorry to give you all this trouble now—but the engraver wants all copy in by or around Aug. 1st—the other song will not be quite as hard to make [out.] Will send it in a week or so, unless you want it sooner.

Give our best regards to Mrs. Roberts & Janet—we hope to see you all again soon.

Sincerely,
Chas E. Ives

Don't forget the bill.

At beat 3 & 4 (meas #23) & all measure #24—a passage for I V is in the piano bass clef staff which should go in S.Q. Staff—treble clef

295. 19 July 1935, to George F. Roberts

Dear Mr. Roberts:

Am sending under separate cover, the last song for the publisher—and then I won't cause you any more trouble till next fall. It's for voice (or voices) one piano but 2 players—Primo & Secondo—was the way they used to put it. I think you won't find it as hard to make out as some of the others. It's built mostly on a chord cycle—have put the letters A.B.C. etc. over the chords that have the same notes—where not filled in.

Please have the "Greek" song photostated and sent me with my copy (also this one) as soon as ready. I'll get them back to you in a day or so, and the Photo Co. can send them to the engraver, [in] San Francisco. He is anxious to get them as soon as possible after Aug. 1st. Hope you & the family are well. Edie is in bed with bad glands.

Chas E. Ives

296. 31 July 1935, to George F. Roberts

Dear Mr. Roberts:

Am sending back the Greek Song—it is a good job—only a few corrections,—bow marks etc.—In measure #29 p. 7 have made F# a quarter note and B-flat an eighth note, as the last syllable of honored is bad to sing.

Please ask the Q. Photo. Co. to mail, just as soon as possible

1 copy to the Golden West Music Press, 368–Ninth St., San Francisco, Calif, and 1 to Henry Cowell, Menlo Park, Calif.

Hope the Antipodes, is not giving much trouble—send it on as soon as convenient—also don't forget to send bill.

The family send best wishes to Mrs. Roberts and Janet,

Sincerely,
Chas E. Ives

• • •

By the summer of 1935 John Kirkpatrick had begun to perform the "Emerson" movement of the *Concord* Sonata in his recitals, and plans were under way to include it on a program in New York's Town Hall the following January. The pianist's desire to meet Ives and play for him only deepened as his knowledge of the sonata grew and he began to work more systematically on its remaining movements. And although he was well enough to see old friends like Roberts and his family that summer, Ives did not yet feel up to having Kirkpatrick visit.

297. Ca. July 1935, from John Kirkpatrick, Greenwich, Connecticut

My dear Mr. Ives,

I have been meaning to send you the enclosed prospectus and set of programs for some time—but why I haven't got around to it I don't know, especially since you have been on my mind a great deal for the past year or so, since I received Mrs. Ives's very kind letter. I hope the intervening time has been kind to you and that your health is once more a joy rather than a concern.

I had the greatest pleasure playing Emerson in the series, which we did in three places, New Canaan, Greenwich and Princeton. We had hoped to place it in more—but at that we found our hands full. The reception of Emerson was extremely interesting and, one can imagine, quite mixed, ranging all the way from the lady who mutters, "absolutely inexcusable," to the gentleman who told me he felt as if he were looking face to face at times into your soul and at times into Emerson's.

Now I must write you again because I am to give a recital next season in Town Hall, Jan. 28,—the program planned as:

Griffes—sonata
Copland—piano variations
Ives—Emerson
—
Harris—sonata
Gottschalk—3 creole pieces

and I would value inestimably your critique of my performance, which still has much to outgrow.

If it is convenient to you, I could come up to Redding any time—I have a car, a trusty old Ford station wagon, or if you don't yet feel quite like receiving visitors, I would equally appreciate your thought.

sincerely,
John Kirkpatrick

• • •

Ives sometimes chastised his favored editors and copyists for not billing him adequately for their work. As he had with Harrison and Becker, Ives took matters into his own hands with Roberts in the letters below and sent a check for his work on the songs.

298. 2 August 1935, to George F. Roberts

Dear Mr. Roberts:

Am sending the "Antipodes" back under separate cover.—Another good job of yours. The last part of last measure top of last page; is troublesome—think if arpeggio marks before up chords—& after down ones within your curve line, which is a help, will make this clear—also accidentals in last time as in first.

The 2nd chord (Secondo Bass) from end (last measure) is C, G, D-flat. I copied this wrong.

One piano for 4 hands—Primo [*bass and treble clefs*] Secondo [*bass and treble clefs*], after just Imo, IIdo will do.

Please have Q.P. Co. mail positives (unbound) to Gold West M.P. Same place as the other ones were—and to Henry Cowell.

You won't forget I owe you a bill.

Best wishes to all
Chas E. Ives

299. 20 August 1935, to George F. Roberts

Dear Mr. Roberts:

You are a good musician—but are you a good business man? As I've been told more than once that I'm neither—I won't call you names. But I owe you for some good work, and have no bill—I don't remember what the last bill covered etc.; so am taking a chance & sending a Ck. for $50.—if it is more than this, please let me know.—if too much please just credit it.

We hope you & the family have been keeping well through the hot summer, and that we will see you all again here before long.

Yours—sincerely
Chas E. Ives

• • •

The surviving correspondence between Ives and Kirkpatrick is one-sided: many more of Kirkpatrick's letters to Ives are extant. The letter of 28 September 1935 implies that Ives had written to him, via Edith, that he planned to arrange for Kirkpatrick to visit in spite of the state of his health. The pianist's place in the career of Ives's music was becoming larger and more important as he continued gathering information about the composer and his works. Ives answers the questions posed in Letter 300 in part in pencil notes on the letter itself, and more extensively in his sketch for a reply. The dialogue over the relative importance of the different versions of the movements of the sonata casts a fascinating light on the developing relationship between the two men.

300. 28 September 1935, from John Kirkpatrick, Greenwich, Connecticut

My Dear Mr. Ives,

I have been meaning to write you ever since receiving your daughter's very kind letter, but have been deterred by a measure of disappointment in not being able to report any progress on Hawthorne and Thoreau. I want very much to play the whole sonata some time, but this summer I had to do a little pot boiling and just didn't have time to get at it.

I was very sorry to hear that you were still in ill health and hope the summer has set you up. Of course I would be immensely flattered to visit you, doctor's orders or better judgement notwithstanding, but don't let any degree of eagerness on my part have any influence in what, for all I know, might be unwise.

In the meantime could I bother you about a bit of documentation?

1. Would my recital be the first public performance in New York of Emerson? [*Ives writes in pencil,* "another unknown man," *and,* "No Keith Corelli"]

2. Could you let me have the dates of composition of the various parts of the sonata? The music of Emerson seems to be first and the epilogue (obviously after 1914) last. (Perhaps an accompanying questionnaire would simplify some of the bother.)

3. Are there any sketches of Emerson which antedate the version printed? [*Ives:* "yes—2 pages here—some in NY"] The epilogue indicates a conception for large orchestra, which leads me to suspect a first sketch of clearer polyphonic intention, taken down for two hands in the printed version. If such exists I would like to study it. In this connection, may I permit myself a comment on the later 4 transcriptions from Emerson? These seem to me an exposition of certain substances which don't form properly part of the actual musical texture, but which hang about the music in no less necessary a way. The printed version is so strongly organized a lyric and rhythmic continuity that what remains is to plumb its nature and evolve a manner of presentation. The transcriptions offer invaluable clues to the musical intent but provide more additional notes than can well be taken care of. [*Ives:* "yes to some extent piano & O[rchestra] got away from E[merson] & sonata did not"] It seems as if Shakespeare, in one pentameter verse, had put words for all the implications of the substance expressed in the verse.—whereas the thing to do is to express all the richness of implication and connotation with just those ten syllables, which of course, presupposes

the great actor. (which shows that all this may be just a burst of self justification on the part of an interpreter, who hopes to do just that). But anyhow that's how I can't help feeling toward them.

4. Does Emerson contain any examples of melody built on pre-existing words? [*Ives:* "No"] I suspect this from the way your songs are often quite indifferent about vocal or instrumental presentation—the horn solo in "in the Night"—etc. also from seeing Adolf Weiss's piano sonata (starting from fish-shaped Paumonok; . . .) before which he evidently saw considerable of you, and which I suspect as an Ivesism on his part. I should love to know if I'll be playing any quotations from Compensation or Self Reliance.

My program is still exactly the same:

Griffes—sonata
Copland—Variations
Ives—Emerson
(intermission)
Harris—sonata
Gottschalk—Souvenir de Porto Rico (Marche des Gibaros)
Danza
El Cocoye (grand caprice cubain)

the Gottschalk is great fun—they have a certain childish exuberance that's very compelling.

I'm taking part in Copland's one man show at the New School on the 11th. He and I are playing two of my two-piano arrangements, the Ode and the Salon Mexico, and I'm playing the variations. After that I'll be working on Emerson more, so it ought to be in a good state around the 17th or so. Nov. 5 I have a recital at Princeton (the Present Day Club) and I expect to do the whole program just as it is.

More documentation:

5. Have you any other piano works beside the 1st and 2nd sonatas?

[*Ives:* "(some shorter pieces)—3rd sonata I wrote ab[out]—5–6 yrs 6 or 8 years ago—looked at it later—wrote N.G.—However I"]

Please give my kindest regards to Mrs. Ives and thank Miss Edith for her letter, and accept my best wishes for your well being,

Sincerely,
John Kirkpatrick

301. Ca. 28 September 1935, excerpts from four sketches for Harmony Ives to John Kirkpatrick

He its he always glad to find one interested in plumbing the foundations—whatever

Dear Mr. Kirkpatrick:

Mr. I thanks you for your letter—he says it's good to find a man ~~musician~~ who is as much interested in the things of the substance as the notes. He says it seems to him now, that the movement in the sonata book is nearer the ~~real~~ Emerson (that is—of course his real Emerson) than either Orchestra & piano overture ~~with sketch~~ plan which you ask about which preceded it, or the transcriptions which have ~~more of some of both~~ more of the ~~instrumental idea first~~ score idea suggestions from it than was needed & some ~~other developments later.~~ Mr. I feels that it ~~may be~~ is better ~~to go by the just stay~~ to play by ~~the old~~ book & not bother with the transcriptions. (Except possibly play some of the fuller meas which . . .

[*From the second sketch:* The printed Emerson it seems to me is nearer the real Emerson "just homely-thinking, meditation & contemplation—little or nothing to please the bodily senses, "easy listening" little to stimulate—either by repetition, or too much reference—to the custom & habit of mind & ear—neither too usual—or too unusual—just like E]

In neither the E or T movements are there any quotations or attempts to picture any particular work or thought—but rather trying to keep to general impression of the great indefinite things—composite picture of him—rather ~~than program~~ as in t[he] preface—but the Hawthorne & Alcotts—have what are supposed to be more definite suggestions of incidents & stories—for instance the Demon Dancer around the pipe—Celestial RR—etc.—& old man Alcott's—the great talker—sonorous thought & the old Alcott ~~house~~ place.

The ~~overture~~ orchestra, piano sketch as a kind of overture or concerto was not fully scored & never finished—I can find only one page & part of another here, I think there may be some more of it in a trunk in N.Y.—I doubt if there [*sic*] worth study but will look for them when we get back probably the later part of Nov. and if found will be glad to let you have them & ~~at any t~~ also I hope to see you then.

[*From the third sketch:* You ask about the transcriptions? The first was mostly from a sketch of an Emerson or orchestra and piano Overture. Around that time 1910–11 I had the overture habit and started to make a series of them to be over "Men of Literature." But they either were not completed or ended up in something else. Some of the things in the Emerson score things, went into the sonata the next year.]

The transcriptions & score may be better or worse music as such, than the printed movement—but they grow ~~grew~~ rather away at times too far away from Emerson—as it seems to me now.—They have too much of that "grit & dagger" [*in the second sketch:* "jilt and dagger"] which E. had & which he said he missed in too ~~many~~ Washington I[rving]—J. R. Lowell"—also, some things that are seem to ~~more~~ have more to do with music, as such, than with Emerson.—for instance, in the top RH line, in the last half of the 2nd brace on first page Transcription, the chords in the sketch, were left out—apparently thought according to a marginal note, were rather too sensuous for Emerson—they might ~~make~~ cause it to please the ladies too easily"—& some other place—end of 3rd–4th braces p. 6—etc—also viola figure on top brace p. 4 of (transcriptions) continues till the cadenza over the next page—& the figures in the violins 2nd meas. of IV transcription p. 12. I remember Robert Schmitz said when somebody ~~played~~ it (I think it was [one of] Schmitz's pupils played it, he filled in with some of this part from the Transcription—& Schmitz said it went we—for instance—playing the top brace of p. 11–p. 15

I am glad to have you do anything ~~that Keith Corelli played that like~~ in any way, you think best—as long as it seems natural to you & doesn't disturb the line of the whole sonata—I haven't played it for some time but I remember, that I didn't play it or didn't feel it exactly this same way all the time. Some times more of the transcriptions seem better—far more often they didn't.

Another thing the transcriptions were arranged for short pieces or kind of studies & were not to take the place of the other—the coda to some of them had to be made & has no place in the sonata.

Emerson's thought was not rigid or pigeon holed—It is said he seldom gave the same lecture in the same way—the mood of the time had its place—& ~~he came~~ to Danbury to lecture once, my grandmother heard him—after his essays were published—one was Spiritual Laws—she had studied & knew it by heart—but she was rather startled & some what put [out] to ~~hear him omit~~ find it so much different than the printed edition—so there you are!

[*From the fourth sketch:* I appreciate greatly the trouble and work you have given this music—especially when you know that it is liable to disturb some people, or do something else that nice music won't do—

[I remember, just after finishing the E movement playing it to an old friend of mine, ~~who~~ He said "that music is homely, awkward, and lanky,—so was Emerson. It won't please the ladies much—neither did E." Be that as it may—it takes at least some courage and, as well as some bodily labor & strength ~~of body~~, patience & time—and you have my ~~grateful &~~ sincere thanks for playing it. . . .

[You ask about other piano music beside the 1st & 2nd sonatas

[Some time in the winter of 26–27, I finished a one movement piece—which I called the "3rd Sonata." The last time I played it over it didn't seem satisfactory—~~Sometime~~ I may get it out again ~~some day~~ & if may not seem better ~~I'll~~ have it copied—have put it away for a while.

[There are some shorter pieces, which I haven't played in some years; most of them are old and of doubtful value; and others ~~which~~ went into chamber music pieces, of these some are in legible photostat copies, and I will be glad to have them sent you.]

Dates of Comp (see his letter last page)

Music

Emerson completed in the summer of 1912

Hawth. completed Oct 12 1911

Alcotts completed 1915

1911

Thor completed 1915

Essays—all 1919

printed when sonata was engraved in fall of 1919

4 trans from Em.

1st arranged, sometime ~~between~~ after 1915 & before 1918 mostly from ~~the~~ uncompleted sketch for score.

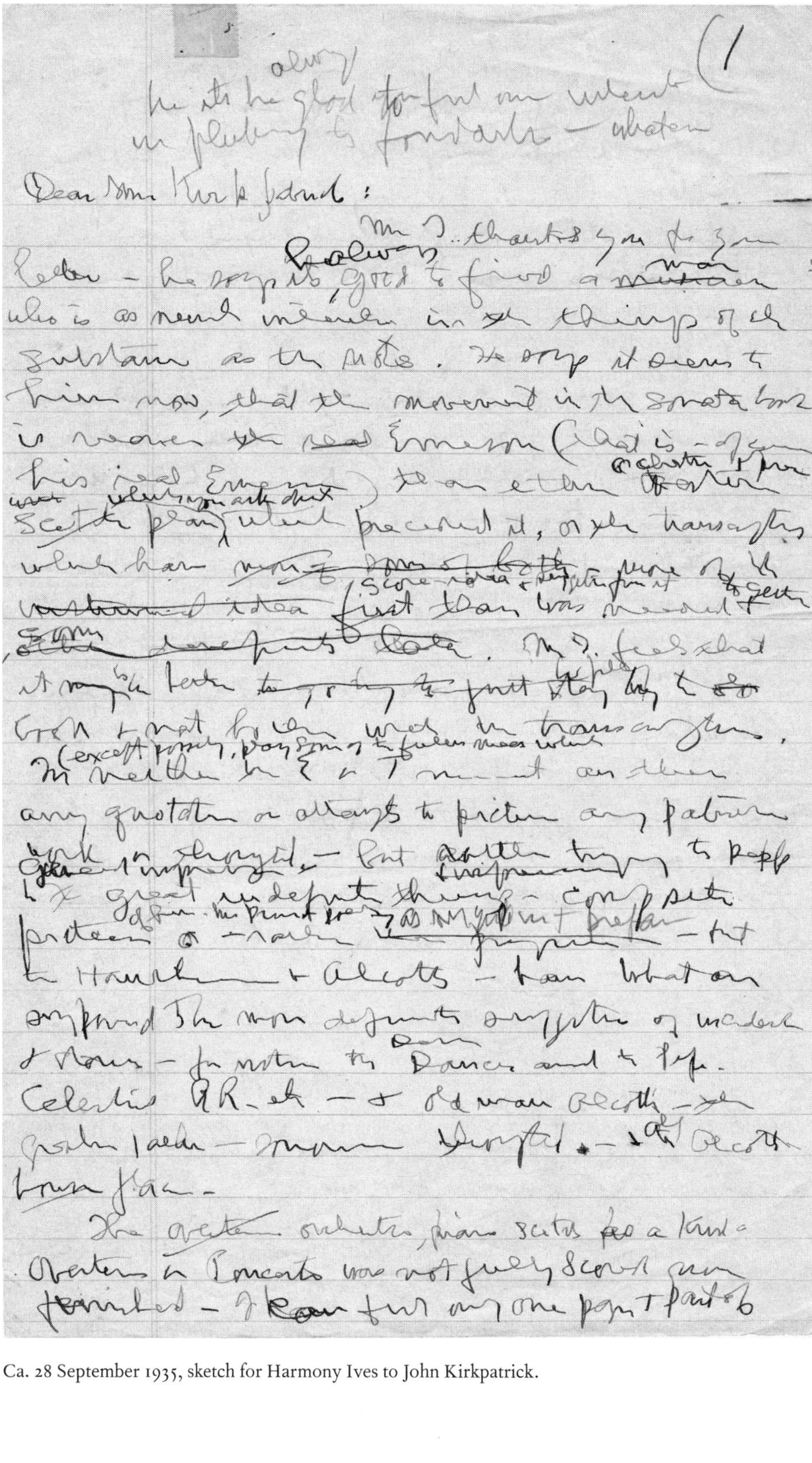

Ca. 28 September 1935, sketch for Harmony Ives to John Kirkpatrick.

The other trans were made a year or two after the sonata was printed—& the 4 were copied and put together as in photo-copy.

302. 25 October 1935, from John Kirkpatrick, Greenwich, Connecticut

My dear Mr. Ives,

Thank you ever so much for all the invaluable documentation, and please thank Mrs. Ives for me for her painstaking transcription of it. I feel as if I had put the whole household to considerable trouble, but I must confess that I am so glad to have it all I can't feel the least bit sorry. Please save the page and part of a page—I'm sure they will reveal much.

I'm sorry I'm not the sort of person who can exemplify the spontaneously improvisatory element that is so important in your music. I have to decide what notes I'm going to play and play just those, short of the kind of relearning that takes some time. I suppose all that is in a way the very antithesis of creative action, bringing in the element of the well rehearsed circus act, which always goes off like clockwork and always exactly the same. One simply does one's best to keep the muscular habits from getting out of hand away from the spiritual causation, and keep them one. But that is why I necessarily prefer the finely crystallized plastique of the printed version to the transcriptions where the expression is certainly more direct and full but the shape more vague and complicated.

I think I told you I would be playing Emerson here in Greenwich for the college club on the 4th. It is at Mrs. Bolling's and unfortunately her piano while really excellent of its vintage is too old to achieve the necessary orchestral illusion. So I'm playing just the Griffes and Harris sonatas and the Gottschalk group. This has decided me to make a sudden foray down to Princeton tonight, after Harris's one man show at the New School, to make the acquaintance of the piano of the present day club, where I play Nov. 13. I hope it will do justice to Emerson.

Hoping to have the pleasure of seeing you sometime soon—and with best wishes for your well being,

sincerely,
John Kirkpatrick

P.S. I was looking over some of the songs this morning before breakfast and found a marvelous way to give the last chord of the hymn on the piano—you remember that the 114 version gives [*see example 2a*] the original for string sextet gives [*see example 2b*]—well—do this: [*see example 2c*] or maybe [*see example 2d*] but anyway keep the B-natural from before and make a chord of only 2 notes and it mixes perfectly.

• • •

Kirkpatrick's performances of "Emerson" began to attract the notice of other composers and performers of new music. In the following letter Kirkpatrick describes the reactions of Roy Harris and George Antheil, which presaged the critical reaction to the premiere of the whole work, still four years in the future. Kirkpatrick's desire to arrive at an authoritative perfor-

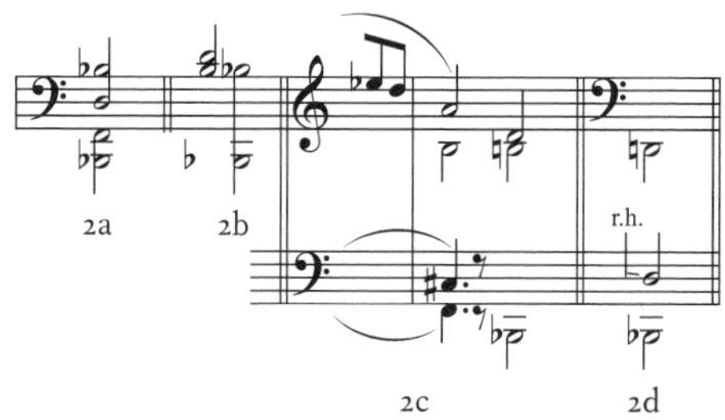

2. (a) Final measure of Ives's "Hymn"; (b) final measure of the version for strings; (c–d) two realizations of the measure by John Kirkpatrick.

mance of the sonata drove him to examine and digest all of its source material—a process that would eventually lead to the grander project of cataloguing all of Ives's manuscripts.

303. November 1935, from John Kirkpatrick, Greenwich, Connecticut

My dear Mr. Ives,

Here is the Princeton Program of last week with my apologies for not getting it to you sooner (I always seem to be just a week late in these matters).

Emerson went quite well except for a few unpardonably conspicuous wrong notes, and made quite an impression. Roy Harris was there and was particularly taken with it—exclaimed: "marvelous composer!" Of course there were the bewildered and dissenting voices too. I didn't achieve quite the rhapsodic ecstasy I got that time I wrote you about when I played it over for George Antheil, but the form was much stronger than ever before.

Roy's sonata went, as a whole, better than ever except that the scherzo started itself off before I had intended—and never quite regained poise. I won't let that happen again!

I must confess that, without wishing to become importunate, I can't help becoming more and more impatient about collating Emerson with the remains of the old overture. I find that I need more and more of the sort of minutely detailed practicing that leads one, for instance, to learn the left hand part through an entire piece, then the right, just to clean out all the silly little unnecessary motions and mistakes that one might not have noticed,—and all those corrections have to be salted down into subconscious habits. So all the changes in text or fingering should have been made about a month before, or one runs the danger of being suddenly pulled back from the superconsious to the conscious, that is if one has been lucky enough to achieve the superconscious at all.

In that way, there are two passages that worry me:—the first line on page 6 and the Beethoven chords on p. 17 (I don't think their inner voices have found their final or most appropriate spacing)—and I suspect and hope that the overture will throw some light on the polyphonic intentions involved. Everything else is perfectly satisfactory and reveals more and more new beauties with each performance. Only those two bits seem sketchier and sketchier. I suspect it's merely a question of choosing the proper degree of literalness in rendering the orchestra. So I necessarily become more and more anxious to see the "page and part of another" that you found and whatever there may be in town.

By the way, was Hawthorne one of those Men of Literature overtures, and is there a surviving score of him?

Please give my kindest regards to Mrs. Ives and to Miss Edith, and accept my best wishes for your well being,

Sincerely
John Kirkpatrick

304. Ca. November 1935, sketches for Ives to John Kirkpatrick

[*Sketch 1*]

I can't make it all out. Hard to read all of it—glad to have you have—but doubt if it will be of much help—although it may in some places

a*sending ~~6~~ 7—pages of Overture "score sketch
b*seems more like Piano Concerto (with sort of cadenzas)
*—quite a little of Overture—not in sonata
*—because not in sonata, may not mean that it ought to be—or that it was left out by mistake
*—a few things notes or lines, originally in piano copy, were left out when this copy was engraved (see page ~~in back of~~ of pasted in old book)

*The Overture (what is left) and sonata (in book) are in some ways more like 2 separate & different pieces on some of the same texts, than the same piece in different forms.

In the two places you speak of 1st line p. 6 & the bottom of p. 15—The first—these measures may have been in the overture, but are not in the pages that I can find—but it probably was—as in the copy from which the sonata was engraved, there was a lower set of notes in LH. which were crossed out of the engraver's copy—I can't make them out exactly, but probably cut out as some other things were—probably or perhaps, because they didn't seem quite essential enough to pay for the difficulty in playing & listening that they might cause. (Am enclosing this & other pages from the copies of engraver's copy—Do whatever you think best

The second place, you speak of "Beethoven ch[ords"] on p. 17—You find a part of this page in the score—beginning etc. as marked. These chords are but the knocks on the portal & are played more as such than as music.—They have no inner counterpoint but I remember there was a kind of blur up in the middle of the 2nd chord, & why the F was let out in second time I don't know.

You can see at the beginning of the overture page here that the orchestra gave some of these knocks & then the piano & ~~then~~ another time the clar & Tpt gave it in unison & the piano had an off figure, which was suggested from the score in the Trans p [13] but is not the same.

You ask if Hawthorne was ~~first for orch or~~ is arrangement from a score—no—It was first as it is in book—for piano only—though at times, had another piano or player in mind—but I don't remember his putting in appearance.

But I was working on a symphony about this time[14] & in the Scherzo, I put some of the H movement in, mostly the parts having to do with Celestial R.R. Later on I made a short fantasy for piano from the sym. score, which had some of the Hawthorne—This piece as I remember didn't seem quite satisfactory—& I have no copy ~~(will ask N.M. to send you copy).~~

[*Sketch 2*]

Dear Mr. K

Mr. Ives thanks you for your letter and will answer it in more detail as soon as he is able to—he has not been at all well ~~in good shape~~ since we've been back in N.Y.

~~Some~~ About half a dozen pages or parts ~~of pages~~ that we've been able to find of it ~~Emerson Overture~~ (though Mr. I says it seems to be more of a concerto with an overdose of cadenzas) will be forwarded to you from the Photo Stat Co. here.

~~There is He hopes~~ They are indistinct hard to make out and Mr I ~~hopes you~~ thinks they won't be of much help to you—in these pages there is much ~~less~~ which didn't go into the sonata—He hopes they won't cause you much trouble or bother.

Under separate cover, ~~some pages of the orchestral score~~ the remains of the old O. which you ask for, are being sent.

305. January 1936, from John Kirkpatrick, New York

My dear Mrs. Ives,

I am taking the liberty of sending you several announcements of my recital, in case you might like to send then to some of your friends.

Please thank Mr. Ives for me for the photographs of the remains of the old Emerson overture. They have been quite invaluable in a great many details.

I hope you will be able to come though I hesitate to persuade you against staying with Mr. Ives.

I sincerely hope to have the pleasure of meeting you some day.

With best wishes, I remain–

faithfully yours
John Kirkpatrick

• • •

The following fragmentary sketch, which probably dates from January 1936, shows Ives's gratitude to Kirkpatrick. Ives responded to Kirkpatrick's efforts with increased financial assistance for his performances.

14. Symphony no. 4.

306. Ca. 23 January 1936, incomplete sketch for Harmony Ives to John Kirkpatrick

. . . the fine good work & the hard work you and the younger composers like Copland, Cowell, Harris, Antheil and others like them are doing now. Too many emasculated, soft-eared, lady birds in the press and easy chairs have too much influence in (against) music today—especially American music. The worse your concert makes them feel, the better—also the music—these are Mr. I's words—but I agree with him.

307. 1 February 1936, from John Kirkpatrick, Greenwich, Connecticut

My dear Mr. Ives,

I have just received the statement from Mr. Copley's office and it seems there is still due $180.61. When I wrote accepting your very generous offer, I did not expect the deficit to be so large, so please do not consider the figure submitted as any indication of expectations but rather as a simple statement of my obligation, toward the fulfillment of which I would, of course, immensely appreciate whatever you might like to contribute.

Thanks very much for the telegram.

I enclose a few program notes. I was sorry not to submit the note on Emerson to you before printing, but since Christmas I have had two separate colds, one very bad, which slowed everything up so much that the notes weren't ready until the last moment (until Monday—the type setter who was working on them fortunately lives in Stamford, so he brought two sets of proof sheets with him on the evening train and gave one to me at the Greenwich station; after reading them I telephoned the corrections to him at Stamford, and they were printed Tuesday morning). I tried not to take too many liberties.

As always you have my sincerest wishes that you may soon be in good health again,—a wish that, I must confess, is not without a measure of selfishness on my part, for I look forward confidently to the pleasure of meeting you some time.

Please give my kindest regards to Mrs. Ives and to Miss Edith.

Thanking you again for all your numerous kindnesses (the Emerson photographs are invaluable)

I remain,
Faithfully yours,
John Kirkpatrick

308. 5 February 1936, from John Kirkpatrick, Greenwich, Connecticut

My dear Mr. Ives,

I am at a loss to begin to indicate to you my appreciation of your generous gift. [presumably a check for the Town Hall concert balance] I can only say that, great as is the joy it gives me (as a kind of luminous deus ex machina fulfillment of a rather complicated act of devotion, the many mundane ramifications of which have been a whole education), it is still far less than the joy of the music itself, which has proved an inexhaustible source of every imaginable kind of beauty and truth.

Just now I'm working at Hawthorne and just this afternoon got an éclair on the rhythmic nature of a passage that had baffled me. I hope to be playing at it in a few months.

With deep gratitude and always with best wishes

Sincerely,
John Kirkpatrick

• • •

Lou Harrison (1917–2003) was another important editor and performer of Ives's music in the late 1930s and 1940s. Like many of his generation, Harrison came to know and work with Ives via Henry Cowell. The Harrison correspondence also provides another example of how Ives developed close relationships with some correspondents, came to rely on their help, and aided them as well.

At Cowell's suggestion, an eighteen-year-old Lou Harrison wrote to Ives asking for copies of his music, which was otherwise almost impossible to get. In response, Ives sent him a large crate containing photostatic copies of much of his piano, chamber, and orchestral music, much of it still in manuscript.[15] Harrison later called the experience of growing up with these scores an open invitation to musical freedom, a kind of musical park that one could explore endlessly.[16]

309. 25 March 1936, from Lou Harrison, San Francisco

Dear Mr. Ives

I am a student at State College in San Francisco. It seems that there are favorable opportunities to perform your works on what we have as student recitals and in theory and history classes. I am very anxious to learn your two piano sonatas but the question of copies in all modern music is so difficult. But Henry Cowell gives me a ray of hope by telling me that I might obtain a copy of each of the sonatas from you. If this were possible I should be deeply grateful, and the works would reach a number of ears. I'm really very anxious to learn the works (if possible) and would greatly appreciate having the copies from which to work.

Hopefully—
Lou Harrison

15. See Letter 318.

16. H. Wiley Hitchcock and Vivian Perlis, eds., *An Ives Celebration: Papers and Panels of the Charles Ives Centennial Festival-Conference* (Urbana: University of Illinois Press, 1977), 200; see also Harrison's description of receiving the crate of music in the same volume, 81–83.

• • •

Just as Ives and Harrison began to correspond, one of the darkest episodes in Ives's life unfolded: the arrest and conviction of Henry Cowell in 1936 on charges in of having sexual relationships with several boys as young as seventeen.[17] The Iveses were utterly unprepared for the news, and unable to understand and deal with it, perhaps especially because of Ives's bad health that summer.[18] It is interesting that only Harmony's clearly upset letters describing the incident survive; there are no sketches reacting to the incident in Ives's hand. Harmony's letters to Charlotte Ruggles show her desire to return to more mundane and less troubling subjects.

310. 3 July 1936, Harmony Ives to Charlotte Ruggles

Dear Mrs. Ruggles,

Have you heard this hideous thing about Henry Cowell—that he has been guilty of Oscar Wilde practices—a crime in California, must stand trial & probably receive a long sentence? Mr. Becker wrote me—fearing to write to Charlie whom I shall not tell until I have confirmation. John Becker heard about it by chance in Chicago a week ago & said he was told it had been in the papers. If true I think it is the saddest thing in our experience. I had no inkling of this defect, had you? I mean I shouldn't have been surprised to have found Henry's standards of relations between men and women different than ours tho' I knew of nothing. The pity of this!—of course it is disease—"a quirk of nature," as Mr. Becker said—Do you know anything?—Mr Becker said he understood he was out on bail.

We were sorry not to have another glimpse of you in N.Y. I telephoned Mrs. Watson's apt. April 1st to find someone else in it!

How are you and Carl?—We are about as usual. I am dreading this disclosure to Charlie—it is the only secret I've ever had from him. John Becker wrote as having no doubt of the fact but I can't bring myself to believe it.

With love and best wishes

Ever yours
Harmony Ives

311. 12 July 1936, Harmony Ives to Charlotte Ruggles

Dear Mrs. Ruggles,

Thank you for writing. In the mail with your letter was one from Henry addressed to me which contained a letter to be given to Charlie if I saw fit. It was a strange letter—admitting his commission of the offense but with no <u>suggestion</u> of contrition—there

17. Hicks, *Henry Cowell, Bohemian,* 134–35.

18. See Letters 164–66.

was in fact, a spirit of bravado it seemed to me—his "spirit was undaunted" (stock phrase) & and he is "absolutely contented." Is he contented with himself do you suppose? Anyway, I told Charlie & he & I feel just as you do. A thing more abhorrent to Charlie's nature couldn't be found. We think these things are too much condoned. He will never willingly, see Henry again—he can't—he doesn't want to hear of the thing—the shock used him up and he hasn't had a long breath since I told him but he will get used to it—isn't it almost shocking the things we "get used to"? He said characteristically "I thought he was a man & he's nothing but a G—— D—— sap!"

I can't write anymore—the letter from Henry was largely about the carrying on of New Music—he has planned it out as you of course know—He said Mr. Ruggles and Mr. Luenning wanted to do it from Bennington but Strang is to do it & Henry's name left on. We want to see New Music go on.

It is grand to hear of all the composing going on and aren't you proud to have [a] son who can farm? I should be above all things. Love to all.

As ever yours,
Harmony Ives

• • •

Just as Cowell's arrest largely stopped his work on Ives's music, Kirkpatrick was expanding his inquiry into more areas of the works and writing letters describing his elation at each new discovery. In the following letter, the idea of making a complete list of Ives's works surfaces for the first time. It would be almost forty years before Kirkpatrick's catalogue of the Ives materials was finally finished.

312. 22 July 1936, from John Kirkpatrick, Greenwich, Connecticut

My dear Mr. Ives,

I have been meaning to write to you ever since receiving Mrs. Ives's very kind note of May 27, but have put it off because I wanted very much to send you a sample of what I was doing with the songs, and it seemed that no sooner had I made a fair copy of one of them than I would promptly become dissatisfied with the presentation of some passage, and so never sent any.

I was terribly sorry to hear that you were still unwell. I hope the summer is proving a beneficial one.

Two weeks ago I went up to Boston to see Slonimsky, and borrowed nearly everything he had of yours. The chamber music scores particularly throw all sorts of necessary light on the songs, but I must confess that though they satisfied temporarily my avidity for knowledge of your music, the total effect was quite opposite and the enlarged horizon only created more avidity, so that I find myself now in the absurdly importunate desire of wanting to make a list of your manuscripts as a preliminary step to a list of your works or to any satisfactory complete collation of any one work. The only songs I feel on sure ground with, for instance, are those where I feel I have the whole apparatus: of the Hymn, pencil autograph, later score, 114, New Music—they all explain each other and each contains, in some passage a most preferable version or most applicable to the piano. The end of the Byron Incantation stumps me, because I prefer the old 114 version of "shall my soul be upon" to either the score or the New Music, but I have only the 1st 4 measures of the original autograph (on the bottom of the second half of Calcium Night, you remember), and so really can't judge confidently.

The last few days I've been making a piano arrangement of Greenland's Icy Mountains in the 4th Symphony—it comes out fairly well. Isn't that one of the "Fugues for organ and strings, 1892–5"?—was it changed at all when it was incorporated into the symphony?—and is the original ms. still extant?

I would greatly appreciate it if some day I could make a little call, however brief. I do not mean to intrude, and on the other hand I think my interest in your music is plenty strong enough not to need the stimulation of personal contact, and you are so good about answering my bothersome questionnaires that I don't think there's anything I'd feel I had to ask you on the spot.—It's just simply that I'd like to see you.

Please give my kindest regards to Mrs. Ives and to miss Edith,

Sincerely,
John Kirkpatrick

• • •

Beneath the anger and sense of betrayal toward Cowell, one can also see an attempt to understand the event that had separated two men who had become very close musical and personal friends, but clearly the Iveses had no conceptual frame within which the news could be contained. Ives's anger softened over time: eventually he participated in the drive to free Cowell, and the two reconciled after his release and pardon.[19]

313. August 1936, Harmony Ives to Evelyn Becker

Dear Mrs. Becker—

It is kind of you to ask Edith & Sarah to stop off at St. Paul & they would arrange to but the trip has been given up. We got a little nervous about having them go along [alone?] & also thought it might be hot so they are going to Cape Cod with my sister instead. Thank you just as much & I hope the girls will meet before long.

I thought you might be interested to see the enclosed—& will you return it? I take no stock in what he [Cowell] wrote Mrs. Wrinett [?] Brown—To me his complacent attitude

19. Leta E. Miller and Rob Collins have recently discovered two sketches written by Ives in May 1937 for a letter to Cowell. The pencil sketches, which are in the first person, are possibly drafts for a letter that Cowell mentioned receiving from Ives on 29 May 1937 in a letter to his stepmother. It is clear in these sketches that Ives's anger at Cowell had faded and that he was still supportive of both Cowell and *New Music.* Miller and Collins, "The Cowell-Ives Relationship: A New Look at Cowell's Prison Years," *American Music* 23, no. 4 (Winter 2005): 473–92.

is terrible—we shall send no money or gifts & shall not write—The thing fills us with a deep physical repulsion which is almost nausea & we do not talk about it tho' there are bursts! Mr. Ives says he feels that one who professed to be a friend has come up behind him & given him a blow & he feels angry and wants to hit him! "I may not be a Christian" he says, but it is the treachery & evil he hates. This "illness" idea may be right but behind the illness is a defective personality or he wouldn't have been liable to it—don't you think so? It is all horrid & his idea that he is coming out & back into the same relations with people is going to get some jolts I think. We feel about the "gifts", etc. that if a man is a man he would take his punishment & not have it sweetened.

Mr. Ives says about "New Music" that it may be best to have it run by a committee—perhaps of five—if so Mr. Becker should certainly be one—but he thinks to proceed slowly is best & not do anything immediate.

Our love to you all

Sincerely yours
Harmony Ives

• • •

Cowell's imprisonment was also a serious problem for *New Music,* which he had run almost single-handedly for years. A new management structure with a new editor and more active board of directors was needed immediately. It fell to Ives, who declined any substantial involvement in editorial decisions because of his health, to help craft an arrangement that satisfied all involved.

314. 10 October 1936, from John Becker, St. Paul

Dear Charles and Edith:

We were so glad to get your letter. Mary Cecelia and all of us too, are so sorry you could not come West and have a visit with us.

I was very glad to get your slant about my attitude relative to being [on] the Editorial Board [of *New Music*], and I am glad that Henry evidently thought that I meant what I said and sent the attached letter, suggesting as you will note, that Strang[20] and Riegger and I be on this Board.

I think that it would be a very good idea if you wrote Strang how you felt about it. I am inclined to believe as you, that Strang is not quite strong enough for the job, but there is nothing we can do about it right now.

Dr. Sokoloff conducted a performance of my orchestra here last night and he really did a marvelous job, and received a tremendous ovation. He told the audience that my orchestra was "a miracle."

I just received a letter from Chicago telling me to come down to talk over with the

20. Cowell had proposed that Gerald Strang take over day-to-day management of *New Music.*

group, the possibility of doing my new Ballet down there in the Spring, but I feel that I just can't afford to spend the money because, after all, one does not know how long this thing will last.

We have been squeezing every penny until it hollers and we have had so many debts that we have had to clean up and if this thing did flop, we would not have a fortune to go on.

Evelyn and the children join me in sending Mrs. Ives, Edith and you all of our love.

Your old friend,
John J. Becker

P.S. I sure will be happy to have your printed score of the "Three Places in New England" and you can bet your life that we are going to give it in performance—and it will be a good one—if I have to conduct it myself, which I probably will. Be sure to write something on the score when you send it.

315. Ca. 10 October 1936, Henry Cowell to John Becker, San Quentin, California

Dear John:

I am glad to have your two letters, enclosed together—glad because it shows your genuine interest in New Music. Interest is not very great when everything is accepted and taken for granted; constructive criticism is something that is really helpful.

Your idea seems to me better than the one now proposed. The reason that we had not, in discussion, adopted some plan whereby the Eastern and middle members of the proposed board would have a final say-so about the music is, of course, because of the great trouble of sending everything to everyone. It would be genuinely impractable [*sic*].

But I believe that the idea of weeding out the self-evidently undesirable works, which no one approves of (this is easy to do—we get lots of very amateurish and no-good works submitted) and then sending the others to the members of a central board is very good. I would propose that there be only one member of such a board for each section—You for the middle, Strang for the west (he is willing to undertake the central operation of the thing) and probably Riegger for the East.

Ives has declined to serve in any capacity since his eyes are worse, and he cannot see well enough to read scores. [*In a footnote:* Ives is, of course, still behind New Music, however, and accepted Strang's editorship.] Ruggles would simply turn down all scores, and ask to have the publication discontinued, as he would find nothing suitable! And for such a central body, the fewer the better, anyway. Then, all those who have been asked in an advisory capacity can still be there.

What do you think of this? It is the same as your plan, with a few minor details changed. Remember, the matter is not yet set. If the letter you had from Strang gave you the impression that everything has been worked out, it was a wrong one. Although, of course, it must always be borne in mind that I cannot, on account of being here, be in constant touch with him, and cannot always know just what is taking place at each moment. He writes me, of course, very often, and I answer him when I can.

It might be a good idea for the three main editors to have marks for passing manuscripts with more or less approval, so that the results can be weighed better. In all such things, and for the final arrangements, do please correspond with Gerry Strang—write him as freely as you would if you knew him personally; for if you did, I feel sure you would like him and his wife both greatly, and there are no psychological or temperamental vagrancies to contend with there, so that one has to be reserved, as there are in so many cases.

Perhaps you will feel like letting him know what I have said here (or enclose this to him if you wish). Of course, I do not have the say—I only make suggestions. There is, at present, a certain amount of music which was ready in advance for New Music, and to which it is committed; by the time that is used up (and there is no reason it should not be supplemented at once with some other works) the new plan should be completely worked out. I am sure Strang feels, as I do, that any plan which has been suggested is only held to until a better one is worked out.

As ever heartily yours,
Henry

316. October 1936, from John Becker, St. Paul

Dear Charles:

Enclosed you will find a copy of a letter from Gerald Strang.[21] As you see, they have followed my plan through, and I feel that the quotation from Henry's letter is O.K. If they wish to have a new Editor each year I can see no reason for not doing so. The point that I wanted to make was that I would not serve on any Editorial Board and then have nothing to say about the ultimate publication. This seems to me to be a start in the right direction and I believe that if worse comes to worse, having our hands in it this way, we may be able to save the situation.

The past week has been a very hectic one. Last Tuesday, I came close to being killed in an accident. It was only a miracle that kept me from going into Lake Superior; and Evelyn is very sorrowful these days, because of the very serious illness of her mother, who today seems to have made a turn for the better. I am afraid, after all, that life is but a vicious circle.

Let me hear from you soon and give Mrs. Ives and Edith our love, and believe me

Your affectionate friend,
John Becker

• • •

Ives often wrote short personal letters to his close friends at Christmas. For those like Becker who were in chronic need of financial support, the season provided an excuse for Ives to send along a check as well.

21. Strang's letter was written on 11 October 1936. Becker's correspondence is held by the New York Public Library.

317. December 1936, to John Becker

Dear John:

We send kindest remembrances & best wishes to you all—from the bottom of our hearts,—and hope you are all well.

Edie has been quite seriously sick for nearly 2 months—but is better & sitting up this week for the first time.

Please don't mind my sending the enclosed—hope it will be of a little help in getting your music in shape—that's the important thing—

Excuse this scrawl—I can't see it well enough to know how bad it is—but I'm tired of writing by proxy.

Love to all & from all

Yours
Chas E. Ives

• • •

It was a few months before Ives responded to Lou Harrison's request for copies of music that he might perform and study, but the wait was well worth it in terms of what Ives finally sent. In 1936 Ives's nephew Chester was again living in New York with the Iveses; he serves as transcriber in the following letter.

318. 17 December 1936, Chester Ives to Lou Harrison

I am writing for my uncle. He asks me to say that some chamber music pieces which were on hand were shipped to you today by express from the Quality Photo Print Company, 521 Fifth Ave. N.Y.[22] Copies of the violin sonatas, etc. are being made and will be sent you in a few days.

Mr. Ives says that he hopes you will not feel in any way obligated to have any of his music played just because so much is being sent, or if it bothers the players too much which is often the case. But he greatly appreciates your interest and generosity in taking the time and trouble about it.

With the other music he is having sent a published score of his A New England Symphony.[23] He asks you to accept it with his compliments and kindest regards,—it is the only score of his which is without mistakes of the pen—That it is free from mistakes "of the mind and heart" he won't swear to.

With his best wishes,
I am, sincerely yours,

22. Ives typically paid for copies made by Quality Photoprint Studio himself.

23. An alternative title for *Three Places in New England*.

Chester Ives
for Charles E. Ives

P.S. If parts or duplicate copies of any of the music should be wanted—unless for immediate use—Mr. Ives will be very glad to have the Photo Print Co. send you any that you would like. They say that they could probably get them to you within ten days or so. This may be more convenient for you than having them made in San Francisco.

• • •

Soon after Harrison received the crate of music, he began to perform it in and around San Francisco. The chorales Harrison mentions are the three "Harvest Home" Chorales, in a copy by George Roberts.

319. 16 February 1937, from Lou Harrison, San Francisco

Dear Ives,

A tale of woe & some of joy. We were working hard on the projected set of concerts and we were going to play some of your music, when the flu struck us all save one. We have been ill almost ever since, January was a nitemare. By this time the Youth Congress had convened and, covered expenses leaving the concerts unnecessary.

Nevertheless, I am pleased to tell you that three enthusiasts, a clarinetist, a violinist, & a pianist, want to do the Largo in the 4th book of chamber music on March 22nd in Berkeley. The clarinetist & violinist would both like parts and, the clarinetist being taken with the piece wondered if he might ask for the score. I have not sent on the vols. to New Music Mss. Library yet because I am still studying them, but don't fear, they will get there.

You are most kind. I am very grateful for the scores you sent me, especially the symphony and the three chorals which I had not heard of. I am most fascinated by the chorals, they bring Bach up to date, and make something entirely new and beautiful in religious music. I can't tell you what things of yours I like the best because the next time I look at another work it becomes a favorite, and so on. Are you still writing? I hope so.

Never fear, the world will see as time goes on that there are no "mistakes of mind or heart" in your symphony, it's too accurately realized a vision to swerve far from the truth that was in your heart when you did it. The whole work amazes me, especially the lovely last movement.

Hoping that the flu hasn't touched you and that all is well.

Gratefully
Lou Harrison

• • •

The following correspondence with Becker highlights Ives's role as advisor and financial safety net. Here Ives seeks to play down Becker's fear that he was being slighted even by other champions of modernist composition such as Slonimsky. The correspondence between Moss Ives and Becker, mentioned in Letters 320 and 321, concerns their shared interest in Catholicism.

320. Ca. 1 March 1937, to John Becker

Dear John:

My brother was here Saturday and got your letter. He much appreciates it, and said he was going to write you. Thanks.

Don't mind what these lady-bird prima donna conductors, Greek or Latin) say, do, or—they all want it easy—play it pretty, please the ladies & make a living.

I would be glad to help out in the fund for traveling expenses—in the project you speak of in your letter. If you can let me know how much it will be, a month or so ahead, so I can arrange it—or at least do all I can.

Tues. A.M. Expected yesterday to have Edie's help in writing, but she is sick again this A.M. and Mrs. Ives is in Hartford taking care of her sister who has been very ill—why doesn't "the Creator" make better human bodies!!—Can you see this—I can see the blot! Will finish on other side this afternoon.

Friday: Yesterday, thought I'd get a stenog. to come in so I could write a decent letter—but had one of those short of breath days & couldn't talk, except when flat on back—so will finish with paw—later on when I can sit up & dictate will send you a good letter

Haven't seen Nicolas Slonimsky in 2 years or more—had heard he was writing a book, but not what about—he hasn't asked me for any information. I shall write him. If it is a book about living composers, and doesn't give you as big a place as anybody, he is way off! And will show him your letter.[24]

You were in the "American Composers" book—Stanford Univ. Press—and I thought all similar books. I haven't seen any of the book and directories that you speak of—or any other for that matter. I don't subscribe or answer their questionnaires. Some time ago I had the office send some copies of articles from magazines etc. but not recently.

As to what New Music should publish I can't be of any help—in fact I haven't looked at any of the issues for several years. I am sorry to be so useless but—, I don't know about any of the music of any of the men whom you mention tho' I do recall that Carl Ruggles & Henry Cowell said that Leuning was a weak sister.

However, it is important that the work of New Music as a matter of principle be kept going. We all send our best wishes to you & Mrs. Becker & all the children

Chas

24. Becker had written an angry letter (Becker to Ives, 15 February 1937 [CIP, 27/5]) in which he complained that he was being ignored in books on modern music and that Slonimsky had asked him only for his birth date for an upcoming book on contemporary composers.

321. 12 March 1937, from John Becker, St. Paul

Dear Charles:

I was so glad to get your letter and certainly appreciate your willingness to find some way to help finance the plan to conduct some of the more important orchestras of the WPA in the country, in contemporary works.

I am afraid however, that it would really be too expensive. I may be able to raise a few dollars among some friends but it would be so few that it would be but a drop in the bucket.

In talking it over with one of the Federal assistants, we decided that the orchestras that we should reach would be: Boston, New York, Philadelphia, Syracuse, Buffalo, possibly Hartford, Chicago, Milwaukee, and St. Paul.

This would take at least $1500.00 and maybe more in view of the fact that I would have to be at each place for quite a long time in order to have rehearsals so that we would give a decent performance. So, I really believe that we will have to give it up.

Again I want to tell you how nice it was to get your letter. You need not worry that I cannot read your letters. A letter from you always pulls me out of the depths.

Evelyn, Mary Cecelia and the children send their love to you all and we hope that all of you are well.

I am still hoping that something may arise to necessitate my coming to Washington so that I may be able to pay you a little visit.

I suppose your brother, by now, has heard from the Archbishop. He was tremendously interested in his book.[25]

Affectionately,

• • •

John Kirkpatrick's correspondence with the Iveses became more personal over time, although he always retained a degree of respectful formality that balanced his repeated requests to talk with Ives in person. In the following letter he suggests a specialist who he hoped would be able to treat the cataracts that Ives had been suffering from since the summer of 1936.[26] The letter also demonstrates the extent to which Kirkpatrick conceived of the project of studying and performing Ives's works as a spiritual quest.

322. 4 April 1937, from John Kirkpatrick, Greenwich, Connecticut

My dear Mrs. Ives—

For a moment I thought I had some useful information for you. My aunt is having some cataracts treated by a remarkable doctor who has some way of dissolving them—but I

25. Moss Ives's book *The Ark and the Dove: The Beginning of Civil and Religious Liberties in America* (New York: Longmans, Green and Co., 1936) argues that tolerance of Catholicism in colonial Maryland was an important influence on the establishment of religious freedom in the United States.

26. Ives, *Memos*, 335.

have just called her up for his address and she tells me that they can be treated that way only when they haven't yet crossed the line of vision—and as you say Mr. Ives's impair his sight, I'm afraid they would be too far developed.

However here I am writing you just the same—so I might as well give you his address—Dr. Edward Davis, 40 East 61st Street—it might come in handy—he is evidently a unique specialist in cataracts, has published a book on the subject and has been remarkably successful with his methods. I have no doubt Mr. Ives has always had the best of medical attention, but somehow one can't help wondering if another mind could bring new light.

I still stubbornly look forward to the great pleasure of making the acquaintance of you all some time in the future. I would appreciate it greatly if some day when Mr. Ives seems unusually well, you would just call me up—the chances are about 3 to 1 that I would be free (except this next week which is completely full, particularly with the Coolidge festival in Washington)—you can always catch me at ten in the morning.

I can't tell you how anxious I am not only to meet Mr. Ives but to see just what the extent of his manuscripts comprises—it really gives one pause to read, in Miss Edith's letter of 35:[27] "About half a dozen pages are all that are found." Of course to you all, living in the midst of that creation, it seems a commonplace, and your natural modesty tends to belittle its importance and to resent slightly the prospect of being catalogued as a national or public monument. But to us whose job is the tonal realization of that creation (the liberation, for all who can hear, of the spiritual forces and truths in the music) every least scrap of documentation is invaluably precious. There are many many songs that I am supposedly actively at work on now, except for the holding up of certain decisions which wait for seeing all the existing versions. And there are many passages in Hawthorne and Thoreau that don't entirely explain themselves from the printed page. And then there is the question of Mr. Ives's growth himself. Composers are notoriously kaleidoscopic and see things they have written years before in quite a different light—hence the value of the manuscripts dating from the time of actual composition.

But I'm afraid this is getting tiresome—I feel like Thoreau: that I can't possibly exaggerate enough to make a clear statement of the way I feel about it—"it" being that the truths in Mr. Ives's music have got to be unfurled for an airing, and that working out the best possible adjustment or presentation for the chosen tonal medium is of prime importance in the unfurling.

You all have, as always, my dearest thoughts and best wishes.

John Kirkpatrick

323. 28 April 1937, from John Kirkpatrick, Greenwich, Connecticut

My dear Mrs. Ives,

Here is a case in point—in connection with the program last night, in which you notice the little question blank—Someone sent in: "If Mr. Ives's songs are so beautiful, why are they

27. See Letter 304.

heard so seldom?" Roy [Harris], in answer, spoke of how they were written so many years before their time and were printed years before they could be generally understood, when they were considered quite mad, and how an unfortunate tradition had persisted that they were unplayable. I am sure that represents the point of view of most musicians toward them, and that the only thing necessary for their wider spread is simply just to let them be seen in their best possible pianistic and optical presentation.

I am sorry to be so self-propagandist, and to continue so redundantly the burthen of my last letter, but you know how I feel about all this.

I hope Mr. Ives is better. When will you be coming out to the country? This April hasn't been so good, but it should be beautiful in May. Please let me know, and I would greatly appreciate it if I could make a brief call before you leave town. I shall soon be taking up Hawthorne again which will be a great pleasure.

Faithfully yours,
John Kirkpatrick

• • •

Younger composers, intrigued and inspired by the growing corpus of compositions by Ives being published and performed in the 1930s, took up the task of promoting his works and wrote to him in hope of meeting him or obtaining otherwise unavailable scores. Some, like Elie Siegmeister (1909–91), were also drawn to his politics, which they understood as leftist. When Siegmeister wrote to Ives in June 1937, he sent a copy of the article on Ives that he had written for the *Soviet Music Encyclopedia* and an issue of *Unison*, a leftist journal published by the American Music League. He also mentioned discussing Ives's music with the critic Olin Downes, who professed interest but knew little of it. Siegmeister immediately volunteered to arrange informal performances.[28]

324. Ca. 15 June 1937, sketch in Edith Ives's hand for Ives to Elie Siegmeister

My dear Mr. Siegmeister:—

I am writing for my father as he is not well.

It was a great pleasure to him to have your kind and interesting letter. He greatly appreciates your interest in his music. He has heard your music spoken of with great respect & he hopes it will be often heard and appreciated.

Your paper for the Russian book is admirable. Father says there is a fine & natural feel behind it—well written—and that you have a gift for making details interesting that some writers would make dull.

He is sincerely grateful to you for all you have done.

This is but a note of acknowledgment & appreciation & thanks for your letter. Just as soon as father has a good day when he can attend to things more as he would like to

28. Siegmeister to Ives, 15 June 1937 (CIP, 32/1).

he will write you in some detail of those things of which you ask & also go over what photostat copies there are of the music here & the list of negatives & have some sent to you.

With our best wishes, I am
Sincerely yours

• • •

John Kirkpatrick finally met the Iveses in person on 12 May 1937. In a letter of the following July, he recalls the visit with pleasure and pens one of the most intimate reactions to the *Concord* Sonata Ives ever received. The correspondence contains many letters responding to the *Concord*, but none before this one came from a performer who had devoted the time and energy necessary to master the piece. Kirkpatrick's understanding of the sonata was singular, and his reaction to it is carefully considered and written in terms that show his assimilation of Ives's prose as well as his music.

Kirkpatrick's remark on Ives's seeming good health at the time of their May meeting points out a paradox. Though his condition was fragile and mercurial, there were times when he seemed quite robust and full of life.[29] This makes sense considering the cyclic nature of Ives's illness; he had few visitors during his health slumps.

325. 25 July 1937, from John Kirkpatrick, Greenwich, Connecticut

My dear Mr. Ives,

You have probably been wondering what's happened to me—though I'm afraid I have already given you in the past sufficient reason for knowing me as a very poor correspondent. The truth is that I felt ashamed to write and not report some progress on the Concord Sonata, and all spring things have been pulling me this way and that away from it—so it has been a great joy to get a lot of work done on it this past month. I think I see all the problems involved clearly now and I know just about how I want to color Hawthorne and Thoreau—I can't play it all yet but I hope to have it together in another month. One thing makes me very happy—I find that I have been making something of a phobia out of the final passage of Hawthorne—but now that I understand it better and can really practice on it, I find it not particularly difficult.

My admiration for the work as a whole grows immeasurably now that I can see it in the round. I don't know any long work that is so triumphantly sure in the instinctive justness of its timing—and it's not a piece that has anything to do with nice balances, but the kind of rhapsodic outburst of strong substances that ordinarily makes for disappointing proportion as in Emanuel Bach or betrays the effort of adjustment as in Beethoven. But this treats its subjects in great free round shapes of music that move or plunge into each other with obvious spontaneity, and yet when one gets off at a distance and looks at it in perspective,

29. See Dane Rudhyar's description of Ives in Perlis, *Charles Ives Remembered*, 171.

there is no aspect of it that does not offer an ever fresh variety of interesting cross relation and beautifully significant proportion.

I really can't wait for the time when I can play it all through up to tempo, just for the pleasure of feeling the flow of the whole complete shape.

By the way, one thing I meant to ask you: was I right in spotting the "human faith melody" (Essays, p. 54) in my program notes?—and was it intentional or organic that they (those two themes) occur in both Emerson and Hawthorne?—because now it seems to me as if you must have noticed in 1915 that that had happened and decided to make a movement out of those two elements which would unify the whole layout.

Did any more pages of the old Emerson overture turn up, beyond what you sent me in photostat?—and do you think there is anything left of the first manuscripts of Hawthorne and Thoreau?

I never got to write you how much I enjoyed seeing you in May. It was a great pleasure to meet you all and talk with you, and I was sorry only that I didn't get to play Emerson for you. There's a rather amusing story about that—The day before, I played a recital at the Rye Country Day School, and was all set to drive down right from there to Philadelphia for a few days visit, but got picked up on the parkway for passing a cop (they have an absurd 35m limit there, and I was doing 41), and was brought to the rather uncomfortable realization that I hadn't yet gotten around to getting my this year's driving license. So he took me down to the police station and it seems I couldn't legally drive the car away not having a license. I took it all very philosophically, half by nature, and half probably because it's a pose I rather enjoy in that kind of predicament, and told him I had no doubt it was all happening for some reason that neither of us knew now. Not knowing just whom to impose on, I called up my dear friend Mrs. Perkins to ask if her chauffeur could bring someone down, and after a moment's consultation she said that she and Mr. Perkins would enjoy the evening's drive after supper and would come down themselves. It all seemed so unreal—being arrested driving a station wagon in one's morning coat, and being rescued by a bank chairman-of-the-board-of-directors—that I couldn't help thinking it really must be for some significant reason that I was being kept in Greenwich,—and the next morning I was so sure it was what it really was, that when the phone rang I knew as precisely as one knows anything that it was Mrs. Ives. Strange are the ways of God and man.

I hope you have been having a profitable summer, and that your health is much better. I must confess I was surprised to see you looking so well in May, and took it to mean a sudden amelioration which I hope has continued. Certainly if anybody has the right to health as perfect freedom of action for the expression of vigorous and ideal thought for the good of humanity, you have.

You remember,—you mentioned the Psalm that superimposes G minor on C major—I heard it several days later at the Federal Theatre, by Lehman Engel's madrigal singers—marvelous piece![30] It seemed to me a sublime conception and an absolutely flawless realization—the proportional relation of the fugato to the end perpendicular sections was so natural—it had such outer brevity and economy and such inner glow and universality. I

30. Engel's Madrigal Singers performed Ives's Psalm 67 at the W.P.A. Theatre of Music in New York on 6 May 1937. See Sinclair, *Descriptive Catalogue*, 270.

was very glad to have had my ears somewhat opened to that kind of medium—I have been doing some coaching for voice pupils of Ann Luckey (the same Ann Luckey who collaborated with me 3 years ago in that series) and I have been making them do some Thomas Morley—particularly one very intricate 5 part canzonet "I follow, lo, the footing" with lots of close stretti. It might be fun to have them do the Psalm. Isn't it 6 voices, 3 men and 3 women?

By the way, I have been rather expecting those shorter piano pieces you mentioned. What happened to them? I haven't ceased being very anxious to see them.

I have thought much about what you said in regard to your feeling about sharps and flats, and I find now that I want to change much less in the way I would like to write your music down. I still insist though that in places you needlessly obscure what are obviously the simple harmonic underpinnings. For instance in Maple Leaves, "The most are gone now . . . "—by all that's holy the A-sharp–F is a perfect fourth and that B-flat minor–C minor–B-flat minor progression is much stronger and more important than the E–B pedal around the accompaniment—so the latter shouldn't disturb the natural spelling of the former. At least that's the way I see it now.

I have worked out a way of doing the flute passage at the end of Thoreau that I think you will like.

Please give my kindest regards to Mrs. Ives and to Miss Edith.

Hoping to see you soon again, I remain, ever faithfully yours,
John Kirkpatrick

• • •

In August Ives sketched a short reply to a letter Kirkpatrick had sent on 16 May, in which he invited the Iveses to a recital. The sketch reveals how deliberately Ives wrote in the voice of the person who would eventually transcribe a given letter. Here, Edith was originally to have been the writer, but the revision projects Harmony's voice. While the changes themselves were cosmetic, Ives's need to make them indicates the care he took in his correspondence and the extent of his control over it.

326. 5 August 1937, sketch for Harmony Ives to John Kirkpatrick

J. Kirkpatrick

~~Father~~ Mr. I want to thank you very very much for your kind & interesting letter, —he greatly appreciates it. He has not been as well this summer as he was last spring—but just as soon as he has a good day he wants ~~to write you a good letter~~ go over the music referred to, & have it sent you—or photostats made for all the copies [that] may not be here.

Mother We thank you for the invitation to the concert, in which you played MacDowell's Sonata—we were sorry not to have gone, but have just left for Redding. Father Mr. I says "I am deeply grateful for your help your interest your playing & your <u>friendship.</u>" He sends kindest wishes in which we all join

Sincerely

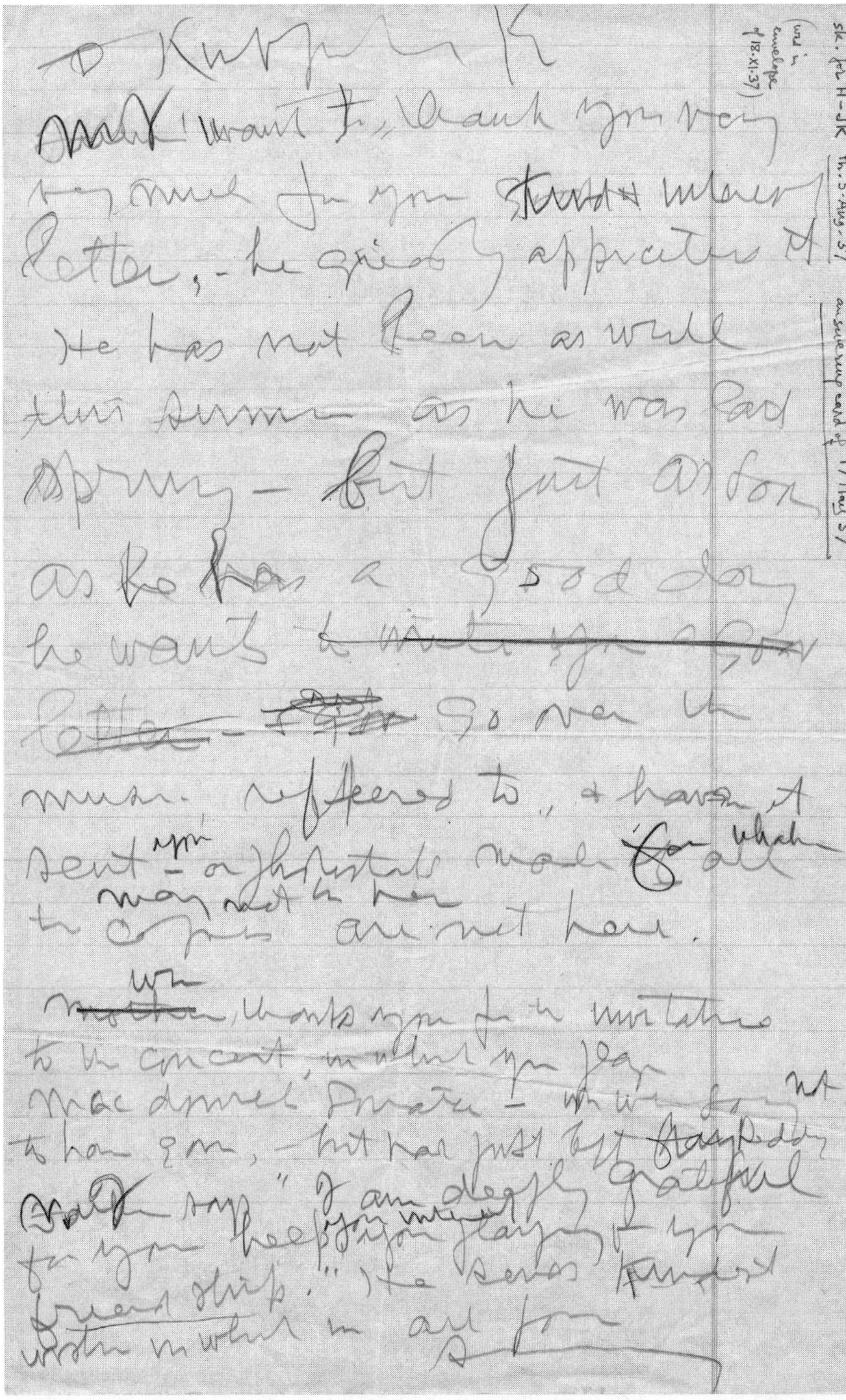

5 August 1937, sketch for Harmony Ives to John Kirkpatrick.

• • •

Mordecai Bauman, a baritone, made the premiere recordings of Ives's songs "Ann Street," "Charlie Rutlage," "Evening," "The Greatest Man," "Resolution," and "Two Little Flowers" for *New Music* in 1938.[31]

327. Late 1937, sketch for Edith Ives to Mordecai Bauman[32]

B

Father thanks you very much sends you many thanks for your letter & suggestion that some of the songs be recorded. He knows what a remarkably fine singer Mr. Bauman is— ~~and it is fortunate he is willing to make the record.~~

~~As to suggesting~~ Father thinks that rather than have him select suggest the songs—it will be better to have Mr. B and the pianist do whatever they feel like doing—as to selecting & singing & playing (over)—any of the ones published by NM & Cos Cob Press would do—though they are more in the "old book 114 Songs" which he would just as well remain silent rather not have sung in public.

Someday—Father says, I would rather like to have some of the songs like "The Masses," "An Election," "West London" Paracelsus recorded, sung—possibly as much for their subject matter & a something behind the words as the music. But the piano parts are arrangements of scores—& it would probably make trouble recording.

[*Additional material for 2nd paragraph:*] Father says, "the older he gets the more he feels it is better to let men ~~doing~~ do things in their own way—rather than the composer ~~shuffling~~ squinting around back—I remember when younger it used to make me mad to have the composer tell you what to play & exactly how to play it—I guess I ended up doing everything they told me not to do.

• • •

Carl Ruggles suffered from intermittent prostatitis, and in 1938 a nearly fatal occurrence required surgery. Charlotte Ruggles immediately wrote to the Iveses for help with paying for the hospital stay that brought a gradual improvement.[33] Carl's recovery was welcome news to the Iveses, who were dealing with Charles's health problems as well. Ives's dreamlike description of conducting Ruggles's music with a baseball bat at his imagined funeral is an intriguing metaphor for the spirit Ives felt American music should embody.

31. Sinclair, *Descriptive Catalogue*, 339.

32. This sketch has no recipient indicated. It is possible that Ives wrote to an unnamed third party about the proposed record.

33. Two undated letters from Charlotte Ruggles to Harmony Ives from March 1938 (CIP, 32/11). The second letter thanks the Iveses for sending a check to cover the hospitalization. Marilyn J. Ziffrin, *Carl Ruggles: Composer, Painter, Storyteller* (Urbana: University of Illinois Press, 1994), 149.

328. 18 April 1938, from Carl Ruggles, Coral Gables, Florida

Dear Harmony and Charles:

Home from hospital, and getting stronger every day. It has been a terrible experience, but the surgeon says I will be better than I have been for years, which is gratifying news. Charlotte has been wonderful through it all, but she is always wonderful. And you and Harmony have been wonderful in helping us through this tragic time. I can never express my gratitude.

Before I was taken ill, I had been holding a Seminar in Modern Composition at the University here. It was tremendously interesting. Two of the students showed real talent, which is a high percentage, don't you think so Charles? Just think, that of all the students that have taken composition at Yale—and in fact all the rest of the universities—you are the only one that came through. That is my profound belief.

When I think of your magnificent music, and the dirty half-wit conductors, it burns me up. Just to show you: The University Orchestra is really excellent, about 80 players. They wanted to play my "Men and Mountains." But old Volpe the conductor said: "No, it's too difficult, and strange." The truth is he couldn't read the score. And all the young players crazy to try it. And they could have done it sure. Mike graduates June 1st and we shall leave immediately for Arlington. Deepest love to you all,

as ever,
Carl

P.S. Mike is going to pitch professional ball for Nashville Tenn. this summer and I think it's fine don't you?[34]

329. May 1938, to Carl Ruggles[35]

Dear Carl:

Your letter brought great news—it was a relief to us. I knew you weren't a-going to die—but I was a-going to your funeral and conduct Sun Treader & Men & Mt's"—not with a "baton" but with a ball-bat—and Micah would stand up & pitch—and after those in-shoots, and liners got goin, down the tuba et al . . . , they would finally learn how to play music for men—not "lilly ears.["]

Carl—you and I can thank the All-mighty for the greatest blessings man can have—our blessed perfect wives.

God bless you all—

ever yours
Chas.

34. Ruggles's son Micah played for a minor league team in Tennessee that summer.

35. Harmony's letter of 9 May 1938 to Charlotte Ruggles (Letter 266) was mailed in the same envelope.

• • •

In the spring of 1938 Kirkpatrick booked New York's Town Hall for the following January for the recital in which he would give the premiere of the full *Concord* Sonata. Ives responded to the letter from aboard the ship on which he was traveling to England for a few months of rest.[36] Contrary to Kirkpatrick's assumption that the trip indicated an improvement in Ives's health, it was intended as a rest cure for Ives and, particularly, for Harmony. Ives described the situation leading up to the trip in a letter to John Becker on 30 June: "I had one of those usual, chronic low swings, am used to them, but this lasted longer than usual—but Mrs. Ives has been in quite a serious condition—it worried me—the doctors were afraid of a bad nervous breakdown."[37]

330. 13 May 1938, from John Kirkpatrick, Stamford, Connecticut

Dear Mr. Ives,

At last the stage seems fairly set for the Concord Sonata. The other day my dear friend Mrs. Perkins remarked that she thought it was about time I did another Town Hall recital, and several days after that when I asked her if she really meant it and if all the ramifications could be accounted for, she was still of the same mind. So Copley has a date for me, January 30, a Monday evening. The program hasn't changed in some time—Beethoven's Waldstein, Ives's Concord. It adds up to about 70 minutes, which is just about right. I haven't ever really played either Hawthorne or Thoreau yet, but they're both old acquaintances and even ripe conceptions with me, and I know exactly what I want to do with them, so I'm confident they'll be well in shape. I did most of the ground work of Hawthorne last year.

Of course it all makes me very happy—not only the imminent fruition of old efforts—but the somewhat disgraceful fact that I never work so well as when there's a performance in the offing.

The series which I started here in January suffered quite an interruption when I fell and turned my ankle and sprained my right hand on March 6. It gave rise among other things to a lot of left hand practicing and to the recital of which I enclose a copy of the invitation. It was a lot of fun and made a nice party. The right hand is perfectly well again and the series was resumed last Tuesday. I think I may combine the latter programs in some way—it seems absurd to have that kind of thing running into July—but I haven't decided how much. I hope to trot out Hawthorne and Thoreau in some shape or other, just to get them out before an audience now as soon as possible and be that much ahead. I'm doing the Waldstein next Tuesday, the 17th, and I think the rest will follow about as indicated on the enclosed revised programs. If Mrs. Ives and Edith might like to attend some of them, if it isn't too far to come, I should be delighted to have them.

I have been meaning to write you in appreciation of your kindness in allowing Roy

36. See Letters 266–67.

37. For the full text, see Letter 170.

[Harris] to include the 67th Psalm in his book, but at first I was waiting from some word from him and then gently slipped into the limbo of good intentions. I'm afraid both of us are equally unsatisfactory correspondents. I see they're going to do it at the Westminster Choir School festival at Princeton, end of this month. I'm taking part in the festival on the 27th—Aaron Copland and I are playing my arrangement of his Symphonic Ode (2 pianos).

How is your health these days? I hope the early spring was a comfort. Did you find the time to hunt up those pieces you mentioned? I am still very anxious to see them. Do you feel well enough to have me make a brief call some day? I should love to see you all and of course there are always lots of things I want to ask you. And when you look at the map, Redding seems hardly around the corner from Stamford.

Please remember me to Mrs. Ives and Edith, and accept my heartfelt wishes for your well-being. When I think of you I wish I had the powers of Phineas Quimby—or of Jesus (that particular power).[38]

Sincerely
John Kirkpatrick

• • •

The following letter documents the first-known full performance of the *Concord* Sonata, given by John Kirkpatrick, still reading from the music, on a small, private lecture-recital series in Stamford, Connecticut.

331. 22 June 1938, from John Kirkpatrick, Stamford, Connecticut

Dear Mr. Ives,

Thank you so much for your radiogram from the ship. I quite envy you a summer in England. I have been there for just 2 weeks, in 1931, and want very much to see it again and longer some time.

I take it the fact of your voyaging is an indication that your health is considerably better, which makes me very glad.

Last night, in our little series here, we got to the American impressionists, and I trotted out the whole Concord Sonata—not yet from memory—but it was nice to feel its unity. The program was:

Griffes–Sonata
Three poems of Fiona MacLeod (Miss Luckey)
Ives—Barn Dance from "Washington's Birthday" (record)
Concord. Mass, 1840–60

I don't know how you like being dubbed an impressionist—labeling things that way so often leads to limiting one's conception of them—but one has to have some kind of

38. Phineas Quimby (1802–1866) formulated a theory and practice of mental healing that influenced Mary Baker Eddy, the founder of the Christian Science movement.

designation for a period—and then there's an awful lot that's really impressionist in your music.

Hawthorne went really very well, and made a big impression. Thoreau still eludes me somewhat, but now that I've trotted it out I see it much more clearly—what to correct and how. (I don't mean correcting the notes but my timings and colorings).

Miss Luckey wanted very much to do some of the songs too, but she has had an unexpectedly busy couple of weeks and simply couldn't get in enough work on them.

I look forward eagerly to seeing you in the fall, and perhaps playing the sonata for you. The Town Hall date is all secured, so it's all up to me now.

Please remember me to Mrs. Ives and to Edith,

with all best wishes, sincerely,
John Kirkpatrick

• • •

As the premiere of the *Concord* approached, Ives began the discussion with Lehman Engel of Arrow Music Press that eventually led to the publication of its second edition in 1947. Even as his works began to appear in other publications, Ives remained dedicated to *New Music* and active in its financial support.

332. Ca. 23 August 1938, excerpts from sketches for Ives to Lehman Engel

[*Sketch 1*]

Dear Mr. Engel:

Your letter of June 22nd was not forwarded—I found it only on our return among some of the other mail which should have been forwarded, and I'm sorry not to have answered before.

I will be glad to have something of mine published, as you propose, for the new catalogue. Also I'll be glad to pay for the work—though I don't feel quite right in paying for mine only, when quite probably there is much music of others, especially of the younger men, which ought to be published. So what I want to do—and will do if I may—is to send you the same amount for other music that mine comes to.

I think it would be better if you and your associates on the board would select whatever of my music you think advisable for this issue. As I remember, you have several manuscript copies of things of mine which have not been published—and if there are others which you haven't and would like to see, I will be glad to have them sent.

[*Sketch 2*]

Another thing is that I will probably have to arrange with someone to correct the proofs—my eye condition makes it very uncertain what I can do when. Some days I can see almost nothing for long periods—at other times I can see well enough for an hour or so a day. If I could have plenty of time and there is no hurry, could probably do the correcting with the help of some of the family.

As to the music, some of the chamber numbers for small orchestra or other groups perhaps might do—perhaps the 2nd Orchestral Set, though as I remember, there are several mistakes in the copy, and some of the instrumentation will have to be changed. I hear the E-flat clarinet is seldom used now, and some of the parts in the lower trumpets will have to be put into the horn or trombone parts. The lower range of the trumpets is weaker than the old trumpets, though the new trumpets' upper notes are much better and higher. Details like this may take some time to attend to. Among the old overture scores there is one and also a 2nd String Quartet which you might be willing to consider.

I would like to have more and better copies of either of these, though I'm afraid very few if any orchestras or quartets would or could possibly play them without a great deal of time and effort and trouble and cussin' (while playing)—and perhaps there is somewhere one man [who] might buy one after he's had a good dinner.

You may have copies of these scores—the 2nd String Quartet is put [in] vol. 6 of t he chamber music books. However I guess it's better for these to wait a few years—for with the exception of men like you and your friends and associates, there are still too many (though the number is getting less every year nowadays, 'tis said) among musicians who are "lillyears" et al, who look at music as a baby doll looks at a nice pansy. They all sing the same nice chorus = write it easy to play, easy to hear, easy to sell and please the ladies (male and female)—even Rollo knows that! But for that matter, the other nice chamber music sets, etc. will make Mabel feel just as badly—but not for so long a time—before rest!

Now, having gotten this "gab" off my chest, I won't talk about the pansies any more—as there is a matter of some importance which I think I spoke to you about in a general way last year, which I would like to take up with you in some detail, and find how you and your board may feel about it.

[*Sketch 3*]

Also there is a matter I've had in mind, a kind of plan which from a business side may help the work of your new A[rrow] M[usic] P[ress] organization and the <u>New Music Editions</u> and <u>Recordings;</u> perhaps not—but at any rate if you would like me to I'll write you about it in some detail, later on.

[*Sketch 4*]

It seems to me that aims and general purpose of your <u>Arrow Music Press</u> and of the <u>New Music Edition</u> about fundamentally (if not in detail) the same. We're all in the same boat, so to say. And I think that, if some practical way could be worked so that the two could combine or at least cooperate, the "cause" which both have in mind would [be] helped and the work more efficiently done than working separately and at cross purposes. I don't know how the editors and others interested in <u>New Music</u> feel about this plan, and I don't think there's any good of writing them until I hear from you.

333. 27 August 1938, from Lehman Engel, Arrow Music Press, New York

Dear Mr. Ives:

I have seldom been as touched as I was by your letter of August 23rd. We are all so very happy to know that you will publish a score in the Press and we were pleased beyond telling to have your generous offer to publish an equal amount of music by a young composer. We will be glad to recommend composers or works to you in about two weeks but I am rather wondering at this writing if you might not rather be interested in publishing a work by Henry Cowell. If you prefer a young man to Henry Cowell we can easily recommend several who are in no position to pay for the publication of their own music. But it seems to me that you were a friend of Cowell and this idea might appeal to you.

I do hope that all of you enjoyed your vacation abroad and I will hope to see you when you are able to have company in New York. I have done some work on your manuscript choruses, that is, toward getting them in order, and I will want to show them to you. Also I have gone through your prose notes and will have some recommendations to make regarding these.

As for myself, I have composed a sinfonietta, a set of ten choruses to Blake's Songs of Innocence and music for Maurice Evans' Hamlet.

We would be very much interested to have your plan about our Press and New Music Editions so please send it along at any time that you feel like writing a letter. With most cordial greetings to your wife, daughter and yourself, and again my deepest thanks,

Lehman Engel

• • •

In the following letters the baritone Mordecai Bauman writes to Ives to ask if there is an orchestration of "Charlie Rutlage," and Ives proposes that Bernard Herrmann make an arrangement based on an earlier chamber piece that had been adapted in the composition of the song. This process highlights the complex interrelationship between the different incarnations of Ives's pieces. Herrmann's orchestration would restore aspects of Ives's original conception of the piece that were lost in his piano vocal score.[39]

334. 2 October 1938, from Mordecai Bauman, New York

My Dear Charles Ives,

I have been asked to sing in December with the Federal Symphony Orchestra and would like to include "Charlie Rutlage" on my program. I wonder whether you have an orchestration of it for full symphony orchestra or if there is any way I can get one made. I am really very anxious to do it. I am going to use it at my Town Hall concert in March. Would

39. Ives himself planned to make an orchestrated version of this piece for his Orchestral Set no. 5, "The Other Side of Pioneering"; see Sinclair, *Descriptive Catalogue*, 355.

you let me know as soon as possible about the orchestration of "Charlie Rutlage," because I must give the people in charge a definite answer?

I made a recording of your songs for New Music and I wonder if you have heard them and whether or not you feel them at all adequate. They weren't made under the best of circumstances. I met Bernard Herrmann the other day and he told me you had taken a trip to Scotland this summer. I was very glad to hear of your improved health and hope it continues.

If the occasion ever arises when I can come and pay you a friendly visit and chat with you I shall be very honored.

Yours,
Mordecai Bauman

335. Ca. 2 October 1938, sketch for Harmony Ives to Mordecai Bauman

Mr. I deeply app. your singing of his songs & thanks you sincerely for all you have done. We have heard enthusiastic comments from those who have heard you sing them. We have only a very poor Victrola here, and as Mr. Ives's hearing has bothered him lately, we are waiting to hear the record on a good machine, & he is looking forward to hearing them.

Mr. Ives wishes me to thank you for your letter. He is sorry there is no orch. score for the song Charlie Rutlage, but thinks it can be readily scored—that is, without much difficulty. I am sorry that Mr. Ives, on account of his general health and eye condition, is unable to do work of this kind nowadays. But he thinks that Bernard Herrmann might be willing to do this score, & he would do it well. We will write him immediately.

As Mr. I remembers, a part, or at least some things in the middle passages of the song, were suggested by an old piece for brass band (A Runaway Horse on Main St.—Fair Week). This will be sent to Mr. Herrmann. It may be of some help.

We hope to have the pleasure of seeing you when we are back in town this winter. With Mr. Ives's best wishes I remain,

• • •

Ives's suggestions to Herrmann on the orchestration of "Charlie Rutlage" show the deferential manner with which he approached those who worked on his pieces as editors, arrangers, or performers. His comments also point out the importance for Ives of a personal connection to his music. He even couches his ideas about the sound of cowboy music in the context of his cousin's description of life on a "cowboy ranch."

336. 6 October 1938, Harmony Ives to Bernard Herrmann

Dear Mr. Herrmann,

We hope you are well & have had a good summer. Our trip went pretty well tho we had lots of bad weather & foggy passages both ways.

Mr. Ives has received a letter from Mr. Mordecai Bauman asking if "Charlie Rutlage" is or could be arranged for voice and symphony orchestra as he wants to sing it at a symphony concert in New York in December. This has never been so arranged & Mr. Ives, who as you know cannot undertake these things nowadays on account of his eyesight, wonders if you would be willing to do it—but, he says, "if you will, you must be a good boy and let him put it on a business basis—as it will [take] some time and trouble on your part."

As he remembers, a part, or at least passages in the middle section, were suggested by an earlier score for brass band—"A Runaway Horse on Main St"—he will send you a copy, if you would like,—it may be of some help.

On the enclosed copy of the song there are a few suggestions. The 1st & last pages for the most part might be a kind of strumming accompaniment by strings alone. Mr. Ives remembers getting a kind of banjo effect by having one half of the strings pizz. & the other half separate short bows. A low tympani or two might beat time with the basso as a kind of Indian tom-tom (Mr. Ives had a cousin who lived on a cowboy ranch some 40 years ago who said the cowboys nearly always had an Ind. tom-tom beating when they sang & usually some banjos). The middle section, the runaway horse part, would be for full orchestra & plenty of drums. A piccolo or E-flat clarinet might play the cowboy yelling song "Whopee to yi yo" etc. (page 20 marked)

Mr. Ives says you must not feel obligated to do this as he knows how busy you are but he would be pleased to have you.

With our best wishes & hoping to see you when we get back, I am,

Yours sincerely,
Harmony T. Ives

• • •

In the course of further discussion of the "Rutlage" project, we see evidence of the awakening critical interest in Ives's music, in part due to the efforts of performers like Bauman. One such interested critic was Olin Downes, who wrote for the *New York Times* from the late 1920s through the mid 1950s.[40]

337. 18 October 1938, from Mordecai Bauman, New York

Dear Charles Ives,

I have been in touch with Bernard Herrmann and he tells me that he will orchestrate the Charlie Rutlage. He is doing the orchestration and also making it available for a smaller combination.

40. Some of Downes's reviews are reprinted in Burkholder, *Charles Ives and His World*, 292–94, 326–28, 340–42, 351, 352–53.

My friend Elie Siegmeister tells me that Olin Downes has asked to meet you. Last year Mr. Siegmeister and myself played and sang a number of your songs for him that he expressed great enthusiasm for. I'm very glad that Mr. Downes is beginning to show an interest in your music.

I hope this letter finds you well.

Sincerely,
Mordecai Bauman

• • •

During his imprisonment, Cowell made a couple of careful attempts to resume contact with the Iveses; the letter below to their mutual friend, Mary Bell, is an example. His manner indicates a sensitivity to Ives's need for time to absorb and accept what has happened.

338. 19 January 1939, Henry Cowell to Mary Bell, San Quentin, California

Dear Mary,

I was delighted to get your fine Christmas letter and card, and to know what you are doing now. I didn't know your address, but took a chance on your old one, and sent you a Christmas card, which I hope you received. It is a great pleasure to know that you made a record of some of the Ives songs—this is splendid. I wish that you could do them all, on records, so that they might be made available in this form! It would be a real service to American music to have someone do this while Ives is still here to imbue the singer with his ideas personally; and you are one of the few people who sees him now, as you say you expected to see them soon when you wrote me. I often think of him; I do not hear from him, as I know he cannot write himself, but had a very fine note from him last year here. I wish that you would tell him that I think of him very often, if you do see him. And give him my staunchest greetings. I am sure he understands that the reason I do not write to him is not because I have lost interest in the subject! It has been with the greatest delight that I see the march forward of understanding of his work on the part of the ever-widening public, and it gives me a tremendous satisfaction to feel that I have played a part in bringing his works to the attention of those who now accept them as of great value. . . .

As ever with hearty greetings,
Henry

339. 2 February 1939, Harmony Ives to Mary Bell

Dear Miss Bell—

We did hope to see you 'ere this but Mr. Ives has been too used up—when you get back we hope for an opportunity.

I return Henry's letter—that matter has been such a blow to Mr. Ives that we never speak of it.

With our best wishes
Most truly yours—
Harmony Ives

• • •

John Kirkpatrick and Mina Hager presented the premieres of "Autumn," "Berceuse," "Down East," "The Side Show," and "Two Little Flowers" on what he called a "one-man-show" of Ives's music at Town Hall on 24 February 1939.[41] During the planning of the concert, Ives suggested that Mordecai Bauman sing in addition to Miss Hager. Kirkpatrick took this suggestion as an assertion that Ives felt that his songs would be better sung by a man. But the context strongly implies that his primary motive for suggesting Bauman was loyalty to a singer who had already been promoting his music. Ives's fragmentary sketches addressing the concert are below; the second is in Edith's voice.

340. 2 February 1939, sketches for Harmony Ives to John Kirkpatrick

[*Sketch 1*]

Madrigal next time

Bauman

<u>and</u> also

Miss Hager

telephone write

get in touch with

Bauman—If any extra expense will take care of that later

[*Sketch 2*]

won't try to have Madrigal this time but would like to have Bauman—sing a few songs—& also Miss Hager. He doesn't mean that all of songs are better if sung by men—only some are.

Bauman has for several years been singing Father's songs—& has done much in their behalf—and he knows quite a number of them. What songs does Miss Hager sing—might suggest "The Rainbow," "Evening" among others, might suggest others later.

41. Sinclair, *Descriptive Catalogue*, 678.

341. 4 February 1939, from John Kirkpatrick, Stamford, Connecticut

Dear Mr. Ives,

I don't know how to thank you—You are making possible one of my fondest ambitions, to do a one-man-show of your music.

I am very sorry that everything seems to have gone through in such a hurry and that, having this sore throat and not being able to get into town either yesterday or today, I couldn't see Mr. Baumann. You're right that in general your songs are more stuff for a man to sing than a woman. When I tentatively asked Miss Hager, I had in mind particularly the "Hymn" and "Where the Eagle Never Sees," both of which I feel would suffer considerably from having their voice parts lowered an octave—and so I got thinking of the whole program in terms of just the two of us. And now Mr. Gilman is anxious to put an announcement of it in tomorrow's [New York] Herald and Mr. Copley insists on a good-sized ad in Sunday's papers, so I'm afraid it will have to stay that way.

I'm terribly sorry to have to disappoint you in this request, and also not to have the pleasure of doing some of them with Mr. Bauman, as I have heard the best possible reports about him. Perhaps we can get together some other time. I don't think you need fear for any lack of variety in the program—the enormous variety in the music itself will take care of that—And Miss Hager is really a first-rate artist—(I was remarking to Paul Rosenfeld that a good Ives singer would have to have both profundity and zip—and she has—besides a very beautiful voice and the kind of musicianship that's both accurate and resilient.)

I hope you'll be feeling better as the days go on.

How grand about publishing the sonata!—I remember your saying you still had the plates. I imagine it would be quite simple to correct them, much as you did the New Music reprints. I haven't heard yet from Lehman Engel.[42]

Looking forward to the immense joy of playing the sonata again—

faithfully yours,
John Kirkpatrick

342. 9 February 1939, from John Kirkpatrick, New York

Dear Mr. Ives,

I find that the programs have to go to print this afternoon, as Monday is a holiday—so that leaves no time for changing the reverse. I tried to work out something last night in line with what you suggested but I am ashamed to say I was so dead tired I couldn't think straight. I did however send the printer a special delivery to have him omit your name in connection with the songs to your verses or Mrs. Ives's.

42. This is one of the earliest overt references to the second edition of the *Concord* Sonata; see Letters 332 and 333.

You are of course perfectly right in wanting to present the whole thing in as broad and universal a light as possible, and I see that I am more wrong than I at first thought. Perhaps I am not yet big enough to feel natural doing a big thing in a big way—Doing a big thing at all is, I guess, something for me to handle, so I tend to be limited and specific in the way of doing it. Perhaps some day I'll grow up. I am terribly sorry to have given you so much bother about all this and ashamed to have shown myself not yet up to presenting something to your heart's content. Now that I know you so much better, I hope that I shall start to grow in that direction, as indeed my years of working on the Concord Sonata have been a rich experience of gradually growing up to its comprehension.

Hoping that your health will continue to be better, and with all best wishes—

Sincerely,
John Kirkpatrick

343. 26 February 1939, from Lehman Engel, New York

Dear Mr. Ives:

I don't remember when I have spent such a moving evening at a concert as I did at the concert of your music at the Town Hall this past week.

It is not only important for you as a composer that concerts (many of them) such as this one be given but it is even more important to all other American composers to have it realized first that there is a Charles Ives among them and secondly it is important for them that their potential public know how fine a thing American music can be.

I don't remember when I have heard music which moved me as deeply as yours did and I openly wanted you to know how grateful I am.

With warmest greetings to your wife, daughter and you,

Cordially yours,
Lehman Engel

• • •

In May 1939 the musicologist and composer Charles Seeger wrote to Ives asking for information about his life and works that could be used in an article on him and Carl Ruggles for the *Magazine of Art*. The sketch for Ives's reply, in Edith's voice, follows.

344. Ca. 1 May 1939, sketch for Edith Ives to Charles Seeger

Seegar—

I am w——

He was very glad to hear from you, and he hopes you & Mrs. Segar have been well; ~~He says~~ He greatly appreciates your interest and kind thought of writing the article ~~as~~ sugested in your letter. He says, "I always enjoyed walking down the mountain arm in arm with Carl Ruggles." ~~We haven't heard from Mr. R.~~ When we last heard from Mr. & Mrs. R they were in Florida & Mr. Ruggles in better health than this winter—his serious illness last year gave us great anxiety.

~~Under separate cover Father is having sent~~ The data asked for is being sent under sep. cover. He is sorry that most of the MSS is in Redding—but it happens that the Photostat office has on hand a couple of the chamber music volumes—& will write them to send it to you.

The typewritten copy of the compiled comment, notices, etc. is only up to 1935—with copies since then, to bring it up to date, father has not kept together or [in] very good order—but we will have copies made of whatever is here, & they will [be] forwarded probably in a few days.

Father says that it is "he & not you who is doing the "imposing" "To look ~~over~~," he says, "through all these "leaves of ~~he won't say grass but~~ not grass "not yet" approaches an imposition—but he says don't bother to return anything—whatever of these bundles you may want to keep—please do so with his compliments and best wishes. Or if it happens there is any of the rest of his music you do not have—but would like to see—he will be glad to have them sent any time.

Again he wants to thank you for your troubles & all you are doing—and sends his best wishes & kindest regards to both of you.

• • •

This letter from Ruth Crawford Seeger (1901–53) documents the only direct contact Ives had with the composer. She may or may not have known that it was through his financial support that her scores had been published in Henry Cowell's *New Music*.

345. 30 May 1939, from Ruth Crawford Seeger

Dear Mrs. Ives—

In case my husband has been so busy simultaneously taking a government trip through the South and working on the Ives-Ruggles article, that he has not been able to write you, I want to send you our thanks for all the material you sent us, and for your kindness in making us a present of the scores. We are delighted and proud to have them.

We will of course see that the magazine reaches you as soon as it is out. And wish so much that we could come along with the magazine, for it has been always one of our strong regrets that, though having such close bonds to Charles Ives both in music trends and friends, our paths have never crossed.

With best regards to you both, an appreciation to Mr. Ives for his warm friendly letter,

Very cordially,
Ruth Crawford Seeger

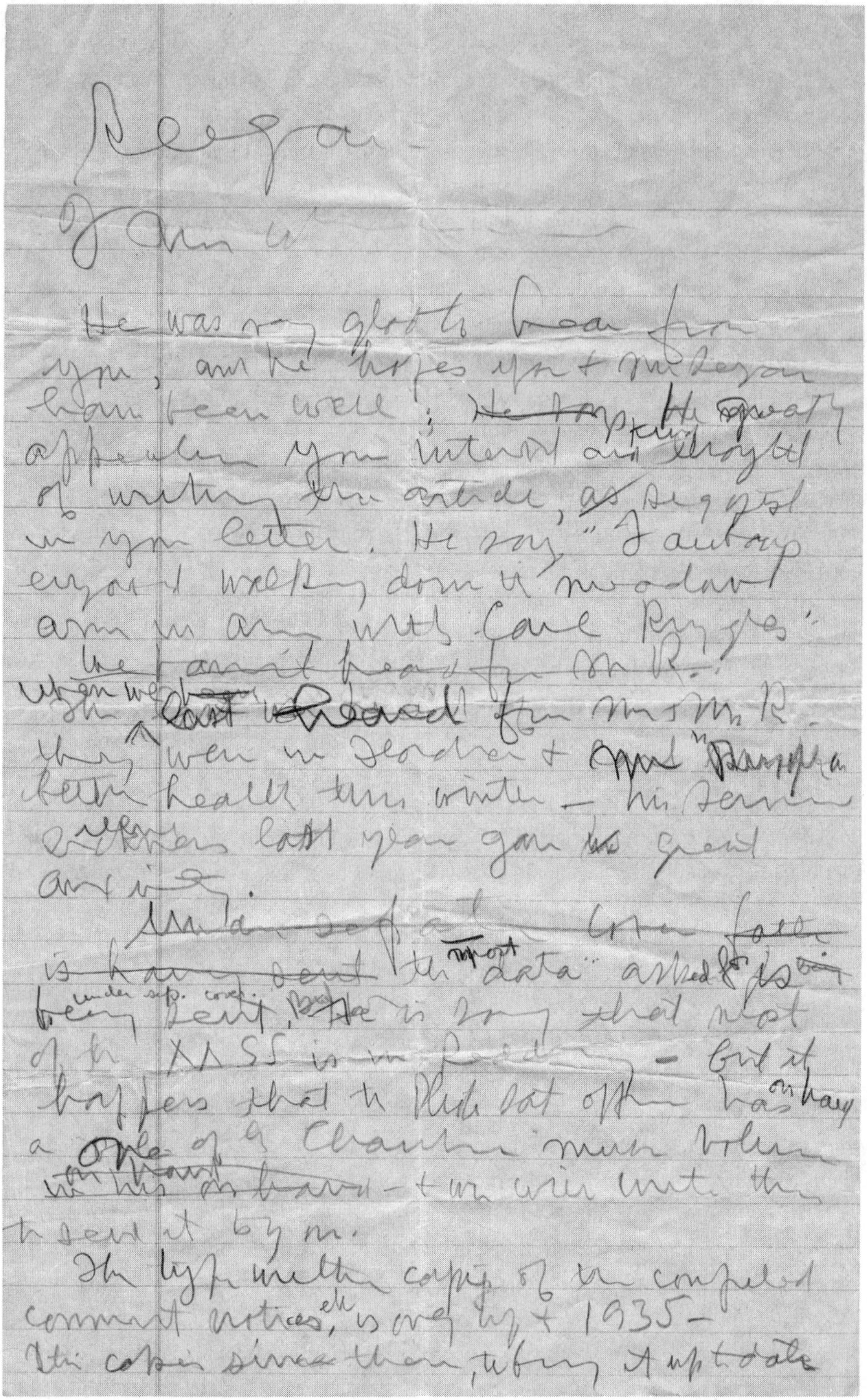

Seeger—

Of Ann St—

He was very glad to hear from you, and he hopes you + Mrs Seeger have been well; ~~He says~~ He greatly appreciates your interest and kind thought of writing the article, ~~as~~ suggested in your letter. He says "I always enjoyed walking down the meadow arm in arm with Carl Ruggles."

~~We haven't heard from Mr R.~~ When we ~~last~~ heard from Mrs Mr R. they were in Florida + appear in "better health this winter — his serious sickness last year gave us great anxiety.

~~[illegible]~~ is ~~having sent~~ the report "data" asked for is being sent under sep. cover. He is sorry that most of the MSS is in Redding — but it happens that the Phila. [illegible] office has on hand a copy of a Chamber music volume ~~in his [illegible]~~ — + we will write them to send it to you.

The type written copies of the compiled comment, notices, etc. is only up to 1935 — [illegible] copies since then, to bring it up to date

Ca. 1 May 1939, sketch for Edith Ives to Charles Seeger.

• • •

Radiana Pazmor sang a group of Ives's songs at a concert in the "Evenings on the Roof" series in Los Angeles in the summer of 1939. This concert series was produced by Peter and Frances Yates, at first in their home, and later at a larger venue. It was one of the most important forums for the presentation of new music in Los Angeles in the 1930s and 1940s.[43]

346. 27 June 1939, from Radiana Pazmor, Hollywood

Dear Mr. Ives,

The Ives evening went off on the whole remarkably well. We had a full house, very enthusiastic. Dr. Klemperer came and stayed until the end of the program, which he rarely does. He really was interested and asked to look at the score of the America Suite; Mrs. Yates left it for him at his office today. We are going to repeat the program on July 9, for we know of quite a few people who wanted to come and were prevented by various circumstances.

Again let me say what a joy it was to prepare this program. The songs "wear" so well! I am beginning to enjoy singing "September," which at first was my bêté noir. (I feel sure you will appreciate this "true confession.") For "Majority," I have real veneration, I think it a great song from every point of view. As I had expected, the one most often mentioned by the G.P. ("general public," meaning laymen not particularly well acquainted with the contemporary idiom) is "White Gulls," and I think "two little flowers" comes next. I have not spoken with anyone who did not feel sympathetic toward the songs, which rather surprised me on the part of some of the people who came simply because I was singing (you know the type.) I think I may say that we won some friends for Ives which is what we set out to do.—Every one of the songs I sang meant something very real to me and I hope I may sing them often.

We all wished that you might have been there. Mrs. Yates will write later, she says, and sends her greetings meanwhile (I spoke with her on the phone today).

As they say in France, "homage" to you dear Mr. Ives, from
Radiana Pazmor

• • •

Dane Rudhyar (1895–1985), although now little remembered, was one of the leading figures in American modernist composition in the late 1920s. Active as a composer and writer on music, he was particularly important as a promoter of the spiritual and intuitive side of dissonant composition.[44] Although Rudhyar's version of spiritualism leaned more toward theosophy and what Carol Oja calls "a trans-Asian mix of religious philosophies," he and Ives shared a reverence for American transcendentalism.[45]

43. For a full account of the series and its history, see Dorothy Crawford, *Evenings On and Off the Roof* (Berkeley: University of California Press, 1995).

44. For a thorough discussion of Rudhyar, see Oja, *Making Music Modern*, 97–110.

45. Ibid., 98.

347. 10 August 1939, from Dane Rudhyar, Santa Fe

My dear Mr. Ives

It is a year now since I have heard from you and I hope it has been a pleasant and happy one for you. I have been most happy to see that at last your star has risen and that New York music circles have really begun to appreciate your great work to their great value and significance in the growth of a real American music.

You may have received this winter a booklet written about my works by an author Alfred Morang—also some papers about the Transcendental Movement in painting (and I hope eventually in all arts) which I have helped to initiate here. It is now 100 years since the Transcendentalist Club in Boston was really functioning (started in 1836 with Emerson, Thoreau, Alcott, etc.—as you well know) and I think it is significant that we should have started something of the same name on these high plateaux where perhaps the new American Culture will be developing away from the materialistic tumult of Eastern cities.

My associates are not all aware of their high mission, or they are shy about it. But 3 or 4 are well aware and I am trying to spread the ideas through lectures, pending the publication of the revised MS. of my book (first written last year) "The Transcendentalist Movement in Painting"—which carries a chapter on the general Transcendental Movement. I feel the time is ready. Interest in Thoreau, Alcott, etc. is greater than ever. The true American Tradition is becoming slowly better known.

That is why I am working toward various centers of cultural activities along that line. I initiated the "American Foundation for Transcendental Painting" here last Fall, duly incorporated as a non-profit corporation in New Mexico. In California I incorporated with my wife and a couple of associates a "Foundation for Personality Integration," to center around matters of Psychological integration leading to real creativeness, transcendental [in] its reliance upon philosophical Principles and Archetypes. I also hope that a "New Music Foundation" can be incorporated to handle matters related to New Music and Strang probably wrote you about it as we discussed the matter at length and I suggested the idea to him.

I hope that a chain of such focal points can be established permanently in all key states for this broad Transcendental Movement in the arts and in human conduct. I am planning the first permanent center here in Santa Fe and bought 2 ½ acres of restricted land on the outskirts of the city in a real estate development which is not only very sound but bids fair to lay the lines of a new residential Santa Fe. Marvelous views of the Sangre de Cristo mountains, all facilities and utilities and great spaces. An inspiring location.

I have applied for a governmental building loan on a 20 year basis to build a small but fine house for my wife and myself to live in as permanently as our lives allow. This house will be deeded to the Foundation for Transcendental Painting for use after our deaths and later we hope to build on the same site (2 ½ acres are quite large) a Gallery for a permanent collection of significant paintings of that "Transcendental" type—all this to be kept later for the Foundation and at once to serve as official headquarters and center of informal meetings. (The Azsuna School of Arts is also serving that purpose. I give lectures there and it is also permanently located and incorporated here).

I thought I had enough money to swing the building loan, but unfortunately my wife's health, which has been bad and a cause of great worry for some years now, has grown worse. She may have to have serious and expensive treatment, and I must keep the little cash I have saved to complete the purchase, for medical care—especially as I am none too well myself and unable to work long hours.

In this emergency I have thought of you, who have been so kind and so generous in the past. I wonder if it would not be possible to loan me four hundred dollars to swing the governmental loan (some cash is needed before they give it, then payments of $40 a month take care of payments on capital, interests, insurance and taxes). What I would like to do would be to pay you back after one year, say beginning with Fall 1940 at the rate of $20 per month for two years (total $450, principal and interests). If you wished it, I could make payments in other ways, or to organizations you are interested in. But this plan would be quite safe. It could be guaranteed by my monthly salary from the Clancy Publications in New York from which I am getting from $175 to $200 a month, sometimes more.

I do not know whether such a loan would be feasible, but it would be a great help if it were. I would not take the liberty of suggesting it for myself personally, but I feel the proposition will give to our Transcendental Movement here a better foundation and greater permanency. And I know how deeply you feel connected with the Movement of last century. Thus I lay down the need before you and let the matter speak for itself.

Has your Concord Sonata been recorded for phonograph? If so please let me know where, so I can get it at once. A composer from Rochester, Burrill Philips, heard it played in New York last year with your songs and told me yesterday, driving through Santa Fe, that it had been the greatest spiritual experience of his year. I am so happy people are knowing you at last for what you are.

The enclosed papers may interest you. I want you to know that I take every opportunity to talk about your work. I hope that more phonographic records will be available for easy demonstrations. If I really had all the biographic material available about you I would love to write a small book about you. Would you like me to do so? If so, I might even try to come to New York especially to get the materials. Please let me know

Always resolutely yours,
Dane Rudhyar

348. Ca. 10 August 1939, sketch for Harmony Ives to Dane Rudhyar

Thansy!

I am writing ——

We were glad to hear from you again and to know that things are going on well with you—but we were so sorry to know that Mrs. R is not well—we sincerely hope she finds her way back to good health. Mr. I says he hasn't yet been able to say conclusively which is the worst for mankind—bad health or bad music!—but ~~both cause profane words~~

He will be glad [to] help as you suggest but will not be able to send on the check ($400) to you until after Sept. 1st. He says he thinks it safe to say that it will [be] received before Sept 10.

He greatly appreciates the big work you have in the making & the high ideals behind it.

He thanks you sincerely for the kind thoughts & interest in his music—and for suggesting & being willing to write a book about it—For a few years back several musicians and writers have suggested and offered to do this—but Mr. I has never seemed quite like having it done—

But recently he has been told quite often & seriously that something of this kind should be done. So perhaps later on in the year he may do something about it—and will let you know—a book with a few leading articles, (one Mr. I would very much like to have by you) has been suggested, together with a general reviews, list of compositions & some biographical data etc., which are quite often asked for.

With kindest remembrances
May you both find better health in the mountain air & spaces
Sincerely
C

• • •

Paul Rosenfeld (1890–1946) was one of the most important critics to support American modernist composers, and Ives clearly appreciated the honesty of his criticism and the strength of his willingness to expect that American concert music be held to the highest standard.[46] Although Rosenfeld's cosmopolitan, intellectual lifestyle and Jewish heritage made him very different from Ives, the two men shared a Yale education, and the affinity the older composer had for the writing of the younger critic may in part stem from this important shared background.

349. 26 March 1940, from Paul Rosenfeld, New York

Dear Mrs. Ives:

I'm making a little study of "nationalism" in American music, therefore this letter to yourself. By "nationalism" I mean the consequences of the saturation of composers with their folk-music to the point where it becomes an integral part of their nature, rathermore than the consequences of a later acquisition of its elements: this saturation appears to me to have occurred in Mr. Ives. What particularly absorbs me is the question whether the "nationalistic" composers have reflected upon their musical "conduct" and what forms their reflections took: and I'm writing to ask whether you think Mr. Ives might care to tell me about any reflections which he himself has made? I'd be most grateful for any light he'd care to cast.

With kindest greetings,
Sincerely
Paul Rosenfeld

46. For a substantial discussion of Rosenfeld's criticism, see ibid., 302–10.

350. Ca. March 1940, sketch for Harmony Ives to Paul Rosenfeld

I am sorry to say Mr. I is not at all well—he cannot write or attend to things nowadays as he would like to—It is a great trial for him to be in this condition. We do hope for better days when he may have the pleasure of seeing you—~~and shaking you by the hand!~~

He feels deeply grateful for your generous interest, your sympathy & friendship—and for being included in ~~your~~ those fine works of art of yours in prose.

[*The next section is crossed out and reworked on page 2—both versions are given here:*]

Some years ago Mr. I wrote a kind of short paper—more of a memorandum—somewhat, he thinks along the lines your letter brings up—how much a man's music comes into being [?] how far from his life experience and how much from reflecting life the mountains [?] & forests etc.

[*Page 2*]

the music itself—

Ever since your letter came, we've been looking for the paper but can't seem to find it—so I won't delay any longer before writing.

I can say that Mr. I's music came from a saturation that started early in life not only of folk music but of his life experiences—~~how much of art is natural and how much of other sources is difficult to say~~—but it all came naturally and I think nature at least nature [?] if not all natural from his heart and mind. How far he says he wonders the music reflects his conduct and how far he reflects its conduct.

But your letter ~~suggests~~ brings up a deep and fundamental subject—and he wishes he could go into it more—he hopes to when he is better. Anyway, if the paper . . .

[*Second version, page 2 of sketch*]

Some years ago Mr. I wrote a paper—though, he says, hardly more than some memoranda–~~somewhat~~ which he thinks ~~along the~~ had something to do with the matter your letter suggests.—A music's source—how much comes into being from life experiences—and how much from reflecting about its material and conduct.

I should say in Mr. I's case—~~somewhat~~ more of the former—as most all of his music is spontaneous and natural to him and to nature.

Mr. I's "saturation" started early in his life—and came not only from folk music" he was brought up on but to a very great extent from the life "around him and "in him"—also there is in his music—something reflecting a kind of "inheritance" from his forebears and father—a natural interest in wanting to make his own paths around the hills and mountains.—a trail all nature if not all natural.

Ever since your letter came we have been trying to find the paper referred to above—but afraid it is not here—so I will not delay in answering your letter—(but if found, we will be glad to send it to you

Mr I hopes it may not be long before he may "take your hand" and thank you in person for all your kindness.

[*Page 3: revisions of opening paragraph*]

Rosenfeld–

Mr. I says he thanks you from the bottom of his [heart] and as much as one man can thank another man, who has done something that the other man did not think—never expected to be done—that is in the remarkable way you have of writing about his and the others' music, to think your own way, and the way of a true poet who thinks as a . . . [*The paragraph stops here.*]

Mr. I has been hoping to be able to write you personally and as he would like—but he is not at all [well] & I am writing for him to have you know that he thanks you ~~from the bottom of his heart~~ as much as a man can for your interest in his music both in the previous article and that in the book Dis[coveries] of a Mu[sic] C[ritic]. The way you get down through the technical examination to the bottom and spirit of a thing astounds him. He says your writing itself stirs him as though a singer of great music and is all your own. He hopes sometime to tell you so in person. Please accept our appreciation. Sincere thanks—

Truly yours

• • •

As the relationship between him and John Kirkpatrick deepened, Ives devoted more financial support to his performances in general. Kirkpatrick continued to investigate the corners of the Ives oeuvre that he had not yet explored. In the following letter he asks about the first piano sonata, a logical step for the man who premiered the second. For reasons unknown, Kirkpatrick never performed the earlier work as a whole, and it was almost nine years after this letter that William Masselos premiered it in an edition prepared by Lou Harrison.

351. 28 March 1940, from John Kirkpatrick, Riverside, Connecticut

Dear Mr. Ives—

I can't thank you enough for your very generous contribution to this last brainstorm of mine. It was a very welcome and deeply touching expression, and I tried to call you up about it but it seemed you all were to be away till Thursday (today).

It went pretty well—had its ups and downs as usual, but there were enough things that are pleasantly rememberable in retrospect to give the feeling of having accomplished at least a little something. Both [Hunter] Johnson and [Robert] Palmer were there—Johnson & a buddy of his had hitch-hiked up from North Carolina just for the occasion.

Hope to be seeing you all again before too long—by the way, any time you might feel like sending a copy of the first sonata, it would be very much appreciated. Now that you've divulged the "argument" I can't wait to see the music.

With all best wishes—and again many many thanks.

Sincerely,
John Kirkpatrick

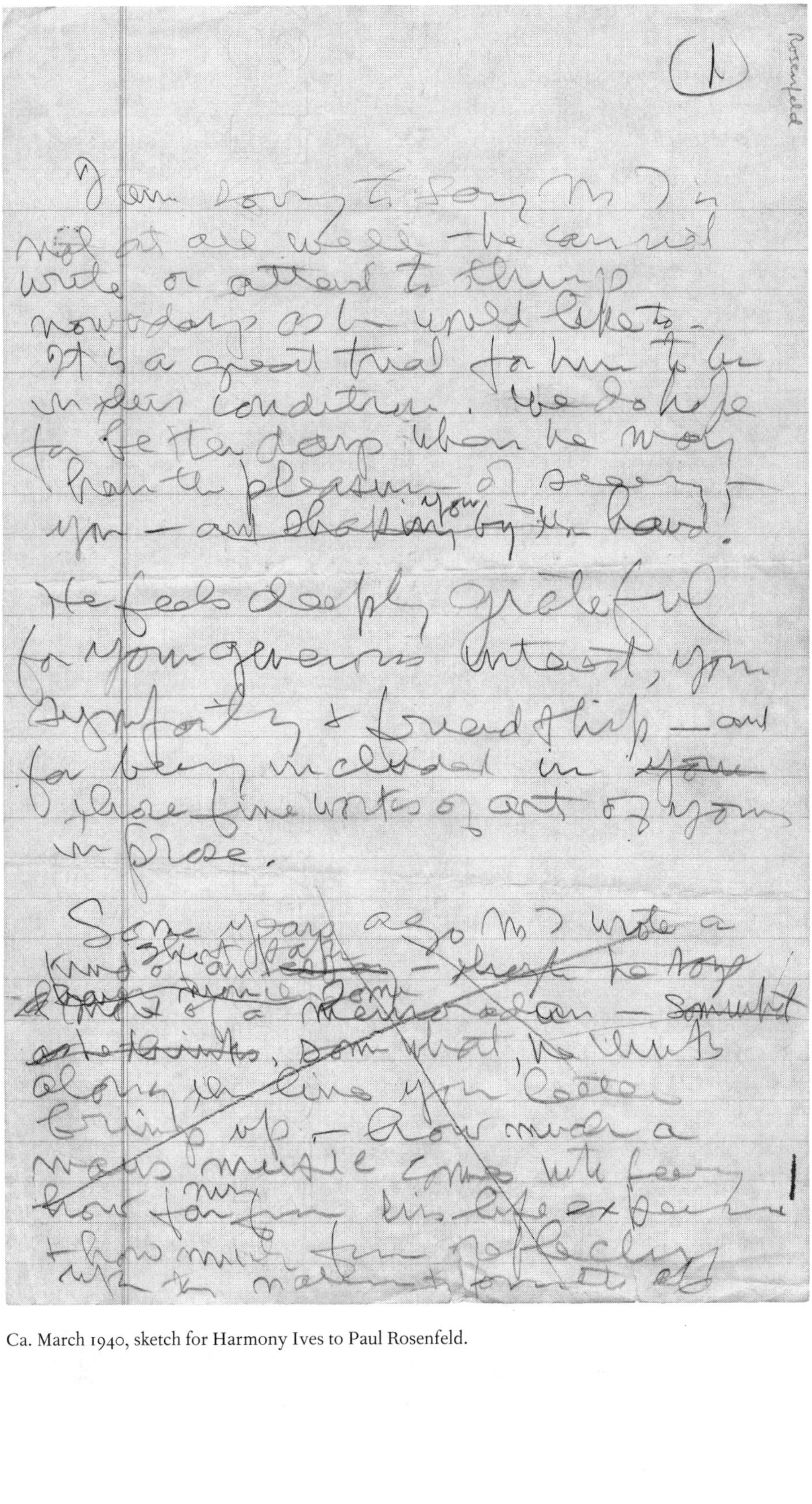

Rosenfeld

(1)

I am sorry to say Mr I is not at all well — he cannot write or attend to things nowadays as he would like to. It is a great trial for him to be in these condition. We do hope for better days when he may have the pleasure of seeing you — and ~~shaking~~ you by the hand!

He feels deeply grateful for your generous interest, your sympathy & friendship — and for being included in ~~your~~ those fine works of art of yours in prose.

~~Some years ago Mr I wrote a kind of short essay — sketch to try of a memorandum — somewhat as he thinks, somewhat, he thinks along the lines your letter brings up — how much a man's music comes into feeling how far from his life experience & how much from reflecting upon the nature of art~~

Ca. March 1940, sketch for Harmony Ives to Paul Rosenfeld.

• • •

In 1940 Henry Cowell's family, along with many prominent musicians and supporters from across the country, mounted an eventually successful drive to free Cowell. There is indirect evidence that Ives participated in this effort: the following letter from Johanna Magdalena Berger thanks Ives for his letter on Cowell's behalf and announces his parole.

352. 24 May 1940, from Johanna Magdalena Berger, New York

Dear Mr. Ives:

Henry Cowell asked me to-day to thank you for your letter on his behalf. He has been paroled and will live with the composer-pianist Percy Grainger and wife. . . . He will be here in about a month.

I had over 40 wonderful letters from prominent people all over the states. Henry would like to thank all his friends personally, but he is frightfully busy with the details of getting out and he is trying to select and train in men to continue the work [of] the conservatory of music he has founded there.

Most Sincerely
Johanna Magdalena Berger

• • •

Although Ives's financial resources had somewhat diminished in the 1940s from their high point at the end of his insurance career, he still maintained a considerable level of generosity toward even fairly remote acquaintances such as Dane Rudhyar.

353. Ca. 14 October 1940, sketch for Harmony Ives to Dane Rudhyar

Rudhyer Rudyar

We were glad to have your letter, but very sorry to know of your illness, & that things have not been going well with you. Mr. I says, "But there is one thing that you have got to do whether you want to or not—(you see in this matter I'm the boss—) I do not want you to send me any interest at any time—& also no repayment in any way—until the time comes that it is perfectly convenient for you to do so—if that time doesn't come till you are with Father Transcendental on the mountains of the next world—it will be fine with me."

We do wish you both health & happiness, as much as is possible in this maudlin world & send kindest wishes—

• • •

In October 1940 Charles Seeger wrote asking Ives to contribute a chamber score for inclusion in the that year's supplement to the *Boletin Latino-Americano de Música,* edited by Francisco Curt Lange in Uruguay.[47] Scores were requested to be previously unpublished and about five pages long. At the bottom of the typed form letter that solicited the score, Seeger wrote by hand, "Greetings, Very important that you be represented!!" Ives produced two sketches for a response to the letter; the first, below, is in a neutral voice that may be intended for Edith; the second is more clearly in Edith's voice.

354. Ca. October 1940, sketch for Edith Ives to Charles Seeger

Seeger—

I am ——

He was very glad to hear from you again & thanks you for the letter about the Inter-American music.

~~We hope Mrs. S & you are well and that things are going as you would like, in spite of this scourged world today.~~

See [*congruency sign*]

Don't bother to have these copies sent back—they are all in photostat negatives. Even if nothing is published Mr. Ives would be glad to have Mr. Lange or you keep whatever either of you would care to in your libraries.

We have never received the book or magazine in which your article about Carl Ruggles's & Mr. Ives's music was to have been. Perhaps there has been some delay in publishing—but if it has been issued, we would like very much to know how we can secure a copy, and would much appreciate it if you, when convenient, would send us the name of the book and the publisher's address. We do hope Mrs. Seeger and you are well and that things have been going as you would wish, in spite of this scourged world of today.

With kindest wishes to you both,
I am
[*congruency sign*]

Under separate cover we are sending what copies of the chamber music are here—only about a dozen pieces in 2 or 3 bound volumes—Mr. Ives says that these may be more than enough—for Mr. Lange to look over at present—however, there are 40 pieces of chamber music in all—& we will be glad to send more later or if they should be wanted. . . .

• • •

After Seeger had sent the copy of his article on Ives and Ruggles, Ives sketched a letter thanking him for and reacting to it. The offer to send copies of the photostatic copies of Ives's scores to Buenos Aires is likely a mistaken response to Seeger's suggestion that Ives contribute to the volume Lange was editing in Uruguay.

47. This request eventually led to the publication of *The Unanswered Question* in the *Boletin* in 1941.

355. Undated sketch for Harmony Ives to Charles Seeger

Seeger

Many thanks for sending the article. We deeply appreciate it. Mr. Ives says he thanks you from the bottom of his heart & your fine way of writing is a kind of work of art in itself. He realizes the time, the care, and the thought you have generously given to it. And it did him good to have Carl "backed up again" with so much deep discernment and enthusiasm. Someday when there are fewer aural cowards among musicians Carl'[s] great tonal mountains will be bringing the people to their summits.[48]

Mr. I will be glad to send later on some of his music as you suggest to the Library of Congress. It may take some little [time] to get it together—though the published music he will have the publishers send soon.

There happens to be another copy here of one of the Chamber orchestra sets we sent you last week—which could be sent to Buenos Aires as you suggest. And if you think best, Some of the other music—

Again we thank you for all you have done—Someday we would like to have the complete copy and hope it may be published before long.

With kindest regards
to you & Mrs. Seeger
C

• • •

The premiere of the *Concord* Sonata and the subsequent positive critical response to it created a demand for the piece that could not be met by the few remaining copies of the first edition. As I mentioned above, the idea of a new edition, to be published by Arrow Music Press, dated from 1939. Working with George Roberts, Ives began to prepare a second edition of the sonata in the early 1940s. Because of his poor health, problems caused by wartime shortages, and the complexity of the task of revision, the edition was not published until 1947.[49]

356. 21 November 1940, sketch for Ives to George F. Roberts

Roberts

It seems from an Arrow Press letter ~~from Arrow Press~~ that there must be some misunderstanding about the corrected copy of the Piano Sonata. It says that neither you nor the engraver were able to decipher it and also that you had made a clear copy, apparently of the whole sonata, which, was sent to me some months ago. This is all wrong as ~~you know~~ we

48. This is probably a reference to Ruggles's *Men and Mountains*.

49. For a brief discussion of the genesis of the second edition of the sonata, see Geoffrey Block, *Ives: Concord Sonata* (Cambridge: Cambridge University Press, 1996), 27–30.

both know—~~how the engraver got so mixed up~~ Possibly the engraver got somewhat mixed up about it all.

I remember when we went all over it together last spring it was quite clear to you—you made corrections in ink and the few passages & pages which you copied were all well & correctly done & put in their right places.

I am sorry to give you this trouble but if you ~~could~~ will let me know as soon as convenient what the situation is, then we can try & get things straightened out.

Mrs. Ives & I send our kindest and best wishes to you all—is Mary Lou still a soprano ~~soloist?~~ and a prima donna![50]

357. 6 January 1941, Harmony Ives to Carl Ruggles

Dear Carl—

We want to thank you & Charlotte for your card and message—it was pleasant to hear from you.

Charlie wants me to tell you that he has a score of "In the Night" (Theatre Set) but the copy is torn. He will send it to you and ask New Music to send you another copy also. If you need parts & will let him know how many, especially the strings, he will be glad to send them.

When you asked him for Chamber Music last year he ordered some sent from the photostat studio, but thro' some mistake he finds now they weren't sent. There are about 40 pieces of Chamber music and if you will let us know what groups of instruments you will want them for he will be glad to have some sent.

He says "It is not only important to have the piano piece published but also important to have every note you have ever written published, whether you want it or not." And he wants to say to Charlotte & Micah "but not to you because if so he may hear a cuss word from Florida"—"The man to whom the world of music owes a great debt is Carl Ruggles—but it may not be fully paid 'til he and an old friend from Redding and "uncle Deac" are walking up that New England mountain in the next world."

It is good to know that you are back on the job as that means you are well & we hope things are going as you all wish in spite of the scourged world.

Kindest remembrances from us both & Edie to you all!

As ever yours
Harmony T. Ives

358. 1 February 1941, from Carl Ruggles, Coral Gables, Florida

Dear Harmony and Charles:

Thank you Harmony for your beautiful letter and Charles's message and tribute. Tell Charles—that outside of my immediate family—I can think [*see example 3a*] of no one

50. Mary Lou was Roberts's younger daughter.

3a. One measure of orchestral reduction from Carl Ruggles's *Men and Mountains*.

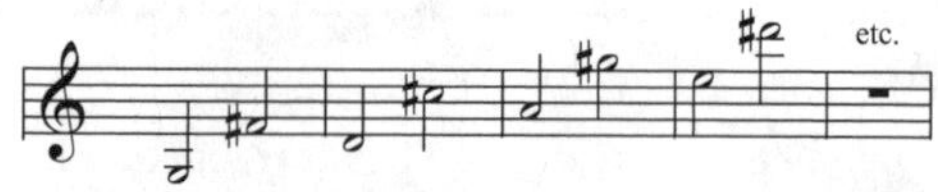

3b. Interval and rhythm drills by Carl Ruggles.

3c. Ruggles notes, "They have a tough time with this rhythm."

with whom I'd rather walk up that New England Mountain. Every Thursday evening I have a class of about 30 of the best players of the symphony here. The class is for the study of new music. I have had to prepare their ears—in a way—to the sound of "strange intervals," also the technique of playing them. Exercises like this: [*see examples 3b and 3c*]

We tried over the "Cage." I had to make the parts. It sounded beautiful. The harmony of chords founded on 4ths was a new experience for them. First the English H. played the solo, then a young singer sang it very well. I wish you had been there Charles. They were all so happy about it. It is, I think, the way to make music.

I shall be more than glad to have anything Charles thinks I can use. I think the short pieces would be best at first, as it takes many rehearsals to balance dissonances. I had 16 rehearsals on my Angels. They all want to let go on the tone. If one plays C natural sharp and another C sharp sharp it's just too bad, or if one plays louder than the other.

If you can send me the following instrumentation it will be o.k. Flute, Oboe, E. Horn, Cls, Bsns, Hrns, Trpts, Trombones, Piano, Bells, 1st Violins (5 parts), 2nd Violins (5), Violas (3), Cellos (3), C. Bass (2). Please send parts for "Theatre Set."

I hope we can give a little concert later, perhaps in May.

Just Ives and Ruggles, The New England Renaissance.

I've always thought how wonderful it would be to have an orchestral concert of Charles's and my works. It would knock them cold.

All our love to you all from us all,
Carl Ruggles

• • •

After Henry Cowell was released from San Quentin, his contact with Ives resumed, although the tone of the correspondence was somewhat more restrained than it had been. In the fall of 1941 Cowell wrote with the news that he was to be married. The relief that the announcement brought to the Iveses, perhaps particularly Harmony, is obvious in the joyful tone of their reply, and the warmth that they obviously still felt for Cowell flooded back into their correspondence with him.

359. 15 September 1941, from Henry Cowell, New York

Dear Mrs. Ives:

I wish to tell you and Mr. Ives of my forthcoming marriage to Sidney Robert[s]on, to take place very soon, probably before October. I am sure you will be happy for me over this event, to which I look forward with such intensity. I do not believe that you have met Sidney; she is a musician, plays the piano well, and has collected folk-songs through the country. She is very successful in being on friendly terms with country people, and wins them over completely. She is thirty-seven years old, of old American stock, with a bit of New Orleans French blood.

I had a conversation with Harold Spivacke, the music librarian of Congress, and he told me that he is establishing a manuscript library of the works of certain important Americans. He wishes to preserve the original pencil sketches, and other more or less illegible hand-written manuscripts of such composers as will cooperate. I am very pleased to send them my own manuscripts, the original forms of those of which I now have better copies. He hopes very much indeed that he can obtain this sort of material from Mr. Ives, and asked me to write you about it. He said that he wrote you once before, but obtained photostated or duplicated copies rather than originals, which is not what he wanted for this particular section of the Library of Congress. I shall ask you please to be good enough to write him directly, and make any arrangements that you and Mr. Ives may wish.

I am very busy—am working now as chief consultant of the music editorial project of the Pan American Union in Washington, coming to New York about half the time. During the New York half, I attend to New Music, and shall teach again at the New School.

With earnest hopes for Mr. Ives' health, and with best wishes to you both, sincerely,
Henry

• • •

This letter is interesting in that it is in Harmony's hand except for the signature, which is in Ives's shaky-pen handwriting. But after Ives's signature, Harmony appears to be writing her own note in her own voice.

360. 18 September 1941, Harmony Ives to Henry Cowell

Dear Henry—

It was great to hear your good news—Our kindest wishes to you both—May the marriage bring a happiness which will last thro' to the end of eternity, then on—

We take great pleasure in enclosing our wedding present—for we can't enclose a book case or a sofa—& then Mrs. Cowell can select something for the family home which won't be a duplicate. That problem we learned by recent experience. Edie, at her wedding, received about 20 flower pots & not one salt cellar.

We will write Mr. Spivake—There are some of the old copies around somewhere—although some are probably lost—

When we get back to N.Y. next Winter we hope to be able to see you both.

Again our kindest wishes to you & Miss Robert[s]on now and forever
Chas. E. Ives

Congratulations and greetings
H.T.I.

361. 2 March 1942, from Henry Cowell, New York

Dear Mr. Ives

New Music publications during 1941, with your aid, showed profit for the first time, and we are able to disburse about $96.00 to the composers, which comes out about $1.00 per share, plus expenses of sending. I enclose your check with special pleasure, although we both know so well that the only reason we have been able to make this disbursement to composers is through your continued support.

The check is on "N.M. Recordings," as the N.M. Board voted to combine the accounts for greater strength, but until we can legally change the name of the account, all checks are drawn in the name of N.M. Recordings.

Your Sonata sounded wonderfully at the Szigeti recital; my wife and I were greatly moved by it.[51] I saw Edith, which gave me much pleasure—

W best greetings to you and Mrs. Ives
Sincerely
Henry Cowell

• • •

The entry of the United States into World War II generated a strong patriotic response from Ives. Unable to contribute to the war effort directly, he revised the lyrics of his song "He Is There," which had been written during World War I, to fit the new situation, and titled it "They Are There." Ives wrote on many occasions of his passionate hope that this new song, which in fact he usually called the "War Song March," would raise morale among the troops and on the home front. The fervency with which Ives performed the song in the recordings he made of it in 1943 are ample demonstration of his intense feeling about it.[52] To prepare the song for publication, Ives turned again to George Roberts. The instructions for making the new piece out of the old one offer a glimpse into the way that Ives approached the physical process of score revision.

51. The recital Cowell mentions was given on 25 February 1942 in Carnegie Hall by Joseph Szigeti, violin, and Andor Foldes, piano. They performed Ives's Fourth Violin Sonata; Rossiter, *Charles Ives and His America*, 293.

52. *Ives Plays Ives* (New World Records, 2006) includes three enthusiastic takes of Ives playing and singing the song on 24 April 1943 in New York.

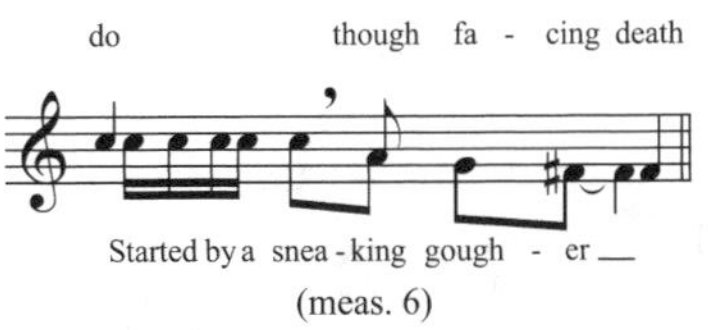
do though fa - cing death
Started by a snea - king gough - er
(meas. 6)

4. One measure of Ives's sketch for "They Are There."

362. 19 October 1942, Harmony Ives to George F. Roberts

Mr. Ives and I are sorry not to have seen you & yours this summer—of course the gas and tire situations affected you as it has all of our friends We hope you have all been well—

Mr. Ives has had a good many requests for a war song & also for copies of the old war song "He is there!" He says as his composing days are over he has taken that song in the old book, cut out the first two verses, revised the words of the 3rd a little and added to it as a second & last verse words taken from another war song written just after the first war started & fitted it into this music calling it "They are There!"

Mr. Ives says (I quote) "I would much appreciate it if you would copy out the voice parts as on the lead pencil sheet, but put the two parts together on one clef. The notes of the 1st verse stems up & when they differ from the 1st verse notes put them in small notes and have all the notes for the last verse in the usual size for if only one verse is sung it will probably be the last—measure below suggests the plan [*see example 4*]. Then cut out the piano part throughout also obbligato parts and paste your copy of the voice parts over the piano part on a larger sheet. It may help if measures are numbered as in copies sent—When this is ready please ask the Quality Photoprint to send for them and make two regular size positives & one larger copy—send one of the regular size copies to you and the other two copies here—Then I will check them over & send to you for final copy, together with optional coda, to send to the publishers.

Then you might make a copy of these two verses each on a separate clef (similar to the one in the lead pencil) as the publisher may think it better to have a staff for each verse.

There are almost no changes in the piano part, in a few measures only nos. 10, 23, 29 just a note or two. In the voice parts a few differences from the printed copy caused by the words—mostly in nos. 6, 10, 11, 18, 23.

There is an optional 2nd piano part, which may be played if a chorus is singing—it might be printed separately on the last page of the printed copy if the publishers want it. I n this 2nd piano part, there is an optional coda beginning in meas. 48 which may be printed in smaller notes at the end of the printed copy. I won't bother you now with these—will send them on later if wanted by the publisher. I am sorry to trouble you with all this & my copy isn't very clear & I am afraid rather hard to make out. All this would make it seem like a song hard to sing but it isn't—only for prima donnas—Mary Lou could sing it right off!"

Our kindest remembrances to you all.

Sincerely yours
Harmony T. Ives

P.S. The music copies & type-written words are being sent under separate cover.

• • •

In the last years of his life, Ives received many valedictory statements and appreciations of his talent and accomplishments in music. But few could have been as touching as the letter his daughter sent him on his sixty-eighth birthday.

363. 30 October 1942, from Edith Ives Tyler, New York

Dearest Daddy:—

This note was meant to reach you on your birthday, but the confusions brought on by George's illness has delayed it for ten days. If it had been ten years—and in a certain sense it has been delayed for twenty-eight years!—The sentiments would still be the same. You see, this is a few pages of fan mail from your own daughter.

When people all live under the same roof together they often find it difficult or awkward to express their really deep feelings about each other. The "everydayness" of life then makes one's sentiments sound a little melodramatic. And because of this it seems to me that people must all too often go through life without receiving in actual words from those close to them, the admiration, love, and thanks, for the many blessings they have bestowed. And I just made up my mind that that wasn't going to happen to you!

And now that I have the page before me and the pen in my hand, though, I find it hard to choose just the right words in which to tell you that you are, and have ever been, the dearest, sweetest father a girl could ever have. It seems to me that just the right words to say this in have not yet been invented,—or brought out of the spiritual world into concrete form for the use of mankind. So you'll just have to feel what I mean when I say these things. And I know you will, because your music comes from that very world where one doesn't use words—that is, words that we use in this particular sphere of living. It is all more like a language of intuition and thought than spoken sounds.

You are so very modest and sweet, Daddy, that I don't think you realize the full import of the words people use about you, "A great man." A lot of them say that because of what they see of you in your music, but those who have been fortunate enough to know you personally, say those words about you and mean them in every sense—not just about the wonderful genius you have. They know that even if God hadn't given you the gift to create those fine thoughts into a form of music that is glorious and challenging, you would still be a great man.

Daddy, I have had a chance to see so many men lately—fine fellows, and no doubt the cream of our generation. But I have never in all my life come across one who could measure up to the fine standard of life and living that you believe in, and that I have always seen you put into action no matter how many counts were against you. What you have done all your life takes a man—the kind of man that God wants all men to be. You have fire and imagination that is truly a divine spark, but to me the great thing about this is that never once have you tried to turn your gift to your own ends. Instead you have continually given to humanity right from your heart, asking nothing in return;—and all too often getting nothing. The thing that makes me happiest about your recognition today is to see the bread you have so generously cast upon most ungrateful waters, finally beginning to return to you. All that great love is flowing back to you at last. Don't refuse it because it comes so late, Daddy. As I once said to you, it is a wonderful thing to know that you have a friend in every part of this world. Someday, I hope, all the nations will catch up to you in that respect!

People who profess to be "in the know" often say, albeit admiringly, "Geniuses are simple men." I say, no, they are men of great simplicity. They are so busy going to the heart of things that they have no time or energy to spend on the trivial things of this world. And because of this they are nearly always misunderstood by all the little trivial people, who have to be around to look after the trivial things! I guess you know all about that, don't you Daddy? You see, I have a pretty keen idea of why you like to wear comfortable old clothes and mix up your food!

People rave and exclaim over the very wonderful fact that you were able to be a successful business man as well as a great composer. Your daughter—and her mother too, I know,—will never cease to hold in her heart the great wonder of your love and understanding as a father and husband. Daddy, I never hear a minister read that passage from the Bible "Be not forgetful to entertain strangers, for thereby some have entertained angels unawares" without putting a different meaning on it than is directly declared in the words, and thinking of you. You see, in this world even those who live together are in a certain sense ever to be "strangers" to each other, much as they may long to be closer. And I cannot hear those words without looking for the hidden "stranger" in someone close to me. We are so much more apt to see the "angel" in a real stranger, than in someone who is nearby all the time. So when I hear those words I think of you, and I know that mother and I have been blessed to be able to "entertain" through a lifetime a very dear, fine angel—you. (I'll argue with the word "unawares" though! Rather I would say that we may often have seemed unawares, but in our hearts we knew all the time.)

I don't know how to thank you for being such a wonderful and comforting father to me. There are no words for it. But your whole life has been an inspiration of faith for me. Knowing that you are there, has made me able to bear many things and solve many things that would otherwise have overwhelmed me. I don't think there is a greater thing a father can do for a daughter than that. And I thank you for that courageous faith with all my heart.

Just one word more. I want to tell you—as I know mother does too—how very patient, uncomplaining, and courageous I think you have been all through these long years of physical pain. No matter how we try, I don't believe we will ever know the full extent of what you have gone through in this matter, nor how much of the suffering you have kept to yourself. But we have understood enough to see again—in this part of your life—the great, fine man shining through. So don't feel downcast because physical troubles often keep you from doing many things you want to do;—you are always doing bigger and finer and stronger things than you realize,—things that men with perfect health seldom come up to. And don't ever feel you've been a burden to mother or me. You have been our mainstay, our guide and the sun of our world! We've leaned against you and turned to you for everything—and we have never been made to turn away empty-handed. So you see, if anyone has been a burden it's been us!

And now,—happy birthday, Daddy dear! I've never yet found a present that money could buy that you wanted, so the only thing I could think of to do was to sit down and thank you for all the things you've given me.

Always love, from the second* oldest fan you've ever had—
Edie

P.S. *Mother is the first one!

E.I.T.

• • •

Roberts completed the revisions to "They Are There" in November 1942 and sent the finished copy to Ives. In the summer of 1943 the League of Composers asked Ives for a patriotic score that might be played by the New York Philharmonic at a concert sponsored by the League that fall. Ives asked Henry Cowell to do an orchestration of the of the piece, to be called "War Song March." Cowell subsequently turned the job over to Lou Harrison, at least in part as a way to get Harrison some money.

364. 21 November 1942, Harmony Ives to George F. Roberts

Dear Mr. Roberts,

Mr. Ives has just received the copies of the War Song from Quality Photostat and says you did the job well—"but you made one important mistake—you didn't send the bill with it. So," he says, "correct this mistake soon."

Also he says, when convenient please send back his copy as there are "one or two notes & a possible cuss-word" which may or may not go in, after he has looked it over again.

Hoping you are all well & with our kindest best wishes
I am
Sincerely yours
Harmony T. Ives

365. 27 July 1943, from Henry Cowell, New York

Dear Mr. Ives:

The War March material arrived safely, and the prints are ready at the Quality Photo Print Shop. It seems to me that this song will be easily adaptable for full symphonic orchestra, and I am sure that the chorus will present no major difficulty.

I have asked to help me prepare this a brilliant young composer who has already been in correspondence with you, namely Lou Harrison, formerly of California but now temporarily in New York. We shall prepare the score together and then give it to Mr. Carl Pagano to copy the orchestral parts, if this is agreeable to you. Do you wish to examine the score before the parts are copied?

As compensation I should be very happy if I could give to Mr. Harrison anything which you had in mind to offer me for this work. I am sure Mr. Harrison really needs the money. I am most enthusiastic about doing this work, which puts across [illegible word] music and ideas!

With affectionate greetings to you and Mrs. Ives, I am,

Very sincerely yours,
Henry

366. Ca. 27 July 1943, sketch for Harmony Ives to Henry Cowell

Henry

Thank you [for] your letter of the 27th—which was just received today. Mr. Ives is sorry to have to bother you & Mr. Kerr[53] with this troublesome job, but he ~~deeply~~ much appreciates your willingness to take care of it. We presume by this time you have photostat copies of the 5 pages of the old score. If not call up the photo office—they have not as yet sent an enlarged copy of these here. Probably it would be well to have a large photo copy of the complete score made & sent here, ~~so that~~ before the ~~ink~~ final ink copy is made by Mr. Pagano—there are a few places which Mr. I thinks he ought to look over if possible—as he couldn't see any of the old copy. Some days he can't even see the enlarged copy—& if he can't within a day or so after it is received, he will let it go and not cause a delay. Also there are some ~~things~~ corrections etc. of the song part which Edie copied in that ~~ought~~ probably ought to be checked again. We are glad that Mr. Harrison will help out in this—Mr. I sends his kindest greetings to him–& will be very glad to see that you both are fully compensated for all you are doing.

(Last para[graph])
Mr. Ives hopes that some of your music could be played on this concert—& also something of Mr. Harrison

Two copies of the song—2nd piano part were enclosed, as it was thought it would save time if Mr. Pagano could have one on hand—please ask the Quality Photo. to send you a duplicate of the score pages ~~to you~~ also.

• • •

Ives must have sketched the following letter to Artur Rodzinski (1892–1958), who was taking over as head of the New York Philharmonic for the 1943 season, sometime in late August or early September of that year because he refers to the orchestration of the "War Song March" that Lou Harrison completed for Ives that August.[54] Ives writes to suggest works that

53. Ives probably confused Lou Harrison with Harrison Kerr, who had been the chair of the *New Music* editorial board in 1939–40.

54. Sinclair, *Descriptive Catalogue*, 313.

might be played on the League of Composers concert mentioned above. His suggestions are the accessible and easily rehearsed second symphony, which would be premiered by the Philharmonic under Leonard Bernstein in 1951, and the newly orchestrated march. The description of the symphony as a war piece adds a layer of meaning not otherwise obvious in the work. Ives's offer to hire a chorus at his own expense so that the "War Song March" could be performed on the proposed concert shows his dedication to it.

367. Late August 1943, sketch for Harmony Ives to Artur Rodzinski

Rodzinski 2nd Symphony

I am ——

He greatly appreciated your interest in asking wanting wishing to see some of his orchestral scores. You are the first conductor of N.Y. Phil who ever asked to see any of his music. He is sorry that ~~so much of it~~ so many of the movements are but in not very clear manuscript copies–& mostly ~~some of it~~ rather hard to make out (read)—the last movement of the 4th symphony especially is ~~rather~~ illegible (not very legible)—a clear copy will be made later & sent to you. The only symphony which has been entirely completely published and so now fine & clearly in legible shape is the 3 Places in N.E. Mr. Ives will have a copy sent you as it will not cause eye trouble, which he asks you to accept with his compliments and best wishes. This 2nd symphony, completed some 40 years ago—will take but little rehearsal time ~~will not~~ can be played quite readily with out trouble—which can't be said for many of the other scores. It reflects this country's days of fret storm & stress for liberty"—and the 2nd theme of the last movement that of Steven Foster's sadness for the "Slaves." The clear ink copy of this has been lost. Mr. I is having another made & will be glad to have it sent to you.

Earlier in the summer, the League of Composers ask[ed] Mr. I to send some music to you via the Philharmonic—with score & parts by Sept. 15.—"Music based on a patriotic idea, such as an anthem or battle song, or requiem." ~~Mr. I says~~ A battle song march was composed during the 1st War, but 2 verses the words have been brought more up to date. The score and parts for orchestra and voices will be sent from the copy bureau in N.Y. before the 15th. A later letter from the League says that they are not sure that there will be a chorus at this concert or broadcast. Although this march could be played without voices, it reflects several old war songs, a hymn [three illegible words] Mr. Ives & everybody who has seen or heard it, feel, that the words should be heard—& if the Phil, or the C.B.S. can not provide or arrange for a chorus Mr. I will be glad to supply one as it is a unison, not difficult, Probably 20 or 25 men singers & 10 to 15 women voices will be enough. Perhaps some of the other composers have . . .

[*The remainder of this sketch has apparently been lost.*]

• • •

Also written in 1943, a second undated and incomplete sketch for a letter to a famous conductor, this one to Serge Koussevitzky (1874–1951), demonstrates Ives's desire to be involved in the war effort and shows how much his understanding of the spiritual history of America was caught up in his conceptions of his own compositions. In 1943 Koussevitzky commissioned Roy Harris (1898–1979) to write a patriotic piece for the Boston Symphony. Ives responded to that commission with a flood of suggestions for patriotic sets or groupings of movements drawn from his works, and he suggested programmatic interpretations for each. The sketch looks to have been written very quickly and without much revision. Ives was overflowing with ideas for these sets and added movements between lines and in the margin. The fragmentary nature of the sketch implies that the letter was never sent or was revised in sketches that do not survive.

368. Ca. 1943 sketch for Harmony Ives to Serge Koussevitzky

Kuss A viTZKey!

I ——

Mr. I was very glad to hear that you are to play a work for orchestra which Roy Harris is to compose ~~and which is to reflect & help struggle to posed in these cursed war Days~~ which will be a help to Humanity in this cursed war. Mr. I was somewhat surprised, as something ~~along this~~ of this character should be commissioned by a sym orchestra—as during the first war, a friend of Mr. I suggested to some of the orchestra leaders of that time, that it happened that there were movements in some of Mr. Ives's symphonies, which reflected & were as he said, kinds of a musical landscapes of the wars of freedom in this country from 1776 to now. But none of the conductors seemed to get the idea. If you would be interested in seeing copies of 3 or 4 of these movements, we will be glad to send you complimentary copies—They were to be played together & will take about the time of most symphonies.

I Gen. Putnams Camp. a Revolutionary Memory

II. Last movement 2nd sym—a reflection [of] the Days before the Civil war a kind of expression of S[tephen] F[oster's] sadness for slavery (as well as) Stephen Foster

III. Decoration Day (from Holiday Symphony)—Freedom from slavery

IV A war march—for chorus & orchestra—another war today's war for Freedom—world freedom today.

—If these were not a part of this country's history—perhaps the US wouldn't have [?] helping the world towards a Freedom as it is today.

P.S. If "4th of July" 3rd movement Symphony Holidays could be played 1st (and at end—Thanksgiving, 4th movement sy Holiday) (also the St. Gaudens of 3 Places in N.E. in a way emblematic of the fight against slavery)—it would help the whole plan—(but it may take more rehearsing than can be given in these days.

. . . that I ought to present these. I would not feel like suggesting these things if I didn't feel that the subject matter did not come first & I feel does reflect something the thoughts

fundamentally from the thoughts, life, spirit, and character of our forefathers—all of which went through generations in which freedom for the people through action and sacrifice—deeply & endowed in their country's history since 1620—& as seen and felt in its various fights for freedom, from 1776 till today. These struggles for liberty, physical, mental, individual, & spiritual are a kind of natural & continued organic movement in the life of the country through generations.

• • •

In December 1943 Ives wrote thanking Cowell for his and Harrison's work on the "War Song March" orchestration, chastising him for not sending a bill for the work, and complaining because the Philharmonic had not performed the piece. Both Ives's sketch and the letter as Harmony transcribed and sent it are included here. The closing of the sketch, "hence, the pyramids" is a mystery, but it is not an isolated piece of nonsense, as the crossed-out sentence after the salutation seems to be. The same phrase, "hence the pyramids," occurs, also as a seeming non sequitur, in a letter to David Twichell, Ives's future brother-in-law, from 1903.[55] Twichell was a fellow member of the Yale class of 1898, and this connection may explain the origin of the mysterious pyramids, which are suggestive of the symbolism of Yale's fraternities and the even more elusive and powerful secret societies.[56] Ives and Twichell both belonged to the sophomore society called Hé Boulé. Semimystical symbolism and coded language were (and still are) typical of these groups, so it seems logical to suggest that the phrase in the letter to Twichell is a bit of Hé Boulé–speak or a catchphrase from Yale of the 1890s. Perhaps it was nostalgia or an indication of the comradeship Ives felt for Cowell that prompted him to include it. In any case, Ives or Harmony edited the reference out of the final draft of the following letter, which she addressed to Cowell's wife, Sidney—one wonders what the Cowells would have made of it.

369. 8 December 1943, sketch for Ives to Henry Cowell

Dear Henry—~~Now you know the right way to spell you = for Henry Benedict van Roekk mit farm—he is a carrot trader~~

You won't be a celebrated musician until you learn how to send out bills—righto—ask Wally Damrosch, Josy Hoffman, Vick Herbert et al—so am enclosing the payment of ~~the~~ an unsent bill—if it is not enough more will be sent—~~and~~ if it is too much—more will be sent! A ba koi I have felt that for all the good work Mr. Harrison did, $65 is not enough—$100 is nearer right, so am enclosing a ck. To make this up—please send it to him with my kindest wishes.

Only 1 more thing then I'll shut up & let you finish the 9th symph. That old lady soci-

55. See Letter 36.

56. Alexandra Robbins gives a fascinating account of the Yale secret societies and their symbolism in *Secrets of the Tomb.*

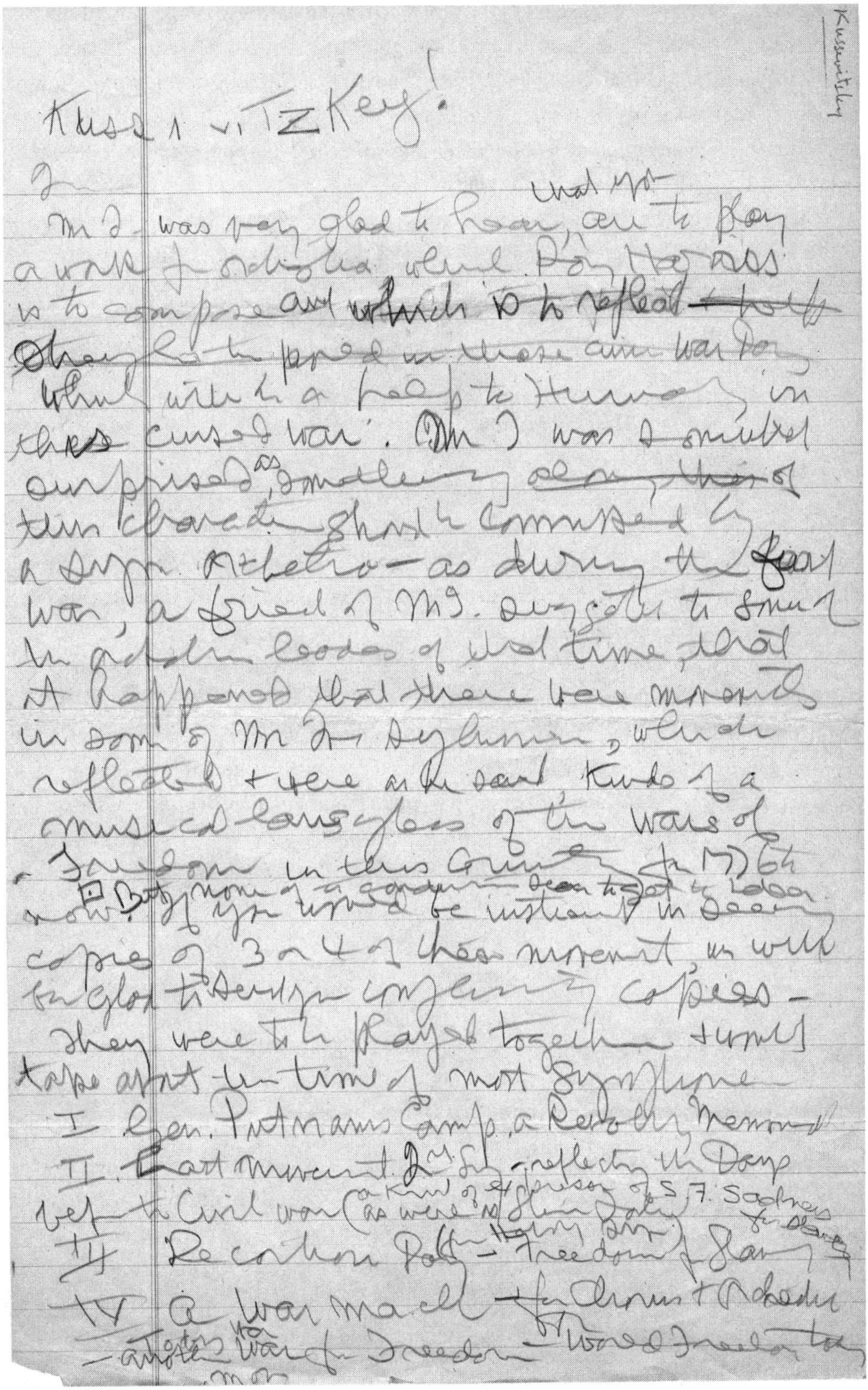

Undated sketch (probably 1943) for Harmony Ives to Serge Koussevitzky.

ety for pretty easy wavers—excuse moi—Phil orch. is old name, won't play that Rough neck war song march of mine they will feel a club on the jaw—not heart they haven't any. The sym[phony players] probably think that the music in a war song is important—it is of no importance——the words—especially the cuss words are a part of the fight—Tell them to yell them out. They ought to get some "yellers" to help but if not, trumpets ~~will help~~ & trombones should ~~blatt out this~~ do the blatting.

If they won't get a chorus let the conductor yell out the words—so for the 2nd verse—as the Tpt & Trombones play the tune—& the bass drum can do the conducting—exciting any way!

When a man gets to be in his 70th year—he has a right to be foolish—hence the pyramids!

370. 8 December 1943, Harmony Ives to Sidney Cowell

Dear Mrs. Cowell,

Thank you for you letter from Shady—I know you must have hated to leave—we who have had a much longer interval are not yet ready to leave here but we must—about the only consolation I have in leaving is the thought of what an awful nuisance we would be to our neighbors if we got snowed in here—

Mr. Ives sends this to Henry "You won't be a celebrated musician unless you learn to send out bills—ask Wally Damrosch, Josy Hoffman Vicky Herbert—et al. So enclosed is payment of your unsent bill for your fine work & help—if it is not enough, more will be sent—if it is too much–more will be sent!—A ba Koi!—I have felt that for all the good work Mr. Harrison did $65. was not enough so please send him the enclosed cheque for $35.00 to him—$100. is nearer right with my kindest wishes"

We shall hope to see you soon—I will telephone you when we are settled.

Sincerely always
Harmony T. Ives

371. 12 December 1943, from Henry Cowell, New York

Dear Mr. Ives:

1000 thanks for the checks for Mr. Harrison and myself—he was absolutely floored by it, and said "it doesn't seem possible that there ARE such people!" To me, it is harder to believe that there are any other sorts, however, the reason I never send bills is probably because I never had any desire to follow in the footsteps of the gang you wrote about—"Wally Dam. Josey Hoff, Vick Herbert, etc."

We shall hope to hear from you when you get settled back in town. We hope to go to the country for Christmas.

Our love to you both,
Henry

• • •

After playing Ives's Third Violin Sonata in 1941, Sol Babitz and Ingolf Dahl began to prepare a performing edition of the work to be published in *New Music*. The edition languished for years, in part because of a dispute between Ives and the editors over whether to retain Ives's bitonal notation for it.[57] The following letter comes from near the end of the process, and, once again, Ives steps in with additional funding to get the edition out.

372. 20 January 1944, Harmony Ives to Henry Cowell

Dear Henry,

Mr. Ives hasn't been at all well lately—says he "can't tend to nothin'"

Your letter in regards to the copy of the 3rd Violin Sonata was just found here with some others mislaid and not forwarded to Redding—Mr. Ives says he is sorry for the trouble this has given you—Encloses $150. in two cheques which New Music paid for copy—balance will be sent when due.

This reminded Mr. Ives that he had forgotten to forward the monthly cheques for N.M. fund for 1944—hereby enclosed.

Over a month ago I wrote for Mr. Ives to the Independent Music Publishers, 205 East 42nd St. asking to have another copy of the War Song March score made. They replied (letter signed by L. S. Abramson) that this was impossible without the master sheet which they did not have—will you, when convenient have this sent to them?

When Mr. Ives is feeling better, we hope to see you both

With our best wishes
Ever sincerely yours
Harmony T. Ives

• • •

Lehman Engel performed several of Ives's choral works with his group, the Madrigal Singers, and worked to promote Ives's music in general in the 1940s. He kept up a lively correspondence with the Iveses during World War II. The following two letters from Harmony to Engel show the effect of the war on the progress of the chronically delayed second edition of the *Concord* Sonata, on which work effectively stopped between 1944 and 1946. These are two of many letters in which Ives, who sketched the letters for Harmony to transcribe, tries to get performances of his "War Song March," which he saw as his contribution to the war effort. The march is one of the few pieces of which Ives repeatedly and avidly seeks performances in the correspondence. The reference to a "slaveland dungeon" points out the con-

57. The sonata was finally issued in *New Music* 24, no. 2 (January 1951). For details on the publication, see Sinclair, *Descriptive Catalogue*, 154. Some correspondence between Ives and Babitz and Dahl is reproduced in Burkholder, *Charles Ives and His World*, 247–50.

nection in Ives's mind between World War II (indeed, perhaps all war) and the Civil War, which assumed such an important place in his personal mythology.

373. 4 March 1944, Harmony Ives to Lehman Engel

Dear Mr. Engel

We were glad to hear from you & thank you for your kind letter. We will have copies of Mr. Ives's published music sent to Mr. Cecil Smith and Mr. Ives asks him to accept them with his compliments & best wishes.

Mr. Ives felt "very very badly" not to have seen you when you were here a while ago—he says to tell you that the next time you are here he is going to see you no matter what condition he is in. He hopes things will go well with you "in these cursed days."

He is going to have a copy of the score of his old war song sent to you. "It is for orchestra, chorus (mostly unison) & drum corps. But the words have been brought more up to date—that is beating up Hitler instead of the Kaiser"—Many who have heard the song or seen the words feel that it will be a real help & something that is needed in these days & that it ought to be sung often. The League of Composers sent it to the N.Y. Philharmonic with the performance note (see enclosure) but as yet it has not been played. Mr. Ives says it is not at all difficult to sing that the orchestral part is not easy & at times rough & tough—so too many symphony conductors are afraid to play anything they can't turn into polite easy sounds for the soft ears" he rather doubts that the Philharmonic will put it over—

He says "if the chorus is not large it would go well enough with 2 pianos the fife and drum corps coming in at the chorus & perhaps a few brass band players around the corner may join in—it is not a song for pretty voices—if the words are yelled out, regardless—so much the better"

We often think and speak of you and hope your plans will work out to your satisfaction—glad to hear of the commission—with our warmest wishes—Sincerely,

Harmony T Ives.

374. 10 July 1944, Harmony Ives to Lehman Engel

Dear Mr. Engel

We were glad to hear from you & to know that you are, as Mr. Ives says "still in music and not in a slaveland dungeon"—

As to the sonata, the final proofs of the corrected pages were returned to the Arrow Press last Fall—Since then we have heard nothing from them 'til a letter came from Mr. Kerr a month or so ago.[58] In it he says:—

"I am very sorry about the long delay in regard to the Concord Sonata, but the engraver, Mr. McRich, who has worked on it from the beginning has been forced out of busi-

58. Harrison Kerr, besides chairing *New Music* board in 1939–40, was one of the founders of the American Music Center.

ness and has no engraving tools available. Since they are imported, it is impossible for him to obtain any new ones and we frankly do not know where to turn for someone to complete the work. The engraving situation is a nearly impossible one & I fear that we shall have to get someone from out of town. I am writing today to the one who does the work for Mr. Cowell hoping he might undertake to finish the job. War time conditions make printing more & more difficult and we are not certain how long it will be before we have to stop altogether"—

So that is the situation.

Perhaps you did not receive the copy of the War Song which we thought was sent to you from the Photostat Co. last winter—So a copy will be sent you under separate cover. More copies are to be made soon of the old score for orchestra, two pianos & drum corps & we will have a copy of that sent you too. So many who have heard or seen this War Song feel that it would be a help in these days if sung more often. Recently we heard of a soldier boy who felt that the song made him want "to fight harder" and that "the Peoples New Free World" idea helps to put the war aims in a definite & big way—and that the soldiers he showed it to felt the same way.

It was good to hear that things are going along with you as well as can be expected in these days of upheaval. I'd like to see you in all those fancy outfits—I hope some of them at least are of a thin texture—we are melting & goodness knows what Washington is.

With kindest greetings from us both

Cordially yours
Harmony T. Ives

P.S. There is not a complete photostat copy of the War Song here, after all, so we will have a new one made & sent which may take a week or two.

• • •

As Ives's fame increased in the mid-1940s, he began to get more requests for his music. The next several letters exemplify this growing demand and demonstrate Ives's accommodation of those who asked him for copies of his scores.

375. 18 July 1944, from Robert Dark, Santa Rosa, California

Dear Mr. Ives:

This request is no doubt unusual and something which may not exactly please or meet with your approval.

I am trying to obtain a copy of your "Concord Sonata" and also copies of the score for you "Largo for Strings," "Theatre Set," and possibly two chamber music works scored so as to utilize the piano.

I am wondering if it would be possible to obtain these works through you or if you could advise by return mail where they may be obtained.

Here lies the reason. As for myself I was formerly a concert pianist using a professional name and toured Europe five years and was a pupil of Rachmaninoff, Dohnanyi and others.

I have been in the Service for over three years. I am now stationed here at the Santa Rosa Army Air Field and am the Base Public Relations Officer.

We also have a very fine Little Symphony Orchestra here under the direction of Corporal Floyd Stancliff formerly of the Bakersfield and Los Angeles Symphony Orchestras. The group is excellent and as far as we are able to learn the only symphonic group of any major importance in the armed forces.

Now we get to brass tacks. I am scheduling the orchestra for a tour of several large cities in the early fall and I will appear as soloist with them and will also play solo concerts once more. We would like very much to include some of your works in our repetoire [*sic*] but to date have been unable to locate any of your works through the San Francisco music stores. I am wondering if you could possibly help us out in this matter or advise us who might. I am particularly anxious to feature works of little known or rather composers who have not had the general audience that their work deserves. I prefer the works of American composers.

May I not hear from you by return mail relative to this matter?

Yours truly,
Robert L. Dark, JR,
2nd Lt., Air Corps.

376. 28 July 1944, sketch for Harmony Ives to Robert Dark

I am ——

He appreciates your interest in his music and is glad to have copies of the published music sent to you—and he asks you to please accept them with his compliments & best wishes. Later on Largo for Strings and some of the chamber music with piano will be sent—but, as these are only photostat copies of the manuscripts, it will probably take a few weeks ~~to have work like this done~~ as, under present conditions, it seems difficult to have work of this kind done without delay. Also the score of a "War Song March" for chorus and orchestra is to be reprinted soon. There are no complete copies of the Concord Sonata left, but a 2nd edition is being published by the Arrow Music Press for American Music Center N.Y. & will probably be ready later in the year.

If parts ~~copies~~ are wanted for any of the above, we will be glad to have them sent on.

With our cordial greetings

377. Sketch for Harmony Ives to American Music Center (on the same page as Letter 376)

(Helen Power)

Please have a copy each of all of Mr. Ives's music which is published by the New Music Editions & Arrow Press (except the score 4th of July" of which there is only one copy left) sent to Lt. . . .

Please have the bills for these & postage sent here to Mr. Ives.

Thanking you for you help

378. Sketch for Harmony Ives to C. C. Birchard & Co. (on the same page as Letters 376 and 377)

Please have a copy of the score of Mr. Ives's Three Places in New England" sent to Lt. Robert L. Dark

Please send the bills for this and postage here to Mr Ives.

379. 17 August 1944, from Dorothea Persichetti, Money Island, Toms River, New Jersey

Dear Mr. Ives,

My husband and I are planning four hand (one piano) programs for the winter season and would like very much using something of yours should you have anything for four hands. I would appreciate your letting me know if anything is available and how we might see it if it is not published.

Very sincerely,
Dorothea Persichetti
(Mrs. Vincent Persichetti)[59]

380. Ca. 17 August 1944, sketch for Harmony Ives to Dorothea Persichetti

Perichitte lette[r?] Money Is. NJ

I am ——

He thanks you for your letter & much appreciates your interest in his music. There were 2 or 3 piano pieces as he remembers for 2 players written quite a good many years ago & but no complete copies of any of them have been found. If any can be, we will have clear copies made & sent you. A movement ~~in both 1st & 2nd piano sonatas were started for 2 pianos—one rather as a kind of~~ one of his piano sonatas started for 2 players—but not final copied as such—the old copy is some where around, he thinks, & if it is found a clean copy also will be made and sent.

In one of the chamber volumes there is a movement called On The Antipodes for 2 players—with voice (over). . . . This chamber volume will be sent you & Mr. Ives asks you no matter if it is played to accept it with his compliments and best wishes

no matter whether anything is played or not

[*On the back of page, a revision from "(over)":*]
though if played with a Trp. (or Clar) taking the voice part, it goes well enough—& saves a singer a hard job" ~~it was first intended with Tpt and a program or usher[?] declaiming the words"~~

59. The American composer and pianist Vincent Persichetti (1915–87) and his wife, Dorothea, performed a substantial body of works for four-hand piano, including many of his own compositions.

• • •

John Kirkpatrick continued to pursue multiple Ives-related projects in the mid-1940s, and his semiregular progress-report letters provide glimpses of the spread and influence of the music. They also hint at connections that were explored but didn't pan out, such as Martha Graham's (1894–1991) interest in creating choreography to an unidentified Ives score.

381. 31 August 1944, from John Kirkpatrick, Georgetown, Connecticut[60]

Dear Mr. and Mrs. Ives,

I have been meaning all summer to send you the enclosed stuff, and report generally on whatever Ives-escapades I've been up to. It's been very stupid of me to procrastinate so,—here it is almost the end of summer.

The copy of the 2nd violin sonata has been under way for some time. I think I did the 1st movement last summer, the 2nd some time during the winter, and the 3rd got done last June. I didn't mean it as an "editing," but as a kind of preliminary tentative editing,—something to work from. There's an excellent fiddler up at Smith College, at Northampton, Miss Louise Rood. She's known mostly as a violist, but I've heard her do some wonderful violin playing too. Her whole approach to music typifies (for me) the best in what one might call U.S. art. I sent her a copy, and we've been trying to get together on it and have a reading-over session, but either one thing or another has intervened. She's been teaching at the Smith summer session, and her mother has been very ill, and I haven't been up there very much this summer,—and what with the gasoline situation making one's movements have to coincide with train and bus schedules (but isn't it marvelous the way the air force can give the kids so much practice-flight experience!). But we hope to get at it as soon as I get back to South Hadley (in about 2 weeks). I want very much to see how she'd go at the bowings. She knows a lot about country fiddling.

I've had bad luck with the copy too. This outfit, the Independent Music Publishers, really a blueprint place, filled my order for five copies, and then went and lost the original sheets. They say it's the first time that's ever happened with them (which I believe), and they're following up whatever leads they can think of to retrieve them. They seem very embarrassed.

About the copy, I've tried to use "common sense" in regard to the pencil notations. I remember once, some time ago, you told me that they were part of a projected orchestration, and to use my own judgement about putting them in or leaving them out. Then later, perhaps in a more inclusive mood, you said to put them all in. So I've put in all except those that seemed to just get too much in the way. For instance, in the slow part in the middle of the 1st movement (top of page 3 in this copy) they're grand,—but in the passage beginning page 11, line 3, measure 5, they'd make (on the piano) an unnecessary

60. Windways, Kirkpatrick's country house, was located in Georgetown, Connecticut, about six miles from Ives's home in West Redding.

muddle. Maybe the barn dance did get into a muddle at that point, but anyway I prefer your first version without them. In the next-to-last measure (that gets repeated), I'm not at all sure I have the rhythm of the violin as you intend, but I should think those repetitions had best be written out with slight variations, something like the round-and-round fade-out in General Booth.

I'm returning the photostat copy you gave me for Martha Graham. You remember I asked you for one, because I'd suggested it to her as something for a dance. Both she and her partner, Erick Hawkins, finally came to the conclusion that it was too rich, or too complete a kind of music to compose dance to. I can see the point—All one would want to do would be to listen to it—it doesn't need anything else. So sometime ago, Erick gave me back the copy. They were both very appreciative of your sending it to them.

The enclosed double-post-card about The Valley Music Press was got out a year ago. It was the brain-child of Ross Finney, at Smith, and Jack [John] Ver[r]all, at Mount Holyoke. Now Jack's in the army, and Ross, before he left for some intelligence work, asked me to take over the policy-direction of it. I've just finished score and parts of a marvelous piece for flute and strings by Hunter Johnson, "For an Unknown Soldier." We've brought out a good suite for solo viola by John Duke, and are planning on Jack's String quartet and Ross's new piano sonata, and I want very much to bring out a wonderful song of Elliott Carter's on a poem of Hart Crane. (The financial principle is that, with the small yearly grant from the two colleges, the Press pays half the printing cost, the composer the other half, and, it being a non-profit organization, the composer reaps the gravy).

The programs are most all my Ives-playings since last Fall. Hope [Kirkpatrick's wife] hasn't been doing any singing at all. I don't know if I told you that we were disappointed last fall in our hopes of an addition to the family, but now it seems that, come Christmastime, if all goes well, our union will be blessed. And all seems to be going very well. Last fall we were both under the weather. I seem to have caught a bug on the way back from the Alton recital (Nov. 19), and by the time of the N.Y. one (Nov. 23) I wasn't sure I could get through with it, but we didn't call the doctor and tried to use simple home common sense, and it went pretty well considering, at least it must have been in a way exciting, because I ended up with 104 degrees. So I spent the next almost 3 weeks in bed with what was tentatively diagnosed as virus-pneumonia (nothing like the real kind, which I've never had, thanks be!)

The series of five (this June) was at Smith College, and was my contribution to piecing out the end of Ross Finney's Music-in-America course (first semester of the summer session) after he was due to leave. Isn't it insidious the way that sort of presentation gets one into pigeon- holing things with labels and tags! Especially when so much first-rate music (and art) is a conglomeration of almost self-contradictory qualities. Take good old Carl, for instance,—the splendid freedom of his musical inspiration, and the almost pedantic preoccupation with his non- repetition-of-notes principle—the startling "modern" quality of his dissonant harmony, and the unmistakably "romantic" Wagner-Strauss derivation of his melodic contour. And of course, nobody has ever combined in their music more diverse elements than Ives!

We hope to be seeing you both again before we go back to South Hadley. I'm taking part in a pair of "victory-concerts" this week-end in New York, and Mother's back with us

Sunday to spend a few days here, but later on, next week, if Mr. Ives has a good day, we'd love to drop in.

With all best wishes from us both,
affectionately,
John Kirkpatrick

• • •

By the mid-1940s Lou Harrison had become involved in running *New Music* as a member of the board and, in 1945, as its editor. Ives also relied increasingly on Harrison's editorial abilities; indeed, in 1947 Ives asked Harrison to be "his eyes" in a never-realized project of a complete edition of his works still in manuscript.[61] Ives's strong reaction to World War II surfaces again in the following letters, as does the theme of anticommercialism that runs throughout his writings. That Harrison's opinion, as expressed in Letter 383, echoed Ives's thoughts in this area was highly gratifying to the older composer.

In the following sketch Ives addresses two works that Harrison edited, the Second String Quartet and the "War Song March," for chorus and orchestra. In preparation for a planned performance of the quartet on Peter Yates's "Evenings on the Roof" concert series in Los Angeles, Harrison proofread the parts made by Ives's copyist, Carl Pagano. The performance seems not to have been given; the quartet premiered in 1946 at the Columbia University Ives festival. There is no record of the performance "thirty years ago" that Ives mentions. It was likely an informal run-through.

382. Ca. October 1944, sketch for Harmony Ives to Lou Harrison

Harrison

We intended writing you before this but Mr. I has not been well enough to attend to anything. It was kind of you to take up the matter, with the Music Center, of having parts made for his 2nd S.Q. Would you be willing to check these over after Mr. Pagano has finished them and have them sent to Mr. Yates?—though it would be well, before sent out to have negatives ~~copies~~ made at Quality Photostat Co. Mr. Ives is very sorry to have to bother you with all this—but it is almost impossible for him to do much ~~things~~ nowadays and on account of his eye condition—he has cataracts on both eyes—he cannot see well enough to make corrections. Mr. Pagano does accurate work but it is always safer to have parts checked over, and Mr. I thinks that these parts should be especially clearly made, as this Q is very difficult to play—he also feels it is almost an imposition to expect this be played in these troubled days. However players today are not quite so afraid of hard jobs ~~work~~ as they were 30 years ago—when this Q was played—or "played at" Mr. I says is a better term—and it almost caused a fight—though probably the badly made part copies were ~~probably~~ partly responsible for this.

61. Leta Miller and Frederic Lieberman, *Lou Harrison: Composing a World* (New York: Oxford University Press, 1998), 17.

There have been ~~a number of~~ many inquiries about the war song—~~that it is felt that~~ they all feel that if sung often it would be of help in these days—the last verse especially seems to appeal to most everybody—including soldier boys—but just as soon as Mr. I gets in better ~~shape~~ he will try to see what should be done, as to copies etc.—and will write you. He hopes what he is asking you to do, will not will not give you too much trouble—and please be sure to let him know what he will owe you for all you do—

With our best wishes & kindest greetings

He hopes the music is carrying you high & that you have time for your own composition—may they be well & often played.

• • •

The reconstruction of several measures in the quartet, described below, was not an uncommon experience for the editors of Ives's scores, even while they worked under his loose supervision. As long as Ives trusted his collaborator, he seems to have enjoyed the communal composition.[62]

383. 23 October 1944, from Lou Harrison, New York

Dear Mr. Ives,

It was a great pleasure & very instructive to me to proofread the parts to your second quartet. There is no better way, I am sure, to get to really know a piece & I am very devoted to the work as a result.

Mr. Yates, at my suggestion is going to perform it on his series this year in Los Angeles. I am going to suggest that it be recorded privately during the time of its best performance. I think it is something in the nature of immorality to allow great music to languish on shelves or to neglect to make a record whenever possible.

I am, of course, nearly 2 generations removed from you & in any sensible society I should be able to hear your major works frequently under the most sympathetic conditions. My generation, however, has missed hearing almost all the important music of the 20th century because we arrived to "musical responsibility" just after the initial & somewhat superficial enthusiasm had vanished & reaction had firmly set in. Some of us are painfully aware that we have been quite forcibly prevented from receiving our heritage & are determined to stand against the dry-rot of the mind that seems to be afflicting the age & the rampant prostitution of a great creative art to purely commercial ends. If we are left with no faith in human dignity or human achievement then what would be the use in any of us "youngsters" writing music or painting pictures? As I see it the musical "industry" in the U.S. is rapidly reducing anyone who has a sense of music as a meaningful art to the curious position of a stylite, or at best, a cloistered medieval monk.

I hadn't meant to rave but it strikes me as so terrible that I can say that I have heard

62. No parts with Harrison's corrections survive.

only about 4 or 5 performances of your music, about the same number of Schoenberg & only one recording of Ruggles, that I am really exercised on the matter. After all, it is you & Schoenberg who have made the most in your music for the pleasure & instruction of the age & it is nothing short of a social curse that prevents the young from such knowledge.

I hope that someday our orchestras & instrumentalists may be led by a composer instead of a Chicago gangster. It would help a great deal. Meantime we bide time & get what smaller performances we can of the music we really want to hear.

End of things I've wanted to tell you for some time.

I enclose a bill which I trust will be agreeable with you.

Hoping this letter finds you in good health.

My best regards to yourself and Mrs. Ives—

P.S. I took the liberty of reconstructing several measures in the 4tet where there was an obvious omission & the sketches were likewise vague—in all cases I used only material used before, or of a similar nature & affixed my initials.

To
Mr. Charles E. Ives
for proofreading & corrections of parts to Second Str. 4tet
24 pages—$6.00[63]
on October 23, 1944
From Lou Harrison
237 Bleeker St.
NYC 14

384. Ca. November 1944, sketch for Harmony Ives to Lou Harrison

Harrison

Mr. Ives was quite affected by your letter. During most of his life he has felt as you do, that not only music but all art, can attribute many of its weak parts to the commercial tread striding too much around in it—; though in some periods its lowering influence is worse than in others—today it is apparently down again. But, he says, with men ~~like you~~ of courage and independence like you, who are not afraid to think for themselves, stand up, do & say what they believe in regardless, better times will come.

You know how to write music Mr. I says, but you don't know how to write bills. All you have done, in these old quartet parts, is worth several times more than $6.—it is worth at least 4 times more—hence the enclosed Ck. We hope things are going as well with you as can be expected in these troubled days. With our kindest greetings,

I am —

63. Ives sent Harrison twenty-four dollars for proofreading the quartet parts, not the six dollars for which he had asked.

P.S. We have received no bill from Mr. Pagano, please ask him if you can conveniently to send his bill here. Or as we have not his address ~~here you might send us his address.~~

* * *

In June 1941 Peter Yates, who ran the Los Angeles modern music concert series "Evenings on the Roof," wrote to Ives to ask if the recording rights to the *Concord* Sonata had been assigned. His wife, Frances Mullen Yates, had been performing movements of the work since 1938, and the Yateses hoped to make a private recording of the whole piece. This caused some consternation for Ives, who felt that Kirkpatrick should be the first one to record the work. Ultimately, Yates's repeated inquiries about the sonata helped push Kirkpatrick to make his premiere recording.

385. 25 November 1944, second sketch for Harmony Ives to John Kirkpatrick

J.K. We hope the concert on the 13th—especially Carl's music went well and to your satisfaction. We were very sorry not to have been able to go.

In several letters during the last 3 or 4 years Mr. Peter Yates of Los Angeles has asked Mr. I. if Mrs. Y could be allowed to make records of the "Concord" Sonata. Mr. I has each time replied that~~ as he remembers~~, all rights for recording this sonata for public use had been given to you. In a letter just received from Mr. Y. He says "———"

Please let us know what you think about all this, and whatever you feel is best to do Mr. I ~~is agreeable to.~~

Love to you both

386. 28 November 1944, from John Kirkpatrick, Mount Holyoke College, South Hadley, Massachusetts

Dear Mrs. Ives,

Your letter touches me more deeply than I can tell you. I have taken the liberty of sending a copy of it to Mr. Lieberson, and enclose a copy of my letter to him. But first I telephoned Miss Halmans,[64] who was very much under the impression that if Columbia is interested, they would not want a private recording in circulation, and who will push negotiations with Lieberson, whom she knows very well. I'll let you know any upshoot.

Miss Rood & I are playing the 2nd Fiddle sonata at the Modern Museum Apr. 29th. More about that later.

Hastily—I'm already late to a lesson.

Best love from us both,
John Kirkpatrick

64. Ray and Bella Halmans were Kirkpatrick's artistic agents.

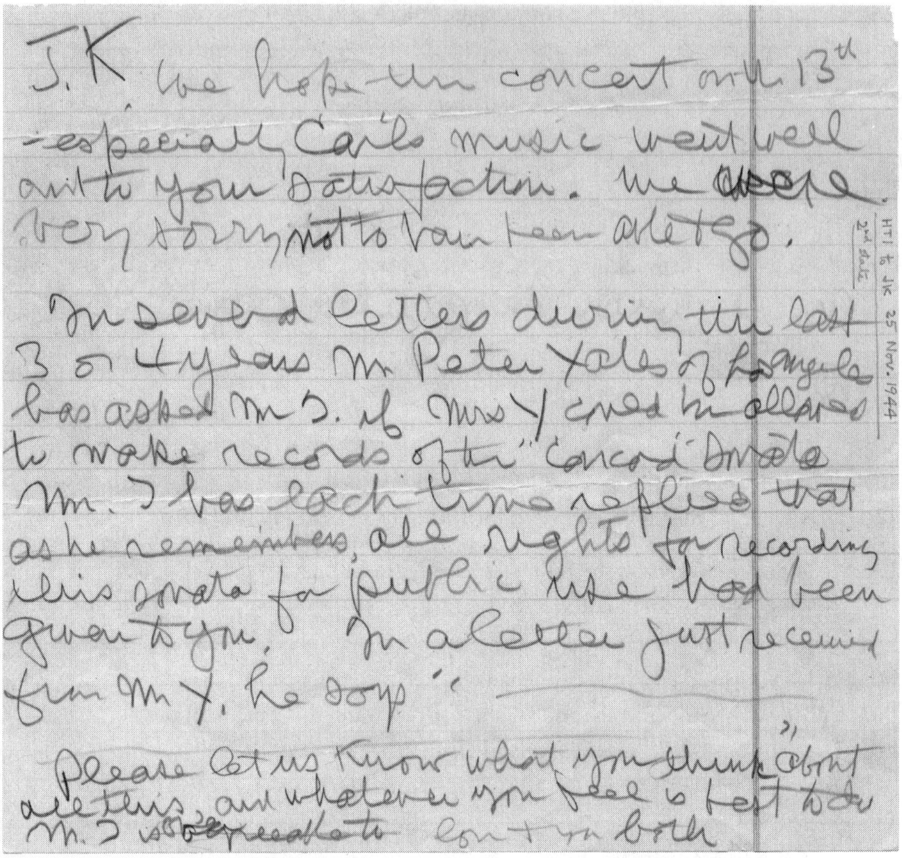
J.K. We hope the concert on the 13th
—especially Carl's music went well
and to your satisfaction. We were
very sorry not to have been able to go.

In several letters during the last
3 or 4 years Mr. Peter Yates of Los Angeles
has asked Mr. I. if Mrs Y could be allowed
to make records of the "Concord Sonata"
Mr. I has each time replied that
as he remembers, all rights for recording
this sonata for public use had been
given to you. In a letter just received
from Mr Y. he says "

Please let us know what you think about
all this, and whatever you feel is best to do
Mr. I is agreeable to [illegible] for both

HTI to JK 25 Nov. 1944
2nd draft

25 November 1944, second sketch for Harmony Ives to John Kirkpatrick.

387. 28 November 1944, John Kirkpatrick, South Hadley, Massachusetts, to Goddard Lieberson, Columbia Records

Dear Mr. Lieberson,

The enclosed letter has just come from Mrs. Ives, and since you were the first person ever to broach the subject of recording the Concord Sonata, I thought the whole matter ought certainly to be referred to you.

As I remember, I wrote you some years ago that I was too dissatisfied with my performance of it to want to commit it to phonographic scrutiny, and that I would let you know when it had improved. Since then it has gone on improving steadily, even to the point where I could confidently stand behind it in both unity and detail. Of course, as one's ability grows one's horizon recedes, so it has never occurred to me to bring up the subject again myself, feeling always that further degrees of improvement were just around the corner.

In the meantime, I must confess, I have been quite unappreciatively oblivious of the extent to which Mr. Ives was holding everything up in behalf of my eventually doing it, so you can imagine how deeply touched I am at receiving such expressions of confident trust.

Now that Mrs. Ives's letter has brought the subject to the brink of decision, the appropriate moment has come to ask you whether or not you are still interested in making this recording, and, in either case, what thoughts you might entertain about Mr. and Mrs. Yates's project.

With all good wishes,
sincerely yours,
John Kirkpatrick

• • •

After the initial push from Ives, Kirkpatrick and his representatives worked quickly to negotiate a recording date for the sonata with Columbia Records. The pianist was troubled by denying Frances Yates the opportunity of recording the sonata and seems to have been glad to be able to say that the record company required that his recording be exclusive.

388. 3 December 1944, from John Kirkpatrick, South Hadley, Massachusetts

Dear Mrs. Ives,

There has been quite a little upshot opening up some very pleasant vistas. Day before yesterday I had a letter from Miss Halmans saying: "Bella (Miss Halmans' sister, Mrs. Postma—they've always worked together) and I have just had lunch with Goddard Lieberson and he is definitely interested in having you record the Ives sonata as well as the Stephen Foster group. . . . He is not in any immediate rush to make these recordings but is ready to do so any time after the first of the year. . . . Now we think it will be quite in order for you to write Mrs. Ives that you would like to take up the exclusive privilege of recording the sonata for Columbia, thereby denying Mrs. Yates of California the private recording. . . . " And yesterday a note came from Lieberson: "Dear John, You will by now have a report from Ray and Bella Halmans. I would like to record the Concord Sonata whenever you are able to. I assume that either you or the Misses Halmans will let me know about any further developments."

Lieberson says nothing about exclusivity of privilege, and Ray seems to treat the question as if taking it for granted that I will assume the full responsibility of Mr. Ives's very kind offer of "all rights." Of course I would be perfectly delighted to do just that, and do my best to justify it by the performance, but in the meantime I couldn't help thinking it might seem a little kinder to Mrs. Yates if some of the responsibility for the decision couldn't be laid at the door of Columbia. So I have written to Lieberson as Enclosed.

And really I find it very difficult to discover how I really do feel about Mrs. Yates's project. In principle, she should be just as free, I suppose, to go ahead with her recording as I with mine, and, as a worker in the same field, I hate the idea of shutting that door to her. Ray seems to feel that it's obvious that she shouldn't be allowed to, and whether that's being commercially greedy or simply businesslike I don't know. I may be unduly sentimental in my approach, and making a mountain out of a molehill which would be a commonplace to anyone more familiar with the business implications of the situation. You and Mr. Ives know that I want to do what's best for the music, and maybe that degree of exclusivity is only part of the duty or responsibility which your letter so happily invests me with, and which I should assume completely and courageously, and certainly gratefully. I suppose you would like to write Mr. Yates quite soon. Perhaps I might hear from Lieberson Tuesday.

Enclosed also the announcement card of the Valley Music Press, which I have taken over, and which I mentioned to Mr. Ives when we were up to see you all this summer. I had an idea it might be great fun to do the 2nd Violin Sonata, if Mr. Ives be willing. Miss Rood and I will be working at it and working out bowings and all in preparation to playing it in April, and I think I could guarantee both a practical and a sympathetic editing. I'm not at all sure though that the Valley Press could ensure it the widest possible diffusion. We're sending out 500 of these double mailing cards (mostly to college music departments), and the American Music Center handles our stuff in New York. Our financial arrangement is that the composer and the press each pay half the printing cost (unless the composer happens to want to assume all of it). In the former case, receipts are halved between the composer and the press; in the latter case, receipts go to the composer until he is paid back for the printing cost, then halved. It's all quite simple and efforts on the part of those implicated are entirely without salary, so it can cheerfully operate with a tiny outlay. Both Smith College and this one are granting an annual subsidy each of $100 for an experimental period until it may become self-supporting.

With our best love to you both, and many many thanks again to Mr. Ives for so thoughtfully watching over my interests,

sincerely
John Kirkpatrick

389. 12 December 1944, from John Kirkpatrick, South Hadley, Massachusetts

Dear Mrs Ives,

Ever since my last letter I have been wanting to apologize for its vagueness. Since then I have had no answer to my letter to Lieberson, but I see in today's paper something about some rather formal festivities in connection with resuming N.Y. Philharmonic recordings that probably have been keeping him quite busy. I don't know much about business methods, either of nowadays or of the past, but anyway I'm sure that in Mr. Ives's office letters were taken care of more promptly. But on the other hand, I certainly have no right to pass opinions, as you know how negligent a correspondent I can be.

In the intervening silence, though, I've been able to see more clearly what I had suspected—that my attitude is considerably hypocritical. I am cheerfully party to what seems to be the business expediency of an exclusive right of recording, but air my regrets at doing so, and want somebody else to take the responsibility. I think I should take the responsibility and if Mr. & Mrs. Yates think me unkind, that's all right. I'm terribly sorry at the way all this shilly- shallying on my part has held up what must have been your natural desire to send Mr. Yates a prompt answer. Please thank Mr. Ives for me again for his placing such a unique privilege in my hands, and also for his patience with my general slowness.

I've been starting up practicing again, and it is really such a joy as defies description. The Hawthorne movement goes much better than ever before.

I'll keep you posted, of course, on any further exchanges of correspondence with Lieberson.

With our best love to you both.

Sincerely,
John Kirkpatrick

• • •

In 1944 Elliott Carter and Henry Cowell proposed forming a society in honor of Ives on his seventieth birthday. The letter Ives sketched in reply shows both his modesty and his gratitude. His suggestion that the society be expanded to include other composers such as Cowell, Carter, and Ruggles reveals his conception that the composers writing modern music were a unified group dedicated to a single cause. The sketch revisions here show how Ives made multiple drafts even in simple correspondence and demonstrate one of Ives's most common methods of rewriting material. After the fourth paragraph he writes an "X." He then writes another draft of the marked paragraph after the body of the sketch is complete.

390. Ca. 20 October 1944, second sketch for Harmony Ives to Elliott Carter

Carter

Mr. Ives was deeply affected by your kind letter on his birthday and says he cannot find words to express his great appreciation of all you, Henry, and other kind friends are doing in his behalf <u>but</u> he feels that he doesn't deserve it all—and to have a society named after him is not fair to many other American composers—and also that it will bring you all too much trouble and take too much of your time,—

Just now he is so overcome and so embarrassed that he doesn't know what he ought to do about it all. When Henry wrote that an informal committee had been formed, he felt somewhat embarrassed about that—but a Charles Ives Society—that's too much, he says, it shouldn't be not only his name but the names of all American composers your committee approves of can be nailed all over it."

He is not at all well, as you may know, and can't do things he would like to, or take an active part in any work and couldn't go to meetings, and he feels he should not let his generous friends put themselves so much out for his sake.

He says, there are other composers he says, who need your help too—among them Carl Ruggles, and in the next generation Henry Cowell and a younger friend of his Elliot

Carter," whom you probably know may have met, and also others whose music should be widely known and often played. (X)[65]

He doesn't feel quite right about having a society named after him—(he says it makes him feel "sort of like a hog")—some of his friends on the high way may infer, as has happened before, that he is an old fraud; he doesn't stand up enough ~~for his old friends~~—that one is his music."

However, later on when he ~~feels~~ is better able to attend to things—and hears whatever you, Henry and other friends think ought be done, he will try to do. But he does, from the bottom of his heart, thank you all for your generous friendship and interest.

65. Ives refers to Cowell and Carter in the third person here as a joke.

• 8 •

FINAL YEARS

(1945–1954)

The last decade of his life saw Ives's health decline more steadily. He was able to write fewer letters, even through sketching and transcription, and Harmony Ives wrote more of their letters herself. The growing acceptance of the music, highlighted by the award of the Pulitzer Prize for the Third Symphony in 1947 and Leonard Bernstein's performance of the Second Symphony with the New York Philharmonic in 1951, was a source of great satisfaction. It also increased the volume of mail at a time when neither of the Iveses was fully able to cope with the flow. Nevertheless, Ives's final years were a valedictory period in his life. The work of past and current champions of his music, such as Cowell, Slonimsky, Harrison, and Kirkpatrick, had come to fruition, and momentum for widespread acceptance of the music seemed to be growing. The friendships that had developed over the years of seemingly thankless work had deepened into another source of comfort even in the face of the inexorable progression of old age.

In the following letter John Kirkpatrick mentions the continuing evolution of his version of the *Concord* Sonata. This was not the same as the first edition or the published second edition (1947). Through studying the manuscript sources for the sonata, Kirkpatrick had developed his own performing edition of it, one that he continued to use even after the publication of Ives's corrections in the second edition.

391. 15 February 1945, from John Kirkpatrick, South Hadley, Massachusetts

Dear Mr. Ives,

Here are some programs—5 down, one to go.

The master sheets of that editing of the 2nd violin sonata have been found, and I have ordered some copies sent to you. Saw a review of the California performance of it in Modern Music—evidently they did only the last 2 movements. Can't wait to get back to working at it with Louise Rood.

Did you see, in this last Modern Music, Lou Harrison's rhapsody about Carl's Evocations?[1] Makes him out to be a saintly, angelic creature (which, of course, he is, at heart).

I find that, for Sunday's performance, I'm still slipping in more and more of the revi-

1. Lou Harrison, "Ruggles, *Evocations*," *Modern Music* 22, no. 2 (January–February 1945): 109.

sions than I used to. By the way, I've never asked you if there are further subsequent revisions, since the set of proof sheets which Mrs. Ives so kindly brought down to Georgetown a couple years ago. Are there, or is that "up to date"? And is there any further quotation on the imminence of the projected Arrow Press reprint?

Haven't had any further communications from Goddard Lieberson about the recording, but suppose no news is good news, especially with the rush they're all in since the resumption of recordings.

Of course, on the trip, everybody loved the Alcotts.

Sorry to make this so brief—must catch the mail.

Best love from us both,
John Kirkpatrick

Daisy[2] gets lovelier and lovelier. She smiles, coos, and gurgles.

• • •

During the preparation of the second edition of the sonata, Kirkpatrick often asked to see the latest revisions Ives had made. Ives's response in the letter below shows how elusive and ephemeral the work was for him. Although he was very much interested in producing a sound and error-free edition that would best represent his understanding of the piece, he was reluctant ever to say that any one version had achieved that goal. Ives's performance of the work reflected an ideal that could exist only within his mind. And this ideal form changed with time and context as a landscape changes with the position of the sun and the time of year or as one's interpretation of an essay changes with one's mood and experience.

392. 16 March 1945, sketch for Harmony Ives to John Kirkpatrick

Kirkpatrick

I am sorry to say Mr. I has not been at all well for some time or he would have answered your kind letters before.

You are too generous in sending all those copies of the 2nd V[iolin]. S[onata]. and Mr. I says you <u>must</u> let him know what those bills were whether you want to or not.

Thank you also for your programs & he hopes "that the Sonata is not knocking all the nice old ladies out of their "boxes."

We think you have the final corrected & revised copies—these are not ~~all~~ very important—it depends sometimes, on the time of day it is played heard—at sunrise that wide chord—and at sunset maybe with an overtone, towards a star. He has felt that some music, like a landscape, though fundamentally the same, may have changing colors during a cosmic horizon, and as^{X} over

One page in the Emerson a copy we are enclosing, might had be better to go in the

2. Daisy was Kirkpatrick's daughter.

record and also in the Alcotts choose few overtones after the chords in the "Concord sky" Two in the top brace p. 55–one in the 3rd brace p. 56. Mr. Ives usually likes to play these & were left out in only copy ~~by mistake of a "old copier"~~[3]—these 2 pages are also being sent. As Mr. I remembers most of the other corrections or revisions are not exactly important.

The Arrow Press are having a difficult time in having the plates printed—but this 2nd Edition will probably be ~~done~~ ready later in the year.

We send our love to Daisy & ask her to give part of it to her Daddy & Momma"

Mamma & Daddy

We hear often from those who have heard you

[*In the bottom margin, upside down, Ives writes a revision referred to with the* [X] above:]

you know the oak tree in May doesn't always play the same tune way that it plays (shouts out) in October.

393. 18 March 1945, from John Kirkpatrick, South Hadley, Massachusetts

Dear Mrs. Ives,

Thanks so much for your good letter. We are very sorry to hear that Mr. Ives hasn't been so well, and hope that the spring will set him up again. We've been enjoying the premature almost-summer weather and wishing we could get to Windways as early as you all will probably get to Redding.[4]

I haven't yet got the bill for the copies of the violin sonata, but I will send it on to Mr. Ives dutifully and gratefully if reluctantly.

I think I told you that I had suggested April 6th to the Columbia outfit for the recording. It now seems that Monday the 2nd would be much better, so I [have] just written them suggesting this change.

Thanks for the four extra pages of proof-sheets. I've been putting in the little overtones "in the Concord Sky" for the last couple of years, ever since you brought that set of proof-sheets to Windways. Yes, they sound lovely, only I thought they were a little more the awestruck bewonderment of the children at all the philosophizing goins-on. In Emerson, I do more of a combining of the original and revised versions. For instance in page 6, in the ascent at the end of line 1, I fill in the rhythm of the original printing with the harmonies of the revision but not with all the detail. Otherwise I just do page 6 just as in the revision. The suggested G natural at "(almost as a recitative through here)" doesn't yet convince me, but I'll keep trying it over. It may just be my Scotch sales-resistance, or simply that I get so fond of all these effects as I've been doing them. Page 17 is pretty much the same way. (Yes, I had noticed that F needed a natural in front of it.) I could never understand why Mr. Ives cut out the aftermath of the phrase (original p. 16) that starts in the middle of the

3. This probably refers to Ives himself.

4. Windways was Kirkpatrick's country house; see Letter 381.

3rd line ("Broadly . . . "). Played with the most important top notes doubled with the octave below, and a little faster than 72, and with appropriate chiaroscuro, I think it's one of the best things in the whole sonata. (Oh yes, and with the final bass G–F# doubled with the octave below). In Emerson I'm always including more and more of the revised details, but that one has never ceased to seem to me to be just right. Also I've been surprised at how my overall tempo has quickened. Six years ago I was doing it in about 47 minutes, now it's about 38. I suppose the more familiar it becomes, the less time has to be taken for transitions of idea. After this recording is over I'll be curious to play over the recordings of those 1939 performances, which I haven't listened to for several years (really not completely since 1939)

Oh yes, another thing, I think it will get conveniently on 9 sides, (It won't go on 8 with the sides limited, as it appears they have to be, to 4' 20"), so I thought it would be great fun to put "In the Inn" on the 10th side. Is that all right by Mr. Ives?

You are sweet to keep such an interest in Daisy's doings. She is a perfect angel. Can you believe that since she was born she has never kept us awake with crying a single night! She reserves all her tantrums for the daytime, and we are so impressed and grateful. Yes, we'll have to take her to pay a call next summer on Uncle Charlie and Aunt Harmony.

With best love from all three of us,

sincerely,
John[5]

• • •

Though Ives was reluctant to be pinned down on a final version of the *Concord*, he did not view it as an open field for improvisation. Some details were quite important to him, as is implicit in his desire both to record his performance of the piece, particularly "Emerson," and to make such substantial changes in the second edition.

394. Ca. 18 March 1945, sketch for Harmony Ives to John Kirkpatrick

Mr. I is very afraid ~~is sorry that~~ the "Concord" is giving ~~so mu~~ you ~~so~~ too much trouble & taking too much of your time. Do whatever you think best as to the records, but he does hope that p. 17 ~~16 old copies~~ can be recorded as it is in the "revised copy." ~~Of the old page 16 copy He has always played it.~~ As he remembers this was more as it was in the old Concerto score—and as he usually liked to ~~played it~~ play it.

He will be very glad to håve "In the Inn" also in the recordings

(Instead of as in page number 16 in book)

5. This is the first letter Kirkpatrick signed using only his first name.

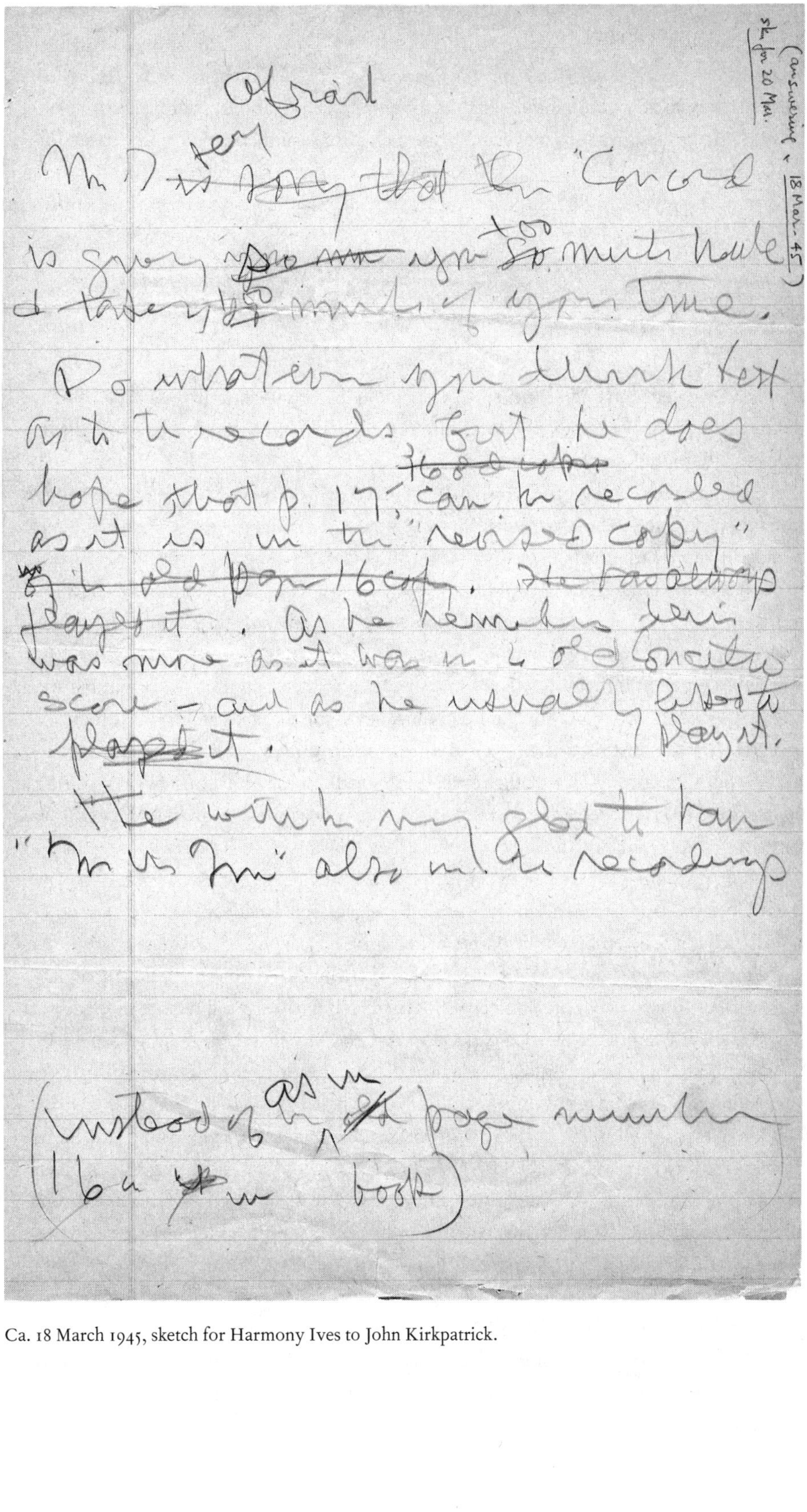
(answering 18 Mar. 45)
sk. for 20 Mar.

Ofrand

Mr I very "Concord

is going you too much trouble

Do whatever you think best
as to the records. But he does
hope that p. 17, can be recorded
as it is in the "revised copy".
As he remembers this
was more as it was in the old Concertina
score — and as he usually liked to
play it.

He would be very glad to have
"In the Inn" also in the recordings

(instead of as in page number
16 in book)

Ca. 18 March 1945, sketch for Harmony Ives to John Kirkpatrick.

• • •

Kirkpatrick's meticulous study of the *Concord* Sonata was most often apparent to Ives through the pianist's voluminous requests for details, clarifications, source material, and answers to the many questions that arose from such a dense and complex work. In the following letter, however, Kirkpatrick responds to hearing his own first recording of the work and in the process gives insight into his conception of the piece and the process of recording it.

395. 18 December 1945, from John Kirkpatrick, South Hadley, Massachusetts

Dear Friends,

Life has been very full and hectic, and lots of good intentions to write you have contributed to paving hell. We trust you have been well and could enjoy at West Redding the marvelous spells of Indian summer we had up here.

Daisy gets more and more wonderful every day. As you see, she's taken up improvisation in tone-clusters. She's just started to take steps with much guidance and we wouldn't wonder if she'll fare forth on her own steam and balance pretty soon. She doesn't use any words yet, consciously, but recognizes and obeys many, and her syllabifications become more and more varied. Really she is so good and cooperative and luminous that we can't understand how we deserved her.

I never wrote you that towards the end of October the Columbia outfit sent me an advance set of the Concord Sonata. I had time, at the time, to play it all over just once, and go over again just the parts I wanted to hear again, and then I had to send it back to them—but I got a good idea of the result, with which I was quite agreeably surprised. Of course these electrical recordings of a piano don't sound too much like a piano, but I was surprised at how much of the intended effect they do achieve with the sound they have. (The only piano recordings I've ever heard that did sound exactly like a piano—so that they'd fool you—were the old Edison records, which aren't made any more.)

Also I hadn't remembered the performance as being as good as it evidently was, which was a most agreeable shock. All I could remember from that nightmarish day of replayings were the few wrong notes we had to leave in, and in the overall picture they seem to have hardly any importance. I had expected, from the way that day felt in retrospect, that the recording would sound either a little hysterical or a little tired, but most of it comes out very much as I would have liked it to.

One thing that amused me no end was the speed with which I did most of Hawthorne. I guess that for years I've been laboring under a slight phobia of not being able to play Hawthorne fast enough—I imagine the music, much of it, at a pretty terrific pace—and all my workouts on it have had that end in mind. But I never imagined being able to play it at the speed I heard myself playing it at. But playing those sides over again, I really didn't think it was too fast. It was clear.

And what a wonderful piece it is! That was the first time I've ever heard it as a listener (though not quite freely so), and it is certainly a most rewarding experience. Its essential qualities seemed so much more intense and concentrated than I've been conscious of, having to be so occupied with the physical problems of it. And I don't think it was the critical scrutiny that I was listening with that was responsible for the impression that there were no "valleys" in the continuity of interest. It sings and sings.

I still haven't gotten together with Louise Rood on the 2nd Violin Sonata. We hope to this spring. Both of us have just had too much to do, especially as she is the one outside member of the Bennington Quartet, which rehearses frequently. But we hope to get at it, and perform it up here (either at Smith or here) (or both) this coming spring.

Our next big event (I should type it: BIG EVENT), Daisy's successor, is due the very end of January, and everything is apparently going ideally and right according to schedule. After which, of course, life will be still fuller and reasonably hecticker.

The two enclosed programs will amuse you. The Wilson College 75th anniversary experiment was great fun, particularly resuscitating lots of stuff I haven't played for years. At Oneonta, I tried playing the whole book of [MacDowell's] Woodland Sketches for the first time. I'm very fond of them as a collection, but in a few of their juxtapositions they don't set each other off ideally. The Alcotts sounds marvelous after the hunting sonata (or after almost anything!). On my A.A.C. tour of the 6 colleges next month, I'm putting it after Carl's 4th Evocation.

I meant to write you also that I had a lovely visit over-night with Carl and Charlotte up at Arlington the last weekend in September.[6] They both looked fine and were in wonderful spirits. They wrote me from Coral Gables just a month ago that Mike was about to be let out of the army.

Hope's family are all coming up here to celebrate Christmas with us, so Daisy will be the center of lots of affection and excitement.

All best things and love from us both,
John [*in pencil in Ives's hand:* Kirkpatrick]

P.S. On the recording, "In the Inn" (on the 10th side) came out very well, particularly the approach to the Chorus. They've sent me no word about when it might be released.

• • •

On 5 April 1946 Lou Harrison conducted the New York Little Symphony in the world premieres of Ives's Third Symphony and his own "Motet for the Day of Ascension," along with Carl Ruggles's "Portals." Ives had completed the symphony in 1911, but the clean ink copy of the score was lost when he sent it to Walter Damrosch, then conductor of the New York Symphony. For the performance, Harrison had to edit a clean copy of the score from the photostatic manuscript copy he had long had. Using only this source and his knowledge of Ives's style, Harrison prepared a score. Ives's input in the process was minimal. After the successful premiere, Harrison's edition, again with minimal corrections from Ives, was published in 1947 by Arrow Music Press, not *New Music*, as Harrison suggests. Harrison also had a private recording made of the performance.

6. Carl and Charlotte Ruggles lived in a converted schoolhouse in Arlington, Vermont.

396. 14 April 1946, from Lou Harrison, New York

Dear Mrs. Ives—

Thank you for your very kind letter. I am glad you felt the performance went well.

Now the copy (in blueprint) of the new manuscript is in my hands and in several days I will send it, with little marks on it for Mr. Ives' perusal. I have made slight changes in dynamics here and there which seemed needed for instrumental balance. They are merely suggestions arrived at during rehearsals, some are given by the musicians themselves.

As soon as it is possible for Mr. Ives to alter or O.K. this copy we would like to put it in print immediately in New Music Edition, if this idea meets with Mr. Ives's approval. I fancy the work will enjoy a quite wide circulation and a number of performances in the near future. When the edition is issued I want to send the score, reviews of its first performance and Mr. Downes's excellent article in this week's Times to several persons who might see to playings.[7] I am almost sure a performance might be had from Pierre Monteux (among others) with the San Francisco Symphony, and it would be a good one—I will write him and my friend Alfred Frankenstein who is critic of the S.F. Chronicle.

Mr. Baroné wishes me to do another work of Mr. Ives next season. He will take Town Hall for the occasion and use more strings.[8] I would like to do one of the "undone" pieces again, so when it is over we will have parts, score and editing. In this way some of those pieces not published or copied might get into circulation.

Elliot says you would wish a copy of the records I had taken. I will order a copy made for you and send them to Redding when I get them.[9] The copy of Mr. Ives's symphony is $12.00 and includes "Portals" at no extra charge since it seems to occupy an unused side of the three discs. The performance of "Portals" is sheer mud in several places, but enough of its grand outlines remain to make it worth having around anyway. The "terrible truth" of the whole evening is at any rate on records.

I wonder if something might be done about collecting Mr. Ives's writings into a little volume—I never tire of the notes and essays he appends to scores and think a volume of them would be a great pleasure.

My very best to you both—I hope the climate in Redding is pleasant and your stay cheerful.

Devotedly,
Lou Harrison

• • •

Ives had an ambivalent relationship with recording technology. He had a very old-fashioned phonograph in the late 1930s—a letter mentions needing "wooden needles" for it—but per-

7. Olin Downes, "Tardy Recognition: Emergence of Charles Ives as Strongly Individual Figure in American Music," *New York Times,* 14 April 1946. The article is reproduced in Burkholder, *Charles Ives and His World,* 403–7.

8. Joseph Baroné was the regular conductor of the New York Little Symphony.

9. Elliott Carter was involved in the preparations for the Little Symphony concert and also with an all-Ives concert at Columbia University in May 1946.

haps he kept it in Manhattan. In any case, Ives very rarely listened to recordings because he had a hearing condition that made them seem distorted to him.[10]

397. 21 April 1946, Harmony Ives to Lou Harrison

Dear Mr. Harrison,

As we have no Victrola here could the records be sent for the time being to the music center?[11] I may be in New York for a short time in June or July, and could then have them sent to 74th Street.

I enclose my cheque for them and Mr. Ives is sending his cheque to you as he feels that all your work on the parts, etc. has not been by any means compensated. He wants you to accept it with his best wishes.

As to the score on account of his eye condition it may take some time for him to go over it. As he remembers there are one or two measures in the old sketch that he did not put in exactly as they were when it was fully scored and if he can find them in the old copy he will send them when he returns the score.

We are sending under separate cover some data you may like for reference and to save your time.

I think the idea of making a collection of his marginal notes etc. a good one—they are characteristic—He says "I'd have to see 'em."

We are so glad your splendid conducting got such good notice.

Mr. Ives will be glad to have the symphony go into New Music Edition and will want [to] take the cost of it and not have it come out of his regular contribution which is for the music of other composers not his.

It is beautiful here—Mr. Ives gets into the woods behind the house. I get my welcome from the wild flowers. I love the early ones—Arbutus & hepaticas & blood root.

Mr. Ives says "Say again how much we appreciate all he has done."

With many thanks
Sincerely yours
Harmony T. Ives

* * *

This letter consists mostly of detailed questions about corrections for the Third Symphony score. It also presages the nervous breakdown Harrison would suffer in May 1947. Harrison's powerful homesickness for the West Coast comes through wistfully in his conversation with Harmony about spring flowers.

10. See Letters 150, 153, 159, 169, and 175. See also Harmony Ives to Bernard Herrmann, 7 October 1936, and Charles Ives to Bernard Herrmann, 19 October 1936 (both in CIP, 30/4).

11. The American Music Center was set up in 1939 to aid in the distribution and promotion of scores by American composers. It became the New York distributor for the *New Music Edition*.

398. 16 May 1946, from Lou Harrison, New York

Dear Mrs. Ives,

Please forgive my long delay in writing. I have had the flu "Bug" that is getting everyone this season & also had to tend to several other matters which I had to lay aside during the concert preparation period.

Firstly I want to express my thanks and gratitude to Mr. Ives for his generous aid in this whole matter, and more immediately for his recent cheque which mounts it to more than ample payment on any labours at part copying and the like. Especially considering the pleasure and instruction I had from that beautiful work.

I also want to thank you for your helpful and sympathetic letters—they make hopeful many hours & days when I have not been feeling too well about the state either of the world or a number of the people in it. It is a delight (and somewhat of a faith) for me to know you and Mr. Ives.

The festival of Mr. Ives music at Columbia was wonderful indeed! Finally I feel that the only music that really moves me wholly and not only in part is Mr. Ives and Carl Ruggles'. The selection was good and the pieces were, for the most part very well played. The 2nd 4tet about which I have been very curious for several years is a masterpiece—rich and enormously imaginative. Its complex idiom becomes absolutely clear and communicative in performance, and with the exception of Schoenberg's 3rd I can think of no other 4tet of our time to touch it. Schoenberg's piece is even a little callous and, consequently, fragile, so that it really doesn't have the open, humanistic beauty a first-rate work should have. I was deeply stirred (in Mr. Ives's 4tet) by that slowly marching passage in the last movement where all the heavenly bodies, and indeed possibly, the heavenly hosts too do really seem to move by.

With this I am sending the Third Symphony with my marks in red (or sometimes circled in red) I trust most of them will be quite clear as they are, but several I would like to draw attention to with a word of explanation.

At the end of Mv. I, 2 ms. before 24, where flute & oboe change to 4/2 I conducted both 4 and 3 at the same time and the passage was clear—it was not nearly so clear the other night when both beats were not given—so a little note might be made about this.

The repetitions of several measures in Mv. II are marked in the original copy but were so faint that they seem to have been missed in this copy.

The climax of the last Mvt. seems to be the most problematic point. My suggestions for the climax chord itself include one D♯ of the many found in the original score but also the saving of the D naturals found in the song version of the same passage. My reasoning and experience during the performance is this: the lowest D being sharp is not heard (despite the horn doubling on it) as a separate note, but does majestically reinforce (as 3rd partial) the G♯ in the bass, which is the note that gives the spot its poignance, as well as emphasizing the upper D naturals by making an unheard clash up there. The effect, at any rate, as I have circled it here, is very telling in performance—I therefore urge its consideration. Two measures later is the insert taken directly from the song version—only reduced from a single measure of 10/8 to one of 7/8 and one of 3/8 for playing and conducting ease.

Whether I mistook Mr. Ives's intention in the very next measure I do not know. The score bore a marking solo over the top note of the octaves in the cello part, which is playing the beautiful chorale. I presumed, since the flute was scored in unison with it that a single solo cello was meant—so I had it done so with the other celli playing together at their notes an octave lower as in the score. The soloist played with full-blown tone & I boosted the flute volume up to audibility and the two instruments intoned the hymn together against the other instruments—the result, coming after the full sound of the climax measures was, as you may remember, extremely lovely. I tell all this only because I still don't know whether Mr. Ives meant it this way or not—also because I have marked the necessary "gli altri" if he did—and changed the flute dynamics. The pizz. at this point is in the original but got left out in the copy—many small marks of that kind are so, and some of the circled notes as well.

At the close the same solo cello problem arises—I again took it literally (and poetically) to be a kind of gentle representation of a human voice, a kind of pastor leading the "amen," and so brought the full cello choir in only on the final low B-flat as marked.

I hope this is all clear and not confusing to Mr. Ives. If we can get the whole thing in shape and in print by fall, at least (says he hopefully!!) It will be much played next season—I'm sure—& so is everyone else.

I am glad that Mr. Ives is able to be out in the open—nothing is so cheering and revitalizing as seeing growth around one & smelling the air & feeling the ground running about one.

I am still a little mystified by some of the eastern flowers, & trees too for that matter. On my native west coast there exists an equivalent kind for each that is here but the change is sometimes an outright masquerade & so I simply don't see some plants whose western relatives I am intimate with. From my childhood in Oregon I am recollecting more and more now that I am once again in a place very much like it. My intervening years in the wonderful Mediterranean land of California almost made me forget a landscape that knows seasons. I also still haven't figured out why seeds never got across the "rockies" so that nature had to reinvent everything on either side!

My best love to you both,
Lou Harrison

• • •

In the sketches for the next several letters Ives began to play games with Harrison's name, calling him "Lew Harry Sun" and, perhaps paternally, "Son Harrylou." The further discussion of the editing of the Third Symphony demonstrates the level of supervision Ives exercised over such work in the late 1940s.

399. 28 June 1946, Harmony Ives to Lou Harrison

Dear Mr. Harrison,

We are sending under separate cover the 3rd symphony score.

Mr. Ives has not been able to go all over it in detail but he is sure that whatever you have done is well done. There are only 3 measures in which a note or two has been put in as in the old sketch copy.

These are:

P. 17—Flute 2nd meas.
P. 20—Horn 3rd meas.
P. 26—Flute 2nd & 3rd meas.
Also P. 18—Flute last meas. "G" not "F"

Then at the end of the last movement in the last two measures in the staff over the 1st violin, is the ad lib. part for the "distant church bells." Mr. Ives says—"a piano off stage perhaps—but better small chimes, celesta or a glockenspiel—These minor chord bell notes were originally put in partly as a remembrance of the bells of the three churches in old Danbury—father would sometimes get the sextons to ring them together, as they made almost a minor triad—the first ring was the bell going up—the 2nd the swing back, which made a somewhat lower tone, or at least seemed to at a distance, as I remember"

However, he says, do whatever seems best—they don't always have to be played especially in a small hall.

The lead pencil slip pinned onto the last page was to be put in when the good ink copy (now lost) was made some 30 years ago—but he is not sure that it was. He feels that possibly it would be well to have a footnote explaining how the bell chords could be played.

We have just received a letter from Mr. Wigglesworth kindly suggesting that this score, also the 3rd Violin Sonata & four other scores be published by New Music Edition.[12] We will write him that the proposal is very acceptable to Mr. Ives. Mr. Pagano's copy could well be used for the 3rd symphony, it is a fine copy—as good as an engraved copy.

Mr. Ives says he wants so much to help in behalf of your music—says how about publishing your "Day of Ascension Motet"?—And also that you must send him a bill from time to time for the work you have done for him in his music scores etc.

As you probably know Schirmer has asked to publish the 3rd Symphony & the 2nd Violin Sonata—but Mr. Ives doesn't want them to publish anything that his old friends New Music Edition & the Arrow Press would want.

Our thanks and kindest wishes,

Faithfully yours
Harmony T. Ives

• • •

Harrison's success with the Third Symphony encouraged him to push for the publication and performance of more Ives works in order to build on the momentum finally established. The symphony seemed headed toward more widespread acceptance: Bernard Herrmann conducted it on his radio program in July, and Harrison implies below that he planned to do so again in

12. Frank Wigglesworth (1918–96) succeeded Lou Harrison as chairman of the *New Music* board and served until he won the Prix de Rome in 1951; Mead, *Henry Cowell's New Music,* 370–72.

August.[13] Meanwhile, anticipating more performances than most material published in *New Music* normally received, Harrison, Elliott Carter, and Frank Wigglesworth had decided to have the symphony published by the more commercial firm Arrow Music Press, which shared office space with *New Music* at the American Music Center in New York. Harrison had begun to think about editing the First Piano Sonata, which he eventually did for a performance by William Masselos in 1949. This letter also documents an aspect of the Ives legend that was very attractive to younger composers in the 1940s: the mysterious allure of other, yet unknown works by Ives, waiting to be discovered in the barn in West Redding.

400. 24 July 1946, from Lou Harrison, New York

Dear Mrs. Ives—

Thank you & Mr. Ives for being so quick about the 3rd symphony. I am giving it to Mr. Pagano to complete corrections.

Mr. Hermann is playing it late in Aug. & before that time he and I will get everything completely cleared up. Then it should be published.

Mr. Carter, Mr. Wigglesworth & I think it would perhaps be best that it should appear in Arrow Press, so that royalties could more easily be collected & the like. As you know, <u>New Music</u> is not well prepared to deal with such a widespread success as this work is going to be next year & Arrow Press, having a licensing& collecting agreement would find it convenient.

I am very glad that the 3rd is going to be played so much and reach such a broad public—I hope that in not many years the 4 Ives symphonies will be as played & enjoyed as the 4 Brahms are, they should be, anyway.

For some time, now, I have been wanting to clear up the 1st Piano Sonata. My own copy I loaned to a pianist from whom I find it difficult to get back. I wonder if it would be possible for me to have another copy so that I can get to work on it. My plan is to make a copy as complete & clear as possible & try to get a Town Hall performance for it this coming season. I've already interviewed several pianists but think a clear copy might more easily do the trick.

Also, in our <u>New Music</u> plan for 4 "tangent editions" of Mr. Ives's works wouldn't it be good to substitute this sonata for the 3rd Symphony which will be "Arrow"?

I've loved the First Sonata for years & in several ways am more attached to it than to the Concord (though who can resist that giant?) & I very much want it to be known.

Another matter, & here please believe I should understand if what I suggest were for one reason or another not feasible to you & Mr. Ives. <u>About the Barn.</u> Mr. Wigglesworth & I would like awfully to be allowed to come up & go through what is there, put it in order & gloat over what treasures must be there to be found. When it is all in order, & after whatever use toward publication & performance is made of the material, I think it should be established as a special library somewhere—perhaps the Library of Congress.

At any rate, <u>what is in that mysterious edifice?</u>

13. Sinclair, *Descriptive Catalogue,* 13.

I am very touched by Mr. Ives's kindness in offering to publish my own music, & indeed am grateful for the concern he so indicates about my composition. But the truth is, that while in the past I have twice been represented in New Music, I am now unsure that anything I have written is yet ready for the unblushing declaration of print.

After the performance of my "Motet for the Day of Ascension" I ripped it apart & have not yet assembled it quite wholly. This piece, I want to explain, in case the intention was unclear, is part of a work in progress now called "The Daily Book" which I intend as a book of ritual pieces celebrating whatever of interest happened to happen on each day: celebrations both sacred & civil, though.

My very best wishes to you & Mr. Ives—I hope the weather in Redding has not been as wet as in N.Y. this last week.

Is Mr. Ives feeling better these days? I hope so!

Love
from
Lou Harrison

Please forgive my pencil, I have written in haste.

• • •

Here we see Ives's slightly ambivalent attitude toward his First Piano Sonata and further evidence of John Kirkpatrick's importance to Ives as a performer and editor of his works. As was implicit in the discussions with Peter and Frances Yates mentioned above, Ives had essentially given Kirkpatrick a permanent right to be first in the performance, recording, and editing of his keyboard music. The transcription below follows Harmony's final copy of the letter.

401. 9 August 1946, Harmony Ives to Lou Harrison

[*Salutation in sketch:*] From Jabby Gibow to son harrylou put all music in Garbage Can! but thank you for let her! Now bee Dam Serious!

Dear Lou Harrison,

Thank you so much for your kind letter.

Mr. Ives was glad to hear of your interest in the 1st piano sonata as he always liked to play it—even now he does sometimes & says it has "a kind of tendency often to cheer him up with a shadow thought of the old days." He feels a clear copy of it should be made—But a year or more ago John Kirkpatrick said he wanted to play it and to make a clear copy of it as he did of the 2nd Violin Sonata. He is so busy nowadays & will be more so at Cornell where he goes in Sept. that perhaps he may not want to attend to this now and if not Mr. Ives would be very glad to have you do it—We will communicate with Mr. Kirkpatrick and let you know. The photostat copy was not fully corrected and is not, in a few places, exactly as Mr. Ives used to play it. Some of the pages from the old copy were lost when the photostat copy was made but were found later and he put them in a copy he has here—it is difficult for him to see them now but probably you can. The rag time movements were first for two players but he can find only a few pages—also a few revisions were made some years ago— These details we can take up with you later on, if Kirkpatrick can't undertake the work now.

As to "the barn"—it was quite cleaned out some time ago & Mr. Ives had photostats made of the MSS that seemed worth keeping—He has to do more sorting as his eyesight permits and later on will have some of these photostats sent to you—He appreciates you & Mr. Wigglesworth's kind thoughts of going over & clearing up these "barn mysteries."

Mr. Ives feels very strongly that all you have done as to his music, especially the 3rd Symphony has not been sufficiently compensated and he encloses a cheque which he says you must accept with his renewed Thanks.

With our warmest & best wishes
Sincerely
Harmony T. Ives

P.S. We have just heard from the Music Center that the published copies of the 2nd movement of the 4th symphony have been sold out. As requests for these are still coming in Mr. Ives thinks it would be well, as soon as possible to have more copies printed from the old plates which he thinks are in the Los Angeles office of New Music Edition. When these are done please have the bills sent to him.

Also, apparently in the second printing of the "Washington's Birthday" Score (Holiday Symphony) the printed description, or rather programme, on the last page was left out. Mr. Ives feels it is important to have this in. Will you have it printed on a separate sheet which can be inserted in the copies of the score now on hand. Of course the expense of this Mr. Ives would want to assume too—We can find no copy but probably there is one in the New York office—We will try & find one somewhere.

We are sorry to bother with all this but suppose these matters should be attended to.

• • •

After Harrison premiered the Third Symphony, Ives won the Pulitzer Prize for Music in 1947 for the work. The recognition and publicity from this award prompted many letters of congratulation to Ives. Some, like the following one from a college classmate, reconnected him with people he had scarcely seen or heard from in almost half a century. This letter points out how far Ives's life had taken him from the society in which he was so intimately involved in the 1890s. Even the connections of his business life seem remote.

402. 8 May 1947, from Robert Graham Dun Douglas,[14] New York

Dear Dasher:[15]

I have in front of me a photograph taken from the New York Times newspaper and underneath is the name of Charles E. Ives, composer. I am not sure whether it is Charles Ives or

14. Douglas graduated from Yale with Ives in 1898.

15. Dasher was one of Ives's nicknames at Yale; see Letter 100.

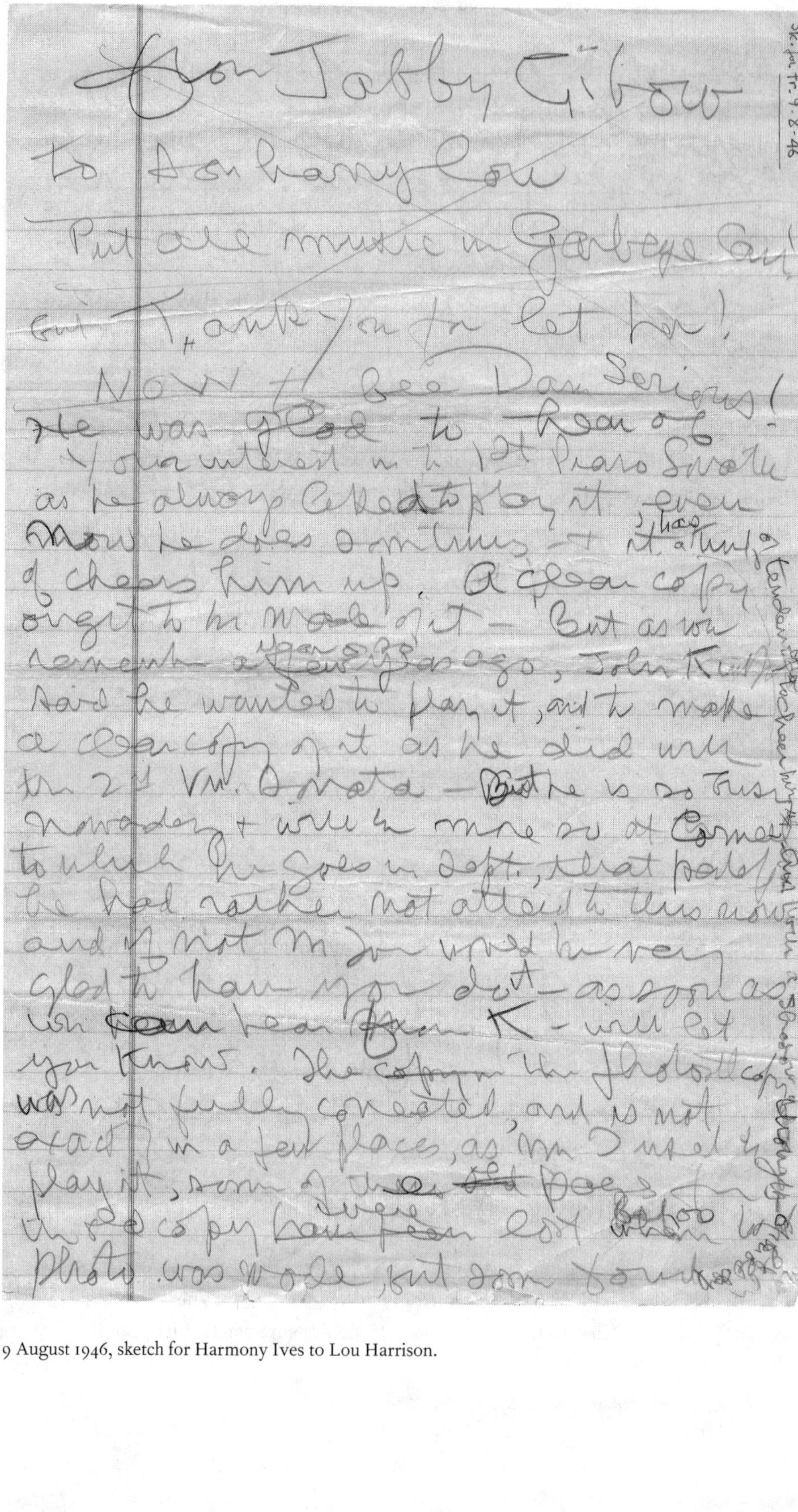
Sk. for fr. 9-8-46

~~Lou Tabby Gibbon~~

~~to Aon harry Lou~~

~~Put all music in Garbage Can!~~

But Thank you for that too!

NOW to Bea Dan Serious!

~~He~~ was glad to hear of your interest in the 1st Piano Sonata as he always liked to play it even now he does sometimes & it has a kind of cheers him up. A clean copy ought to be made of it — But as you remember a few years ago, John Kirkpatrick said he wanted to play it, and to make a clean copy of it as he did with the 2nd Vn. Sonata — But he is so busy nowadays & will be more so at Cornell to which he goes in Sept., that perhaps he had rather not attend to this now and if not Mr. Ives would be very glad to have you do it — as soon as we ~~hear~~ hear from K — will let you know. The ~~copy~~ the photostat copy was not finally corrected, and is not exact in a few places, as Mr I used to play it, some of the ~~old~~ pages in the old copy ~~have been~~ were lost before the photo was made, but some found

9 August 1946, sketch for Harmony Ives to Lou Harrison.

a picture of Sir Walter Raleigh. Anyhow, Charlie, I congratulate you in getting recognition for your music. I am not capable of discussing your music because I find it difficult to keep a tune, but it is very gratifying that you received even belated recognition.

I see Julian Myrick quite often as I go down to East Hampton, and he and I frequently speak of you.

Please tell Mrs. Ives that I have a very distinct recollection of one cold winter's day at Saranac Lake, New York, of a very beautiful young lady in a coon skin coat and cap. That was the year that Dave Twichell, Walter Megis and I went up to the Saranac Club, and the lady was the present Mrs. Ives.

It would be awfully nice to see you again if I can locate you. I was just talking to Fred Gilbert and he gave me your address as Redding, Conn. I hope this reaches you.

Fred is suffering a great deal and I feel very sorry for him. He had some stomach trouble in India or China after graduation, and then later in England he had a recurrence of the trouble, and about three months ago he was hit again with the same thing. Fred says he suffers a good deal and I know he does. His address is Hotel Margaret, 97 Columbia Heights, Brooklyn, New York, in case you ever feel like writing him.

Seth Milliken was badly hurt when the elevator in the University Club misbehaved. It seems he broke the bone above the knee and it was his lame leg. Perhaps that was fortunate. He seems to be getting on all right. Seth is really a sterling fellow.

Walter Megis telephoned me but I was out of town—at East Hampton. He was on his way from Florida, probably to Canada.

Every now and then I see Julian Ripley, Jack Lockman, Mull Mullally and Henry Fletcher, but not many '98 men turn up at the Yale Club, and I am not old enough yet to join the others in the over-stuffed chairs of the University Club.

With very kind regards.
Faithfully yours,
Graham
R. G. D. Douglas

• • •

Ives's sketches for a reply to Ruggles's letter of congratulation for the Pulitzer Prize offer a window into several aspects of his world and the characters he projected in the correspondence. In the first sketch, Ives writes in Edith's voice and dwells on Harmony's health problems. The childlike tone Ives gives to Edith is interesting given that by 1947 she was married and had a child. The second sketch is in Ives's own voice and is a clear instance of the exaggerated "Ives character," with the its dialect and self-deprecation.

403. 21 May 1947, two sketches for a letter to Carl Ruggles

[*Sketch 1, in Edith Ives Tyler's voice*]

Dear uncle Carl & aunt Charlotte

I am writing for mother who usually has to write for Daddy as his hands shake so much, he does not like to bother his friends with the snake tracks his pen makes. Mother has not been at all well for some time, she is very tired out and her heart condition is not good. We are much worried about her. They do want to see you both and do very much hope to when mother gets better.

Daddy thanks you for your congratulations as to Pulitzer Prize "glingo"—he says—your music is too great for a prize—and you ought to be glad.

We all send you our love—and Daddy's grandson is here and joins in.

[*Sketch 2, in Ives's voice*]

Dear Carl—

Just a few snake tracks from an "ole feller's" shaky paw, to tell you, that you are the best composer in Europe, Asia, Africa, and America—but if you should get a Pulitzer Prize swished on you, then that would mean that "you ain't"—

We were glad to hear that you and Charlotte are back in old New England where the Rocky Hills and plumy elms sing out "over the river."

We hope that we will see you both coming up Umpawaug hill some time this summer, ~~to stay here for a while.~~

With our love to you both,

• • •

Also intriguing are the differences between the sketch in Edith's voice and the final copy of the letter in which Ives sent Becker a check drawn on the Pulitzer Prize money. Edith retains all the wording from her father's sketch for the letter, but she includes information about a "breakdown" in her health or nerves that was severe enough to disrupt her life for a year. Such a condition did not fit with the childlike, simple Edie of Ives's sketches in her voice.

404. 14 September 1947, sketch for Edith Ives Tyler to John Becker

Becker

Dear Dr. Becker

Daddy was glad to hear that your music was well played & much appreciated. He says Nicolas Slonimsky has deep penetration into the fundamental spirit of music ~~more so that~~

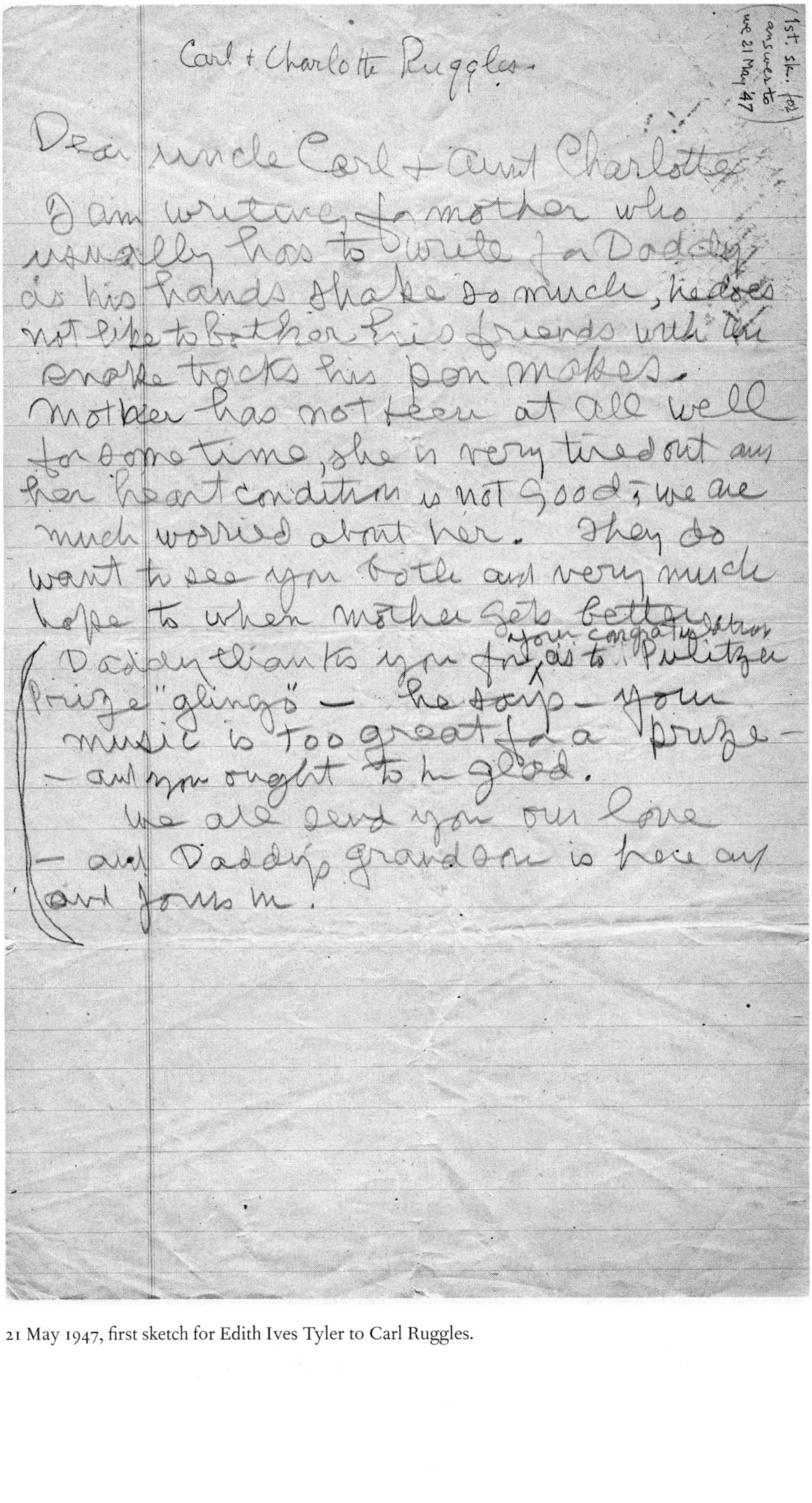

Carl + Charlotte Ruggles.

1st. sk. for answer to we 21 May '47

Dear uncle Carl + aunt Charlotte

I am writing for mother who usually has to write for Daddy as his hands shake so much, he does not like to bother his friends with the snake tracks his pen makes.

Mother has not been at all well for some time, she is very tired out and her heart condition is not good; we are much worried about her. They do want to see you both and very much hope to when mother gets better.

Daddy thanks you for your congratulations as to Pulitzer Prize "glingo" — he says — your music is too great for a prize — and you ought to be glad.

We all send you our love — and Daddy's grandson is here and joins in.

21 May 1947, first sketch for Edith Ives Tyler to Carl Ruggles.

~~many some conductors~~ have. Mother has been somewhat better, and therefore Daddy is, but neither can attend to things as they would like to nowadays. [*Here Edith's letter adds:* "Will you please tell Mrs. Becker and Bruce that they will soon be hearing from me about the wonderful Christmas presents they sent Kit?[16] Incredible as it seems I am just writing my last-Christmas notes now! You probably heard of the breakdown I had. All my personal affairs have been at odds and ends for nearly a year as a result."]

Daddy says to tell you that the enclosed check is not from him, but from that 'ole Pulitzer feller'.

• • •

In May 1947 Lou Harrison was hospitalized after a severe nervous breakdown. Upon being alerted to the condition by John Cage, Ives sent $250 (equivalent to approximately $2,060 in 2003)[17] to Harrison to cover the cost of his treatment. Ives wrote to Harrison that as recognition for his editing and conducting the Third Symphony, he was sending him half of the $500 he had received with the Pulitzer Prize. As we have seen, Ives also gave "half of the money" to composer John Becker, and he gave "half" again to *New Music*—for a net loss of $250.

405. 13 May 1947, from John Cage, New York

Dear Mr. Ives:

Lou Harrison, our mutual friend, has been very ill lately, and at the advice of his doctor and analyst, Richard M. Brickner, 1000 Park Avenue, New York City, is at present receiving custodial care at Stony Lodge, Ossining-on-the-Hudson, New York. His illness is diagnosed as a curable case of schizophrenia. He must remain at Stony Lodge until he is granted admittance to the Psychoanalytic Clinic at 722 W. 168, N.Y.C. When he is in the latter hospital, there will be no charge for his treatment, which, I understand, will be excellent. While he is at Stony Lodge, however, the charges amount to about ten dollars a day.

Being one of his closest friends, I have taken the responsibility of arranging for the payment of bills connected with this illness; I, myself, am not able to help, since I just manage to pay my own bills. I am, therefor, approaching his friends whom I have reason to believe might be both willing and able to be of assistance in this matter.

The first bill from Stony Lodge covers a period of nine days ending May 15th and amounts to $96.42. Lou may need to stay there two or three weeks, dependent as I mentioned on his gaining admittance to the other hospital.

Would you be willing to assume all or any part of this expense? I am certain that Lou will want to repay as soon as he is well and working those who help him at this time. He

16. Kit was the nickname for her son, Charles Ives Tyler.

17. Samuel H. Williamson, "What Is the Relative Value?" Economic History Services, April 2004, www.eh.net/hmit/compare/ (accessed 27 October 2005).

does not know that I am asking for this assistance. Any details which you want to know can be given by me, or by Dr. Brickner, whose address I have given, or by Dr. Berger at Stony Lodge.

The day I took Lou to Stony Lodge, he asked me to write to you concerning the work which you had given him to do in connection with your compositions. Naturally, he is unable to do it at present. If there is urgency about this, I will be glad to take care of either the return of MSS to you or their transmission to someone else. Otherwise, he might continue that work when he is well.

I look forward to a reply at your convenience,

Very Sincerely,
John Cage

406. Ca. 13 May 1947, sketch for Harmony Ives to John Cage

I am writing ——

We are sorry to hear of Lou Harrison's Illness. It happens that we had this cheque made out to him before your letter came. It represents one half of the amount of the Pulitzer award that Mr. Ives recently received. Mr. Ives feels that Lou had done so much in behalf of the 3rd Symphony that he wants to share this part of the award with him. Will you tell him this is not a present but a recognition of his help? and give him our love.

We hope to hear good news of him and Mr. Ives says he will be glad to help if necessary in further expenses.

407. Late May 1947, from John Cage, Massachusetts

Dear Mrs. Ives:

Please pardon my writing in pencil and on this paper: I am in the country.

I want to thank you for your very kind letter and say that the check is at Stony Lodge and that Lou seems to be improving. I saw him Monday on my way here.

I will keep you informed as to his progress. I will return to New York Friday and see him again then.

Please accept my very sincere appreciation of your letter. It is very beautiful.

408. Ca. 13 May 1947, from John Cage, New York

Dear Mrs. Ives,

Through Mrs. Cowell, I hear that extended work on Mr. Ives Compositions is to be done. It is my feeling that Lou will be able to do this and that he might even devote weekends to it immediately. He is recovering quickly and is in full possession of his mental faculties (he remains somewhat unstable emotionally but that too will be improved). At any rate, he will be in need of work which would be as congenial to him. Please let me know what your needs are, the work to be done, etc. And I will discuss it with Lou. Or, you might even write directly to him at the Psychiatric Institute & Hospital. . . .

Very sincerely,
John Cage

• • •

409. 2 July 1947, from Lou Harrison, New York

Dear Mr. and Mrs. Ives,

I want to thank you for your kindness with regard to the Pulitzer award, and to congratulate you on a long deserved recognition. I am proud to have the honor of having been the first to do that beautiful work. I constantly remember that during the first several rehearsals I was so moved and astonished by sections of it that I was unable to continue and had to stop and explain to the musicians. It is clear that the piece is among the major productions of American music, and I look forward to a long and vigorous life for it.

When I last had the pleasure of seeing you I was already teetering over the edge of a severe nervous collapse. For the last several months I have been under care and treatment. As a result I have been unable to do anything about the sonatas and other works you entrusted to my care. I believe that Frank Wigglesworth now has the Trio and the Browning Overture. He may have the rest as well. If not, it is all safe at my apartment and can be easily reached should some immediate need arise. When I get better I want to continue proof reading. However, I do not know just how soon I will be back into condition and perhaps you would wish someone to do the works now so that they may more speedily reach publication. If you would let me know I could arrange for this.

My projected article on Mr. Ives has suffered delay as well but I include it among my recovery projects and may soon begin work.

Trusting that you are both enjoying life this pleasant Summer,
and thanks again,
Sincerely,
Lou Harrison

• • •

The much-delayed second edition of the *Concord* Sonata finally appeared late in 1947. Ives's desire to receive no royalties for the piece and to have no fees charged for performance or recording of the work was his standard position in such matters. He typically donated royalties that would have been paid to him to help support other modernist composers or performers.

410. 20 September 1947, Harmony Ives to Lehman Engel

Dear Mr. Engel

The final proofs of the "Concord Sonata" were returned to Mr. Turner yesterday—Mr. Ives is sorry for the delay but it is difficult for him to attend to things nowadays as he would like to.

There is one matter that he has not felt quite right about—he feels very strongly that no performance fees should be charged as the time and hard work that has to be given in preparing a work which has so many difficulties does not justify a fee—as he says it took John Kirkpatrick over 10 years of almost daily practice to play this as he thought it should be played so he does hope that the fee notice printed at the bottom of the first page will be taken out—He feels badly to trouble you so much but says he thinks in this matter he should take this stand so please let him and he asks that you keep for the Arrow Press, from whatever profits may be due him any amount which you feel would be lost by omitting the playing fees—he wants you to take "more than enough and not less than enough"—& if you don't he adds that the next time he sees you "you may walk away with a black eye!"

Enclosed is a cheque for $500. (date Oct. 25th) This makes $1,500. now sent for the cost of publishing and if there is any balance please let him know what it is and he will send it as soon as he can.

He deeply appreciates all you have so kindly done in behalf of his music and hopes things are going well with you.

With our cordial best wishes
Sincerely yours,
Harmony T. Ives

P.S. He wants to acknowledge and thank you for your telegram of congratulations on his receiving the Pulitzer Award.

• • •

By the late 1940s Ives received many more requests for his music from mainstream performers. In the following drafts for letters to the organist E. Power Biggs (1906–77), Ives burnishes the legend of his youth as a slightly subversive organist who enjoyed the athletic thrill of a fast pedal variation. The first sketch replies to Biggs's request for organ works by giving a general recollection of the works Ives had composed for organ many years previously. The second letter addresses the "Variations on 'America,'" which Biggs edited and played for the first time on his national radio show on 4 July 1948.[18]

18. E. Power Biggs to Harmony Ives, 13 July 1948 (CIP, 27/9).

411. Ca. 15 April 1948, sketch for Harmony Ives to E. Power Biggs

Biggs Boston

I am ——

He cannot attend to things nowadays as he would like to. He deeply appreciates your interest in his music and for offering to play some of his organ works.

He has not composed anything for organ for over 40 years, ~~and~~ apparently most of it has been mislaid or lost—~~only 2~~ we can find only 2—Variations on America, and a short prelude ["Adeste Fideles" in an organ prelude]—photostat copies will be sent under separate cover. Mr. Ives did compose an organ sonata nearly 50 years ago. He ~~has~~ does not remember seeing it for many years, it may have been left in the library of some of th[e] ~~churches~~ churches he played in at the time, if it can be found will send it to you. He remembers playing at an organ recital ~~he thinks when he was organist & choir leader with Central Pres Ch in NY The 3rd movement & 4th movements of~~ some 30 years ago, The 3rd movement "The Alcotts" and the 4th "Thoreau" of his 2nd Piano Sonata though he can't find these arrangements for organ here but a ~~copy of the published~~ published copy of this piano sonata will be sent with the 2 organ pieces [*congruency sign*] Mr. Ives sends his sincere thanks for offering to play something of his in your broadcast recitals, and he hopes it will not give too much trouble.

(over)

[*congruency sign*] The 1st & 3rd movements of his 3rd Symphony are partly from ~~som~~ early organ pieces. The published score of this symphony will also be sent you.

He asks you to accept these with his compliments & best wishes.

P.S. The Variations on America is a kind of reflection of those youthful days and playing the pedal variations near the end Mr. Ives says gave him almost as much fun as playing baseball.

• • •

412. Undated sketch for Harmony Ives to E. Power Biggs

[*The top three inches of the first sheet of foolscap is torn off.*]

. . . of you to go to the trouble of playing this youthful opus of his. But he says that it is his ~~part~~ duty not yours to have a clear copy made so please have the bill for this sent to him here.

It was so long ago ~~that~~ when he first ~~wrote~~ played this work, that recollections of his earliest performances are not fully remembered.

Sometimes some of the audiences would join in when "America" would appear to their ears, and some would almost march down the aisle. Mr. Ives's father would occasionally play with him; but always insisted that the 4th variation should be omitted, because it was, in his father's opinion, a kind of Polonaise which had no place in our country and also was in a rather sad minor key. The Brass Band journey in and the loud pedal variations were considered more appropriate. Sometimes, when America would appear to their ears, some of the listeners would join in, even if it occasionally made the boys go marching down the aisles. Usually as he remembers many of the boys had more fun, watching the feet play the pedal variations than in listening to the music.

It was played in Brewster, NY—not Maine.

Mr. Ives is sorry he can't remember more ~~interesting that~~ about these old performances and be of more help to you. He sends you his sincere thanks—and he hopes it will not take too much of your time or give you too much trouble.

With our best wishes

• • •

When Paul Rosenfeld died in 1946, Jerome Mellquist began to gather together essays for a book honoring the critic. Ives's reply to the request that he contribute an essay to the book follows.[19] Note that the normal references to Ives in the third person have been crossed out and the first person has been substituted. Ives probably intended to send the letter in the first person through an overt transcription by Harmony, like the one in Letter 239 to Aaron Copland. Ives would occasionally do this with letters he considered important. The hand in the sketch appears to be Ives's but, with few revisions, is comparatively neat for the late 1940s. There are two passages on the page in cursive that are not in Ives's hand.

413. Ca. April 1948, second sketch for Ives to Jerome Mellquist

Mellquist re Rosenfeld

Tribute to Paul Rosenfeld

[*In a different hand:*] He asks me to write for him / He says as follows—

I am ——

~~He is~~ I am very sorry not to be able to attend to things nowadays as ~~he~~ I would like to, and it makes ~~him~~ me feel especially badly not to write the article you requested as to Mr. Rosenfeld's wonderful integrity about music and his fight for an American tradition.

~~Mr. Ives~~ I deeply—very deeply, appreciate all Mr. Rosenfeld has written in behalf of ~~his~~ my music—and ~~that he~~ tho' I cannot contribute to the "mosaic, ~~he~~ I hope~~s~~ no one will think that ~~he is~~ I am not very grateful to Mr. Rosenfeld. ~~Mr. Ives~~ I have always felt that Rosenfeld was a great man in the arts, and had that gift of almost immediate insight into the ~~wider~~ larger side of music even if it brought a technical process to which he was unaccustomed—a penetrative discernment into the fundamental & inner meanings, even when heard for the first time. It seems to ~~Mr. Ives~~ me that Rosenfeld strongly felt that among music's greatest powers was that which would help bring more and more to

19. Jerome Mellquist and Lucie Wiese, eds., *Paul Rosenfeld: Voyager in the Arts* (New York: Creative Age Press, 1948).

humanity the deeper & higher things in life and in a way the finer sides in the common life of all people.

At the end of one of the chapters in his Book "Discoveries of a Music Critic" (Harcourt Brace Co. NY) he says . . .

[*In another hand:*] ~~I appreciate~~ what you are doing for his memory will be gratefully appreciated.

• • •

During the last decade of his life, Ives received fan letters from a wide variety of correspondents with varying degrees of knowledge of his music. Particularly affecting are those from composers who wrote to tell him of the important influence of his music on their lives and works.

414. 3 May 1948, from Robert Palmer, Ithaca, New York

Dear Mr. Ives:

I am a younger composer whose name you may know through our mutual friend John Kirkpatrick who teaches here at Cornell with me. I have known John for over ten years and he has done much for me in many ways, and has often spoken to me of your music.

It has been one of my lifelong ambitions to be able to see you and tell you face to face how much your music has meant to me during the few years I have known it, and how much your integrity and sincerity of expression both in your music and your philosophical ideas as expressed in the various prose comments often published with your scores have meant too.

I don't suppose my comments can have much meaning for you, separated as we are by age, background, environment and many other things that would make communication difficult, but I want to say that I feel very strongly part of the kind of native expression that I think you were the very first man to create on this continent, and that your work, your writings, and what you stand for are a never failing source of spiritual and emotional strength to me. Although I may never see you, I felt I must express to you directly what you and your music, which expresses so incomparably our native soul, have meant to me.

Sincerely yours,
Robert Palmer

415. 8 June 1948, Harmony Ives to Robert Palmer

Dear Mr. Palmer

Mr. Ives is sorry not to have acknowledged your very kind note sooner—He hasn't been well and we had to be away from home for some time seeing doctors and things get very behind hand.

He wants me to say that your note meant a great deal to him.

He is able to see very few people but hopes he may be well enough some day to meet you. To know that his music has meant so much to you gives him happiness. He says he senses from your letter that you have an innate perception & feeling that will help to enrich the life of music and deepen its help to mankind.

He wants you to have a copy of the 2nd edition of his Concord Sonata, just published & we are sending you one with his compliments & best wishes.

Thanking you again for your kindness
I am
Sincerely yours
Harmony T. Ives

416. 6 January 1949, from Wallingford Riegger, New York

Dear Charles Ives:

It is with perhaps justifiable pride that I send you the enclosed announcement, with the featuring of your 75th anniversary along with Schönberg's. Believe it or not, last May I got wind of elaborate plans for the performance of Schönberg this season, by both the League of Composers and the ISCM—on a/c of his 75 anniversary. It occurred to me to look up the date of your birth—with the result that you see in the folder. The League also is taking cognizance of "native talent" in like manner.

Of course both organizations were grateful when I pointed out the oversight—but it all goes to show how we still have not "grown up."

Well, here's wishing you the best of things possible under the circumstances, and plenty of performances (not 50 years from now!)

As ever,
cordially,
Wallingford Riegger

• • •

Lou Harrison continued to edit selected Ives manuscripts, and after the Third Symphony he turned to the First Piano Sonata, which had been a source of considerable mystery and interest to many who knew only the *Concord*. Much of the impetus for this edition of the sonata came from William Masselos, who had undertaken to learn and perform the sonata after seeing Harrison's photostatic copy of the manuscript. As was true with the symphony, Ives's editorial comment on the work Harrison did was minimal.

417. 1 February 1949, from Lou Harrison, New York

Dear Mr. Ives,

Through this last month I have been working very hard on the copying and clearing of your First Piano Sonata. During this Mr. Masselos has been learning the work for its performance on the seventeenth. I am pleased to no end with the results. Mr. Masselos is really superb and seems to me to understand the idiom very well. I am quite sure that the two performances of it that he has scheduled for this season will be excellent ones. He is planning to present the work later in the season under the auspices of the International Society of Contemporary Music on their Spring Festival.

As to what I did. All the corrections and amendation that you noted above and below the original score and all additions of no matter what difficulty are included in the present version. I felt that you would not want the vigor or richness of the work impeded by any considerations of easiness or convenience and have proceeded on that principle, especially since Mr. Masselos was also anxious that your full wishes in this matter be carried out. As it stands all five movements are complete and in legible copy. I have not made a printing copy but did not do so since I am sure whatever printer you might care to have publish the work would naturally have to have an autographer anyway. So I have made transparencies in a simple hand copy that can be reproduced for examination and whatever corrections you might wish to make. Mr. Masselos and I will get a copy to you as soon as possible. I trust that you will find what we have done acceptable. We have both worked hard at it. Indeed I hope that in the event of publication you might permit that Mr. Masselos make pianistic suggestions and other editorial comments, but of course we both want to adhere to your desires in this.

My copying work amounted to thirty five large pages with six staff systems to a page in order to make fewer page turns for learning and give better the sense of extended lines and phrases. I hope that you will find the rate of four dollars a page agreeable since there were so many of them difficult to figure out. This amounts to one hundred forty dollars.

We all share a great pleasure these days in the interest and use of your music, which seems to be broadening and deepening among the general public and look forward to its continuance. Henry Cowell tells me that you are having an increasing number of good playings and bids for publication. Nothing could be better for American music. I join in celebrating you and wish you the best of health and happiness.

My love to you and to Mrs. Ives.,

Sincerely,
Lou Harrison

418. 10 February 1949, Harmony Ives to Lou Harrison

Dear Lou Harrison

Mr. Ives feels much obliged to you for doing the First Sonata. It must have been a lot of work. There is still a small amount of change to be done before it is ever published & he hopes to be able to see you again after a while to show you—He has been feeling rather below par lately—I hope to be at the concert on the 17th with the Ruggles and maybe will see you—I hope so.

With our warm best wishes & hoping you are very well

Sincerely yours
Harmony T. Ives

I enclose Mr. Ives cheque

• • •

In the later correspondence, Harmony Ives's voice emerges more distinctly, especially in letters to friends like the Becker and Ruggles families. These letters reveal her personality more clearly than those that Ives wrote in her voice and tend to focus more on the passing of the seasons, the doings of other friends, and her pride at the recognition that was finally coming to her husband.

419. 1 March 1949, Harmony Ives to John and Evelyn Becker

Dear John and Evelyn

We have certainly been very remiss about writing—we haven't been down sick but neither have we been very well and I have so much writing to do answering all Charlie's demanding mail that we get off very few personal letters. We have seen the Ruggles twice since we came & Henry once so you see our life is very quiet—Charlie just doesn't feel equal to the effort—Edie & Kit are bright spots.

We have had such a wonderful mild winter—yesterday a picturesque snow storm which stayed on the trees & even our block was beautiful for a few hours—but we have had no winter really & I'm glad—winter is fun only for the very young I feel.

The Ruggles seem to be enjoying their winter here pretty much tho' Carl said the last time we saw him that he is longing for the time to come to go home to Vermont—doesn't like N.Y. any more. Charlotte says they go out very little—I think neither of them is very strong. Carl was very sick last year. They are happy over their son's being appointed principal of the school where he has been dean. We were interested to hear your account of Gene's excellent progress—such a satisfaction to see a child developing so well.

Charlie's First Piano Sonata was played on the 17th of Feb—by a young man—William Masselos—very good pianist—I went with Carl & Charlotte—my only concert of the season—"Evocations" was performed also—lovely. The Sonata made a real hit—cheers & bravos & long applause. It was great fun—of course the rag time movements are quite tremendous—the audience were mostly young people as so many of the audiences are now whenever the newer music is played—they eat it up. Charlie's Sonata isn't exactly "newer" as it was completed in 1909 but it sounded so.

We are glad you are better than you were—Charlie is in his 75th year & I will soon be 73 so we are old people and I have to confess we feel it—we just have to let things go—things we used to like to do now seem only an effort—fortunately we are quite content by our own fireside.

I believe Henry is much better than last year when he was in pain all the time with his sciatica. Sidney is so interested in all that he does—a good help meet.

We both send our love and best wishes to you & yours

As ever sincerely
Harmony T. Ives

• • •

Some of the most interesting reactions to Ives's music come from those who knew him personally before they were able to hear his works performed. These letters often comment on the extent to which Ives himself was revealed or present in his compositions.

420. 3 April 1949, from Gertrude Sanford, West Redding, Connecticut

Dear Mrs. Ives—

I have been sitting here thinking about Mr. Ives' 1st sonata and the performance on Sunday last, and have been wondering if all composers reflect so much of their personality in their music. Not having known any others, I couldn't say, but during that concert, I could hear and see Mr. Ives so plainly that it was positively uncanny. There were parts in it when I could have giggled and other parts which almost brought the tears. All I can say is—thank goodness I was able to hear it and enjoy it. I did have such a good time even though I was indisposed part of the time! . . .

It was such fun to see Kit. He is a darling little fellow—and so bright and friendly. I am wondering whether he still has his "trigger?" Can't say I blame Mr. Ives feelings much on that score. The youngsters at school brought all sorts of guns and pistols to play with at recess time, and things finally became so involved, that I forbid them in school. I think that the movies are mostly responsible for that, along with those awful comic (?) books. . . .

I do hope it won't be long before you will be enjoying some of this good old Redding air. There's nothing like it!

Many, many thanks to you for a fine week end and my best love to you both.

Gertrude

• • •

Meanwhile, in California Peter Yates continued to promote Ives's music in his criticism and in the concert series he produced in Los Angeles. The correspondence between Yates and Ives shows an interesting dimension of conflict between East- and West-Coast communities of new music. The clearest manifestation of this divide was Yates's continuing drive to obtain permission for his wife to record the *Concord* Sonata, which certainly colors his reactions to the Kirkpatrick recording below. Much of this criticism of Kirkpatrick's performance stems from Yates's reliance on the original edition of the *Concord,* from which his recorded performance and the newly published second edition diverged considerably. Yates seems not to have known that Kirkpatrick's changes all derived from his study of Ives's manuscripts and the composer's own revisions. But it is also interesting that no letter survives in which Ives writes to Yates explaining this. Perhaps he wished to avoid the conflict altogether.

421. 20 October 1949, from Peter Yates, Los Angeles

Dear Friends:

Deliberately and hopefully I waited five years between the last season when we played your music and the present season, to let the audience grow up and so that when they heard the music again it would come to them all fresh. It did. Except the piano solo in the first movement of the violin sonata, which the pianist was too unsure of himself to play well. Then the feet started scuffling and folks remembered they had a cough. But the rest of the time they were working so hard listening they didn't know what it was hit them; they didn't even know if they liked it; they just strained silent and listened. I sat beside Szigeti, the violinist, and Temianka, the leader of the Paganini Quartet.[20] Szigeti came because he played your fourth sonata, you remember, and has never heard any other of your music. He just decided that he ought to hear, it was his job to hear enough of your music to know why that sonata is the way it is. But he had heard the Kirkpatrick recording and didn't know whether he could sit through a performance. When he told me that I didn't remind him that his recording of the Fourth Violin Sonata is every bit as bad, and that those two recordings have done more harm than good. That's probably why he came late. He knew he should come and he didn't want to come but his conscience wouldn't let him get out of it. He came after the violin sonata in time for the second group of songs and that made him settle down to stay. After the first movement of the Concord he leaned over to tell me how much more than the recording he was hearing, the bigger dimensions and more varied ranges of tone, the structure and projection of it. During the Hawthorne Temianka said it sounded like Scriabin, but Szigeti said, No, it's bigger and all vital. They couldn't accept all the changes of pace and the breaks in continuity but at the end I found out that Szigeti had heard beyond these temporary hesitations as to whether he liked what he was hearing. He had discovered what I thought nobody knew but myself, that the Copland Piano Sonata, which is Copland's best piece, is just a thinned down, watered down, curtailed timid adventure into Concord-land. I never said it to anybody, because people wouldn't understand it if I were to tell them Copland's best music is just a few slivers off your log. Then Szigeti began discovering more and more what he had heard: in the Alcotts he discovered the method was montage. I had to argue with him about that and try to explain that montage is a Paris notion with no background, but you like Bartok lay in the folk eloquence like embroidered flowers into a thick dense texture of polyphony woven out of three main themes. I didn't care too much to win the argument because I could see he was beginning to hear it now, the whole of it, all one piece, with the montage lying on top and the pauses and changes of pace all explained. I never really hear a big piece of music until after it's finished and I think neither does he. But you could tell that audience, like him, had been hit with something it couldn't quite swallow or choke up, really hit by it this time for the first time. The other times they didn't know what to make of it even if they stood up for it and even those who asked to hear it again and came to the house for another hearing didn't make it out. But this time it had them so they couldn't get rid of it. The funniest or

20. Henri Temianka (1906–92) was the founder of the Paganini Quartet and a conductor as well as a violinist.

saddest thing was the critic in the Times who couldn't get rid of it so much that after he had congratulated us for putting it over as a program wasn't happy until he had cussed it all out in the same language that critics from generation to generation have always used to talk about music that is too big for them. Poor fellow, he knew it and couldn't get rid of it. That review will shame him, and he knows it, with nearly everyone who sat there in the audience.

It's probably as well we couldn't get the quartet ready for this concert. Two quartets gave it up. Then I turned it over to Sol, who went through eight players before he had to put it off, but in doing so he heard it himself so thoroughly he sold himself on it.[21] We'll keep at it now we have the parts and get it done, though that may take a couple of years. Not so long now, though, because the effect of that concert on the audience has gone all over town. In October we'll do a half -hour of it on a local radio broadcast. The request came the next day. And we may even be given two programs running for the Concord. Meantime Frances will be playing the Concord again for our audiences in Tucson and Tempe, Arizona, who asked for it, nervously, but they did ask for it.

Sol played the Third Sonata better than ever before, and the pianist when he had got himself together after that first solo went at it better and better, with a good clanging tone that the music needs and not too much pedal, that Sol talked him out of. They will go out and play it for Szigeti, who wants to hear it now, and go do two movements on the radio. If we had done the quartet as well as the sonatas the audience would have been too weak to go home. This isn't music you can listen to and let it run over you like Schumann or Chopin or Debussy. It makes you work, sweat, and think.

I knew from the moment I went out on the stage and began talking about you and your music that the bars were down for the first time. I wanted to get over that horrible embarrassment that seems to hit an American audience when it hears music so much in its own language that it can't feel, well it doesn't matter anyhow, it's all foreign and esthetic, the way they usually react to new music. So I called it red underwear music. I said hearing it was like coming home from college after the first year and finding your grandfather sitting in his red underwear or auntie on the stoop in her rocker smoking her corncob pipe. That hit them, because it was such an overstatement that after I had said it they couldn't so easily any more be embarrassed. They laughed, eased up and thought, oh it can't be so bad as that. And of course it wasn't. But I think back to the time Sol played the first sonata and the audience couldn't accept what happened to The Old Oaken Bucket or the sunrise of the third movement. This time they were prepared for it and could accept it.

The concert was broadcast and a tape recording made. If the tape is as good as that of the Diabelli Variations which Frances played last spring, we'll have some records made for you. I had known ever since we heard the first reports about the [Kirkpatrick *Concord* Sonata] recording that something was wrong. Finally we heard the record and were shocked not only by the bad mechanical sound but by the playing. But I didn't write you about it, I could only grieve and wonder how people in the east could hear this sort of a

21. Sol Babitz, a violinist who often performed on Yates's concert series, had prepared an edition of Ives's Third Violin Sonata that was published by *New Music* in 1951. He also recorded the work for Alco Records. Sinclair, *Descriptive Catalogue,* 154. See Letter 372.

performance and still be excited, when anyone who heard the record could make nothing much of what was played. Now we have set Frances's performance against the recording, and Szigeti's answer is what we all feel. People who had heard the record heard the music this time, and found out how much more was in it. Somehow Frances will have to make another recording and get it issued for the sake of the music. We cannot understand what Kirkpatrick has done to the music, play Emerson without character and Hawthorne like a horse race without nuance and make so little of Alcotts and lose the walking theme in Thoreau. This is for yourselves of course, not for publication; but another record must be made. And we cannot understand how Kirkpatrick could mangle the first movement as he has with doubled octaves and pianistic apparatus in the first movement, as if to say it's good music but it isn't written correctly. I warned the audience that the present published version is not all your own.

I think the time has come when the public, having now amazingly swallowed Bartok and being in the act of getting hold of Schoenberg—our Schoenberg program seemed to most listeners the most natural music in the world—will now start to get an ear-hold onto you. The reason is that enough musicians are learning how to play Bartok and now learning to play Schoenberg, and when a few more do better by your music than Kirkpatrick or Szigeti or Janssen have done by it the public will hear your music too because musicians will be learning how to play it too.[22] I was interested to notice that the device of bringing in the theme naked at the end of the movement in the third sonata is the same that musicologists have discovered in Bartok's later quartets. Every time something new is discovered in another composer we find it was already done by you. I told the audience that also. They really got an earful.

The Saturday Review has an article about you. I haven't heard whether they will use it but they haven't sent it back. I'll do you up later in my column, but I decided to wait until I could judge the effect of this program.

Frances will write you also, when she is a bit rested. Both of us send you our love and renewed devotion.

Affectionately,
Peter Yates

P.S.—The songs which we substituted for the quartet and which were sung by a very young, attractive, soprano the best we have had for your music since Radiana Pazmor, called Marni Nixon, included White Gulls, The Circus Band (a new one for us), and Rough Wind.

• • •

The following is one of the most suggestive and tantalizing fragments in the correspondence: a letter from the daughter of Horatio Parker, Ives's musically conservative composition pro-

22. Werner Janssen conducted the Janssen Symphony of Los Angeles, which made the premiere recording of the "St. Gaudens" movement of *Three Places in New England* in 1949 for Artist Records. See Sinclair, *Descriptive Catalogue*, 41.

fessor at Yale. There is no other evidence of a relationship between the Ives and Parker families, but this letter, written more than fifty years after Ives graduated, suggests that the relationship between the former student and teacher was much more cordial than Ives later allowed. The Parker piece mentioned is for soprano and alto soloists, chorus, and chamber ensemble; it was published in 1913.

422. 11 November 1949, from Isabel Parker Semler, New Canaan, Connecticut

Dear Mrs Ives,

We did so enjoy our visit with you and Mr. Ives. I have wanted to write you before but Mother has not been very well and the time flies.

She has asked me to send Mr. Ives my father's 'Seven Greek Pastoral Scenes' which she thinks he will enjoy reading.

Our warmest regards to you both—

Ever sincerely yours,
Isabel Parker Semler

• • •

The next pair of letters might also be considered fan mail. They document the effect that Ives's music had on people across the country and very near home. The letters also reveal some of the ways the music became more widely known despite the relatively small, though growing, number of performances given and recordings available.

423. 25 November 1949, from Richard T. Gore, Wooster, Ohio

Dear Mr. Ives:

I am writing you not to add one more encomium to the many you have already received, but because I want to say something in reply to what you have said to me in your music. I am not at all telepathetic, but I am certainly grateful for the chain of circumstances that caused me to spend a month at the Concord Summer School of Music in 1935 and, while there, to wander through the woods of Walden Pond, see the sight of Thoreau's hut, go boating on the river, inspect Emerson's garden and the Alcott's house, little knowing that there would some day be a musical connection. (Evidently Thomas Whitney Surette did not know of your sonata; at any rate, he never mentioned it.)

As soon as we got the recording by Mr. Kirkpatrick—who went to Cornell University to teach piano the same year I left as organist—I got a score as well, and have lived with both, on and off, ever since. Last Tuesday I addressed some fellow-townsmen on You and Your Music, played and sang "Charlie Rutlage" and played "The Alcotts" and "Thoreau" for them. Their reactions were surprisingly good, in general. One doubtful lady said—and I knew you would enjoy this naive remark—"That was very stimulating, but now couldn't you play some music?" I have already been asked to give the same sort of talk-play for another group.

What interests me about your free use of the twelve tones of the octave is not that you were doing it years before Schönberg had formulated his technique, but that you did it so much better, so much more freely and imaginatively. Schönberg and his school are the prisoners of their own theories; they are also prisoners of the 19th century in form, phrasing, and orchestration. Your music is unshackled.

Being an organist I am, almost by definition, a worshiper of J. S. Bach. I have played all his organ works and heard nearly half of his cantatas. But since his time there has not been a single organ composer who can match him for originality and nobility of thought. I understand you have composed for the organ. How can I get a copy of some organ piece of yours?

When you finished the "Concord Sonata" I was seven years old. I have had many moving musical experiences in my two score years, but making the acquaintance of your music has been uniquely so. Thank you, sir!

Sincerely yours,
Richard T. Gore
Professor of Music[23]

424. 10 April 1950, from Emma M. Smith, New York

Dear Mrs. Ives:

Last Wednesday afternoon I attended the last of a series of concerts at Town Hall and heard Bill Masselos play your husband's Piano Sonata Number One. It was one of the most delightful two hours I have spent this winter, and later at dinner Mr. Masselos said he would send me your address so I could write you about it. I was particularly interested in the old hymn tunes which ran through the sonata. Mr. Tangeman said that you were one of the Twichell family from Hartford, and I think our families must have known each other. My father was William Moody, president of the Northfield Schools, and my grandfather was D. L. Moody the evangelist (Moody & Sankey) which makes those hymn tunes so familiar to me! One hears these so seldom now.

I understand Mr. Ives is not well, but we are such close neighbors I should love to have you both over for a cocktail someday. And we could reminisce about many more old hymns. I enclose the program for your interest.

Sincerely,
Emma M. Smith

• • •

Along with letters from casual listeners and professional promoters of Ives's music came an increasing number of requests for information from scholars and other students. Because of

23. Gore taught at the College of Wooster Conservatory of Music.

his health and the sheer volume of mail he was receiving by the early 1950s, Ives was able to give only cursory replies that would often include copies of his published music or digests of printed commentary and biographical information. The following pair of letters illustrates such an exchange.

425. 28 June 1950, from Joseph H. Soifer, Hartford, Connecticut

Dear Mr. Ives:

This letter is written at the suggestion of Dr. Isadore Freed, Chairman of the Composition Department of the Julius Hartt School of Music in Hartford.

I am a candidate for a Master of Music degree, with a major in Music Education, at that institution. As my advisor, Dr. Freed has been most helpful in the planning and development of my thesis, the title of which is "Implications of the Folk Spirit in the Works of Contemporary American Composers."

Both in my thesis work and as a member of the Music Educator's Eastern Conference Contemporary Music Committee, I am anxious to help clarify the atmosphere in the relations between the contemporary composers and the music educators. Certainly one area where there is a common meeting ground is that of contemporary works that have either American folk music thematic origins or works written in a completely American folk idiom.

Would you be willing to indicate those of your works which you feel are most representative of the above mentioned classifications? Both in quality and numbers, our high school and college choral and instrumental groups are achieving new heights of musical accomplishments and your choice of representative works might be pointed in that direction.

I would appreciate any remarks you wish to make on any aspects of the subject and would, of course, be grateful for program material on any of the works.

Cordially yours,
Joseph H. Soifer

426. Ca. 28 June 1950, sketch for Harmony Ives to Joseph H. Soifer

I am ——

He regrets he cannot attend to things nowadays as he would like to—~~But~~ So under separate cover we are enclosing some data which we hope will give you ~~what~~ most of the information you ask for, for ~~your~~ the thesis. Mr. Ives ~~will be~~ is ~~glad~~ to have ~~sent you at the school copies of the published complimentary~~ complimentary copies of all his published music sent to ~~you&~~ Hartt the school.

He greatly appreciates your interest in, and the help your thesis will give as to the "American folk music thematic origins."

Mr. Ives [is] sorry he cannot be of more extensive help now.

He sends his kind regards to you & Dr. Freed

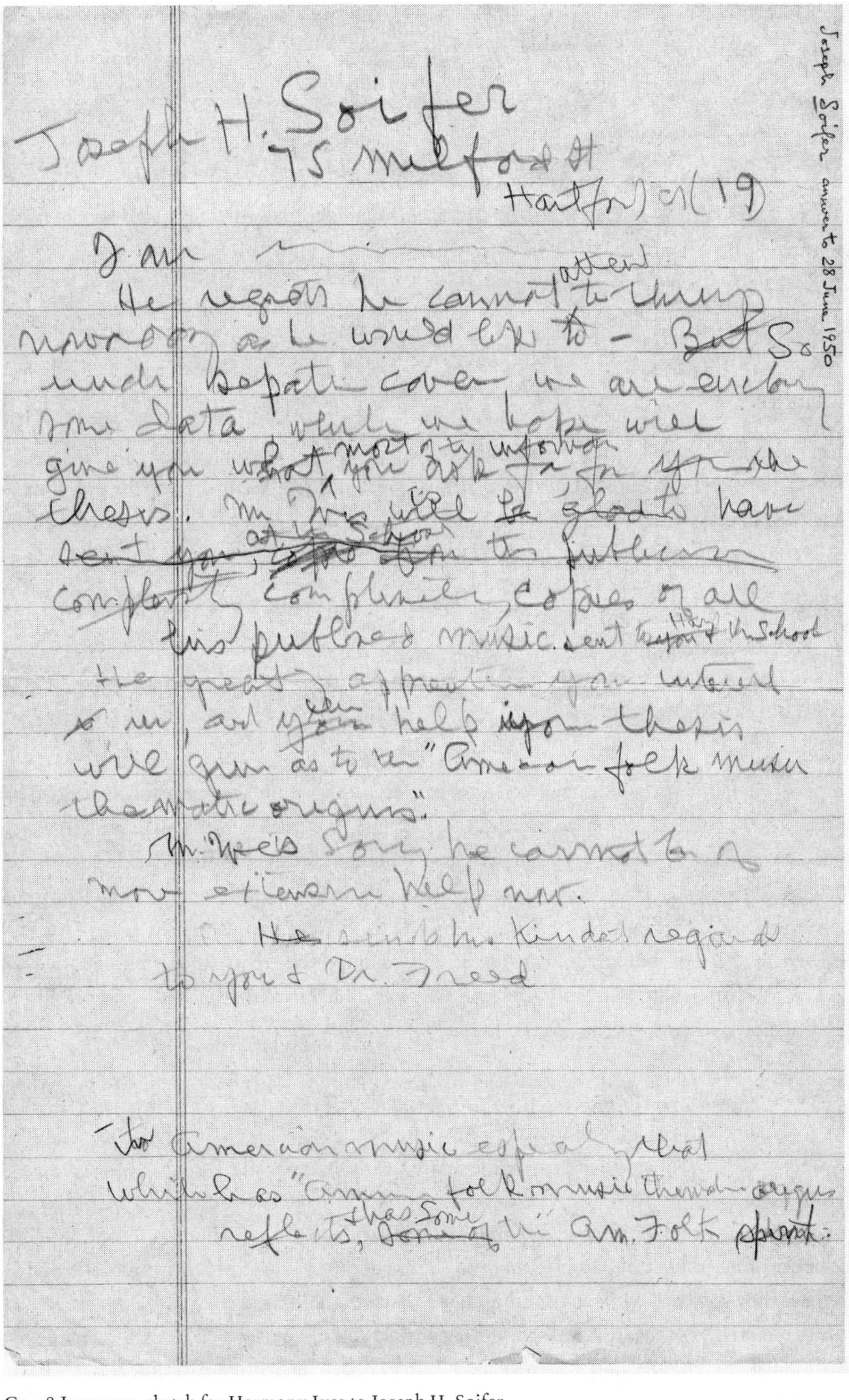

Joseph H. Soifer
75 Milford St
Hartford Ct (19)

Joseph Soifer answer to 28 June 1950

Ca. 28 June 1950, sketch for Harmony Ives to Joseph H. Soifer.

—to American music especially that which has "American folk music thematic origins reflects, & has some of ~~some of~~ the Am. Folk spirit.

• • •

Occasionally, even as late as 1950, Ives wrote in his own hand to close friends like John Becker. These letters were usually quite short and often poked derisive fun at the state of the handwriting.

427. 26 July 1950, to John Becker

Dear John,

Harmony is not well so these snake tracks have to go down on you.

We hope you will enjoy your trip to "Italia." Please don't get mad at me for sending the enclosed check—but don't give it to "Verdi"

With "very best" to all of you, now and forever.

Chas.

Am having recordings of my S.Q. #2 sent you.

• • •

In the summer of 1950 CBS canceled Bernard Herrmann's radio program and disbanded his orchestra. Popular music was to be substituted. Thus, Herrmann wrote Ives ostensibly to tell him that he would be unable to record the Third Symphony with the group as had been planned. The letter also reads as a veiled request for funding to sustain the group for as long as it would take to do the recording. Ives was quite upset at the demise of the orchestra: here was another case of the ruin of music at the hands of commerce. The request for support, however, in this case went unanswered. By this time Ives was reluctant to take on new responsibilities; his ongoing philanthropy was considerable.

428. 20 August 1950, from Bernard Herrmann, New York

My dear Mrs. Ives,

I do hope that you will forgive this long delay in writing to you.—but a series of hard luck has pursued me this past month—C.B.S. has decided to disband their orchestra and replace the programs with dance music. It was hard indeed to see my Sunday symphony series replaced with recordings—but the expense of television is the excuse for the move.—So at the moment, although I have a salary, I do not have an orchestra. So I feel that I have no right to ask Charles to refuse any one else the right to record the 3rd Symphony. I have called all the recording companies I know to ask them if they would be interested—they said no.—So there it is, as much as I love the symphony and would love to record it, no one seems willing to let me do it (unless of course I pay for it my self—which I can hardly afford to do) so I must bow out in favor of someone who is more fortunate. I envy him the opportunity, for you know how much the 3rd Symphony means to me and the number of times I have performed it.—But you must do what you think best for the symphony and Mr. Ives's music.

I do hope that you are both well and that I will be able to see you both before long. I should love to come up to see you either in the country or the city—I shall be in the city at the above address until Oct. 15. My plans are vague after that. I need six more weeks to finish the orchestration of the opera, but see no way just now how to get them. It is maddening to be so close to the final pages and yet so far.

Please forgive the depressing tone of this letter, I do not mean to inflict my woes on any friends, but it is hard indeed to see such a wonderful orchestra, created with so much blood and sweat go down the drain. So please forgive me. I know you both understand and will have understanding. So please see if we can have a meeting before long.

Keep well and don't let the above upset you, I felt as we are friends I must tell you the facts.

As ever
Bernard Herrmann

429. Ca. 20 August 1950, sketch for Harmony Ives to Bernard Herrmann

Herrmann

We both were deeply depressed & sorrowful to hear that your orchestra is to depart. Mr. Ives says ~~"it is caused by~~ just that damned commercialism that is lowering and weakening music & other arts to substitute dance music for what you have been doing is an insult not only to music but to "America." We have had several letters angered by this emasculation of music—as several say, lowering it to mediocrity & ~~vul~~ too much vulgarity, for the soft ear's ~~eissies~~ velvet pocket books."

We do want to see you—but Mr. Ives is not at all well now, & just as soon as he is better, I will let you know & hope you can come to Redding.

If you think it advisable possible to have the symphony recorded before your orchestra leaves Mr. Ives would be glad to help out in the expenses, as your letter infers it could be done this way.

Mr. Ives sends his kindest hand shake to his old young friend.

• • •

Peter Yates continued to send letters describing the programming of Ives's pieces in the "Evenings on the Roof" series into the early 1950s. His quest to have Frances Yates record the *Concord* Sonata continued as well. Yates's questions in the following letter point out how many of Ives's pieces remained to be edited, disseminated, and performed.

430. 11 October 1950, from Peter Yates, Los Angeles

Dear Friends:

One of our singers would like to do Aeschuylus and Sophocles and has asked me whether the parts for it are available. If these have not been made, please let me know; we'll see whether we can have it done ourselves.

Monday evening the Coriolan Quartet played your Second Quartet—at last, after all the years I have been trying to get it done. The performance was a bit stiff and not, in my opinion, polyphonically free enough. The first movement was at least clearly defined; the second came off very well and brought a chuckle from the audience; the third, which I consider one of the greatest movements in 20th century music, was quite well done; some preferred it to the recorded version. On the whole it was a very satisfactory job and would have gone even better, if the group had not first had to tackle one of the few—perhaps the only—rather ungrateful quartets by Mozart, a beautiful piece which does not jell.

Some of the audience were well pleased, especially by the last movement. A good many were well roughed up. This is always a good sign. The only review I have seen was rather silly. Two other critics (weeklies) were better pleased; I hope their reviews will show it.

The quartet will repeat the program next month at the University of California at LA. All going well, this should allow time for clearing up difficulties. I am going to sit in on a rehearsal and try to persuade them they should allow the polyphony to go a little more free. I should add that they all admire the Second Quartet and enjoy playing it.

Frances outdid herself playing the Concord for the LA County Museum series. This performance was broadcast and later rebroadcast from a tape recording. One way or another a good many people heard it; and for the second time the reception here was thoroughly enthusiastic.

Several people have asked Frances to record it on a long-playing record. I think she should, but first we want to consult you about it. Kirkpatrick has had his recording out for two years without competition. Frances after all has waited a good while and played it many times. It seems to me she deserves her turn to bring her own very different version before the larger public. Please let us know your opinion.

A young eastern pianist, Gordon Manley, was here lately. Frances played the Concord for him, and we showed him the Three Page Sonata. He was full of excitement after hearing the Concord. He came back the next afternoon and read the little sonata through three times and decided to play it for his Carnegie Hall program this winter.

I wrote an article about the new issues of the four Schoenberg quartets (for which I also wrote material to accompany the recordings) and the six Bartok quartets and your Second Quartet, grouping these as the central body of 20th century chamber music. The article was sent to the Saturday Review of literature, which has previously used a couple of my articles. This time, however, Slonimsky got there first, with an article just about Bartok and Schoenberg. I'll probably have to use my article in my own column. There aren't many magazines in the country right now which will consider using material of this sort. Too bad, because I believe the Second Quartet deserves to be praised not simply by itself but in company with the best music of its time.

The next question is, of course: what about the First Quartet? Neither quartet was in the six books of chamber music I gave to the library.

And the next: has the First Piano Sonata been printed? I know that it has been played in New York.

There are several questions to be answered. I don't like to trouble you with letter writing, but some of these questions can't be answered by anyone else.

We are grateful to you for sending us the quartet scores and the recordings. At least I am sure you had them sent, though there was no indication of it on or in either package. The recordings are on loan and with the Concord have made you two more devotees. I must get a record player so that I can enjoy them myself. It's hard to afford all the luxuries we want.

Our boys are big now and do their share of the housework, leaving Frances more time and rest for music. For ten years she had no time for teaching; now she has two good classes, one at the music school and one at home. Her playing is broadening wonderfully. The Beethoven sonata she played with the Concord at the Museum was one of the best performances I have heard. Maybe I'm prejudiced.

Henry Cowell's visit this summer, when he taught at the University of So. California, gave us great pleasure. I admire him more the more I know him. No one does more than he to help and encourage younger composers. Almost single-handed he has given American music self- awareness. We were happy to learn from him that when he last saw you you were both in better health.

Frances sends her greetings.

Cordially,
Peter Yates

• • •

In February 1951 Leonard Bernstein conducted Ives's Second Symphony with the New York Philharmonic in a concert that was also later broadcast on radio. At the time this was among the most prestigious performances of an Ives piece that had ever been mounted, and after it praise and commentary poured in from sources close at hand and farther afield.

431. 10 March 1951, from Bigelow Ives, Danbury, Connecticut

Dear Aunt Harmony—

I am enclosing four clippings on the concert taken from the Danbury News: 1 reporting on the concert, 2 announcing the forthcoming radio broadcast, 3 reporting on the broadcast, and 4 my letter of correction of the 3rd article.

In the first article the reporter was under the mistaken impression that there was only one concert presentation—and that on Friday evening. She also made the mistake of inserting my name & Evelyn's in it, which certainly was not necessary—and thereby ignored the fact that Mrs. Charles Ives <u>certainly</u> attended the concert, not to mention the Redding Ryders—and numerous members of the Ives family. Neither did I like to read that Uncle Charley had "been discovered several years ago by the late Lawrence Gillman."

The second article was so brief as to allow no space for errors.

The third article, by the same reporter, was written in a burst of enthusiasm immediately after she had heard the broadcast—and in a general tone, reflects a gratifying appreciation of Uncle Charley's music by one who is largely under-exposed to music beyond the point of Cesar Franck. The errors were several in number: 1 There was no Brahms on the program—it was Cesar Franck, 2 she completely missed the point about the final dissonant chord. Of course it was played by the entire orchestra—each musician being told to play whatever note struck his own fancy—not as she put it, "one final trumpet blast." Nor, did I like to see it characterized as "an idiosyncrasy" of grand-father's—an unfortunate choice of words, 3 the most grievous errors of all are contained in the final paragraph, and are perhaps best explained in my letter to the editor—which they published four days later. Being limited to 200 words I felt it best to confine my correction to the errors of the last paragraph, ignoring the "trumpet blast" story. In order to assure publication of the letter I also thought it would be helpful if I gave them a kind pat on the back for their interest and sincere effort. It really showed a commendable improvement in editorial standards locally—for of late we have had nothing but the most disheartening array of banal news stories in our local newspaper. . . . The writer of the local articles on Uncle Charley's music, however, is a girl a few years older than ourselves—and a very good personal friend of ours. She's been on the staff of the News for about 30 years or better—largely unappreciated by the younger and brash new set of editors. Her work has always been a cut above the average—and she is constantly striving to improve and widen her standards of taste—on an under-paid salary. I chastize myself for not having the foresight to procure a seat for her at Carnegie that Sunday afternoon. She is a true music lover and has not had the opportunity to hear a major symphony orchestra more than once or twice in her life. I think she does remarkably well under such limitations.

The broadcast was heard here in Danbury under the best conditions—it came in so well over our set that we found it remarkably comparable to a seat at Carnegie. Immediately after its conclusion the phone started ringing and we were kept busy listening to the exuberant expressions of appreciation from a host of friends and strangers alike. I felt a deep pride in our old home town—that it could still be roused to an awareness of its great Yankee heritage. One fellow told me that his whole family—grandparents, parents, and children—gathered around the radio which was placed on the kitchen table. Sunday dinner had been swept aside. The older men had just returned from church (Congregational) where they had been singing in the choir. Before the symphony was half way through—Grandfather had jumped to his feet to pound his fists on the table and shout with joy, "By god, that's the kind of music I always knew there was in America—but I've never heard before!" Everyone who called us said about the same thing in substance. So as long as Uncle Charley's music is played the spirit of New England will continue to live and maintain real vitality.

Mother just called to say that Sarane had written today, announcing that Efram Kurtz plans to conduct the Houston Symphony playing the 2nd Symphony—sometime this month. Bernstein will be visiting Kurtz at the time—and will aid in the rehearsals. That's really wonderful news—to think that the renaissance is spreading so fast and wide! Now how about something besides the 2nd Symphony! . . .

Mother says that you report managing to stay on a pretty even keel and that Uncle Charley feels a lot better by virtue of having a trim beard once more. I think it's a rotten shame that the operation had to be postponed so long. It must be very trying for you—after getting nerved up to it so nicely—and then have this let down with its prolonged waiting. . . .

Affectionately,
Bigelow

• • •

Harmony Ives's note to Leonard Bernstein after the performance of the Second Symphony reflects her gratitude for the performance and also suggests the level of her happy surprise that Ives's work was finally being recognized.

432. 11 March 1951, Harmony Ives to Leonard Bernstein

Dear Mr. Bernstein:

It was a wonderful and thrilling experience to hear Mr. Ives 2nd Symphony as you conducted it on February 22nd. I have been familiar with it—in snatches—for forty years and more and to hear the whole performed at last was a big event in my life. People did like it, didn't they? Someone wrote in the New Yorker recently of Mr. Ives music that its hearers are participators in it.

Mr. Ives has had many letters and he wants me to say to you that "the enthusiasm with which it was received was due so much to your devoted interpretation and wonderful conducting." Mr. Richard Bales, conductor of the orchestra at the National Gallery of Art in Washington, wrote that he "just wanted to yell when he wasn't on the verge of tears."

Mr. Ives heard the broadcast tho' he does not hear well over the radio and it took him back so to his father and his youth that he had tears in his eyes. You will be interested to know that his comment on the allegro movements was "too slow"—otherwise he was satisfied.

He thanks you from the bottom of his heart for getting this symphony played and for your skillful and artistic and masterly conducting.

I am so glad I had the pleasure of meeting you. I hope your Sabbatical year will be a happy and fruitful one.

With all our good wishes
Sincerely yours
Harmony T. Ives

P.S. Mr. Ives will be glad to send you the data on his music of which he spoke if you will let him know where to send it.

• • •

Patricia Travers was a violinist who recorded the Second Violin Sonata with Otto Herz for Columbia Records in 1950. That she met Ives in connection with her performance of the work is remarkable at this point in his life.

433. 29 April 1951, from Patricia Travers, Clifton, New Jersey

Dear Mr. Ives,

I received a statement today from Columbia which shows that to date more than 1300 copies of your sonata have been sold. This of course was very gratifying to me, but imagine my surprise when I found enclosed a check for $52, together with an explanation that this sum represented royalties due to you but which you had ordered the recording company to pay to me.

I am accepting these royalties only because I know that it is your wish; and in connection with that please let me say how grateful I am to you, and how honored and proud I feel at this beautiful expression of your kindly regard.

I suppose you have heard the recording. I have played it over many times, and I am so happy to have this permanent memento of our short personal meeting last year.

With kindest regards to Mrs. Ives and yourself, I remain,

Sincerely,
Patricia Travers

• • •

In the early 1950s health concerns weighed on both the Iveses and hampered their ability to respond even to longtime correspondents like Peter Yates. The following incomplete sketch may be for a long-delayed reply to his letter of 11 October 1950.

434. May 1951, sketch for Edith Ives Tyler to Peter Yates

~~Yeats~~ Peter Yates—

I am very sorry to have to tell you that father & mother are not at all well Mother has had a serious operation last month—but is recovering now & ~~left~~ & was well enough to leave the hospital last week—it was a severe strain—it brought father so low in body & mind that he was in a serious condition——he is a little better now—but he can't attend to things at all—or answer letters. He says one of the first he wants to write is to you. He deeply appreciates your wonderfully interesting letter & all you are so kindly doing in behalf of the music. We were so glad to hear that Mrs. Yates is better & we send you both our kindest remembrances—& Daddy says "now & forever."

P.S. We will have sent complimentary copies of the recent publications and recordings of

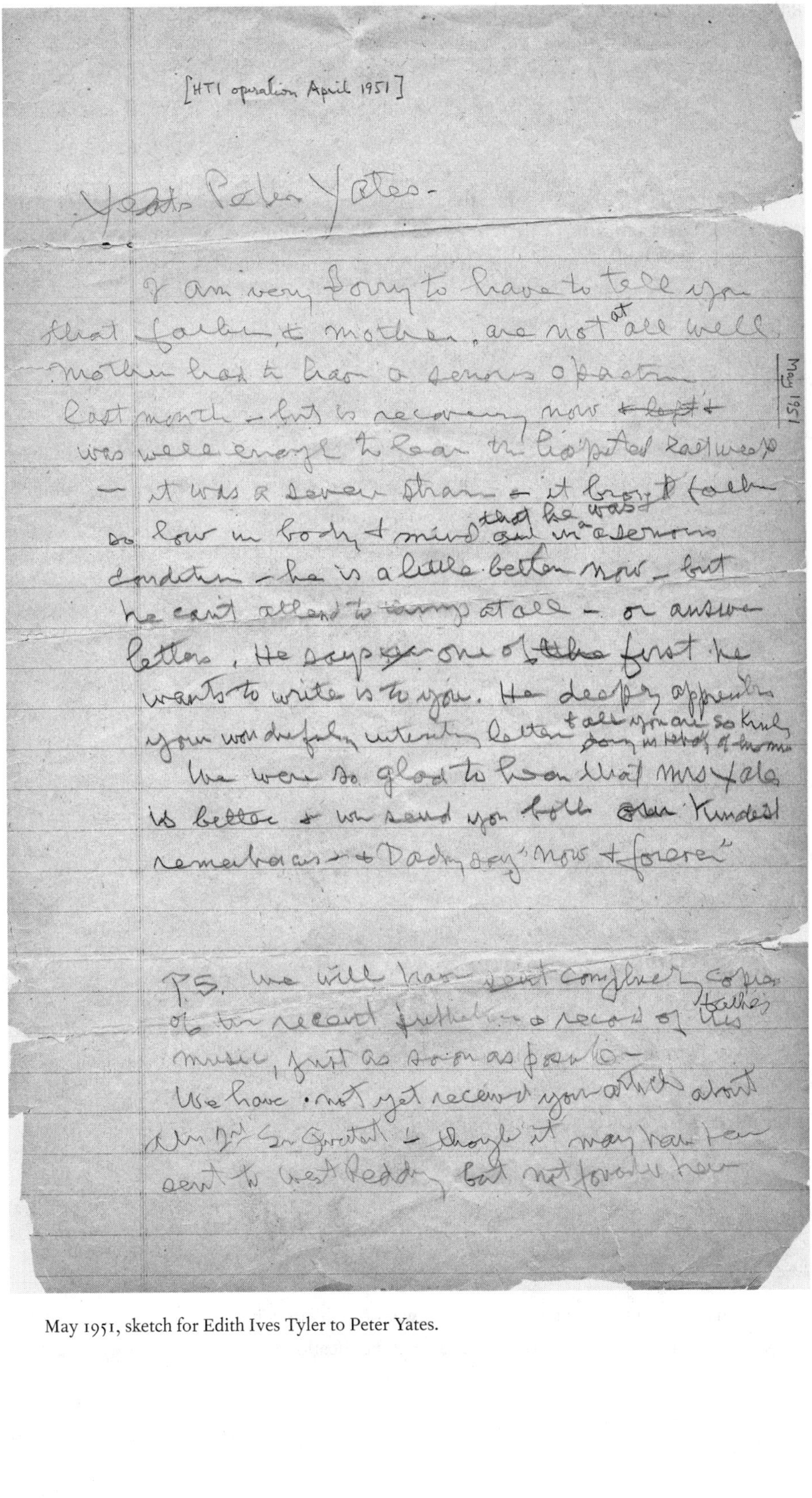
[HTI operation April 1951]

~~Yeats~~ Peter Yates—

I am very sorry to have to tell you that father & mother, are not at all well. Mother had to have a serious operation last month—but is recovering now & was well enough to leave the hospital last week—it was a severe strain & it brought father so low in body & mind that he was in a serious condition—he is a little better now—but he can't attend to ~~things~~ at all—or answer letters. He says one of ~~the~~ first he wants to write is to you. He deeply appreciates your wonderfully interesting letter & all you are so kind ~~doing in behalf of his music~~

We were so glad to hear that Mrs Yates is better & we send you both ~~our~~ kindest remembrances—& Daddy says "now & forever"

P.S. We will have ~~sent~~ complimentary copies of the record ~~published~~ a record of father's music, just as soon as possible—

We have not yet received your article about the 2nd Sn Quartet—though it may have been sent to West Redding but not forwarded here

May 1951

May 1951, sketch for Edith Ives Tyler to Peter Yates.

father's music, just as soon as possible—we have not yet received your article about the 2nd Str Quartet—though it may have been sent to West Redding, but not found here

• • •

Well into his seventies, Ives very rarely received visitors, and so it is a mark of the warmth of his friendship with Slonimsky that the Iveses welcomed him and his family to Redding in April 1952. The description of the visit in Slonimsky's letter of thanks provides a nicely balanced portrait of Ives's humor, spirituality, and ardent musical joy.

435. 3 April 1952, from Nicolas Slonimsky, Boston

Dear Mr. Ives:

We thoroughly enjoyed the afternoon we spent at your home last week. Dorothy and Electra got a great kick out of your jokes, limericks, etc. And, of course, I always get a great deal of spiritual nourishment talking to you about your works.

I hope you can find for me the article you wrote for Pro Musica and a copy of your ¼ composition [Three Quarter-Tone Pieces for two pianos]. I wonder also whether your intervalic studies in major sevenths and, I think, in minor ninths can be found.[24]

I enclose an interesting clipping about the conducting classes of Pierre Monteux, which include your Third Symphony.

With our best regards to Mrs. Ives,

As ever,
Cordially yours,
Nicolas Slonimsky

P.S. Electra exclaimed, "My God!" when I handed her your surprise gift. She will write you if she can summon enough courage to overcome her shyness.

• • •

Ives provided support for his friends in ventures not directly connected with him. For instance, he helped fund the Black Mountain Music Press, a project that Lou Harrison headed while he taught at the experimental school in western North Carolina. The edition of an Ives piece by the press seems not to have materialized.

436. 10 July 1952, from Lou Harrison, Black Mountain, North Carolina

Dear Mr. Ives,

It has been a long time since I've written & I want to tell you what a pleasure it has been working on your scores as they one by one reach publication & performance. I was much

24. This is perhaps the song "Soliloquy."

moved by Mr. Bernstein's performance of the Second Symphony, which is a splendid work, full of warmth and humor; am delighted, as I'm sure you are, by the recordings, especially (I think) that very good one of the chamber combinations & small orchestra works (Over the Pavements, The Unanswered Question & others) & much look forward to hearing the Robert Browning Overture, on which Henry Cowell & I are currently working.

I don't believe I ever thanked you for your kindness in suggesting me several years ago for the National Academy of Arts and Letters Creative grant which helped me so much. I do now, & too, for your kindness in assigning me as royalty recipient so generously & also for the very generous present you sent me through Henry Cowell.

This year I happily received a Guggenheim Fellowship & am at work on several large works which I hope to complete within the year. It is very gratifying to me & enables me to concentrate on composing.

I have been living & teaching at Black Mt. College, Black Mt. North Carolina since last fall, & late this spring myself & one of the students founded the Black Mt. College Music Press. It is founded to publish the smaller works of contemporary composers, in as fine & inventive a way as possible. We want to include a work of yours if you will give us permission to do so.

Editions will each be small & on the best paper & we want to make the music beautiful to look at as well. Our first two issues will be made this month & will honor the two composers teaching on campus this summer, Stephan Wolpe & John Cage.

We are planning to make the Press self-sustaining & it is possible by reason of faculty & students doing almost all the work of it together right here on campus.

We do, however, need help to get started on our first two issues, which together will cost $130.00. I wonder if it would be possible for you to advance us this sum so that we can begin, &, at the same time give us permission to publish a work of yours so that we can select among the smaller ones that would be possible for us to print? Have you a special favorite among those that you might want to suggest? We would welcome very warmly both the permission & the suggestion.

Thank you again for your kindness, Mr. Ives.

My very best to you & Mrs Ives & with continued wishes for your health & happiness.

Sincerely,
Lou Harrison

P.S. As well as direct from the College we are arranging to have distribution through the American Music Center in New York.

P.S. #2 I enclose our little college announcement of the middle of the year.

437. 24 July 1952, Harmony Ives to Lou Harrison

Dear Lou Harrison

We were glad to hear from you again—we were glad too to hear that you got the fellowship and hope it will give you a year of creative work.

Mr. Ives is glad to help in the issue of Black Mt. Music Press & sends the enclosed cheque with his best wishes. If you wish to publish anything of his later he will be glad to have you select something as you know the length & number of instruments suitable for the edition.

I remember so well how beautifully you conducted the Third Symphony—

Remember me to Mr. Cage whom I remember meeting.

Mr. Ives and I are about as usual tho' the heat pretty much used us up. He wants me to say again how much he thanks you for all you have done in behalf of his music.

As ever
sincerely yours
Harmony T. Ives

438. Late July 1952, from Lou Harrison, Black Mountain, North Carolina

Dear Mrs. Ives,

Thank you for your kind letter & Mr. Ives for his generous & instant aid. The two first editions look to me as though they will be beautiful the way they are planned.

I have here a page that I hope Mr. Ives will remember, which is titled "Varied Air & Variations," & in which a widely skipping melodic line is written in much heavier pencil & with indication to "follow the stone wall around the mountain." It is adventurous and polyphonic in texture. In considering it as a possibility I noticed that it must in some way be connected with the "Protests" because there is another repeat & ending for this. Now, are these the "Protests" published in the anniversary edition of New Music some years back? If so, & this is a part it should be issued as a supplement, otherwise we would like to consider it as a separate item. Also, would Mr. Ives allow us to publish it with the original & most poetic annotations with which it abounds?

We had a tremendous rainstorm here the last two days which helps our flourishing farm (on which the college is based in a very genuine sense).

Thank you for remembering my conducting of Mr. Ives's Third Symphony. It was among my "most pleasures" & I hope to have another pleasure of the kind if I am invited this year to guest-conduct the Winston-Salem Orchestra here in North Carolina when (if they are capable of it) I want to conduct another "unheard" work by Mr. Ives. If one of the more complex works is unsuitable I will select a simpler one.

I am glad you have survived the heat, which can be oppressive, I know, & are in good health.

My best to you & Mr. Ives,

sincerely
Lou Harrison

• • •

The next two letters, from around January 1953, represent a kind of transfigured echo to the responses Ives received when he sent out the *Concord* Sonata mostly to strangers more than thirty years earlier. Now, though, strangers wrote asking fervently for the music, praising it, and describing the influence it had made in their musical lives.

439. Ca. December 1952, from John Ardoin, Denton, Texas

Dear Mr. Ives,

I am a composition student at North Texas State College. For some time now I have tried with no luck to obtain a copy of your Concord Mass. Sonata. I believe the one printing that was available (Knickerbocker Press—1920) has long been out of print and currently there is not a modern edition.

If there were any possible way that you might help me to obtain a copy, I should be very grateful. I have long regarded this work as a criterion to work forward to. Recently I had to write a paper on the Freeing of Music. If you will allow me to I should like to tell you my feelings of the Concord Sonata. I wrote, "Here is a work of complete freedom in every aspect of tonal and metric elements. The music itself, easily transfers the feeling of its liberation directly to the listener, giving him a completely, usually unexplainable, new listening sensation. This is simply the next part of the cycle in the freeing of music. The music is only releasing the inhibitions of the listener as it itself was freed from the inhibitions of the composer."

I wish I could tell you in words what this work has meant to me. But my feeling and devotion to it go far deeper.

I hope you will forgive me for taking up your time with this letter. I debated a long time whether or not I should even bother you with it. But any help you might give in helping me to obtain this score I shall always appreciate and remember.

Sincerely yours,
John Ardoin

440. 22 January 1953, from John Ardoin, Denton, Texas

Dear Mr. and Mrs. Ives,

First let me thank you so much for your wonderful letter. I fastened it in my score so that I might see it whenever I use the music. I would like to say so much more than simply thank you for your gift. I assure you it will always be one of my most cherished memories. As you sent me two copies, I hope you won't mind my sharing one of them with my composition teacher Miss Violet Archer. Perhaps you know of her. She is a graduate of Yale also and a pupil of Hindemith when she studied there. Your music also means a great deal to her and she was quite thrilled to have a copy of the Concord Sonata on Columbia. It is one of my prize records.

I want to tell you that your letter and the scores arrived on the same day that we had a composition recital and I felt that your letter brought me great luck for the soprano didn't flat and the pianist missed only a few notes! I am enclosing the program for you to see.

Again let me express my deepest thanks for the music. I shall never forget your generosity.

Sincerely,
John Ardoin

• • •

Among the sadder of the missed opportunities documented in the correspondence is the ultimately unsuccessful effort on the part of faculty of the Yale School of Music to have the university confer an honorary doctorate on Ives. Technicalities and his failing health prevented him from accepting the award, which would have been much appreciated as a sort of valediction from an institution that was very important to Ives and to Harmony's side of the family.

441. 24 March 1953, from Richard Donovan, New Haven

Dear Mr. Ives:

Several of us here on the Yale Music Faculty have been greatly interested in having Yale confer upon you an Honorary Degree. Accordingly we formally presented the matter to the committee on Honorary Degrees some weeks ago. We were informed however it was not possible this year owing to the rule of long standing that no Honorary Degree may be presented to any member of a class holding a reunion in the same year. Unfortunately your class of 1898 is holding a reunion here in June. We have made an effort to have the rule waived in this case, but apparently no exception could be made.

Probably experience has shown that such a rule is wise and necessary. Nevertheless, the unforeseen technicality was a great disappointment to your admirers among the Yale musicians.

We shall certainly try again.

With best wishes, I am,
Very sincerely yours,
Richard Donovan

442. 6 April 1953, Harmony Ives to Richard Donovan

Dear Mr. Donovan,

I am writing for Mr. Ives who, as you know, is not well and it is difficult for him to do so.

He asks me to say how deeply he appreciates the fact that you & other friends of his at The Yale School of Music suggested him as a recipient of a degree from his Alma Mater—He would have considered it a great honor.

We understand the degree cannot be presented in absentia and whether Mr. Ives could undertake what would be to him the ordeal of appearing I have my doubts.

With a further expression of his gratitude

I am
Sincerely yours
Harmony T. Ives

• • •

The last large Ives project that Henry Cowell undertook was to write, along with his wife, Sidney, the first book-length biography of Ives, and the only one to have significant direct input from the composer himself. Harmony's letter here suggests the level of detail and clarification the Iveses provided for the book and shows her distinct personality, as opposed to the character Ives projects in the letters he wrote in her voice.

443. 11 October 1953, Harmony Ives to Sidney Cowell

Dear Sidney,

Your questions are easy to answer—"Thanksgiving day" 4th movement of "Holidays Symphony"—

We were not in Europe at the time of Nicolas Slonimsky's concerts.—The dates of our three trips are—1924 in England 2 mos. (Mr. Ives first trip abroad). May 1932–July 1933, & 1938 2 mos. in Scotland & Eng.

We are hanging on loathe to go—It is so beautiful now—Our reservoir fed by springs is very low—we hope to be able to stay thro' the month.

We are wondering why we get no response from the Music Center on our orders—we have sent several asking that all bills be sent here but have received no acknowledgments nor invoices—John Kirkpatrick told us that Ray Green is no longer there.

I have known two melon-eating cats—doesn't somehow go with their fierce natures does it?

We are pretty well but both of us get used up rather easily—no wonder at our ages.

Our best to you both
Harmony T. Ives

• • •

In 1954 the Yale faculty did offer an honorary doctorate to Ives. Nearing the end of his life, he was unable to attend the ceremony to accept the award.

444. 4 March 1954, Harmony Ives to Reuben Holden

Dear Mr. Holden,

Mr Ives received your letter telling of the decision of the President of the Fellows of Yale to confer on him an honorary degree in June. He greatly appreciates it and wishes he might be able to accept.

But his health is not good and I have been waiting to consult his physician whom I have not been able to see until this week. He says and we feel that Mr. Ives is not equal to going through the ceremony.

It is too bad—it would have crowned his career to have an honor from his Alma Mater—but he has your letter and the knowledge that he was chosen means much to him.

Our association with Yale covers many years. His great grandfather, Isaac Ives, graduated there and he had an Uncle Joseph in 1855 (who didn't graduate) and my father Joseph Twichell was for many years a member of the Corporation and my three brothers graduates.

With renewed assurance of his deep appreciation,

Sincerely yours,

This has been a hard letter to write—great regret.

• • •

The following letter provides another example of the type of information Ives gave the Cowells for their biography. "TSIAJ," meaning "This Scherzo Is a Joke," is the marking Ives appended to the fast movement of his String Trio, which employs a dense fabric of overlapping quotations to comic effect.

445. 11 April 1954, Harmony Ives to Sidney Cowell

Dear Sidney—

You are right as to TSIAJ—only we thought it labeled a fast movement & the "S" stood for scherzo. Mr. Ives says it is a poor joke anyway & of no importance—I wish he felt like even poor jokes these days—Carl [Ruggles] telephoned—They are returning to go home—

Our best to you both
H.T.I.

• • •

Charles Ives died on 19 May as a result of a stroke that followed successful hernia surgery. The death was unexpected, and Harmony was devastated. Her stunned responses to the many letters of condolence she received are among the most touching letters in the correspondence. Ives's funeral was private and small. Of all the musical friends and associates, only John Kirkpatrick attended. He wrote the following letter to describe the service to Carl and Charlotte Ruggles, who could not make the trip from Vermont. Kirkpatrick included this letter as the "Envoi" to his "Temporary Mimeographed Catalogue" of Ives's works.

446. 21 May 1954, John Kirkpatrick to Carl and Charlotte Ruggles

Charles Ives died Wednesday morning, 19 May 1954, around 2:30 A.M., at the Roosevelt hospital, New York. Though the service was announced as private (2:30 Friday), I took the liberty of asking if I might come. Carl and Charlotte Ruggles were in Arlington, Vermont, and it would have been very difficult for them to take the trip. The following letter was an attempt to give them some feeling of having been there.

Friday evening, 21 May 54,
on train between Westport and New York and plane between New York and Ithaca . . .

Dear Carl and Charlotte,

Having just come from Charlie's funeral . . . here's as much as I remember. . . . It seems that Charlie's operation was his old double hernia, and that his doctor had been worried about it, feeling that it would be dangerous for them to come up to Redding again without having it put in order. Actually the operation itself was a complete success, and all the incisions were healing quicker than they had dared to expect, and he was continuing to improve in spite of his mounting irritation at having to stay in the hospital so long. . . . But then Tuesday he had something like a stroke, and from then on they didn't have much hope.

Edie told me that she and Harmony were with him for several hours before the end . . . and that they all held hands quietly and it was a time of the kind of luminous serenity that animates his greatest music. Edie said something like—he seemed as if transfigured, that it was a kind of intimate communion of unspoken awareness she could never have imagined (I forgot how she put it), a kind of serenity resolving all the tensions of his life, that somehow persisted intact quite a bit after he had quietly stopped breathing. Edie said that Harmony derives great comfort from this (that his actual going was so deeply calm and happy).—but that otherwise Harmony had felt the general strain heightened by the way she could never be alone with him. . . .

. . . I took the early plane from Ithaca and made the train from Grand Central in good time. In driving to the house, George told me . . . about the operation and what a tragic disappointment it had been. When we got to the house, Harmony looked exhausted and numb . . . but generally she looks quite well. Charlie's face looked clear and serene. Harmony said something like that she was so happy I was there . . . and I said that I had wondered if perhaps I might be seeing you, but that of course the trip from Arlington to West Redding wasn't exactly easy, and that I would try to represent you as well as I could.

Then most of the time before lunch I spent in Charlie's little room that has the piano in it—some of the time with George, some with Edie, some with the Rev. Mr. Twichell (Harmony's brother—she didn't want anyone else to do the service). . . .

Lunch was just Harmony, George and Edie, the Twichells and myself. It was so touching the way various neighbors had sent various things:—a batch of individual chicken pies (worthy of a grand cordon bleu!), a wonderful tuna and tomato salad, a cherry pie, etc. Harmony passed up the pie and went to sit beside Charlie. . . . You remember how the dining room is in relation to the rest of the house—well, the coffin was on the other side of the living room, between the front door and the big window that overlooks the hills. . . .

Then pretty soon people started arriving. First Mrs. Moss Ives and four . . . of her sons, Mrs. Hall (Harmony's sister) and her two sons and their wives, . . . Mr. Myrick, a Mrs. Ryder (I met her husband later afterward) who is a local organist (lovely big-hearted person) who was to play the hymn, Abide With Me. . . . there were in all about 25 or 30. They were finally seated around the edge of the living room and pretty much filling the dining room (I was back near the door to Charlie's music room).

Mr. Twichell read passages quite beautifully . . . Psalms and St. Paul. Mrs. Ryder played Abide With Me very beautifully and turned aside at the end to hide her tears. I told her afterward that it was more beautiful than I could have done it (that's true).

Not having been to many kinds of funerals, I had sort of wondered if by any remote chance any additional prayers might conceivably be asked from whoever might feel like venturing anything. Naive as such a thought might be, still I have always been impressed with one thing my grandmother used to say—that it was far better to have the right clothes and not go. So all during the service a few thoughts were formulating themselves (which turned out not to be called for). But since I had told Harmony that I'd try to represent you as well as I could, perhaps my communicating these random thoughts to you may get something off your chest (even in silence), as they did off mine. It would have gone something like this:— "Dear Father, we thank Thee for the wondrous things that Charlie has meant to so many souls, and for the much more that he still may mean to those who are to come. We bless Thy Holy Name that the complacent were upset. We bless Thy Holy Name that the new song was sung unto the Lord. We bless Thy Holy Name that the new paths he struck out were sanctified by his devotion to Thee, and that it has pleased Thee to bestow this blessing on the spirit of adventure in all who love Thee. Bless his heart. Bless his soul. May he rejoice once again in the strength of his youth. May he have the joy of knowing some of those he longed to know, some of those whom he so worthily glorified. Bless his wise and loving companion in this earthly life, bless and comfort her. Bless his work. May his achievement be held in honor among mankind, and may it continue to give courage and inspiration to those who need them. Bless us all, and, if it be Thy will, may we have the joy of knowing him again in whatever circumstances it may please Thee to assign us. These things we ask in the name of our Savior. Amen."

After the service there was an interim of milling around while some left and others got ready to go to the cemetery. Looking at Charlie's face again from the distance moved me to murmur to Harmony's sister, Mrs. Hall: "Even the sight of his face still makes one giggle inwardly!"—to which she agreed with enthusiastic nods and smiles. But nearer to, before they closed the coffin, there seemed more to be a kind of serene, elusive mystery.

I went with Chester Ives and his mother (Mrs. Moss Ives) and a cousin, a charming Mrs. Van Wyck from Norwalk (née Amelia Ives). The cemetery is geographically quite beautiful—a huge tract, all little hills and slopes, laid out by Charlie's grandfather Ives in the sixties. It was raining then but there was an awning over the plot, and it was all quite brief. Pall bearers from the hearse to the grave were nephews and neighbors. Not all the flowers had been brought from the house, and it made just a graceful abundance. . . . after the closing prayer we all got back in the cars, most to return to the house.

On the way back, Mrs. Van Wyck . . . told a story about Charlie's father (which she said was news to Charlie himself when she told it to him). It seems that the first 3 children (of Charlie's grandfather Ives) were treated to music lessons by a generous uncle, but none of them took to it, and the uncle was discouraged and didn't try it on little George. But then one day they were all going on a picnic and George didn't want to—he wanted to stay and mow somebody's lawn to get a little more money toward buying a flute. So the uncle quickly changed his mind and (as you know) little George trained a band in the Civil War.

Back at the house . . . Harmony looked deeply relieved and relaxed, and somehow quite radiant. In saying goodbye to her, she thanked me again for coming, and I was moved to try to thank her for all that we all owed her for what she had made possible in the bloom of his work (I forget how I put it)—and she said she'd tell all that to Charlie.

In retrospect . . . it seemed clearer to me than ever before that Charlie was probably here for a purpose, that the complacent patterns had to be upset, and that the specially shaped personality . . . had necessarily to have all kinds of corresponding disadvantages—for instance, the tragic enforced seclusion of one who (I firmly believe) was really temperamentally gregarious—or the dogged continuance of rebellion long after the complacent conventions had been overthrown. . . . Anyway, it will be fascinating to see what develops in the way of regard for Charlie's music (inherently it so invites any and all kinds of reactions, both to and from). . . . But let us thank God for its core of unshakeable reality, so warmly human, so sure in form, so high in impulse. What a great example!

447. 26 May 1954, Harmony Ives to John and Evelyn Becker

Dear John & Evelyn

Thank you for your heartfelt note—The love and sympathy & prayers of old friends are a help.

My beloved has left me & my life is emptied of its contents—but it has been such a wonderful life with him that I know how I have been blessed,

The simple service at Redding with my brother reading such beautiful scripture & a simple prayer & a dear neighbor playing just once "Abide with Me!" was what he would have wished. John Kirkpatrick was there & I was so glad of that—Charlie had failed very much this winter & probably a life of invalidism was spared him but I cannot get myself together as yet—

Do pray for us—without the hope of life immortal what were this life?

Ever with love
Harmony

• • •

Even after his death, something about Ives seems to have pushed against rigid institutions. As they had just before his death, faculty in the Yale School of Music tried to get an exception to the rules concerning the granting of honorary degrees for Ives—this time to the rule against granting degrees posthumously. As this request, too, was denied, Harmony was sent the citations that would have been read in the event that award had been allowed.

448. 9 June 1954, Reuben Holden, secretary, Yale University, to Richard Donovan, New Haven

Dear Mr. Donovan:

As you gathered, the Corporation voted against conferring the degree on Mr. Ives posthumously. I regret this very much as I thought it would be very much in order myself.

I am, however, sending Mrs. Ives your very excellent citation which would have been used had he been able to receive the degree. Thanks so much for all your help.

I should further add that the Corporation in voting down the proposal last Saturday admitted that they had made a mistake in not having awarded the degree long ago.

Very sincerely yours,
Reuben A. Holden

[*Proposed citations to be read at the Yale ceremony:*]

CHARLES EDWARD IVES, American composer, whose recent death removed one of our most important creative artists, was a member of the Class of 1898. A native of Connecticut, he received his formal musical training at Yale where, even at an early age, his highly original music marked him as a composer far in advance of his time. This unique discoverer of new tonal resources succeeded in creating a musical fabric acknowledged to be indigenous to America. It is fitting that Yale should honor one of her most distinguished (sons) (graduates).

Another possibility:

The recent death of the composer, CHARLES EDWARD IVES, of the Class of 1898, has deprived America of one of her most gifted creative artists. A native of Connecticut, Mr. Ives received his formal training at Yale where, even at an early age, his highly original music marked him as a composer far in advance of his time. This unique discoverer of new tonal resources succeeded in creating a musical fabric acknowledged to be indigenous to America. It is fitting that Yale should honor a (son) (graduate) who has contributed so significantly to the culture of his country.

449. 15 June 1954, Harmony Ives to Richard Donovan

Dear Mr Donovan—

Mr. Holden sent me a copy of the citation you had prepared if my husband had been able to receive his honorary degree.

It made me sad to read it & think he could not see it—I like it very much.

We realized all you had done to bring about the offer from the President and Fellows and thank you greatly.

Sincerely yours,
Harmony T. Ives

450. 13 June 1954, Harmony Ives to Carl and Charlotte Ruggles

Dearest Carl & Charlotte,

I got your telegram—I need all your love & sympathy—oh—this desperate loneliness—

Charlie has been so long my joy & my care that my life seems emptied of its contents and I do not know how I shall fill it. I am staying on here to make some attempt to get things in order to empty this house. Henry [Cowell] is coming in tomorrow to help me to bring some order into the chaos in the top floor—Charlie never threw anything away & the accumulation is awesome.

Charlie had what the surgeon called an intolerable hernia condition that had to be corrected but we expected him to recover—for two days he did remarkably well but his heart weakened & the end came.

A sonnet I read in The Spectator has helped me—"We knew joy / unchanging and thro' this unchanging joy / I apprehended the joy unchangeable."

You two devoted souls can sense my sorrow—I cannot believe what has happened to me—that I shall see him no more—

We had a simple service at Redding, my brother officiating—just family & neighbors—John Kirkpatrick was there which gave me comfort—and now he lies near his father in the old Wooster Cemetery in Danbury.

Oh, but these partings are hard even if one has a sustaining faith

With our love—& I mean <u>our</u>
As ever
Harmony

451. Before 22 June 1954, from Germaine Schmitz, San Francisco

Dear Friend:

Your earlier answer to my letter had caused me great worry foreshadowing the realization that your fears were typically justified.

With all my heart I am with you in your loss, shared by every friend and all the musicians of the world alike.

Numerous were the splendid eulogies which we read in newspapers and magazines. They remembered with warmth Mr. Ives's vast contributions to the musical scene, and recalled, as well, his ever kindly, generous, and patient personal touch. They realized, as we have often had occasion to in the many years past, that it [is] so often almost too late that great men receive recognition in their lifetime—it is a constant but hapless procrastination of the spirit.

Yet, like all great men of ideas These are the food that they live for with little concern for recognition or the lack of their full worth.

I meant to send this note to you sooner but Ill health in my immediate family caused me worry and great fatigue, but all is better now.

Please dear friend, accept my deepest sympathies, and my warm personal thoughts and wishes.

Sincerely
Germaine Schmitz

452. 22 June 1954, Harmony Ives to Germaine Schmitz

Dear Germaine,

Thank you for writing—I greatly appreciated your affectionate letter.

Mr. Ives has for so long been my joy & my care that my life seems emptied of its contents and I do not know how I shall fill it. To be his wife has been a blessed and wonderful experience.

I am staying on here as I must empty this house & feel I must get some of the preliminaries done before moving the furniture in the fall. It is a sad and tiring thing to do.

You, too have known this desperate loneliness and I thank you for your sympathy.

Affectionately yours
Harmony T. Ives

453. 22 June 1954, from Carl and Charlotte Ruggles, Arlington, Vermont

Dearest Harmony:

You have been in our hearts, our prayers and our thoughts these past tragic days—We wish so much that we were near to perhaps assuage in some small measure the grief and loneliness of your great loss.

Right after the telegram Carl was ill and has said so many times that a Great White Light had gone out of his life. Charlie and Carl are alike in so many ways that I have always felt spiritually very near you. You have always been a great inspiration to me and a help when the days were long and down—A very beautiful letter from John telling us of the service and a prayer he said in his heart when he said "Good Bye" We were with you my dear & I know "we shall meet Beyond the River" Carl is out under the trees feeling some better The iris, lupin & day lilies all swaying in the high wind—Love to Edie and our devotion & dearest love to you

always
Charlotte

All my love to you dear Harmony.

Carl

APPENDIX

LIST OF LETTERS AND FORMATS

(Copy)	indicates that the CIP holds a photocopy
ALS	a signed letter in the hand of the sender
AL	an unsigned letter in the hand of the sender
TLS	a typed letter, signed
Typed, no sig.	usually indicates a typed copy of a letter, possibly a carbon
JKT	Transcription by John Kirkpatrick

All references to the Charles Ives Papers are given by box and folder number (for example, 32/10 indicates box 32, folder 10) or by the designation "Correspondence Addendum.

1. CHILDHOOD, HOPKINS, AND YALE (1881–1903)

All letters are written by Charles Ives unless otherwise noted and are in his hand. Letters 1–7 were mailed from Westbrook, Connecticut, unless otherwise noted. Letters 8–36 were mailed from New Haven, Connecticut, unless otherwise noted. Letters 1–35 are in CIP, 33/1. Letter 36 is in 32/10.

1. Ca. 10 September 1881 to Sarah H. Ives (Danbury, Connecticut) [ALS]
2. 18 July 1886, to George Ives [ALS]
3. 14 August 1889, to George Ives [ALS]
4. 20 August 1889, to George Ives [ALS]
5. 27 August 1889, to Sarah H. Ives (Danbury, Connecticut) [ALS]
6. 19 August 1890, to George Ives [ALS], and Amelia Brewster to George Ives [ALS]
7. 31 August 1889 [1890], to Amelia Brewster [ALS]
8. 9 May 1893, to George Ives (New Haven) [ALS]
9. 5 July 1893, to George Ives [ALS]
10. 12 July 1893, to George Ives [ALS]
11. 22 August 1893, to George Ives (stationery: "The Colonies[,] Chicago") [ALS]
12. 30 September 1893, to George Ives (incomplete) [AL]
13. 4 October 1893, to Mollie Ives [ALS]
14. 30 October 1893, to George Ives [ALS]
15. 19 November 1893, to George Ives [ALS]
16. 3 December 1893, to George Ives [ALS]
17. 10 December 1893, to George Ives [ALS]
18. 17 December 1893, to George Ives [ALS]

19. 11 February 1894, to George Ives [ALS]
20. 20 February 1894, to George Ives [ALS]
21. 24 February 1894, to George Ives [ALS]
22. 29 March 1894, to George Ives [ALS]
23. 1 April 1894, to George Ives [ALS]
24. 12 April 1894, to George Ives [ALS]
25. 29 April 1894, to George Ives [ALS]
26. 2 May 1894, to George Ives [ALS]
27. 4 March 1895, from Charles W. Whittlesey [ALS] (in John Kirkpatrick Papers, MSS 56, 87/97).
28. 6 May 1894, to George Ives [ALS]
29. 8 May 1894, to George Ives [ALS]
30. 13 May 1894, to George Ives [ALS]
31. 28 September 1894, from George Ives (Danbury, Connecticut) [ALS]
32. 30 September 1894, to George Ives (written on the back of the paper of Letter 31) [ALS]
33. 24 October 1894, to George Ives [ALS]
34. 29 October 1894, to George Ives [ALS]
35. 20 January 1895, to Mollie Ives [ALS]
36. September or October 1903, to David Twichell (New York) [ALS]

2. COURTSHIP AND MARRIAGE (1907–1908)

All letters are by Charles Ives or Harmony Twichell. Unless otherwise noted, Ives's letters are mailed from New York City, Twichell's from Hartford, Connecticut. All letters are in CIP, Correspondence Addendum, which contains all letters acquired after cataloguing was completed.

37. July 1907, from Harmony Twichell (New York) [ALS]
38. 25 October 1907, from Harmony Twichell [ALS]
39. 26–27 October 1907 (postmarked 27 October), from Harmony Twichell [ALS]
40. 27 October 1907, Sunday morning, from Harmony Twichell [ALS]
41. 27 October 1907, Sunday afternoon, from Harmony Twichell [ALS]
42. 28 October 1907, Monday, from Harmony Twichell [ALS]
43. 28 October 1907, from Harmony Twichell [ALS]
44. 29 October 1907, from Harmony Twichell [ALS]
45. 7 November 1907, from Harmony Twichell [ALS]
46. 8 November 1907, P.M. from Harmony Twichell [ALS]
47. 22 November 1907, to Harmony Twichell [ALS]
48. 24 November 1907, to Harmony Twichell [ALS]
49. 25 November 1907, to Harmony Twichell [ALS]
50. 26 November 1907, to Harmony Twichell [ALS]
51. 6 December 1907, A.M.from Harmony Twichell (Hartford, Connecticut) [ALS]
52. 6 December 1907, P.M., from Harmony Twichell [ALS]
53. 25 December 1907, from Harmony Twichell [ALS]
54. 1 April 1908, from Harmony Twichell [ALS]
55. 14 April 1908, from Harmony Twichell [ALS]

56. 11 May 1908, from Harmony Twichell [ALS]
57. 13 May 1908, to Harmony Twichell [ALS]
58. 20 May 1908, to Harmony Twichell [ALS]
59. 25 May 1908, to Harmony Twichell [ALS]
60. 26 May 1908, Tuesday, to Harmony Twichell [ALS]

3. CALL AND RESPONSE (1911–1936)

All letter sketches by Ives are in his hand unless otherwise indicated. All letters are in the CIP. All letters from Ives were mailed from New York or West Redding unless otherwise noted.

61. 14 December 1911, to Walter Damrosch [typed, no sig.; 29/1]
62. 24 June 1915, to Walter Damrosch [typed, no sig.; 29/1]
63. 28 June 1915, from Walter Damrosch (Long Island, New York) [ALS; 29/1]
64. Ca. 1936, sketch for Harmony Ives to Walter Damrosch [29/1]
65. Ca. 8 March 1921, from John Spencer Camp (Hartford, Connecticut) [ALS; 27/10]
66. 9 March 1921, from Charles Wakefield Cadman (Los Angeles) [TLS; 27/10]
67. 11 April 1921, to Charles Wakefield Cadman [TLS; 27/10]
68. 10 March 1921, from Walter Goldstein (New Orleans) [TLS; 29/13]
69. Sketch for Ives to Goldstein on back of Letter 68 [29/13]
70. 3 January 1922 [1923], from George R. Falconer (New York) [29/7]
71. 8 August 1922, from William Ames Fisher (Oliver Ditson Company, Boston) [TLS; 29/7]
72. 9 August 1922, from Deane Dossert (New York) [ALS; 29/1]
73. Ca. 3 April 1921, from Roland Diggle (stationery: Roland Diggle, Mus. Doc. / Organist—Composer . . . Los Angeles, California) [ALS; 29/1]
74. Ca. 14 August 1922, from Roland Diggle, (Los Angeles) [ALS; 29/1]
75. 17 August 1922, from A. de Blanek, (stationery: Conservatorio Nacional / de Musica / Avenida de Italia No. 47 / Habana) [ALS; 29/1]
76. 21 August 1922, from Karl H. Eschman (Granville, Ohio) [TLS; 29/6]
77. Ca. 21 August 1922, sketch for Ives to Karl H. Eschman [29/6]
78. 29 September 1922, from Bessie Bartlett Frankel (stationery: The National Federation of Music Clubs / United States of America / Department of Extension / Mrs. Cecil Frankel, Chairman / . . . Los Angeles, California) [TLS; 29/7]
79. 7 May 1923, from Mrs. Cecil (Bessie Barlett) Frankel [TLS; 29/7]
80. 4 December 1922, from Leon R. Maxwell (New Orleans) [TLS; 30/17]
81. 11 December 1922, to Leon R. Maxwell [typed, no sig.; 30/17]
82. 21 January 1924, from Leon R. Maxwell (New Orleans) [TLS; 30/17]
83. 28 December 1922, from Caroline D. Hewitt (New York) [ALS; 30/6]
84. 6 January 1923, from Mrs. Donald T. Baker (Long Island, New York) [ALS; 27/3]
85. 5 March 1923, from E. Linwood Lehman (Charlottesville, Virginia) [TLS; 30/15]
86. 18 April 1923, from Charles Ditson (New York) [TLS; 29/1]
87. 4 May 1923, from Muriel W. Humphrey (Middletown, Connecticut) [ALS; 30/8]
88. 20 May 1923, from Percy Goetschius (New York) [ALS; 29/13]
89. 25 May 1923, from Charles Holman-Black (Paris) [TLS; 30/8]

90. 6 May 1923, from Louis Sajous (stationery: Fraternal Association of Musicians, New York City) [TLS; 31/14]
91. 1 November 1928, from G. Francesco Malipiero (Casa Malipiero, Asolo (Treviso), Italy) [TLS; 30/17]
92. 23 November 1928, to G. Francesco Malipiero [typed, no sig.; 30/17]
93. 17 June 1920, from William Lyon Phelps (New Haven) [ALS (copy); 31/6]
94. 4 July 1920, from William Lyon Phelps (Huron City, Michigan) [ALS; 31/6]
95. 21 December 1920, to William Lyon Phelps [typed, no sig.; 31/6]
96. 27 August 1921, from John Cornelius Griggs (stationery: Canton Christian College / Canton, China) [ALS; 29/14]
97. Ca. 3 January 1930, sketch for Ives to John C. Griggs [29/14]
98. 12 October 1922, from W. Woods Chandler (Simsbury, Connecticut) [ALS; 27/12]
99. 16 November 1922, from Franklin Carter Jr. (Greenwich, Connecticut) [ALS; 27/12]
100. 19 March 1923, from Arthur (Pop) Baldwin (Cleveland) [typed copy; 27/3]
101. 5 May 1920, from Henry D. Sedgwick (Cambridge, Massachusetts) [ALS; 31/17]
102. 10 March 1923, to Henry D. Sedgwick [Correspondence Addendum].
103. 20 April 1923, from Henry D. Sedgwick (Cambridge, Massachusetts) [ALS; 31/17]
104. 15 March 1921, from Elizabeth Sprague Coolidge (Lakewood, New Jersey) [TLS; 27/12]
105. Ca. 15 March 1921, sketch for Ives to Elizabeth Sprague Coolidge [27/12]
106. 26 May 1920, from Henry F. Gilbert (Cambridge, Massachusetts) [ALS; 29/11]
107. 28 May 1920, sketch for Ives to Henry F. Gilbert [29/11]
108. 10 April 1921, from Henry H. Bellamann (Columbia, South Carolina) [TLS; 27/8]
109. Ca. 10 April 1921, to Henry H. Bellamann [typed, no sig.; 27/8]
110. 4 July 1921, to Henry H. Bellamann [ALS; 27/8]
111. 22 June 1921, to Edwin Stringham [typed, no sig.; 32/7]
112. 18 April 1921, from Arnold Capleton (Prague) [ALS; 27/10]
113. 24 June 1921, to Arnold Capleton [typed, no sig.; 27/10]
114. 15 August 1921, from Arnold Capleton (Prague) [ALS; 27/10]
115. 15 August 1921, from Clifton Furness (Indianapolis) [ALS; 29/9]
116. Ca. 15 August 1921, sketch for Ives to Clifton Furness [29/9]
117. 11 October 1921, to Clifton Furness [typed, no sig.; 29/9]
118. 10 December 1923, from Arnold Capleton (Prague) [ALS; 27/10]

4. HEALTH (1907–1954)

119. 17 October 1907, from Harmony Twichell(Hartford, Connecticut) [ALS; Correspondence Addendum]
120. 13 January 1908, from Harmony Twichell (Hartford, Connecticut) [ALS; Correspondence Addendum]
121. 30 January 1908, from Harmony Twichell (Danbury, Connecticut) [ALS; Correspondence Addendum]
122. 31 January 1908, from Harmony Twichell (Danbury, Connecticut) [ALS; Correspondence Addendum]

123. 6 February 1908, P.M., from Harmony Twichell (Hartford, Connecticut) [ALS; Correspondence Addendum]
124. 11 March 1908, from Harmony Twichell (Lakewood, New Jersey) [ALS; Correspondence Addendum]
125. 8 June 1916, from Harmony Ives (Hartford, Connecticut) [ALS; Correspondence Addendum]
126. 4 September 1918, to C. C. Whittelsey, Assistant Personnel Secretary, Y.M.C.A. Ambulance Corps [typed, no sig.; 32/16]
127. 19 November 1918, Julian Myrick to Rockland Tyng, New York Board of Taxes and Assessments (New York) [typed, no sig.; 30/18]
128. 2 August 1920, from Julian Myrick (New York) [TLS; 30/18]
129. 9 January 1922, to Henry H. Bellamann [TLS (copy); 27/8]
130. 22 June 1926, from Julian Myrick (New York) [TLS; 30/18]
131. 5 June 1929, from Julian Myrick (New York) [TLS; 30/18]
132. 18 June 1929, to T. Carl Whitmer [ALS; 32/14]
133. Ca. 22 July 1929, sketch for Ives to Julian Myrick [30/18]
134. 22 July 1929, from Julian Myrick (New York) [ALS; 30/18]
135. Ca. 22 July 1929, sketch for Ives to Julian Myrick [30/18]
136. 30 December 1929, to T. Carl Whitmer [ALS (copy); 32/14]
137. 16 January 1930, to Nicolas Slonimsky [ALS (copy); 32/1]
138. 17 February 1930, to Nicolas Slonimsky [ALS (copy); 32/1]
139. 21 June 1930, from Julian Myrick (New York) [TLS; 30/18]
140. Ca. 30 September 1930, to Julian Myrick [ALS (copy); 30/18]
141. 30 September 1930, Harmony Ives to Julian Myrick [ALS (copy); 30/18]
142. Summer or fall 1930, from Mrs. E. Robert Schmitz (Paris) [ALS; 31/15]
143. 13 January 1931, to T. Carl Whitmer [ALS (copy); 32/14]
144. 29 January 1931, from Julian Myrick (New York) [TLS; 30/18]
145. 29 April 1931, Harmony Ives to John Becker [ALS (copy); 27/4: the originals of the Becker correspondence are in the New York Public Library. The CIP holds copies of most of the letters from Ives to Becker (in 27/6) and transcriptions (in 27/4, 5) of the whole run of correspondence by John Kirkpatrick. I have cited these below.]
146. Ca. 6 April 1932, Edith Ives to John Becker [ALS (copy); 27/4]
147. December 1933, to Nicolas Slonimsky [ALS (copy); 32/4]
148. 4–5 August 1934, to John Becker [ALS (copy); 27/4]
149. 7 August 1934, to Nicolas Slonimsky [in Ives's and Edith's hands (copy); [32/4]
150. December 1934, to John Becker [ALS (copy); 27/4]
151. 27–29 January 1935, to John Becker [ALS (copy); 27/4]
152. March 1935, to John Becker [in Ives's hand (copy); 27/4]
153. Spring 1935, to Henry Cowell [ALS (copy); 28/5]
154. 8 June 1935, to John Becker [ALS (copy); 27/4]
155. Ca. 17 June 1935, to John Becker [ALS (copy); 27/4]
156. 3 September 1935, to John Becker [ALS (copy); 27/4]
157. Ca. 18 September 1935, to John Becker [ALS (copy); 27/4]
158. 15 October 1935, to George F. Roberts [JKT; 31/8]
159. November 1935, to Nicolas Slonimsky [ALS (copy); 32/4]

160. Ca. 2 November 1935, to John Becker [ALS (copy); 27/4]
161. Ca. 17 November 1935, to John Becker [ALS (copy); 27/4]
162. 21 January 1936, from Dr. Elliott Joslin (Boston) [ALS; 30/10]
163. Ca. October 1936, sketch for Ives to Elliott Joslin [30/10]
164. Ca. 3 July 1936, to John Becker [ALS (copy); 27/4]
165. Ca. 18 June 1936, sketches for Ives to Nicolas Slonimsky [32/5]
166. 6 July 1936, Harmony Ives to Nicolas Slonimsky [JKT; 32/5]
167. 1–5 March 1937, to John Becker [ALS (copy); 27/5]
168. January 1938, to John Becker [ALS (copy); 27/5]
169. 14 October 1937, Edith Ives to Radiana Pazmor [ALS; 31/3]
170. 30 June 1938, to John Becker (London) [ALS (copy); 27/5]
171. 11 October 1938, Edith Ives to John Becker [ALS (copy); 27/5]
172. 16 October 1938, Edith Ives to Lehman Engel [ALS (copy); 29/4]
173. Ca. 27 July 1939, to John Becker [ALS (copy); 27/4]
174. 17 January 1941, Harmony Ives to Evelyn Becker [ALS (copy); 27/5]
175. March 1942, two sketches for Harmony Ives to Joseph Szigeti [32/8]
176. 6 September 1943, Edith Ives Tyler to John Becker [ALS (copy); 27/5]
177. 16 March 1944, Harmony Ives to Charlotte Ruggles [JKT; 31/12]
178. 2 April 1944, Harmony Ives to Carl Ruggles [JKT; 31/12]
179. Ca. 10 September 1947, sketch for Harmony Ives to Friede Rothe [31/9]
180. Ca. 4 May 1949, sketch for Harmony Ives to Norris A. Pynn [31/5]
181. 15 November 1950, Harmony Ives to Carl and Charlotte Ruggles [JKT; 31/12]
182. 9 July 1951, Harmony Ives to Nicolas Slonimsky [JKT; 32/5]
183. 16 September 1951, Harmony Ives to Carl and Charlotte Ruggles [JKT; 31/12]
184. 19 March 1952, Harmony Ives to John Becker [ALS (copy); 27/5]
185. 24 March 1953, Harmony Ives to Carl and Charlotte Ruggles [JKT; 31/12]
186. 2 January 1954, Harmony Ives to John and Evelyn Becker [ALS (copy); 27/5]

5. COLLABORATORS AND CHAMPIONS (1923–1933)

187. 22 January 1923, from Clifton Furness (New York) [ALS; 29/9]
188. 4 October 1923, from E. Robert Schmitz (New York) [ALS; 31/15]
189. Ca. 4 October 1923, sketch for Ives to E. Robert Schmitz [31/15]
190. 9 December 1923, to E. Robert Schmitz [typed, no sig., with corrections in Ives's hand; 31/15]
191. 27 March 1924, to Carl Engel [typed, no sig., with a note in Ives's hand; 29/2]
192. 6 April 1924, from Clifton Furness (Evanston, Illinois) [ALS; 29/9]
193. Ca. early 1926, to the dean of Harvard College [typed copy; 27/11]
194. 19 February 1927, from Elliott Carter (Cambridge, Massachusetts) [ALS; 27/11]
195. 27 July 1927, from Henry Cowell (Menlo Park, California) [TLS (copy); 28/1]
196. 16 August 1927, to Henry Cowell [marked "copy"; 28/1]
197. 9 September 1927, to Katherine Heyman [TLS (copy); 30/7]
198. 7 October 1927, from John Kirkpatrick (New York) [ALS; 30/13]
199. 10 October 1927, to John Kirkpatrick [typed, no sig.; 30/13]

200. 16 October 1927, from John Kirkpatrick (New York) [ALS; 30/13]
201. January 1928, from Elliott Carter (Cambridge, Massachusetts) [27/11]
202. 11 January 1928, to Hans Barth [typed, no sig., with corrections in Ives's hand; 27/3]
203. 6 February 1928, to John Kirkpatrick [typed, no sig.; 30/13]
204. 28 February 1928, from Henry Cowell (New York) [TLS (copy); 28/1]
205. 10 April 1928, from Henry Cowell (New York) [TLS (copy); 28/1]
206. Ca. 24 April 1928, to Henry Cowell [ALS (copy); 28/1]
207. 12 August 1928, to Henry Cowell [ALS (copy); 28/1]
208. 20 August 1928, from Henry Cowell (Menlo Park, California) [TLS (copy; 28/1]
209. 11 October 1928, to Henry Cowell [TLS (copy); 28/1]
210. 24 November 1928, from Henry Cowell (Menlo Park, California) [TLS (copy); 28/1]
211. 31 January 1929, from Hans Barth (New York) [TLS; 27/3]
212. 1 April 1929, to Hans Barth [typed, no sig.; 27/3]
213. 14 July 1929, sketch for Ives to Nicolas Slonimsky [32/1]
214. 28–29 August 1929, to Henry Cowell [ALS (copy); 28/1]
215. 31 August 1929, from Henry Cowell (Menlo Park, California) [TLS; 28/1]
216. 5 September 1929, from Henry Cowell (Menlo Park, California) [typed, no sig. (copy). Ives has written "from Cowell" in the top margin; 28/1]
217. 15 October 1929, from Henry Cowell (Menlo Park, California) [TLS (copy); 28/1]
218. 17 April 1930, to Henry Cowell (Richmond, Virginia) [ALS (copy); 28/1]
219. 9 May 1930, from Nicolas Slonimsky (Jamaica Plain, Massachusetts) [TLS; 32/1]
220. 27 May 1930, to Nicolas Slonimsky [ALS (copy); 32/1]
221. 8 June 1930, to Nicolas Slonimsky [ALS (copy); 32/1]
222. Ca. July 1930, sketch for Ives to E. Robert Schmitz [31/16]
223. 24 December 1930, from Nicolas Slonimsky (Jamaica Plain, Massachusetts) [TLS; 32/1]
224. 26 December 1930, to Nicolas Slonimsky [ALS (copy); 32/1]
225. 30 December 1930, to Nicolas Slonimsky [ALS (copy); 32/1]
226. 7 July 1931, from Morton Gould (Richmond Hill, New York) [TLS; 29/14]
227. 13 July 1931, from Henry Cowell (Menlo Park, California) [TLS(copy); 28/2]
228. 19 July 1931, sketch for telegram to Henry Cowell [28/2]
229. Ca. 1931, sketches for Ives to Ashbel Barney [32/3]
230. Ca. 13 January 1932, to Nicolas Slonimsky [ALS (copy); 32/3]
231. 15 February 1932, from Pedro Sanjuan (Havana) [ALS; 31/14]
232. 9 August 1932, from Pedro Sanjuan (Havana) [ALS; 31/14]
233. 4 May 1932, from Lehman Engel (New York) [TLS; 29/3]
234. 16 June 1932, first sketch and letter from Edith Ives to Lehman Engel (London) [29/3]
235. 21 July 1932, to Aaron Copland [ALS (copy); 27/13]
236. 29 July 1933, from Radiana Pazmor (Middlebury, Vermont) [ALS; 31/3]
237. Ca. 29 July 1933, sketch for Ives to Radiana Pazmor [31/3]
238. 10 August 1933, from Radiana Pazmor (stationery: The Overland Route) [ALS; 31/3]
239. 10 October 1933, Harmony Ives to Aaron Copland [in Harmony Ives's hand except for the signature (copy); 27/13]

6. TRAVEL (1930–1938)

240. Ca. 12 October 1930, to Nicolas Slonimsky (stationery: Canadian Pacific Hotels / Château Frontenac / Québec) [ALS (copy); [32/2]
241. 17 September 1931, to Nicolas Slonimsky (stationery: A letter for you written at the Kedgemakooge Rod and Gun Club, a delightful summer inn located on the shady bank of Kedge makooge Lake in the heart of the lake region of Nova Scotia. Here one finds recreation throughout the vacation. [ALS (copy); 32/2]
242. 15 April 1932, sketch for Edith Ives to E. Robert Schmitz [in Edith Ives's hand; 31/16]
243. Mid-July 1932, to Nicolas Slonimsky (London) [ALS (copy); 32/3]
244. 15 August 1932, postcard to John Becker (Burg Reichenstein, Germany) [ALS (copy); 27/5]
245. 19 September 1932, from Nicolas Slonimsky [TLS, with additions and corrections in Slonimsky's hand; 32/3]
246. Mid-October 1932, to Nicolas Slonimsky (stationery: Hôtel du Lac / Interlaken [Switzerland]) [ALS (copy); 32/3]
247. Ca. November 1932, letter on two postcards to Carl Ruggles (Interlaken, Switzerland) [ALS (copy); 31/11]
248. 22 October 1932, to Clifton Furness (Interlaken, Switzerland) [copy in Furness's hand; 32/3]
249. 20 November 1932, sketch for Edith Ives to E. Robert Schmitz (stationery: Hôtel du Lac / Interlaken) [on the back of a sketch for Letter 248; 31/16]
250. 22 November 1932, Edith Ives to John Becker (stationery: Hôtel du Lac / Interlaken) [JKT; 27/5]
251. December 1932, to Nicolas Slonimsky (Taormina, Sicily) [on a Christmas card, no salutation, ALS (copy); 32/3]
252. Christmas 1932, to T. Carl Whitmer (Taormina, Sicily) [ALS (copy); 32/15]
253. Christmas 1932, sketch for Edith Ives to Bernard Herrmann (Taormina, Sicily) (stationery: Hôtel du Lac / Interlaken) [30/4]
254. December 1932, sketch for Edith Ives to Jerome Moross [on the same sheet as Letter 253; 30/4]
255. 8 January 1933, to Mary Bell (Taormina, Sicily) [postcard, in Ives's hand; 27/7]
256. 5 February 1933, to Nicolas Slonimsky (Taormina, Sicily) [ALS (copy); 52/3]
257. 28 February 1933, to Mary Bell (Taormina, Sicily) [ALS; 27/7]
258. 28 March 1933, Harmony Ives to John Becker (Rome) [ALS (copy); 27/5]
259. May 1933, to Nicolas Slonimsky (London) [ALS (copy); 32/3]
260. June 1933, to John Becker (London) [ALS (copy); 27/5]
261. July 1933, to T. Carl Whitmer [ALS (copy); 32/15]
262. June or July 1934, to Henry Cowell [ALS (copy); 28/5]
263. August 1934, to Henry Cowell (on the S.S. *Pennland* en route to Scotland) [ALS (copy); 28/5]
264. 12–16 August 1934, to John Becker (on the S.S. *Pennland* en route to Scotland) [ALS (copy); 27/5]
265. September or October 1934, to Henry Cowell (England) [ALS (copy); 28/5]
266. 9 May 1938, Harmony Ives to Charlotte Ruggles [JKT; 31/11]
267. 22 June 1938, to E. Robert Schmitz (London) [AL (copy); 31/16]

268. 11 December 1933, from John Kirkpatrick (Greenwich, Connecticut) [TLS; 30/13]
269. Ca. 3 January 1934, to Nicolas Slonimsky [ALS (copy); 32/4]
270. 5 January 1934, from Nicolas Slonimsky (Boston) [TLS; 32/4]
271. 11 January 1934, to Nicolas Slonimsky [ALS (copy); 32/4]
272. 5 January 1934, from John Kirkpatrick (Greenwich, Connecticut) [TLS; 30/13]
273. 18 January 1934, from John Kirkpatrick (Greenwich, Connecticut) [TLS; 30/13]
274. 27–30 April 1934, to Henry Cowell [ALS (copy); 28/5]
275. 10 May 1934, from Wallingford Riegger (New Music Quarterly Recordings, New York) [ALS; 31/13]
276. 13 May 1934, sketch for Ives to Wallingford Riegger [31/13]
277. May 1934, undated and incomplete sketch for Ives to Wallingford Riegger [31/13]
278. 16 May 1934, from Wallingford Riegger (New Music Quarterly Recordings, New York) [ALS; 31/13]
279. Ca. 12 May 1934, to George F. Roberts [JKT; 31/8]
280. 15 May 1934, from Charles Martin (New York) [excerpt, typed copy probably made for Ives, with marginalia by Ives; 29/11]
281. 24–28 May 1934, to Aaron Copland [ALS (copy); 27/13]
282. 15 June 1934, to George F. Roberts [JKT; 31/8]
283. 28 June 1934, from Aaron Copland (Lavinia, Minnesota) [ALS; 27/13]
284. 12 July 1934, from John Kirkpatrick (Greenwich, Connecticut) [TLS; 30/13]
285. 9 November 1934, from Radiana Pazmor (New York) [ALS; 31/3]
286. 13 November 1934, Edith Ives to Radiana Pazmor [ALS (copy); 31/3]
287. 1 December 1934, from Radiana Pazmor (New York) [ALS; 31/3]
288. 3 December 1934, Edith Ives to Radiana Pazmor [ALS; 31/3]
289. December 1934, sketch for Ives to Radiana Pazmor [31/3]
290. 15 December 1934, from Carl Ruggles (Arlington, Vermont) [ALS; 31/11]
291. Early June 1935, to George F. Roberts [JKT; 31/8]
292. 20 June 1935, to George F. Roberts [ALS (copy); 31/8]
293. 24 June 1935, to George F. Roberts [JKT; 31/8]
294. 10 July 1935, to George F. Roberts [JKT; 31/8]
295. 19 July 1935, to George F. Roberts [JKT; 31/8]
296. 31 July 1935, to George F. Roberts [ALS (copy of letter and envelope, which has some musical sketching in Ives's hand on the back, including tetrachord divisions of the major and minor scales with the half steps marked in the minor); 31/8]
297. Ca. July 1935, from John Kirkpatrick (Greenwich, Connecticut) [TLS; 30/13]
298. 2 August 1935, to George F. Roberts [JKT; 31/8]
299. 20 August 1935, to George F. Roberts [JKT; 31/8]
300. 28 September 1935, from John Kirkpatrick (Greenwich, Connecticut) [TLS, with pencil annotations by Ives; 30/13]
301. Ca. 28 September 1935, excerpts from four sketches for Harmony Ives to John Kirkpatrick [30/13;final letter, John Kirkpatrick Papers, MSS 56, 18/203]
302. 25 October 1935, from John Kirkpatrick (Greenwich, Connecticut) [TLS; 30/13]

303. November 1935, from John Kirkpatrick (Greenwich, Connecticut) [TLS; 30/13]
304. Ca. November 1935, sketches for Ives to John Kirkpatrick [30/13]
305. January 1936, from John Kirkpatrick (New York) [30/13]
306. Ca. 23 January 1936, incomplete sketch for Harmony Ives to John Kirkpatrick [30/13]
307. 1 February 1936, from John Kirkpatrick (Greenwich, Connecticut) [TLS; 30/13]
308. 5 February 1936, from John Kirkpatrick (Greenwich, Connecticut) [30/13]
309. 25 March 1936, from Lou Harrison (San Francisco) [ALS; 31/2]
310. 3 July 1936, Harmony Ives to Charlotte Ruggles [JKT; 31/11]
311. 12 July 1936, Harmony Ives to Charlotte Ruggles [JKT; 31/11]
312. 22 July 1936, from John Kirkpatrick (Greenwich, Connecticut) [ALS; 30/13]
313. August 1936, Harmony Ives to Evelyn Becker [JKT; 27/4]
314. 10 October 1936, from John Becker (St. Paul) [JKT; 27/4]
315. Ca. 10 October 1936, Henry Cowell to John Becker (San Quentin, California) [JKT from Becker's copy; 27/4]
316. October 1936, from John Becker (St. Paul) [JKT from Becker's carbon copy; 27/5]
317. December 1936 to John Becker [JKT; 27/5]
318. 17 December 1936, Chester Ives to Lou Harrison [ALS; 30/2]
319. 16 February 1937, from Lou Harrison (San Francisco) [ALS; 30/2]
320. Ca. 1 March 1937, to John Becker [ALS, in Ives's hand and voice until "of course you were in all similar books" through the end, where the hand switches to Harmony's (copy); 27/5]
321. 12 March 1937, from John Becker (St. Paul) [JKT from Becker's carbon copy; 27/5]
322. 4 April 1937, from John Kirkpatrick (Greenwich, Connecticut) [TLS; 30/13]
323. 28 April 1937, from John Kirkpatrick (Greenwich, Connecticut) [TLS; 30/13]
324. Ca. 15 June 1937, sketch in Edith Ives's hand for Ives to Elie Siegmeister [32/1]
325. 25 July 1937, from John Kirkpatrick (Greenwich, Connecticut) [TLS; 30/13]
326. 5 August 1937, sketch for Harmony Ives to John Kirkpatrick [30/13]
327. Late 1937, sketch for Edith Ives to Mordecai Bauman [27/3]
328. 18 April 1938, from Carl Ruggles (Coral Gables, Florida) [ALS; 31/11]
329. May 1938, to Carl Ruggles [ALS (copy); 31/11]
330. 13 May 1938, from John Kirkpatrick (Stamford, Connecticut) [TLS; 30/14]
331. 22 June 1938, from John Kirkpatrick (Stamford, Connecticut) [TLS; 30/14]
332. Ca. 23 August 1938, excerpts from three sketches for Ives to Lehman Engel [nos. 1 and 2 in Ives's hand and voice, no. 3 in Edith Ives's hand but Ives's voice in the first person; 29/3]
333. 27 August 1938, from Lehman Engel (Arrow Music Press, New York) [ALS; 29/3]
334. 2 October 1938, from Mordecai Bauman (New York) [ALS; 27/3]
335. Ca. 2 October 1938, sketch for Harmony Ives to Mordecai Bauman [in Harmony Ives's hand; 27/3]
336. 6 October 1938, Harmony Ives to Bernard Herrmann [TLS (copy); 30/4]
337. 18 October 1938, from Mordecai Bauman (New York) [27/3]
338. 19 January 1939, Henry Cowell to Mary Bell (San Quentin, California) [TLS (copy); 27/7]
339. 2 February 1939, Harmony Ives to Mary Bell [ALS; 27/7]
340. 2 February 1939, sketches for Harmony Ives to John Kirkpatrick [30/14]
341. 4 February1939, from John Kirkpatrick (Stamford, Connecticut) [ALS; 30/14]
342. 9 February 1939, from John Kirkpatrick (New York) [ALS; 30/14]

343. 26 February 1939, from Lehman Engel (New York) [TLS; 29/4]
344. Ca. 1 May 1939, sketch for Edith Ives to Charles Seeger [31/18]
345. 30 May 1939, from Ruth Crawford Seeger [ALS; 31/18]
346. 27 June 1939, from Radiana Pazmor (Hollywood) [ALS; 31/3]
347. 10 August 1939, from Dane Rudhyar (Santa Fe) [ALS; 31/10]
348. Ca. 10 August 1939, sketch for Harmony Ives to Dane Rudhyar [31/10]
349. 26 March 1940, from Paul Rosenfeld (New York) [TLS; 31/9]
350. Ca. March 1940, sketch for Harmony Ives to Paul Rosenfeld [31/9]
351. 28 March 1940, from John Kirkpatrick (Riverside, Connecticut) [ALS; 30/14]
352. 24 May 1940, from Johanna Magdalena Berger (New York) [ALS; 27/9]
353. Ca. 14 October 1940, sketch for Harmony Ives to Dane Rudhyar [31/10]
354. Ca. October 1940, sketch for Harmony Ives to Charles Seeger [31/18]
355. Undated sketch for Harmony Ives to Charles Seeger [31/18]
356. 21 November 1940, sketch for Ives to George F. Roberts [31/8]
357. 6 January 1941, Harmony Ives to Carl Ruggles [JKT; 31/11]
358. 1 February 1941, from Carl Ruggles (Coral Gables, Florida) [ALS; 31/11]
359. 15 September 1941, from Henry Cowell (New York) [TLS (copy); 28/6]
360. 18 September 1941, Harmony Ives to Henry Cowell [ALS (copy); 28/6]
361. 2 March 1942, from Henry Cowell (New York) [ALS (copy); 28/6]
362. 19 October 1942, Harmony Ives to George F. Roberts [in Harmony Ives's hand except for the musical example; 31/8]
363. 30 October 1942, from Edith Ives Tyler (New York) [ALS; Correspondence Addendum]
364. 21 November 1942, Harmony Ives to George F. Roberts [JKT; 31/8]
365. 27 July 1943, from Henry Cowell (New York) [TLS (copy); 28/7]
366. Ca. 27 July 1943, sketch for Harmony Ives to Henry Cowell [28/7]
367. Late August 1943, sketch for Harmony Ives to Artur Rodzinski [31/9]
368. Undated sketch for Harmony Ives to Serge Koussevitzky [30/12]
369. 8 December 1943, sketch for Ives to Henry Cowell [28/7]
370. 8 December 1943, Harmony Ives to Sidney Cowell [ALS (copy); 28/7]
371. 12 December 1943, from Henry Cowell (New York) [TLS (copy); 28/7]
372. 20 January 1944, Harmony Ives to Henry Cowell [ALS; 28/7]
373. 4 March 1944, Harmony Ives to Lehman Engel [ALS (copy); 29/5]
374. 10 July 1944, Harmony Ives to Lehman Engel [ALS (copy); 29/5]
375. 18 July 1944, from Robert Dark (Santa Rosa, California) [TLS; 29/1]
376. 28 July 1944, sketch for Harmony Ives to Robert Dark [29/1]
377. Sketch for Harmony Ives to American Music Center [same page as Letter 376; 29/1]
378. Sketch for Harmony Ives to C. C. Birchard and Co. [same page as Letter 376; 29/1]
379. 17 August 1944, from Dorothea Persichetti (Money Island, Toms River, New Jersey) [ALS; 31/4]
380. Ca. 17 August 1944, sketch for Harmony Ives to Dorothea Persichetti [31/4]
381. 31 August 1944, from John Kirkpatrick (Georgetown, Connecticut) [TLS; 30/14]
382. Ca. October 1944, sketch for Harmony Ives to Lou Harrison [30/2]
383. 23 October 1944, from Lou Harrison (New York) [ALS; 30/2]
384. Ca. November 1944, sketch for Harmony Ives to Lou Harrison [30/2]
385. 25 November 1944, second sketch for Harmony Ives to John Kirkpatrick [30/14]

386. 28 November 1944, from John Kirkpatrick (Mount Holyoke College, South Hadley, Massachusetts) [ALS; 30/14]
387. 28 November 1944, John Kirkpatrick (South Hadley, Massachusetts) to Goddard Lieberson, Columbia Records, New York [typed copy; 30/14]
388. 3 December 1944, from John Kirkpatrick (South Hadley, Massachusetts) [TLS; 30/14]
389. 12 December 1944, from John Kirkpatrick (South Hadley, Massachusetts) [ALS; 30/14]
390. Ca. 20 October 1944, second sketch for Harmony Ives to Elliott Carter [27/11]

8. FINAL YEARS (1945–1954)

391. 15 February 1945, from John Kirkpatrick (South Hadley, Massachusetts) [TLS; 30/14]
392. 16 March 1945, sketch for Harmony Ives to John Kirkpatrick [30/14]
393. 18 March 1945, from John Kirkpatrick (South Hadley, Massachusetts) [TLS; 30/14]
394. Ca. 18 March 1945, sketch for Harmony Ives to John Kirkpatrick [30/14]
395. 18 December 1945, from John Kirkpatrick (South Hadley, Massachusetts) [TLS; 30/14]
396. 14 April 1946, from Lou Harrison (New York) [ALS; 30/2]
397. 21 April 1946, Harmony Ives to Lou Harrison [ALS; 30/2]
398. 16 May 1946, from Lou Harrison (New York) [ALS; 30/3]
399. 28 June 1946, Harmony Ives to Lou Harrison [30/3]
400. 24 July 1946, from Lou Harrison (New York) [ALS;30/3]
401. 28 June 1946, Harmony Ives to Lou Harrison [ALS; 30/3]
402. 8 May 1947, from Robert Graham Dun Douglas (New York) [TLS; 29/1]
403. 21 May 1947, two sketches for a letter to Carl Ruggles [31/12]
404. 14 September 1947, sketch for Edith Ives Tyler to John Becker [section from final letter from JK's transcription;27/5]
405. 13 May 1947, from John Cage (New York) [TLS; 30/3]
406. Ca. 13 May 1947, sketch for Harmony Ives to John Cage [30/3]
407. Late May 1947, from John Cage (Massachusetts) [ALS; 30/3]
408. Ca. 13 May 1947, from John Cage (New York) [TLS; 30/3]
409. 2 July 1947, from Lou Harrison (New York) [TLS; 30/3]
410. 20 September 1947, Harmony Ives to Lehman Engel [ALS (copy); 29/5]
411. Ca. 15 April 1948, sketch for Harmony Ives to E. Power Biggs [27/9]
412. Undated sketch for Harmony Ives to E. Power Biggs [27/9]
413. Ca. April 1948, second sketch for Ives to Jerome Mellquist [31/7]
414. 3 May 1948, from Robert Palmer (Ithaca, New York) [ALS; 31/2]
415. 8 June 1948, Harmony Ives to Robert Palmer [JKT; 31/2]
416. 6 January 1949, from Wallingford Riegger [New York] [ALS] [31/13]
417. 1 February 1949, from Lou Harrison (New York) [TLS; 30/3]
418. 10 February 1949, Harmony Ives to Lou Harrison [ALS; 30/3]
419. 1 March 1949, Harmony Ives to John and Evelyn Becker [JKT; 27/5]
420. 3 April 1949, from Gertrude Sanford (West Redding, Connecticut) [ALS; 31/14]
421. 20 October 1949, from Peter Yates (Los Angeles) [TLS; 32/18]
422. 11 November 1949, from Isabel Parker Semler (New Canaan, Connecticut) [ALS; 31/19]

423. 25 November 1949, from Richard T. Gore (Wooster, Ohio) [TLS; 29/14]
424. 10 April 1950, from Emma M. Smith (New York) [ALS; 32/6]
425. 28 June 1950, from Joseph H. Soifer (Hartford, Connecticut) [TLS; 32/6]
426. Ca. 28 June 1950, sketch for Harmony Ives to Joseph H. Soifer [32/6]
427. 26 July 1950, to John Becker [ALS (copy); 27/5]
428. 20 August 1950, from Bernard Herrmann (New York) [ALS; 30/5]
429. Ca. 20 August 1950, sketch for Harmony Ives to Bernard Herrmann [30/5]
430. 11 October 1950, from Peter Yates (Los Angeles) [TLS; 32/18]
431. 10 March 1951, from Bigelow Ives (Danbury, Connecticut) [ALS; 30/9]
432. 11 March 1951, Harmony Ives to Leonard Bernstein [typed copy; 28/7]
433. 29 April 1951, from Patricia Travers (Clifton, New Jersey) [ALS; 32/9]
434. May 1951, sketch for Edith Ives Tyler to Peter Yates [32/18]
435. 3 April 1952, from Nicolas Slonimsky (Boston) [ALS; 32/5]
436. 10 July 1952, from Lou Harrison (Black Mountain, North Carolina) [ALS; 30/3]
437. 24 July 1952, Harmony Ives to Lou Harrison [ALS; 30/3]
438. Late July 1952, from Lou Harrison (Black Mountain, North Carolina) [ALS; 30/3]
439. Ca. December 1952, from John Ardoin (Denton, Texas) [TLS; 27/1]
440. 22 January 1953, from John Ardoin (Denton, Texas) [TLS; 27/1]
441. 24 March 1953, from Richard Donovan (New Haven) [typed, no sig.; 29/1]
442. 6 April 1953, Harmony Ives to Richard Donovan [ALS; 29/1]
443. 11 October 1953, Harmony Ives to Sidney Cowell [ALS (copy); 28/8]
444. 4 March 1954, Harmony Ives to Reuben Holden [typed, no sig.; 29/1]
445. 11 April 1954, Harmony Ives to Sidney Cowell [ALS (copy); 28/8]
446. 21 May 1954, John Kirkpatrick to Carl and Charlotte Ruggles [retyped by Kirkpatrick in 1960; 30/14]
447. 26 May 1954, Harmony Ives to John and Evelyn Becker [JKT; 27/5]
448. 9 June 1954, Reuben Holden, secretary, Yale University, to Richard Donovan (New Haven) [TLS; 29/1]
449. 15 June 1954, Harmony Ives to Richard Donovan [ALS; 29/1]
450. 13 June 1954, Harmony Ives to Carl and Charlotte Ruggles [JKT; 31/12]
451. Before 22 June 1954, from Germaine Schmitz (San Francisco) [ALS; 31/16]
452. 22 June 1954, Harmony Ives to Germaine Schmitz [JKT; 31/16]
453. 22 June 1954, from Carl and Charlotte Ruggles (Arlington, Vermont) [ALS; 31/12]

SELECTED BIBLIOGRAPHY

PERSONAL PAPERS

The Charles Ives Papers are in the Irving S. Gilmore Music Library of Yale University, Mss. 14. Material acquired since the cataloguing of the Charles Ives Papers is in the Addendum.

The John Kirkpatrick Papers are in the Irving S. Gilmore Music Library of Yale University, MSS 56.

PRINTED SOURCES

Barr, Cyrilla. *Elizabeth Sprague Coolidge: American Patron of Music.* New York: Schirmer Books, 1998.

Bernardin de Saint Pierre, Jacques-Henri. *Paul and Virginia.* 1771. Translated with an introduction by John Donovan. London: Peter Owen, 1982.

Blitzstein, Marc. "The Young Americans in Music." *La Revue Musicale,* no. 163 (February 1936): 145–48.

Block, Geoffrey. *Ives: Concord Sonata* (Cambridge: Cambridge University Press, 1996), 27–30.

Block, Geoffrey, and J. Peter Burkholder, eds. *Charles Ives and the Classical Tradition.* New Haven: Yale University Press, 1996.

———. "Selected Reviews: 1888–1951." In *Charles Ives and His World,* edited by J. Peter Burkholder, 273–362. Princeton: Princeton University Press, 1996.

Broyles, Michael. "Charles Ives and the American Democratic Tradition." In *Charles Ives and His World,* edited by J. Peter Burkholder, 135–40. Princeton: Princeton University Press, 1996.

Bukoff, Ronald Nick. "Charles Ives, a History and Bibliography of Criticism (1920–1939), and Ives's Influence on Bernard Herrmann, Elie Siegmeister, and Robert Palmer." Ph.D. diss., Cornell University, 1988.

Burkholder, J. Peter. *All Made of Tunes: Charles Ives and the Uses of Musical Borrowing.* New Haven: Yale University Press, 1995.

———. *Charles Ives: The Ideas behind the Music.* New Haven: Yale University Press, 1985.

———, ed. *Charles Ives and His World.* Princeton: Princeton University Press, 1996.

Catalogue of the Officers and Graduates of Yale University in New Haven, Connecticut, 1701–1924. New Haven: Yale University, 1924.

Copland, Aaron. "One Hundred and Fourteen Songs." *Modern Music* 11, no. 2 (January– February, 1934): 59–64.

Cowell, Henry. "Why the Ultra-Modernists Frown on Krenek's Opera." *Singing and Playing* 4, no. 2 (February 1929): 15, 35. Cited in Bruce Saylor, *The Writings of Henry Cowell: A Descriptive Bibliography.* New York: Institute for American Music, 1977.

———, ed. *American Composers on American Music: A Symposium.* With a New Introduction. New York: Frederick Ungar, 1962.

Cowell, Henry, and Sidney Cowell. *Charles Ives and His Music.* 1955; reprint with additional material, New York: Oxford University Press, 1969.
Crawford, Dorothy. *Evenings On and Off the Roof.* Berkeley: University of California Press, 1995.
Dennison, Sam, ed. *American Orchestral Music: Nationalists and Traditionalists in Early Twentieth-Century America.* Boston: G. K. Hall, 1992.
Devore, Richard Owen. "Stylistic Diversity within the Music of Five Avant-Garde American Composers, 1929–1945." Ph.D. diss., University of Iowa, 1985.
Downes, Irene, ed. *Olin Downes on Music: A Selection from His Writings during the Half- Century 1906–1955.* New York: Simon and Schuster, 1957.
Downes, Olin. "Tardy Recognition: Emergence of Charles Ives as Strongly Individual Figure in American Music." *New York Times,* 14 April 1946, 53.
Feder, Stuart. *Charles Ives: "My Father's Song."* New Haven: Yale University Press, 1992.
Franco-American Musical Society Quarterly Bulletin, 1924–25.
Goldbeck, Fred. "Musiciens Américains à la 'Spirale.'" *La Revue Musicale,* no. 165 (April 1936): 293.
Goodman, Peter W. *Morton Gould: American Salute.* Portland, Ore.: Amadeus Press, 2000.
Hall, Helen. *Unfinished Business: In Neighborhood and Nation.* New York: Macmillan, 1972.
Harrison, Lou. "Ruggles, *Evocations.*" *Modern Music* 22, no. 2 (January–February 1945): 109.
Hicks, Michael. *Henry Cowell, Bohemian.* Urbana: University of Illinois Press, 2002.
Hitchcock, H. Wiley. *Ives.* Oxford Studies of Composers Series, no. 14. London: Oxford University Press, 1977.
Hitchcock, H. Wiley, and Vivian Perlis, eds. *An Ives Celebration: Papers and Panels of the Charles Ives Centennial Festival-Conference.* Urbana: University of Illinois Press, 1977.
Ives, Charles. *Eighteen Songs. New Music* 9, no. 1 (October 1935).
———. *Essays Before a Sonata, The Majority, and Other Writings.* Edited by Howard Boatwright. New York: W. W. Norton, 1961.
———. *129 Songs.* Edited by H. Wiley Hitchcock. Music of the United States of America, vol. 12. Middleton, Wis.: A-R Editions, 2004.
———. *Memos.* Edited with appendices by John Kirkpatrick. New York: W. W. Norton, 1972.
———. *Piano Sonata No. 2, "Concord Mass., 1840–1860."* 2nd ed. 1947; reprint, New York: Associated Music Publishers, 1970.
Ives, Moss. *The Ark and the Dove: The Beginning of Civil and Religious Liberties in America* New York: Longmans, Green and Co., 1936.
Johnson, Owen. *Stover at Yale.* With an introduction by Judith Ann Schiff. New Haven: The Yale Bookstore, 1997.
Kennedy, Sidney R., Julien A. Ripley, and Henry B. Wright, eds. *Decennial Record Class of Eighteen Hundred and Ninety-Eight Yale College.* New Haven: Tuttle, Morehouse and Taylor, 1910.
Kennedy, William Bruce. "Rhyme and Reason: An Evaluation of Lehman Engel's Contribution to the Criticism of the Music Theatre." Ph.D. diss., Kent State University, 1987.
Kohlenberg, Randy B. *Harrison Kerr: Portrait of a Twentieth-Century American Composer.* Composers of North America, no. 23. Lanham, Md.: Scarecrow Press, 1997.
Lardner, Ring. *You Know Me Al: A Busher's Letters.* 1914; reprint, New York: Charles Scribner's Sons, 1960.
Lawton, Mary. *Schumann-Heink: The Last of the Titans.* New York: Macmillan, 1929.
Lichtenwanger, William, ed. *Oscar Sonneck and American Music.* Urbana: University of Illinois Press, 1983.
Lord, Frank Atkins, ed. *Yale Class Book [18]98.* New Haven: O. A. Dorman Co., 1898.
Lombroso, Cesare. *The Man of Genius.* New York: Charles Scribner's Sons, 1895.

Lutz, Tom. *American Nervousness, 1903: An Anecdotal History*. Ithaca: Cornell University Press, 1991.

Martin, Sherrill V. *Henry F. Gilbert: A Biobibliography*. Westport, Conn.: Praeger, 2004.

Mead, Rita. *Henry Cowell's New Music 1925–1936: The Society, the Music Editions, and the Recordings*. Ann Arbor, Mich.: UMI Editions, 1981.

Mellquist, Jerome, and Lucie Wiese, eds. *Paul Rosenfeld: Voyager in the Arts*. New York: Creative Age Press, 1948.

Miller, Leta E., and Rob Collins. "The Cowell-Ives Relationship: A New Look at Cowell's Prison Years," *American Music* 23, no. 4 (Winter 2005): 473–92.

Miller, Leta, and Frederic Lieberman. *Lou Harrison: Composing a World*. New York: Oxford University Press, 1998.

New Grove Dictionary of Music and Musicians. 2nd ed. Edited by Laura Macy. www.grovemusic.com.

Oja, Carol. *Making Music Modern: New York in the 1920s*. New York: Oxford University Press, 2000.

Owens, Tom C. "Charles Ives and His American Context: Images of Americanness in the Arts." Ph.D. diss., Yale University, 1999.

———, ed. "Selected Correspondence: 1881–1954." In *Charles Ives and His World*, edited by J. Peter Burkholder, 199–272. Princeton: Princeton University Press, 1996.

Patterson, Donald L., and Janet L. Patterson. *Vincent Persichetti: A Bio-Bibliography*. Westport, Conn.: Greenwood Press, 1988.

Perlis, Vivian, ed. *Charles Ives Remembered: An Oral History*. 1974; reprint, New York: Da Capo Press, 1994.

Phelps, William Lyon. *Autobiography with Letters*. New York: Oxford University Press, 1939.

Pro Musica Quarterly, 1925–29.

Reese, Gustave, ed. *A Birthday Offering to Carl Engel*. New York: G. Schirmer, 1943.

Robbins, Alexandra. *Secrets of the Tomb: Skull and Bones, the Ivy League, and the Hidden Paths of Power*. Boston: Little, Brown, 2002.

Rossiter, Frank. *Charles Ives and His America*. New York: Liveright, 1975.

Saylor, Bruce. *The Writings of Henry Cowell: A Descriptive Bibliography*. New York: Institute for American Music, 1977.

Sherwood, Gayle. "Charles Ives and Our National Malady." *Journal of the American Musicological Society* 54, no. 3 (Fall 2001): 555–84.

———. "The Choral Works of Charles Ives: Chronology, Style, Reception." Ph.D. diss., Yale University, 1995.

Sinclair, James. *Descriptive Catalogue of the Music of Charles Ives*. New Haven: Yale University Press, 2002.

Slonimsky, Nicolas. *Music since 1900*. 4th ed. New York: Charles Scribner's Sons, 1971.

Smith, Steven C. *A Heart at Fire's Center: The Life and Music of Bernard Herrmann*. Berkeley: University of California Press, 1991.

Swafford, Jan. *Charles Ives: A Life with Music* New York: W. W. Norton, 1996.

Tick, Judith. "Charles Ives and Gender Ideology." In *Musicology and Difference: Gender and Sexuality in Music Scholarship*, edited by Ruth Solie, 83–102. Berkeley: University of California Press, 1994.

———. *Ruth Crawford Seeger: A Composer's Search for American Music*. New York: Oxford University Press, 1997.

Verdi, Giuseppe. Letter to Ricordi, 18 March 1899, Istituto di Studio Verdiani, Parma. Quoted in Mary Jane Phillips-Matz, *Verdi: A Biography*. New York: Oxford University Press, 1993, 750.

Waterhouse, John C. G. *La musica di Gian Francesco Malipiero*. Turin: Nuova Eri Edizione RAI, 1990.

Williamson, Samuel H. "What Is the Relative Value?" Economic History Services, April 2004, www.eh.net/hmit/compare/ (accessed 27 October 2005).

Yale Daily News, 1893–98.
Ziffrin, Marilyn. *Carl Ruggles: Composer, Painter, and Storyteller*. Urbana: University of Illinois Press, 1994.

RECORDINGS

Ives, Charles. *Ives Plays Ives*, CRI CD 810, 1999; reissue, New World Records, 2006.
———. "Emerson" Piano Concerto, edited by David Porter, performed by Alan Feinberg and the National Symphony Orchestra of Ireland, conducted by James Sinclair, Naxos CD8.559175.

INDEX